THE NORTON MIX

AMERICAN HISTORY

★

EDITORS

KAREN DUNN-HALEY
GENERAL EDITOR
UNIVERSITY OF CALIFORNIA, DAVIS

STEVE DAVIS
LONE STAR COLLEGE, KINGWOOD

MATTHEW SCHOENBACHLER
UNIVERSITY OF NORTH ALABAMA

WENDY WALL
BINGHAMTON UNIVERSITY

THE NORTON MIX

AMERICAN HISTORY

A CUSTOM READER AND TEXTBOOK

American Political &
Social History II

Lauren Kozakiewicz

NORTON CUSTOM
W. W. NORTON & COMPANY, INC.
NEW YORK • LONDON

W. W. Norton & Company has been independent since its founding in 1923, when William Warder Norton and Mary D. Herter Norton first published lectures delivered at the People's Institute, the adult education division of New York City's Cooper Union. The Nortons soon expanded their program beyond the Institute, publishing books by celebrated academics from America and abroad. By mid-century, the two major pillars of Norton's publishing program—trade books and college texts—were firmly established. In the 1950s, the Norton family transferred control of the company to its employees, and today—with a staff of four hundred and a comparable number of trade, college, and professional titles published each year—W. W. Norton & Company stands as the largest and oldest publishing house owned wholly by its employees.

Bibliographies for these titles can be accessed here: http://wwnorton.com/college/history/AmericanHistory Biblio/

Printed in the United States of America

Editor: Jon Durbin
Custom editor: Katie Hannah
Associate editor: Justin Cahill
Managing editor, College: Marian Johnson
Project editor: Erica Wnek
Editorial assistant: Elizabeth Dana
Production associate: Diana Spiegle
Design director: Rubina Yeh
Book designers: Chris Welch, Hope Miller Goodell
Text permissions editor: Nancy Rodwan
Photo researcher: Stephanie Romeo
Copyeditor: Mike Fleming
Proofreaders: Barbara Necol, Ann Kirschner
Composition: Westchester Publishing Services
Manufacturing: RR Donnelley

ISBN 978-0-393-27843-9

W. W. Norton & Company, Inc., 500 Fifth Avenue, New York, NY 10110
www.wwnorton.com
W. W. Norton & Company, Ltd., Castle House, 75/76 Wells Street, London WIT3QT

CONTENTS

PREFACE

This book has been compiled by your instructor from a larger set of documents selected by the editors of *The Norton Mix: American History*. Rather than assign an already-published compilation that might include documents you will never use in class, your instructor has created a customized book that will provide you with a greater value than a standard textbook because it includes just those materials that you'll need for this particular course.

The flexible nature of the *Mix* has allowed your instructor to determine the book's content and the sequence of the individual selections to suit the course you're taking. Your instructor has chosen from more than 270 documents, a list derived in part from an extensive research study that W. W. Norton's editors conducted to identify the most frequently assigned readings in American history courses. Approximately one third of these are the "core documents" in American history, ranging from the Declaration of Independence to Martin Luther King Jr.'s "Letter from Birmingham Jail." Further, we've made available numerous documents illustrating everyday life in various historical periods, as well as a broad array of visual images—engravings, paintings, cartoons, and photographs. Some sources have been translated from Spanish, including an 1863 Los Angeles speech on the origins of Cinco de Mayo celebrations. As one example of an attempt to provide a balance of offerings, Benjamin Franklin's *Albany Plan*, a standard source, is available in the *Mix*; so is Franklin's *Drinker's Dictionary*, a less-known source comically dealing with an aspect of everyday life in the colonies. Your professor has chosen from among these and other selections to create a book that will work for your course and provide you with a great value.

The editors have sought to cover a variety of topics touching on political, economic, cultural, and social change in the three major chronological eras that are covered by most university and college American history courses: the colonial period through the early national period; the antebellum period through the Gilded Age and the rise of urban America; and the twentieth century to the present. Some of the sources in the *Mix* are presented in full, and some are excerpted from speeches, articles, journals, chapters, and books. Selections average six pages in length—some are short and concise, while a few longer selections (up to twenty pages) will expose you to a larger context and give you practice reading and determining meaning within longer documents.

For the most part, we have remained faithful to the original sources. Ways of speaking, writing, and spelling have changed over time, and these nuances are themselves of historical interest. We hope that you will come to recognize that language is not static and that it is as representative of different historical periods as, say, clothing or music or social customs. Nonetheless, in cases where archaic spelling might hinder your ability to read and comprehend a document, the editors have made modest changes in order to modernize the text. We have excerpted documents with the same goal in mind, attempting to capture each document's full flavor but eliminating unnecessary detail when this seemed appropriate. We have used footnotes to explain unfamiliar terms, people, places, and events. In cases where the original document itself includes footnotes, our additional editorial notations are marked with "[Ed.]" for clarity. For words that may be unfamiliar to you, we encourage you to consult a good dictionary.

Your instructor may have also included excerpts from essays and articles by contemporary historians. These secondary sources reveal how historians interpret the past, and they invite you to consider how you might come to alternative interpretations. While learning the language of a discipline is an important skill and one that we hope you will develop, this collection is not meant to immerse student readers in historical theory and the language of the historical profession. Rather, the secondary sources have been selected to give you a clear introduction to specific historical topics as well as the opportunity to question historians' assertions and interpretations. We hope that this approach will provide a solid foundation and will spark an interest in reading more works of historical nonfiction, such as biographies. Some readers may even think about becoming historians themselves.

Most colleges and universities, either through a general education curriculum or other institutional means, expect you to graduate with critical thinking and information literacy skills. *The Norton Mix: American History* encourages the practical development of these skills in the course of studying American history. The headnotes and study questions in this collection are designed to help give you firm critical footing as you approach the selected documents and images. Providing basic historical context, the headnotes introduce the author's background and viewpoint, sometimes in relation to contrasting positions. Study questions at the end of each selection are meant to guide you from a basic understanding of content to an *analysis* of facts and an exploration of the writer's point of view, circumstances, and potential biases. We hope that the result will be plenty of lively, intelligent discussion in your classrooms.

Over a century ago, historian Henry Adams complained that "nothing in education is so astonishing as the amount of ignorance it accumulates in the form of inert facts." This collection of primary and secondary sources is meant to help you understand that history is more than mere names and dates to be memorized. Bringing the past alive, each primary source was selected to immerse you in the historical moment, to raise intriguing questions, and to give you a sense of the real lives behind "inert facts."

Karen Dunn-Haley, General Editor
Stephen K. Davis, Editor
Matthew Schoenbachler, Editor
Wendy Wall, Editor
May 2013

CHAPTER 1

AMERICA'S GILDED AGE

From *Give Me Liberty! Seagull Fourth Edition*

Eric Foner

Credits: photo 1: Library of Congress; photo 2: Museum of the City of New York, The Jacob Riis Collection; photo 3: Courtesy of the author; photo 4: Library of Congress; photo 5: Smithsonian Institution, National Anthropological Archives; photo 6: Smithsonian Institution, National Anthropological Archives; photo 7: Thomas Pollock Anshutz, *The Ironworker's Noontime*, 1880, Fine Arts Museum of San Francisco, Gift of Mr. and Mrs. John D. Rockefeller 3rd, 1979.7.4; photo 8: Bettmann/Corbis.

Table 1: U.S. Bureau of the Census, *Historical Statistics of the United States* (Washington D.C., 1975), 134.

1

America's Gilded Age 1870–1890

FOCUS QUESTIONS

- What factors combined to make the United States a mature industrial society after the Civil War?
- How was the West transformed economically and socially in this period?
- Was the Gilded Age political system effective in meeting its goals?
- How did the economic development of the Gilded Age affect American freedom?
- How did reformers of the period approach the problems of an industrial society?

An immense crowd gathered in New York Harbor on October 28, 1886, for the dedication of *Liberty Enlightening the World*, a fitting symbol for a nation now wholly free. The idea for the statue originated in 1865 with Édouard de Laboulaye, a French educator and the author of several books on the United States, as a response to the assassination of Abraham Lincoln. The statue, de Laboulaye hoped, would celebrate both the historic friendship between France and the United States and the triumph, through the Union's victory in the Civil War, of American freedom. Measuring more than 150 feet from torch to toe and standing atop a huge pedestal, the edifice was the tallest man-made structure in the Western Hemisphere. It exceeded in height, newspapers noted with pride, the Colossus of Rhodes, a wonder of the ancient world.

In time, the Statue of Liberty, as it came to be called, would become Americans' most revered national icon. For over a century it has stood as a symbol of freedom. The statue has offered welcome to millions of immigrants—the "huddled masses yearning to breathe free" celebrated in a poem by Emma Lazarus inscribed on its base in 1903. In the years since its dedication, the statue's familiar image has been reproduced by folk artists in every conceivable medium and has been used by advertisers to promote everything from cigarettes and lawn mowers to war bonds. As its use by Chinese students demanding democracy in the Tiananmen Square protests of 1989 showed, it has become a powerful international symbol as well.

The year of the statue's dedication, 1886, also witnessed the "great upheaval," a wave of strikes and labor protests that touched every part of the nation. The 600 dignitaries (598 of them men) who gathered on what is now called Liberty Island for the dedication hoped the Statue of Liberty would inspire renewed devotion to the nation's political and economic system. But for all its grandeur, the statue could not conceal the deep social divisions and fears about the future of American freedom that accompanied the country's emergence as the world's leading industrial power. Nor did the celebrations address the crucial questions that moved to the center stage of American public life during the 1870s and 1880s and remained there for decades to come: What are the social conditions that make freedom possible, and what role should the national government play in defining and protecting the liberty of its citizens?

THE SECOND INDUSTRIAL REVOLUTION

Between the end of the Civil War and the early twentieth century, the United States underwent one of the most rapid and profound economic revolutions any country has ever experienced. There were numerous causes for this explosive economic growth. The country enjoyed abundant natural resources, a growing supply of labor, an expanding market for manufactured goods, and the availability of capital for investment. In addition, the federal government actively promoted industrial and agricultural development. It enacted high tariffs that protected American industry from foreign competition, granted land to railroad companies to encourage construction, and used the army to remove Indians from western lands desired by farmers and mining companies.

THE INDUSTRIAL ECONOMY

The rapid expansion of factory production, mining, and railroad construction in all parts of the country except the South signaled the transition from Lincoln's America—a world centered on the small farm and artisan workshop—to a mature industrial society. Americans of the late nineteenth century marveled at the triumph of the new economy. "One can hardly believe," wrote the philosopher John Dewey, "there has been a revolution in history so rapid, so extensive, so complete."

By 1913, the United States produced one-third of the world's industrial output—more than the total of Great Britain, France, and Germany combined. Half of all industrial workers now labored in plants with more than 250 employees. On the eve of the Civil War, the first industrial revolution, centered on the textile industry, had transformed New England into a center of manufacturing. But otherwise, the United States was still primarily an agricultural nation. By 1880, for the first time, the Census Bureau found a majority of the workforce engaged in non-farming jobs. The traditional dream of economic independence seemed obsolete. By 1890, two-thirds of Americans worked for wages, rather than owning a farm, business, or craft shop. Drawn to factories by the promise of employment, a new working class emerged in these years. Between 1870 and 1920, almost 11 million

CHRONOLOGY

1872	Crédit Mobiler scandal
1873	Mark Twain and Charles Dudley Warner's *Gilded Age*
1876	Battle of the Little Bighorn
1877	Reconstruction ends
	Munn v. Illinois
	Great Railroad Strike
1879	Henry George's *Progress and Poverty*
1883	Civil Service Act
	Railroads create time zones
	William Graham Sumner's *What Social Classes Owe to Each Other*
1884	*Elk v. Wilkins*
1886	Haymarket affair
	Wabash v. Illinois
1887	Interstate Commerce Commission created
	Dawes Act
1888	Edward Bellamy's *Looking Backward*
1890	Sherman Antitrust Act
	Jacob Riis's *How the Other Half Lives*
	Massacre at Wounded Knee
1894	Henry Demarest Lloyd's *Wealth against Commonwealth*
1895	*United States v. E. C. Knight Co.*
1896	Utah gains statehood
1899	Thorstein Veblen's *The Theory of the Leisure Class*
1905	*Lochner v. New York*

Americans moved from farm to city, and another 25 million immigrants arrived from overseas.

Most manufacturing now took place in industrial cities. New York, with its new skyscrapers and hundreds of thousands of workers in all sorts of manufacturing establishments, symbolized dynamic urban growth. After merging with Brooklyn in 1898, its population exceeded 3.4 million. The city financed industrialization and westward expansion, its banks and stock exchange funneling capital to railroads, mines, and factories. But the heartland of the second industrial revolution was the region around the Great Lakes, with its factories producing iron and steel, machinery, chemicals, and packaged foods. Pittsburgh had become the world's center of iron and steel manufacturing. Chicago, by 1900 the nation's second-largest city, with 1.7 million inhabitants, was home to factories producing steel and farm machinery and giant stockyards where cattle were processed into meat products for shipment east in refrigerated rail cars. Smaller industrial cities also proliferated, often concentrating on a single industry—cast-iron stoves in Troy, New York, silk in Paterson, New Jersey, furniture in Grand Rapids, Michigan.

Table 1 INDICATORS OF ECONOMIC CHANGE, 1870–1920

	1870	*1900*	*1920*
Farms (millions)	2.7	5.7	6.4
Land in farms (million acres)	408	841	956
Wheat grown (million bushels)	254	599	843
Employment (millions)	14	28.5	44.5
In manufacturing (millions)	2.5	5.9	11.2
Percentage in workforce[a]			
Agricultural	52		27
Industry[b]	29		44
Trade, service, administration[c]	20		27
Railroad track (thousands of miles)	53	258	407
Steel produced (thosuands of tons)	0.8	11.2	46
GNP (billions of dollars)	7.4	18.7	91.5
Per capita (in 1920 dollars)	371	707	920
Life expectancy at birth (years)	42	47	54

[a] Percentages are rounded and do not total 100.
[b] Includes manufacturing, transportation, mining, and construction.
[c] Includes trade, finance, and public administration.

RAILROADS AND THE NATIONAL MARKET

The railroad made possible what is sometimes called the "second industrial revolution." Spurred by private investment and massive grants of land and money by federal, state, and local governments, the number of miles of railroad track in the United States tripled between 1860 and 1880 and tripled again by 1920, opening vast new areas to commercial farming and creating a truly national market for manufactured goods. In 1886, the railroads adopted a standard national gauge (the distance separating the two tracks), making it possible for the first time for trains of one company to travel on any other company's track. By the 1890s, five transcontinental lines transported the products of western mines, farms, ranches, and forests to eastern markets and carried manufactured goods to the West. The railroads reorganized time itself. In 1883, the major companies divided the nation into the four time zones still in use today.

The growing population formed an ever-expanding market for the mass production, mass distribution, and mass marketing of goods, essential elements of a modern industrial economy. The spread of national brands like Ivory soap and Quaker Oats symbolized the continuing integration of the economy. So did the growth of national chains, most prominently the Atlantic and Pacific Tea Company, better known as A & P grocery stores. Based in Chicago, the national mail-order firms Montgomery Ward and Sears, Roebuck & Co. sold clothing, jewelry, farm equipment, and numerous other goods to rural families throughout the country.

THE SPIRIT OF INNOVATION

A remarkable series of technological innovations spurred rapid communication and economic growth. The opening of the Atlantic cable in 1866 made it possible to send electronic telegraph messages instantaneously between the United States and Europe. During the 1870s and 1880s, the telephone, typewriter, and handheld camera came into use.

Scientific breakthroughs poured forth from research laboratories in Menlo Park and Orange, New Jersey, created by the era's greatest inventor, Thomas A. Edison. During the course of his life, Edison helped to establish entirely new industries that transformed private life, public entertainment, and economic activity, including the phonograph, lightbulb, motion picture, and a system for generating and distributing electric power. He opened the first electric generating station in Manhattan in 1882 to provide power to streetcars, factories, and private homes, and he established, among other companies, the forerunner of General Electric to market electrical equipment. The spread of electricity was essential to industrial and urban growth, providing a more reliable and flexible source of power than water or steam. However, it was not Edison

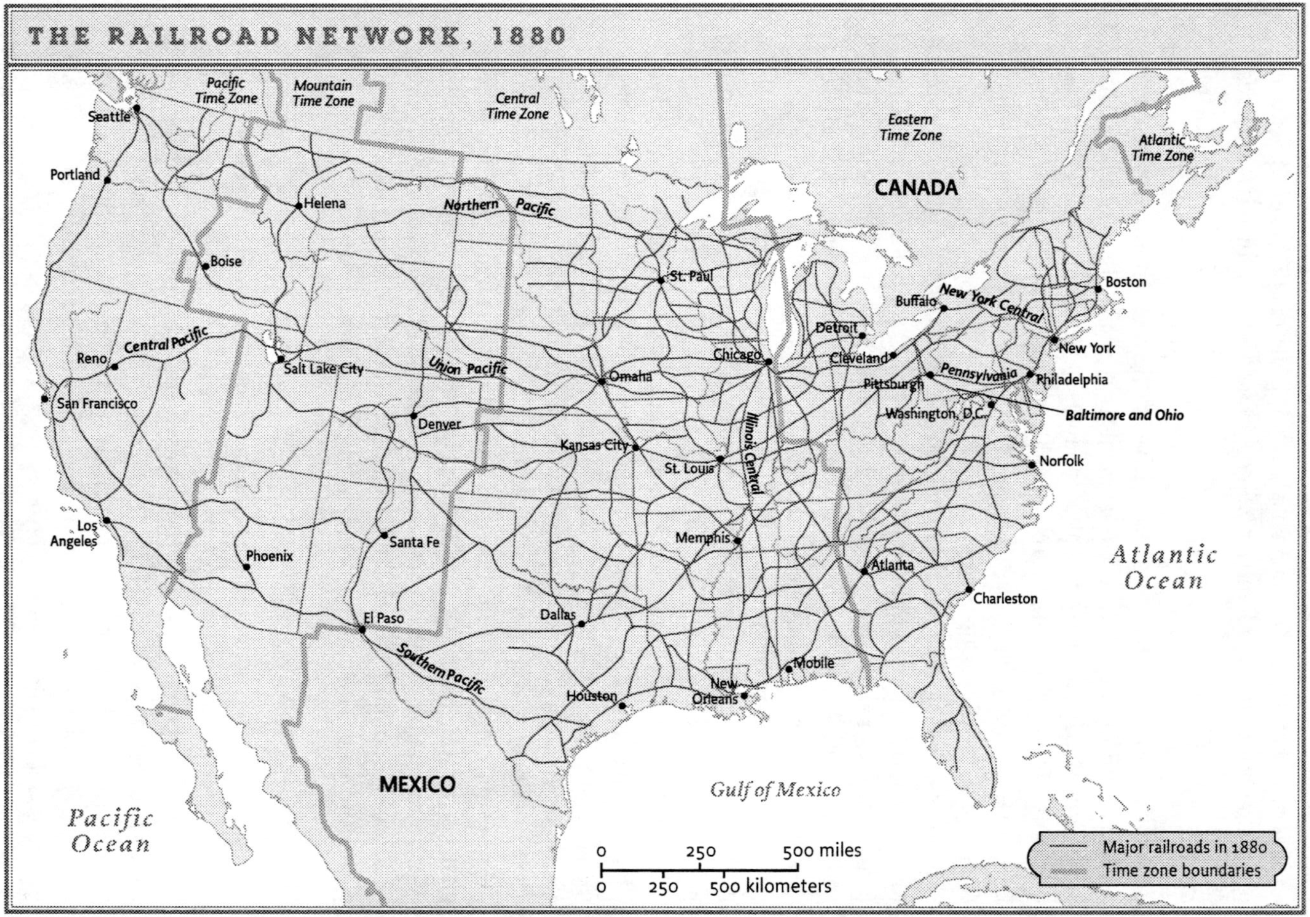

By 1880, the transnational rail network made possible the creation of a truly national market for goods.

but another inventor, Nikola Tesla, an ethnic Serb born in modern-day Croatia who emigrated to the United States at the age of twenty-eight, who developed an electric motor using the system of alternating current that overcame many of the challenges of using electricity for commercial and industrial purposes.

COMPETITION AND CONSOLIDATION

Economic growth was dramatic but highly volatile. The combination of a market flooded with goods and the federal monetary policies (discussed later) that removed money from the national economy led to a relentless fall in prices. The world economy suffered prolonged downturns in the 1870s and 1890s. Indeed, before the 1930s, the years from 1873 to 1897 were known throughout the world as the Great Depression.

Businesses engaged in ruthless competition. Railroads and other companies tried various means of bringing order to the chaotic marketplace. They formed "pools" that divided up markets between supposedly competing firms and fixed prices. They established "trusts"—legal devices whereby the affairs of several rival companies were managed by a single director. Such efforts to coordinate the economic activities of independent companies generally proved short-lived, disintegrating as individual firms continued their intense pursuit of profits.

To avoid cutthroat competition, more and more corporations battled to control entire industries. Many companies fell by the wayside or were gobbled up by others. The process of economic concentration culminated between 1897 and 1904, when some 4,000 firms vanished into larger corporations that served national markets and exercised an unprecedented degree of control over the marketplace. By the time the wave of mergers had been completed, giant corporations like U.S. Steel (created by financier J. P. Morgan in 1901 by combining eight large steel companies into the first billion-dollar economic enterprise), Standard Oil, and International Harvester (a manufacturer of agricultural machinery) dominated major parts of the economy.

THE RISE OF ANDREW CARNEGIE

In an era without personal or corporate income taxes, some business leaders accumulated enormous fortunes and economic power. Under the aggressive leadership of Thomas A. Scott, the Pennsylvania Railroad—for a time the nation's largest corporation—forged an economic empire that stretched across the continent and included coal mines and oceangoing steamships. With an army of professional managers to oversee its far-flung activities, the railroad pioneered modern techniques of business organization.

Another industrial giant was Andrew Carnegie, who emigrated with his family from his native Scotland at the age of thirteen and as a teenager worked in a Pennsylvania textile factory. During the depression that began in 1873, Carnegie set out to establish a "vertically integrated" steel company—that is, one that controlled every phase of the business from raw materials to transportation, manufacturing, and distribution. By the 1890s, he dominated the steel industry and had accumulated a fortune worth hundreds of millions of dollars. Carnegie's complex of steel factories at Homestead, Pennsylvania, were the most technologically advanced in the world.

Carnegie's father, an immigrant Scottish weaver who had taken part in popular efforts to open the British political system to working-class participation, had instilled in his son a commitment to democracy and social equality. From his mother, Carnegie learned that life was a ceaseless struggle in which one must strive to get ahead or sink beneath the waves. His life reflected the tension between these elements of his upbringing. Believing that the rich had a moral obligation to promote the advancement of society, Carnegie denounced the "worship of money" and distributed much of his wealth to various philanthropies, especially the creation of public libraries in towns throughout the country. But he ran his companies with a dictatorial hand. His factories operated nonstop, with two twelve-hour shifts every day of the year except the Fourth of July.

THE TRIUMPH OF JOHN D. ROCKEFELLER

If any single name became a byword for enormous wealth, it was John D. Rockefeller, who began his working career as a clerk for a Cleveland merchant and rose to dominate the oil industry. He drove out rival firms through cutthroat competition, arranging secret deals with railroad companies, and fixing prices and production quotas. Rockefeller began with "horizontal" expansion—buying out competing oil refineries. But like Carnegie, he soon established a vertically integrated monopoly, which controlled the drilling, refining, storage, and distribution of oil. By the 1880s, his Standard Oil Company controlled 90 percent of the nation's oil industry. Like Carnegie, Rockefeller gave much of his fortune away, establishing foundations to promote education and medical research. And like Carnegie, he bitterly fought his employees' efforts to organize unions.

These and other industrial leaders inspired among ordinary Americans a combination of awe, admiration, and hostility. Depending on one's point of view, they were "captains of industry," whose energy and vision pushed the economy forward, or "robber barons," who wielded power without any accountability in an unregulated marketplace. Most rose from modest backgrounds and seemed examples of how inventive genius and business sense enabled Americans to seize opportunities for success. But their dictatorial attitudes, unscrupulous methods, repressive labor policies, and exercise of

Next!, *a cartoon from the magazine Puck, September 7, 1904, depicts the Standard Oil Company as an octopus with tentacles wrapped around the copper, steel, and shipping industries, as well as a state house and Congress. One tentacle reaches for the White House.*

power without any democratic control led to fears that they were undermining political and economic freedom. Concentrated wealth degraded the political process, declared Henry Demarest Lloyd in *Wealth against Commonwealth* (1894), an exposé of how Rockefeller's Standard Oil Company made a mockery of economic competition and political democracy by manipulating the market and bribing legislators. "Liberty and monopoly," Lloyd concluded, "cannot live together."

WORKERS' FREEDOM IN AN INDUSTRIAL AGE

Striking as it was, the country's economic growth distributed its benefits very unevenly. For a minority of workers, the rapidly expanding industrial system created new forms of freedom. In some industries, skilled workers commanded high wages and exercised considerable control over the production process. A worker's economic independence now rested on technical skill rather than ownership of one's own shop and tools as in earlier times. What was known as "the miner's freedom" consisted of elaborate work rules that left skilled underground workers free of managerial supervision on the job. Through their union, skilled iron- and steelworkers fixed output quotas and controlled the training of apprentices in the technique of iron rolling. These workers often knew more about the details of production than their employers did.

Such "freedom," however, applied only to a tiny portion of the industrial labor force and had little bearing on the lives of the growing army of semi-skilled workers who tended machines in the new factories. For most workers, economic insecurity remained a basic fact of life. During the depressions of the 1870s and 1890s, millions of workers lost their jobs or were forced to accept reductions of pay. The "tramp" became a familiar figure on the social landscape as thousands of men took to the roads in search of work. Many industrial workers labored sixty-hour weeks with no pensions, compensation for injuries, or protections against unemployment. Although American workers received higher wages than their counterparts in Europe, they also experienced more dangerous working conditions. Between 1880 and 1900, an average of 35,000 workers perished each year in factory and mine accidents, the highest rate in the industrial world.

Much of the working class remained desperately poor and to survive needed income from all family members. In 1888, the *Chicago Times* published a series of articles by reporter Nell Cusack under the title "City Slave Girls," exposing wretched conditions among the growing number of women working for wages in the city's homes, factories, and sweatshops. The articles unleashed a flood of letters to the editor from women workers. One woman singled out domestic service—still the largest employment category for women—as "a slave's life," with "long hours, late and early, seven days in the week, bossed and ordered about as before the war."

SUNSHINE AND SHADOW: INCREASING WEALTH AND POVERTY

At the other end of the economic spectrum, the era witnessed an unprecedented accumulation of wealth. Class divisions became more and more visible. In frontier days, all classes in San Francisco, for example, lived near the waterfront. In the late nineteenth century, upper-class families built mansions on Nob Hill and Van Ness Avenue (known as "millionaire's row"). In eastern cities as well, the rich increasingly resided in their own exclusive neighborhoods and vacationed among members of their own class at exclusive resorts like Newport, Rhode Island. The growing urban middle class of professionals, office workers, and small businessmen moved to new urban and suburban neighborhoods linked to central business districts by streetcars and commuter railways. "Passion for money," wrote the novelist Edith Wharton in *The House of Mirth* (1905), dominated society. Wharton's book traced the difficulties of Lily Bart, a young woman of modest means pressured by her mother and New York high society to "barter" her beauty for marriage to a rich husband in a world where "to be poor . . . amounted to disgrace."

By 1890, the richest 1 percent of Americans received the same total income as the bottom half of the population and owned more property than the

Baxter Street Court, *1890, one of numerous photographs by Jacob Riis depicting living conditions in New York City's slums.*

remaining 99 percent. Many of the wealthiest Americans consciously pursued an aristocratic lifestyle, building palatial homes, attending exclusive social clubs, schools, and colleges, holding fancy-dress balls, and marrying into each other's families. In 1899, the economist and social historian Thorstein Veblen published *The Theory of the Leisure Class*, a devastating critique of an upper-class culture focused on "conspicuous consumption"—that is, spending money not on needed or even desired goods, but simply to demonstrate the possession of wealth. One of the era's most widely publicized spectacles was an elaborate costume ball organized in 1897 by Mrs. Bradley Martin, the daughter of a New York railroad financier. The theme was the royal court of prerevolutionary France. The Waldorf-Astoria Hotel was decorated to look like the palace of Versailles, the guests wore the dress of the French nobility, and the hostess bedecked herself with the actual jewels of Queen Marie Antoinette.

Not that far from the Waldorf, much of the working class lived in desperate conditions. Matthew Smith's 1868 best-seller *Sunshine and Shadow in New York* opened with an engraving that contrasted department store magnate Alexander T. Stewart's two-million-dollar mansion with housing in the city's slums. Two decades later, Jacob Riis, in *How the Other Half Lives* (1890), offered a shocking account of living conditions among the urban poor, complete with photographs of apartments in dark, airless, overcrowded tenement houses.

THE TRANSFORMATION OF THE WEST

Nowhere did capitalism penetrate more rapidly or dramatically than in the trans-Mississippi West, whose "vast, trackless spaces," as the poet Walt Whitman called them, were now absorbed into the expanding economy. At the close of the Civil War, the frontier of continuous white settlement did not extend very far beyond the Mississippi River. To the west lay millions of acres of fertile and mineral-rich land roamed by giant herds of buffalo whose meat and hides provided food, clothing, and shelter for a population of more than 250,000 Indians.

In 1893, the historian Frederick Jackson Turner gave a celebrated lecture, "The Significance of the Frontier in American History," in which he argued that on the western frontier the distinctive qualities of American culture were forged: individual freedom, political democracy, and economic mobility. The West, he added, acted as a "safety valve," drawing off those dissatisfied with their situation in the East and therefore counteracting the threat of social unrest. Turner's was one of the most influential interpretations of American history ever developed. But his lecture summarized attitudes toward the West that had been widely shared among Americans long before 1893. Ever since the beginning of colonial settlement in British North America, the West—a region whose definition shifted as the population expanded—had been seen as a place of opportunity for those seeking to improve their condition in life.

Many Americans did indeed experience the westward movement in the way Turner described it. From farmers moving into Ohio, Indiana, and Illinois in the decades after the American Revolution to prospectors who struck it rich in the California gold rush of the mid-nineteenth century, millions of Americans and immigrants from abroad found in the westward movement a path to economic opportunity. But Turner seemed to portray the West as an empty space before the coming of white settlers. In fact, of course, it was already inhabited by Native Americans, whose dispossession was essential to the opening of land for settlement by others. Moreover, the West was hardly a uniform paradise of small, independent farmers. Beginning in the eighteenth century, for example, California was the site of forced Indian labor on missions established by members of religious orders, a system that helped establish the pattern of large agricultural landholdings in that region. Landlords, railroads, and mining companies in the West also utilized Mexican migrant and indentured labor, Chinese working on long-term contracts, and, until the end of the Civil War, African-American slaves.

A DIVERSE REGION

The West, of course, was hardly a single area. West of the Mississippi River lay a variety of regions, all marked by remarkable physical beauty—the "vast, trackless" Great Plains, the Rocky Mountains, the desert of the Southwest, the Sierra Nevada, and the valleys and coastline of California and the Pacific Northwest. It would take many decades before individual settlers and corporate business enterprises penetrated all these areas. But the process was far advanced by the end of the nineteenth century.

The political and economic incorporation of the American West was part of a global process. In many parts of the world, indigenous inhabitants—the

Mapuche in Chile, the Zulu in South Africa, aboriginal peoples in Australia, American Indians—were pushed aside (often after fierce resistance) as centralizing governments brought large interior regions under their control. In the United States, the incorporation of the West required the active intervention of the federal government, which acquired Indian land by war and treaty, administered land sales, regulated territorial politics, and distributed land and money to farmers, railroads, and mining companies.

In the twentieth century, the construction of federally financed irrigation systems and dams would open large areas to commercial farming. Ironically, the West would become known (not least to its own inhabitants) as a place of rugged individualism and sturdy independence. But without active governmental assistance, the region could never have been settled and developed.

FARMING ON THE MIDDLE BORDER

Even as sporadic Indian wars raged, settlers poured into the West. Territorial and state governments eager for population, and railroad companies anxious to sell land they had acquired from the government, flooded European countries and eastern cities with promotional literature promising easy access to land. More land came into cultivation in the thirty years after the Civil War than in the previous two and a half centuries of American history. Hundreds of thousands of families acquired farms under the Homestead Act, and even more purchased land from speculators and from railroad companies that had been granted immense tracts of public land by the federal government. A new agricultural empire producing wheat and corn for national and international markets arose on the Middle Border (Minnesota, the Dakotas, Nebraska, and Kansas), whose population rose from 300,000 in 1860 to 5 million in 1900. The farmers were a diverse group, including native-born easterners, blacks escaping the post-Reconstruction South, and immigrants from Canada, Germany, Scandinavia, and Great Britain. Although ethnic diversity is generally associated with eastern cities, in the late nineteenth century the most multicultural state in the Union was North Dakota.

Despite the promises of promotional pamphlets, farming on the Great Plains was not an easy task. Difficulties came in many forms—from the poisonous rattlesnakes that lived in the tall prairie grass to the blizzards and droughts that periodically afflicted the region. Much of the burden fell on women. Farm families generally invested in the kinds of labor-saving machinery that would bring in cash, not machines that would ease women's burdens in the household (like the backbreaking task of doing laundry). While husbands and sons tended to devote their labor to cash crops, farm wives cared for animals, grew crops for food, and cooked and cleaned. A farm woman in Arizona described her morning chores in her diary: "Get up, turn out my chickens, draw a pail of water . . . make a fire, put potatoes to cook, brush and sweep half inch of dust off floor, feed three litters of chickens, then mix biscuits, get breakfast, milk, besides work in the house, and this morning had to go half mile after calves." On far-flung homesteads, many miles from schools, medical care, and sources of entertainment, farm families suffered from loneliness and isolation—a problem especially severe for women when their husbands left, sometimes for weeks at a time, to market their crops.

BONANZA FARMS

John Wesley Powell, the explorer and geologist who surveyed the Middle Border in the 1870s, warned that because of the region's arid land and limited rainfall, development there required large-scale irrigation projects. The model of family farming envisioned by the Homestead Act of 1862 could not apply: no single family could do all the work required on irrigated farms—only cooperative, communal farming could succeed, Powell maintained.

Despite the emergence of a few "bonanza farms" that covered thousands of acres and employed large numbers of agricultural wage workers, family farms still dominated the trans-Mississippi West. Even small farmers, however, became increasingly oriented to national and international markets,

California Harvest Scene—Dr. Glenn's Farm in Colusa County, *an engraving from 1876, illustrates the large scale of operations and heavy investment in machinery common on western "bonanza" farms.*

specializing in the production of single crops for sale in faraway places. At the same time, railroads brought factory-made goods to rural people, replacing items previously produced in farmers' homes. Farm families became more and more dependent on loans to purchase land, machinery, and industrial products, and more and more vulnerable to the ups and downs of prices for agricultural goods in the world market. Agriculture reflected how the international economy was becoming more integrated. The combination of economic depressions and expanding agricultural production in places like Argentina, Australia, and the American West pushed prices of farm products steadily downward. From Italy and Ireland to China, India, and the American South, small farmers throughout the world suffered severe difficulties in the last quarter of the nineteenth century. Many joined the migration to cities within their countries or the increasing international migration of labor.

The future of western farming ultimately lay with giant agricultural enterprises relying heavily on irrigation, chemicals, and machinery—investments far beyond the means of family farmers. A preview of the agricultural future was already evident in California, where, as far back as Spanish and Mexican days, landownership had been concentrated in large units. In the late nineteenth century, California's giant fruit and vegetable farms, owned by corporations like the Southern Pacific Railroad, were tilled not by agricultural laborers who could expect to acquire land of their own, but by migrant laborers from China, the Philippines, Japan, and Mexico, who tramped from place to place following the ripening crops.

THE COWBOY AND THE CORPORATE WEST

The two decades following the Civil War also witnessed the golden age of the cattle kingdom. The Kansas Pacific Railroad's stations at Abilene, Dodge City, and Wichita, Kansas, became destinations for the fabled drives of millions of cattle from Texas. A collection of white, Mexican, and black men who conducted the cattle drives, the cowboys became symbols of a life of freedom on the open range. Their exploits would later serve as the theme of many a Hollywood movie, and their clothing inspired fashions that remain popular today. But there was nothing romantic about the life of the cowboys, most of whom were low-paid wage workers. (Texas cowboys even went on strike for higher pay in 1883.) The days of the long-distance cattle drive ended in the mid-1880s, as farmers enclosed more and more of the open range with barbed-wire fences, making it difficult to graze cattle on the grasslands of the Great Plains, and two terrible winters destroyed millions of cattle. When the industry recuperated, it was reorganized in large, enclosed ranches close to rail connections.

The West was more than a farming empire. By 1890, a higher percentage of its population lived in cities than was the case in other regions. The economic focus of California's economy remained San Francisco, a major manufacturing and trading center. The explosive growth of southern California began in the 1880s, first with tourism, heavily promoted by railroad companies, followed by the discovery of oil in Los Angeles in 1892. Large corporate enterprises appeared throughout the West. The lumber industry, dominated by small-scale producers in 1860, came under the control of corporations that acquired large tracts of forest and employed armies of loggers. Western mining, from Michigan iron ore and copper to gold and silver in California, Nevada, and Colorado, fell under the sway of companies that mobilized eastern and European investment to introduce advanced technology. Gold and silver rushes took place in the Dakotas in 1876, Idaho in 1883, and Alaska at the end of the century. But as in California after 1848, the independent prospector working a surface mine with his pick and shovel quickly gave way to deep-shaft corporate mining employing wage workers.

A similar process occurred in New Mexico, where traditional life based on sheep farming on land owned in common by Mexican villagers had continued more or less unchanged after the United States acquired the area in the Mexican War. The existence of these Spanish and Mexican communal landholdings may have influenced John Wesley Powell's recommendations concerning communal farming. Railroads reached the area in the 1870s, bringing with them eastern mining companies and commercial ranchers and farmers. Because courts only recognized Mexican-era land titles to individual plots of land, communal landholdings were increasingly made available for sale to newcomers. By 1880, three-quarters of New Mexico's sheep belonged to just twenty families. Unable to continue as sheep raisers, more and more Hispanic residents went to work for the new mines and railroads.

CONFLICT ON THE MORMON FRONTIER

The Mormons had moved to the Great Salt Lake Valley in the 1840s, hoping to practice their religion free of the persecution that they had encountered in the East. They envisioned their community in Utah as the foundation of a great empire they called Deseret. Given the widespread unpopularity of Mormon polygamy and the close connection of church and state in Mormon theology, conflict with the both the federal government and the growing numbers of non-Mormons moving west became inevitable. In 1857, after receiving reports that the work of federal judges in Utah was being obstructed by the territorial governor, the Mormon leader Brigham Young, President James Buchanan removed Young and appointed a non-Mormon to replace him. Young refused to comply, and federal troops entered the Salt Lake Valley, where they remained until the beginning of the Civil War. During this time of tension, a group of Mormons attacked a wagon train of non-Mormon settlers

VOICES OF FREEDOM

From Ira Steward, "A Second Declaration of Independence" (1879)

At a Fourth of July celebration in Chicago in 1879, Ira Steward, the most prominent labor leader associated with the movement for the eight-hour day, invoked the legacy of the Declaration of Independence and the abolition of slavery during the Civil War to discuss labor's grievances.

Resolved, That the practical question for an American Fourth of July is not between freedom and slavery, but between wealth and poverty. For if it is true that laborers ought to have as little as possible of the wealth they produce, South Carolina slaveholders were right and the Massachusetts abolitionists were wrong. Because, when the working classes are denied everything but the barest necessities of life, they have no decent use for liberty. . . .

Slavery is . . . the child of poverty, instead of poverty the child of slavery: and freedom is the child of wealth, instead of wealth the child of freedom. The only road, therefore, to universal freedom is the road that leads to universal wealth.

Resolved, That while the Fourth of July was heralded a hundred years ago in the name of Liberty, we now herald this day in behalf of the great economic measure of Eight Hours, or shorter day's work for wageworkers everywhere . . . because more leisure, rest and thought will cultivate habits, customs, and expenditures that mean higher wages: and the world's highest paid laborers now furnish each other with vastly more occupations or days' work than the lowest paid workers can give to one another. . . . [And] if the worker's power to buy increases with his power to do, granaries and warehouses will empty their pockets, and farms and factories fill up with producers. . . .

And we call to the workers of the whole civilized world, especially those of France, Germany, and Great Britain, to join hands with the laborers of the United States in this mighty movement. . . .

On the . . . issue of eight hours, therefore, or less hours, we join hands with all, regardless of politics, nationality, color, religion, or sex; knowing no friends or foes except as they aid or oppose this long-postponed and world-wide movement.

And for the soundness of our political economy, as well as the rectitude of our intentions, we confidently and gladly appeal to the wiser statesmanship of the civilized world.

From Andrew Carnegie, "Wealth" (1889)

One of the richest men in Gilded Age America, Andrew Carnegie promoted what he called the Gospel of Wealth, the idea that those who accumulated money had an obligation to use it to promote the advancement of society. He explained his outlook in this article in the North *American Review*, one of the era's most prominent magazines.

The problem of our age is the proper administration of wealth, so that the ties of brotherhood may still bind together the rich and poor in harmonious relationship. The conditions of human life have not only been changed, but revolutionized, within the past few hundred years. In former days there was little difference between the dwelling, dress, food, and environment of the chief and those of his retainers. The Indians are to-day where civilized man then was. When visiting the Sioux, I was led to the wigwam of the chief. It was just like the others in external appearance, and even within the difference was trifling between it and those of the poorest of his braves. The contrast between the palace of the millionaire and the cottage of the laborer with us to-day measures the change which has come with civilization.

This change, however, is not to be deplored, but welcomed as highly beneficial. It is essential for the progress of the race, that the houses of some should be homes for all that is highest and best in literature and the arts, and for all the refinements of civilization, rather than that none should be so.

In bestowing charity, the main consideration should be to help those who will help themselves. He is the only true reformer who is as careful and as anxious not to aid the unworthy as he is to aid the worthy, and, perhaps, even more so, for in alms-giving more injury is probably done by rewarding vice than by relieving virtue.

The best means of benefiting the community is to place within its reach the ladders upon which the aspiring can rise—parks, and means of recreation, by which men are helped in body and mind; works of art, certain to give pleasure and improve the public taste, and public institutions of various kinds, which will improve the general condition of the people;—in this manner returning their surplus wealth to the mass of their fellows in the forms best calculated to do them lasting good.

Thus is the problem of Rich and Poor to be solved. The laws of accumulation will be left free; the laws of distribution free. Individualism will continue, but the millionaire will be but a trustee for the poor.

Such, in my opinion, is the true Gospel concerning Wealth.

QUESTIONS

1. Why does Ira Steward appeal to other countries for assistance and understanding?

2. Why does Carnegie think it is better to build public institutions than to give charity to the poor?

3. How do the views of Steward and Carnegie about how the economy should operate compare?

traveling through Utah and intending to settle in California. What came to be called the Mountain Meadows Massacre resulted in the death of all the adults and older children in the wagon train—over 100 persons. Only a handful of young children survived. Nearly twenty years later, one leader of the assault was convicted of murder and executed.

After the Civil War, sporadic conflict continued between Mormon families, who spread out across the Southwest, and Native Americans as well as other settlers. The issues were the same as in other parts of the West—white settlers encroaching on Indian land, conflicts between farmers and ranchers over water and other resources—but were exacerbated by powerful cultural differences (Mormons, for example, saw the freewheeling lifestyle of cowboys as the embodiment of immorality). Mormon leaders sought to avoid further antagonizing the federal government. In the 1880s, Utah banned the practice of polygamy, a prohibition written into the state constitution as a requirement before Utah gained admission as a state in 1896. (Polygamy persists to this day among some fundamentalist Mormons living in isolated areas.)

THE SUBJUGATION OF THE PLAINS INDIANS

The incorporation of the West into the national economy spelled the doom of the Plains Indians and their world. Their lives had already undergone profound transformations. In the eighteenth century, the spread of horses, originally introduced by the Spanish, led to a wholesale shift from farming and hunting on foot to mounted hunting of buffalo. New Indian groups migrated to the Great Plains to take advantage of the horse, coalescing into the great tribes of the nineteenth century—the Cheyenne, Comanche, Crow, Kiowa, and Sioux. Persistent warfare took place between the more established tribes and newcomers, including Indians removed from the East, who sought access to their hunting grounds.

Most migrants on the Oregon and California Trails before the Civil War encountered little hostility from Indians, often trading with them for food and supplies. But as settlers encroached on Indian lands, bloody conflict between the army and Plains tribes began in the 1850s and continued for decades.

In 1869, President Ulysses S. Grant announced a new "peace policy" in the West, but warfare soon resumed. Drawing on methods used to defeat the Confederacy, Civil War generals like Philip H. Sheridan set out to destroy the foundations of the Indian economy—villages, horses, and especially the buffalo. Hunting by mounted Indians had already reduced the buffalo population—estimated at 30 million in 1800—but it was army campaigns and the depredations of hunters seeking buffalo hides that rendered the vast herds all but extinct. By 1886, an expedition from the Smithsonian Institution in Washington had difficulty finding twenty-five "good specimens." "A cold wind blew across the prairie when the last buffalo fell," said the Sioux leader Sitting Bull, "a death-wind for my people."

"LET ME BE A FREE MAN"

The army's relentless attacks broke the power of one tribe after another. In 1877, troops commanded by former Freedmen's Bureau commissioner O. O. Howard pursued the Nez Percé Indians on a 1,700-mile chase across the Far West. The Nez Percé (whose name was given them by Lewis and Clark in 1805 and means "pierced noses" in French) were seeking to escape to Canada after fights with settlers who had encroached on tribal lands in Oregon and Idaho. After four months, Howard forced the Indians to surrender, and they were removed to Oklahoma.

Two years later, the Nez Percé leader, Chief Joseph, delivered a speech in Washington to a distinguished audience that included President Rutherford B. Hayes. Condemning the policy of confining Indians to reservations, Joseph adopted the language of freedom and equal rights before the law so powerfully reinforced by the Civil War and Reconstruction. "Treat all men alike," he pleaded. "Give them the same law. . . . Let me be a free man—free to travel, free to stop, free to work, free to trade where I choose, free to . . . think and talk and act for myself." The government eventually transported the surviving Nez Percé to another reservation in Washington Territory. Until his death in 1904, Joseph would unsuccessfully petition successive presidents for his people's right to return to their beloved Oregon homeland.

Indians occasionally managed to inflict costly delay and even defeat on army units. The most famous Indian victory took place in June 1876 at Little Bighorn, when General George A. Custer and his entire command of 250 men perished. The Sioux and Cheyenne warriors, led by Sitting Bull and Crazy Horse, were defending tribal land in the Black Hills of the Dakota Territory. Reserved for them in an 1868 treaty "for as long as the grass shall grow," their lands had been invaded by whites after the discovery of gold. In the Southwest, Cochise, Geronimo, and other leaders of the Apache, who had been relocated by the government a number

Sitting Bull, probably the best-known Native American of the late nineteenth century, in a photograph from 1885.

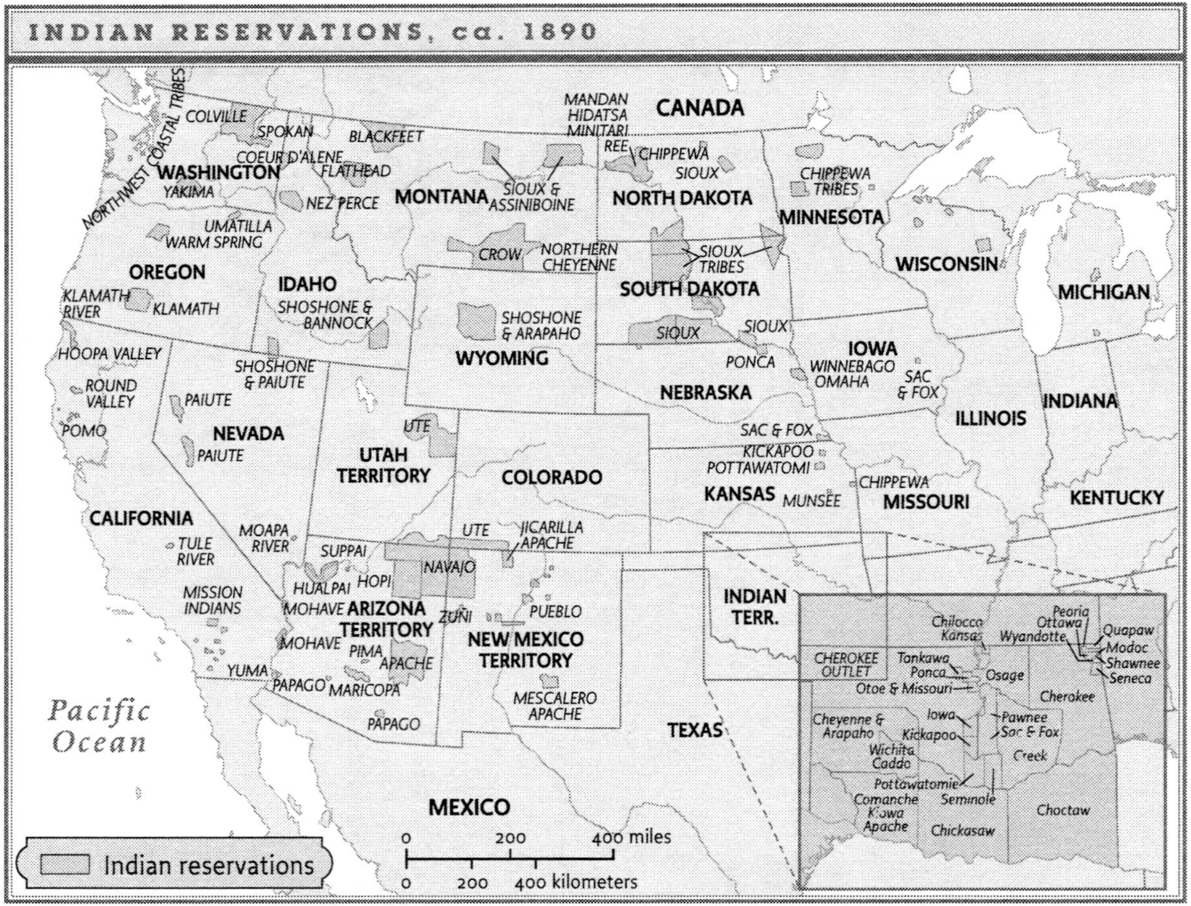

By 1890, the vast majority of the remaining Indian population had been removed to reservations scattered across the western states.

of times, led bands that crossed and recrossed the border with Mexico, evading the army and occasionally killing civilians. They would not surrender until the mid-1880s.

Another casualty was the Comanche empire, centered in modern-day New Mexico and Colorado. Beginning in the mid-eighteenth century, the Comanche dominated much of the Great Plains and Southwest. The Comanche had subordinated local Indian groups to their power, imposed a toll on trade routes like the Santa Fe Trail, and dealt for a time as an equal with the Spanish, French, and American governments. Their power was not finally broken until the 1870s.

These events delayed only temporarily the onward march of white soldiers, settlers, and prospectors. Between the end of the Civil War and 1890, eight new western states entered the Union (Nebraska, Colorado, North and South Dakota, Montana, Washington, Idaho, and Wyoming). Railroads now crisscrossed the Great Plains, farmers and cattlemen exploited land formerly owned by Indians, and the Plains tribes had been concentrated on reservations, where they lived in poverty, preyed upon by unscrupulous traders and government agents. A strong opponent of the reservation system, Sitting Bull escaped to Canada after the army defeated the Sioux, but he returned and was imprisoned in 1881. He was released in 1883 and for a time became part of Buffalo Bill's Wild West Show, a popular traveling extravaganza complete with mock Indian attacks and shooting and riding exhibitions. For most Americans, Indians were now simply objects of curiosity or entertainment.

REMAKING INDIAN LIFE

"The life my people want is a life of freedom," Sitting Bull declared. The Indian idea of freedom, however, which centered on preserving their cultural and political autonomy and control of ancestral lands, conflicted with the interests and values of most white Americans. Nearly all officials believed that the federal government should persuade or force the Plains Indians to surrender most of their land and to exchange their religion, communal property, nomadic way of life, and gender relations for Christian worship, private ownership, and small farming on reservations with men tilling the fields and women working in the home.

In 1871, Congress eliminated the treaty system that dated back to the revolutionary era, by which the federal government negotiated agreements with Indians as if they were independent nations. This step was supported by railroad companies that found tribal sovereignty an obstacle to construction and by Republicans who believed that it contradicted the national unity born of the Civil War. The federal government pressed forward with its assault on

Boys from the Lakota tribe on their arrival (left) and during their stay at Carlisle, a boarding school that aimed to "civilize" Indians, by J. N. Choate, a local photographer.

Indian culture. The Bureau of Indian Affairs established boarding schools where Indian children, removed from the "negative" influences of their parents and tribes, were dressed in non-Indian clothes, given new names, and educated in white ways.

THE DAWES ACT

The crucial step in attacking "tribalism" came in 1887 with the passage of the Dawes Act, named for Senator Henry L. Dawes of Massachusetts, chair of the Senate's Indian Affairs Committee. The Act broke up the land of nearly all tribes into small parcels to be distributed to Indian families, with the remainder auctioned off to white purchasers. Indians who accepted the farms and "adopted the habits of civilized life" would become full-fledged American citizens. The policy proved to be a disaster, leading to the loss of much tribal land and the erosion of Indian cultural traditions. Whites, however, benefited enormously. When the government made 2 million acres of Indian land available in Oklahoma, 50,000 white settlers poured into the territory to claim farms on the single day of April 22, 1889. Further land rushes followed in the 1890s. In the half century after the passage of the Dawes Act, Indians lost 86 million of the 138 million acres of land in their possession in 1887.

INDIAN CITIZENSHIP

Many laws and treaties in the nineteenth century offered Indians the right to become an American citizen if they left the tribal setting and assimilated into American society. But tribal identity was the one thing nearly every Indian wished to maintain, and very few took advantage of these offers. Thus, few Indians were recognized as American citizens. Western courts ruled that the citizenship rights guaranteed by the Fourteenth and Fifteenth Amendments did not apply to them, and in *Elk v. Wilkins* (1884) the U.S. Supreme Court agreed, even though John Elk had left his tribe in Oklahoma and lived among white settlers in Nebraska. The Court questioned whether any Indian had achieved the degree of "civilization" required of American citizens.

By 1900, roughly 53,000 Indians had become American citizens by accepting land allotments under the Dawes Act. The following year, Congress granted citizenship to 100,000 residents of Indian Territory (in present-day Oklahoma). The remainder would have to wait until 1919 (for those who fought in World War I) and 1924, when Congress made all Indians American citizens.

THE GHOST DANCE AND WOUNDED KNEE

Some Indians sought solace in the Ghost Dance, a religious revitalization campaign reminiscent of the pan-Indian movements led by earlier prophets like Neolin and Tenskwatawa. Its leaders foretold a day when whites disappear, the buffalo would return, and Indians could once again practice their ancestral customs "free from misery, death, and disease." Large numbers of Indians gathered for days of singing, dancing, and religious observances. Fearing a general uprising, the government sent troops to the reservations. On December 29, 1890, soldiers opened fire on Ghost Dancers encamped near Wounded Knee Creek in South Dakota, killing between 150 and 200 Indians, mostly women and children.

The events at Wounded Knee also arose from immediate circumstances. During the 1890 congressional elections, Democrats had accused Republicans of mismanaging Indian affairs and Republicans responded that Indians were barbarians who posed a danger to white settlers. The Republican administration of Benjamin Harrison had sent some 9,000 troops into South Dakota—the largest military mobilization since the Civil War—to deal with a nonexistent Indian "uprising." The Wounded Knee massacre was widely applauded in the press. An Army Court of Inquiry essentially exonerated the troops and their commander, and twenty soldiers were later awarded the Medal of Honor, a recognition of exceptional heroism in battle, for their actions at Wounded Knee. Like federal efforts to exert control over the Mormons in Utah, the suppression of the Ghost Dance revealed the limits on Americans' efforts to seek in the West the freedom to practice nonmainstream religions.

The Wounded Knee massacre marked the end of four centuries of armed conflict between the continent's native population and European settlers and their descendants. By 1900, the Indian population had fallen to 250,000, the lowest point in American history. A children's book about Indians published around this time stated flatly, "The Indian pictured in these pages no longer exists." Yet despite everything, Indians survived, and in the twentieth century their numbers once again would begin to grow.

SETTLER SOCIETIES AND GLOBAL WESTS

The conquest of the American West was part of a global process whereby settlers moved boldly into the interior of regions in temperate climates around the world, bringing their familiar crops and livestock and establishing mining and other industries. Countries such as Argentina, Australia, Canada, and New Zealand, as well as the United States, are often called "settler societies," because immigrants from overseas quickly outnumbered and displaced the original inhabitants—unlike in India and most parts of colonial Africa, where fewer Europeans ventured and those who did relied on the labor of the indigenous inhabitants.

In the late nineteenth century, even as the population of the American West grew dramatically, the Argentine military occupied the Pampas, opening a vast area for cattle raising and wheat cultivation. In 1885, Canada marked the completion of its first transcontinental railroad, although the more severe climate limited the number of western settlers to a much smaller population than in the American West (and as a result, the displacement of Indians did not produce as much conflict and bloodshed). In many settler societies, native peoples were subjected to cultural reconstruction similar to policies in the United States. In Australia, the government gathered the Aboriginal populations—their numbers devastated by disease—in "reserves" reminiscent of American Indian reservations. Australia went further than the United States in the forced assimilation of surviving Aboriginal peoples. The government removed large numbers of children from their families to be adopted by whites—a policy only abandoned in the 1970s and for which the prime minister formally apologized in 2008 in a national moment of reconciliation called Sorry Day.

POLITICS IN A GILDED AGE

The era from 1870 to 1890 is the only period of American history commonly known by a derogatory name—the Gilded Age, after the title of an 1873 novel by Mark Twain and Charles Dudley Warner. "Gilded" means covered with a layer of gold, but it also suggests that the glittering surface covers a core of little real value and is therefore deceptive. Twain and Warner were referring not only to the remarkable expansion of the economy in this period but also to the corruption caused by corporate dominance of politics and to the oppressive treatment of those left behind in the scramble for wealth. "Get rich, dishonestly if we can, honestly if we must," was the era's slogan, according to *The Gilded Age.*

THE CORRUPTION OF POLITICS

As they had earlier in the nineteenth century, Americans during the Gilded Age saw their nation as an island of political democracy in a world still dominated by undemocratic governments. In Europe, only France and Switzerland enjoyed universal male suffrage. Even in Britain, which prided itself on its tradition of political liberty, most of the working class could not vote until the passage of the Reform Act of 1884. As late as the eve of World War I, the House of Lords, an unelected body of hereditary aristocrats, could veto any legislation passed by the House of Commons.

Nonetheless, the power of the new corporations, seemingly immune to democratic control, raised disturbing questions for the American understanding of political freedom as popular self-government. Political corruption was rife. "The galleries and lobbies of every legislature," observed an Illinois Republican leader, "are thronged with men seeking to procure an advantage" for one corporation or another. In Pennsylvania's legislature, the "third house" of railroad lobbyists supposedly exerted as much influence as the elected chambers. In the West, many lawmakers held stock or directorships in lumber companies and railroads that received public aid.

Urban politics fell under the sway of corrupt political machines like New York's Tweed Ring, which plundered the city of tens of millions of dollars. "Boss" William M. Tweed's organization reached into every neighborhood. He forged close ties with railroad men and labor unions, and he won support from the city's immigrant poor by fashioning a kind of private welfare system that provided food, fuel, and jobs in hard times. A combination of political reformers and businessmen tired of paying tribute to the ring ousted Tweed in the early 1870s, although he remained popular among the city's poor, who considered him an urban Robin Hood.

At the national level, many lawmakers supported bills aiding companies in which they had invested money or from which they received stock or salaries. The most notorious example of corruption came to light during Grant's presidency. This was Crédit Mobilier, a corporation formed by an inner ring of Union Pacific Railroad stockholders to oversee the line's government-assisted construction. Essentially, it enabled the participants to sign contracts with themselves, at an exorbitant profit, to build the new line. The arrangement was protected by the distribution of stock to influential politicians, including Speaker of the House Schuyler Colfax, who was elected vice president in 1868. In another example of corruption, the Whiskey Ring of the Grant administration united Republican officials, tax collectors, and whiskey manufacturers in a massive scheme that defrauded the federal government of millions of tax dollars.

THE POLITICS OF DEAD CENTER

In national elections, party politics bore the powerful imprint of the Civil War. Republicans controlled the industrial North and Midwest and the agrarian West and were particularly strong among members of revivalist churches, Protestant immigrants, and blacks. Organizations of Union veterans formed a bulwark of Republican support. Every Republican candidate for president from 1868 to 1900 had fought in the Union army. (In the 1880 campaign, all four candidates—Republican James A. Garfield, Democrat Winfield Scott Hancock, Prohibitionist Neal Dow, and James B. Weaver of the Greenback-Labor Party, discussed later—had been Union generals during the war.) By 1893, a lavish system of pensions for Union soldiers and their widows and children consumed more than 40 percent of the federal budget. Democrats, after 1877, dominated the South and did well among Catholic voters, especially Irish-Americans, in the nation's cities.

The parties were closely divided. In three of the five presidential elections between 1876 and 1892, the margin separating the major candidates was less than 1 percent of the popular vote. Twice, in 1876 and 1888, the candidate with an electoral-college majority trailed in the popular vote. The congressional elections of 1874, when Democrats won control of the House of Representatives, ushered in two decades of political stalemate. A succession of one-term presidencies followed: Rutherford B. Hayes (elected in 1876), James A. Garfield (succeeded, after his assassination in 1881, by Chester A. Arthur), Grover Cleveland in 1884, Benjamin Harrison in 1888, and Cleveland, elected for the second time, in 1892. Only for brief periods did the same party control the White House and both houses of Congress. More than once, Congress found itself paralyzed as important bills shuttled back and forth between the House and Senate, and special sessions to complete legislation became necessary. Gilded Age presidents made little effort to mobilize public opinion or exert executive leadership. Their staffs were quite small. Grover Cleveland himself answered the White House doorbell.

In some ways, American democracy in the Gilded Age seemed remarkably healthy. Elections were closely contested, party loyalty was intense, and 80 percent or more of eligible voters turned out to cast ballots. It was an era of massive party rallies and spellbinding political oratory. James G. Blaine was

POLITICAL STALEMATE, 1876–1892

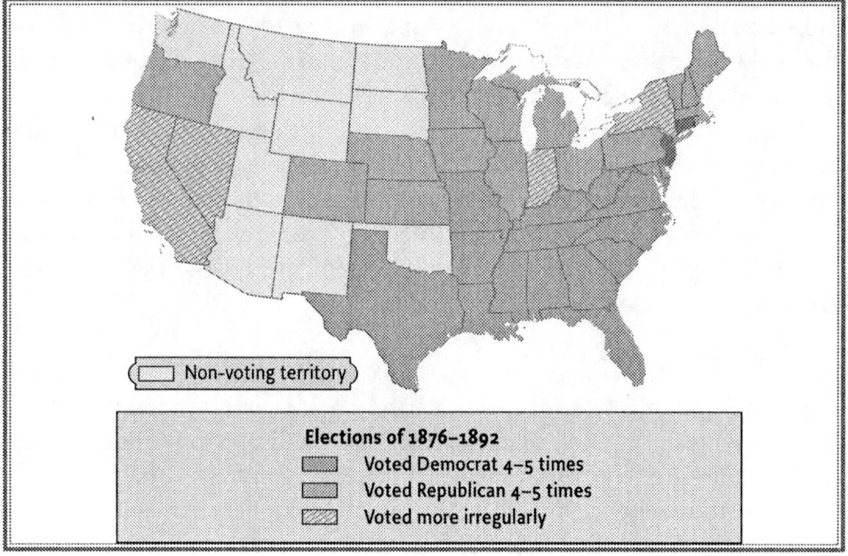

among the members of Congress tainted by the Crédit Mobilier scandal, but Robert G. Ingersoll's speech before the Republican national convention of 1876 nearly secured Blaine's nomination for president by depicting him as a "plumed knight" who had raised his "shining lance" against the country's enemies.

GOVERNMENT AND THE ECONOMY

The nation's political structure, however, proved ill equipped to deal with the problems created by the economy's rapid growth. Despite its expanded scope and powers arising from the Civil War, the federal government remained remarkably small by modern standards. Activities from education to medical care, business regulation, civil and criminal prosecutions, and many others were almost entirely under the control of local and state governments or private institutions. The federal workforce in 1880 numbered 100,000 (today, it exceeds 2.5 million).

Nationally, both parties came under the control of powerful political managers with close ties to business interests. Republicans strongly supported a high tariff to protect American industry, and throughout the 1870s they pursued a fiscal policy based on reducing federal spending, repaying much of the national debt, and withdrawing greenbacks—the paper money issued by the Union during the Civil War—from circulation. Democrats opposed the high tariff, but the party's national leadership remained closely linked to New York bankers and financiers and resisted demands from debt-ridden agricultural areas for an increase in the money supply. In 1879, for the first time since the war, the United States returned to the gold standard—that is, paper currency became exchangeable for gold at a fixed rate.

By reducing competition from foreign manufactured goods and leaving the banks, not the government, in control of issuing money, Republican economic policies strongly favored the interests of eastern industrialists and bankers. These policies worked to the disadvantage of southern and western farmers, who had to pay a premium for manufactured goods while the prices they received for their produce steadily declined.

REFORM LEGISLATION

Gilded Age national politics did not entirely lack accomplishments. Inspired in part by President Garfield's assassination by a disappointed office seeker, the Civil Service Act of 1883 created a merit system for federal employees, with appointment via competitive examinations rather than political influence. Although it applied at first to only 10 percent of the more than 100,000 government workers, the act marked the first step in establishing a professional civil service and removing officeholding from the hands of political machines. (However, since funds raised from political appointees had helped to finance the political parties, civil service reform had the unintended result of increasing politicians' dependence on donations from business interests.)

In 1887, in response to public outcries against railroad practices, Congress established the Interstate Commerce Commission (ICC) to ensure that the rates railroads charged farmers and merchants to transport their goods were "reasonable" and did not offer more favorable treatment to some shippers over others. The ICC was the first federal agency intended to regulate economic activity, but since it lacked the power to establish rates on its own—it could only sue companies in court—it had little impact on railroad practices. Three years later, Congress passed the Sherman Antitrust Act, which banned all combinations and practices that restrained free trade. The measure posed a significant threat to corporate efforts to dominate sectors of the economy. But the courts primarily used it as a way to suppress labor unions. Nonetheless, these laws helped to establish the precedent that the national government could regulate the economy to promote the public good.

POLITICAL CONFLICT IN THE STATES

The nation had to weather the effects of drastic economic change and periodic economic crises without leadership from Washington. At the state and local levels, however, the Gilded Age was an era of political ferment and conflict over the proper uses of governmental authority. In the immediate aftermath of the Civil War, state governments in the North, like those in the Reconstruction South, greatly expanded their responsibility for public health, welfare, and education, and cities invested heavily in public works such as park construction and improved water and gas services. Those who suffered from economic change called on the activist state created by the war to redress their own grievances.

Third parties enjoyed significant if short-lived success in local elections. The Greenback-Labor Party proposed that the federal government stop taking "greenback" money out of circulation. This, it argued, would make more funds available for investment and give the government, not private bankers, control of the money supply. It also condemned the use of militias and private police against strikes. In the late 1870s, the party controlled local government in a number of industrial and mining communities and contributed to the election of twenty-one members of Congress independent of the two major parties.

The policies of railroad companies produced a growing chorus of protest, especially in the West. Farmers and local merchants complained of excessively high freight rates, discrimination in favor of large producers and shippers, and high fees charged by railroad-controlled grain warehouses. Critics of the railroads came together in the Patrons of Husbandry, or Grange, which moved to establish cooperatives for storing and marketing farm output in the hope of forcing the carriers "to take our produce at a fair price." Founded in 1867, the Grange claimed more than 700,000 members by the mid-1870s. Its members called on state governments to establish fair freight rates and warehouse charges. In several states, the Grange succeeded in having commissions established to investigate—and, in some cases, regulate—railroad practices.

At the same time, the labor movement, revitalized during the Civil War, demanded laws establishing eight hours as a legal day's work. Seven northern legislatures passed such laws, but since most lacked strong means of enforcement they remained dead letters. But the efforts of farmers and workers to use the power of the state to counteract the inequalities of the Gilded Age inspired a far-reaching debate on the relationship between political and economic freedom in an industrial society.

FREEDOM IN THE GILDED AGE

THE SOCIAL PROBLEM

As the United States matured into an industrial economy, Americans struggled to make sense of the new social order. Debates over political economy engaged the attention of millions of Americans, reaching far beyond the tiny academic world into the public sphere inhabited by self-educated workingmen and farmers, reformers of all kinds, newspaper editors, and politicians. This broad public discussion produced thousands of books, pamphlets, and articles on such technical issues as land taxation and currency reform, as well as widespread debate over the social and ethical implications of economic change.

Many Americans sensed that something had gone wrong in the nation's social development. Talk of "better classes," "respectable classes," and "dangerous classes" dominated public discussion, and bitter labor strife seemed to have become the rule. During the Gilded Age, Congress and a number of states established investigating committees to inquire into the relations between labor and capital. Their hearings produced powerful evidence of distrust between employees and employers. In 1881, the Massachusetts Bureau of Labor Statistics reported that virtually every worker it interviewed in Fall River, the nation's largest center of textile production, complained of overwork, poor housing, and tyrannical employers.

FREEDOM, INEQUALITY, AND DEMOCRACY

The appearance of what Massachusetts cotton manufacturer Edward Atkinson called "a permanent factory population" living on the edge of poverty alongside a growing class of millionaires posed a sharp challenge to traditional definitions of freedom. Did America's promise still lie in the opportunity it offered ordinary citizens to achieve economic autonomy? "The great curse of the Old World—the division of society into classes," declared *The Nation*, had come to America. It became increasingly difficult to view wage labor as a temporary resting place on the road to economic independence, or the West as a haven for the dispossessed small producers of the East.

Given the vast expansion of the nation's productive capacity, many Americans viewed the concentration of wealth as inevitable, natural, and justified by progress. By the turn of the century, advanced economics taught that wages were determined by the iron law of supply and demand and that wealth rightly flowed not to those who worked the hardest but to men with business skills and access to money. The close link between freedom and equality, forged in the Revolution and reinforced during the Civil War, appeared increasingly out of date. The task of social science, wrote iron manufacturer Abram Hewitt, was to devise ways of making "men who are equal in liberty" content with the "inequality in . . . distribution" inevitable in modern society.

Among the first to take up this challenge were the self-styled "liberal" reformers. (Their beliefs were quite different from those called liberals in modern America, who advocate that an activist government try to address social needs.) This group of editors and professionals broke with the Republican Party in 1872 and helped to bring about a change in northern opinion regarding Reconstruction. But their program was not confined to the South. Like the men who led the movement for a new constitution in the 1780s, Gilded Age

The Ironworkers' Noontime, *painted in 1880–1881 by Thomas Anshutz, an artist born in West Virginia, whose family owned iron factories. Unlike artists who depicted factories and workers earlier in the century, Anshutz does not try to reconcile nature and industry (there are no reminders of the natural environment). Nor does he emphasize the dignity of labor. The workers seem dwarfed by the factory, and some seem exhausted.*

reformers feared that with lower-class groups seeking to use government to advance their own interests, democracy was becoming a threat to individual liberty and the rights of property. Some urged a return to the long-abandoned principle that voting should be limited to property owners. During the 1830s, Alexis de Tocqueville had reported that opponents of democracy "hide their heads." By the 1870s, wrote one observer, "expressions of doubt and distrust in regard to universal suffrage are heard constantly . . . [at] the top of our society."

SOCIAL DARWINISM IN AMERICA

The idea of the natural superiority of some groups to others, which before the Civil War had been invoked to justify slavery in an otherwise free society, now reemerged in the vocabulary of modern science to explain the success and failure of individuals and social classes. In 1859, the British scientist Charles Darwin published *On the Origin of Species*. One of the most influential works of science ever to appear, it expounded the theory of evolution whereby plant and animal species best suited to their environment took the place of those less able to adapt.

In a highly oversimplified form, language borrowed from Darwin or developed by his followers, such as "natural selection," "the struggle for existence," and "the survival of the fittest," entered public discussion of social problems in the Gilded Age. According to what came to be called Social Darwinism, evolution was as natural a process in human society as in nature, and government must not interfere. Especially misguided, in this view, were efforts to uplift those at the bottom of the social order, such as laws regulating conditions of work or public assistance to the poor. The giant industrial corporation, Social Darwinists believed, had emerged because it was better adapted to its environment than earlier forms of enterprise. To restrict its operations by legislation would reduce society to a more primitive level.

Even the depressions of the 1870s and 1890s did not shake the widespread view that the poor were essentially responsible for their own fate. Charity workers and local governments spent much time and energy distinguishing the "deserving" poor (those, like widows and orphans, destitute through no fault of their own) from the "undeserving," a far larger number. Failure to advance in society was widely thought to indicate a lack of character, an absence of self-reliance and determination in the face of adversity. As late as 1900, half the nation's largest cities offered virtually no public relief, except to persons living in poorhouses. To improve their lot, according to the philosophy of Social Darwinism, workers should practice personal economy, keep out of debt, and educate their children in the principles of the marketplace, not look to the government for aid.

The era's most influential Social Darwinist was Yale professor William Graham Sumner. For Sumner, freedom meant "the security given to each man" that he can acquire, enjoy, and dispose of property "exclusively as he chooses," without interference from other persons or from government. Freedom thus defined required frank acceptance of inequality. Society faced two and only two alternatives: "liberty, inequality, survival of the fittest; not-liberty, equality, survival of the unfittest." In 1883, Sumner published *What Social Classes Owe to Each Other*. His answer, essentially, was nothing: "In a free state," no one was entitled to claim "help from, and cannot be charged to [offer] help to, another." Government, Sumner believed, existed only to protect "the property of men and the honor of women," not to upset social arrangements decreed by nature.

LIBERTY OF CONTRACT

The growing influence of Social Darwinism helped to popularize an idea that would be embraced by the business and professional classes in the last quarter of the nineteenth century—a "negative" definition of freedom as limited government and an unrestrained free market. Central to this social vision was the idea of contract. "The laws of contract," wrote one reformer, "are the foundation of civilization." Labor contracts reconciled freedom and authority in the workplace. So long as labor relations were governed by contracts freely arrived at by independent individuals, neither the government nor unions had a right to interfere with working conditions, and Americans had no grounds to complain of a loss of freedom.

Demands by workers that the government enforce an eight-hour day, provide relief to the unemployed, or in other ways intervene in the economy struck liberals as an example of how the misuse of political power posed a threat to liberty. "The right of each man to labor as much or as little as he chooses, and to enjoy his own earnings, is the very foundation stone of . . . freedom," wrote Chicago newspaper editor Horace White. The principle of free labor, which originated as a celebration of the independent small producer in a society of broad equality and social harmony, was transformed into a defense of the unrestrained operations of the capitalist marketplace.

THE COURTS AND FREEDOM

In elevating liberty of contract from one element of freedom to its very essence, the courts played a significant role. The Fourteenth Amendment had empowered the federal government to overturn state laws that violated citizens' rights. By the 1880s, liberty of contract, not equality before the law for former slaves, came to be defined as the amendment's true meaning. State and federal courts regularly struck down state laws regulating economic enterprise as an interference with the right of the free laborer to choose his employment and working conditions, and of the entrepreneur to utilize his property as he saw fit. For decades, the courts viewed state regulation of business—especially laws establishing maximum hours of work and safe working conditions—as an insult to free labor.

At first, the Supreme Court was willing to accept laws regulating enterprises that represented a significant "public interest." In *Munn v. Illinois*, an 1877 decision, it upheld the constitutionality of an Illinois law that established a state board empowered to eliminate railroad rate discrimination and set maximum charges. Nine years later, however, in *Wabash v. Illinois*, the Court essentially reversed itself, ruling that only the federal government, not the states, could regulate railroads engaged in interstate commerce, as all important lines were. The decision led directly to the passage of the Interstate Commerce Act of 1887. But on virtually every occasion when cases brought by the ICC against railroads made their way to the Supreme Court, the company emerged victorious.

The courts generally sided with business enterprises that complained of a loss of economic freedom. In 1885, the New York Court of Appeals invalidated a state law that prohibited the manufacture of cigars in tenement dwellings on the grounds that such legislation deprived the worker of the "liberty" to work "where he will." Although women still lacked political rights, they were increasingly understood to possess the same economic "liberty," defined in this way, as men. On the grounds that it violated women's freedom, the Illinois Supreme Court in 1895 declared unconstitutional a state law that outlawed the production of garments in sweatshops and established a forty-eight-hour work week for women and children. In the same year, in *United States v. E. C. Knight Co.*, the U.S. Supreme Court ruled that the Sherman Antitrust Act of 1890, which barred combinations in restraint of trade, could not be used to break up a sugar refining monopoly, since the Constitution empowered Congress to regulate commerce, but not manufacturing. Their unwillingness to allow regulation of the economy, however, did not prevent the courts from acting to impede labor organization. The Sherman Act, intended to prevent business mergers that stifled competition, was used by judges primarily to issue injunctions prohibiting strikes on the grounds that they illegally interfered with the freedom of trade.

In a 1905 case that became almost as notorious as *Dred Scott* and gave the name "Lochnerism" to the entire body of liberty of contract decisions, the Supreme Court in *Lochner v. New York* voided a state law establishing ten hours per day or sixty per week as the maximum hours of work for bakers. The law, wrote Associate Justice Rufus Peckham for the 5-4 majority, "interfered with the right of contract between employer and employee" and therefore infringed upon individual freedom. By this time, the Court was invoking "liberty" in ways that could easily seem absurd. In one case, it overturned as a violation of "personal liberty" a Kansas law prohibiting "yellow-dog" contracts, which made nonmembership in a union a condition of employment. In another, it struck down state laws requiring payment of coal miners in money rather than paper usable only at company-owned stores. Workers, observed mine union leader John P. Mitchell, could not but feel that "they are being guaranteed the liberties they do not want and denied the liberty that is of real value to them."

LABOR AND THE REPUBLIC

"THE OVERWHELMING LABOR QUESTION"

As Mitchell's remark suggests, public debate in the late nineteenth century more than at almost any other moment in American history divided along class lines. The shift from the slavery controversy to what one politician called "the overwhelming labor question" was dramatically illustrated in 1877, the year of both the end of Reconstruction and the first national labor walkout—the Great Railroad Strike. When workers protesting a pay cut paralyzed rail traffic in much of the country, militia units tried to force them back to work.

After troops fired on strikers in Pittsburgh, killing twenty people, workers responded by burning the city's railroad yards, destroying millions of dollars in property. General strikes paralyzed Chicago and St. Louis. The strike revealed both a strong sense of solidarity among workers and the close ties between the Republican Party and the new class of industrialists. President Rutherford B. Hayes, who a few months earlier had ordered federal troops in the South to end their involvement in local politics, ordered the army into the North. The workers, the president wrote in his diary, were "put down by force."

"The days are over," declared the *New York Times*, "in which this country could rejoice in its freedom from the elements of social strife which have long abounded in the old countries." In the aftermath of 1877, the federal government constructed armories in major cities to ensure that troops would be on hand in the event of further labor difficulties. Henceforth, national power would be used not to protect beleaguered former slaves, but to guarantee the rights of property.

THE KNIGHTS OF LABOR AND THE "CONDITIONS ESSENTIAL TO LIBERTY"

The 1880s witnessed a new wave of labor organizing. At its center stood the Knights of Labor. The Knights were the first group to try to organize unskilled workers as well as skilled, women alongside men, and blacks as well as whites (although even the Knights excluded the despised Asian immigrants on the West Coast). The group reached a peak membership of nearly 800,000 in 1886 (making it the largest labor organizaion of the nineteenth century) and involved millions of workers in strikes, boycotts, political action, and educational and social activities.

Labor reformers of the Gilded Age put forward a wide array of programs, from the eight-hour day to public employment in hard times, currency reform, anarchism, socialism, and the creation of a vaguely defined "cooperative commonwealth." All these ideas arose from the conviction that the social conditions of the 1880s needed drastic change. Americans, declared Terence V. Powderly, head of the Knights of Labor, were not "the free people that we imagine we are."

The labor movement launched a sustained assault on the understanding of freedom grounded in Social Darwinism and liberty of contract. Because of unrestrained economic growth and political corruption, the Knights charged, ordinary Americans had lost control of their economic livelihoods and their own government. Reaching back across the divide of the Civil War, labor defined employers as a new "slave power." Concentrated capital, warned George E. McNeill, a shoemaker and factory worker who became one of the movement's most eloquent writers, had become "a greater power than that of the state." "Extremes of wealth and poverty," he warned, threatened the very existence of democratic government. The remedy was to "engraft republican principles into our industrial system" by guaranteeing a basic set of economic rights for all Americans.

Labor raised the question whether meaningful freedom could exist in a situation of extreme economic inequality. On July 4, 1886, the Federated Trades of the Pacific Coast rewrote the Declaration of Independence. Workers, the new Declaration claimed, had been subjected not to oppressive government but to "the unjust domination of a special class." It went on to list among mankind's inalienable rights, "Life and the means of living, Liberty and the conditions essential to liberty."

MIDDLE-CLASS REFORMERS

Dissatisfaction with social conditions in the Gilded Age extended well beyond aggrieved workers. Supreme Court justice John Marshall Harlan in the late 1880s spoke of a "deep feeling of unease," a widespread fear that the country "was in real danger of another kind of slavery that would result from the aggregation of capital in the hands of a few individuals." Alarmed by fear of class warfare and the growing power of concentrated capital, social thinkers offered numerous plans for change. In the last quarter of the century, more than 150 utopian or cataclysmic novels appeared, predicting that social conflict would end either in a new, harmonious social order or in total catastrophe. One popular novel of the era, *Caesar's Column* (1891) by Ignatius Donnelly, ended with civilized society destroyed in a savage civil war between labor and capital.

Of the many books proposing more optimistic remedies for the unequal distribution of wealth, the most popular were *Progress and Poverty* (1879) by Henry George, *The Cooperative Commonwealth* (1884) by Laurence Gronlund, and Edward Bellamy's *Looking Backward* (1888). All three were among the century's greatest best-sellers, their extraordinary success testifying to what George called "a wide-spread consciousness . . . that there is something *radically* wrong in the present social organization." All three writers, though in very different ways, sought to reclaim an imagined golden age of social harmony and American freedom.

PROGRESS AND POVERTY

Although it had no direct impact on government policy, *Progress and Poverty* probably commanded more public attention than any book on economics in American history. An antislavery newspaper editor in California in the 1850s and 1860s, Henry George had witnessed firsthand the rapid monopolization of land in the state. His book began with a famous statement of "the problem" suggested by its title—the growth of "squalor and misery" alongside material

The Great Labor Parade of September 1, *from* Frank Leslie's Illustrated Newspaper, *September 13, 1884. A placard illustrates how the labor movement identified Gilded Age employers with the Slave Power of the pre–Civil War era.*

progress. His solution was the "single tax," which would replace other taxes with a levy on increases in the value of real estate. The single tax would be so high that it would prevent speculation in both urban and rural land. No one knows how many of Henry George's readers actually believed in this way of solving the nation's ills. But millions responded to his clear explanation of economic relationships and his stirring account of how the "social distress" long thought to be confined to the Old World had made its appearance in the New.

Freedom lay at the heart of George's analysis. The "proper name" for the political movement spawned by his book, he once wrote, was "freedom men," who would "do for the question of industrial slavery" what the Republican Party had done for the slavery of blacks. George rejected the traditional equation of liberty with ownership of land (since the single tax in effect made land the "common property" of the entire society). In other ways, however, his definition of freedom was thoroughly in keeping with mainstream thought. Despite calling for a single massive public intervention in the economy, George saw government as a "repressive power," whose functions in the "co-operative society" of the future would be limited to enhancing the quality of life—building "public baths, museums, libraries, gardens," and the like.

THE COOPERATIVE COMMONWEALTH

Quite different in outlook was *The Cooperative Commonwealth,* the first book to popularize socialist ideas for an American audience. Its author, Laurence Gronlund, was a lawyer who had emigrated from Denmark in 1867. Socialism—the belief that private control of economic enterprises should be replaced by government ownership in order to ensure a fairer distribution of the benefits of the wealth produced—became a major political force in western Europe in the late nineteenth century. In the United States, however, where access to private property was widely considered essential to individual freedom, socialist beliefs were largely confined to immigrants, whose writings, frequently in foreign languages, attracted little attention.

Gronlund began the process of socialism's Americanization. While Karl Marx, the nineteenth century's most influential socialist theorist, had predicted that socialism would come into being via a working-class revolution, Gronlund portrayed it as the end result of a process of peaceful evolution, not violent upheaval. He thus made socialism seem more acceptable to middle-class Americans who desired an end to class conflict and the restoration of social harmony.

BELLAMY'S UTOPIA

Not until the early twentieth century would socialism become a significant presence in American public life. As Gronlund himself noted, the most important result of *The Cooperative Commonwealth* was to prepare an audience for Edward Bellamy's *Looking Backward,* which promoted socialist ideas while "ignoring that name" (Bellamy wrote of nationalism, not socialism). Bellamy lived virtually his entire life in the small industrial city of Chicopee Falls, Massachusetts. In *Looking Backward,* his main character falls asleep in the late nineteenth century only to awaken in the year 2000, in a world where cooperation has replaced class strife, "excessive individualism," and cutthroat competition. Inequality has been banished and with it the idea of liberty as a condition to be achieved through individual striving free of governmental restraint. Freedom, Bellamy insisted, was a social condition, resting on interdependence, not autonomy.

From today's vantage point, Bellamy's utopia—with citizens obligated to labor for years in an Industrial Army controlled by a single Great Trust—seems a chilling social blueprint. Yet the book inspired the creation of hundreds of nationalist clubs devoted to bringing into existence the world of 2000 and left a profound mark on a generation of reformers and intellectuals. Bellamy held out the hope of retaining the material abundance made possible by industrial capitalism while eliminating inequality. In proposing that the state guarantee economic security to all, Bellamy offered a far-reaching expansion of the idea of freedom. "I am aware that you called yourself free in the nineteenth century," a resident of the year 2000 tells Bellamy's Rip Van Winkle. But "the meaning of the word could not then have been at all what it is at present," or it could not have been applied to a society in which so many lived in a state of "galling personal dependence upon others as to the very means of life."

PROTESTANTS AND MORAL REFORM

Mainstream Protestants played a major role in seeking to stamp out sin during the Gilded Age. What one historian calls a "Christian lobby" promoted political solutions to what it saw as the moral problems raised by labor conflict and the growth of cities, and threats to religious faith by Darwinism and other scientific advances.

Unlike the pre–Civil War period, when "moral suasion" was the preferred approach of many reformers, powerful national organizations like the Women's Christian Temperance Union, National Reform Association, and Reform Bureau now campaigned for federal legislation that would "christianize the government" by outlawing sinful behavior. Among the proposed targets were the consumption of alcohol, gambling, prostitution, polygamy, and birth control. Most of these groups spoke less about improving society than stamping out the sins of individuals. In a striking departure from the prewar situation, southerners joined in the campaign for federal regulation of individual behavior, something whites in the region had previously strongly opposed, fearing it could lead to action against slavery. The key role played by the white South in the campaign for moral legislation helped earn the region a reputation as the Bible Belt—a place where political action revolved around religious principles. Although efforts to enact a national law requiring businesses to close on Sunday failed, the Christian lobby's efforts in the 1880s and 1890s set the stage for later legislation such as the Mann Act of 1910, banning the transportation of women across state lines for immoral purposes (an effort to suppress prostitution), and Prohibition.

A SOCIAL GOSPEL

Most of the era's Protestant preachers concentrated on attacking individual sins like drinking and Sabbath-breaking and saw nothing immoral about the pursuit of riches. But the outlines of what came to be called the Social Gospel were taking shape in the writings of Walter Rauschenbusch, a Baptist minister in New York City, Washington Gladden, a Congregational clergyman in Columbus, Ohio, and others. They insisted that freedom and spiritual self-development required an equalization of wealth and power and that unbridled competition mocked the Christian ideal of brotherhood.

The Social Gospel movement originated as an effort to reform Protestant churches by expanding their appeal in poor urban neighborhoods and making them more attentive to the era's social ills. The movement's adherents established missions and relief programs in urban areas that attempted to alleviate poverty, combat child labor, and encourage the construction of better working-class housing. They worked with the Knights of Labor and other groups demanding health and safety laws. Some suggested that a more cooperative organization of the economy should replace competitive capitalism. Within American Catholicism, as well, a group of priests and bishops emerged who attempted to alter the church's traditional hostility to movements for social reform and its isolation from contemporary currents of social thought. With most of its parishioners working men and women, they argued, the church should lend its support to the labor movement. These developments suggested the existence of widespread dissatisfaction with the "liberty of contract" understanding of freedom.

THE HAYMARKET AFFAIR

The year of the dedication of the Statue of Liberty, 1886, also witnessed an unprecedented upsurge in labor activity. Inspired by a successful strike by western railroad unions against lines controlled by the powerful financier Jay Gould, workers flooded into the Knights of Labor. Its membership, only 100,000 in 1885, rose more than sevenfold in the following year. On May 1, 1886, some 350,000 workers in cities across the country demonstrated for an eight-hour day. Having originated in the United States, May 1, or May Day as it came to be called, soon became an annual date of parades, picnics, and protests, celebrated around the world by organized labor.

The most dramatic events of 1886 took place in Chicago, a city with a large and vibrant labor movement that brought together native-born and immigrant workers, whose outlooks ranged from immigrant socialism and anarchism to American traditions of equality and anti-monopoly. In 1885, the iron moulders union—one of the most powerful organizations of skilled industrial workers in the country—had organized a strike against a wage reduction at the great McCormick plant that produced agricultural machinery. The company brought in strikebreakers and private police, who battled in the streets with the strikers. Fearing chaos, the mayor and prominent business leaders persuaded the company to settle on the union's terms. But in February 1886, after the company installed new machinery that reduced its dependence on the iron moulders' traditional skills, it announced that henceforth the factory would operate on a nonunion basis. The result was a bitter, prolonged strike.

This time, Chicago's city government sided with the company. On May 3, 1886, four strikers were killed by police when they attempted to prevent strikebreakers from entering the factory. The next day, a rally was held in Haymarket Square to protest the killings. Near the end of the speeches, someone—whose identity has never been determined—threw a bomb into the crowd, killing a policeman. The panicked police opened fire, shooting several bystanders and a number of their own force. Soon after, police raided the offices of labor and radical groups and arrested their leaders. Employers took the opportunity to paint the labor movement as a dangerous and un-American force, prone to violence and controlled by foreign-born radicals. Eight anarchists were charged with plotting and carrying out the bombing. Even though the evidence against them was extremely weak, a jury convicted the "Haymarket martyrs." Four were hanged, one committed suicide in prison, and the remaining three were imprisoned until John Peter Altgeld, a pro-labor governor of Illinois, commuted their sentences in 1893.

Seven of the eight men accused of plotting the Haymarket bombing were foreign-born—six Germans and an English immigrant. The last was Albert Parsons, a native of Alabama who had served in the Confederate army in the Civil War and edited a Republican newspaper in Texas during Reconstruction. Fearing violence because of his political views and the fact that his wife, Lucy Parsons, was black, Albert Parsons moved to Chicago during the 1870s. Having survived the Ku Klux Klan in Reconstruction Texas, Parsons perished on the Illinois gallows for a crime that he, like the other "Haymarket martyrs," did not commit.

LABOR AND POLITICS

The Haymarket affair took place amid an outburst of independent labor political activity. One study has identified more than 100 local political tickets associated with the Knights of Labor between 1886 and 1888, from Anniston, Alabama, to Whitewater, Wisconsin. Their major aim was to end the use of public and private police forces and court injunctions against strikes and labor organizations. At least sixty achieved some kind of electoral success. In Kansas City, a coalition of black and Irish-American workers and middle-class voters elected Tom Hanna as mayor. He proceeded to side with unions rather than employers in industrial disputes.

The most celebrated labor campaign took place in New York City, where in 1886, somewhat to his own surprise, Henry George found himself thrust into the role of labor's candidate for mayor. George's aim in running was to bring attention to the single tax on land. The labor leaders who organized the United Labor Party had more immediate goals in mind, especially stopping the courts from barring strikes and jailing unionists for conspiracy. George ran a spirited campaign, speaking at factories, immigrant associations, and labor parades and rallies. A few days after the dedication of the Statue of Liberty, New Yorkers flocked to the polls to elect their mayor. Nearly 70,000 voted for George, who finished second, eclipsing the total of the Republican candidate, Theodore Roosevelt, and coming close to defeating Democrat Abram Hewitt.

In a political system that within living memory had witnessed the disappearance of the Whig Party, the rise and fall of the Know-Nothings, and the emergence of the Republicans, the events of 1886 suggested that labor might be on the verge of establishing itself as a permanent political force. In fact, that year marked the high point of the Knights of Labor. Facing increasing employer hostility and linked by employers and the press to the violence and radicalism associated with the Haymarket events, the Knights soon declined. The major parties, moreover, proved remarkably resourceful in appealing to labor voters.

Thus, America's Gilded Age witnessed deep and sometimes violent divisions over the definition of freedom in a rapidly industrializing society. The battle between upholders of Social Darwinism and laissez-faire, who saw freedom as the right of individuals to pursue their economic interests without outside restraint, and those who believed in collective efforts to create "industrial freedom" for ordinary Americans, would continue for many decades. In the early twentieth century, reformers would turn to new ways of addressing the social conditions of freedom and new means of increasing ordinary Americans' political and economic liberty. But before this, in the 1890s, the nation would face its gravest crisis since the Civil War, and the boundaries of freedom would once again be redrawn.

Chapter Review

REVIEW QUESTIONS

1. The American economy thrived because of federal involvement, not the lack of it. How did the federal government actively promote industrial and agricultural development in this period?
2. Why were railroads so important to America's second industrial revolution? What events demonstrate their influence on society and politics as well as the economy?
3. Why did organized efforts of farmers, workers, and local reformers largely fail to achieve substantive change in the Gilded Age?
4. Describe the involvement of American family farmers in the global economy after 1870 and its effects on their independence.
5. According to *The Gilded Age* by Mark Twain and Charles Dudley Warner, the era's slogan was "Get rich, dishonestly if we can, honestly if we must." Explain how this was true of the politics of the era.
6. How did American political leaders seek to remake Indians and change the ways they lived?
7. Explain how social thinkers misapplied Charles Darwin's ideas to justify massive disparities in wealth and power and to deny government a role in equalizing opportunity.
8. How did social reformers such as Edward Bellamy, Henry George, and advocates of the social gospel conceive of liberty and freedom differently than the proponents of the liberty of contract ideal and laissez faire?
9. In what ways did the West provide a "safety valve" for the problems in the industrial East? In what ways did it reveal some of the same problems?

KEY TERMS

- standard gauge
- trusts
- vertical integration
- horizontal expansion
- "captains of industry" v. "robber barons"
- "The Significance of the Frontier in American History"
- bonanza farming
- Gospel of Wealth
- Dawes Act
- Ghost Dance
- Sherman Antitrust Act
- Interstate Commerce Commission
- Patrons of Husbandry
- Social Darwinism
- liberty of contract
- Knights of Labor
- Social Gospel
- Haymarket Affair

wwnorton.com/studyspace

VISIT STUDYSPACE FOR THESE RESOURCES AND MORE:

- Author Videos
- A chapter outline
- A practice quiz
- Interactive maps
- Multimedia documents

CHAPTER 2

FREEDOM'S BOUNDARIES, AT HOME AND ABROAD

From *Give Me Liberty! Seagull*
Fourth Edition

Eric Foner

Credits: photo 1: Kansas State Historical Society; photo 2: Library of Congress; photo 3: Library of Congress; photo 4: Library of Congress; photo 5: Library of Congress; photo 6: Courtesy of the Bernice Pauahi Bishop Museum Archives; photo 7: North Wind Picture Archives/Alamy.

Table 1: Arwin D. Smallwood, *The Atlas of African-American History and Politics* (New York, 1998), 106.

2

Freedom's Boundaries, at Home and Abroad 1890–1900

FOCUS QUESTIONS

- What were the origins and the significance of Populism?
- How did the liberties of blacks after 1877 give way to legal segregation across the South?
- In what ways did the boundaries of American freedom grow narrower in this period?
- How did the United States emerge as an imperial power in the 1890s?

One of the most popular songs of 1892 bore the title "Father Was Killed by a Pinkerton Man." It was inspired by an incident during a bitter strike at Andrew Carnegie's steelworks at Homestead, Pennsylvania, the nineteenth century's most widely publicized confrontation between labor and capital. The strike pitted one of the nation's leading industrial corporations against a powerful union, the Amalgamated Association, which represented the skilled iron- and steelworkers among the complex's 3,800 employees.

Homestead's twelve steel mills were the most profitable and technologically advanced in the world. The union contract gave the Amalgamated Association a considerable say in their operation, including the right to approve the hiring of new workers and to regulate the pace of work. To Carnegie and Henry Clay Frick, his partner and chairman of the Carnegie Steel Company, the union's power increasingly seemed an intolerable infringement on management's rights. In 1892, they decided to operate the plant on a nonunion basis. Frick surrounded the factory with a fence topped by barbed wire, constructed barracks to house strikebreakers, and fired the entire workforce. Henceforth, only workers who agreed not to join the union could work at Homestead. In response, the workers, including the unskilled laborers not included in the Amalgamated Association, blockaded the steelworks and mobilized support from the local community. The battle memorialized in song took place on July 6, 1892, when armed strikers confronted 300 private policemen from the Pinkerton Detective Agency. Seven workers and three Pinkerton agents were killed, and the Pinkertons were forced to retreat. Four days later, the governor of Pennsylvania dispatched 8,000 militiamen to open the complex on management's terms. The strikers held out until November, but the union's defeat was now inevitable. In the end, the Amalgamated Association was destroyed.

The Carnegie corporation's tactics and the workers' solidarity won the strikers widespread national sympathy. "Ten thousand Carnegie libraries," declared the *St. Louis Post-Dispatch*, "would not compensate the country for the evils resulting from Homestead." The strike became an international cause célèbre as well. British newspapers pointed out that their country restricted the use of private police forces far more severely than the United States. Britons, they claimed, understood economic liberty better than Americans.

Homestead demonstrated that neither a powerful union nor public opinion could influence the conduct of the largest corporations. The writer Hamlin Garland, who visited Homestead two years after the strike, found the workforce sullen and bitter. He described a town "as squalid and unlovely as could be imagined," with dingy houses over which hung dense clouds of black smoke. It was "American," he wrote, "only in the sense in which [it] represents the American idea of business."

In fact, two American ideas of freedom collided at Homestead—the employers' definition, based on the idea that property rights, unrestrained by union rules or public regulation, sustained the public good, and the workers' conception, which stressed economic security and independence from what they considered the "tyranny" of employers. The strife at Homestead also reflected broader battles over American freedom during the 1890s. Like the Homestead workers, many Americans came to believe that they were being denied economic independence and democratic self-government, long central to the popular understanding of freedom.

During the 1890s, millions of farmers joined the Populist movement in an attempt to reverse their declining economic prospects and to rescue the government from what they saw as control by powerful corporate interests. The 1890s witnessed the imposition of a new racial system in the South that locked African-Americans into the status of second-class citizenship, denying them many of the freedoms white Americans took for granted. Increasing immigration produced heated debates over whether the country should reconsider its traditional self—definition as a refuge for foreigners seeking greater freedom on American shores. At the end of the 1890s, in the Spanish-American War, the United States for the first time acquired overseas possessions and found itself ruling over subject peoples from Puerto Rico to the Philippines. Was the democratic republic, many Americans wondered, becoming an empire like those of Europe? Rarely has the country experienced at one time so many debates over both the meaning of freedom and freedom's boundaries.

THE POPULIST CHALLENGE

THE FARMERS' REVOLT

Even as labor unrest crested, a different kind of uprising was ripening in the South and the trans-Mississippi West, a response to falling agricultural prices and growing economic dependency in rural areas. Like industrial workers, small farmers faced increasing economic insecurity. In the South, the sharecropping system locked millions of tenant farmers, white and black, into perpetual poverty. The interruption of cotton exports during the Civil War had led to the rapid expansion of production in India, Egypt, and Brazil. The glut of cotton on the world market led to declining prices (from 11 cents a pound in 1881 to 4.6 cents in 1894), throwing millions of small farmers deep into debt and threatening them with the loss of their land. In the West, farmers who had mortgaged their property to purchase seed, fertilizer, and equipment faced the prospect of losing their farms when unable to repay their bank loans. Farmers increasingly believed that their plight derived from the high freight rates charged by railroad companies, excessive interest rates for loans from merchants and bankers, and the fiscal policies of the federal government that reduced the supply of money and helped to push down farm prices.

Through the Farmers' Alliance, the largest citizens' movement of the nineteenth century, farmers sought to remedy their condition. Founded in Texas in the late 1870s, the Alliance spread to forty-three states by 1890. The farmers' alternatives, said J. D. Fields, a Texas Alliance leader, were "success and freedom, or failure and servitude." At first, the Alliance remained aloof from politics, attempting to improve rural conditions by the cooperative financing and marketing of crops. Alliance "exchanges" would loan money to farmers and sell their produce. But it soon became clear that farmers on their own could not finance this plan, and banks refused to extend loans to the exchanges. The Alliance therefore proposed that the federal government establish warehouses where farmers could store their crops until they were sold. Using the crops as collateral, the government would then issue loans to farmers at low interest rates, thereby ending their dependence on bankers and merchants. Since it would have to be enacted by Congress, the "subtreasury plan," as this proposal was called, led the Alliance into politics.

THE PEOPLE'S PARTY

In the early 1890s, the Alliance evolved into the People's Party (or Populists), the era's greatest political insurgency. The party did not just appeal to farmers. It sought to speak for all the "producing classes" and achieved some of its greatest successes in states like Colorado and Idaho, where it won the support of miners and industrial workers. But its major base lay in the cotton and wheat belts of the South and West.

CHRONOLOGY

1867	Alaska purchased
1874	Women's Christian Temperance Union founded
1879–1880	Kansas Exodus
1882	Chinese Exclusion Act
1883	*Civil Rights Cases*
1885	Josiah Strong's *Our Country*
1886	AFL established
1890	National American Woman Suffrage Association organized
1891	Populist Party organized
1892	Homestead strike
1893	Hawaii's Queen Liliuokalani overthrown
	Economic depression begins
1894	Coxey's Army marches to Washington
	Pullman strike
	Immigration Restriction League established
1895	Booker T. Washington's Atlanta speech
1896	*Plessy v. Ferguson*
	The National Association of Colored Women established
1897	William McKinley inaugurated president
1898	Spanish-American War
	Anti-Imperialist League
1899–1903	Philippine War
1900	Gold Standard Act
1901–1904	*Insular Cases*

Building on the Farmers' Alliance network of local institutions, the Populists embarked on a remarkable effort of community organization and education. To spread their message they published numerous pamphlets on political and economic questions, established more than 1,000 local newspapers, and sent traveling speakers throughout rural America. Wearing "a huge black sombrero and a black Prince Albert coat," Texas Populist orator "Cyclone" Davis traveled the Great Plains accompanied by the writings of Thomas Jefferson, which he quoted to demonstrate the evils of banks and large corporations. At great gatherings on the western plains, similar in some ways to religious revival meetings, and in small-town southern country stores, one observer wrote, "people commenced to think who had never thought before, and people talked who had seldom spoken. . . . Little by little they commenced to theorize upon their condition."

Here was the last great political expression of the nineteenth-century vision of America as a commonwealth of small producers whose freedom rested on the ownership of productive property and respect for the dignity of labor. "Day by day," declared the *People's Party Paper* of Georgia in 1893, "the power of the individual sinks. Day by day the power of the classes, or the corporations, rises. . . . In all essential respects, the republic of our fathers is dead."

But although the Populists used the familiar language of nineteenth-century radicalism, they were hardly a backward-looking movement. They embraced the modern technologies that made large-scale cooperative enterprise possible—the railroad, the telegraph, and the national market—while

A group of Kansas Populists, perhaps on their way to a political gathering, in a photograph from the 1890s.

looking to the federal government to regulate them in the public interest. They promoted agricultural education and believed farmers should adopt modern scientific methods of cultivation. They believed the federal government could move beyond partisan conflict to operate in a businesslike manner to promote the public good—a vision soon to be associated with the Progressive movement and, many years later, politicians like Jimmy Carter and Barack Obama.

THE POPULIST PLATFORM

The Populist platform of 1892, adopted at the party's Omaha convention, remains a classic document of American reform. Written by Ignatius Donnelly, a Minnesota editor and former Radical Republican congressman during Reconstruction, it spoke of a nation "brought to the verge of moral, political, and material ruin" by political corruption and economic inequality. "The fruits of the toil of millions," the platform declared, "are boldly stolen to build up colossal fortunes . . . while their possessors despise the republic and endanger liberty." The platform put forth a long list of proposals to restore democracy and economic opportunity, many of which would be adopted during the next half-century: the direct election of U.S. senators, government control of the currency, a graduated income tax, a system of low-cost public financing to enable farmers to market their crops, and recognition of the right of workers to form labor unions. In addition, Populists called for public ownership of the railroads to guarantee farmers inexpensive access to markets for their crops. A generation would pass before a major party offered so sweeping a plan for political action to create the social conditions of freedom.

THE POPULIST COALITION

In some southern states, the Populists made remarkable efforts to unite black and white small farmers on a common political and economic program. The obstacles to such an alliance were immense—not merely the heritage of racism and the political legacy of the Civil War, but the fact that many white Populists were landowning farmers while most blacks were tenants and agricultural laborers. Unwelcome in the southern branches of the Farmers' Alliance, black farmers formed their own organization, the Colored Farmers' Alliance. In 1891, it tried to organize a strike of cotton pickers on plantations in South Carolina, Arkansas, and Texas. The action was violently suppressed by local authorities and landowners, some of them sympathetic to the white Alliance but unwilling to pay higher wages to their own laborers.

In general, southern white Populists' racial attitudes did not differ significantly from those of their non-Populist neighbors. Nonetheless, recognizing the need for allies to break the Democratic Party's stranglehold on power in the South, some white Populists insisted that black and white farmers shared common grievances and could unite for common goals. Tom Watson, Georgia's leading Populist, worked the hardest to forge a black-white alliance. "You are kept apart," he told interracial audiences, "that you may be separately fleeced of your earnings. . . . This race antagonism perpetuates a monetary system which beggars both." While many blacks refused to abandon the party of Lincoln, others were attracted by the Populist appeal. In 1894, a coalition of white Populists and black Republicans won control of North Carolina, bringing to the state a "second Reconstruction" complete with increased spending on public education and a revival of black officeholding. In most of the South, however, Democrats fended off the Populist challenge by resorting to the tactics they had used to retain power since the 1870s—mobilizing whites with warnings about "Negro supremacy," intimidating black voters, and stuffing ballot boxes on election day.

The Populist movement also engaged the energies of thousands of reform-minded women from farm and labor backgrounds. Some, like Mary Elizabeth Lease, a former homesteader and one of the first female lawyers in Kansas, became prominent organizers, campaigners, and strategists. Lease was famous for her speeches urging farmers to "raise less corn and more hell" (although she apparently never actually uttered those exact words, which would have been considered inappropriate for a woman in public). "We fought England for our liberty," Lease declared, "and put chains on four million blacks. We wiped out slavery and . . . began a system of white wage slavery worse than the first." During the 1890s, referendums in Colorado and Idaho approved extending the vote to women, while in Kansas and California the proposal went down in defeat. Populists in all these states endorsed women's suffrage.

Populist presidential candidate James Weaver received more than 1 million votes in 1892. The party carried five western states, with twenty-two electoral votes, and elected three governors and fifteen members of Congress. In his inaugural address in 1893, Lorenzo Lewelling, the new Populist governor of Kansas, anticipated a phrase made famous seventy years later by Martin Luther King Jr.: "I have a dream. . . . In the beautiful vision of a coming time I behold the abolition of poverty. A time is foreshadowed when . . . liberty, equality, and justice shall have permanent abiding places in the republic."

THE GOVERNMENT AND LABOR

Were the Populists on the verge of replacing one of the two major parties? The severe depression that began in 1893 led to increased conflict between capital and labor and seemed to create an opportunity for expanding the Populist vote. Time and again, employers brought state or federal authority to bear to protect their own economic power or put down threats to public order.

POPULIST STRENGTH, 1892

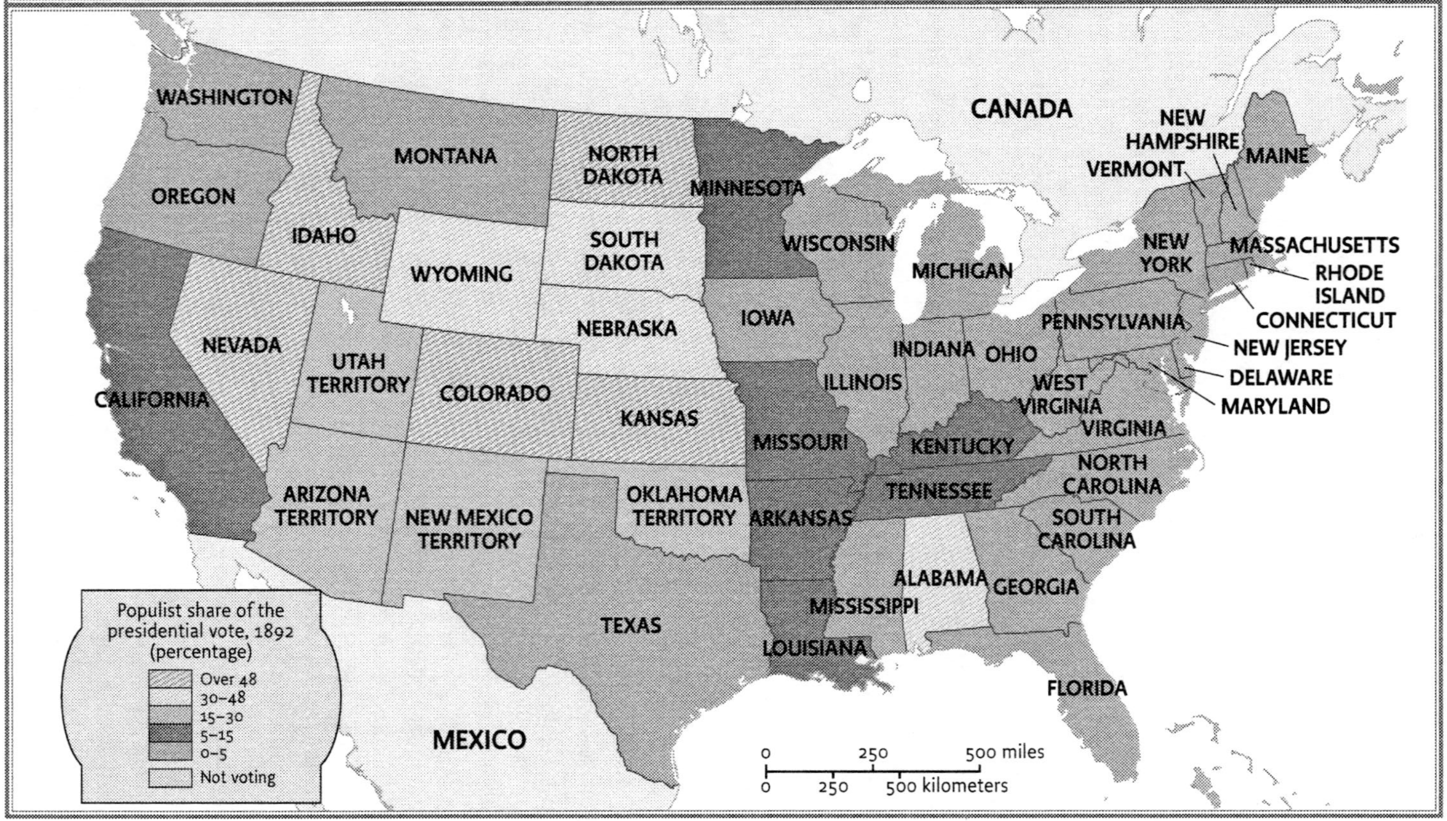

Even before the economic downturn, in 1892, the governor of Idaho declared martial law and sent militia units and federal troops into the mining region of Coeur d'Alene to break a strike. In May 1894, the federal government deployed soldiers to disperse Coxey's Army—a band of several hundred unemployed men led by Ohio businessman Jacob Coxey, who marched to Washington demanding economic relief.

Also in 1894, workers in the company-owned town of Pullman, Illinois, where railroad sleeping cars were manufactured, called a strike to protest a reduction in wages. The American Railway Union, whose 150,000 members included both skilled and unskilled railroad laborers, announced that its members would refuse to handle trains with Pullman cars. When the boycott crippled national rail service, President Grover Cleveland's attorney general, Richard Olney (himself on the board of several railroad companies), obtained a federal court injunction ordering the strikers back to work. Federal troops and U.S. marshals soon occupied railroad centers like Chicago and Sacramento.

The strike collapsed when the union's leaders, including its charismatic president, Eugene V. Debs, were jailed for contempt of court for violating the judicial order. In the case of *In re Debs*, the Supreme Court unanimously confirmed the sentences and approved the use of injunctions against striking labor unions. On his release from prison in November 1895, more than 100,000 persons greeted Debs at a Chicago railroad depot.

POPULISM AND LABOR

In 1894, Populists made determined efforts to appeal to industrial workers. Populist senators supported the demand of Coxey's Army for federal unemployment relief, and Governor Davis Waite of Colorado, who had edited a labor newspaper before his election, sent the militia to protect striking miners against company police. In the state and congressional elections of that year, as the economic depression deepened, voters by the millions abandoned the Democratic Party of President Cleveland.

In rural areas, the Populist vote increased in 1894. But urban workers did not rally to the Populists, whose core issues—the subtreasury plan and lower mortgage interest rates—had little meaning for them and whose demand for higher prices for farm goods would raise the cost of food and reduce the value of workers' wages. Moreover, the revivalist atmosphere of many Populist gatherings and the biblical cadences of Populist speeches were alien to the largely immigrant and Catholic industrial working class. Urban working-class voters in 1894 instead shifted en masse to the Republicans, who claimed that raising tariff rates (which Democrats had recently reduced) would restore prosperity by protecting manufacturers and industrial workers from the competition of imported goods and cheap foreign labor. In one of the most decisive shifts in congressional power in American history, the Republicans gained 117 seats in the House of Representatives.

BRYAN AND FREE SILVER

In 1896, Democrats and Populists joined to support William Jennings Bryan for the presidency. A thirty-six-year-old congressman from Nebraska, Bryan won the Democratic nomination after delivering to the national convention an electrifying speech that crystallized the farmers' pride and grievances. "Burn down your cities and leave our farms," Bryan proclaimed, "and your cities will spring up again as if by magic; but destroy our farms and grass will grow in the streets of every city in the country." Bryan called for the "free coinage" of silver—the unrestricted minting of silver money. In language ringing with biblical imagery, Bryan condemned the gold standard: "You shall not press down upon the brow of labor this crown of thorns. You shall not crucify mankind upon a cross of gold."

At various points in the nineteenth century, from debates over "hard" versus "soft" money in the Jacksonian era to the greenback movement after the Civil War, the "money question" had played a central role in American politics. Bryan's demand for "free silver" was the latest expression of the view that increasing the amount of currency in circulation would raise the prices farmers received for their crops and make it easier to pay off their debts. His nomination wrested control of the Democratic Party from long-dominant leaders like President Grover Cleveland, who were closely tied to eastern businessmen.

There was more to Bryan's appeal, however, than simply free silver. A devoutly religious man, he was strongly influenced by the Social Gospel movement and tried to apply the teachings of Jesus Christ to uplifting the "little people" of the United States. He championed a vision of the government helping ordinary Americans that anticipated provisions of the New Deal of the 1930s, including a progressive income tax, banking regulation, and the right of workers to form unions.

Many Populists were initially cool to Bryan's campaign. Their party had been defrauded time and again by Democrats in the South. Veteran Populists feared that their broad program was in danger of being reduced to "free silver." But realizing that they could not secure victory alone, the party's leaders endorsed Bryan's candidacy. Bryan broke with tradition and embarked on a nationwide speaking tour, seeking to rally farmers and workers to his cause.

THE CAMPAIGN OF 1896

Republicans met the silverite challenge head on, insisting that gold was the only "honest" currency. Abandoning the gold standard, they insisted, would destroy business confidence and prevent recovery from the depression by

THE PRESIDENTIAL ELECTION OF 1896

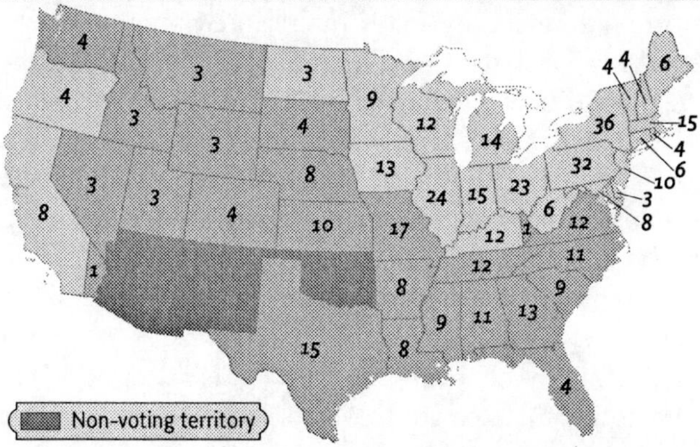

	Party	Candidate	Electoral Vote (Share)	Popular Vote (Share)
	Republican	McKinley	271 (61%)	7,104,779 (51%)
	Democrat	Bryan	176 (39%)	6,502,925 (47%)
	Minor parties			315,398 (2%)

making creditors unwilling to extend loans, since they could not be certain of the value of the money in which they would be repaid. The party nominated for president Ohio governor William McKinley, who as a congressman in 1890 had shepherded to passage the strongly protectionist McKinley Tariff.

The election of 1896 is sometimes called the first modern presidential campaign because of the amount of money spent by the Republicans and the efficiency of their national organization. Eastern bankers and industrialists, thoroughly alarmed by Bryan's call for monetary inflation and his fiery speeches denouncing corporate arrogance, poured millions of dollars into Republican coffers. (McKinley's campaign raised some $10 million; Bryan's around $300,000.) While McKinley remained at his Ohio home, where he addressed crowds of supporters from his front porch, his political manager Mark Hanna created a powerful national political machine that flooded the country with pamphlets, posters, and campaign buttons.

The results revealed a nation as divided along regional lines as in 1860. Bryan carried the South and West and received 6.5 million votes. McKinley swept the more populous industrial states of the Northeast and Midwest, attracting 7.1 million. The Republican candidate's electoral margin was even greater: 271 to 176. The era's bitter labor strife did not carry over into the electoral arena; indeed, party politics seemed to mute class conflict rather than to reinforce it. Industrial America, from financiers and managers to workers, now voted solidly Republican, a loyalty reinforced when prosperity returned after 1897.

According to some later critics, the popular children's classic *The Wonderful Wizard of Oz*, published by L. Frank Baum in 1900, offered a commentary on the election of 1896 and its aftermath. In this interpretation, the Emerald City (where everything is colored green, for money) represents Washington, D.C., and the Wizard of Oz, who remains invisible in his palace and rules by illusion, is President McKinley. The only way to get to the city is via a Yellow Brick Road (the color of gold). The Wicked Witches of the East and West represent oppressive industrialists and mine owners. In the much-beloved film version made in the 1930s, Dorothy, the all-American girl from the heartland state of Kansas, wears ruby slippers. But in the book her shoes are silver, supposedly representing the money preferred by ordinary people.

Whatever Baum's symbolism, one thing was clear. McKinley's victory shattered the political stalemate that had persisted since 1876 and created one of the most enduring political majorities in American history. During McKinley's presidency, Republicans placed their stamp on economic policy by passing the Dingley Tariff of 1897, raising rates to the highest level in history, and the Gold Standard Act of 1900. Not until 1932, in the midst of another economic depression, would the Democrats become the nation's majority party. The election of 1896 also proved to be the last presidential election with extremely high voter turnout (in some states, over 90 percent of those eligible). From then on, with the South solidly Democratic and the North overwhelmingly Republican, few states witnessed vigorous two-party campaigns. Voter participation began a downhill trend, although it rose again from the mid-1930s through the 1960s. Today, only around half the electorate casts ballots.

THE SEGREGATED SOUTH

THE REDEEMERS IN POWER

The failure of Populism in the South opened the door for the full imposition of a new racial order. The coalition of merchants, planters, and business entrepreneurs who dominated the region's politics after 1877 called themselves Redeemers, since they claimed to have redeemed the region from the alleged horrors of misgovernment and "black rule." On achieving power, they had moved to undo as much as possible of Reconstruction. State budgets were slashed, taxes, especially on landed property, reduced, and public facilities like hospitals and asylums closed. Hardest hit were the new public school systems. Louisiana spent so little on education that it became the only state in the Union in which the percentage of whites unable to read and write actually increased between 1880 and 1900. Black schools, however, suffered the most, as the gap between expenditures for black and white pupils widened steadily.

"What I want here is Negroes who can make cotton," declared one planter, "and they don't need education to help them make cotton."

New laws authorized the arrest of virtually any person without employment and greatly increased the penalties for petty crimes. "They send [a man] to the penitentiary if he steals a chicken," complained a former slave in North Carolina. As the South's prison population rose, the renting out of convicts became a profitable business. Every southern state placed at least a portion of its convicted criminals, the majority of them blacks imprisoned for minor offenses, in the hands of private businessmen. Railroads, mines, and lumber companies competed for this new form of cheap, involuntary labor. Conditions in labor camps were often barbaric, with disease rife and the death rates high. "One dies, get another" was the motto of the system's architects. The Knights of Labor made convict labor a major issue in the South. In 1892, miners in Tennessee burned the stockade where convict workers were housed and shipped them out of the region. Tennessee abolished the convict lease system three years later but replaced it with a state-owned coal mine using prison labor that reaped handsome profits for decades.

THE FAILURE OF THE NEW SOUTH DREAM

During the 1880s, Atlanta editor Henry Grady tirelessly promoted the promise of a New South, an era of prosperity based on industrial expansion and agricultural diversification. In fact, while planters, merchants, and industrialists prospered, the region as a whole sank deeper and deeper into poverty. Some industry did develop, including mining in the Appalachians, textile production in the Carolinas and Georgia, and furniture and cigarette manufacturing in certain southern cities. The new upcountry cotton factories offered jobs to entire families of poor whites from the surrounding countryside. But since the main attractions for investors were the South's low wages and taxes and the availability of convict labor, these enterprises made little contribution to regional economic development. With the exception of Birmingham, Alabama, which by 1900 had developed into an important center for the manufacture of iron and steel, southern cities were mainly export centers for cotton, tobacco, and rice, with little industry or skilled labor. Overall, the region remained dependent on the North for capital and manufactured goods. In 1900, southern per capita income amounted to only 60 percent of the national average. As late as the 1930s, President Franklin D. Roosevelt would declare the South the nation's "number one" economic problem.

BLACK LIFE IN THE SOUTH

As the most disadvantaged rural southerners, black farmers suffered the most from the region's condition. In the Upper South, economic development offered some opportunities—mines, iron furnaces, and tobacco factories

Coal miners, in a photograph by Lewis Hine. Mining was one occupation in which blacks and whites often worked side by side.

employed black laborers, and a good number of black farmers managed to acquire land. In the rice kingdom of coastal South Carolina and Georgia, planters found themselves unable to acquire the capital necessary to repair irrigation systems and machinery destroyed by the war. By the turn of the century, most of the great plantations had fallen to pieces, and many blacks acquired land and took up self-sufficient farming. In most of the Deep South, however, African-Americans owned a smaller percentage of the land in 1900 than they had at the end of Reconstruction.

In southern cities, the network of institutions created after the Civil War—schools and colleges, churches, businesses, women's clubs, and the like—served as the foundation for increasingly diverse black urban communities. They supported the growth of a black middle class, mostly professionals like teachers and physicians, or businessmen like undertakers and shopkeepers serving the needs of black customers. But the labor market was rigidly divided along racial lines. Black men were excluded from supervisory positions in factories and workshops and white-collar jobs such as clerks in offices. A higher percentage of black women than white worked for wages, but mainly as domestic servants. They could not find employment among the growing numbers of secretaries, typists, and department store clerks.

THE KANSAS EXODUS

Overall, one historian has written, the New South was "a miserable landscape dotted only by a few rich enclaves that cast little or no light upon the poverty surrounding them." Trapped at the bottom of a stagnant economy, some blacks sought a way out through emigration from the South. In 1879 and 1880, an estimated 40,000 to 60,000 African-Americans migrated to Kansas, seeking political equality, freedom from violence, access to education, and economic opportunity. The name participants gave to this migration—the Exodus, derived from the biblical account of the Jews escaping slavery in Egypt—indicated that its roots lay in deep longings for the substance of freedom. Those promoting the Exodus, including former fugitive slave Benjamin "Pap" Singleton, the organizer of a real estate company, distributed flyers and lithographs picturing Kansas as an idyllic land of rural plenty. Lacking the capital to take up farming, however, most black migrants ended up as unskilled laborers in towns and cities. But few chose to return to the South. In the words of one minister active in the movement, "We had rather suffer and be free."

Despite deteriorating prospects in the South, most African-Americans had little alternative but to stay in the region. The real expansion of job opportunities was taking place in northern cities. But most northern employers refused to offer jobs to blacks in the expanding industrial economy, preferring to hire white migrants from rural areas and immigrants from Europe. Not until the outbreak of World War I in Europe in 1914 cut off immigration did northern employers open industrial jobs to blacks, setting in motion the Great Migration. Until then, the vast majority of African-Americans remained in the South.

THE DECLINE OF BLACK POLITICS

Neither black voting nor black officeholding came to an abrupt end in 1877. Blacks continued to cast ballots in large numbers, although Democrats solidified their control of state and local affairs by redrawing district lines and substituting appointive for elective officials in counties with black majorities. A few blacks even served in Congress in the 1880s and 1890s. Nonetheless, political opportunities became more and more restricted. Not until the 1990s would the number of black legislators in the South approach the level seen during Reconstruction.

For black men of talent and ambition, other avenues—business, the law, the church—increasingly seemed to offer greater opportunities for personal advancement and community service than politics. The banner of political leadership passed to black women activists. The National Association of Colored Women, founded in 1896, brought together local and regional women's clubs to press for both women's rights and racial uplift. Most female activists emerged from the small urban black middle class and preached the necessity of "respectable" behavior as part and parcel of the struggle for equal rights. They aided poor families, offered lessons in home life and childrearing, and battled gambling and drinking in black communities. Some poor blacks resented middle-class efforts to instruct them in proper behavior. But by insisting on the right of black women to be considered as "respectable" as their white counterparts, the women reformers challenged the racial ideology that consigned all blacks to the status of degraded second-class citizens.

For nearly a generation after the end of Reconstruction, despite fraud and violence, black southerners continued to cast ballots. In some states, the Republican Party remained competitive. In Virginia, a coalition of mostly black Republicans and anti-Redeemer Democrats formed an alliance known as the Readjuster movement (the name derived from their plan to scale back, or "readjust," the state debt). They governed the state between 1879 and 1883. Tennessee and Arkansas also witnessed the formation of biracial political coalitions that challenged Democratic Party rule. Despite the limits of the Populists' interracial alliance, the threat of a biracial political insurgency frightened the ruling Democrats and contributed greatly to the disenfranchisement movement. In North Carolina, for example, the end of the Populist-Republican coalition government in 1898—accomplished by a violent campaign that culminated in a riot in Wilmington in which scores of blacks were killed—was quickly followed by the elimination of black voting.

THE ELIMINATION OF BLACK VOTING

Between 1890 and 1906, every southern state enacted laws or constitutional provisions meant to eliminate the black vote. Since the Fifteenth Amendment prohibited the use of race as a qualification for the suffrage, how were such measures even possible? Southern legislatures drafted laws that on paper appeared color-blind, but that were actually designed to end black voting. The most popular devices were the poll tax (a fee that each citizen had to pay in order to retain the right to vote), literacy tests, and the requirement that a prospective voter demonstrate to election officials an "understanding" of the state constitution. Six southern states also adopted a "grandfather clause," exempting from the new requirements descendants of persons eligible to vote before the Civil War (when only whites, of course, could cast ballots in the South). The racial intent of the grandfather clause was so clear that the Supreme Court in 1915 invalidated such laws for violating the

Fifteenth Amendment. The other methods of limiting black voting, however, remained on the books.

Some white leaders presented disenfranchisement as a "good government" measure—a means of purifying politics by ending the fraud, violence, and manipulation of voting returns regularly used against Republicans and Populists. But ultimately, as a Charleston newspaper declared, the aim was to make clear that the white South "does not desire or intend ever to include black men among its citizens." Democrats persistently raised the threat of "Negro domination" to justify the denial of the right to vote. Although election officials often allowed whites who did not meet the new qualifications to register, numerous poor and illiterate whites also lost the right to vote, a result welcomed by many planters and urban reformers. Louisiana, for example, reduced the number of blacks registered to vote from 130,000 in 1894 to 1,342 a decade later. But 80,000 white voters also lost the right. Disenfranchisement led directly to the rise of a generation of southern "demagogues," who mobilized white voters by extreme appeals to racism. Tom Watson, who as noted before had tried to forge an interracial Populist coalition in the 1890s, reemerged early in the twentieth century as a power in Georgia public life through vicious speeches whipping up prejudice against blacks, Jews, and Catholics.

As late as 1940, only 3 percent of adult black southerners were registered to vote. The elimination of black and many white voters, which reversed the nineteenth-century trend toward more inclusive suffrage, could not have been accomplished without the approval of the North. In 1891, the Senate defeated a proposal for federal protection of black voting rights in the South. Apart from the grandfather clause, the Supreme Court gave its approval to disenfranchisement laws. According to the Fourteenth Amendment, any state that deprived male citizens of the franchise was supposed to lose part of its representation in Congress. But like much of the Constitution, this provision was consistently violated so far as African-Americans were concerned. As a result, southern congressmen wielded far greater power on the national scene than their tiny electorates warranted. As for blacks, for decades thereafter, they would regard "the loss of suffrage as being the loss of freedom."

THE LAW OF SEGREGATION

Along with disenfranchisement, the 1890s saw the widespread imposition of segregation in the South. Laws and local customs requiring the separation of the races had numerous precedents. They had existed in many parts of the pre–Civil War North. Southern schools and many other institutions had been segregated during Reconstruction. In the 1880s, however, southern race relations remained unsettled. Some railroads, theaters, and hotels admitted blacks

In Plessy v. Ferguson *(1896), the U.S. Supreme Court ruled that laws establishing racial segregation did not violate the equal protection clause of the Fourteenth Amendment, so long as facilities were "separate but equal." In fact, this was almost never the case, as illustrated by these photographs of the elementary schools for black and white children in South Boston, Virginia, in the early twentieth century.*

and whites on an equal basis while others separated them by race or excluded blacks altogether.

In 1883, in the *Civil Rights Cases*, the Supreme Court invalidated the Civil Rights Act of 1875, which had outlawed racial discrimination by hotels, theaters, railroads, and other public facilities. The Fourteenth Amendment, the Court insisted, prohibited unequal treatment by state authorities, not private businesses. In 1896, in the landmark decision in *Plessy v. Ferguson*, the Court gave its approval to state laws requiring separate facilities for blacks and whites. The case arose in Louisiana, where the legislature had required railroad companies to maintain a separate car or section for black passengers. A Citizens Committee of black residents of New Orleans came together to challenge the law. To create a test case, Homer Plessy, a light-skinned African-American, refused a conductor's order to move to the "colored only" part of his railroad car and was arrested.

To argue the case before the Supreme Court, the Citizens Committee hired Albion W. Tourgée, who as a judge in North Carolina during Reconstruction had waged a courageous battle against the Ku Klux Klan. "Citizenship is national and knows no color," he insisted, and racial segregation violated the Fourteenth Amendment's guarantee of equal protection before the law. But in an 8-1 decision, the Court upheld the Louisiana law, arguing that segregated facilities did not discriminate so long as they were "separate but equal." The lone dissenter, John Marshall Harlan, reprimanded the majority with an oft-quoted comment: "Our constitution is color-blind." Segregation, he insisted, sprang from whites' conviction that they were the "dominant race" (a phrase used by the Court's majority), and it violated the principle of equal liberty. To Harlan, freedom for the former slaves meant the right to participate fully and equally in American society.

SEGREGATION AND WHITE DOMINATION

As Harlan predicted, states reacted to the *Plessy* decision by passing laws mandating racial segregation in every aspect of southern life, from schools to hospitals, waiting rooms, toilets, and cemeteries. Some states forbade taxi drivers to carry members of different races at the same time. Despite the "thin disguise" (Harlan's phrase) of equality required by the Court's "separate but equal" doctrine, facilities for blacks were either nonexistent or markedly inferior. In 1900, no public high school for blacks existed in the entire South. Black elementary schools, one observer reported, occupied buildings "as bad as stables."

More than a form of racial separation, segregation was one part of an all—encompassing system of white domination, in which each component—disenfranchisement, unequal economic status, inferior education—reinforced the others. The point was not so much to keep the races apart as to ensure that when they came into contact with each other, whether in politics, labor relations, or social life, whites held the upper hand. For example, many blacks could be found in "whites-only" railroad cars. But they entered as servants and nurses, not as paying customers entitled to equal treatment.

An elaborate social etiquette developed, with proper behavior differentiated by race. One sociologist who studied the turn-of-the-century South reported that in places of business, blacks had to stand back and wait until whites had been served. They could not raise their voices or in other ways act assertively in the presence of whites, and they had to "give way" on the streets. In shops, whites but not blacks were allowed to try on clothing.

Segregation affected other groups as well as blacks. In some parts of Mississippi where Chinese laborers had been brought in to work the fields after the Civil War, three separate school systems—white, black, and Chinese—were established. In California, black, Hispanic, and American Indian children were frequently educated alongside whites, but state law required separate schools for those of "mongolian or Chinese descent." In Texas and California, although Mexicans were legally considered "white," they found themselves barred from many restaurants, places of entertainment, and other public facilities.

THE RISE OF LYNCHING

Those blacks who sought to challenge the system, or who refused to accept the demeaning behavior that was a daily feature of southern life, faced not only overwhelming political and legal power but also the threat of violent reprisal.

Table 1 STATES WITH OVER 200 LYNCHINGS, 1889–1918

State	*Number of Lynchings*
Georgia	386
Mississippi	373
Texas	335
Louisiana	313
Alabama	276
Arkansas	214

In every year between 1883 and 1905, more than fifty persons, the vast majority of them black men, were lynched in the South—that is, murdered by a mob. Lynching continued well into the twentieth century. By mid-century, the total number of victims since 1880 had reached nearly 5,000. Some lynchings occurred secretly at night; others were advertised in advance and attracted large crowds of onlookers. Mobs engaged in activities that shocked the civilized world. In 1899, Sam Hose, a plantation laborer who killed his employer in self-defense, was brutally murdered near Newman, Georgia, before 2,000 onlookers, some of whom arrived on a special excursion train from Atlanta. A crowd including young children watched as his executioners cut off Hose's ears, fingers, and genitals, burned him alive, and then fought over pieces of his bones as souvenirs. Law enforcement authorities made no effort to prevent the lynching or to bring those who committed the crime to justice.

Like many victims of lynchings, Hose was accused after his death of having raped a white woman. Many white southerners considered preserving the purity of white womanhood a justification for extralegal vengeance. Yet in nearly all cases, as activist Ida B. Wells argued in a newspaper editorial after a Memphis lynching in 1892, the charge of rape was a "bare lie." Born a slave in Mississippi in 1862, Wells had become a schoolteacher and editor. Her essay condemning the lynching of three black men in Memphis led a mob to destroy her newspaper, the *Memphis Free Press*, while she was out of the city. Wells moved to the North, where she became the nation's leading antilynching crusader. She bluntly insisted that given the conditions of southern blacks, the United States had no right to call itself the "land of the free."

Although many countries have witnessed outbreaks of violence against minority racial, ethnic, or religious groups, widespread lynching of individuals over so long a period was a phenomenon unknown elsewhere. Canada, for example, has experienced only one lynching in its history—in 1884, when a mob from the United States crossed the border into British Columbia to lynch an Indian teenager who had fled after being accused of murder.

Years later, black writer Blyden Jackson recalled growing up in early-twentieth-century Louisville, Kentucky, a city in many ways typical of the New South. It was a divided society. There was the world "where white folks lived . . .

the Louisville of the downtown hotels, the lower floors of the big movie houses . . . the inner sanctums of offices where I could go only as a humble client or a menial custodian." Then there was the black world, "the homes, the people, the churches, and the schools," where "everything was black." "I knew," Jackson later recalled, "that there were two Louisvilles and . . . two Americas."

POLITICS, RELIGION, AND MEMORY

As the white North and South moved toward reconciliation in the 1880s and 1890s, one cost was the abandonment of the dream of racial equality spawned by the Civil War and written into the laws and Constitution during Reconstruction. In popular literature and memoirs by participants, at veterans' reunions and in public memorials, the Civil War came to be remembered as a tragic family quarrel among white Americans in which blacks had played no significant part. It was a war of "brother against brother" in which both sides fought gallantly for noble causes—local rights on the part of the South, preservation of the Union for the North. Slavery increasingly came to be viewed as a minor issue, not the war's fundamental cause, and Reconstruction as a regrettable period of "Negro rule" when former slaves had power thrust upon them by a vindictive North. This outlook gave legitimacy to southern efforts to eliminate black voting, lest the region once again suffer the alleged "horrors" of Reconstruction.

Southern governments erected monuments to the Lost Cause, a romanticized version of slavery, the Old South, and the Confederate experience. Religion was central to the development of Lost Cause mythology—it offered a way for white southerners to come to terms with defeat in the Civil War without abandoning white supremacy. According to the Lost Cause, Confederate leaders like Robert E. Lee and Thomas "Stonewall" Jackson were sterling representatives of Christian virtue, while the Yankees had represented the forces of evil. The death of the Confederacy, in many sermons, was equated with the death of Christ, who gave his life for the sins of mankind.

Even as white northern Protestants abandoned concern for racial justice and embraced the idea of sectional reconciliation, southern churches played a key role in keeping the values of the Old South alive by refusing to reunite with northern branches. In the 1840s, the Methodist and Baptist churches had divided into northern and southern branches. Methodists would not reunite until well into the twentieth century; Baptists have yet to do so. In the North and South, school history textbooks emphasized happy slaves and the evils of Reconstruction, and the role of black soldiers in winning the war was all but forgotten. In fact, when a group of black veterans attempted to participate in a Florida ceremony commemorating the fiftieth anniversary of the outbreak of the Civil War in 1911, a white mob tore the military insignias off their jackets and drove them away.

REDRAWING THE BOUNDARIES

The effective nullification of the laws and amendments of Reconstruction and the reduction of blacks to the position of second-class citizens reflected nationwide patterns of thought and policy. As the nineteenth century drew to a close, American society seemed to be fracturing along lines of both class and race. The result, commented economist Simon Patten, was a widespread obsession with redrawing the boundary of freedom by identifying and excluding those unworthy of the blessings of liberty. "The South," he wrote, "has its negro, the city has its slums. . . . The friends of American institutions fear the ignorant immigrant, and the workingman dislikes the Chinese." As Patten suggested, many Americans embraced a more and more restricted definition of nationhood. The new exclusiveness was evident in the pages of popular periodicals, filled with derogatory imagery depicting blacks and other "lesser" groups as little more than savages and criminals incapable of partaking in American freedom.

THE NEW IMMIGRATION AND THE NEW NATIVISM

The 1890s witnessed a major shift in the sources of immigration to the United States. Despite the prolonged depression, 3.5 million newcomers entered the United States during the decade, seeking jobs in the industrial centers of the

A cartoon from the magazine Judge *illustrates anti-immigrant sentiment. A tide of newcomers representing the criminal element of other countries washes up on American shores, to the consternation of Uncle Sam.*

North and Midwest. Over half arrived not from Ireland, England, Germany, and Scandinavia, the traditional sources of immigration, but from southern and eastern Europe, especially Italy and the Russian and Austro-Hungarian empires. The "new immigrants" were widely described by native-born Americans as members of distinct "races," whose lower level of civilization explained everything from their willingness to work for substandard wages to their supposed inborn tendency toward criminal behavior. They were "beaten men from beaten races," wrote economist Francis Amasa Walker, representing "the worst failures in the struggle for existence." American cities, said an Ohio newspaper, were being overrun by foreigners who "have no true appreciation of the meaning of liberty" and therefore posed a danger to democratic government.

Founded in 1894 by a group of Boston professionals, the Immigration Restriction League called for reducing immigration by barring the illiterate from entering the United States. Such a measure was adopted by Congress early in 1897 but was vetoed by President Cleveland. Like the South, northern and western states experimented with ways to eliminate undesirable voters. Nearly all the states during the 1890s adopted the secret or "Australian" ballot, meant both to protect voters' privacy and to limit the participation of illiterates (who could no longer receive help from party officials at polling places). Several states ended the nineteenth-century practice of allowing immigrants to vote before becoming citizens and adopted stringent new residency and literacy requirements. None of these measures approached the scope of black disenfranchisement in the South or the continued denial of voting rights to women. But suffrage throughout the country was increasingly becoming a privilege, not a right.

CHINESE EXCLUSION AND CHINESE RIGHTS

The boundaries of nationhood, expanded so dramatically in the aftermath of the Civil War, slowly contracted. Leaders of both parties expressed vicious opinions regarding immigrants from China—they were "odious, abominable, dangerous, revolting," declared Republican leader James G. Blaine. Between 1850 and 1870, nearly all Chinese immigrants had been unattached men, brought in by labor contractors to work in western gold fields, railroad construction, and factories. In the early 1870s, entire Chinese families began to immigrate, leading Congress in 1875 to exclude Chinese women from entering the country. California congressman Horace Page, the bill's author, insisted that it was intended to preserve the health of white citizens by barring Chinese prostitutes. But immigration authorities enforced the Page law so as to keep out as well the wives and daughters of arriving men and of those already in the country.

Beginning in 1882, Congress temporarily excluded immigrants from China from entering the country altogether. Although non-whites had long been barred from becoming naturalized citizens, this was the first time that race had been used to exclude an entire group of people from entering the United States. Congress renewed the restriction ten years later and made it permanent in 1902.

At the time of exclusion, 105,000 persons of Chinese descent lived in the United States. Nearly all of them resided on the West Coast, where they suffered intense discrimination and periodic mob violence. In the late-nineteenth-century West, thousands of Chinese immigrants were expelled from towns and mining camps, and mobs assaulted Chinese residences and businesses. Drawing on the legislation of the Reconstruction era, Chinese victims sued local governments for redress when their rights were violated and petitioned Congress for indemnity. Their demands for equal rights forced the state and federal courts to define the reach of the Fourteenth Amendment. For example, between 1871 and 1885, San Francisco provided no public education for Chinese children. In 1885, the California Supreme Court, in *Tape v. Hurley*, ordered the city to admit Chinese students to public schools. The state legislature responded by passing a law authorizing segregated education, and the city established a school for Chinese. But Joseph and Mary Tape, who had lived in the United States since the 1860s, insisted that their daughter be allowed to attend her neighborhood school like other children. "Is it a disgrace to be born a Chinese?" Mary Tape wrote. "Didn't God make us all!" But her protest failed. Not until 1947 did California repeal the law authorizing separate schools for the Chinese.

The U.S. Supreme Court also considered the status of Chinese-Americans. In *Yick Wo v. Hopkins* (1886), the Court unanimously ordered San Francisco to grant licenses to Chinese-operated laundries, which the city government had refused to do. To deny a person the opportunity to earn a living, the Court declared, was "intolerable in any country where freedom prevails." Twelve years later, in *United States v. Wong Kim Ark*, the Court ruled that the Fourteenth Amendment awarded citizenship to children of Chinese immigrants born on American soil.

Yet the justices also affirmed the right of Congress to set racial restrictions on immigration. And in its decision in *Fong Yue Ting* (1893), the Court authorized the federal government to expel Chinese aliens without due process of law. In his dissent, Justice David J. Brewer acknowledged that the power was now directed against a people many Americans found "obnoxious." But "who shall say," he continued, "it will not be exercised tomorrow against other classes and other people?" Brewer proved to be an accurate prophet. In 1904, the Court cited *Fong Yue Ting* in upholding a law barring anarchists from entering the United States, demonstrating how restrictions on the rights of one group can become a precedent for infringing on the rights of others.

Exclusion profoundly shaped the experience of Chinese-Americans, long stigmatizing them as incapable of assimilation and justifying their isolation from mainstream society. Congress for the first time also barred groups of whites from entering the country, beginning in 1875 with prostitutes and convicted felons, and in 1882 adding "lunatics" and those likely to become a "public charge." "Are we still a [place of refuge] for the oppressed of all nations?" wondered James B. Weaver, the Populist candidate for president in 1892.

THE EMERGENCE OF BOOKER T. WASHINGTON

The social movements that had helped to expand the nineteenth-century boundaries of freedom now redefined their objectives so that they might be realized within the new economic and intellectual framework. Prominent black leaders, for example, took to emphasizing economic self-help and individual advancement into the middle class as an alternative to political agitation.

Symbolizing the change was the juxtaposition, in 1895, of the death of Frederick Douglass with Booker T. Washington's widely praised speech at the Atlanta Cotton Exposition that urged blacks to adjust to segregation and abandon agitation for civil and political rights. Born a slave in 1856, Washington had studied as a young man at Hampton Institute, Virginia. He adopted the outlook of Hampton's founder, General Samuel Armstrong, who emphasized that obtaining farms or skilled jobs was far more important to African-Americans emerging from slavery than the rights of citizenship. Washington put this view into practice when he became head of Tuskegee Institute in Alabama, a center for vocational education (education focused on training for a job rather than broad learning).

Booker T. Washington, advocate of industrial education and economic self-help.

In his Atlanta speech, Washington repudiated the abolitionist tradition that stressed ceaseless agitation for full equality. He urged blacks not to try to combat segregation: "In all the things that are purely social we can be as separate as the fingers, yet one as the hand in all things essential to mutual progress." Washington advised his people to seek the assistance of white employers who, in a land racked by labor turmoil, would prefer a docile, dependable black labor force to unionized whites. Washington's ascendancy rested in large part on his success in channeling aid from wealthy northern whites to Tuskegee and to black politicians and newspapers who backed his program. But his support in the black community also arose from a widespread sense that in the world of the late nineteenth century, frontal assaults on white power were impossible and that blacks should concentrate on building up their segregated communities.

THE RISE OF THE AFL

Within the labor movement, the demise of the Knights of Labor and the ascendancy of the American Federation of Labor (AFL) during the 1890s reflected a similar shift away from a broadly reformist past to more limited goals. As the Homestead and Pullman strikes demonstrated, direct confrontations with the large corporations were likely to prove suicidal. Unions, declared Samuel Gompers, the AFL's founder and longtime president, should not seek economic independence, pursue the Knights' utopian dream of creating a "cooperative commonwealth," or form independent parties with the aim of achieving power in government. Rather, the labor movement should devote itself to negotiating with employers for higher wages and better working conditions for its members. Like Washington, Gompers spoke the language of the era's business culture. Indeed, the AFL policies he pioneered were known as "business unionism." Gompers embraced the idea of "freedom of contract," shrewdly turning it into an argument against interference by judges with workers' right to organize unions.

During the 1890s, union membership rebounded from its decline in the late 1880s. But at the same time, the labor movement became less and less inclusive. Abandoning the Knights' ideal of labor solidarity, the AFL restricted membership to skilled workers—a small minority of the labor force—effectively excluding the vast majority of unskilled workers and, therefore, nearly all blacks, women, and new European immigrants. AFL membership centered on sectors of the economy like printing and building construction that were dominated by small competitive businesses with workers who frequently were united by craft skill and ethnic background. AFL unions had little presence in basic industries like steel and rubber, or in the large-scale factories that now dominated the economy.

THE WOMEN'S ERA

Changes in the women's movement reflected the same combination of expanding activities and narrowing boundaries. The 1890s launched what would later be called the "women's era"—three decades during which women, although still denied the vote, enjoyed larger opportunities than in the past for economic independence and played a greater and greater role in public life. By now, nearly every state had adopted laws giving married women control over their own wages and property and the right to sign separate contracts and make separate wills. Nearly 5 million women worked for wages in 1900. Although most were young, unmarried, and concentrated in traditional jobs such as domestic service and the garment industry, a generation of college-educated women was beginning to take its place in better-paying clerical and professional positions.

Through a network of women's clubs, temperance associations, and social reform organizations, women exerted a growing influence on public affairs. Founded in 1874, the Women's Christian Temperance Union (WCTU) grew to become the era's largest female organization, with a membership by 1890 of 150,000. Under the banner of Home Protection, it moved from demanding the prohibition of alcoholic beverages (blamed for leading men to squander their wages on drink and treat their wives abusively) to a comprehensive program of economic and political reform, including the right to vote. Women, insisted Frances Willard, the group's president, must abandon the idea that "weakness" and dependence were their nature and join assertively in movements to change society. "A wider freedom is coming to the women of America," she declared in an 1895 speech to male and female strikers in a Massachusetts shoe factory. "Too long has it been held that woman has no right to enter these movements. So much for the movements. Politics is the place for woman."

At the same time, the center of gravity of feminism shifted toward an outlook more in keeping with prevailing racial and ethnic norms. The earlier "feminism of equal rights," which claimed the ballot as part of a larger transformation of women's status, was never fully repudiated. The movement continued to argue for women's equality in employment, education, and politics. But with increasing frequency, the native-born, middle-class women who dominated the suffrage movement claimed the vote as educated members of a "superior race."

A new generation of suffrage leaders suggested that educational and other voting qualifications did not conflict with the movement's aims, so long as they applied equally to men and women. Immigrants and former slaves had been enfranchised with "ill-advised haste," declared Carrie Chapman Catt, president of the National American Woman Suffrage Association (created in 1890 to reunite the rival suffrage organizations formed after the Civil War). Indeed, Catt suggested, extending the vote to native-born white women would help to counteract the growing power of the "ignorant foreign vote" in the North and the dangerous potential for a second Reconstruction in the South. Elitism within the movement was reinforced when many advocates of suffrage blamed the "slum vote" for the defeat of a women's suffrage referendum in California. In 1895, the same year that Booker T. Washington delivered his Atlanta address, the National American Woman Suffrage Association held its annual convention in that segregated city. Eight years later, the association met in New Orleans, where the delegates sang "Dixie" and listened to speeches by former Confederate officers that denounced blacks as barbarians. Like other American institutions, the organized movement for women's suffrage had made its peace with nativism and racism.

BECOMING A WORLD POWER

THE NEW IMPERIALISM

In the last years of the 1890s, the narrowed definition of nationhood was projected abroad, as the United States took its place as an imperial power on the international stage. In world history, the last quarter of the nineteenth century is known as the age of imperialism, when rival European empires carved up large parts of the world among themselves. For most of this period, the United States remained a second-rate power. In 1880, the sultan of Turkey (head of the Ottoman empire) decided to close three foreign embassies to reduce expenses. He chose those in Sweden, Belgium, and the United States. In that year, the American navy was smaller than Denmark's or Chile's. When European powers met at the Berlin Congress of 1884–1885 to divide most of Africa among themselves, the United States attended because of its relationship with Liberia but did not sign the final agreement.

Throughout the nineteenth century, large empires dominated much of the globe. Some were land-based, like the Russian, Ottoman, and Chinese empires, and others included territories on several continents linked by sea, such as the British, French, and Spanish. After 1870, a "new imperialism" arose, dominated by European powers and Japan. Belgium, Great Britain, and France consolidated their hold on colonies in Africa, and newly unified Germany acquired colonies there as well. The British and Russians sought to increase their influence in Central Asia, and all the European powers struggled to dominate parts of China. By the early twentieth century, most of Asia, Africa, the Middle East, and the Pacific had been divided among these empires. The justification for this expansion of imperial power was that it would bring modern "civilization" to the supposedly backward peoples of the non-European world. The natives, according to their colonial occupiers, would be instructed in Western values, labor practices, and the Christian religion. Eventually, they would be accorded the right of self-government, although no one could be sure how long this would take. In the meantime, "empire" was another word for "exploitation."

AMERICAN EXPANSIONISM

Territorial expansion, of course, had been a feature of American life from well before independence. But the 1890s marked a major turning point in America's relationship with the rest of the world. Americans were increasingly aware of themselves as an emerging world power. "We are a great imperial Republic destined to exercise a controlling influence upon the actions of mankind and to affect the future of the world," proclaimed Henry Watterson, an influential newspaper editor.

Until the 1890s, American expansion had taken place on the North American continent. Ever since the Monroe Doctrine, to be sure, many Americans had considered the Western Hemisphere an American sphere of influence. There was persistent talk of acquiring Cuba, and President Grant had sought to annex the Dominican Republic, only to see the Senate reject the idea. The last territorial acquisition before the 1890s had been Alaska, purchased from Russia by Secretary of State William H. Seward in 1867, to much derision from those who could not see the purpose of American ownership of "Seward's icebox." Seward, however, was mostly interested in the Aleutian Islands, a part of Alaska that stretched much of the way to Asia and that, he believed, could be the site of coaling stations for merchant ships plying the Pacific.

Most Americans who looked overseas were interested in expanded trade, not territorial possessions. The country's agricultural and industrial production could no longer be entirely absorbed at home. By 1890, companies like Singer Sewing Machines and John D. Rockefeller's Standard Oil Company aggressively marketed their products abroad. Especially during economic downturns, business leaders insisted on the necessity of greater access to foreign customers. Middle-class American women, moreover, were becoming more and more desirous of clothing and food from abroad, and their demand for consumer goods such as "Oriental" fashions and exotic spices for cooking spurred the economic penetration of the Far East.

THE LURE OF EMPIRE

One group of Americans who spread the nation's influence overseas were religious missionaries, thousands of whom ventured abroad in the late nineteenth century to spread Christianity, prepare the world for the second coming of Christ, and uplift the poor. Inspired by Dwight Moody, a Methodist evangelist, the Student Volunteer Movement for Foreign Missions sent more than 8,000 missionaries to "bring light to heathen worlds" across the globe. Missionary work offered employment to those with few opportunities at home, including blacks and women, who made up a majority of the total.

A cartoon in Puck, *December 1, 1897, imagines the annexation of Hawaii by the United States as a shotgun wedding. The minister, President McKinley, reads from a book entitled* Annexation Policy. *The Hawaiian bride appears to be looking for a way to escape. Most Hawaiians did not support annexation.*

A small group of late-nineteenth-century thinkers actively promoted American expansionism, warning that the country must not allow itself to be shut out of the scramble for empire. In *Our Country* (1885), Josiah Strong, a prominent Congregationalist clergyman, sought to update the idea of manifest destiny. Having demonstrated their special aptitude for liberty and self-government on the North American continent, Strong announced, Anglo-Saxons should now spread their institutions and values to "inferior races" throughout the world. The economy would benefit, he insisted, since one means of civilizing "savages" was to turn them into consumers of American goods.

Naval officer Alfred T. Mahan, in *The Influence of Sea Power upon History* (1890), argued that no nation could prosper without a large fleet of ships engaged in international trade, protected by a powerful navy operating from overseas bases. Mahan published his book in the same year that the census bureau announced that there was no longer a clear line separating settled from unsettled land. Thus, the frontier no longer existed. "Americans," wrote Mahan, "must now begin to look outward." His arguments influenced the outlook of James G. Blaine, who served as secretary of state during Benjamin Harrison's presidency (1889–1893). Blaine urged the president to try to acquire Hawaii, Puerto Rico, and Cuba as strategic naval bases.

Although independent, Hawaii was already closely tied to the United States through treaties that exempted imports of its sugar from tariff duties and provided for the establishment of an American naval base at Pearl Harbor. Hawaii's economy was dominated by American-owned sugar plantations that employed a workforce of native islanders and Chinese, Japanese, and Filipino laborers under long-term contracts. Early in 1893, a group of American planters organized a rebellion that overthrew the Hawaii government of Queen Liliuokalani. On the eve of leaving office, Harrison submitted a treaty of annexation to the Senate. After determining that a majority of Hawaiians did not favor the treaty, Harrison's successor, Grover Cleveland, withdrew it. In July 1898, in the midst of the Spanish-American War, the United States finally annexed the Hawaiian Islands. In 1993, the U.S. Congress passed, and President Bill Clinton signed, a resolution expressing regret to native Hawaiians for "the overthrow of the Kingdom of Hawaii . . . with the participation of agents and citizens of the United States."

The depression that began in 1893 heightened the belief that a more aggressive foreign policy was necessary to stimulate American exports. Fears of economic and ethnic disunity fueled an assertive nationalism. In the face of social conflict and the new immigration, government and private organizations in the 1890s promoted a unifying patriotism. These were the years when rituals like the Pledge of Allegiance and the practice of standing for the playing of "The Star-Spangled Banner" came into existence. Americans had long honored the Stars and Stripes, but the "cult of the flag," including an official Flag Day, dates to the 1890s. New, mass-circulation newspapers also promoted nationalistic sentiments. By the late 1890s, papers like William Randolph Hearst's *New York Journal* and Joseph Pulitzer's *New York World*—dubbed the "yellow press" by their critics after the color in which Hearst printed a popular comic strip—were selling a million copies each day by mixing sensational accounts of crime and political corruption with aggressive appeals to patriotic sentiments.

THE "SPLENDID LITTLE WAR"

All these factors contributed to America's emergence as a world power in the Spanish-American War of 1898. But the immediate origins of the war lay not at home but in the long Cuban struggle for independence from Spain. Ten years of guerrilla war had followed a Cuban revolt in 1868. The movement for independence resumed in 1895. As reports circulated of widespread suffering caused by the Spanish policy of rounding up civilians and moving them into detention camps, the Cuban struggle won growing support in the United States.

Demands for intervention escalated after February 15, 1898, when an explosion—probably accidental, a later investigation concluded—destroyed the American battleship *Maine* in Havana Harbor, with the loss of nearly 270 lives. The yellow press blamed Spain and insisted on retribution. After Spain rejected an American demand for a cease-fire on the island and eventual Cuban independence, President McKinley in April asked Congress for a declaration of war. The purpose, declared Senator Henry Teller of Colorado, was to aid Cuban patriots in their struggle for "liberty and freedom." To underscore the government's humanitarian intentions, Congress adopted the Teller Amendment, stating that the United States had no intention of annexing or dominating the island.

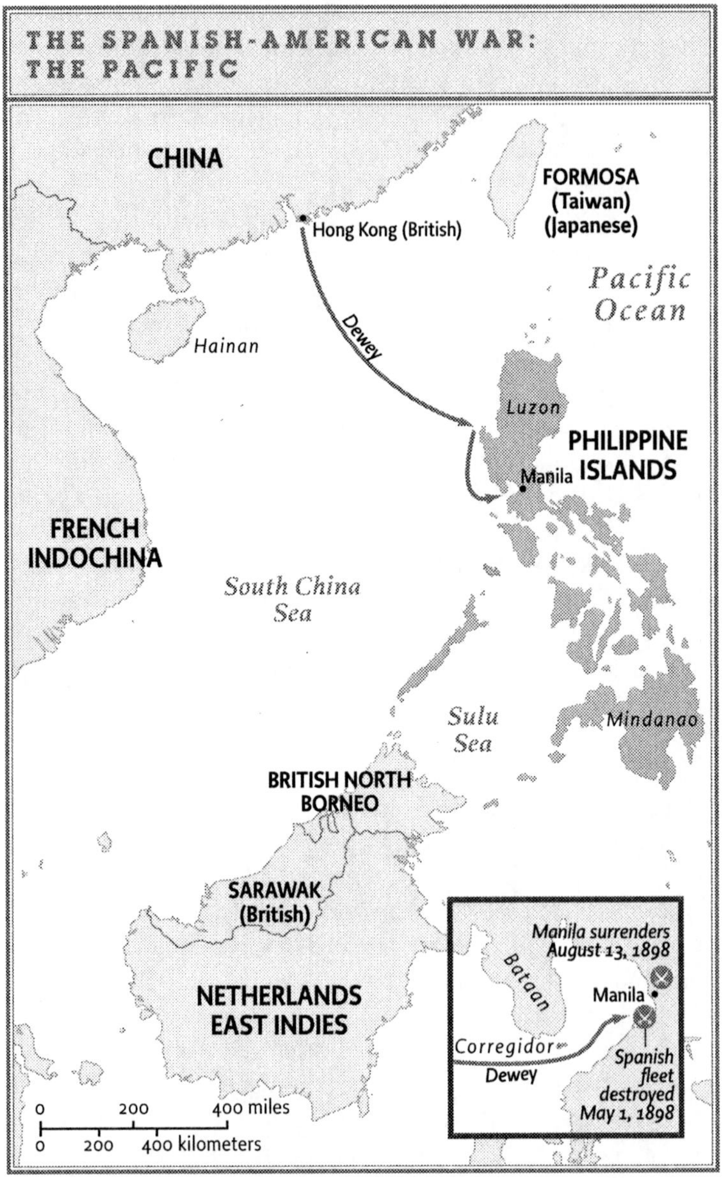

In both the Caribbean and the Pacific, the United States achieved swift victories over Spain in the Spanish-American War.

THE SPANISH-AMERICAN WAR: THE CARIBBEAN

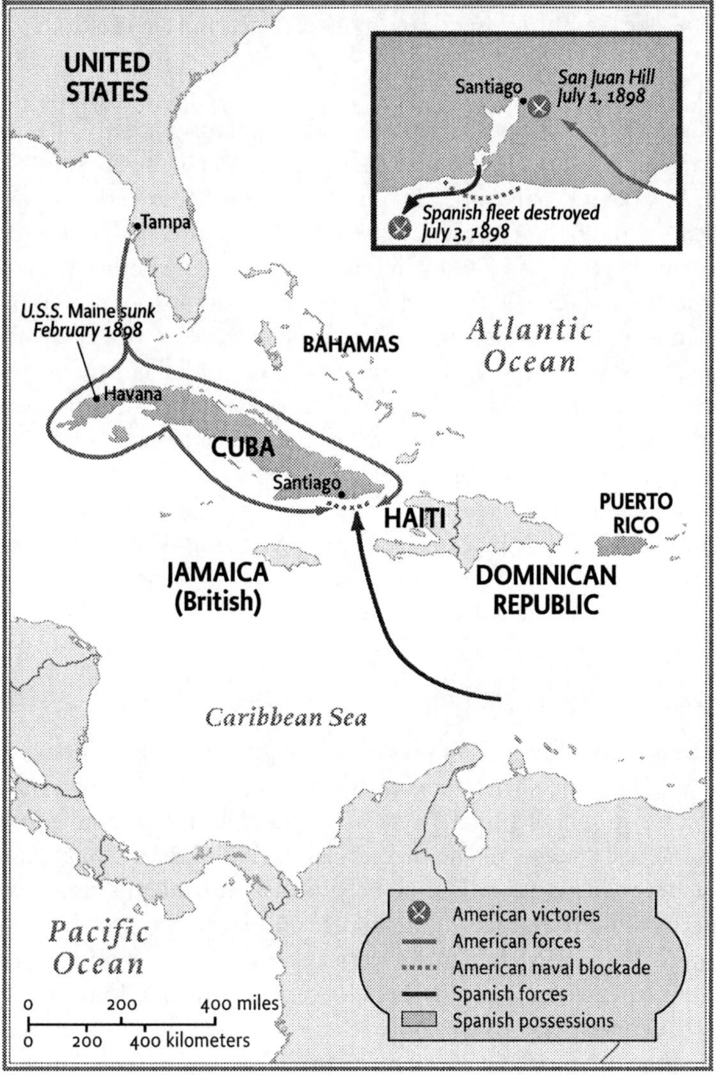

Secretary of State John Hay called the Spanish-American conflict a "splendid little war." It lasted only four months and resulted in fewer than 400 American combat deaths. Having shown little interest in imperial expansion before 1898, McKinley now embraced the idea. The war's most decisive engagement, in fact, took place not in Cuba but at Manila Bay, a strategic harbor in the Philippine Islands in the distant Pacific Ocean. Here, on May 1, the American navy under

Admiral George Dewey defeated a Spanish fleet. Soon afterward, soldiers went ashore, becoming the first American army units to engage in combat outside the Western Hemisphere. July witnessed another naval victory off Santiago, Cuba, and the landing of American troops on Cuba and Puerto Rico.

ROOSEVELT AT SAN JUAN HILL

The most highly publicized land battle of the war took place in Cuba. This was the charge up San Juan Hill, outside Santiago, by Theodore Roosevelt's Rough Riders. An ardent expansionist, Roosevelt had long believed that a war would reinvigorate the nation's unity and sense of manhood, which had suffered, he felt, during the 1890s. A few months shy of his fortieth birthday when war broke out, Roosevelt resigned his post as assistant secretary of the navy to raise a volunteer cavalry unit, which rushed to Cuba to participate in the fighting. Roosevelt envisioned his unit as a cross section of American society and enrolled athletes from Ivy League colleges, western cowboys, representatives of various immigrant groups, and even some American Indians. But with the army still segregated, he excluded blacks from his regiment. Ironically, when the Rough Riders reached the top of San Juan Hill, they found that black units had preceded them—a fact Roosevelt omitted in his reports of the battle, which were widely reproduced in the popular press. His exploits made Roosevelt a national hero. He was elected governor of New York that fall and in 1900 became McKinley's vice president.

AN AMERICAN EMPIRE

With the backing of the yellow press, the war quickly escalated from a crusade to aid the suffering Cubans to an imperial venture that ended with the United States in possession of a small overseas empire. McKinley became convinced that the United States could neither return the Philippines to Spain nor grant them independence, for which he believed the inhabitants unprepared. In an interview with a group of Methodist ministers, the president spoke of receiving a divine revelation that Americans had a duty to "uplift and civilize" the Filipino people and to train them for self-government. In the treaty with Spain that ended the war, the United States acquired the Philippines, Puerto Rico, and the Pacific island of Guam. As for Cuba, before recognizing its independence, McKinley forced the island's new government to approve the Platt Amendment to the new Cuban constitution (drafted by Senator Orville H. Platt of Connecticut), which authorized the United States to intervene militarily whenever it saw fit. The United States also acquired a permanent lease on naval stations in Cuba, including what is now the facility at Guantánamo Bay.

The Platt Amendment passed the Cuban Congress by a single vote. Cuban patriots were terribly disappointed. José Martí had fomented revolution in

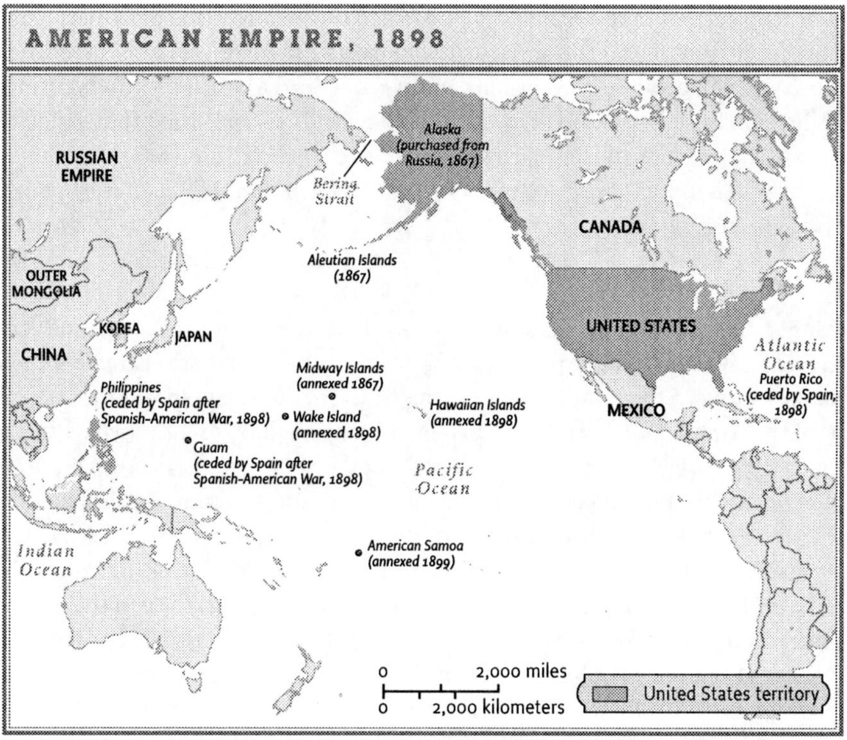

As a result of the Spanish-American War, the United States became the ruler of a far-flung overseas empire.

Cuba from exile in the United States and then traveled to the island to take part in the uprising, only to be killed in a battle with Spanish soldiers in 1895. "To change masters is not to be free," Martí had written. And the memory of the betrayal of 1898 would help to inspire another Cuban revolution half a century later.

American interest in its new possessions had more to do with trade than gaining wealth from natural resources or large-scale American settlement. Puerto Rico and Cuba were gateways to Latin America, strategic outposts from which American naval and commercial power could be projected throughout the hemisphere. The Philippines, Guam, and Hawaii lay astride shipping routes to the markets of Japan and China. In 1899, soon after the end of the Spanish-American War, Secretary of State John Hay announced the Open Door policy, demanding that European powers that had recently divided China into commercial spheres of influence grant equal access to American exports. The Open Door referred to the free movement of goods and money, not people. Even as the United States banned the immigration of Chinese into this country, it insisted on access to the markets and investment opportunities of Asia. Such economic ambitions could easily lead to military intervention. When Chinese nationalists in the 1900 Boxer Rebellion killed thousands of Christian Chinese and beseiged foreign embassies in Beijing, the United States contributed more than 3,000 soldiers to the international force that helped to suppress the rebellion.

THE PHILIPPINE WAR

Many Cubans, Filipinos, and Puerto Ricans had welcomed American intervention as a way of breaking Spain's long hold on these colonies. Large planters looked forward to greater access to American markets, and local elites hoped that the American presence would fend off radical changes proposed by rebellious nationalist movements. Nationalists and labor leaders admired America's democratic ideals and believed that American participation in the destruction of Spanish rule would lead to social reform and political self-government.

But the American determination to exercise continued control, direct or indirect, led to a rapid change in local opinion, nowhere more so than in the Philippines. Filipinos had been fighting a war against Spain since 1896. After Dewey's victory at Manila Bay, their leader, Emilio Aguinaldo, established a provisional government with a constitution modeled on that of the United States. But once McKinley decided to retain possession of the islands, the Filipino movement turned against the United States. The result was a second war, far longer (it lasted from 1899 to 1903) and bloodier (it cost the lives of more than 100,000 Filipinos and 4,200 Americans) than the Spanish-American conflict. Today, this is perhaps the least remembered of all American wars. At the time, however, it was closely followed and widely debated in the United States. Press reports of atrocities committed by American troops—the burning of villages, torture of prisoners of war, and rape and execution of civilians—tarnished the nation's self-image as liberators. "We do not intend to free the people of the Philippines," complained Mark Twain. "We have gone there to conquer."

The McKinley administration justified its policies on the grounds that its aim was to "uplift and civilize and Christianize" the Filipinos (although most residents of the islands were already Roman Catholics). William Howard Taft, who became governor-general of the Philippines in 1901, believed it might take a century to raise Filipinos to the condition where they could appreciate "what Anglo-Saxon liberty is."

Once in control of the Philippines, the colonial administration took seriously the idea of modernizing the islands. It expanded railroads and harbors, brought in American schoolteachers and public health officials, and sought to modernize agriculture (although efforts to persuade local farmers to substitute corn for rice ran afoul of Filipino climate and cultural traditions). The United States, said President McKinley, had an obligation to its "little brown brothers." Yet in all the new possessions, American policies tended to serve the interests of land-based local elites—native-born landowners in the Philippines, American sugar planters in Hawaii and Puerto Rico—and such policies bequeathed enduring poverty to the majority of the rural population. Under American rule, Puerto Rico, previously an island of diversified small farmers, became a low-wage plantation economy controlled by absentee corporations. By the 1920s, its residents were among the poorest in the entire Caribbean.

CITIZENS OR SUBJECTS?

American rule also brought with it American racial attitudes. In an 1899 poem, the British writer Rudyard Kipling urged the United States to take up the "white man's burden" of imperialism. American proponents of empire agreed that the domination of non-white peoples by whites formed part of the progress of civilization. Among the soldiers sent to the Philippines to fight Aguinaldo were a number of black regiments. Their letters from the front suggested that American atrocities arose from white troops applying to the Filipino population the same "treatment for colored peoples" practiced at home. "Is America any better than Spain?" wondered George W. Prioleau, a black cavalryman who had fought at San Juan Hill.

America's triumphant entry into the ranks of imperial powers sparked an intense debate over the relationship among political democracy, race, and American citizenship. The American system of government had no provision for permanent colonies. The right of every people to self-government was one of the main principles of the Declaration of Independence. The idea of an "empire of liberty" assumed that new territories would eventually be admitted as equal states and their residents would be American citizens. In the aftermath of the Spanish-American War, however, nationalism, democracy, and American freedom emerged more closely identified than ever with notions of Anglo-Saxon superiority.

Leaders of both parties, while determined to retain the new overseas possessions, feared that people of what one congressman called "an alien race and foreign tongue" could not be incorporated into the Union. The Foraker Act of 1900 declared Puerto Rico an "insular territory," different from previous territories in the West. Its 1 million inhabitants were defined as citizens of Puerto Rico, not the United States, and denied a future path to statehood. Filipinos occupied a similar status. In a series of cases decided between 1901 and 1904 and known collectively as the Insular Cases, the Supreme Court held that the Constitution did not fully apply to the territories recently acquired by the United States—a significant limitation of the scope of American

VOICES OF FREEDOM

From Josiah Strong, Our Country (1885)

The Congregational minister Josiah Strong promoted both the Social Gospel—a desire, grounded in religious belief, to solve the nation's social problems—and an updated version of manifest destiny and American expansionism strongly connected to ideas of racial superiority and a Christian missionary impulse.

It seems to me that God, with infinite wisdom and skill, is training the Anglo-Saxon race for an hour sure to come in the world's future. Heretofore there has always been in the history of the world a comparatively unoccupied land westward, into which the crowded countries of the East have poured their surplus populations. But the widening waves of migration, which millenniums ago rolled east and west from the valley of the Euphrates meet to-day on our Pacific coast. There are no more new worlds. The unoccupied arable lands of the earth are limited, and will soon be taken. The time is coming when the pressure of population on the means of subsistence will be felt here as it is now felt in Europe and Asia. Then will the world enter upon a new stage of its history—*the final competition of races, for which the Anglo-Saxon is being schooled.* Long before the thousand millions are here, the mighty *centrifugal* tendency, inherent in this stock and strengthened in the United States, will assert itself. Then this race of unequaled energy, with all the majesty of numbers and the might of wealth behind it—the representative, let us hope, of the largest liberty, the purest Christianity, the highest civilization—having developed peculiarly aggressive traits calculated to impress its institutions upon mankind, will spread itself over the earth. If I read not amiss, this powerful race will move down upon Mexico, down upon Central and South America, out upon the islands of the sea, over upon Africa and beyond. And can any one doubt that the result of this competition of races will be the "survival of the fittest"?

Some of the stronger races, doubtless, may be able to preserve their integrity; but, in order to compete with the Anglo-Saxon, they will probably be forced to adopt his methods and instruments, his civilization and his religion.

From "Aguinaldo's Case against the United States" (1899)

Emilio Aguinaldo, who led the Filipino armed struggle for independence against Spain and then another war against the United States when President McKinley decided to annex the Philippines, explained his reasons for opposing American imperialism in an article in the widely read magazine, the North American Review. He contrasted American traditions of self-government with the refusal to grant this right to the Philippines.

We Filipinos have all along believed that if the American nation at large knew exactly, as we do, what is daily happening in the Philippine Islands, they would rise en masse, and demand that this barbaric war should stop [and] . . . she would cease to be the laughing stock of other civilized nations, as she became when she abandoned her traditions and set up a double standard of government—government by consent in America, government by force in the Philippine Islands. . . .

You have been deceived all along the line. You have been greatly deceived in the personality of my countrymen. You went to the Philippines under the impression that their inhabitants were ignorant savages. . . . We have been represented by your popular press as if we were Africans or Mohawk Indians. . . .

You repeat constantly the dictum that we cannot govern ourselves. . . . With equal reason, you might have said the same thing some fifty or sixty years ago of Japan; and, little over a hundred years ago, it was extremely questionable, when you, also, were rebels against the English Government, if you could govern yourselves. . . . Now, the moral of all this obviously is: Give us the chance; treat us exactly as you demanded to be treated at the hands of England when you rebelled against her autocratic methods.

Now, here is a unique spectacle—the Filipinos fighting for liberty, the American people fighting them to give them liberty. . . . You entered into an alliance with our chiefs at Hong Kong and at Singapore, and you promised us your aid and protection in our attempt to form a government on the principles and after the model of the government of the United States. . . . In combination with our forces, you compelled Spain to surrender. . . . Joy abounded in every heart, and all went well . . . until . . . the Government at Washington . . . commenc[ed] by ignoring all promises that had been made and end[ed] by ignoring the Philippine people, their personality and rights, and treating them as a common enemy. . . . In the face of the world you emblazon humanity and Liberty upon your standard, while you cast your political constitution to the winds and attempt to trample down and exterminate a brave people whose only crime is that they are fighting for their liberty.

QUESTIONS

1. How does Strong justify the idea of world domination by Anglo-Saxons?

2. Why does Aguinaldo think that the United States is betraying its own values?

3. How do these documents reflect different definitions of liberty?

freedom. Congress, the Court declared, must recognize the "fundamental" personal rights of residents of the Philippines and Puerto Rico. But otherwise it could govern them as it saw fit for an indefinite period of time. Thus, two principles central to American freedom since the War of Independence—no taxation without representation, and government based on the consent of the governed—were abandoned when it came to the nation's new possessions.

In the twentieth century, the territories acquired in 1898 would follow different paths. Hawaii, which had a sizable population of American missionaries and planters, became a traditional territory. Its population, except for Asian immigrant laborers, became American citizens, and it was admitted as a state in 1959. After nearly a half-century of American rule, the Philippines achieved independence in 1946. Until 1950, the U.S. Navy administered Guam, which remains today an "unincorporated" territory. As for Puerto Rico, it is sometimes called "the world's oldest colony," because ever since the Spanish conquered the island in 1493 it has lacked full self-government. Congress extended American citizenship to Puerto Ricans in 1917. Puerto Rico today remains in a kind of political limbo, poised on the brink of statehood or independence. The island has the status of a commonwealth. It elects its own government but lacks a voice in Congress (and in the election of the U.S. president) and key issues such as defense and environmental policy are controlled by the United States.

An advertisement employs the idea of a White Man's Burden (borrowed from a poem by Rudyard Kipling) as a way of promoting the virtues of Pears' Soap. Accompanying text claims that Pears' is "the ideal toilet soap" for "the cultured of all nations," and an agent of civilization in "the dark corners of the earth."

DRAWING THE GLOBAL COLOR LINE

Just as American ideas about liberty and self-government had circulated around the world in the Age of the American Revolution, American racial attitudes had a global impact in the age of empire. The turn of the twentieth century was a time of worldwide concern about immigration, race relations, and the "white man's burden," all of which inspired a global sense of fraternity among "Anglo-Saxon" nations. Chinese exclusion in the

United States strongly influenced anti-Chinese laws adopted in Canada, and American segregation and disenfranchisement became models for Australia and South Africa as they formed new governments; they read in particular the proceedings of the Mississippi constitutional convention of 1890, which pioneered ways to eliminate black voting rights.

One "lesson" these countries learned from the United States was that the "failure" of Reconstruction demonstrated the impossibility of multiracial democracy. The extremely hostile account of Reconstruction by the British writer James Bryce in his widely read book *The American Commonwealth* (published in London in 1888) circulated around the world. Bryce called African-Americans "children of nature" and insisted that giving them the right to vote had been a terrible mistake, which had produced all kinds of corruption and misgovernment. His book was frequently cited by the founders of the Australian Commonwealth (1901) to justify their "white Australia" policy, which barred the further immigration of Asians. The Union of South Africa, inaugurated in 1911, saw its own policy of racial separation—later known as apartheid—as following in the footsteps of segregation in the United States. South Africa, however, went much further, enacting laws that limited skilled jobs to whites and dividing the country into areas where black Africans could and could not live. Even American proposals that did not become law, such as the literacy test for immigrants vetoed by President Cleveland, influenced measures adopted overseas. The United States, too, learned from other countries. The Gentleman's Agreement that limited Japanese immigration early in the twentieth century followed a similar arrangement between Japan and Canada.

"REPUBLIC OR EMPIRE?"

The emergence of the United States as an imperial power sparked intense debate. Opponents formed the Anti-Imperialist League. It united writers and social reformers who believed American energies should be directed at home, businessmen fearful of the cost of maintaining overseas outposts, and racists who did not wish to bring non-white populations into the United States. Among its prominent members were E. L. Godkin, the editor of *The Nation*, the novelist William Dean Howells, and the labor leader George E. McNeill. The league held meetings throughout the country and published pamphlets called Liberty Tracts, warning that empire was incompatible with democracy. America's historic mission, the league declared, was to "help the world by an example of successful self-government," not to conquer other peoples. A "republic of free men," anti-imperialists proclaimed, should assist the people of Puerto Rico and the Philippines in their own "struggles for liberty," rather than subjecting them to colonial rule.

In 1900, Democrats again nominated William Jennings Bryan to run against McKinley. The Democratic platform opposed the Philippine War for placing the United States in the "un-American" position of "crushing with military force" another people's desire for "liberty and self-government." George S. Boutwell, president of the Anti-Imperialist League, declared that the most pressing question in the election was the nation's future character—"republic or empire?"

But without any sense of contradiction, proponents of an imperial foreign policy also adopted the language of freedom. Anti-imperialists were the real "infidels to the gospel of liberty," claimed Senator Albert Beveridge of Indiana, because America ventured abroad not for material gain or national power, but to bring "a new day of freedom" to the peoples of the world. America's was a "benevolent" imperialism, rooted in a national mission to uplift backward cultures and spread liberty across the globe. Beveridge did not, however, neglect more practical considerations. American trade, he insisted, "henceforth must be with Asia. The Pacific is our ocean. . . . Where shall we turn for consumers of our surplus? Geography answers the question. China is our natural customer." And the Philippines held the key to "the commercial situation of the entire East." Riding the wave of patriotic sentiment inspired by the war, and with the economy having recovered from the depression of 1893–1897, McKinley in 1900 repeated his 1896 triumph.

At the dawn of the twentieth century, the United States seemed poised to take its place among the world's great powers. Writers at home and overseas confidently predicted that American influence would soon span the globe. In his 1902 book *The New Empire*, Brooks Adams, a grandson of John Quincy Adams, predicted that because of its economic power, the United States would soon "outweigh any single empire, if not all empires combined." Years would pass before this prediction was fulfilled. But in 1900, many features that would mark American life for much of the twentieth century were already apparent. The United States had surpassed Britain, France, and Germany in industrial production. The merger movement of 1897–1904 left broad sections of the economy under the control of giant corporations. The political system had stabilized. The white North and South had achieved reconciliation, while rigid lines of racial exclusion—the segregation of blacks, Chinese exclusion, Indian reservations—limited the boundaries of freedom and citizenship.

Yet the questions central to nineteenth-century debates over freedom—the relationship between political and economic liberty, the role of government in creating the conditions of freedom, and the definition of those entitled to enjoy the rights of citizens—had not been permanently answered. Nor had the dilemma of how to reconcile America's role as an empire with traditional ideas of freedom. These were the challenges bequeathed by the nineteenth century to the first generation of the twentieth.

Chapter Review

REVIEW QUESTIONS

1. What economic and political issues gave rise to the Populist Party and what changes did the party advocate?
2. How did employers use state and federal forces to protect their own economic interests, and what were the results?
3. Compare and contrast the goals, strategies, and membership of the American Federation of Labor and the Knights of Labor.
4. Who were the Redeemers, and how did they change society and politics in the New South?
5. Explain how changes in the politics, economics, social factors, and spread of violence affected the situation of blacks in the New South.
6. How did religion and the idea of the Lost Cause give support to a new understanding of the Civil War?
7. What ideas and interests motivated the United States to create an empire in the late nineenth century?
8. Compare the arguments for and against U.S. imperialism. Be sure to consider the views of Josiah Strong and Emilio Aguinaldo.
9. What rights did Chinese immigrants and Chinese Americans gain in these years, and what limitations did they experience? How did their experiences set the stage for other restrictions on immigration?

KEY TERMS

The People's Party or Populists
Coxey's Army
"free coinage" of silver
Kansas Exodus
disenfranchisement
Plessy v. Ferguson
"separate but equal"
lynching
the Lost Cause
"new immigrants"
Immigration Restriction League
Washington's Atlanta Speech
American Federation of Labor
"women's era"

Alfred T. Mahan
"yellow press"
U.S.S. *Maine*
Platt Amendment
Open Door policy
"white man's burden"
Insular Cases
Anti-Imperialist League

wwnorton.com/studyspace

VISIT STUDYSPACE FOR THESE RESOURCES AND MORE:

- Author Videos
- A chapter outline
- A practice quiz
- Interactive maps
- Multimedia documents

CHAPTER 3

THE PROGRESSIVE ERA

From *Give Me Liberty! Seagull Fourth Edition*

Eric Foner

3

The Progressive Era 1900–1916

FOCUS QUESTIONS

- Why was the city such a central element in Progressive America?
- How did the labor and women's movements challenge the nineteenth-century meanings of American freedom?
- In what ways did Progressivism include both democratic and anti-democratic impulses?
- How did the Progressive presidents foster the rise of the nation-state?

It was late afternoon on March 25, 1911, when fire broke out at the Triangle Shirtwaist Company. The factory occupied the top three floors of a ten-story building in the Greenwich Village neighborhood of New York City. Here some 500 workers, mostly young Jewish and Italian immigrant women, toiled at sewing machines producing ladies' blouses, some earning as little as three dollars per week. Those who tried to escape the blaze discovered that the doors to the stairwell had been locked—the owners' way, it was later charged, of discouraging theft and unauthorized bathroom breaks. The fire department rushed to the scene with high-pressure hoses. But their ladders reached only to the sixth floor. As the fire raged, onlookers watched in horror as girls leapt from the upper stories. By the time the blaze had been put out, 46 bodies lay on the street and 100 more were found inside the building.

The Triangle Shirtwaist Company was typical of manufacturing in the nation's largest city, a beehive of industrial production in small, crowded

City of Ambition, 1910, by the photographer Alfred Stieglitz, captures the stark beauty of New York City's new skyscrapers. Photo © 2013 Georgia O'Keeffe Museum/Artists Rights Society (ARS), New York.

factories. New York was home to 30,000 manufacturing establishments with more than 600,000 employees—more industrial workers than in the entire state of Massachusetts. Triangle had already played a key role in the era's labor history. When 200 of its workers tried to join the International Ladies' Garment Workers Union (ILGWU), the owners responded by firing them. This incident helped to spark a general walkout of female garment workers in 1909—the Uprising of the 20,000. Among the strikers' demands was better safety in clothing factories. The impoverished immigrants forged an alliance with middle- and upper-class female supporters, including members of the Women's Trade Union League, which had been founded in 1903 to help bring women workers into unions. Alva Belmont, the ex-wife of railroad magnate William Vanderbilt, contributed several of her cars to a parade in support of the striking workers. By the time the walkout ended early in 1911, the ILGWU had won union contracts with more than 300 firms. But the Triangle Shirtwaist Company was not among them.

The Triangle fire was not the worst fire disaster in American history (seven years earlier, over 1,000 people had died in a blaze on the *General Slocum* excursion boat in New York Harbor). But it had an unrivaled impact on public consciousness. More than twenty years later, Franklin D. Roosevelt would refer to it in a press conference as an example of why the government needed to regulate industry. In its wake, efforts to organize the city's workers accelerated, and the state legislature passed new factory inspection laws and fire safety codes.

Triangle focused attention on the social divisions that plagued American society during the first two decades of the twentieth century, a period known as the Progressive era. These were years when economic expansion produced millions of new jobs and brought an unprecedented array of goods within reach of American consumers. Cities expanded rapidly—by 1920, for the first time, more Americans lived in towns and cities than in rural areas. Yet severe inequality remained the most visible feature of the urban landscape, and persistent labor strife raised anew the question of government's role in combating social inequality. The fire and its aftermath also highlighted how traditional gender roles were changing as women took on new responsibilities in the workplace and in the making of public policy.

The word "Progressive" came into common use around 1910 as a way of describing a broad, loosely defined political movement of individuals and groups who hoped to bring about significant change in American social and political life. Progressives included forward-looking businessmen who realized that workers must be accorded a voice in economic decision making, and labor activists bent on empowering industrial workers. Other major contributors to Progressivism were members of female reform organizations who hoped to protect women and children from exploitation, social scientists who believed that academic research would help to solve social problems, and members of an anxious middle class who feared that their status was threatened by the rise of big business.

Everywhere in early-twentieth-century America the signs of economic and political consolidation were apparent—in the power of a small directorate of Wall Street bankers and corporate executives, the manipulation of democracy by corrupt political machines, and the rise of new systems of managerial control in workplaces. In these circumstances, wrote Benjamin P. DeWitt, in his 1915 book *The Progressive Movement*, "the individual could not hope to compete. . . . Slowly, Americans realized that they were not free."

As this chapter will discuss, Progressive reformers responded to the perception of declining freedom in varied, contradictory ways. The era saw the expansion of political and economic freedom through the reinvigoration of the movement for woman suffrage, the use of political power to expand workers' rights, and efforts to improve democratic government by weakening the power of city bosses and giving ordinary citizens more influence on legislation. It witnessed the flowering of understandings of freedom based on individual fulfillment and personal self-determination—the ability to participate fully in the ever-expanding consumer marketplace and, especially for women, to enjoy economic and sexual freedoms long considered the province of men. At the same time, many Progressives supported efforts to limit the full enjoyment of freedom to those deemed fit to exercise it properly. The new system of white supremacy born in the 1890s became fully consolidated in the South. Growing numbers of native-born Americans demanded that immigrants abandon their traditional cultures and become fully "Americanized." And efforts were made at the local and national levels to place political decision making in the hands of experts who did not have to answer to the electorate. Even as the idea of freedom expanded, freedom's boundaries contracted in Progressive America.

AN URBAN AGE AND A CONSUMER SOCIETY

FARMS AND CITIES

The Progressive era was a period of explosive economic growth, fueled by increasing industrial production, a rapid rise in population, and the continued expansion of the consumer marketplace. In the first decade of the twentieth century, the economy's total output rose by about 85 percent. For the last time in American history, farms and cities grew together. As farm prices recovered from their low point during the depression of the 1890s, American agriculture entered what would later be remembered as its "golden age." The expansion of urban areas stimulated demand for farm goods. Farm families poured into the western Great Plains. More than 1 million claims for free government land were filed under the Homestead Act of 1862—more than in the previous forty years combined. Between 1900 and 1910, the combined population of Texas and Oklahoma rose by nearly 2 million people, and Kansas, Nebraska, and the Dakotas added 800,000. Irrigation transformed the Imperial Valley of California and parts of Arizona into major areas of commercial farming.

But it was the city that became the focus of Progressive politics and of a new mass-consumer society. Throughout the industrialized world, the number of great cities multiplied. The United States counted twenty-one cities whose population exceeded 100,000 in 1910, the largest of them New York, with 4.7 million residents. The twenty-three square miles of Manhattan Island were home to over 2 million people, more than lived in thirty-three of the states. Fully a quarter of them inhabited the Lower East Side, an immigrant neighborhood more densely populated than Bombay or Calcutta in India.

The stark urban inequalities of the 1890s continued into the Progressive era. Immigrant families in New York's downtown tenements often had no electricity or indoor toilets. Three miles to the north stood the mansions of Fifth Avenue's Millionaire's Row. According to one estimate, J. P. Morgan's financial firm directly or indirectly controlled 40 percent of all financial and industrial capital in the United States. Alongside such wealth, reported the Commission on Industrial Relations, established by Congress in 1912, more than one-third of the country's mining and manufacturing workers lived in "actual poverty."

The city captured the imagination of artists, writers, and reformers. The glories of the American landscape had been the focal point of nineteenth-century painters (exemplified by the Hudson River school, which produced canvases celebrating the wonders of nature). The city and its daily life now became their preoccupation. Painters like George W. Bellows and John Sloan and photographers such as Alfred Stieglitz and Edward Steichen captured the electric lights, crowded bars and theaters, and soaring skyscrapers of the urban landscape. With its youthful, exuberant energies, the city seemed an expression of modernity itself.

THE MUCKRAKERS

Others saw the city as a place where corporate greed undermined traditional American values. At a time when more than 2 million children under the age of fifteen worked for wages, Lewis Hine photographed child laborers to draw attention to persistent social inequality. A new generation of journalists writing for mass-circulation national magazines exposed the ills of industrial and urban life. *The Shame of the Cities* by Lincoln Steffens (published as a series in *McClure's Magazine* in 1901–1902 and in book form in 1904) showed how party bosses and business leaders profited from political corruption. *McClure's* also hired Ida Tarbell to expose the arrogance and economic machinations of John D. Rockefeller's Standard Oil Company. Published in two volumes in 1904, her *History of the Standard Oil Company* was the most substantial product of what Theodore Roosevelt disparaged as "muckraking"—the use of journalistic skills to expose the underside of American life.

A photograph by Lewis Hine, who used his camera to chronicle the plight of child laborers, of a young spinner in a southern cotton factory.

Major novelists of the era took a similar unsparing approach to social ills. Theodore Dreiser's *Sister Carrie* (1900) traced a young woman's moral corruption in Chicago's harsh urban environment. Perhaps the era's most influential novel was Upton Sinclair's *The Jungle* (1906), whose description of unsanitary slaughterhouses and the sale of rotten meat stirred public outrage and led directly to the passage of the Pure Food and Drug Act and the Meat Inspection Act of 1906.

IMMIGRATION AS A GLOBAL PROCESS

If one thing characterized early-twentieth-century cities, it was their immigrant character. The "new immigration" from southern and eastern Europe had begun around 1890 but reached its peak during the Progressive era. Between 1901 and the outbreak of World War I in Europe in 1914, some 13 million immigrants came to the United States, the majority from Italy, Russia, and the Austro-Hungarian empire. In fact, Progressive-era immigration formed part of a larger process of worldwide migration set in motion by industrial expansion and the decline of traditional agriculture. Poles emigrated not only to Pittsburgh and Chicago but to work in German factories and Scottish mines. Italians sought jobs in Belgium, France, and Argentina as well as the United States. As many as 750,000 Chinese migrated to other countries each year.

During the years from 1840 to 1914 (when immigration to the United States would be virtually cut off, first by the outbreak of World War I and

CHRONOLOGY

1889	Hull House founded
1898	Charlotte Perkins Gilman's *Women and Economics*
1901	Socialist Party founded in United States
	President McKinley assassinated
1902	President Theodore Roosevelt assists in coal strike
1903	Women's Trade Union League founded
	Ford Motor Company established
1904	Northern Securities dissolved
1905	Industrial Workers of the World established
1906	Upton Sinclair's *The Jungle* Meat Inspection Act
	Pure Food and Drug Act
	Hepburn Act
1908	*Muller v. Oregon*
1909	Uprising of the 20,000
1911	Triangle Shirtwaist Company fire
	Society of American Indians founded
1912	Children's Bureau established
	Theodore Roosevelt organizes the Progressive Party
1913	Sixteenth Amendment
	Seventeenth Amendment
	Federal Reserve established
1914	Ludlow Massacre
	Federal Trade Commission established
	Clayton Act

then by legislation), perhaps 40 million persons emigrated to the United States and another 20 million to other parts of the Western Hemisphere, including Canada, Argentina, Brazil, and the Caribbean. This population flow formed one part of a massive shifting of peoples throughout the world, much of which took place in Asia. Millions of persons migrated to Southeast Asia and the South Pacific, mainly from India and China. Millions more moved from Russia and northern Asia to Manchuria, Siberia, and Central Asia.

Numerous causes inspired this massive uprooting of population. Rural southern and eastern Europe and large parts of Asia were regions marked by widespread poverty and illiteracy, burdensome taxation, and declining economies. Political turmoil at home, like the revolution that engulfed Mexico after 1911, also inspired emigration. Not all of these immigrants could be classified as "free laborers," however. Large numbers of Chinese, Mexican, and Italian migrants, including many who came to the United States, were bound to long-term labor contracts. These contracts were signed with labor agents, who then provided the workers to American employers. But all the areas attracting immigrants were frontiers of one kind or another—agricultural, mining, or industrial—with expanding job opportunities.

Most European immigrants to the United States entered through Ellis Island. Located in New York Harbor, this became in 1892 the nation's main facility for processing immigrants. Millions of Americans today trace their ancestry to an immigrant who passed through Ellis Island. The less fortunate, who failed a medical examination or were judged to be anarchists, prostitutes, or in other ways undesirable, were sent home.

At the same time, an influx of Asian and Mexican newcomers was taking place in the West. After the exclusion of immigrants from China in the late nineteenth century, a small number of Japanese arrived, primarily to work as agricultural laborers in California's fruit and vegetable fields and on Hawaii's sugar plantations. By 1910, the population of Japanese origin had grown to 72,000. Between 1910 and 1940, Angel Island in San Francisco Bay—the "Ellis Island of the West"—served as the main entry point for immigrants from Asia.

Far larger was Mexican immigration. Between 1900 and 1930, some 1 million Mexicans (more than 10 percent of that country's population) entered the United States—a number exceeded by only a few European countries. Many Mexicans entered through El Paso, Texas, the main southern gateway into the United States. Many ended up in the San Gabriel Valley of California, where citrus growers searching for cheap labor had earlier experimented with Native American, South Asian, Chinese, and Filipino migrant workers.

By 1910, one-seventh of the American population was foreign-born, the highest percentage in the country's history. More than 40 percent of New York City's population had been born abroad. In Chicago and smaller industrial

An illustration in the 1912 publication The New Immigration *depicts the various "types" entering the United States.*

cities like Providence, Milwaukee, and San Francisco, the figure exceeded 30 percent. Although many newcomers moved west to take part in the expansion of farming, most clustered in industrial centers. By 1910, nearly three-fifths of the workers in the twenty leading manufacturing and mining industries were foreign-born.

THE IMMIGRANT QUEST FOR FREEDOM

Like their nineteenth-century predecessors, the new immigrants arrived imagining the United States as a land of freedom, where all persons enjoyed equality before the law, could worship as they pleased, enjoyed economic opportunity, and had been emancipated from the oppressive social hierarchies of their homelands. "America is a free country," one Polish immigrant wrote home. "You don't have to be a serf to anyone." Agents sent abroad by the American government to investigate the reasons for large-scale immigration reported that the main impetus was a desire to share in the "freedom and prosperity enjoyed by the people of the United States." Freedom, they added, was largely an economic ambition—a desire to escape from "hopeless poverty" and achieve a standard of living impossible at home. While some of the new immigrants, especially Jews fleeing religious persecution in the Russian empire, thought of themselves as permanent emigrants, the majority initially planned to earn enough money to return home and purchase land. Groups like Mexicans and Italians included many "birds of passage," who remained only temporarily in the United States. In 1908, a year of economic downturn in the United States, more Italians left the country than entered.

Table 1 IMMIGRANTS AND THEIR CHILDREN AS PERCENTAGE OF POPULATION, TEN MAJOR CITIES, 1920

City	*Percentage*
New York City	76%
Cleveland	72
Boston	72
Chicago	71
Detroit	65
San Francisco	64
Minneapolis	63
Pittsburgh	59
Seattle	55
Los Angeles	45

The new immigrants clustered in close-knit "ethnic" neighborhoods with their own shops, theaters, and community organizations, and often continued to speak their native tongues. As early as 1900, more than 1,000 foreign-language newspapers were published in the United States. Churches were pillars of these immigrant communities. In New York's East Harlem, even anti-clerical Italian immigrants, who resented the close alliance in Italy between the Catholic Church and the oppressive state, participated eagerly in the annual festival of the Madonna of Mt. Carmel. After Italian-Americans scattered to the suburbs, they continued to return each year to reenact the festival.

Although most immigrants earned more than was possible in the impoverished regions from which they came, they endured low wages, long hours, and dangerous working conditions. In the mines and factories of Pennsylvania and the Midwest, eastern European immigrants performed low-wage unskilled labor, while native-born workers dominated skilled and supervisory jobs. The vast majority of Mexican immigrants became poorly paid agricultural, mine, and railroad laborers, with little prospect of upward economic mobility. "My people are not in America," remarked one Slavic priest, "they are under it."

CONSUMER FREEDOM

Cities, however, were also the birthplace of a mass-consumption society that added new meaning to American freedom. There was, of course, nothing unusual in the idea that the promise of American life lay, in part, in the enjoyment by the masses of citizens of goods available in other countries only to the well-to-do. Not until the Progressive era, however, did the advent of large downtown department stores, chain stores in urban neighborhoods, and retail mail-order houses for farmers and small-town residents make available to consumers throughout the country the vast array of goods now pouring from the nation's factories. By 1910, Americans could purchase, among many other items, electric sewing machines, washing machines, vacuum cleaners, and record players. Low wages, the unequal distribution of income, and the South's persistent poverty limited the consumer economy, which would not fully come into its own until after World War II. But it was in Progressive America that the promise of mass consumption became the foundation for a new understanding of freedom as access to the cornucopia of goods made available by modern capitalism.

Leisure activities also took on the characteristics of mass consumption. Amusement parks, dance halls, and theaters attracted large crowds of city dwellers. The most popular form of mass entertainment at the turn of the century was vaudeville, a live theatrical entertainment consisting of numerous short acts typically including song and dance, comedy, acrobats, magicians, and trained animals. In the 1890s, brief motion pictures were already being introduced into vaudeville shows. As the movies became longer and involved more sophisticated plot narratives, separate theaters developed. By 1910, 25 million Americans per week, mostly working-class urban residents, were attending "nickelodeons"—motion-picture theaters whose five-cent admission charge was far lower than at vaudeville shows.

THE WORKING WOMAN

The new visibility of women in urban public places—at work, as shoppers, and in places of entertainment like cinemas and dance halls—indicated that traditional gender roles were changing dramatically in Progressive America. As the Triangle fire revealed, more and more women were working for wages. Black women still worked primarily as domestics or in southern cotton fields. Immigrant women were largely confined to low-paying factory employment. But for native-born white women, the kinds of jobs available expanded enormously. By 1920, around 25 percent of employed women were office workers or telephone operators, and only 15 percent worked in domestic service, the largest female job category of the nineteenth century. Female work was no longer confined to young, unmarried white women and adult black women. In 1920, of 8 million women working for wages, one-quarter were married and living with their husbands.

The working woman—immigrant and native, working-class and professional—became a symbol of female emancipation. Women faced special limitations on their economic freedom, including wage discrimination and exclusion from many jobs. Yet almost in spite of themselves, union leader Abraham Bisno remarked, young immigrant working women developed a sense of independence: "They acquired the *right to a personality*," something alien to the highly patriarchal family structures of the old country. "We enjoy our independence and freedom" was the assertive statement of the Bachelor Girls Social Club, a group of female mail-order clerks in New York.

The growing number of younger women who desired a lifelong career, wrote Charlotte Perkins Gilman in her influential book *Women and Economics* (1898), offered evidence of a "spirit of personal independence" that pointed to a coming transformation of both economic and family life. Gilman's writings reinforced the claim that the road to woman's freedom lay through the workplace. In the home, she argued, women experienced not fulfillment but oppression, and the housewife was an unproductive parasite, little more than a servant to her husband and children. By condemning women to a life of domestic drudgery, prevailing gender norms made them incapable of contributing to society or enjoying freedom in any meaningful sense of the word.

The desire to participate in the consumer society produced remarkably similar battles within immigrant families of all nationalities between parents and their self-consciously "free" children, especially daughters. Contemporaries, native and immigrant, noted how "the novelties and frivolities of fashion" appealed to young working women, who spent part of their meager wages on clothing and makeup and at places of entertainment. Daughters considered parents who tried to impose curfews or to prevent them from going out alone to dances or movies as old-fashioned and not sufficiently "American." Immigrant parents found it very difficult to adapt to what one Mexican mother called "this terrible freedom in this United States." "The Mexican girls," she told a sociologist studying immigrant life in Los Angeles, "seeing American girls with freedom, they want it too."

THE RISE OF FORDISM

If any individual exemplified the new consumer society, it was Henry Ford. The son of an immigrant Irish farmer, Ford had worked as an apprentice in Michigan machine shops and later as an engineer for the Edison Illuminating Company. Ford did not invent the automobile, but he developed the techniques of production and marketing that brought it within the reach of ordinary Americans. In 1905, he established the Ford Motor Company, one of dozens of small automobile manufacturing firms that emerged in these years. Three years later, he introduced the Model T, a simple, light vehicle sturdy enough to navigate the country's poorly maintained roads. While early European models

The assembly line at the Ford Motor Company factory in Highland Park, Michigan, around 1915.

like the Mercedes aimed at an elite market and were superior in craftsmanship, Ford concentrated on standardizing output and lowering prices.

In 1913, Ford's factory in Highland Park, Michigan, adopted the method of production known as the moving assembly line, in which car frames were brought to workers on a continuously moving conveyor belt. The process enabled Ford to expand output by greatly reducing the time it took to produce each car. In 1914, he raised wages at his factory to the unheard of level of five dollars per day (more than double the pay of most industrial workers), enabling him to attract a steady stream of skilled laborers. Labor conditions in the Ford plant were not as appealing as the wages, however: assembly-line work was monotonous (the worker repeated the same basic motions for the entire day), and Ford used spies and armed detectives to prevent unionization. When other businessmen criticized him for endangering profits by paying high wages, Ford replied that workers must be able to afford the goods being turned out by American factories. Ford's output rose from 34,000 cars, priced at $700 each, in 1910, to 730,000 Model T's that sold at a price of $316 (well within the reach of many workers) in 1916. The economic system based on mass production and mass consumption came to be called Fordism.

THE PROMISE OF ABUNDANCE

As economic production shifted from capital goods (steel, railroad equipment, etc.) to consumer products, the new advertising industry perfected ways of increasing sales, often by linking goods with the idea of freedom. Numerous products took "liberty" as a brand name or used an image of the Statue of Liberty as a sales device. The department-store magnate Edward Filene called consumerism a "school of freedom," since shoppers made individual choices on basic questions of living. Economic abundance would eventually come to define the "American way of life," in which personal fulfillment was to be found through acquiring material goods.

The promise of abundance shifted the quest for freedom to the realm of private life, but it also inspired political activism. Exclusion from the world of mass consumption would come to seem almost as great a denial of the rights of citizenship as being barred from voting once had been. The desire for consumer goods led many workers to join unions and fight for higher wages. The argument that monopolistic corporations artificially raised prices at the expense of consumers became a weapon against the trusts. "Consumers' consciousness," wrote Walter Lippmann, who emerged in these years as one of the nation's most influential social commentators, was growing rapidly, with the "high cost of living" as its rallying cry.

AN AMERICAN STANDARD OF LIVING

The maturation of the consumer economy gave rise to concepts—a "living wage" and an "American standard of living"—that offered a new language for criticizing the inequalities of wealth and power in Progressive America. Father John A. Ryan's influential book *A Living Wage* (1906) described a decent standard of living (one that enabled a person to participate in the consumer economy) as a "natural and absolute" right of citizenship. Ryan had grown up in Minnesota in a family sympathetic to Henry George, the Knights of Labor, and the Populists. His book sought to translate into American terms Pope Leo XIII's powerful statement of 1894, *Rerum Novarum*, which criticized the divorce of economic life from ethical considerations, endorsed the right of workers to organize unions, and repudiated competitive individualism in favor of a more cooperative vision of the good society. Ryan's insistence that economic relationships should be governed by moral standards had a powerful influence on social thought among American Catholics.

The popularity of the idea of an American standard of living reflected, in part, the emergence of a mass-consumption society during the Progressive era. For the first time in the nation's history, mass consumption came to occupy a central place in descriptions of American society and its future. In the Gilded Age, social theorists like Henry George had wondered why economic progress produced both increased wealth and abject misery. The Progressive generation was strongly influenced by the more optimistic writings of Simon W. Patten, a prophet of prosperity. Patten announced the end of the "reign of want" and the advent of a society of abundance and leisure. In the dawning "new civilization," he proclaimed, Americans would enjoy economic equality in a world in which "every one is independent and free."

VARIETIES OF PROGRESSIVISM

For most Americans, however, Patten's "new civilization" lay far in the future. The more immediate task, in the Progressives' view, was to humanize industrial capitalism and find common ground in a society still racked by labor conflict and experiencing massive immigration from abroad. Some Progressives proposed to return to a competitive marketplace populated by small producers. Others accepted the permanence of the large corporation and looked to the government to reverse the growing concentration of wealth and to ensure social justice. Still others would relocate freedom from the economic and political worlds to a private realm of personal fulfillment and unimpeded self-expression. But nearly all Progressives agreed that freedom must be infused with new meaning to deal with the economic and social conditions of the early twentieth century. The "old democracy," wrote Walter Weyl, associate editor of *The New Republic*, a weekly magazine that became the "bible" of Progressive intellectuals, provided no answer to the problems of a world in which the "chief restrictions upon liberty" were economic, not political.

INDUSTRIAL FREEDOM

In Progressive America, complaints of a loss of freedom came not only from the most poorly paid factory workers but from better-off employees as well. Large firms in the automobile, electrical, steel, and other industries sought to implement greater control over the work process. Efficiency expert Frederick W. Taylor pioneered what he called "scientific management"—a program that sought to streamline production and boost profits by systematically controlling costs and work practices. Through scientific study, the "one best way" of producing goods could be determined and implemented. The role of workers was to obey the detailed instructions of supervisors. Not surprisingly, many skilled workers saw the erosion of their traditional influence over the work process as a loss of freedom. "Men and women," complained Samuel Gompers, whose American Federation of Labor (AFL) represented such skilled workers, "cannot live during working hours under autocratic conditions, and instantly become sons and daughters of freedom as they step outside the shop gates."

The great increase in the number of white-collar workers—the army of salespeople, bookkeepers, salaried professionals, and corporate managers that sprang up with the new system of management—also undermined the experience of personal autonomy. For although they enjoyed far higher social status and incomes than manual workers, many, wrote one commentator, were the kind of individuals who "under former conditions, would have been . . . managing their own businesses," not working for someone else.

These developments helped to place the ideas of "industrial freedom" and "industrial democracy," which had entered the political vocabulary in the Gilded Age, at the center of political discussion during the Progressive era. Lack of "industrial freedom" was widely believed to lie at the root of the much-discussed "labor problem." Since in an industrial age the prospect of managing one's own business seemed increasingly remote, many Progressives believed that the key to increasing industrial freedom lay in empowering workers to participate in economic decision making via strong unions. Louis D. Brandeis, an active ally of the labor movement whom President Woodrow Wilson appointed to the Supreme Court in 1916, maintained that unions embodied an essential principle of freedom—the right of people to govern themselves. The contradiction between "political liberty" and "industrial slavery," Brandeis insisted, was America's foremost social problem. Workers deserved a voice not only in establishing wages and working conditions but also in making such managerial decisions as the relocation of factories, layoffs, and the distribution of profits.

THE SOCIALIST PRESENCE

Economic freedom was also a rallying cry of American socialism, which reached its greatest influence during the Progressive era. Founded in 1901, the Socialist Party brought together surviving late-nineteenth-century radicals such as Populists and followers of Edward Bellamy, with a portion of the labor movement. The party called for immediate reforms such as free college education, legislation to improve the condition of laborers, and, as an ultimate goal, democratic control over the economy through public ownership of railroads and factories. It was the task of socialism, said western labor leader John O'Neill, to "gather together the shards of liberty"—the fragments of the American heritage of freedom—scattered by a government controlled by capitalist millionaires.

By 1912, the Socialist Party claimed 150,000 dues-paying members, published hundreds of newspapers, enjoyed substantial support in the American Federation of Labor, and had elected scores of local officials. Socialism flourished in diverse communities throughout the country. On the Lower East Side of New York City, it arose from the economic exploitation of immigrant workers and Judaism's tradition of social reform. Here, a vibrant

Roller skaters with socialist leaflets during a New York City strike in 1916. A "scab" is a worker who crosses the picket line during a strike.

socialist culture developed, complete with Yiddish-language newspapers and theaters, as well as large public meetings and street demonstrations. In 1914, the district elected socialist Meyer London to Congress. Another center of socialist strength was Milwaukee, where Victor Berger, a German-born teacher and newspaper editor, mobilized local AFL unions into a potent political force that elected Emil Seidel mayor in 1910. Seidel's administration provided aid to the unemployed, forced the police to recognize the rights of strikers, and won the respect of middle-class residents for its honesty and freedom from machine domination. Socialism also made inroads among tenant farmers in old Populist areas like Oklahoma, and in the mining regions of Idaho and Montana.

THE GOSPEL OF DEBS

No one was more important in spreading the socialist gospel or linking it to ideals of equality, self-government, and freedom than Eugene V. Debs, the railroad union leader who had been jailed during the Pullman Strike of 1894. For two decades, Debs criss-crossed the country preaching that control of the economy by a democratic government held out the hope of uniting "political equality and economic freedom." As a champion of the downtrodden, Debs managed to bridge the cultural divide among New York's Jewish immigrants, prairie socialists of the West, and native-born intellectuals attracted to the socialist ideal. "While there is a lower class," proclaimed Debs, "I am in it, . . . while there is a soul in prison, I am not free."

Throughout the Atlantic world of the early twentieth century, socialism was a rising presence. Debs would receive more than 900,000 votes for president (6 percent of the total) in 1912. In that year, the socialist *Appeal to Reason*, published in Girard, Kansas, with a circulation of 700,000, was the largest weekly newspaper in the country, and socialist Max Hayes polled one-third of the vote when he challenged Samuel Gompers for the presidency of the AFL. In western Europe, socialism experienced even more pronounced growth. In the last elections before the outbreak of World War I in 1914, socialists in France, Germany, and Scandinavia won between one-sixth and one-third of the vote. "Socialism is coming," declared the *Appeal to Reason*. "It is coming like a prairie fire and nothing can stop it."

AFL AND IWW

Socialism was only one example of widespread discontent in Progressive America. The labor strife of the Gilded Age continued into the early twentieth century. Having survived the depression of the 1890s, the American Federation of Labor saw its membership triple to 1.6 million between 1900 and 1904. At the same time, it sought to forge closer ties with forward-looking corporate leaders willing to deal with unions as a way to stabilize employee relations. AFL president Gompers joined with George Perkins of the J. P. Morgan financial empire and Mark Hanna, who had engineered McKinley's election, in the National Civic Federation, which accepted the right of collective bargaining for "responsible" unions. It helped to settle hundreds of industrial disputes and encouraged improvements in factory safety and the establishment of pension plans for long-term workers. Most employers nonetheless continued to view unions as an intolerable interference with their authority, and resisted them stubbornly.

The AFL mainly represented the most privileged American workers—skilled industrial and craft laborers, nearly all of them white, male, and native-born. In 1905, a group of unionists who rejected the AFL's exclusionary policies formed the Industrial Workers of the World (IWW). Part trade union, part advocate of a workers' revolution that would seize the means of production and abolish the state, the IWW made solidarity its guiding principle, extending "a fraternal hand to every wage-worker, no matter what his religion, fatherland, or trade." The organization sought to mobilize those excluded from the AFL—the immigrant factory-labor force, migrant timber and agricultural workers, women, blacks, and even the despised Chinese on the West Coast. The IWW's most prominent leader was William "Big Bill" Haywood, who had worked in western mines as a youth. Dubbed by critics "the most dangerous man in America," Haywood became a national figure in 1906 when he was kidnapped and spirited off to Idaho, accused of instigating the murder of a former anti-union governor. Defended by labor lawyer Clarence Darrow, Haywood was found not guilty.

THE NEW IMMIGRANTS ON STRIKE

The Uprising of the 20,000 in New York's garment industry, mentioned earlier, was one of a series of mass strikes among immigrant workers that placed labor's demand for the right to bargain collectively at the forefront of the reform agenda. These strikes demonstrated that while ethnic divisions among workers impeded labor solidarity, ethnic cohesiveness could also be a basis

VOICES OF FREEDOM

From Charlotte Perkins Gilman, *Women and Economics* (1898)

***Women and Economics*, by the prolific feminist social critic and novelist Charlotte Perkins Gilman, influenced the new generation of women aspiring to greater independence. It insisted that how people earned a living shaped their entire lives, and that therefore women must free themselves from the home to achieve genuine freedom.**

It is not motherhood that keeps the housewife on her feet from dawn till dark; it is house service, not child service. Women work longer and harder than most men. . . . A truer spirit is the increasing desire of young girls to be independent, to have a career of their own, at least for a while, and the growing objection of countless wives to the pitiful asking for money, to the beggary of their position. More and more do fathers give their daughters, and husbands their wives, a definite allowance,—a separate bank account,—something . . . all their own.

The spirit of personal independence in the women of today is sure proof that a change has come. . . . The radical change in the economic position of women is advancing upon us. . . . The growing individualization of democratic life brings inevitable change to our daughters as well as to our sons. . . . One of its most noticeable features is the demand in women not only for their own money, but for their own work for the sake of personal expression. Few girls today fail to manifest some signs of this desire for individual expression. . . .

Economic independence for women necessarily involves a change in the home and family relation. But, if that change is for the advantage of individual and race, we need not fear it. It does not involve a change in the marriage relation except in withdrawing the element of economic dependence, nor in the relation of mother to child save to improve it. But it does involve the exercise of human faculty in women, in social service and exchange rather than in domestic service solely. . . . [Today], when our still developing social needs call for an ever-increasing . . . freedom, the woman in marrying becomes the house-servant, or at least the housekeeper, of the man. . . . When women stand free as economic agents, they will [achieve a] much better fulfilment of their duties as wives and mothers and [contribute] to the vast improvement in health and happiness of the human race.

From John Mitchell, "The Workingman's Conception of Industrial Liberty" (1910)

During the Progressive era, the idea of "industrial liberty" moved to the center of political discussion. Progressive reformers and labor leaders like John Mitchell, head of the United Mine Workers, condemned the prevailing idea of liberty of contract in favor of a broader definition of economic freedom.

While the Declaration of Independence established civil and political liberty, it did not, as you all know, establish industrial liberty. . . . Liberty means more than the right to choose the field of one's employment. He is not a free man whose family must buy food today with the money that is earned tomorrow. He is not really free who is forced to work unduly long hours and for wages so low that he can not provide the necessities of life for himself and his family; who must live in a crowded tenement and see his children go to work in the mills, the mines, and the factories before their bodies are developed and their minds trained. To have freedom a man must be free from the harrowing fear of hunger and want; he must be in such a position that by the exercise of reasonable frugality he can provide his family with all of the necessities and the reasonable comforts of life. He must be able to educate his children and to provide against sickness, accident, and old age. . . .

A number of years ago the legislatures of several coal producing States enacted laws requiring employers to pay the wages of their workmen in lawful money of the United States and to cease the practice of paying wages in merchandise. From time immemorial it had been the custom of coal companies to conduct general supply stores, and the workingmen were required, as a condition of employment, to accept products in lieu of money in return for services rendered. This system was a great hardship to the workmen. . . . The question of the constitutionality of this legislation was carried into the courts and by the highest tribunal it was declared to be an invasion of the workman's liberty to deny him the right to accept merchandise in lieu of money as payment of his wages. . . . [This is] typical of hundreds of instances in which laws that have been enacted for the protection of the workingmen have been declared by the courts to be unconstitutional, on the grounds that they invaded the liberty of the working people. . . . Is it not natural that the workingmen should feel that they are being guaranteed the liberties they do not want and denied the liberty that is of real value to them? May they not exclaim, with Madame Roland [of the French Revolution], "O Liberty! Liberty! How many crimes are committed in thy name!"

QUESTIONS

1. What does Gilman see as the main obstacles to freedom for women?

2. What does Mitchell believe will be necessary to establish "industrial liberty"?

3. How do the authors differ in their view of the relationship of the family to individual freedom?

Striking New York City garment workers carrying signs in multiple languages, 1913.

of unity, so long as strikes were organized on a democratic basis. The IWW did not originate these confrontations but was sometimes called in by local unionists to solidify the strikers. IWW organizers printed leaflets, posters, and banners in multiple languages and insisted that each nationality enjoy representation on the committee coordinating a walkout. It drew on the sense of solidarity within immigrant communities to persuade local religious leaders, shopkeepers, and officeholders to support the strikes.

The labor conflict that had the greatest impact on public consciousness took place in Lawrence, Massachusetts. The city's huge woolen mills employed 32,000 men, women, and children representing twenty-five nationalities. They worked six days per week and earned an average of sixteen cents per hour. When the state legislature in January 1912 enacted a fifty-four-hour limit to the workweek, employers reduced the weekly take-home pay of those who had been laboring longer hours. Workers spontaneously went on strike, and called on the IWW for assistance.

In February, Haywood and a group of women strikers devised the idea of sending strikers' children out of the city for the duration of the walkout. Socialist families in New York City agreed to take them in. The sight of the children, many of whom appeared pale and half-starved, marching up Fifth

Avenue from the train station led to a wave of sympathy for the strikers. "I have worked in the slums of New York," wrote one observer, "but I have never found children who were so uniformly ill-nourished, ill-fed, and ill-clothed." A few days later, city officials ordered that no more youngsters could leave Lawrence. When a group of mothers and children gathered at the railroad station in defiance of the order, club-wielding police drove them away, producing outraged headlines around the world. The governor of Massachusetts soon intervened, and the strike was settled on the workers' terms. A banner carried by the Lawrence strikers gave a new slogan to the labor movement: "We want bread and roses, too"—a declaration that workers sought not only higher wages but the opportunity to enjoy the finer things of life.

Another highly publicized labor uprising took place in New Orleans, where a 1907 strike of 10,000 black and white dockworkers prevented employers' efforts to eliminate their unions and reduce their wages. This was a remarkable expression of interracial solidarity at a time when segregation had become the norm throughout the South. Other strikes proved less successful. A six-month walkout of 25,000 silk workers in Paterson, New Jersey, in 1913 failed despite publicity generated by the Paterson pageant, in which the strikers reenacted highlights of their struggle before a sympathetic audience at New York's Madison Square Garden.

A strike against the Rockefeller-owned Colorado Fuel and Iron Company was also unsuccessful. Mostly recent immigrants from Europe and Mexico, the strikers demanded recognition of the United Mine Workers of America, wage increases, an eight-hour workday, and the right to shop and live in places not owned by the company. When the walkout began, in September 1913, the mine owners evicted 11,000 strikers and their families from company housing. They moved into tent colonies, which armed militia units soon surrounded. On April 20, 1914, the militia attacked the largest tent city, at Ludlow, and burned it to the ground, killing an estimated twenty to thirty men, women, and children. Seven months after the Ludlow Massacre, the strike was called off.

LABOR AND CIVIL LIBERTIES

The fiery organizer Mary "Mother" Jones, who at the age of eighty-three had been jailed after addressing the Colorado strikers, later told a New York audience that the union "had only the Constitution; the other side had the bayonets." Yet the struggle of workers for the right to strike and of labor radicals against restraints on open-air speaking made free speech a significant public issue in the early twentieth century. By and large, the courts rejected their claims. But these battles laid the foundation for the rise of civil liberties as a central component of freedom in twentieth-century America.

State courts in the Progressive era regularly issued injunctions prohibiting strikers from speaking, picketing, or distributing literature during labor disputes. Like the abolitionists before them, the labor movement, in the name of freedom, demanded the right to assemble, organize, and spread their views. The investigations of the Commission on Industrial Relations revealed the absence of free speech in many factory communities, with labor organizers prohibited from speaking freely under threat of either violence from private police or suppression by local authorities. "I don't think we live in a free country or enjoy civil liberties," Clarence Darrow told the commission.

The IWW's battle for civil liberties breathed new meaning into the idea of freedom of expression. Lacking union halls, its organizers relied on songs, street theater, impromptu organizing meetings, and street corner gatherings to spread their message and attract support. In response to IWW activities, officials in Los Angeles, Spokane, Denver, and more than a dozen other cities limited or prohibited outdoor meetings. To arouse popular support, the IWW filled the jails with members who defied local law by speaking in public. Sometimes, prisoners were brutally treated, as in Spokane, where three died and hundreds were hospitalized after being jailed for violating a local law requiring prior approval of the content of public speeches. In nearly all the free-speech fights, however, the IWW eventually forced local officials to give way. "Whether they agree or disagree with its methods or aims," wrote one journalist, "all lovers of liberty everywhere owe a debt to this organization for . . . [keeping] alight the fires of freedom."

THE NEW FEMINISM

During the Progressive era, the word "feminism" first entered the political vocabulary. One organization, the Feminist Alliance, constructed apartment houses with communal kitchens, cafeterias, and daycare centers, to free women from the constraints of the home. In 1914, a mass meeting at New York's Cooper Union debated the question "What is Feminism?" The meeting was sponsored by Heterodoxy, a women's club located in Greenwich Village that brought together female professionals, academics, and reformers. Feminism, said one speaker, meant women's emancipation "both as a human being and a sex-being." Feminists' forthright attack on traditional rules of sexual behavior added a new dimension to the discussion of personal freedom.

Heterodoxy was part of a new radical "bohemia" (a social circle of artists, writers, and others who reject conventional rules and practices). Its definition of feminism merged issues like the vote and greater economic opportunities with open discussion of sexuality. In New York's Greenwich Village and counterparts in Chicago, San Francisco, and other cities, a "lyrical left" came into being in the prewar years. Its members formed discussion clubs, attended experimental theaters, and published magazines. They confidently expected to preside over the emancipation of the human spirit from the prejudices of the nineteenth century.

One symbol of the new era was Isadora Duncan, who brought from California a new, expressive dance based on the free movement of a body liberated from the constraints of traditional technique and costume. "I beheld the dance I had always dreamed of," wrote the novelist Edith Wharton on seeing a Duncan performance, "satisfying every sense as a flower does, or a phrase of Mozart's." Another sign of artistic revolution was the Armory Show of 1913, an exhibition that exposed New Yorkers to new cubist paintings from Europe by artists previously unknown in the United States, like Pablo Picasso.

The lyrical left made freedom the key to its vision of society. At the famed salon in heiress Mabel Dodge's New York living room, a remarkable array of talented radicals gathered to discuss with equal passion labor unrest, modern trends in the arts, and sexual liberation. Although many Progressives frequented the Dodge salon, there was a world of difference between the exuberant individualism of the lyrical left and most Progressives' preoccupation with order and efficiency. "What [women] are really after," explained Crystal Eastman, is "*freedom.*" A graduate of New York University Law School, Eastman had taken a leading role both in the suffrage movement and in investigating industrial accidents. But her definition of freedom went beyond the vote, beyond "industrial democracy," to encompass emotional and sexual self-determination.

THE RISE OF PERSONAL FREEDOM

During the Progressive era, as journalist William M. Reedy jested, it struck "sex o'clock" in America. The founder of psychiatry, Sigmund Freud, lectured at Clark University in Worcester, Massachusetts, in 1909, and discovered that his writings on infantile sexuality, repression, and the irrational sources of human behavior were widely known "even in prudish America." Issues of intimate personal relations previously confined to private discussion blazed forth in popular magazines and public debates.

For the generation of women who adopted the word "feminism" to express their demand for greater liberty, free sexual expression and reproductive choice emerged as critical definitions of women's emancipation. Greenwich Village became a center of sexual experimentation. The aura of tolerance attracted many homosexuals to the area, and although organized demands for gay rights lay far in the future, the gay community became an important element of the Village's lifestyle. But new sexual attitudes spread far beyond bohemia; they flourished among the young, unmarried, self-supporting women who made sexual freedom a hallmark of their oft-proclaimed personal independence.

THE BIRTH-CONTROL MOVEMENT

The growing presence of women in the labor market reinforced demands for access to birth control, an issue that gave political expression to changing sexual behavior. In the nineteenth century, the right to "control one's body" generally meant the ability to refuse sexual advances, including those of a woman's husband. Now, it suggested the ability to enjoy an active sexual life without necessarily bearing children. Emma Goldman, who had emigrated to the United States from Lithuania at the age of sixteen, toured the country lecturing on subjects from anarchism to the need for more enlightened attitudes toward homosexuality. She regularly included the right to birth control in her speeches and distributed pamphlets with detailed information about various contraceptive devices. "I demand freedom for both sexes," she proclaimed, "freedom of action, freedom in love and freedom in motherhood." Goldman constantly ran afoul of the law. By one count, she was arrested more than forty times for dangerous or "obscene" statements or simply to keep her from speaking.

By forthrightly challenging the laws banning contraceptive information and devices, Margaret Sanger, one of eleven children of an Irish-American

Mothers with baby carriages wait outside Margaret Sanger's birth-control clinic in Brownsville, Brooklyn, 1916.

working-class family, placed the issue of birth control at the heart of the new feminism. In 1911, she began a column on sex education, "What Every Girl Should Know," for *The Call*, a New York socialist newspaper. Postal officials barred one issue, containing a column on venereal disease, from the mails. The next issue of *The Call* included a blank page with the headline: "What Every Girl Should Know—Nothing; by order of the U. S. Post Office."

By 1914, the intrepid Sanger was openly advertising birth-control devices in her own journal, *The Woman Rebel*. "No woman can call herself free," she proclaimed, "who does not own and control her own body [and] can choose consciously whether she will or will not be a mother." In 1916, Sanger opened a clinic in a working-class neighborhood of Brooklyn and began distributing contraceptive devices to poor Jewish and Italian women, an action for which she was sentenced to a month in prison. Few Progressives rallied to her defense. But for a time, the birth-control issue became a crossroads where the paths of labor radicals, cultural modernists, and feminists intersected. The IWW and Socialist Party distributed Sanger's writings. Like the IWW free-speech fights and Goldman's persistent battle for the right to lecture, Sanger's travail was part of a rich history of dissent in the Progressive era that helped to focus enlightened opinion on the ways local authorities and national obscenity legislation set rigid limits to Americans' freedom of expression. Slowly, laws banning birth control began to change. But since access was determined by individual states, even when some liberalized their laws, birth control remained unavailable in many other states.

NATIVE AMERICAN PROGRESSIVISM

Many groups participated in the Progressive impulse. Founded in 1911, the Society of American Indians was a reform organization typical of the era. It brought together Indian intellectuals to promote discussion of the plight of Native Americans in the hope that public exposure would be the first step toward remedying injustice. Because many of the society's leaders had been educated at government-sponsored boarding schools, the society united Indians of many tribal backgrounds. It created a pan-Indian public space independent of white control.

Many of these Indian intellectuals were not unsympathetic to the basic goals of federal Indian policy, including the transformation of communal landholdings on reservations into family farms. But Carlos Montezuma, a founder of the Society of American Indians, became an outspoken critic. Born in Arizona, he had been captured as a child by members of a neighboring tribe and sold to a traveling photographer, who brought him to Chicago. There Montezuma attended school and eventually obtained a medical degree.

In 1916, Montezuma established a newsletter, *Wassaja* (meaning "signaling"), that condemned federal paternalism toward the Indians and called for the abolition of the Bureau of Indian Affairs. Convinced that outsiders exerted too much power over life on the reservations, he insisted that self-determination was the only way for Indians to escape poverty and marginalization: "We must free ourselves. . . . We must be independent." But he also demanded that Indians be granted full citizenship and all the constitutional rights of other Americans. Montezuma's writings had little influence at the time on government policy, but Indian activists would later rediscover him as a forerunner of Indian radicalism.

THE POLITICS OF PROGRESSIVISM

EFFECTIVE FREEDOM

Progressivism was an international movement. In the early twentieth century, cities throughout the world experienced similar social strains arising from rapid industrialization and urban growth. In 1850, London and Paris were the only cities whose population exceeded 1 million. By 1900, there were twelve—New York, Chicago, and Philadelphia in the United States, and others in Europe, Latin America, and Asia. Facing similar social problems, reformers across the globe exchanged ideas and envisioned new social policies. Sun Yat-Sen, the Chinese leader, was influenced by the writings of Henry George and Edward Bellamy. The mayor of Osaka, Japan, called for a new "social economy" that replaced competition with cooperation.

As governments in Britain, France, and Germany instituted old age pensions, minimum wage laws, unemployment insurance, and the regulation of workplace safety, American reformers came to believe they had much to learn from the Old World. The term "social legislation," meaning governmental action to address urban problems and the insecurities of working-class life, originated in Germany but soon entered the political vocabulary of the United States.

Progressives believed that the modern era required a fundamental rethinking of the functions of political authority, whether the aim was to combat the power of the giant corporations, protect consumers, civilize the marketplace, or guarantee industrial freedom at the workplace. Drawing on the reform programs of the Gilded Age and the example of European legislation, Progressives sought to reinvigorate the idea of an activist, socially conscious government. Even in South Carolina, with its strong tradition of belief in local autonomy, Governor Richard I. Manning urged his constituents to modify their view of government as "a threat to individual liberty," to see it instead as "a means for solving the ills of the body politic."

Progressives could reject the traditional assumption that powerful government posed a threat to freedom, because their understanding of freedom was itself in flux. "Effective freedom," wrote the philosopher John Dewey, was far different from the "highly formal and limited concept of liberty" as protection from outside restraint. Freedom was a positive, not a negative, concept—the "power to do specific things." As such, it depended on "the *distribution* of powers that exists at a given time." Thus, freedom inevitably became a political question. "Freedom," wrote Dewey's brilliant young admirer, the writer Randolph Bourne, "means a democratic cooperation in determining the ideals and purposes and industrial and social institutions of a country."

STATE AND LOCAL REFORMS

Throughout the Western world, social legislation proliferated in the early twentieth century. In the United States, with a political structure more decentralized than in European countries, state and local governments enacted most of the era's reform measures. In cities, Progressives worked to reform the structure of government to reduce the power of political bosses, establish public control of "natural monopolies" like gas and water works, and improve public transportation. They raised property taxes in order to spend more money on schools, parks, and other public facilities.

Gilded Age mayors Hazen Pingree and Samuel "Golden Rule" Jones pioneered urban Progressivism. A former factory worker who became a successful shoe manufacturer, Pingree served as mayor of Detroit from 1889 to 1897. He battled the business interests that had dominated city government, forcing gas and telephone companies to lower their rates, and established a municipal power plant. Jones had instituted an eight-hour day and paid vacations at his factory that produced oil drilling equipment. As mayor of Toledo, Ohio, from 1897 to 1905, he founded night schools and free kindergartens, built new parks, and supported the right of workers to unionize.

Since state legislatures defined the powers of city government, urban Progressives often carried their campaigns to the state level. Pingree became governor of Michigan in 1896, in which post he continued his battle against railroads and other corporate interests. Hiram Johnson, who as public prosecutor had secured the conviction for bribery of San Francisco political boss Abraham Ruef, was elected governor of California in 1910. Having promised to "kick the Southern Pacific [Railroad] out of politics," he secured passage of the Public Utilities Act, one of the country's strongest railroad-regulation measures, as well as laws banning child labor and limiting the working hours of women.

The most influential Progressive administration at the state level was that of Robert M. La Follette, who made Wisconsin a "laboratory for democracy." After serving as a Republican member of Congress, La Follette became convinced that an alliance of railroad and lumber companies controlled state politics. Elected governor in 1900, he instituted a series of measures known as the Wisconsin Idea, including nominations of candidates for office through primary elections rather than by political bosses, the taxation of corporate wealth, and state regulation of railroads and public utilities. To staff his administration, he drew on nonpartisan faculty members from the University of Wisconsin.

PROGRESSIVE DEMOCRACY

"We are far from free," wrote Randolph Bourne in 1913, "but the new spirit of democracy is the angel that will free us." Progressives hoped to reinvigorate democracy by restoring political power to the citizenry and civic harmony to a divided society. Alarmed by the upsurge in violent class conflict and the unrestricted power of corporations, they believed that political reforms could help to create a unified "people" devoted to greater democracy and social reconciliation. Yet increasing the responsibilities of government made it all the more important to identify who was entitled to political participation and who was not.

The Progressive era saw a host of changes implemented in the political process, many seemingly contradictory in purpose. The electorate was simultaneously expanded and contracted, empowered and removed from direct influence on many functions of government. Democracy was enhanced by the Seventeenth Amendment—which provided that U.S. senators be chosen by popular vote rather than by state legislatures—by widespread adoption of the popular election of judges, and by the use of primary elections among party members to select candidates for office. Several states, including California under Hiram Johnson, adopted the initiative and referendum (the former allowed voters to propose legislation, the latter to vote directly on it) and the recall, by which officials could be removed from office by popular vote. The era culminated with a constitutional amendment enfranchising women—the largest expansion of democracy in American history.

But the Progressive era also witnessed numerous restrictions on democratic participation, most strikingly the disenfranchisement of blacks in the South, a process supported by many white southern Progressives as a way of ending election fraud. To make city government more honest and efficient, many localities replaced elected mayors with appointed nonpartisan commissions or city managers—a change that insulated officials from machine domination but also from popular control. New literacy tests and residency and registration requirements, common in northern as well as southern states, limited the right to vote among the poor. Taken as a whole, the electoral changes of the

Progressive era represented a significant reversal of the idea that voting was an inherent right of American citizenship. And most white Progressives proved remarkably indifferent to the plight of African-Americans. In the eyes of many Progressives, the "fitness" of voters, not their absolute numbers, defined a functioning democracy.

GOVERNMENT BY EXPERT

"He didn't believe in democracy; he believed simply in government." The writer H. L. Mencken's quip about Theodore Roosevelt came uncomfortably close to the mark for many Progressive advocates of an empowered state. Most Progressive thinkers were highly uncomfortable with the real world of politics, which seemed to revolve around the pursuit of narrow class, ethnic, and regional interests. Robert M. La Follette's reliance on college professors to staff important posts in his administration reflected a larger Progressive faith in expertise. The government could best exercise intelligent control over society through a democracy run by impartial experts who were in many respects unaccountable to the citizenry.

This impulse toward order, efficiency, and centralized management—all in the name of social justice—was an important theme of Progressive reform. The title of Walter Lippmann's influential 1914 work of social commentary, *Drift and Mastery*, posed the stark alternatives facing the nation. "Drift" meant continuing to operate according to the outmoded belief in individual autonomy. "Mastery" required applying scientific inquiry to modern social problems. The new generation of educated professionals, Lippmann believed, could be trusted more fully than ordinary citizens to solve America's deep social problems. Political freedom was less a matter of direct participation in government than of qualified persons devising the best public policies.

JANE ADDAMS AND HULL HOUSE

But alongside this elitist politics, Progressivism also included a more democratic vision of the activist state. As much as any other group, organized women reformers spoke for the more democratic side of Progressivism. Still barred from voting and holding office in most states, women nonetheless became central to the political history of the Progressive era. Women challenged the barriers that excluded them from formal political participation and developed a democratic, grassroots vision of Progressive government. In so doing, they placed on the political agenda new understandings of female freedom. The immediate catalyst was a growing awareness among women reformers of the plight of poor immigrant communities and the emergence of the condition of women and child laborers as a major focus of public concern.

The era's most prominent female reformer was Jane Addams, who had been born in 1860, the daughter of an Illinois businessman. After graduating from college, Addams, who never married, resented the prevailing expectation that a woman's life should be governed by what she called the "family claim"—the obligation to devote herself to parents, husband, and children. In 1889, she founded Hull House in Chicago, a "settlement house" devoted to improving the lives of the immigrant poor. Hull House was modeled on Toynbee Hall, which Addams had visited after its establishment in a working-class neighborhood of London in 1884. Unlike previous reformers, who had aided the poor from afar, settlement-house workers moved into poor neighborhoods. They built kindergartens and playgrounds for children, established employment bureaus and health clinics, and showed female victims of domestic abuse how to gain legal protection. By 1910, more than 400 settlement houses had been established in cities throughout the country.

"SPEARHEADS FOR REFORM"

Addams was typical of the Progressive era's "new woman." By 1900, there were more than 80,000 college-educated women in the United States. Many found a calling in providing social services, nursing, and education to poor families in the growing cities. The efforts of middle-class women to uplift the poor, and of laboring women to uplift themselves, helped to shift the center of gravity of politics toward activist government. Women like Addams discovered that even well-organized social work was not enough to alleviate the problems of inadequate housing, income, and health. Government action was essential. Hull House instigated an array of reforms in Chicago, soon adopted elsewhere, including stronger building and sanitation codes, shorter working hours and safer labor conditions, and the right of labor to organize.

Female activism spread throughout the country. Ironically, the exclusion of blacks from jobs in southern textile mills strengthened the region's movement against child labor. Reformers portrayed child labor as a menace to white supremacy, depriving white children of educations they would need as adult members of the dominant race. These reformers devoted little attention to the condition of black children. Women's groups in Alabama were instrumental in the passage of a 1903 state law restricting child labor. By 1915, every southern state had followed suit. But with textile mill owners determined to employ children and many poor families dependent on their earnings, these laws were enforced only sporadically.

The settlement houses have been called "spearheads for reform." They produced prominent Progressive figures like Julia Lathrop, the first woman to head a federal agency (the Children's Bureau, established in 1912 to investigate the conditions of mothers and children and advocate their interests). Florence

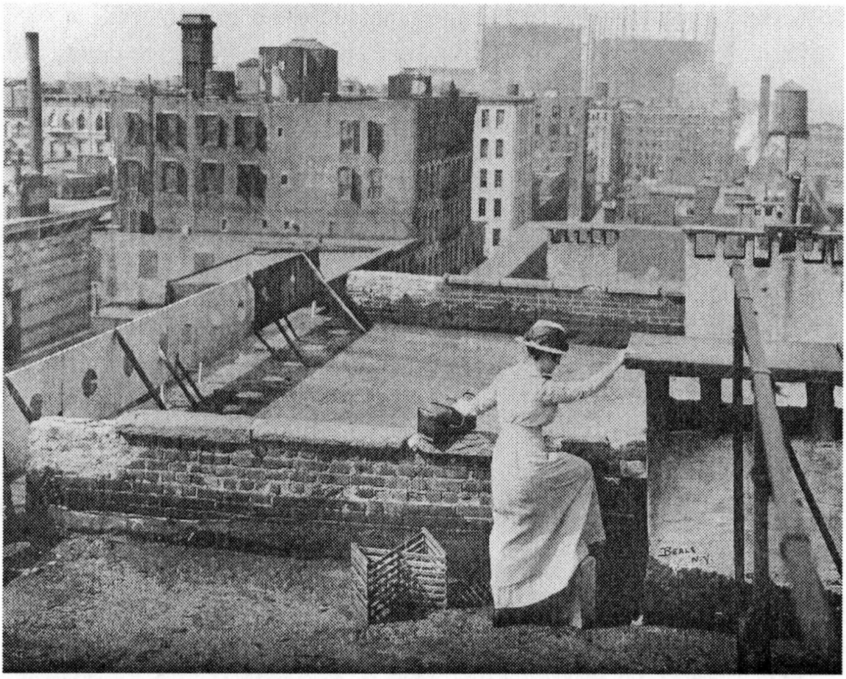

Visiting nurse on a New York City rooftop, 1908. Efforts to uplift the immigrant poor offered new opportunities for professional employment to many women during the Progressive era.

Kelley, the daughter of Civil War–era Radical Republican congressman William D. Kelley and a veteran of Hull House, went on to mobilize women's power as consumers as a force for social change. In the Gilded Age, the writer Helen Campbell had brilliantly exposed the contradiction of a market economy in which fashionable women wore clothing produced by poor women in wretched sweatshops. "Emancipation on the one side," she pointedly observed, "has meant no corresponding emancipation for the other." A generation later, under Kelley's leadership, the National Consumers' League became the nation's leading advocate of laws governing the working conditions of women and children. Freedom of choice in the marketplace, Kelley insisted, enabled socially conscious consumers to "unite with wage earners" by refusing to purchase goods produced under exploitative conditions.

THE CAMPAIGN FOR WOMAN SUFFRAGE

After 1900, the campaign for women's suffrage moved beyond the mostly elite membership of the 1890s to engage a broad coalition ranging from middle-class members of women's clubs to unionists, socialists, and settlement-house workers. For the first time, it became a mass movement. Membership in the National American Woman Suffrage Association grew from 13,000 in 1893 to more than 2 million by 1917. The group campaigned throughout the country for the right to vote and began to enjoy some success. By 1900, more than half the states allowed women to vote in local elections dealing with school issues, and Wyoming, Colorado, Idaho, and Utah had adopted full women's suffrage.

Cynics charged that Wyoming legislators used suffrage to attract more female migrants to their predominantly male state, while Utah hoped to enhance the political power of husbands in polygamous marriages banned by law but still practiced by some Mormons. In Colorado and Idaho, however, the success of referendums in the 1890s reflected the power of the Populist Party, a strong supporter of votes for women. Between 1910 and 1914, seven more western states enfranchised women. In 1913, Illinois became the first state east of the Mississippi River to allow women to vote in presidential elections.

These campaigns, which brought women aggressively into the public sphere, were conducted with a new spirit of militancy. They also made effective use of the techniques of advertising, publicity, and mass entertainment characteristic of modern consumer society. California's successful 1911 campaign utilized automobile parades, numerous billboards and electric signs, and countless suffrage buttons and badges. Nonetheless, state campaigns were difficult, expensive, and usually unsuccessful. The movement increasingly focused its attention on securing a national constitutional amendment giving women the right to vote.

MATERNALIST REFORM

Ironically, the desire to exalt women's role within the home did much to inspire the reinvigoration of the suffrage movement. Many of the era's experiments in public policy arose from the conviction that the state had an obligation to protect women and children. Female reformers helped to launch a mass movement for direct government action to improve the living standards of poor mothers and children. Laws providing for mothers' pensions (state aid to mothers of young children who lacked male support) spread rapidly after 1910. The pensions tended to be less than generous, and local eligibility requirements opened the door to unequal treatment (white widows benefited the most, single mothers were widely discriminated against, and black women were almost entirely excluded). "Maternalist" reforms like mothers' pensions rested on the assumption that the government should encourage women's capacity for bearing and raising children and enable them to be economically independent at the same time. Both feminists and believers in conventional domestic roles supported such measures. The former hoped that these laws would subvert women's dependence on men, the latter that they would strengthen traditional families and the mother-child bond.

Other Progressive legislation recognized that large numbers of women did in fact work outside the home, but defined them as a dependent group (like children) in need of state protection in ways male workers were not. In 1908, in the landmark case of *Muller v. Oregon*, Louis D. Brandeis filed a famous brief citing scientific and sociological studies to demonstrate that because women had less strength and endurance than men, long hours of labor were dangerous for women, while their unique ability to bear children gave the government a legitimate interest in their working conditions. Persuaded by Brandeis's argument, the Supreme Court unanimously upheld the constitutionality of an Oregon law setting maximum working hours for women.

Thus, three years after the notorious *Lochner* decision invalidating a New York law limiting the working hours of male bakers, the Court created the first large breach in "liberty of contract" doctrine. But the cost was high: at the very time that women in unprecedented numbers were entering the labor market and earning college degrees, Brandeis's brief and the Court's opinion solidified the view of women workers as weak, dependent, and incapable of enjoying the same economic rights as men. By 1917, thirty states had enacted laws limiting the hours of labor of female workers. Many women derived great benefit from these laws; others saw them as an infringement on their freedom.

While the maternalist agenda built gender inequality into the early foundations of the welfare state, the very use of government to regulate working conditions called into question basic assumptions concerning liberty of contract. Although not all reformers were willing to take the step, it was easy to extend the idea of protecting women and children to demand that government better the living and working conditions of men as well, by insuring them against the impact of unemployment, old age, ill health, and disability. Brandeis himself insisted that government should concern itself with the health, income, and future prospects of all its citizens.

THE IDEA OF ECONOMIC CITIZENSHIP

Brandeis envisioned a different welfare state from that of the maternalist reformers, one rooted less in the idea of healthy motherhood than in the notion of universal economic entitlements, including the right to a decent income and protection against unemployment and work-related accidents. For him, the right to assistance derived from citizenship itself, not some special service to the nation (as in the case of mothers) or upstanding character (which had long differentiated the "deserving" from the "undeserving" poor).

This vision, too, enjoyed considerable support in the Progressive era. By 1913, twenty-two states had enacted workmen's compensation laws to benefit workers, male or female, injured on the job. This legislation was the first wedge that opened the way for broader programs of social insurance. To avoid the stigma of depending on governmental assistance, contributions from workers' own wages funded these programs in part, thus distinguishing them from charity dispensed by local authorities to the poor. But state minimum wage laws and most laws regulating working hours applied only to women. Women and children may have needed protection, but interference with the freedom of contract of adult male workers was still widely seen as degrading. The establishment of a standard of living and working conditions beneath which no American should be allowed to fall would await the coming of the New Deal.

THE PROGRESSIVE PRESIDENTS

Despite the ferment of Progressivism on the city and state levels, the most striking political development of the early twentieth century was the rise of the national state. The process of nationalization was occurring throughout American life. National corporations dominated the economy; national organizations like the American Medical Association came into being to raise the incomes and respect of professions. The process was even reflected in the consolidation of local baseball teams into the American and National Leagues and the advent in 1903 of the World Series. Only energetic national government, Progressives believed, could create the social conditions of freedom.

Despite creative experiments in social policy at the city and state levels, the tradition of localism seemed to most Progressives an impediment to a renewed sense of national purpose. Poverty, economic insecurity, and lack of industrial democracy were national problems that demanded national solutions. The democratic national state, wrote *New Republic* editor Herbert Croly, offered an alternative to control of Americans' lives by narrow interests that manipulated politics or by the all-powerful corporations. Croly proposed a new synthesis of American political traditions. To achieve the "Jeffersonian ends" of democratic self-determination and individual freedom, he insisted, the country needed to employ the "Hamiltonian means" of government intervention in the economy. Each in his own way, the Progressive presidents—Theodore Roosevelt, William Howard Taft, and Woodrow Wilson—tried to address this challenge.

THEODORE ROOSEVELT

President Theodore Roosevelt addressing a crowd in Evanston, Illinois, in 1902.

In September 1901, the anarchist Leon Czolgosz assassinated William McKinley while the president visited the Pan-American Exposition in Buffalo, New York. At the age of forty-two, Vice President Theodore Roosevelt became the youngest man ever to hold the office of president. Roosevelt was an impetuous, energetic individual with a penchant for what he called the "strenuous life" of manly adventure. In many ways, he became the model for the twentieth-century president, an official actively and continuously engaged in domestic and foreign affairs. Roosevelt regarded the president as "the steward of the public welfare." He moved aggressively to set the political agenda.

When the British writer H. G. Wells visited the United States soon after the turn of the century, he found that "the steady trend towards concentration" had become "the cardinal topic of thought and discussion in the American mind." Roosevelt's program, which he called the Square Deal, attempted to confront the problems caused by economic consolidation by distinguishing between "good" and "bad" corporations. The former, among which he included U.S. Steel and Standard Oil, served the public interest. The latter were run by greedy financiers interested only in profit, and had no right to exist.

Soon after assuming office, Roosevelt shocked the corporate world by announcing his intention to prosecute under the Sherman Antitrust Act the Northern Securities Company. Created by financier J. P. Morgan, this "holding company" owned the stock and directed the affairs of three major western railroads. It monopolized transportation between the Great Lakes and the Pacific. Morgan was outraged. "Wall Street is paralyzed," quipped one newspaper, "at the thought that a President of the United States should sink to enforce the law." In 1904, the Supreme Court ordered Northern Securities dissolved, a major victory for the antitrust movement.

ROOSEVELT AND ECONOMIC REGULATION

Roosevelt also believed that the president should be an honest broker in labor disputes, rather than automatically siding with employers as his predecessors had usually done. When a strike paralyzed the West Virginia and Pennsylvania coalfields in 1902, he summoned union and management leaders to the White House. By threatening a federal takeover of the mines, he persuaded the owners to allow the dispute to be settled by a commission he himself would appoint.

Reelected in 1904, Roosevelt pushed for more direct federal regulation of the economy. Appealing to the public for support, he condemned the misuse of the "vast power conferred by vast wealth." He proposed to strengthen the Interstate Commerce Commission, which the Supreme Court had essentially limited to collecting economic statistics. By this time, journalistic exposés, labor unrest, and the agitation of Progressive reformers had created significant public support for Roosevelt's regulatory program. In 1906, Congress passed the Hepburn Act, giving the ICC the power to examine railroads' business records and to set reasonable rates, a significant step in the development of federal intervention in the corporate economy. That year, as has been noted, also saw the Pure Food and Drug Act, which established a federal agency to police the quality and labeling of food and drugs, and the Meat Inspection Act. Many businessmen supported these measures, recognizing that they would benefit from greater public confidence in the quality and safety of their products. But they were alarmed by Roosevelt's calls for federal inheritance and income taxes and the regulation of all interstate businesses.

JOHN MUIR AND THE SPIRITUALITY OF NATURE

If the United States lagged behind Europe in many areas of social policy, it led the way in the conservation of natural resources. The first national park, Yellowstone in Wyoming, was created by Congress in 1872, partly to preserve an area of remarkable natural beauty and partly at the urging of the Northern Pacific Railroad, which was anxious to promote western tourism. In the 1890s, the Scottish-born naturalist John Muir organized the Sierra Club to help preserve forests from uncontrolled logging by timber companies.

Muir's love of nature stemmed from deep religious feelings. Nearly blinded in an accident in an Indianapolis machine shop where he worked in his twenties, he found in the restoration of his sight an inspiration to appreciate God's creation. He called forests "God's first temples," and wrote that "in God's wilderness lies the hope of the world." In nature, he believed, men could experience directly the presence of God. Muir's outlook blended evangelical Protestantism with a romantic view of nature inspired by the Transcendentalists of the pre–Civil War era—like Henry David Thoreau, he lamented the intrusions of civilization on the natural environment. But unlike the Transcendentalists, Muir developed a broad following. As more and more Americans lived in cities, they came to see nature less as something to conquer and more as a place for recreation and personal growth. Muir's spiritual understanding of nature resonated with these urbanites.

THE CONSERVATION MOVEMENT

In the 1890s, Congress authorized the president to withdraw "forest reserves" from economic development, a restriction on economic freedom in the name of a greater social good. But it was under Theodore Roosevelt that conservation became a concerted federal policy. A dedicated outdoorsman who built a ranch in North Dakota in the 1880s, Roosevelt moved to preserve parts of the natural environment from economic exploitation.

Relying for advice on Gifford Pinchot, the head of the U.S. Forest Service, he ordered that millions of acres be set aside as wildlife preserves and encouraged Congress to create new national parks. The creation of parks like Yellowstone, Yosemite, and Glacier required the removal of Indians who hunted and fished there as well as the reintroduction of animals that had previously disappeared. City dwellers who visited the national parks did not realize that these were to a considerable extent artificially created and managed environments, not primordial nature.

In some ways, conservation was a typical Progressive reform. Manned by experts, the government could stand above political and economic battles, serving the public good while preventing "special interests" from causing irreparable damage to the environment. The aim was less to end the economic utilization of natural resources than to develop responsible, scientific plans for their use. Pinchot halted timber companies' reckless assault on the nation's forests. But unlike Muir, he believed that development and conservation could go hand in hand and that logging, mining, and grazing on public lands should be controlled, not eliminated. Conservation also reflected the Progressive thrust toward efficiency and control—in this case, control of nature itself.

In the view of Progressive conservationists, the West's scarcest resource—water—cried out for regulation. Governments at all levels moved to control the power of western rivers, building dams and irrigation projects to regularize their flow, prevent waste, and provide water for large-scale agriculture and urban development. With such projects came political conflict, as cities like Los Angeles and San Francisco battled with rural areas for access to water. After secretly buying up large tracts of land in the Owens Valley east of the city, for example, the city of Los Angeles constructed a major aqueduct between 1908 and 1913, over the vigorous objections of the valley's residents. By the 1920s, so much water had been diverted to the city that the once thriving farming and ranching businesses of Owens Valley could no longer operate.

TAFT IN OFFICE

Having served nearly eight years as president, Roosevelt did not run again in 1908. His chosen successor was William Howard Taft, a federal judge from Ohio who had served as governor of the Philippines after the Spanish-American War. Taft defeated William Jennings Bryan, making his third unsuccessful race for the White House. Taft's inaugural address expressed the Progressive view of the state: "The scope of a modern government . . . has been widened far beyond the principles laid down by the old 'laissez-faire' school of political writers."

Although temperamentally more conservative than Roosevelt, Taft pursued antitrust policy even more aggressively. He persuaded the Supreme Court in 1911 to declare John D. Rockefeller's Standard Oil Company (one of Roosevelt's "good" trusts) in violation of the Sherman Antitrust Act and to order its breakup into separate marketing, producing, and refining companies. The government also won a case against American Tobacco, which the Court ordered to end pricing policies that were driving smaller firms out of business. In these decisions, the justices announced a new standard for judging large corporations—the "rule of reason"—which in effect implemented Roosevelt's old distinction between good and bad trusts. Big businesses were not, in and of themselves, antitrust violators, unless they engaged in policies that stifled competition.

Taft supported the Sixteenth Amendment to the Constitution, which authorized Congress to enact a graduated income tax (one whose rate of taxation is higher for wealthier citizens). It was ratified shortly before he left office. A 2 percent tax on incomes over $4,000 had been included in a tariff enacted in 1894 but had been quickly declared unconstitutional by the Supreme Court as a "communistic threat to property." The movement to resurrect the income tax united southern and western farmers who wished to reduce government dependence on revenue from the tariff, which they believed discriminated against nonindustrial states, and Progressives who believed that taxation should be based on the ability to pay. A key step in the modernization of the federal government, the income tax provided a reliable and flexible source of revenue for a national state whose powers, responsibilities, and expenditures were growing rapidly.

Despite these accomplishments, Taft seemed to gravitate toward the more conservative wing of the Republican Party. Only a few months after taking office, he signed the Payne-Aldrich Tariff, which reduced rates on imported goods but not nearly as much as reformers wished. Taft's rift with

Progressives grew deeper when Richard A. Ballinger, the new secretary of the interior, concluded that Roosevelt had exceeded his authority in placing land in forest reserves. Ballinger decided to return some of this land to the public domain, where mining and lumber companies would have access to it. Gifford Pinchot accused Ballinger of colluding with business interests and repudiating the environmental goals of the Roosevelt administration. When Taft fired Pinchot in 1910, the breach with party Progressives became irreparable. In 1912, Roosevelt challenged Taft for the Republican nomination. Defeated, Roosevelt launched an independent campaign as the head of the new Progressive Party.

THE ELECTION OF 1912

All the crosscurrents of Progressive-era thinking about what *McClure's Magazine* called "the problem of the relation of the State and the corporation" came together in the presidential campaign of 1912. The four-way contest between Taft, Roosevelt, Democrat Woodrow Wilson, and Socialist Eugene V. Debs became a national debate on the relationship between political and economic freedom in the age of big business. At one end of the political spectrum stood Taft, who stressed that economic individualism could remain the foundation of the social order so long as government and private entrepreneurs

Eugene V. Debs, the Socialist Party candidate, speaking in Chicago during the 1912 presidential campaign.

cooperated in addressing social ills. At the other end was Debs. Relatively few Americans supported the Socialist Party's goal of abolishing the "capitalistic system" altogether, but its immediate demands—including public ownership of the railroads and banking system, government aid to the unemployed, and laws establishing shorter working hours and a minimum wage—summarized forward-looking Progressive thought.

But it was the battle between Wilson and Roosevelt over the role of the federal government in securing economic freedom that galvanized public attention in 1912. The two represented competing strands of Progressivism. Both believed government action necessary to preserve individual freedom, but they differed over the dangers of increasing the government's power and the inevitability of economic concentration. Though representing a party thoroughly steeped in states' rights and laissez-faire ideology, Wilson was deeply imbued with Progressive ideas. "Freedom today," he declared, "is something more than being let alone. The program of a government of freedom must in these days be positive, not negative merely." As governor of New Jersey, Wilson had presided over the implementation of a system of workmen's compensation and state regulation of utilities and railroads.

NEW FREEDOM AND NEW NATIONALISM

Strongly influenced by Louis D. Brandeis, with whom he consulted frequently during the campaign, Wilson insisted that democracy must be reinvigorated by restoring market competition and freeing government from domination by big business. Wilson feared big government as much as he feared the power of the corporations. The New Freedom, as he called his program, envisioned the federal government strengthening antitrust laws, protecting the right of workers to unionize, and actively encouraging small businesses—creating, in other words, the conditions for the renewal of economic competition without increasing government regulation of the economy. Wilson warned that corporations were as likely to corrupt government as to be managed by it, a forecast that proved remarkably accurate.

To Roosevelt's supporters, Wilson seemed a relic of a bygone era; his program, they argued, served the needs of small businessmen but ignored the inevitability of economic concentration and the interests of professionals, consumers, and labor. Wilson and Brandeis spoke of the "curse of bigness." What the nation actually needed, Walter Lippmann countered, was frank acceptance of the benefits of bigness, coupled with the intervention of government to counteract its abuses. Lippmann was expressing the core of the New Nationalism, Roosevelt's program of 1912. Only the "controlling and directing power of the government," Roosevelt insisted, could restore "the liberty of the oppressed." He called for heavy taxes on personal and corporate fortunes and federal regulation of industries, including railroads, mining, and oil.

The Progressive Party platform offered numerous proposals to promote social justice. Drafted by a group of settlement-house activists, labor reformers, and social scientists, the platform laid out a blueprint for a modern, democratic welfare state, complete with woman suffrage, federal supervision of corporate enterprise, national labor and health legislation for women and children, an eight-hour day and "living wage" for all workers, and a national system of social insurance covering unemployment, medical care, and old age. Described by Roosevelt as the "most important document" since the end of the Civil War, the platform brought together many of the streams of thought and political experiences that flowed into Progressivism. Roosevelt's campaign helped to give freedom a modern social and economic content and established an agenda that would define political liberalism for much of the twentieth century.

WILSON'S FIRST TERM

The Republican split ensured a sweeping victory for Wilson, who won about 42 percent of the popular vote, although Roosevelt humiliated Taft by winning about 27 percent to the president's 23 percent. In office, Wilson proved himself a strong executive leader. He established an office at the Capitol so that he could confer regularly with members of Congress about pending legislation, and he was the first president to hold regular press conferences in order to influence public opinion directly and continuously. He delivered messages personally to Congress rather than sending them in written form like all his predecessors since John Adams.

With Democrats in control of Congress, Wilson moved aggressively to implement his version of Progressivism. The first significant measure of his presidency was the Underwood Tariff, which substantially reduced duties on imports and, to make up for lost revenue, imposed a graduated income tax on the richest 5 percent of Americans. There followed the Clayton Act of 1914, which exempted labor unions from antitrust laws and barred courts from issuing injunctions curtailing the right to strike. In 1916 came the Keating-Owen Act outlawing child labor in the manufacture of goods sold in interstate commerce (the Supreme Court would later declare it unconstitutional), the Adamson Act establishing an eight-hour workday on the nation's railroads, and the Warehouse Act, reminiscent of the Populist subtreasury plan, which extended credit to farmers when they stored their crops in federally licensed warehouses.

THE EXPANDING ROLE OF GOVERNMENT

Some of Wilson's policies seemed more in tune with Roosevelt's New Nationalism than the New Freedom of 1912. He abandoned the idea of aggressive trust-busting in favor of greater government supervision of the economy. Wilson presided over the creation of two powerful new public agencies. In 1913, Congress created the Federal Reserve System, consisting of twelve regional banks. They were overseen by a central board appointed by the president and empowered to handle the issuance of currency, aid banks in danger of failing, and influence interest rates so as to promote economic growth. The law was a delayed response to the Panic of 1907, when the failure of several financial companies threatened a general collapse of the banking system. With the federal government lacking a modern central bank, it had been left to J. P. Morgan to assemble the funds to prop up threatened financial institutions. Morgan's actions highlighted the fact that in the absence of federal regulation of banking, power over finance rested entirely in private hands.

A second expansion of national power occurred in 1914, when Congress established the Federal Trade Commission (FTC) to investigate and prohibit "unfair" business activities such as price-fixing and monopolistic practices. Both the Federal Reserve and FTC were welcomed by many business leaders as a means of restoring order to the economic marketplace and warding off more radical measures for curbing corporate power. But they reflected the remarkable expansion of the federal role in the economy during the Progressive era.

By 1916, the social ferment and political mobilizations of the Progressive era had given birth to a new American state. With new laws, administrative agencies, and independent commissions, government at the local, state, and national levels had assumed the authority to protect and advance "industrial freedom." Government had established rules for labor relations, business behavior, and financial policy, protected citizens from market abuses, and acted as a broker among the groups whose conflicts threatened to destroy social harmony. But a storm was already engulfing Europe that would test the Progressive faith in empowered government as the protector of American freedom.

Chapter Review

REVIEW QUESTIONS

1. Identify the main groups and ideas that drove the Progressive movement.
2. Explain how immigration to the United States in this period was part of a global movement of peoples.
3. Describe how Fordism transformed American industrial and consumer society.
4. Socialism was a rising force across the globe in the early twentieth century. How successful was the movement in the United States?
5. Explain why the Industrial Workers of the World (IWW) grew so rapidly and aroused so much opposition.
6. How did immigrants adjust to life in America? What institutions or activities became important to their adjustment, and why?
7. What did Progressive-era feminists want to change in society, and how did their actions help to spearhead broader reforms?
8. How did ideas of women's roles, shared by maternalist reformers, lead to an expansion of activism by and rights for women?
9. How did each Progressive-era president view the role of the federal government?
10. Pick a Progressive-era reform (a movement, specific legislation, and organization) and describe how it shows how Progressives could work for both the expansion of democracy and restrictions on it.

KEY TERMS

muckrakers
child labor
Ellis Island and Angel Island
Fordism
American standard of living
Rerum Novarum
"scientific management"
Industrial Workers of the World
collective bargaining
"New Feminism"
birth-control movement
Society of American Indians
social legislation
Seventeenth Amendment

maternalist reform
Muller v. Oregon
workmen's compensation laws
Pure Food and Drug Act
Conservation Movement
Sixteenth Amendment
New Freedom and New Nationalism
Federal Trade Commission

wwnorton.com/studyspace

VISIT STUDYSPACE FOR THESE RESOURCES AND MORE:

- Author Videos
- A chapter outline
- A practice quiz
- Interactive maps
- Multimedia documents

CHAPTER 4

SAFE FOR DEMOCRACY: THE UNITED STATES AND WORLD WAR I

From *Give Me Liberty! Seagull Fourth Edition*

Eric Foner

Credits: photo 1: Eileen Tweedy/The Art Archive at Art Resource, NY; photo 2: Library of Congress; photo 3: Library of Congress; photo 4: Photographs and Prints Division, Schomburg Center for Research in Black Culture, The New York Public Library, Astor, Lenox, and Tilden Foundations; photo 5: Courtesy of the author; photo 6: Bettmann Corbis.

W.E.B. Du Bois: "Returning Soldiers." W. W. Norton & Co. wishes to thank the Crisis Publishing Co., Inc., the publisher of the magazine of the National Association for the Advancement of Colored People, for the use of this material first published in the May 1919 issue of Crisis Magazine; Table 1: Robert B. Grant, *The Black Man Comes to the City* (Chicago, 1972) 28–30.

4

Safe for Democracy: The United States and World War I 1916–1920

FOCUS QUESTIONS

- In what ways did the Progressive presidents promote the expansion of American power overseas?
- How did the United States get involved in World War I?
- How did the United States mobilize resources and public opinion for the war effort?
- How did the war affect race relations in the United States?
- Why was 1919 such a watershed year for the United States and the world?

In 1902, W. T. Stead published a short volume with the arresting title *The Americanization of the World; or, the Trend of the Twentieth Century.* Stead was an English editor whose sensational writings included an exposé of London prostitution, *Maiden Tribute of Modern Babylon.* He would meet his death in 1912 as a passenger on the *Titanic,* the ocean liner that foundered after striking an iceberg in the North Atlantic. Impressed by Americans' "exuberant energies," Stead predicted that the United States would soon emerge as "the greatest of world-powers." But what was most striking about his work was that Stead located the source of American power less in the realm of military might or territorial acquisition than in the country's single-minded commitment to the "pursuit of wealth" and the relentless international spread of American culture—art, music, journalism, even ideas about religion and gender relations. He foresaw a future in which the United States promoted its interests and values through an unending involvement in the affairs of other nations. Stead proved to be an accurate prophet.

The Spanish-American War had established the United States as an international empire. Despite the conquest of the Philippines and Puerto Rico, however, the country's overseas holdings remained tiny compared to those of Britain, France, and Germany. And no more were added, except for a strip of land surrounding the Panama Canal, acquired in 1903, and the Virgin Islands, purchased from Denmark in 1917. In 1900, Great Britain ruled over more than 300 million people in possessions scattered across the globe, and France had nearly 50 million subjects in Asia and Africa. Compared with these, the American presence in the world seemed very small. As Stead suggested, America's empire differed significantly from those of European countries—it was economic, cultural, and intellectual, rather than territorial.

The world economy at the dawn of the twentieth century was already highly globalized. An ever-increasing stream of goods, investments, and people flowed from country to country. Although Britain still dominated world banking and the British pound remained the major currency of international trade, the United States had become the leading industrial power. By 1914, it produced more than one-third of the world's manufactured goods. Already, Europeans complained of an "American invasion" of steel, oil, agricultural equipment, and consumer goods. Spearheads of American culture like movies and popular music were not far behind.

Europeans were fascinated by American ingenuity and mass production techniques. Many feared American products and culture would overwhelm their own. "What are the chief new features of London life?" one British writer asked in 1901. "They are the telephone, the portable camera, the phonograph, the electric street car, the automobile, the typewriter. . . . In every one of these the American maker is supreme." Meanwhile, hundreds of thousands of Americans traveled abroad each year in the early twentieth century. And American racial and ethnic groups became heavily engaged in overseas politics. Through fraternal, religious, and political organizations based in their ethnic and racial communities, Irish-Americans supported

Irish independence, American Jews protested the treatment of their co-religionists in Russia, and black Americans hoped to uplift Africa. American influence was growing throughout the world.

America's growing connections with the outside world led to increasing military and political involvement. In the two decades after 1900, many of the basic principles that would guide American foreign policy for the rest of the century were formulated. The "open door"—the free flow of trade, investment, information, and culture—emerged as a key principle of American foreign relations. "Since the manufacturer insists on having the world as a market," wrote Woodrow Wilson, "the flag of his nation must follow him and the doors of nations which are closed against him must be battered down."

Americans in the twentieth century often discussed foreign policy in the language of freedom. At least in rhetoric, the United States ventured abroad—including intervening militarily in the affairs of other nations—not to pursue strategic goals or to make the world safe for American economic interests, but to promote liberty and democracy. A supreme faith in America's historic destiny and in the righteousness of its ideals enabled the country's leaders to think of the United States simultaneously as an emerging great power and as the worldwide embodiment of freedom.

More than any other individual, Woodrow Wilson articulated this vision of America's relationship to the rest of the world. His foreign policy, called by historians "liberal internationalism," rested on the conviction that economic and political progress went hand in hand. Thus, greater worldwide freedom would follow inevitably from increased American investment and trade abroad. Frequently during the twentieth century, this conviction would serve as a mask for American power and self-interest. It would also inspire sincere efforts to bring freedom to other peoples. In either case, liberal internationalism represented a shift from the nineteenth-century tradition of promoting freedom primarily by example, to active intervention to remake the world in the American image.

American involvement in World War I provided the first great test of Wilson's belief that American power could "make the world safe for democracy." Most Progressives embraced the country's participation in the war, believing that the United States could help to spread Progressive values throughout the world. But rather than bringing Progressivism to other peoples, the war destroyed it at home. The government quickly came to view critics of American involvement not simply as citizens with a different set of opinions, but as enemies of the very ideas of democracy and freedom. As a result, the war produced one of the most sweeping repressions of the right to dissent in all of American history.

AN ERA OF INTERVENTION

Just as they expanded the powers of the federal government in domestic affairs, the Progressive presidents were not reluctant to project American power outside the country's borders. At first, their interventions were confined to the Western Hemisphere, whose affairs the United States had claimed a special right to oversee ever since the Monroe Doctrine of 1823. Between 1901 and 1920, U.S. marines landed in Caribbean countries more than twenty times. Usually, they were dispatched to create a welcoming economic environment for American companies that wanted stable access to raw materials like bananas and sugar, and for bankers nervous that their loans to local governments might not be repaid.

"I TOOK THE CANAL ZONE"

Just as he distinguished between good and bad trusts, Theodore Roosevelt divided the world into "civilized" and "uncivilized" nations. The former, he believed, had an obligation to establish order in an unruly world. Roosevelt became far more active in international diplomacy than most of his predecessors, helping, for example, to negotiate a settlement of the Russo-Japanese War of 1905, a feat for which he was awarded the Nobel Peace Prize. Closer to home, his policies were more aggressive. "I have always been fond of the West African proverb," he wrote, "'Speak softly and carry a big stick.'" And although he declared that the United States "has not the slightest desire for territorial aggrandizement at the expense of its southern neighbors," Roosevelt pursued a policy of intervention in Central America.

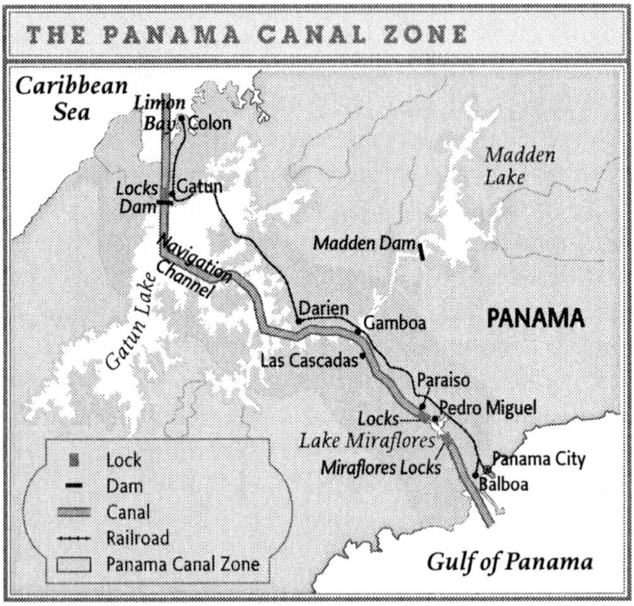

Constructed in the first years of the twentieth century, after Theodore Roosevelt helped engineer Panama's independence from Colombia, the Panama Canal drastically reduced the time it took for commercial and naval vessels to sail from the Atlantic to the Pacific Ocean.

In his first major action in the region, Roosevelt engineered the separation of Panama from Colombia in order to facilitate the construction of a canal linking the Atlantic and Pacific Oceans. The idea of a canal across the fifty-one-mile-wide Isthmus of Panama had a long history. In 1879–1881, the French engineer Ferdinand de Lesseps attempted to construct such a waterway but failed because of inadequate funding and the toll exacted on his workers by yellow fever and malaria. Roosevelt had long been a proponent of American naval development. He was convinced that a canal would facilitate the movement of naval and commercial vessels between the two oceans. In 1903, when Colombia, of which Panama was a part, refused to cede land for the project, Roosevelt helped to set in motion an uprising by conspirators led by Philippe Bunau-Varilla, a representative of the Panama Canal Company. An American gunboat prevented the Colombian army from suppressing the rebellion.

Upon establishing Panama's independence, Bunau-Varilla signed a treaty giving the United States both the right to construct and operate a canal and sovereignty over the Canal Zone, a ten-mile-wide strip of land through which the route would run. A

CHRONOLOGY

1903	United States secures the Panama Canal Zone
1904	Roosevelt Corollary to the Monroe Doctrine
1905	The Niagara movement established
1907	Gentleman's Agreement with Japan
1909	National Association for the Advancement of Colored People organized
1910	Mexican Revolution begins
1914–1919	World War I
1915	*Lusitania* sinks
1916	Madison Grant's *The Passing of the Great Race* Randolph Bourne's "Trans-National America"
1917	Zimmerman Telegram intercepted United States enters the war Espionage Act passed Russian Revolution
1918	Woodrow Wilson's "Fourteen Points" speech Eugene V. Debs convicted under the Espionage Act
1918–1920	Worldwide flu epidemic
1919	Eighteenth Amendment Treaty of Versailles signed
1919–1920	Red Scare
1920	Senate rejects the Treaty of Versailles Nineteenth Amendment
1921	Tulsa Riot

remarkable feat of engineering, the canal was the largest construction project in history to that date. Like the building of the transcontinental railroad in the 1860s and much construction work today, it involved the widespread use of immigrant labor. Most of the 60,000 workers came from the Caribbean islands of Barbados and Jamaica, but others hailed from Europe, Asia, and the United States. In keeping with American segregation policies, the best jobs were reserved for white Americans, who lived in their own communities complete with schools, churches, and libraries. It also required a massive effort to eradicate the mosquitoes that carried the tropical diseases responsible, in part, for the failure of earlier French efforts. When completed in 1914, the canal reduced the sea voyage between the East and West Coasts of the United States by 8,000 miles. "I took the Canal Zone," Roosevelt exulted. But the manner in which the canal had been initiated, and the continued American rule over the Canal Zone, would long remain a source of tension. In 1977, President Jimmy Carter negotiated treaties that led to turning over the canal's operation and control of the Canal Zone to Panama in the year 2000.

THE ROOSEVELT COROLLARY

Roosevelt's actions in Panama reflected a principle that came to be called the Roosevelt Corollary to the Monroe Doctrine. This held that the United States had the right to exercise "an international police power" in the Western Hemisphere—a significant expansion of Monroe's pledge to defend the hemisphere against European intervention. Early in Roosevelt's administration, British, Italian, and German naval forces blockaded Venezuela to ensure the payment of debts to European bankers. Roosevelt persuaded them to withdraw, but the incident convinced him that financial instability in the New World would invite intervention from the Old. In 1904, Roosevelt ordered American forces to seize the customs houses of the Dominican Republic to ensure payment of its debts to European and American investors. He soon arranged an "executive agreement" giving a group of American banks control over Dominican finances. In 1906, he dispatched troops to Cuba to oversee a disputed election; they remained in the country until 1909. Roosevelt also encouraged investment by American corporations like the United Fruit Company, whose huge banana plantations soon dominated the economies of Honduras and Costa Rica.

Roosevelt's successor, William Howard Taft, landed marines in Nicaragua to protect a government friendly to American economic interests. In general, however, Taft emphasized economic investment and loans from American banks, rather than direct military intervention, as the best way to spread American influence. As a result, his foreign policy became known as Dollar Diplomacy. In Honduras, Nicaragua, the Dominican Republic, and even Liberia—the West African nation established in 1816 as a home for freed American slaves—Taft pressed for more efficient revenue collection, stable government, and access to land and labor by American companies.

THE UNITED STATES IN THE CARIBBEAN, 1898–1941

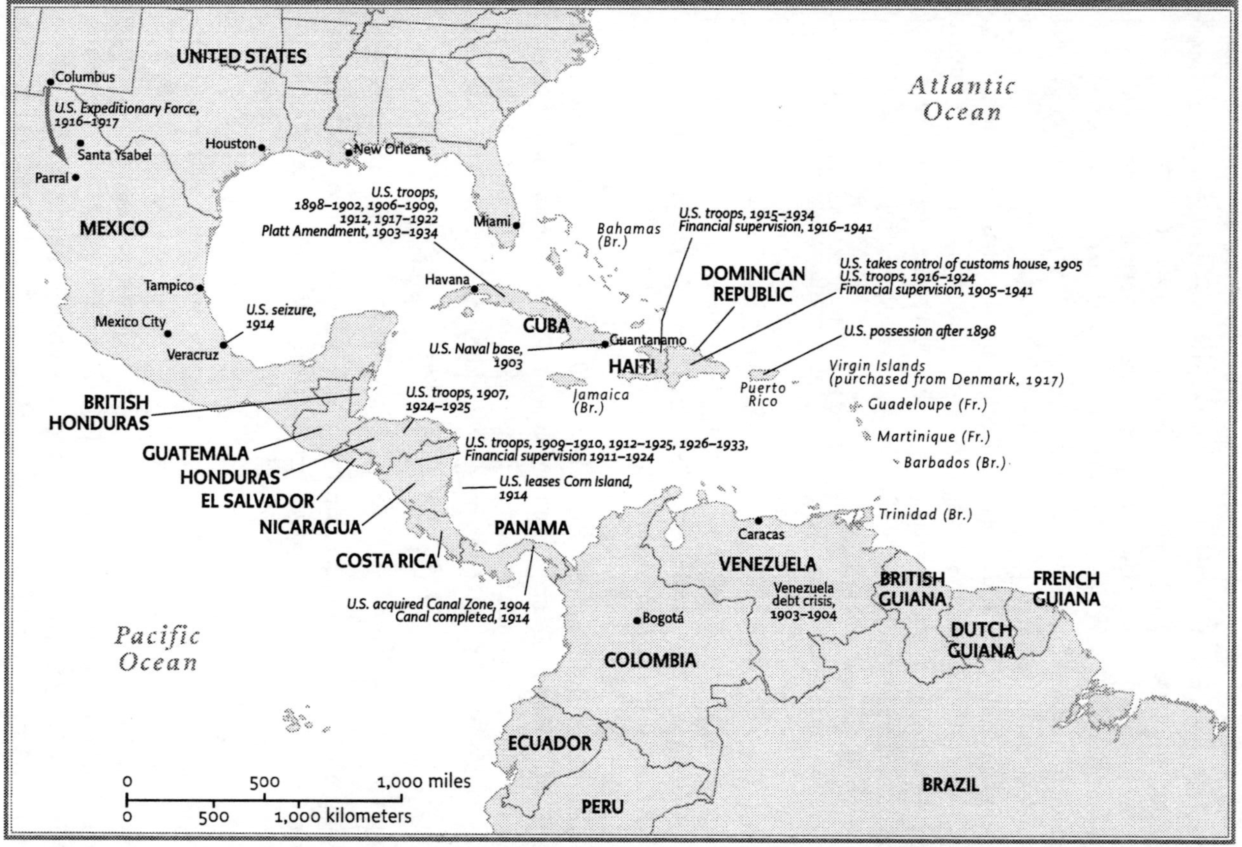

Between 1898 and 1934, the United States intervened militarily numerous times in Caribbean countries, generally to protect the economic interests of American banks and investors.

MORAL IMPERIALISM

The son of a Presbyterian minister, Woodrow Wilson brought to the presidency a missionary zeal and a sense of his own and the nation's moral righteousness. He appointed as secretary of state William Jennings Bryan, a strong anti-imperialist. Wilson repudiated Dollar Diplomacy and promised a new foreign policy that would respect Latin America's independence and free it from foreign economic domination. But Wilson could not abandon the conviction that the United States had a responsibility to teach other peoples the lessons of democracy. Moreover, he believed, the export of American manufactured goods and investments went hand in hand with the spread of democratic ideals. To Wilson, expanding American economic influence served a higher purpose than mere profit. Americans, he told a group of businessmen in 1916, were "meant to carry liberty and justice" throughout the world. "Go out and sell goods," he urged them, "that will make the world more comfortable and happy, and convert them to the principles of America."

Wilson's "moral imperialism" produced more military interventions in Latin America than the foreign policy of any president before or since. In 1915, he sent marines to occupy Haiti after the government refused to allow American banks to oversee its financial dealings. In 1916, he established a military government in the Dominican Republic, with the United States controlling the country's customs collections and paying its debts. American soldiers remained in the Dominican Republic until 1924 and in Haiti until 1934. They built roads and schools, but did little or nothing to promote democracy. Wilson's foreign policy underscored a paradox of modern American history: the presidents who spoke the most about freedom were likely to intervene most frequently in the affairs of other countries.

WILSON AND MEXICO

Wilson's major preoccupation in Latin America was Mexico, where in 1911 a revolution led by Francisco Madero overthrew the government of dictator Porfirio Díaz. Two years later, without Wilson's knowledge but with the backing of the U.S. ambassador and of American companies that controlled Mexico's oil and mining industries, military commander Victoriano Huerta assassinated Madero and seized power.

Wilson was appalled. The United States, he announced, would not extend recognition to a "government of butchers." He would "teach" Latin Americans, he added, "to elect good men." When civil war broke out in Mexico, Wilson ordered American troops to land at Vera Cruz to prevent the arrival of weapons meant for Huerta's forces. But to Wilson's surprise, Mexicans greeted the marines as invaders rather than liberators. Vera Cruz, after all, was where the forces of the conquistador Hernán Cortés had landed in the sixteenth century and those of Winfield Scott during the Mexican War. More than 100 Mexicans and 19 Americans died in the fighting that followed. Huerta left the presidency in 1914, but civil war continued, and neither side seemed grateful for Wilson's interference.

In 1916, the war spilled over into the United States when "Pancho" Villa, the leader of one faction, attacked Columbus, New Mexico, where he killed seventeen Americans. Wilson ordered 10,000 troops into northern Mexico on an expedition that unsuccessfully sought to arrest Villa. Mexico was a warning that it might be more difficult than Wilson assumed to use American might to reorder the internal affairs of other nations, or to apply moral certainty to foreign policy.

AMERICA AND THE GREAT WAR

In June 1914, a Serbian nationalist assassinated Archduke Franz Ferdinand, heir to the throne of the Austro-Hungarian empire, in Sarajevo, Bosnia. (Today, Sarajevo is the capital of Bosnia and Herzegovina.) This deed set in motion a chain of events that plunged Europe into the most devastating war the world had ever seen. In the years before 1914, European nations had engaged in a scramble to obtain colonial possessions overseas and had constructed a shifting series of alliances seeking military domination within Europe. In the aftermath of the assassination, Austria-Hungary, the major power in eastern Europe, declared war on Serbia. Within a little more than a month, because of the European powers' interlocking military alliances, Britain, France, Russia, and Japan (the Allies) found themselves at war with the Central Powers—Germany, Austria-Hungary, and the Ottoman empire, whose holdings included modern-day Turkey and much of the Middle East.

German forces quickly overran Belgium and part of northern France. The war then settled into a prolonged stalemate, with bloody, indecisive battles succeeding one another. New military technologies—submarines, airplanes, machine guns, tanks, and poison gas—produced unprecedented slaughter. In one five-month battle at Verdun, in 1916, 600,000 French and German soldiers perished—nearly as many combatants as in the entire American Civil War. By the time the war ended, an estimated 10 million soldiers, and uncounted millions of civilians, had perished. And the war was followed by widespread famine and a worldwide epidemic of influenza that killed an estimated 21 million people more.

The Great War, or World War I as it came to be called, dealt a severe blow to the optimism and self-confidence of Western civilization. For decades, philosophers, reformers, and politicians had hailed the triumph of reason and human progress. Despite increasingly bitter rivalries between European powers, especially Germany and Britain, as they competed for political and military dominance at home and carved up Asia and Africa into rival empires, mankind seemed to have moved beyond the time when disputes were settled by war. The conflict was also a shock to European socialist and labor movements. Of the two great ideologies that had arisen in the nineteenth century, nationalism and socialism, the former proved more powerful. Karl Marx had called on the "workers of the world" to unite against their oppressors. Instead, they marched off to kill each other.

NEUTRALITY AND PREPAREDNESS

As war engulfed Europe, Americans found themselves sharply divided. British-Americans sided with their nation of origin, as did many other Americans who associated Great Britain with liberty and democracy and Germany with repressive government. On the other hand, German-Americans identified with Germany. Irish-Americans bitterly opposed any aid to the British, a sentiment reinforced in 1916 when authorities in London suppressed the Easter Rebellion, an uprising demanding Irish independence, and executed several of its leaders. Immigrants from the Russian empire, especially Jews, had no desire to see the United States aid the czar's regime. Indeed, the presence of Russia, the world's largest despotic state, as an ally of Britain and France made it difficult to see the war as a clear-cut battle between democracy and autocracy. Many feminists, pacifists, and social reformers, moreover, had become convinced that peace was essential to further efforts to enhance social justice at home. They lobbied vigorously against American involvement. So did large numbers of religious leaders, who viewed war as a barbaric throwback to a less Christian era.

When war broke out in 1914, President Wilson proclaimed American neutrality. But as in the years preceding the War of 1812, naval warfare in Europe reverberated in the United States. Britain declared a naval blockade of Germany and began to stop American merchant vessels. Germany launched submarine warfare against ships entering and leaving British ports. In May 1915, a German submarine sank the British liner *Lusitania* (which was carrying a large cache of arms) off the coast of Ireland, causing the death of 1,198 passengers, including 124 Americans. Wilson composed a note of protest so strong that Bryan resigned as secretary of state, fearing that the president was laying the foundation for military intervention. Bryan had advocated warning Americans not to travel on the ships of belligerents, but Wilson felt this would represent a retreat from the principle of freedom of the seas.

The sinking of the *Lusitania* outraged American public opinion and strengthened the hand of those who believed that the United States must prepare for possible entry into the war. These included longtime advocates of a stronger military establishment, like Theodore Roosevelt, and businessmen with close economic ties to Britain, the country's leading trading partner and the recipient of more than $2 billion in wartime loans from American banks.

Wilson himself had strong pro-British sympathies and viewed Germany as "the natural foe of liberty." By the end of 1915, he had embarked on a policy of "preparedness"—a crash program to expand the American army and navy.

THE ROAD TO WAR

In May 1916, Germany announced the suspension of submarine warfare against noncombatants. Wilson's preparedness program seemed to have succeeded in securing the right of Americans to travel freely on the high seas without committing American forces to the conflict. "He kept us out of war" became the slogan of his campaign for reelection. With the Republican Party reunited after its split in 1912, the election proved to be one of the closest in American history. Wilson defeated Republican candidate Charles Evans Hughes by only twenty-three electoral votes and about 600,000 popular votes out of more than 18 million cast. Partly because he seemed to promise not to send American soldiers to Europe, Wilson carried ten of the twelve states that had adopted woman suffrage. Without the votes of women, Wilson would not have been reelected.

On January 22, 1917, Wilson called for a "peace without victory" in Europe and outlined his vision for a world order including freedom of the seas, restrictions on armaments, and self-determination for nations great and small. Almost immediately, however, Germany announced its intention to resume submarine warfare against ships sailing to or from the British Isles, and several American merchant vessels were sunk. The German government realized that its actions would probably lead Wilson to intervene, but German strategists gambled that the blockade would strangle Britain economically before the arrival of American troops.

In March 1917, British spies intercepted and made public the Zimmerman Telegram, a message by German foreign secretary Arthur Zimmerman calling on Mexico to join in a coming war against the United States and promising to help it recover territory lost in the Mexican War of 1846–1848. A revolution in Russia that same month overthrew the czar and established a constitutional government, making it more plausible to believe that the United States would be fighting on the side of democracy. On April 2, Wilson went before Congress to ask for a declaration of war against Germany. "The world," he proclaimed, "must be made safe for democracy. Its peace must be planted upon the tested foundation of political liberty." The war resolution passed the Senate 82–6 and the House 373–50.

THE FOURTEEN POINTS

Not until the spring of 1918 did American forces arrive in Europe in large numbers. By then, the world situation had taken a dramatic turn. In November 1917, a communist revolution headed by Vladimir Lenin overthrew the Russian government that had come to power the previous spring. Shortly

WORLD WAR I: THE WESTERN FRONT

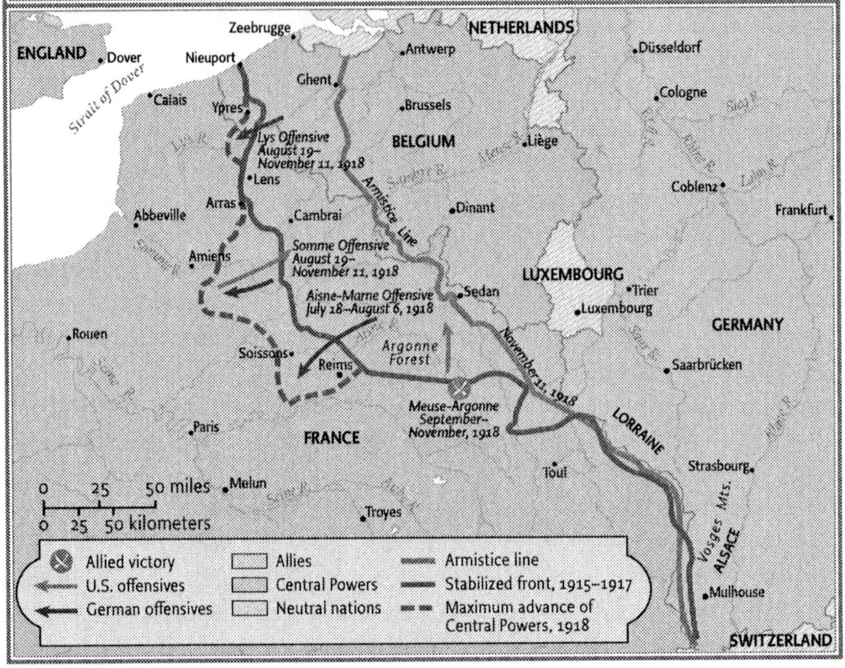

After years of stalemate on the western front in World War I, the arrival of American troops in 1917 and 1918 shifted the balance of power and made possible the Allied victory.

thereafter, Lenin withdrew Russia from the war and published the secret treaties by which the Allies had agreed to divide up conquered territory after the war—an embarrassment for Wilson, who had promised a just peace.

Partly to assure the country that the war was being fought for a moral cause, Wilson in January 1918 issued the Fourteen Points, the clearest statement of American war aims and of his vision of a new international order. Among the key principles were self-determination for all nations, freedom of the seas, free trade, open diplomacy (an end to secret treaties), the readjustment of colonial claims with colonized people given "equal weight" in deciding their futures, and the creation of a "general association of nations" to preserve the peace. Wilson envisioned this last provision, which led to the establishment after the war of the League of Nations, as a kind of global counterpart to the regulatory commissions Progressives had created at home to maintain social harmony and prevent the powerful from exploiting the weak. Although purely an American program, not endorsed by the other Allies, the Fourteen Points established the agenda for the peace conference that followed the war.

The United States threw its economic resources and manpower into the war. When American troops finally arrived in Europe, they turned the tide of battle. In the spring of 1918, they helped to repulse a German advance near Paris and by July were participating in a major Allied counteroffensive. In September, in the Meuse-Argonne campaign, more than 1 million American soldiers under General John J. Pershing helped to push back the outnumbered and exhausted German army. With his forces in full retreat, the German kaiser abdicated on November 9. Two days later, Germany sued for peace. More than 100,000 Americans had died, a substantial number, but they were only 1 percent of the 10 million soldiers killed in the Great War.

THE WAR AT HOME

THE PROGRESSIVES' WAR

Looking back on American participation in the European conflict, Randolph Bourne summed up one of its lessons: "War is the health of the state." Bourne saw the expansion of government power as a danger, but it struck most Progressives as a golden opportunity. To them, the war offered the possibility of reforming American society along scientific lines, instilling a sense of national unity and self-sacrifice, and expanding social justice. That American power could now disseminate Progressive values around the globe heightened the war's appeal.

Almost without exception, Progressive intellectuals and reformers, joined by prominent labor leaders and native-born socialists, rallied to Wilson's support. The roster included intellectuals like John Dewey, journalists such as Walter Lippmann and Herbert Croly, AFL head Samuel Gompers, socialist writers like Upton Sinclair, and prominent reformers including Florence Kelley and Charlotte Perkins Gilman. In *The New Republic*, Dewey urged Progressives to recognize the "social possibilities of war." The crisis, he wrote, offered the prospect of attacking the "immense inequality of power" within the United States, thus laying the foundation for Americans to enjoy "effective freedom."

THE WARTIME STATE

Like the Civil War, World War I created, albeit temporarily, a national state with unprecedented powers and a sharply increased presence in Americans' everyday lives. Under the Selective Service Act of May 1917, 24 million men were required to register with the draft, and the army soon swelled from 120,000 to 5 million men. The war seemed to bring into being the New Nationalist state Theodore Roosevelt and so many Progressives had desired. New federal agencies moved to regulate industry, transportation, labor relations, and agriculture. Headed by Wall Street financier Bernard Baruch, the War Industries Board presided over all elements of war production from the distribution of raw materials to the prices of manufactured goods. To spur efficiency, it established standardized specifications for everything from automobile tires to shoe colors (three were permitted—black, brown, and white). The Railroad Administration took control of the nation's transportation system, and the Fuel Agency rationed coal and oil. The Food -Administration instructed farmers on modern methods of cultivation and promoted the more efficient preparation of meals. Its director, Herbert Hoover, mobilized the shipment of American food to the war-devastated Allies, popularizing the slogan "Food will win the war."

These agencies generally saw themselves as partners of business as much as regulators. They guaranteed government suppliers a high rate of profit and encouraged cooperation among former business rivals by suspending antitrust laws. At the same time, however, the War Labor Board, which included representatives of government, industry, and the American Federation of Labor, pressed for the establishment of a minimum wage, eight-hour workday, and the right to form unions. During the war, wages rose substantially, working conditions in many industries improved, and union membership doubled. To finance the war, corporate and individual income taxes rose enormously. By 1918, the wealthiest Americans were paying 60 percent of their income in taxes. Tens of millions of Americans answered the call to demonstrate their patriotism by purchasing Liberty bonds. Once peace arrived, the wartime state quickly withered away. But for a time, the federal government seemed well on its way to fulfilling the Progressive task of promoting economic rationalization, industrial justice, and a sense of common national purpose.

THE PROPAGANDA WAR

During the Civil War, it had been left to private agencies—Union Leagues, the Loyal Publication Society, and others—to mobilize prowar public opinion. But the Wilson administration decided that patriotism was too important to leave to the private sector. Many Americans were skeptical about whether democratic America should enter a struggle between rival empires. Some vehemently opposed American participation, notably the Industrial Workers of the World (IWW) and the bulk of the Socialist Party, which in 1917 condemned the declaration of war as "a crime against the people of the United States" and called on "the workers of all countries" to refuse to fight. As the major national organization to oppose Wilson's policy, the Socialist Party became a rallying point for antiwar sentiment. In mayoral elections across the country in the fall of 1917, the Socialist vote averaged 20 percent, far above the party's previous total.

All combatants raised money by selling war bonds. In the German poster, the text reads: "The war loan is the way to peace. The enemies want it this way [referring to the mailed fist]. So subscribe." The fist conveys sheer power—it offers an image rather different from the representation of liberty on the American war poster.

In April 1917, the Wilson administration created the Committee on Public Information (CPI) to explain to Americans and the world, as its director, George Creel, put it, "the cause that compelled America to take arms in defense of its liberties and free institutions." Enlisting academics, journalists, artists, and advertising men, the CPI flooded the country with prowar propaganda, using every available medium from pamphlets (of which it issued 75 million) to posters, newspaper advertisements, and motion pictures. It trained and dispatched across the country 75,000 Four-Minute Men, who delivered brief standardized talks (sometimes in Italian, Yiddish, and other immigrant languages) to audiences in movie theaters, schools, and other public venues.

Never before had an agency of the federal government attempted the "conscious and intelligent manipulation of the organized habits and opinions of the masses," in the words of young Edward Bernays, a member of Creel's staff who would later create the modern profession of public relations. The CPI's activities proved, one adman wrote, that it was possible to "sway the ideas of whole populations, change their habits of life, create belief, practically universal in any policy or idea." In the 1920s, advertisers would use what they had learned to sell goods. But the CPI also set a precedent for active governmental efforts to shape public opinion in later international conflicts, from World War II to the Cold War and Iraq.

"THE GREAT CAUSE OF FREEDOM"

The CPI couched its appeal in the Progressive language of social cooperation and expanded democracy. Abroad, this meant a peace based on the principle of national self-determination. At home, it meant improving "industrial democracy." A Progressive journalist, Creel believed the war would accelerate the movement toward solving the "age-old problems of poverty, inequality, oppression, and unhappiness." He took to heart a warning from historian Carl Becker that a simple contrast between German tyranny and American democracy would not seem plausible to the average worker: "You talk to him of our ideals of liberty and he thinks of the shameless exploitation of labor and of the ridiculous gulf between wealth and poverty." The CPI distributed pamphlets foreseeing a postwar society complete with a "universal eight-hour day" and a living wage for all.

While "democracy" served as the key term of wartime mobilization, "freedom" also took on new significance. The war, a CPI advertisement proclaimed, was being fought in "the great cause of freedom." Thousands of persons, often draftees, were enlisted to pose in giant human tableaus representing symbols of liberty. One living representation of the Liberty Bell at Fort Dix, New Jersey, included 25,000 people. The most common visual image in wartime propaganda was the Statue of Liberty, employed especially to rally support among immigrants. "You came here seeking Freedom," stated a caption on one Statue of Liberty poster. "You must now help preserve it." Buying Liberty bonds became a demonstration of patriotism. Wilson's speeches cast the United States as a land of liberty fighting alongside a "concert of free people" to secure self-determination for the oppressed peoples of the world. The idea of freedom, it seems, requires an antithesis, and the CPI found one in the German kaiser and, more generally, the German nation and people. Government propaganda whipped up hatred of the wartime foe by portraying it as a nation of barbaric Huns.

THE COMING OF WOMAN SUFFRAGE

The enlistment of "democracy" and "freedom" as ideological war weapons inevitably inspired demands for their expansion at home. In 1916, Wilson had cautiously endorsed votes for women. America's entry into the war threatened to tear the suffrage movement apart, since many advocates had been associated with opposition to American involvement. Indeed, among those who voted against the declaration of war was the first woman member of Congress, the staunch pacifist Jeannette Rankin of Montana. "I want to stand by my country, but I cannot vote for war," she said. Although defeated in her reelection bid in 1918, Rankin would return to Congress in 1940. She became the only member to oppose the declaration of war against Japan in 1941, which ended her political career. In 1968, at the age of eighty-five, Rankin took part in a giant march on Washington to protest the war in Vietnam.

As during the Civil War, however, most leaders of woman suffrage organizations enthusiastically enlisted in the effort. Women sold war bonds, organized patriotic rallies, and went to work in war production jobs. Some 22,000 served as clerical workers and nurses with American forces in Europe. Many believed wartime service would earn them equal rights at home.

At the same time, a new generation of college-educated activists, organized in the National Woman's Party, pressed for the right to vote with militant tactics many older suffrage advocates found scandalous. The party's leader, Alice Paul, had studied in England between 1907 and 1910 when the British suffrage movement adopted a strategy that included arrests, imprisonments, and vigorous denunciations of a male-dominated political system. How could the country fight for democracy abroad, Paul asked, while denying it to women at home? She compared Wilson to the Kaiser, and a group of her followers chained themselves to the White House fence, resulting in a seven-month prison sentence. When they began a hunger strike, the prisoners were force-fed.

The combination of women's patriotic service and widespread outrage over the mistreatment of Paul and her fellow prisoners pushed the administration toward full-fledged support for woman suffrage. "We have made partners of the women in this war," Wilson proclaimed. "Shall we admit them only to a partnership of suffering and sacrifice and toil and not to a partnership of privilege and right?" In 1920, the long struggle ended with the ratification of the Nineteenth Amendment barring states from using sex as a qualification for the suffrage. The United States became the twenty-seventh country to allow women to vote.

PROHIBITION

The war gave a powerful impulse to other campaigns that had engaged the energies of many women in the Progressive era. Ironically, efforts to stamp out prostitution and protect soldiers from venereal disease led the government to distribute birth-control information and devices—the very action for which Margaret Sanger had recently been jailed.

Prohibition, a movement inherited from the nineteenth century that had gained new strength and militancy in Progressive America, finally achieved national success during the war. Numerous impulses flowed into the renewed campaign to ban intoxicating liquor. Employers hoped it would create a more disciplined labor force. Urban reformers believed that it would promote a more orderly city environment and undermine urban political machines that used saloons as places to organize. Women reformers hoped Prohibition would protect wives and children from husbands who engaged in domestic violence when drunk or who squandered their wages at saloons. Many native-born Protestants saw Prohibition as a way of imposing "American" values on immigrants.

Like the suffrage movement, Prohibitionists first concentrated on state campaigns. By 1915, they had won victories in eighteen southern and midwestern states where the immigrant population was small and Protestant denominations like Baptists and Methodists strongly opposed drinking. But like the suffrage movement, Prohibitionists came to see national legislation as their best strategy. The war gave them added ammunition. Many prominent breweries were owned by German-Americans, making beer seem unpatriotic. The Food Administration insisted that grain must be used to produce food, not distilled into beer and liquor. In December 1917, Congress passed the Eighteenth Amendment, prohibiting the manufacture and sale of intoxicating liquor. It was ratified by the states in 1919 and went into effect at the beginning of 1920.

LIBERTY IN WARTIME

World War I raised questions already glimpsed during the Civil War that would trouble the nation again during the McCarthy era and in the aftermath of the terrorist attacks of 2001: What is the balance between security and freedom? Does the Constitution protect citizens' rights during wartime? Should dissent be equated with lack of patriotism? The conflict demonstrated that during a war, traditional civil liberties are likely to come under severe pressure.

In 1917, Randolph Bourne ridiculed Progressives who believed they could mold the war according to their own "liberal purposes." The conflict, he predicted, would empower not reformers but the "least democratic forces in American life." The accuracy of Bourne's prediction soon become apparent. Despite the administration's idealistic language of democracy and freedom, the war inaugurated the most intense repression of civil liberties the nation has ever known. Perhaps the very nobility of wartime rhetoric contributed to the massive suppression of dissent. For in the eyes of Wilson and many of his supporters, America's goals were so virtuous that disagreement could only reflect treason to the country's values. "It is a fearful thing to lead this great peaceful people into war," Wilson remarked in his speech asking Congress to bring America into the conflict. Even he could not have predicted how significant an impact the war would have on American freedom.

THE ESPIONAGE ACT

For the first time since the Alien and Sedition Acts of 1798, the federal government enacted laws to restrict freedom of speech. The Espionage Act of 1917 prohibited not only spying and interfering with the draft but also "false statements" that might impede military success. The postmaster general barred from the mails numerous newspapers and magazines critical of the administration. The victims ranged from virtually the entire socialist press and many foreign-language publications to *The Jeffersonian*, a newspaper owned by ex-Populist leader Tom Watson, which criticized the draft as a violation of states' rights. In 1918, the Sedition Act made it a crime to make spoken or printed statements that intended to cast "contempt, scorn, or disrepute" on the "form of government," or that advocated interference with the war effort. The government charged more than 2,000 persons with violating these laws. Over half were convicted. A court sentenced Ohio farmer John White to twenty-one months in prison for saying that the murder of innocent women and children by German soldiers was no worse than what the United States had done in the Philippines in the war of 1899–1903.

The most prominent victim was Eugene V. Debs, convicted in 1918 under the Espionage Act for delivering an antiwar speech. Before his sentencing, Debs gave the court a lesson in the history of American freedom, tracing the tradition of dissent from Thomas Paine to the abolitionists, and pointing out that the nation had never engaged in a war without internal opposition. Germany sent socialist leader Karl Liebknecht to prison for four years for opposing the war; in the United States, Debs's sentence was ten years. After the war's end, Wilson rejected the advice of his attorney general that he commute Debs's sentence. Debs ran for president while still in prison in 1920 and received 900,000 votes. It was left to Wilson's successor, Warren G. Harding, to release Debs from prison in 1921.

COERCIVE PATRIOTISM

Even more extreme repression took place at the hands of state governments and private groups. Americans had long displayed the flag (and used it in advertisements for everything from tobacco products to variety shows). But during World War I, attitudes toward the American flag became a test of patriotism. Persons suspected of disloyalty were forced to kiss the flag in public; those who made statements critical of the flag could be imprisoned. During the war, thirty-three states outlawed the possession or display of red or black flags (symbols, respectively, of communism and anarchism), and twenty-three outlawed a newly created offense, "criminal syndicalism," the advocacy of unlawful acts to accomplish political change or "a change in industrial ownership."

"Who is the real patriot?" Emma Goldman asked while on trial for conspiring to violate the Selective Service Act. She answered, those who "love America with open eyes," who were not blind to "the wrongs committed in the name of patriotism." But from the federal government to local authorities and private groups, patriotism came to be equated with support for the government, the war, and the American economic system, while antiwar sentiment, labor radicalism, and sympathy for the Russian Revolution became "un-American." Minnesota established a Commission of Public Safety to root out disloyalty from the state. Local authorities formally investigated residents who failed to subscribe to Liberty Loans. Throughout the country, schools revised their course offerings to ensure their patriotism and required teachers to sign loyalty oaths.

The 250,000 members of the newly formed American Protective League (APL) helped the Justice Department identify radicals and critics of the war by spying on their neighbors and carrying out "slacker raids" in which thousands of men were stopped on the streets of major cities and required to produce draft registration cards. Many private groups seized upon the atmosphere of repression as a weapon against domestic opponents. Employers cooperated with the government in crushing the Industrial Workers of the World (IWW), a move long demanded by business interests. In July 1917, vigilantes in Bisbee, Arizona, rounded up some 1,200 striking copper miners and their sympathizers, herded them into railroad boxcars, and transported them into the desert, where they were abandoned. New Mexico's governor ordered them housed in tents and provided with food and water. Few ever returned to Bisbee. In August, a crowd in Butte, Montana, lynched IWW leader Frank Little. The following month, operating under one of the broadest warrants in American history, federal agents swooped down on IWW offices throughout the country, arresting hundreds of leaders and seizing files and publications.

The war experience, commented Walter Lippmann, demonstrated "that the traditional liberties of speech and opinion rest on no solid foundation." Yet while some Progressives protested individual excesses, most failed to speak out against the broad suppression of freedom of expression. Civil liberties, by and large, had never been a major concern of Progressives, who had always viewed the national state as the embodiment of democratic purpose and insisted that freedom flowed from participating in the life of society, not standing in opposition. Strong believers in the use of national power to improve social conditions, Progressives found themselves ill prepared to develop a defense of minority rights against majority or governmental tyranny. From the AFL to *New Republic* intellectuals, moreover, supporters of the war saw the elimination of socialists and alien radicals as a necessary prelude to the integration of labor and immigrants into an ordered society, an outcome they hoped would emerge from the war.

WHO IS AN AMERICAN?

In many respects, Progressivism was a precursor to major developments of the twentieth century—the New Deal, the Great Society, the socially active state. But in accepting the idea of "race" as a permanent, defining characteristic of individuals and social groups, Progressives bore more resemblance to nineteenth-century thinkers than to later twentieth-century liberals, with whom they are sometimes compared.

THE "RACE PROBLEM"

Even before American participation in World War I, what contemporaries called the "race problem"—the tensions that arose from the country's increasing ethnic diversity—had become a major subject of public concern. "Race" referred to far more than black-white relations. The *Dictionary of Races of Peoples*, published in 1911 by the U.S. Immigration Commission, listed no fewer than forty-five immigrant "races," each supposedly with its own inborn characteristics. They ranged from Anglo-Saxons at the top down to Hebrews, Northern Italians, and, lowest of all, Southern Italians—supposedly violent, undisciplined, and incapable of assimilation.

In 1907, Congress had decreed that an American woman who married an alien automatically forfeited her American citizenship. Popular bestsellers like *The Passing of the Great Race*, published in 1916 by Madison Grant, president of the New York Zoological Society, warned that the influx of new immigrants and the low birthrate of native white women threatened the foundations of American civilization. The new science of eugenics, which studied the alleged mental characteristics of different races, gave anti-immigrant sentiment an air of professional expertise. If democracy could not flourish in the face of vast inequalities of economic power, neither, most Progressives believed, could it survive in a nation permanently divided along racial and ethnic lines.

AMERICANIZATION AND PLURALISM

Somehow, the very nationalization of politics and economic life served to heighten awareness of ethnic and racial difference and spurred demands for "Americanization"—the creation of a more homogeneous national culture. A 1908 play by the Jewish immigrant writer Israel Zangwill, *The Melting Pot*, gave a popular name to the process by which newcomers were supposed to merge their identity into existing American nationality. Public and private groups of all kinds—including educators, employers, labor leaders, social reformers, and public officials—took up the task of Americanizing new immigrants. The Ford Motor Company's famed sociological department entered the homes of immigrant workers to evaluate their clothing, furniture, and food preferences and enrolled them in English-language courses. Ford fired those who failed to adapt to American standards after a reasonable period of time. Americanization programs often targeted women as the bearers and transmitters of culture. In Los Angeles, teachers and religious missionaries worked to teach English to Mexican-American women so that they could then assimilate

VOICES OF FREEDOM

From Eugene V. Debs, Speech to the Jury before Sentencing under the Espionage Act (1918)

The most prominent spokesman for American socialism and a fervent opponent of American participation in World War I, Eugene V. Debs was arrested for delivering an antiwar speech and convicted of violating the Espionage Act. In his speech to the jury, he defended the right of dissent in wartime.

I wish to admit the truth of all that has been testified to in this proceeding. . . . Gentlemen, you have heard the report of my speech at Canton on June 16, and I submit that there is not a word in that speech to warrant the charges set out in the indictment. . . . In what I had to say there my purpose was to have the people understand something about the social system in which we live and to prepare them to change this system by perfectly peaceable and orderly means into what I, as a Socialist, conceive to be a real democracy. . . . I have never advocated violence in any form. I have always believed in education, in intelligence, in enlightenment; and I have always made my appeal to the reason and to the conscience of the people.

In every age there have been a few heroic souls who have been in advance of their time, who have been misunderstood, maligned, persecuted, sometimes put to death. . . . Washington, Jefferson, Franklin, Paine, and their compeers were the rebels of their day. . . . But they had the moral courage to be true to their convictions. . . .

William Lloyd Garrison, Wendell Phillips, Elizabeth Cady Stanton . . . and other leaders of the abolition movement who were regarded as public enemies and treated accordingly, were true to their faith and stood their ground. . . . You are now teaching your children to revere their memories, while all of their detractors are in oblivion.

This country has been engaged in a number of wars and every one of them has been condemned by some of the people. The war of 1812 was opposed and condemned by some of the most influential citizens; the Mexican War was vehemently opposed and bitterly denounced, even after the war had been declared and was in progress, by Abraham Lincoln, Charles Sumner, Daniel Webster. . . . They were not indicted; they were not charged with treason. . . .

I believe in the Constitution. Isn't it strange that we Socialists stand almost alone today in upholding and defending the Constitution of the United States? The revolutionary fathers . . . understood that free speech, a free press and the right of free assemblage by the people were fundamental principles in democratic government. . . . I believe in the right of free speech, in war as well as in peace.

From W. E. B. Du Bois, "Returning Soldiers," *The Crisis* (1919)

Scholar, poet, activist, founder of the National Association for the Advancement of Colored People and editor of its magazine, *The Crisis*, W. E. B. Du Bois was the most prominent black leader of the first half of the twentieth century. He supported black participation in World War I, but he insisted that black soldiers must now join in the struggle for freedom at home.

We are returning from war! *The Crisis* and tens of thousands of black men were drafted into a great struggle. For bleeding France and what she means and has meant and will mean to us and humanity and against the threat of German race arrogance, we fought gladly and to the last drop of blood; for America and her highest ideals, we fought in far-off hope; for the dominant southern oligarchy entrenched in Washington, we fought in bitter resignation. For the America that represents and gloats in lynching, disfranchisement, caste, brutality and devilish insult—for this, in the hateful upturning and mixing of things, we were forced by vindictive fate to fight, also.

But today we return! . . . We sing: This country of ours, despite all its better souls have done and dreamed, is yet a shameful land.

It *lynches.*

And lynching is barbarism of a degree of contemptible nastiness unparalleled in human history. Yet for fifty years we have lynched two Negroes a week, and we have kept this up right through the war.

It *disfranchises* its own citizens.

Disfranchisement is the deliberate theft and robbery of the only protection of poor against rich and black against white. The land that disfranchises its citizens and calls itself a democracy lies and knows it lies.

It encourages *ignorance.*

It has never really tried to educate the Negro. A dominate minority does not want Negroes educated. It wants servants. . . .

It *insults* us.

It has organized a nationwide and latterly a worldwide propaganda of deliberate and continuous insult and defamation of black blood wherever found. . . .

This is the country to which we Soldiers of Democracy return. This is the fatherland for which we fought! But it is *our* fatherland. It was right for us to fight. . . .

We *return fighting.*

Make way for Democracy!

QUESTIONS

1. Why does Debs relate the history of wartime dissent in America?

2. What connections does Du Bois draw between blacks fighting abroad in the war and returning to fight at home?

3. In what ways does each author point up the contradiction between America's professed values and its actual conduct?

American values. Fearful that adult newcomers remained too stuck in their Old World ways, public schools paid great attention to Americanizing immigrants' children. The challenge facing schools, wrote one educator, was "to implant in their children, so far as can be done, the Anglo-Saxon conception of righteousness, law and order, and popular government."

A minority of Progressives questioned Americanization efforts and insisted on respect for immigrant subcultures. At Hull House, teachers offered English-language instruction but also encouraged immigrants to value their European heritage. Probably the most penetrating critique issued from the pen of Randolph Bourne, whose 1916 essay, "Trans-National America," exposed the fundamental flaw in the Americanization model. "There is no distinctive American culture," Bourne pointed out. Interaction between individuals and groups had produced the nation's music, poetry, and other cultural expressions. Bourne envisioned a democratic, cosmopolitan society in which immigrants and natives alike submerged their group identities in a new "trans-national" culture.

With President Wilson declaring that some Americans "born under foreign flags" were guilty of "disloyalty . . . and must be absolutely crushed," the federal and state governments demanded that immigrants demonstrate their unwavering devotion to the United States. The Committee on Public Information renamed the Fourth of July, 1918, Loyalty Day and asked ethnic groups to participate in patriotic pageants. New York City's celebration included a procession of 75,000 persons with dozens of floats and presentations linking immigrants with the war effort and highlighting their contributions to American society. Leaders of ethnic groups that had suffered discrimination saw the war as an opportunity to gain greater rights. Prominent Jewish leaders promoted enlistment and expressions of loyalty. The Chinese-American press insisted that even those born abroad and barred from citizenship should register for the draft, to "bring honor to the people of our race."

THE ANTI-GERMAN CRUSADE

German-Americans bore the brunt of forced Americanization. The first wave of German immigrants had arrived before the Civil War. By 1914, German-Americans numbered nearly 9 million, including immigrants and persons of German parentage. They had created thriving ethnic institutions including clubs, sports associations, schools, and theaters. On the eve of the war, many Americans admired German traditions in literature, music, and philosophy, and one-quarter of all the high school students in the country studied the German language. But after American entry into the war, the use of German and expressions of German culture became a target of prowar organizations. In Iowa, Governor William L. Harding issued a proclamation requiring that all oral communication in schools, public places, and over the telephone be conducted in English. Freedom of speech, he declared, did not include "the right to use a language other than the language of the country."

A vivid example of the anti-German propaganda produced by the federal government to encourage prowar sentiment during World War I.

By 1919, the vast majority of the states had enacted laws restricting the teaching of foreign languages. Popular words of German origin were changed: "hamburger" became "liberty sandwich," and "sauerkraut" was renamed "liberty cabbage." Many communities banned the playing of German music. The government jailed Karl Müch, the director of the Boston Symphony and a Swiss citizen, as an enemy alien after he insisted on including the works of German composers like Beethoven in his concerts. The war dealt a crushing blow to German-American culture. By 1920, the number of German-language newspapers had been reduced to 276 (one-third the number twenty years earlier), and only 1 percent of high school pupils still studied German. The Census of 1920 reported a 25 percent drop in the number of Americans admitting to having been born in Germany.

TOWARD IMMIGRATION RESTRICTION

Even as Americanization programs sought to assimilate immigrants into American society, the war strengthened the conviction that certain kinds of undesirable persons ought to be excluded altogether. The new immigrants, one advocate of restriction declared, appreciated the values of democracy and freedom far less than "the Anglo-Saxon," as evidenced by their attraction to "extreme political doctrines" like anarchism and socialism. Stanford University psychologist Lewis Terman introduced the term "IQ" (intelligence quotient) in 1916, claiming that this single number could measure an individual's mental capacity. Intelligence tests administered to recruits by the army seemed to confirm scientifically that blacks and the new immigrants stood far below native white Protestants on the IQ scale, further spurring demands for immigration restriction.

In 1917, over Wilson's veto, Congress required that immigrants be literate in English or another language. The war accelerated other efforts to upgrade the American population. Some were inspired by the idea of improving the human race by discouraging reproduction among less "desirable" persons. Indiana in 1907 had passed a law authorizing doctors to sterilize insane and "feeble-minded" inmates in mental institutions so that they would not pass their "defective" genes on to children. Numerous other states now followed suit. In *Buck v. Bell* (1927), the Supreme Court upheld the constitutionality of these laws. Justice Oliver Wendell Holmes's opinion included the famous statement, "Three generations of imbeciles are enough." By the time the practice ended in the 1960s, some 63,000 persons had been involuntarily sterilized.

GROUPS APART: MEXICANS, PUERTO RICANS, AND ASIAN-AMERICANS

No matter how coercive, Americanization programs assumed that European immigrants and especially their children could eventually adjust to the conditions of American life, embrace American ideals, and become productive citizens enjoying the full blessings of American freedom. This assumption did not apply to non-white immigrants or to blacks. Although the melting-pot idea envisioned that newcomers from Europe would leave their ethnic enclaves and join the American mainstream, non-whites confronted ever-present boundaries of exclusion.

The war led to further growth of the Southwest's Mexican population. Wartime demand for labor from the area's mine owners and large farmers led the government to exempt Mexicans temporarily from the literacy test enacted in 1917. Mexicans were legally classified as white, and many Progressive reformers viewed the growing Mexican population as candidates for Americanization. Teachers and religious missionaries sought to instruct them in English, convert them to Protestantism, and in other ways promote their assimilation into the mainstream culture. Yet public officials in the Southwest treated them as a group apart. Segregation, by law and custom, was common in schools, hospitals, theaters, and other institutions in states with significant Mexican populations. By 1920, nearly all Mexican children in California and the Southwest were educated in their own schools or classrooms. Phoenix, Arizona, established separate public schools for Indians, Mexicans, blacks, and whites.

Puerto Ricans also occupied an ambiguous position within American society. On the eve of American entry into World War I, Congress terminated the status "citizen of Puerto Rico" and conferred American citizenship on residents of the island. The aim was to dampen support for Puerto Rican independence and to strengthen the American hold on a strategic outpost in the

Caribbean. The change did not grant islanders the right to vote for president, or representation in Congress. Puerto Rican men, nonetheless, were subject to the draft and fought overseas. José de Diego, the Speaker of the House of the island's legislature, wrote the president in 1917 asking that Puerto Rico be granted the democracy the United States was fighting for in Europe.

Even more restrictive were policies toward Asian-Americans. In 1906, the San Francisco school board ordered all Asian students confined to a single public school. When the Japanese government protested, president Theodore Roosevelt persuaded the city to rescind the order. He then negotiated the Gentlemen's Agreement of 1907 whereby Japan agreed to end migration to the United States except for the wives and children of men already in the country. In 1913, California barred all aliens incapable of becoming naturalized citizens (that is, Asians) from owning or leasing land.

THE COLOR LINE

By far the largest non-white group, African-Americans, were excluded from nearly every Progressive definition of freedom. After their disenfranchisement in the South, few could participate in American democracy. Barred from joining most unions and from skilled employment, black workers had little access to "industrial freedom." A majority of adult black women worked outside the home, but for wages that offered no hope of independence. Predominantly domestic and agricultural workers, they remained unaffected by the era's laws regulating the hours and conditions of female labor. Nor could blacks, the majority desperately poor, participate fully in the emerging consumer economy, either as employees in the new department stores (except as janitors and cleaning women) or as purchasers of the consumer goods now flooding the marketplace.

Progressive intellectuals, social scientists, labor reformers, and suffrage advocates displayed a remarkable indifference to the black condition. Israel Zangwill did not include blacks in the melting-pot idea popularized by his Broadway play. Walter Weyl waited until the last fifteen pages of *The New Democracy* to introduce the "race problem." His comment that the chief obstacles to freedom were economic, not political, revealed little appreciation of how the denial of voting rights underpinned the comprehensive system of inequality to which southern blacks were subjected.

Most settlement-house reformers accepted segregation as natural and equitable, assuming there should be white settlements for white neighborhoods and black settlements for black. White leaders of the woman suffrage movement said little about black disenfranchisement. In the South, members of upper-class white women's clubs sometimes raised funds for black schools and community centers. But suffrage leaders insisted that the vote was a racial entitlement, a "badge and synonym of freedom," in the words of Rebecca Felton of Georgia, that should not be denied to "free-born white women." During Reconstruction, women had been denied constitutional recognition because it was "the Negro's hour." Now, World War I's "woman's hour" excluded blacks. The amendment that achieved woman suffrage left the states free to limit voting by poll taxes and literacy tests. Living in the South, the vast majority of the country's black women did not enjoy its benefits.

ROOSEVELT, WILSON, AND RACE

The Progressive presidents shared prevailing attitudes concerning blacks. Theodore Roosevelt shocked white opinion by inviting Booker T. Washington to dine with him in the White House and by appointing a number of blacks to federal offices. But in 1906, when a small group of black soldiers shot off their guns in Brownsville, Texas, killing one resident, and none of their fellows would name them, Roosevelt ordered the dishonorable discharge of three black companies—156 men in all, including six winners of the Congressional Medal of Honor. Roosevelt's ingrained belief in Anglo-Saxon racial destiny (he called Indians "savages" and blacks "wholly unfit for the suffrage") did nothing to lessen Progressive intellectuals' enthusiasm for his New Nationalism. Even Jane Addams, one of the few Progressives to take a strong interest in black rights and a founder of the National Association for the Advancement of Colored People (NAACP), went along when the Progressive Party convention of 1912 rejected a civil rights plank in its platform and barred black delegates from the South.

Woodrow Wilson, a native of Virginia, could speak without irony of the South's "genuine representative government" and its exalted "standards of liberty." His administration imposed racial segregation in federal departments in Washington, D.C., and dismissed numerous black federal employees. Wilson allowed D. W. Griffith's film *Birth of a Nation,* which glorified the Ku Klux Klan as the defender of white civilization during Reconstruction, to have its premiere at the White House in 1915. "Have you a 'new freedom' for white Americans and a new slavery for your African-American fellow citizens?" William Monroe Trotter, the militant black editor of the *Boston Guardian* and founder of the all-black National Equal Rights League, asked the president.

Blacks subject to disenfranchisement and segregation were understandably skeptical of the nation's claim to embody freedom and fully appreciated the ways the symbols of liberty could coexist with brutal racial violence. In one of hundreds of lynchings during the Progressive era, a white mob in Springfield, Missouri, in 1906 falsely accused three black men of rape, hanged them from an electric light pole, and burned their bodies in a public orgy of violence. Atop the pole stood a replica of the Statue of Liberty.

W. E. B. DU BOIS AND THE REVIVAL OF BLACK PROTEST

Black leaders struggled to find a strategy to rekindle the national commitment to equality that had flickered brightly, if briefly, during Reconstruction. No one thought more deeply, or over so long a period, about the black condition and the challenge it posed to American democracy than the scholar and activist W. E. B. Du Bois. Born in Great Barrington, Massachusetts, in 1868, and educated at Fisk and Harvard universities, Du Bois lived to his ninety-fifth year. The unifying theme of his career was Du Bois's effort to reconcile the contradiction between what he called "American freedom for whites and the continuing subjection of Negroes." His book *The Souls of Black Folk* (1903) issued a clarion call for blacks dissatisfied with the accommodationist policies of Booker T. Washington to press for equal rights. Du Bois believed that educated African-Americans like himself—the "talented tenth" of the black community—must use their education and training to challenge inequality.

In some ways, Du Bois was a typical Progressive who believed that investigation, exposure, and education would lead to solutions for social problems. As a professor at Atlanta University, he projected a grandiose plan for decades of scholarly study of black life in order to make the country aware of racism

W. E. B. Du Bois, founder of the NAACP and editor of its magazine, The Crisis, *in his New York office.*

and point the way toward its elimination. But he also understood the necessity of political action.

In 1905, Du Bois gathered a group of black leaders at Niagara Falls (meeting on the Canadian side since no American hotel would provide accommodations) and organized the Niagara movement, which sought to reinvigorate the abolitionist tradition. "We claim for ourselves," Du Bois wrote in the group's manifesto, "every single right that belongs to a freeborn American, political, civil, and social; and until we get these rights we will never cease to protest and assail the ears of America." The Declaration of Principles adopted at Niagara Falls called for restoring to blacks the right to vote, an end to racial segregation, and complete equality in economic and educational opportunity. These would remain the cornerstones of the black struggle for racial justice for decades to come. Four years later, Du Bois joined with a group of mostly white reformers shocked by a lynching in Springfield, Illinois (Lincoln's adult home), to create the National Association for the Advancement of Colored People. The NAACP, as it was known, launched a long struggle for the enforcement of the Fourteenth and Fifteenth Amendments.

The NAACP's legal strategy won a few victories. In *Bailey v. Alabama* (1911), the Supreme Court overturned southern "peonage" laws that made it a crime for sharecroppers to break their labor contracts. Six years later, it ruled unconstitutional a Louisville zoning regulation excluding blacks from living in certain parts of the city (primarily because it interfered with whites' right to sell their property as they saw fit). Overall, however, the Progressive era witnessed virtually no progress toward racial justice. At a time when Americans' rights were being reformulated, blacks, said Moorfield Story, the NAACP's president, enjoyed a "curious citizenship." They shared obligations like military service, but not "the fundamental rights to which all men are entitled unless we repudiate . . . the Declaration of Independence."

CLOSING RANKS

Among black Americans, the wartime language of freedom inspired hopes for a radical change in the country's racial system. With the notable exception of William Monroe Trotter, most black leaders saw American participation in the war as an opportunity to make real the promise of freedom. To Trotter, much-publicized German atrocities were no worse than American lynchings; rather than making the world safe for democracy, the government should worry about "making the South safe for the Negroes." Yet the black press rallied to the war. Du Bois himself, in widely reprinted editorials, called on African-Americans to enlist in the army to help "make our own America a real land of the free."

Black participation in the Civil War had helped to secure the destruction of slavery and the achievement of citizenship. But during World War I, closing ranks did not bring significant gains. The navy barred blacks entirely, and the segregated army confined most of the 400,000 blacks who served in the war to supply units rather than combat. Wilson feared, as he noted in his diary, that the overseas experience would "go to their heads." And the U.S. Army campaigned strenuously to persuade the French not to treat black soldiers as equals—not to eat or socialize with them, or even shake their hands. Contact with African colonial soldiers fighting alongside the British and French did widen the horizons of black American soldiers. But while colonial troops marched in the victory parade in Paris, the Wilson administration did not allow black Americans to participate.

THE GREAT MIGRATION AND THE "PROMISED LAND"

Nonetheless, the war unleashed social changes that altered the contours of American race relations. The combination of increased wartime production and a drastic falloff in immigration from Europe once war broke out opened thousands of industrial jobs to black laborers for the first time, inspiring a large-scale migration from South to North. On the eve of World War I, 90 percent of the African-American population still lived in the South. Most northern cities had tiny black populations, and domestic and service work still predominated among both black men and women in the North. But between 1910 and 1920, half a million blacks left the South. The black population of Chicago more than doubled, New York City's rose 66 percent, and smaller industrial cities like Akron, Buffalo, and Trenton showed similar gains.

Table 1 THE GREAT MIGRATION

City	*Black Population, 1910*	*Black Population, 1920*	*Percent Increase*
New York	91,709	152,467	66.3%
Philadelphia	84,459	134,229	58.9
Chicago	44,103	109,458	148.2
St. Louis	43,960	69,854	58.9
Detroit	5,741	40,838	611.3
Pittsburgh	25,623	37,725	47.2
Cleveland	8,448	34,451	307.8

Many motives sustained the Great Migration—higher wages in northern factories than were available in the South (even if blacks remained confined to menial and unskilled positions), opportunities for educating their children, escape from the threat of lynching, and the prospect of exercising the right to vote. Migrants spoke of a Second Emancipation, of "crossing over Jordan," and of leaving the realm of pharaoh for the Promised Land. One group from Mississippi stopped to sing, "I am bound for the land of Canaan," after their train crossed the Ohio River into the North.

The black migrants, mostly young men and women, carried with them "a new vision of opportunity, of social and economic freedom," as Alain Locke explained in the preface to his influential book, *The New Negro* (1925). Yet the migrants encountered vast disappointments—severely restricted employment opportunities, exclusion from unions, rigid housing segregation, and outbreaks of violence that made it clear that no region of the country was free from racial hostility. More white southerners than blacks moved north during the war, often with similar economic aspirations. But the new black presence, coupled with demands for change inspired by the war, created a racial tinderbox that needed only an incident to trigger an explosion.

RACIAL VIOLENCE, NORTH AND SOUTH

Dozens of blacks were killed during a 1917 riot in East St. Louis, Illinois, where employers had recruited black workers in an attempt to weaken unions (most of which excluded blacks from membership). In 1919, more than 250 persons died in riots in the urban North. Most notable was the violence in Chicago, touched off by the drowning by white bathers of a black teenager who accidentally crossed the unofficial dividing line between black and white beaches on Lake Michigan. The riot that followed raged for five days and involved pitched battles between the races throughout the city. By the time the National Guard restored order, 38 persons had been killed and more than 500 injured.

Violence was not confined to the North. In the year after the war ended, seventy-six persons were lynched in the South, including several returning black veterans wearing their uniforms. In Phillips County, Arkansas, attacks on striking black sharecroppers by armed white vigilantes left as many as 200 persons dead and required the intervention of the army to restore order. The worst race riot in American history occurred in Tulsa, Oklahoma, in 1921, when more than 300 blacks were killed and over 10,000 left homeless after a white mob, including police and National Guardsmen, burned an all-black section of the city to the ground. The violence erupted after a group of black veterans tried to prevent the lynching of a youth who had accidentally tripped and fallen on a white female elevator operator, causing rumors of rape to sweep the city.

THE RISE OF GARVEYISM

World War I kindled a new spirit of militancy. The East St. Louis riot of 1917 inspired a widely publicized Silent Protest Parade on New York's Fifth Avenue in which 10,000 blacks silently carried placards reading, "Mr. President, Why Not Make America Safe for Democracy?" In the new densely populated black ghettos of the North, widespread support emerged for the Universal Negro Improvement Association, a movement for African independence and black self-reliance launched by Marcus Garvey, a recent immigrant from Jamaica. Freedom for Garveyites meant national self-determination. Blacks, they insisted, should enjoy the same internationally recognized identity enjoyed by other peoples in the aftermath of the war. "Everywhere we hear the cry of freedom," Garvey proclaimed in 1921. "We desire a freedom that will lift us to the common standard of all men, . . . freedom that will give us a chance and opportunity to rise to the fullest of our ambition and that we cannot get in countries where other men rule and dominate." Du Bois and other established black leaders viewed Garvey as little more than a demagogue. They applauded when the government deported him after a conviction for mail fraud. But the massive following his movement achieved testified to the sense of betrayal that had been kindled in black communities during and after the war.

1919

A WORLDWIDE UPSURGE

The combination of militant hopes for social change and disappointment with the war's outcome was evident far beyond the black community. In the Union of Soviet Socialist Republics (or Soviet Union), as Russia had been renamed after the revolution, Lenin's government had nationalized landholdings, banks, and factories and proclaimed the socialist dream of a workers' government. The Russian Revolution and the democratic aspirations unleashed by World War I sent tremors of hope and fear throughout the world. Like 1848 and, in the future, 1968, 1919 was a year of worldwide social and political upheaval. Inspired by Lenin's call for revolution, communist-led governments came to power in Bavaria (a part of Germany) and Hungary. General strikes demanding the fulfillment of wartime promises of "industrial democracy" took place in Belfast, Glasgow, and Winnipeg. In Spain, anarchist peasants began seizing land. Crowds in India challenged British rule, and nationalist movements in other colonies demanded independence. "We are living and shall live all our lives in a revolutionary world," wrote Walter Lippmann.

The worldwide revolutionary upsurge produced a countervailing mobilization by opponents of radical change. Even as they fought the Germans, the Allies viewed the Soviet government as a dire threat and attempted to overturn it. In the summer of 1918, Allied expeditionary forces—British, French, Japanese, and Americans—landed in Russia to aid Lenin's opponents in the civil war that had engulfed the country. The last of them did not leave until 1920.

Wilson's policies toward the Soviet Union revealed the contradictions within the liberal internationalist vision. On the one hand, in keeping with the principles of the Fourteen Points and its goal of a worldwide economic open door, Wilson hoped to foster trade with the new government. On the other, fear of communism as a source of international instability and a threat to private property inspired military intervention in Russia. The Allies did not invite the Soviet Union to the Versailles peace conference, and Wilson refused to extend diplomatic recognition to Lenin's government. The Soviet regime survived, but in the rest of the world the tide of change receded. By the fall, the mass strikes had been suppressed and conservative governments had been installed in central Europe. Anticommunism would remain a pillar of twentieth-century American foreign policy.

UPHEAVAL IN AMERICA

In the United States, 1919 also brought unprecedented turmoil. It seemed all the more disorienting for occurring in the midst of a worldwide flu epidemic that killed between 20 and 40 million persons, including nearly 700,000 Americans. Racial violence, as noted above, was widespread. In June, bombs exploded at the homes of prominent Americans, including the attorney general, A. Mitchell Palmer, who escaped uninjured. Among aggrieved American workers, wartime language linking patriotism with democracy and freedom inspired hopes that an era of social justice and economic empowerment was at hand. In 1917, Wilson had told the AFL, "While we are fighting for freedom, we must see to it among other things that labor is free." Labor took him seriously—more seriously, it seems, than Wilson intended. The government, as one machinist put it, had "proclaimed to the World that the freedom and democracy we are fighting for shall be practiced in the industries of America."

By the war's end, many Americans believed that the country stood on the verge of what Herbert Hoover called "a new industrial order." Sidney Hillman, leader of the garment workers' union, was one of those caught up in the utopian dreams inspired by the war and reinforced by the Russian Revolution. "One can hear the footsteps of the Deliverer," he wrote. "Labor will rule and the World will be free." In 1919, more than 4 million workers engaged in strikes—the greatest wave of labor unrest in American history. There were walkouts, among many others, by textile workers, telephone operators, and Broadway actors. Throughout the country, workers appropriated the imagery and rhetoric of the war, parading in army uniforms with Liberty buttons, denouncing their employers as "kaisers," and demanding "freedom in the workplace." They were met by an unprecedented mobilization of employers, government, and private patriotic organizations.

The strike wave began in January 1919 in Seattle, where a walkout of shipyard workers mushroomed into a general strike that for once united AFL unions and the IWW. For five days, a committee of labor leaders oversaw city services, until federal troops arrived to end the strike. In September, Boston policemen struck for higher wages and shorter working hours. Declaring "there is no right to strike against the public safety," Massachusetts governor Calvin Coolidge called out the National Guard to patrol the city and fired the entire police force. In the nation's coalfields, a company manager observed, wartime propaganda had raised unrealistic expectations among workers, who took the promise of "an actual emancipation" too "literally." When the war ended, miners demanded an end to company absolutism. Their strike was ended by a court injunction obtained by Attorney General Palmer.

THE GREAT STEEL STRIKE

The wartime rhetoric of economic democracy and freedom helped to inspire the era's greatest labor uprising, the 1919 steel strike. Centered in Chicago, it united some 365,000 mostly immigrant workers in demands for union recognition, higher wages, and an eight-hour workday. Before 1917, the steel mills were little autocracies where managers arbitrarily established wages and working conditions and suppressed all efforts at union organizing. During the war, workers flooded into the Amalgamated Association, the union that had been nearly destroyed by its defeat at Homestead a generation earlier. By the end of 1918, they had won an eight-hour day. Employers' anti-union activities resumed following the armistice that ended the fighting. "For why this war?" asked one Polish immigrant steelworker at a union meeting. "For why we buy Liberty bonds? For the mills? No, for freedom and America—for everybody. No more [work like a] horse and wagon. For eight-hour day."

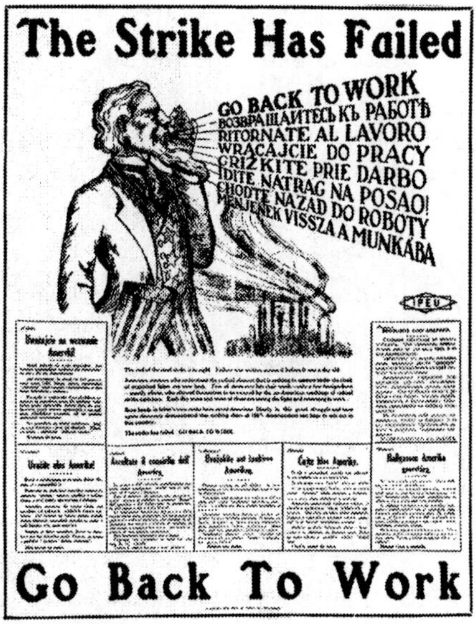

An advertisement placed by a steel company in a Pittsburgh newspaper announces, in several languages, that the steel strike of 1919 "has failed." The use of the figure of Uncle Sam illustrates how the companies clothed their anti-union stance in the language of patriotism.

In response to the strike, steel magnates launched a concerted counterattack. Employers appealed to anti-immigrant sentiment among native-born workers, many of whom returned to work, and conducted a propaganda campaign that associated the strikers with the IWW, communism, and disloyalty. "Americanismvs. Alienism" was the issue of the strike, declared the *New York Tribune*. With middle-class opinion having turned against the labor movement and the police in Pittsburgh assaulting workers on the streets, the strike collapsed in early 1920.

THE RED SCARE

Many Progressives hoped to see the wartime apparatus of economic planning continue after 1918. The Wilson administration, however, quickly dismantled the agencies that had established controls over industrial production and the labor market, although during the 1930s they would serve as models for some policies of Franklin D. Roosevelt's New Deal. Wartime repression of dissent, however, continued. It reached its peak with the Red Scare of 1919–1920, a short-lived but intense period of political intolerance inspired by the post-war strike wave and the social tensions and fears generated by the Russian Revolution.

Convinced that episodes like the steel strike were part of a worldwide communist conspiracy, Attorney General A. Mitchell Palmer in November 1919 and January 1920 dispatched federal agents to raid the offices of radical and labor organizations throughout the country. They carried search warrants so broad that they reminded those with a sense of history of the writs of assistance against which James Otis had eloquently protested as being destructive of liberty in 1761. The Palmer Raids were overseen by the twenty-four-year-old director of the Radical Division of the Justice Department, J. Edgar Hoover. More than 5,000 persons were arrested, most of them without warrants, and held for months without charge. The government deported hundreds of immigrant radicals, including Emma Goldman, the prominent radical speaker. Hoover also began compiling files on thousands of Americans suspected of holding radical political ideas, a practice he would later continue as head of the Federal Bureau of Investigation.

The abuse of civil liberties in early 1920 was so severe that Palmer came under heavy criticism from Congress and much of the press. Secretary of Labor Louis Post began releasing imprisoned immigrants, and the Red Scare collapsed. Even the explosion of a bomb outside the New York Stock Exchange in September 1920, which killed forty persons, failed to rekindle it. (The perpetrators of this terrorist explosion, the worst on American soil until the Oklahoma City bombing of 1995, were never identified.) The reaction to the Palmer Raids planted the seeds for a new appreciation of the importance of civil liberties that would begin to flourish during the 1920s. But in their immediate impact, the events of 1919 and 1920 dealt a devastating setback to radical and labor organizations of all kinds and kindled an intense identification of patriotic Americanism with support for the political and economic status quo. The IWW had been effectively destroyed, and many moderate unions lay in disarray. The Socialist Party crumbled under the weight of governmental repression (the New York legislature expelled five Socialist members, and Congress denied Victor Berger the seat to which he had been elected from Wisconsin) and internal differences over the Russian Revolution.

WILSON AT VERSAILLES

The beating back of demands for fundamental social change was a severe rebuke to the hopes with which so many Progressives had enlisted in the war effort. Wilson's inability to achieve a just peace based on the Fourteen Points compounded the sense of failure. Late in 1918, the president traveled to France to attend the Versailles peace conference. Greeted by ecstatic Paris crowds, he declared that American soldiers had come to Europe "as crusaders, not merely to win a war, but to win a cause . . . to lead the world on the way of liberty." But he proved a less adept negotiator than his British and French counterparts, David Lloyd George and Georges Clemenceau.

While the Fourteen Points had called for "open covenants openly arrived at," the negotiations were conducted in secret. The Versailles Treaty did accomplish some of Wilson's goals. It established the League of Nations, the body central to his vision of a new international order. It applied the principle of self-determination to eastern Europe and redrew the map of that region. From the ruins of the Austro-Hungarian empire and parts of Germany and czarist Russia, new European nations emerged from the war—Finland, Poland, Czechoslovakia, Austria, Hungary, Latvia, Lithuania, Estonia, and Yugoslavia. Some enjoyed ethno-linguistic unity, while others comprised unstable combinations of diverse nationalities.

Despite Wilson's pledge of a peace without territorial acquisitions or vengeance, the Versailles Treaty was a harsh document that all but guaranteed future conflict in Europe. Clemenceau won for France the right to occupy the Saar Basin and Rhineland—iron- and coal-rich parts of Germany. The treaty placed strict limits on the size of Germany's future army and navy. Lloyd George persuaded Wilson to agree to a clause declaring Germany morally responsible for the war and setting astronomical reparations payments (they were variously estimated at between $33 billion and $56 billion), which crippled the German economy.

THE WILSONIAN MOMENT

To many people around the world, the Great War seemed like a civil war among the nations of Europe. The carnage destroyed European claims that theirs was a higher civilization, which gave them the right to rule over more barbaric peoples. In this sense, it helped to heighten the international prestige

World War I and the Versailles Treaty redrew the map of Europe and the Middle East. The Austro-Hungarian and Ottoman empires ceased to exist, and Germany and Russia were reduced in size. A group of new states emerged in eastern Europe, embodying the principle of self-determination, one of Woodrow Wilson's Fourteen Points.

of the United States, a latecomer to the war. Like the ideals of the American Revolution, the Wilsonian rhetoric of self-determination reverberated across the globe, especially among oppressed minorities (including blacks in the United States) and colonial peoples seeking independence. In fact, these groups took Wilson's rhetoric more seriously than he did. Despite his belief in self-determination, he had supported the American annexation of the Philippines, believing that colonial peoples required a long period of tutelage before they were ready for independence.

Nonetheless, Wilsonian ideals quickly spread around the globe—not simply the idea that government must rest on the consent of the governed, but also Wilson's stress on the "equality of nations," large and small, and that international disputes should be settled by peaceful means rather than armed conflict. These stood in sharp contrast to the imperial ideas and practices of Europe. In Eastern Europe, whose people sought to carve new, independent nations from the ruins of the Austro-Hungarian and Ottoman empires, many considered Wilson a "popular saint." The leading Arabic newspaper *Al-Ahram*,

published in Egypt, then under British rule, gave extensive coverage to Wilson's speech asking Congress to declare war in the name of democracy, and to the Fourteen Points, and translated the Declaration of Independence into Arabic for its readers. In Beijing, students demanding that China free itself of foreign domination gathered at the American embassy shouting, "Long live Wilson." Japan proposed to include in the charter of the new League of Nations a clause recognizing the equality of all people, regardless of race. Hundreds of letters, petitions, and declarations addressed to President Wilson made their way to the Paris headquarters of the American delegation to the peace conference. Few reached the president, as his private secretary, Gilbert Close, carefully screened his mail.

Outside of Europe, however, the idea of "self-determination" was stillborn. When the peace conference opened, Secretary of State Robert Lansing warned that the phrase was "loaded with dynamite" and would "raise hopes which can never be realized." Wilson's language, he feared, had put "dangerous" ideas "into the minds of certain races" and would inspire "impossible demands, and cause trouble in many lands." As Lansing anticipated, advocates of colonial independence descended on Paris to lobby the peace negotiators. Arabs demanded that a unified independent state be carved from the old Ottoman empire in the Middle East. Nguyen That Thanh, a young Vietnamese patriot working in Paris, pressed his people's claim for greater rights within the

Mahatma Ghandi, pictured here in 1919, became the leader of the nonviolent movement for independence for India. He was among those disappointed by the failure of the Versailles peace conference to apply the principle of self-determination to the colonial world.

French empire. Citing the Declaration of Independence, he appealed unsuccessfully to Wilson to help bring an end to French rule in Vietnam. W. E. B. Du Bois organized a Pan-African Congress in Paris that put forward the idea of a self-governing nation to be carved out of Germany's African colonies. Koreans, Indians, Irish, and others also pressed claims for self-determination.

The British and French, however, had no intention of applying this principle to their own empires. They rebuffed the pleas of colonial peoples for self-rule. During the war, the British had encouraged Arab nationalism as a weapon against the Ottoman empire and had also pledged to create a homeland in Palestine for the persecuted Jews of Europe. In fact, the victors of World War I divided Ottoman territory into a series of new territories, including Syria, Lebanon, Iraq, and Palestine, controlled by the victorious Allies under League of Nations "mandates." South Africa, Australia, and Japan acquired former German colonies in Africa and Asia. Nor did Ireland achieve its independence at Versailles. Only at the end of 1921 did Britain finally agree to the creation of the Irish Free State, while continuing to rule the northeastern corner of the island. As for the Japanese proposal to establish the principle of racial equality, Wilson, with the support of Great Britain and Australia, engineered its defeat.

THE SEEDS OF WARS TO COME

Du Bois, as noted above, had hoped that black participation in the war effort would promote racial justice at home and self-government for colonies abroad. "We return," he wrote in *The Crisis* in May 1919, "we return from fighting, we return fighting. Make way for Democracy!" But the war's aftermath both in the United States and overseas left him bitterly disappointed. Du Bois concluded that Wilson had "never at any single moment meant to include in his democracy" black Americans or the colonial peoples of the world. "Most men today," he complained, "cannot conceive of a freedom that does not involve somebody's slavery." In 1903, in *The Souls of Black Folk*, Du Bois had made the memorable prediction that "the problem of the twentieth century is the problem of the color-line." He now forecast a "fight for freedom" that would pit "black and brown and yellow men" throughout the world against racism and imperialism.

Disappointment at the failure to apply the Fourteen Points to the non-European world created a pervasive cynicism about Western use of the language of freedom and democracy. Wilson's apparent willingness to accede to the demands of the imperial powers helped to spark a series of popular protest movements across the Middle East and Asia, and the rise of a new anti-Western nationalism. It inspired the May 4 movement in China, a mass protest against the decision at the Versailles peace conference to award certain German concessions (parts of China governed by foreign powers) to Japan. Some leaders, like Nguyen That Thanh, who took the name Ho Chi Minh, turned to communism, in whose name he would lead Vietnam's long and bloody struggle for independence. The Soviet leader Lenin, in fact, had spoken of "the right of nations to self-determination" before Wilson, and with the collapse of the Wilsonian moment, Lenin's reputation in the colonial world began to eclipse that of the American president. But whether communist or not, these movements announced the emergence of anticolonial nationalism as a major force in world affairs, which it would remain for the rest of the twentieth century.

"Your liberalness," one Egyptian leader remarked, speaking of Britain and America, "is only for yourselves." Yet ironically, when colonial peoples demanded to be recognized as independent members of the international community, they would invoke both the heritage of the American Revolution—the first colonial struggle that produced an independent nation—and the Wilsonian language whereby the self-governing nation-state is the most legitimate political institution, and all nations deserve equal respect.

As Du Bois recognized, World War I sowed the seeds not of a lasting peace but of wars to come. German resentment over the peace terms would help to fuel the rise of Adolf Hitler and the coming of World War II. In the breakup of Czechoslovakia and Yugoslavia, violence over the status of Northern Ireland, and the seemingly unending conflict in the Middle East between Arabs and Israelis, the world was still haunted by the ghost of Versailles.

THE TREATY DEBATE

One final disappointment awaited Wilson on his return from Europe. He viewed the new League of Nations as the war's finest legacy. But many Americans feared that membership in the League would commit the United States to an open-ended involvement in the affairs of other countries. Wilson asserted that the United States could not save the world without being continually involved with it. His opponents, led by Senator Henry Cabot Lodge of Massachusetts, argued that the League threatened to deprive the country of its freedom of action.

A considerable majority of senators would have accepted the treaty with "reservations" ensuring that the obligation to assist League members against attack did not supersede the power of Congress to declare war. As governor of New Jersey and as president, Wilson had proved himself to be a skilled politician capable of compromising with opponents. In this case, however, convinced that the treaty reflected "the hand of God," Wilson refused to negotiate with congressional leaders. In October 1919, in the midst of the League debate, Wilson suffered a serious stroke. Although the extent of his illness was kept secret, he remained incapacitated for the rest of his term. In effect, his wife, Edith, headed the government for the next seventeen months. In November 1919 and again in March 1920, the Senate rejected the Versailles Treaty.

American involvement in World War I lasted barely nineteen months, but it cast a long shadow over the following decade—and, indeed, the rest of the century. In its immediate aftermath, the country retreated from international involvements. But in the long run, Wilson's combination of idealism and power politics had an enduring impact. His appeals to democracy, open markets, and a special American mission to instruct the world in freedom, coupled with a willingness to intervene abroad militarily to promote American interests and values, would create the model for twentieth-century American international relations.

On its own terms, the war to make the world safe for democracy failed. Even great powers cannot always bend the world to their purposes. The war brought neither stability nor democracy to most of the world, and it undermined freedom in the United States. It also led to the eclipse of Progressivism. Republican candidate Warren G. Harding, who had no connection with the party's Progressive wing, swept to victory in the presidential election of 1920. Harding's campaign centered on a "return to normalcy" and a repudiation of what he called "Wilsonism." He received 60 percent of the popular vote. Begun with idealistic goals and grand hopes for social change, American involvement in the Great War laid the foundation for one of the most conservative decades in the nation's history.

Chapter Review

REVIEW QUESTIONS

1. Explain the role of the United States in the global economy by 1920.
2. What were the assumptions underlying the Roosevelt Corollary? How did the doctrine affect U.S. relations with European nations and those in the Western hemisphere?

3. What did President Wilson mean by "moral imperialism," and what measures were taken to apply this to Latin America?
4. How did the ratification of both the Eighteenth and Nineteenth Amendments suggest both the restrictive and democratizing nature of Progressivism?
5. Why did Progressives see in the expansion of governmental powers in wartime an opportunity to reform American society?
6. What were the goals and methods of the Committee on Public Information during World War I?
7. What are governmental and private examples of coercive patriotism during the war? What were the effects of those efforts?
8. What were the major causes—both real and imaginary—of the Red Scare?
9. How did World War I and its aftermath provide African-Americans with opportunities?
10. Identify the goals of those pressing for global change in 1919, and of those who opposed them.

KEY TERMS

"liberal internationalism"
Panama Canal Zone
Roosevelt Corollary
Dollar Diplomacy
"moral imperialism"
sinking of the *Lusitania*
Zimmerman Telegram
Fourteen Points
Selective Service Act
War Industries Board
Espionage Act
Sedition Act
National Association for the Advancement of Colored People
Great Migration
Tulsa riot of 1921
Garveyites
flu epidemic
Red Scare of 1919–1920
Versailles Treaty

wwnorton.com/studyspace

VISIT STUDYSPACE FOR THESE RESOURCES AND MORE:

- Author Videos
- A chapter outline
- A practice quiz
- Interactive maps
- Multimedia documents

CHAPTER 5

FROM BUSINESS CULTURE TO GREAT DEPRESSION

From *Give Me Liberty! Seagull Fourth Edition*

Eric Foner

Credits: photo 1: Library of Congress; photo 2: Library of Congress; photo 3: Honolulu Academy of Arts: Gift of Philip H. Roach, Jr., 2001; photo 4: The Art Archive/Culver Picture6s; photo 5: San Diego Museum of Art; photo 6: Washington State Historical Society; photo 7: Photographs and Prints Division, Schomburg Center for Research in Black Culture, The New York Public Library, Astor, Lenox, and Tilden Foundations; photo 8: National Archives.

5

From Business Culture to Great Depression
The Twenties, 1920–1932

FOCUS QUESTIONS

- Who benefited and who suffered in the new consumer society of the 1920s?
- In what ways did the government promote business interests in the 1920s?
- Why did the protection of civil liberties gain importance in the 1920s?
- What were the major flash points between fundamentalism and pluralism in the 1920s?
- What were the causes of the Great Depression, and how effective were the government's responses by 1932?

In May 1920, at the height of the postwar Red Scare, police arrested two Italian immigrants accused of participating in a robbery at a South Braintree, Massachusetts, factory in which a security guard was killed. Nicola Sacco, a shoemaker, and Bartolomeo Vanzetti, an itinerant unskilled laborer, were anarchists who dreamed of a society in which government, churches, and private property had been abolished. They saw violence as an appropriate weapon of class warfare. But very little evidence linked them to this particular crime. One man claimed to have seen Vanzetti at the wheel of the getaway car, but all the other eyewitnesses described the driver quite differently. Disputed tests on one of the six bullets in the dead man's body suggested that it might have been fired from a gun owned by Sacco. Neither fingerprints nor possession of stolen money linked either to the crime. In the atmosphere of anti-radical and anti-immigrant fervor, however, their conviction was a certainty. "I have suffered," Vanzetti wrote from prison, "for things that I am guilty of. I am suffering because I am a radical and indeed I am a radical; I have suffered because I was an Italian, and indeed I am an Italian."

Although their 1921 trial had aroused little public interest outside the Italian-American community, the case of Sacco and Vanzetti attracted international attention during the lengthy appeals that followed. There were mass protests in Europe against their impending execution. In the United States, the movement to save their lives attracted the support of an impressive array of intellectuals, including the novelist John Dos Passos, the poet Edna St. Vincent Millay, and Felix Frankfurter, a professor at Harvard Law School and a future justice of the Supreme Court. In response to the mounting clamor, the governor of Massachusetts appointed a three-member commission to review the case, headed by Abbott Lawrence Lowell, the president of Harvard University (and for many years an official of the Immigration Restriction League). The commission upheld the verdict and death sentences, and on August 23, 1927, Sacco and Vanzetti died in the electric chair. "It is not every prisoner," remarked the journalist Heywood Broun, "who has a president of Harvard throw the switch for him."

The Sacco-Vanzetti case laid bare some of the fault lines beneath the surface of American society during the 1920s. The case, the writer Edmund Wilson commented, "revealed the whole anatomy of American life, with all its classes, professions and points of view and . . . it raised almost every fundamental question of our political and social system." It demonstrated how long the Red Scare extended into the 1920s and how powerfully it undermined basic American freedoms. It reflected the fierce cultural battles that raged in many communities during the decade. To many native-born Americans, the two men symbolized an alien threat to their way of life. To Italian-Americans, including respectable middle-class organizations like the Sons of Italy that raised money for the defense, the outcome symbolized the nativist prejudices and stereotypes that haunted immigrant communities. To Dos Passos, the executions underscored the success of the anti-radical crusade: "They are stronger. They are rich. They hire and fire the politicians, the old judges, . . . the college presidents." Dos Passos's lament was a bitter comment on the triumph of pro-business conservatism during the 1920s.

In popular memory, the decade that followed World War I is recalled as the Jazz Age or the Roaring Twenties. With its flappers (young, sexually liberated

A 1927 photograph shows Nicola Sacco and Bartolomeo Vanzetti outside the courthouse in Dedham, Massachusetts, surrounded by security agents and onlookers. They are about to enter the courthouse, where the judge will pronounce their death sentence.

women), speakeasies (nightclubs that sold liquor in violation of Prohibition), and a soaring stock market fueled by easy credit and a get-rich-quick outlook, it was a time of revolt against moral rules inherited from the nineteenth century. Observers from Europe, where class divisions were starkly visible in work, politics, and social relations, marveled at the uniformity of American life. Factories poured out standardized consumer goods, their sale promoted by national advertising campaigns. Conservatism dominated a political system from which radical alternatives seemed to have been purged. Radio and the movies spread mass culture throughout the nation. Americans seemed to dress alike, think alike, go to the same movies, and admire the same larger-than-life national celebrities.

Many Americans, however, did not welcome the new secular, commercial culture. They resented and feared the ethnic and racial diversity of America's cities and what they considered the lax moral standards of urban life. The 1920s was a decade of profound social tensions—between rural and urban Americans, traditional and "modern" Christianity, participants in the burgeoning consumer culture and those who did not fully share in the new prosperity.

THE BUSINESS OF AMERICA

A DECADE OF PROSPERITY

"The chief business of the American people," said Calvin Coolidge, who became president after Warren G. Harding's sudden death from a heart attack in 1923, "is business." Rarely in American history had economic growth seemed more dramatic, cooperation between business and government so close, and business values so widely shared. After a sharp postwar recession that lasted into 1922, the 1920s was a decade of prosperity. Productivity and economic output rose dramatically as new industries—chemicals, aviation, electronics—flourished and older ones like food processing and the manufacture of household appliances adopted Henry Ford's moving assembly line.

The automobile was the backbone of economic growth. The most celebrated American factories now turned out cars, not textiles and steel as in the nineteenth century. Annual automobile production tripled during the 1920s, from 1.5 to 4.8 million. General Motors, which learned the secret of marketing numerous individual models and stylish designs, surpassed Ford with its cheap, standardized Model T (replaced in 1927 by the Model A). By 1929, half of all American families owned a car (a figure not reached in England until 1980). The automobile industry stimulated the expansion of steel, rubber, and oil production, road construction, and other sectors of the economy. It promoted tourism and the growth of suburbs (already, some commuters were driving to work) and helped to reduce rural isolation.

During the 1920s, American multinational corporations extended their sway throughout the world. With Europe still recovering from the Great War, American investment overseas far exceeded that of other countries. The dollar replaced the British pound as the most important currency of international trade. American companies produced 85 percent of the world's cars and 40 percent of its manufactured goods. General Electric and International Telephone and Telegraph bought up companies in other countries. International Business Machines (IBM) was the world's leader in office supplies. American oil companies built new refineries overseas. American companies took control of raw materials abroad, from rubber in Liberia to oil in Venezuela.

One of the more unusual examples of the global spread of American corporations was Fordlandia, an effort by the auto manufacturer Henry Ford to create a town in the heart of Brazil's Amazon rain forest. Ford hoped to secure a steady supply of rubber for car tires. But as in the United States, where he had compelled immigrant workers to adopt American dress and diet, he wanted to bring local inhabitants up to what he considered the proper standard of life (this meant, for example, forbidding his workers from using alcohol and tobacco and trying to get them to eat brown rice and whole wheat bread instead of traditional

Brazilian foods). Eventually, the climate and local insects destroyed the rubber trees that Ford's engineers, lacking experience in tropical agriculture, had planted much too close together, while the workers rebelled against the long hours of labor and regimentation of the community.

A NEW SOCIETY

During the 1920s, consumer goods of all kinds proliferated, marketed by salesmen and advertisers who promoted them as ways of satisfying Americans' psychological desires and everyday needs. Frequently purchased on credit through new installment buying plans, they rapidly altered daily life. Telephones made communication easier. Vacuum cleaners, washing machines, and refrigerators transformed work in the home and reduced the demand for domestic servants. Boosted by Prohibition and an aggressive advertising campaign that, according to the company's sales director, made it "impossible for the consumer to *escape*" the product, Coca-Cola became a symbol of American life.

Americans spent more and more of their income on leisure activities like vacations, movies, and sporting events. By 1929, weekly movie attendance had reached 80 million, double the figure of 1922. Hollywood films now dominated the world movie market.

CHRONOLOGY

1915	Reemergence of the Ku Klux Klan
1919	*Schenck v. United States*
1920	American Civil Liberties Union established
1921	Trial of Sacco and Vanzetti
1922	Washington Naval Arms Conference
	Cable Act
	Herbert Hoover's *American Individualism*
1923	*Adkins v. Children's Hospital*
	Meyer v. Nebraska
1924	Immigration Act of 1924
	Indian Citizenship Act of 1924
1925	Scopes trial
1927	Charles Lindbergh flies non-stop over the Atlantic
	Sacco and Vanzetti executed
1927–1928	President Coolidge vetoes McNary-Haugen farm bill
1929	Sheppard-Towner Act repealed
	Stock market crashes
1930	Hollywood adopts the Hays code
	Smoot-Hawley Tariff
1932	Reconstruction Finance Corporation established
	Bonus march on Washington

Movies had been produced early in the century in several American cities, but shortly before World War I filmmakers gravitated to Hollywood, a district of Los Angeles, attracted by the open space, year-round sunshine for outdoor filming, and varied scenery. In 1910, two French companies, Pathé and Gaumont, had been the world's leading film producers. By 1925, American releases outnumbered French by eight to one. In the 1920s, both companies abandoned film production for the more profitable business of distributing American films in Europe.

Advertisements, like this one for a refrigerator, promised that consumer goods would enable Americans to fulfill their hearts' desires.

Radios and phonographs brought mass entertainment into Americans' living rooms. The number of radios in Americans' homes rose from 190,000 in 1923 to just under 5 million in 1929. These developments helped to create and spread a new celebrity culture, in which recording, film, and sports stars moved to the top of the list of American heroes. During the 1920s, more than 100 million records were sold each year. RCA Victor sold so many recordings of the great opera tenor Enrico Caruso that he is sometimes called the first modern celebrity. He was soon joined by the film actor Charlie Chaplin, baseball player Babe Ruth, and boxer Jack Dempsey. Ordinary Americans followed every detail of their lives. Perhaps the decade's greatest celebrity, in terms of intensive press coverage, was the aviator Charles Lindbergh, who in 1927 made the first solo nonstop flight across the Atlantic.

André Siegfried, a Frenchman who had visited the United States four times since the beginning of the century, commented in 1928 that a "new society" had come into being, in which Americans considered their "standard of living" a "sacred acquisition, which they will defend at any price." In this new "mass civilization," widespread acceptance of going into debt to purchase consumer goods had replaced the values of thrift and self-denial, central to nineteenth-century notions of upstanding character. Work, once seen as a source of pride in craft skill or collective empowerment via trade unions, now came to be valued as a path to individual fulfillment through consumption and entertainment.

THE LIMITS OF PROSPERITY

"Big business in America," remarked the journalist Lincoln Steffens, "is producing what the socialists held up as their goal—food, shelter, and clothing for all." But signs of future trouble could be seen beneath the prosperity of the 1920s. The fruits of increased production were very unequally distributed. Real wages for industrial workers (wages adjusted to take account of inflation) rose by one-quarter between 1922 and 1929, but corporate profits rose at more than twice that rate. The process of economic concentration continued unabated. A handful of firms dominated numerous sectors of the economy. In 1929, 1 percent of the nation's banks controlled half of its financial resources. Most of the small auto companies that had existed earlier in the century had fallen by the wayside. General Motors, Ford, and Chrysler now controlled four-fifths of the industry.

At the beginning of 1929, the share of national income of the wealthiest 5 percent of American families exceeded that of the bottom 60 percent. A majority of families had no savings, and an estimated 40 percent of the population remained in poverty, unable to participate in the flourishing consumer economy. Improved productivity meant that goods could be produced with fewer workers. During the 1920s, more Americans worked in the professions, retailing, finance, and education, but the number of manufacturing workers declined by 5 percent, the first such drop in the nation's history. Parts of New England were already experiencing the chronic unemployment caused by deindustrialization. Many of the region's textile companies failed in the face of low-wage competition from southern factories, or shifted production to take advantage of the South's cheap labor. Most advertisers directed their messages at businessmen and the middle class. At the end of the decade, 75 percent of American households still did not own a washing machine, and 60 percent had no radio.

THE FARMERS' PLIGHT

Nor did farmers share in the decade's prosperity. The "golden age" of American farming had reached its peak during World War I, when the need to feed war-torn Europe and government efforts to maintain high farm prices had raised farmers' incomes and promoted the purchase of more land on credit. Thanks to mechanization and the increased use of fertilizer and insecticides, agricultural production continued to rise even when government subsidies ended and world demand stagnated. As a result, farm incomes declined steadily and banks foreclosed tens of thousands of farms whose owners were unable to meet mortgage payments.

For the first time in the nation's history, the number of farms and farmers declined during the 1920s. For example, half the farmers in Montana lost their land to foreclosure between 1921 and 1925. Extractive industries, like mining and lumber, also suffered as their products faced a glut on the world market. During the decade, some 3 million persons migrated out of rural areas. Many headed for southern California, whose rapidly growing economy needed new labor. The population of Los Angeles, the West's leading industrial center, a producer of oil, automobiles, aircraft, and, of course, Hollywood movies, rose from 575,000 to 2.2 million during the decade, largely because of an influx of displaced farmers from the Midwest. Well before the 1930s, rural America was in an economic depression.

THE IMAGE OF BUSINESS

Even as unemployment remained high in Britain throughout the 1920s, and inflation and war reparations payments crippled the German economy, Hollywood films spread images of "the American way of life" across the globe. America, wrote the historian Charles Beard, was "boring its way" into the world's consciousness. In high wages, efficient factories, and the mass production of consumer goods, Americans seemed to have discovered the secret of permanent prosperity. Businessmen like Henry Ford and engineers like Herbert Hoover were cultural heroes. Photographers like Lewis Hine and Margaret Bourke-White and painters like Charles Sheeler celebrated the beauty of machines and factories. *The Man Nobody Knows*, a 1925 best-seller by advertising executive Bruce Barton, portrayed Jesus Christ as "the greatest advertiser of his day, . . . a virile go-getting he-man of business," who "picked twelve men from the bottom ranks and forged a great organization."

After the Ludlow Massacre of 1914, John D. Rockefeller himself had hired a public relations firm to repair his tarnished image. Now, persuaded by the success of World War I's Committee on Public Information that it was possible, as an advertising magazine put it, to "sway the minds of whole populations," numerous firms established public relations departments. They aimed to justify corporate practices to the public and counteract its long-standing distrust of big business.

They succeeded in changing popular attitudes toward Wall Street. Congressional hearings of 1912–1914 headed by Louisiana congressman Arsène Pujo had laid bare the manipulation of stock prices by a Wall Street "money trust." The Pujo investigation had reinforced the widespread view of the stock market as a place where insiders fleeced small investors—as, indeed, they frequently did. But in the 1920s, as the steadily rising price of stocks made front-page news, the market attracted more investors. Many assumed that stock values would rise forever. By 1928, an estimated 1.5 million Americans owned stock—still a small minority of the country's 28 million families, but far more than in the past.

THE DECLINE OF LABOR

With the defeat of the labor upsurge of 1919 and the dismantling of the wartime regulatory state, business appropriated the rhetoric of Americanism and "industrial freedom" as weapons against labor unions. Some corporations during the 1920s implemented a new style of management. They provided their employees with private pensions and medical insurance plans, job security, and greater workplace safety. They established sports programs to occupy their employees' leisure time. They spoke of "welfare capitalism," a more socially conscious kind of business leadership, and trumpeted the fact that they now paid more attention to the "human factor" in employment.

At the same time, however, employers in the 1920s embraced the American Plan, at whose core stood the open shop—a workplace free of both government regulation and unions, except, in some cases, "company unions" created and controlled by management. Collective bargaining, declared one group of employers, represented "an infringement of personal liberty and a menace to the institutions of a free people." Prosperity, they insisted, depended on giving business complete freedom of action. This message was reinforced in a propaganda campaign that linked unionism and socialism as examples of the sinister influence of foreigners on American life. Even the most forward-looking companies continued to employ strikebreakers, private detectives, and the blacklisting of union organizers to prevent or defeat strikes.

During the 1920s, organized labor lost more than 2 million members, and unions agreed to demand after demand by employers in an effort to stave off complete elimination. In cities like Minneapolis, New Orleans, and Seattle, once centers of thriving labor movements, unions all but disappeared. Uprisings by the most downtrodden workers did occur sporadically throughout the decade. Southern textile mills witnessed desperate strikes by workers who charged employers with "making slaves out of the men and women" who labored there. Facing the combined opposition of business, local politicians, and the courts, as well as the threat of violence, such strikes were doomed to defeat.

THE EQUAL RIGHTS AMENDMENT

The idealistic goals of World War I, wrote the young Protestant minister Reinhold Niebuhr, seemingly had been abandoned: "We are rapidly becoming the most conservative nation on earth." Like the labor movement, feminists struggled to adapt to the new political situation. The achievement of suffrage in 1920 eliminated the bond of unity between various activists, each "struggling for her own conception of freedom," in the words of labor reformer Juliet Stuart Poyntz. Black feminists insisted that the movement must now demand enforcement of the Fifteenth Amendment in the South, but they won little support from white counterparts. A few prominent feminists, including Elizabeth

Cady Stanton's daughter Harriot Stanton Blatch, joined the rapidly diminishing Socialist Party, convinced that women should support an independent electoral force that promoted governmental protection of vulnerable workers.

The long-standing division between two competing conceptions of woman's freedom—one based on motherhood, the other on individual autonomy and the right to work—now crystallized in the debate over an Equal Rights Amendment (ERA) to the Constitution promoted by Alice Paul and the National Women's Party. This amendment proposed to eliminate all legal distinctions "on account of sex." In Paul's opinion, the ERA followed logically from winning the right to vote. Having gained political equality, she insisted, women no longer required special legal protection—they needed equal access to employment, education, and all the other opportunities of citizens. To supporters of mothers' pensions and laws limiting women's hours of labor, which the ERA would sweep away, the proposal represented a giant step backward. Apart from the National Women's Party, every major female organization, from the League of Women Voters to the Women's Trade Union League, opposed the ERA.

In the end, none of these groups achieved success in the 1920s. The ERA campaign failed, as did a proposed constitutional amendment giving Congress the power to prohibit child labor, which farm groups and business organizations opposed. In 1929, Congress repealed the Sheppard-Towner Act of 1921, a major achievement of the maternalist reformers that had provided federal assistance to programs for infant and child health.

WOMEN'S FREEDOM

If political feminism faded, the prewar feminist demand for personal freedom survived in the vast consumer marketplace and in the actual behavior of the decade's much-publicized liberated young women. Female liberation resurfaced as a lifestyle, the stuff of advertising and mass entertainment, stripped of any connection to political or economic radicalism. No longer one element in a broader program of social reform, sexual freedom now meant individual autonomy or personal rebellion. With her bobbed hair, short skirts, public smoking and drinking, and unapologetic use of birth-control methods such as the diaphragm, the young, single "flapper" epitomized the change in standards of sexual behavior, at least in large cities. She frequented dance halls and music clubs where white people now performed "wild" dances like the Charleston that had long been popular in black communities. She attended sexually charged Hollywood films featuring stars like Clara Bow, the provocative "'It' Girl," and Rudolph Valentino, the original on-screen "Latin Lover." When Valentino died of a sudden illness in 1926, crowds of grieving women tried to storm the funeral home.

Tipsy, *a 1930 painting by the Japanese artist Kobayakawa Kiyoshi, illustrates the global appeal of the "new woman" of the 1920s. The subject, a moga ("modern girl" in Japanese), sits alone in a nightclub wearing Western clothing, makeup, and hairstyle, accompanied by a cigarette and a martini. The title of the work suggests that Kiyoshi does not entirely approve of her behavior, but he presents her as self-confident and alluring.*

What had been scandalous a generation earlier—women's self-conscious pursuit of personal pleasure—became a device to market goods from automobiles to cigarettes. In 1904, a woman had been arrested for smoking in public in New York City. Two decades later, Edward Bernays, the "father" of modern public relations, masterminded a campaign to persuade women to smoke, dubbing cigarettes women's "torches of freedom." The new freedom, however, was available only during one phase of a woman's life. Once she married, what Jane Addams had called the "family claim" still ruled. And marriage, according to one advertisement, remained "the one pursuit that stands foremost in the mind of every girl and woman." Having found a husband, women were expected to seek freedom within the confines of the home, finding "liberation," according to the advertisements, in the use of new labor-saving appliances.

BUSINESS AND GOVERNMENT

THE RETREAT FROM PROGRESSIVISM

In 1924, a social scientist remarked that the United States had just passed through "one of the most critical ten-year periods" in its history. Among the changes was the disintegration of Progressivism as a political movement and body of thought. The government's success in whipping up mass hysteria during the war seemed to undermine the very foundation of democratic thought—the idea of the rational, self-directed citizen. Followers of Sigmund Freud emphasized the unconscious, instinctual motivations of human behavior; scientists pointed to wartime IQ tests allegedly demonstrating that many Americans were mentally unfit for self-government. "The great bulk of people are stupid," declared one advertising executive, explaining why advertisements played on the emotions rather than providing actual information.

During the 1920s, Walter Lippmann published two of the most penetrating indictments of democracy ever written, *Public Opinion* and *The Phantom Public*, which repudiated the Progressive hope of applying "intelligence" to social problems in a mass democracy. Instead of acting out of careful consideration of the issues or even individual self-interest, Lippmann claimed, the American voter was ill-informed and prone to fits of enthusiasm. Not only were modern problems beyond the understanding of ordinary men and women (a sentiment that had earlier led Lippmann to favor administration by experts), but the independent citizen was nothing but a myth. Like advertising copywriters and journalists, he continued, the government had perfected the art of creating and manipulating public opinion—a process Lippmann called the "manufacture of consent."

In 1929, the sociologists Robert and Helen Lynd published *Middletown*, a classic study of life in Muncie, Indiana, a typical community in the American heartland. The Lynds found that new leisure activities and a new emphasis on consumption had replaced politics as the focus of public concern. Elections were no longer "lively centers" of public attention as in the nineteenth century, and voter participation had fallen dramatically. National statistics bore out their point; the turnout of eligible voters, over 80 percent in 1896, had dropped to less than 50 percent in 1924. Many factors helped to explain this decline, including the consolidation of one-party politics in the South, the long period of Republican dominance in national elections, and the enfranchisement of women, who for many years voted in lower numbers than men. But the shift from public to private concerns also played a part. "The American citizen's first importance to his country," declared a Muncie newspaper, "is no longer that of a citizen but that of a consumer."

THE REPUBLICAN ERA

Government policies reflected the pro-business ethos of the 1920s. Recalling the era's prosperity, one stockbroker later remarked, "God, J. P. Morgan and the Republican Party were going to keep everything going forever." Business lobbyists dominated national conventions of the Republican Party. They called on the federal government to lower taxes on personal incomes and business profits, maintain high tariffs, and support employers' continuing campaign against unions. The administrations of Warren G. Harding and Calvin Coolidge obliged. "Never before, here or anywhere else," declared the *Wall Street Journal*, "has a government been so completely fused with business." The two presidents appointed so many pro-business members of the Federal Reserve Board, the Federal Trade Commission, and other Progressive-era agencies that, complained Nebraska senator George W. Norris, they in effect repealed the regulatory system. The Harding administration did support

The policies of President Calvin Coolidge were music to the ears of big business, according to one 1920s cartoonist.

Secretary of Commerce Herbert Hoover's successful effort to persuade the steel industry to reduce the workday from twelve to eight hours. But it resumed the practice of obtaining court injunctions to suppress strikes, as in a 1922 walkout of 250,000 railroad workers protesting a wage cut.

Under William Howard Taft, appointed chief justice in 1921, the Supreme Court remained strongly conservative. A resurgence of laissez-faire jurisprudence eclipsed the Progressive ideal of a socially active national state. The Court struck down a federal law that barred goods produced by child labor from interstate commerce. It even repudiated *Muller v. Oregon* in a 1923 decision (*Adkins v. Children's Hospital*) overturning a minimum wage law for women in Washington, D.C. Now that women enjoyed the vote, the justices declared, they were entitled to the same workplace freedom as men. "This," lamented Florence Kelley, "is a new Dred Scott decision," which, in the name of liberty of contract, "fills those words with the bitterest and most cruel mockery."

CORRUPTION IN GOVERNMENT

Warren G. Harding took office as president in 1921 promising a return to "normalcy" after an era of Progressive reform and world war. Reflecting the prevailing get-rich-quick ethos, his administration quickly became one of the most corrupt in American history. A likeable, somewhat ineffectual individual—he called himself "a man of limited talents from a small town"—Harding seemed to have little regard for either governmental issues or the dignity of the presidency. Prohibition did not cause him to curb his appetite for liquor. He continued a previous illicit affair with a young Ohio woman, Nan Britton. The relationship did not become known until 1927, when Britton published *The President's Daughter*, about their child to whom Harding had left nothing in his will.

Although his cabinet included men of integrity and talent, like Secretary of State Charles Evans Hughes and Secretary of Commerce Herbert Hoover,

Harding also surrounded himself with cronies who used their offices for private gain. Attorney General Harry Daugherty accepted payments not to prosecute accused criminals. The head of the Veterans' Bureau, Charles Forbes, received kickbacks from the sale of government supplies. The most notorious scandal involved Secretary of the Interior Albert Fall, who accepted nearly $500,000 from private businessmen to whom he leased government oil reserves at Teapot Dome, Wyoming. Fall became the first cabinet member in history to be convicted of a felony.

THE ELECTION OF 1924

Harding's successor, Calvin Coolidge, who as governor of Massachusetts had won national fame for using state troops against striking Boston policemen in 1919, was a dour man of few words. But in contrast to his predecessor he seemed to exemplify Yankee honesty. The scandals subsided, but otherwise Coolidge continued his predecessor's policies. He twice vetoed the McNary-Haugen bill, the top legislative priority of congressmen from farm states. This bill sought to have the government purchase agricultural products for sale overseas in order to raise farm prices. Coolidge denounced it as an unwarranted interference with the free market. In 1924, Coolidge was reelected in a landslide, defeating John W. Davis, a Wall Street lawyer nominated on the 103rd ballot by a badly divided Democratic convention. (This was when the comedian Will Rogers made the quip, often repeated in future years, "I am a member of no organized political party; I am a Democrat.")

One-sixth of the electorate in 1924 voted for Robert La Follette, running as the candidate of a new Progressive Party, which called for greater taxation of wealth, the conservation of natural resources, public ownership of the railroads, farm relief, and the end of child labor. Although such ideas had been proposed many times before World War I, Coolidge described the platform as a blueprint for a "communistic and socialistic" America. Despite endorsements from veteran Progressives like Jane Addams and John Dewey and the American Federation of Labor, La Follette could raise no more than $250,000 for his campaign. He carried only his native Wisconsin. But his candidacy demonstrated the survival of some currents of dissent in a highly conservative decade.

ECONOMIC DIPLOMACY

Foreign affairs also reflected the close working relationship between business and government. "Any student of modern diplomacy," declared Huntington Wilson, a State Department official, "knows that in these days of competition, capital, trade, agriculture, labor and statecraft all go hand in hand if a country is to profit." The 1920s marked a retreat from Wilson's goal of internationalism

VOICES OF FREEDOM

From André Siegfried, "The Gulf Between," *Atlantic Monthly* (March 1928)

The French writer André Siegfried in 1928 commented on the rise of an industrial economy and consumer culture and the changes they produced in American society.

Never has Europe more eagerly observed, studied, discussed America; and never . . . have the two continents been wider apart in their aspirations and ideals. . . . Europe, after all, is not very different from what it was a generation ago; but there has been born since then a new America. . . .

The conquest of the continent has been completed, and—all recent American historians have noted the significance of the event—the western frontier has disappeared; the pioneer is no longer needed, and, with him, the mystic dream of the West . . . has faded away. Thus came the beginning of the era of organization: the new problem was not to conquer adventurously but to produce methodically. The great man of the new generation was no longer a pioneer like Lincoln . . . but . . . Henry Ford. From this time on, America has been no more an unlimited prairie with pure and infinite horizons, in which free men may sport like wild horses, but a huge factory of prodigious efficiency. . . .

In the last twenty-five or thirty years America has produced a new civilization. . . . From a *moral point of view,* it is obvious that Americans have come to consider their standard of living as a somewhat sacred acquisition, which they will defend at any price. This means that they would be ready to make many an intellectual or even moral concession in order to maintain that standard.

From a *political point of view,* it seems that the notion of efficiency of production is on the way to taking [precedence over] the very notion of liberty. In the name of efficiency, one can obtain, from the American, all sorts of sacrifices in relation to his personal and even to certain of his political liberties. . . .

Mass production and mass civilization, its natural consequence, are the true characteristics of the new American society. . . . Lincoln, with his Bible and classical tradition, was easier for Europe to understand than Ford, with his total absence of tradition and his proud creation of new methods and new standards, especially conceived for a world entirely different from our own.

From Majority Opinion, Justice James C. McReynolds, in *Meyer v. Nebraska* (1923)

A landmark in the development of civil liberties, the Supreme Court's decision in Meyer v. Nebraska rebuked the coercive Americanization impulse of World War I, overturning a Nebraska law that required all school instruction to take place in English.

The problem for our determination is whether the statute [prohibiting instruction in a language other than English] as construed and applied unreasonably infringes the liberty guaranteed . . . by the Fourteenth Amendment. . . .

The American people have always regarded education and acquisition of knowledge as matters of supreme importance which should be diligently promoted. . . . The calling always has been regarded as useful and honorable, essential, indeed, to the public welfare. Mere knowledge of the German language cannot reasonably be regarded as harmful. Heretofore it has been commonly looked upon as helpful and desirable. [Meyer] taught this language in school as part of his occupation. His right to teach and the right of parents to engage him so to instruct their children, we think, are within the liberty of the Amendment.

It is said the purpose of the legislation was to promote civil development by inhibiting training and education of the immature in foreign tongues and ideals before they could learn English and acquire American ideals. . . . It is also affirmed that the foreign born population is very large, that certain communities commonly use foreign words, follow foreign leaders, move in a foreign atmosphere, and that the children are therefore hindered from becoming citizens of the most useful type and the public safety is impaired.

That the State may do much, go very far, indeed, in order to improve the quality of its citizens, physically, mentally, and morally, is clear; but the individual has certain fundamental rights which must be respected. The protection of the Constitution extends to all, to those who speak other languages as well as to those born with English on the tongue. Perhaps it would be highly advantageous if all had ready understanding of our ordinary speech, but this cannot be coerced by methods which conflict with the Constitution. . . . No emergency has arisen which rendered knowledge by a child of some language other than English so clearly harmful as to justify its inhibition with the consequent infringement of rights long freely enjoyed.

QUESTIONS

1. Why does Siegfried feel Europeans no longer find America understandable?

2. How does the decision in *Meyer v. Nebraska* expand the definition of liberty protected by the Fourteenth Amendment?

3. How do the two excerpts reflect the changes American society experienced in the 1910s and 1920s?

in favor of unilateral American actions mainly designed to increase exports and investment opportunities overseas. Indeed, what is sometimes called the "isolationism" of the 1920s represented a reaction against the disappointing results of Wilson's military and diplomatic pursuit of freedom and democracy abroad. The United States did play host to the Washington Naval Arms Conference of 1922 that negotiated reductions in the navies of Britain, France, Japan, Italy, and the United States. But the country remained outside the League of Nations. Even as American diplomats continued to press for access to markets overseas, the Fordney-McCumber Tariff of 1922 raised taxes on imported goods to their highest levels in history, a repudiation of Wilson's principle of promoting free trade.

Much foreign policy was conducted through private economic relationships rather than governmental action. The United States emerged from World War I as both the world's foremost center of manufacturing and the major financial power, thanks to British and French debts for American loans that had funded their war efforts. During the 1920s, New York bankers, sometimes acting on their own and sometimes with the cooperation of the Harding and Coolidge administrations, solidified their international position by extending loans to European and Latin American governments. They advanced billions of dollars to Germany to enable the country to meet its World War I reparations payments. American industrial firms, especially in auto, agricultural machinery, and electrical equipment manufacturing, established plants overseas to supply the world market and take advantage of inexpensive labor. American investors gained control over raw materials such as copper in Chile and oil in Venezuela. In 1928, in the so-called Red Line Agreement, British, French, and American oil companies divided oil-producing regions in the Middle East and Latin America among themselves.

As before World War I, the government dispatched soldiers when a change in government in the Caribbean threatened American economic interests. Having been stationed in Nicaragua since 1912, American marines withdrew in 1925. But the troops soon returned in an effort to suppress a nationalist revolt headed by General Augusto César Sandino. Having created a National Guard headed by General Anastasio Somoza, the marines finally departed in 1933. A year later, Somoza assassinated Sandino and seized power. For the next forty-five years, he and his family ruled and plundered Nicaragua. Somoza was overthrown in 1978 by a popular movement calling itself the Sandinistas.

THE BIRTH OF CIVIL LIBERTIES

Among the casualties of World War I and the 1920s was Progressivism's faith that an active federal government embodied the national purpose and enhanced the enjoyment of freedom. Wartime and postwar repression,

Prohibition, and the pro-business policies of the 1920s all illustrated, in the eyes of many Progressives, how public power could go grievously wrong.

This lesson opened the door to a new appreciation of civil liberties—rights an individual may assert even against democratic majorities—as essential elements of American freedom. Building on prewar struggles for freedom of expression by labor unions, socialists, and birth-control advocates, some reformers now developed a greater appreciation of the necessity of vibrant, unrestricted political debate. In the name of a "new freedom for the individual," the 1920s saw the birth of a coherent concept of civil liberties and the beginnings of significant legal protection for freedom of speech against the government.

THE "FREE MOB"

Wartime repression continued into the 1920s. Under the heading "Sweet Land of Liberty," *The Nation* magazine in 1923 detailed recent examples of the degradation of American freedom—lynchings in Alabama, Arkansas, and Florida; the beating by Columbia University students of an undergraduate who had written a letter defending freedom of speech and the press; the arrest of a union leader in New Jersey and 400 members of the IWW in California; refusal to allow a socialist to speak in Pennsylvania. Throughout the 1920s, artistic works with sexual themes were subjected to rigorous censorship. The Postal Service removed from the mails books it deemed obscene. The Customs Service barred works by the sixteenth-century French satirist Rabelais, the modern novelist James Joyce, and many others from entering the country. A local crusade against indecency made the phrase "Banned in Boston" a term of ridicule among upholders of artistic freedom. Boston's Watch and Ward Committee excluded sixty-five books from the city's bookstores, including works by the novelists Upton Sinclair, Theodore Dreiser, and Ernest Hemingway.

Hollywood producers feared that publicity over actress Mary Pickford's divorce, actor Wallace Reid's death from a drug overdose, and a murder trial involving actor Fatty Arbuckle would reinforce the belief that movies promoted immorality. In 1930, the film industry adopted the Hays code, a sporadically enforced set of guidelines that prohibited movies from depicting nudity, long kisses, and adultery, and barred scripts that portrayed clergymen in a negative light or criminals sympathetically. (The code in some ways anticipated recent efforts by television networks, music companies, and video game producers to adopt self-imposed guidelines to fend off governmental regulation.) Filmmakers hoped that self-censorship would prevent censorship by local governments, a not uncommon occurrence since the courts deemed movies a business subject to regulation, not a form of expression. Not until 1951, in a case involving *The Miracle*, a film many Catholics found offensive, would the Supreme Court declare movies an artistic form protected by the First Amendment.

Even as Europeans turned in increasing numbers to American popular culture and consumer goods, some came to view the country as a repressive cultural wasteland. Americans, commented the British novelist D. H. Lawrence, who lived for a time in the United States, prided themselves on being the "land of the free," but "the free mob" had destroyed the right to dissent. "I have never been in any country," he wrote, "where the individual has such an abject fear of his fellow countrymen." Disillusionment with the conservatism of American politics and the materialism of the culture inspired some American artists and writers to emigrate to Paris. The Lost Generation of cultural exiles included novelists and poets like Ernest Hemingway, Gertrude Stein, and F. Scott Fitzgerald. Europe, they felt, valued art and culture, and appreciated unrestrained freedom of expression (and, of course, allowed individuals to drink legally).

A "CLEAR AND PRESENT DANGER"

During World War I, the Unitarian minister John Haynes Holmes later recalled, "there suddenly came to the fore in our nation's life the new issue of civil liberties." The arrest of antiwar dissenters under the Espionage and Sedition Acts inspired the formation in 1917 of the Civil Liberties Bureau, which in 1920 became the American Civil Liberties Union (ACLU). For the rest of the century, the ACLU would take part in most of the landmark cases that helped to bring about a "rights revolution." Its efforts helped to give meaning to traditional civil liberties like freedom of speech and invented new ones, like the right to privacy. When it began, however, the ACLU was a small, beleaguered organization. A coalition of pacifists, Progressives shocked by wartime repression, and lawyers outraged at what they considered violations of Americans' legal rights, it saw its own pamphlets defending free speech barred from the mails by postal inspectors.

Prior to World War I, the Supreme Court had done almost nothing to protect the rights of unpopular minorities. Now, it was forced to address the question of the permissible limits on political and economic dissent. In its initial decisions, it dealt the concept of civil liberties a series of devastating blows. In 1919, the Court upheld the constitutionality of the Espionage Act and the conviction of Charles T. Schenck, a socialist who had distributed antidraft leaflets through the mails. Speaking for the Court, Justice Oliver Wendell Holmes declared that the First Amendment did not prevent Congress from prohibiting speech that presented a "clear and present danger" of inspiring illegal actions. Free speech, he observed, "would not protect a man in falsely shouting fire in a theater and causing a panic."

For the next half-century, Holmes's doctrine would remain the basic test in First Amendment cases. Since the Court usually allowed public officials to decide what speech was in fact "dangerous," it hardly provided a stable basis for the defense of free expression in times of crisis. A week after *Schenck v. United States*, the Court unanimously upheld the conviction of Eugene V. Debs for a speech condemning the war. It also affirmed the wartime jailing of the editor of a German-language newspaper whose editorials had questioned the draft's constitutionality.

THE COURT AND CIVIL LIBERTIES

Also in 1919, the Court upheld the conviction of Jacob Abrams and five other men for distributing pamphlets critical of American intervention in Russia after the Bolshevik revolution. This time, however, Holmes and Louis Brandeis dissented, marking the emergence of a court minority committed to a broader defense of free speech. Six years after *Abrams*, the two again dissented when the majority upheld the conviction of Benjamin Gitlow, a communist whose *Left-wing Manifesto* calling for revolution led to his conviction under a New York law prohibiting "criminal anarchy." "The only meaning of free speech," Holmes now declared, was that advocates of every set of beliefs, even "proletarian dictatorship," should have the right to convert the public to their views in the great "marketplace of ideas" (an apt metaphor for a consumer society). In approving Gitlow's conviction, the Court majority observed that the Fourteenth Amendment obligated the states to refrain from unreasonable restraints on freedom of speech and the press. The comment marked a major step in the long process by which the Bill of Rights was transformed from an ineffective statement of principle into a significant protection of Americans' freedoms.

The tide of civil-liberties decision making slowly began to turn. By the end of the 1920s, the Supreme Court had voided a Kansas law that made it a crime to advocate unlawful acts to change the political or economic system, and one from Minnesota authorizing censorship of the press. The new regard for free speech went beyond political expression. In 1930, the Court threw out the conviction of Mary Ware Dennett for sending a sex-education pamphlet, *The Sex Side of Life*, through the mails. Three years later, a federal court overturned the Customs Service's ban on James Joyce's novel *Ulysses*, a turning point in the battle against the censorship of works of literature.

Meanwhile, Brandeis was crafting an intellectual defense of civil liberties on grounds somewhat different from Holmes's model of a competitive market in ideas. In 1927, the Court upheld the conviction of the prominent California socialist and women's rights activist Anita Whitney for attending a convention of the Communist Labor Party where speakers advocated violent revolution.

Brandeis voted with the majority on technical grounds. But he issued a powerful defense of freedom of speech as essential to active citizenship in a democracy: "Those who won our independence believed . . . that freedom to think as you will and to speak as you think are indispensable to the discovery and spread of political truth. . . . The greatest menace to freedom is an inert people." A month after the decision, the governor of California pardoned Whitney, terming freedom of speech the "indispensable birthright of every free American." The intrepid Mrs. Whitney was soon back in court for violating a California law making it a crime to display a red flag. In 1931, the Supreme Court overturned the law as "repugnant to the guaranty of liberty contained in the Fourteenth Amendment." A judicial defense of civil liberties was slowly being born.

THE CULTURE WARS

THE FUNDAMENTALIST REVOLT

Although many Americans embraced modern urban culture with its religious and ethnic pluralism, mass entertainment, and liberated sexual rules, others found it alarming. Many evangelical Protestants felt threatened by the decline of traditional values and the increased visibility of Catholicism and Judaism because of immigration. They also resented the growing presence within mainstream Protestant denominations of "modernists" who sought to integrate science and religion and adapt Christianity to the new secular culture. "The day is past," declared Harry Emerson Fosdick, pastor of New York's First Presbyterian Church and a prominent modernist, "when you can ask thoughtful men to hold religion in one compartment of their minds and their modern world view in another."

Convinced that the literal truth of the Bible formed the basis of Christian belief, fundamentalists launched a campaign to rid Protestant denominations of modernism and to combat the new individual freedoms that seemed to contradict traditional morality. Their most flamboyant apostle was Billy Sunday, a talented professional baseball player who became a revivalist preacher. Between 1900 and 1930, Sunday drew huge crowds with a highly theatrical preaching style and a message denouncing sins ranging from Darwinism to alcohol. He was said to have preached to 100 million people during his lifetime—more than any other individual in history.

Much of the press portrayed fundamentalism as a movement of backwoods bigots. In fact, it was a national phenomenon. Even in New York City, the center of the new modern culture, Fosdick was removed from his ministry in 1924 (whereupon John D. Rockefeller Jr. built the interdenominational Riverside Church for him). Fundamentalism remained an important strain of 1920s culture and politics. Prohibition, which fundamentalists strongly supported,

A 1923 lithograph by George Bellows captures the dynamic style of the most prominent evangelical preacher of the 1920s, Billy Sunday.

succeeded in reducing the consumption of alcohol as well as public drunkenness and drink-related diseases. Not until 1975 would per capita consumption of alcohol reach its pre-Prohibition level of 2.6 gallons per year.

Prohibition, however, remained a deeply divisive issue. The greatest expansion of national authority since Reconstruction, it raised major questions of local rights, individual freedom, and the wisdom of attempting to impose religious and moral values on the entire society through legislation. It divided the Democratic Party into "wet" and "dry" wings, leading to bitter battles at the party's 1924 and 1928 national conventions. Too many Americans deemed Prohibition a violation of individual freedom for the flow of illegal liquor to stop. In urban areas, Prohibition led to large profits for the owners of illegal speakeasies and the "bootleggers" who supplied them. It produced widespread corruption as police and public officials accepted bribes to turn a blind eye to violations of the law. These developments reinforced fundamentalists' identification of urban life and modern notions of freedom with immorality and a decline of Christian liberty.

THE SCOPES TRIAL

In 1925, a trial in Tennessee threw into sharp relief the division between traditional values and modern, secular culture. John Scopes, a teacher in a Tennessee public school, was arrested for violating a state law that prohibited the teaching of Charles Darwin's theory of evolution. His trial became a national sensation. The proceedings were even carried live on national radio.

The Scopes trial reflected the enduring tension between two American definitions of freedom. Fundamentalist Christians, strongest in rural areas of the South and West, clung to the traditional idea of "moral" liberty—voluntary adherence to time-honored religious beliefs. The theory that man had evolved over millions of years from ancestors like apes contradicted the biblical account of creation. Those who upheld the Tennessee law identified evolutionists with feminists, socialists, and religious modernists, all of whom, they claimed, substituted human judgment for the word of God. To Scopes's defenders, including the American Civil Liberties Union, which had persuaded him to violate the law in order to test its constitutionality, freedom meant above all the right to independent thought and individual self-expression. To them, the Tennessee law offered a lesson in the dangers of religious intolerance and the merger of church and state.

The renowned labor lawyer Clarence Darrow defended Scopes. The trial's highlight came when Darrow called William Jennings Bryan to the stand as an "expert witness" on the Bible. Viewing the trial as a "duel to the death" between science and Christianity, he accepted Darrow's challenge. But Bryan revealed an almost complete ignorance of modern science and proved unable to respond effectively to Darrow's sarcastic questioning. Does the serpent really crawl on its belly as punishment for having tempted Eve in the Garden of Evil? When Bryan answered "yes," Darrow inquired how it got around before being cursed—on its tail? Asked whether God had actually created the world in six days, Bryan replied that these should be understood as ages, "not six days of twenty-four hours"—thus opening the door to the very nonliteral interpretation of the Bible fundamentalists rejected.

The jury found Scopes guilty, although the Tennessee supreme court later overturned the decision on a technicality. Shortly after the trial ended, Bryan died and the movement for anti-evolution laws disintegrated. Fundamentalists retreated for many years from battles over public education, preferring to build their own schools and colleges where teaching could be done as they saw fit and preachers were trained to spread their interpretation of Christianity. The battle would be rejoined, however, toward the end of the twentieth century, when fundamentalism reemerged as an important force in politics. To this day, the teaching of the theory of evolution in public schools arouses intense debate in parts of the United States.

THE SECOND KLAN

Few features of urban life seemed more alien to rural and small-town native-born Protestants than their immigrant populations and cultures. The wartime obsession with "100 percent Americanism" continued into the 1920s, a

A Ku Klux Klan gathering in Seattle, Washington, in 1923. The unrobed members of the audience are covering their faces to avoid identification. Unlike the Klan of the Reconstruction era, the second Ku Klux Klan was more powerful in the North and West than in the South.

decade of citizenship education programs in public schools, legally sanctioned visits to immigrants' homes to investigate their household arrangements, and vigorous efforts by employers to instill appreciation for "American values." Only "an agile and determined immigrant," commented the *Chicago Tribune*, could "hope to escape Americanization by at least one of the many processes now being prepared for his special benefit." In 1922, Oregon became the only state ever to require all students to attend public schools—a measure aimed, said the state's attorney general, at abolishing parochial education and preventing "bolshevists, syndicalists and communists" from organizing their own schools.

Perhaps the most menacing expression of the idea that enjoyment of American freedom should be limited on religious and ethnic grounds was the resurgence of the Ku Klux Klan in the early 1920s. The Klan had been reborn in Atlanta in 1915 after the lynching of Leo Frank, a Jewish factory manager accused of killing a teenage girl. By the mid-1920s, it claimed more than 3 million members, nearly all white, native-born Protestants, many of whom held respected positions in their communities. Unlike the Klan of Reconstruction, the organization now sank deep roots in parts of the North and West. It became the largest private organization in Indiana, and for a time controlled the state Republican Party. It was partly responsible for the Oregon law banning private schools. In southern California, its large marches and auto parades made the Klan a visible presence. The new Klan attacked a far broader array of targets than during Reconstruction. American civilization, it insisted, was endangered not only by blacks but by immigrants (especially Jews and Catholics) and all the forces (feminism, unions, immorality, even, on occasion, the giant corporations) that endangered "individual liberty."

CLOSING THE GOLDEN DOOR

The Klan's influence faded after 1925, when its leader in Indiana was convicted of assaulting a young woman. But the Klan's attacks on modern secular culture and political radicalism and its demand that control of the nation be returned to "citizens of the old stock" reflected sentiments widely shared in the 1920s. The decade witnessed a flurry of legislation that offered a new answer to the venerable question "Who is an American?" Some new laws redrew the boundary of citizenship to include groups previously outside it. With women now recognized as part of the political nation, Congress in the Cable Act of 1922 overturned the 1907 law requiring American women who married foreigners to assume the citizenship of the husband—except in the case of those who married Asians, who still forfeited their nationality. Two years later, it declared all Indians born in the United States to be American citizens, although many western states continued to deny the vote to those living on reservations.

Far more sweeping was a fundamental change in immigration policy. Immigration restriction had a long history. The Naturalization Act of 1790 had barred blacks and Asians from naturalization, with the ban lifted for the former in 1870. Beginning in 1875, various classes of immigrants had been excluded, among them prostitutes, the mentally retarded, and those with contagious diseases. Nonetheless, prior to World War I virtually all the white persons who wished to pass through the "golden door" into the United States and become citizens were able to do so. During the 1920s, however, the pressure for wholesale immigration restriction became irresistible. One index of the changing political climate was that large employers dropped their traditional opposition. Fears of immigrant radicalism now outweighed the desire for cheap unskilled labor, especially since mechanization had halted the growth of the industrial labor force and the Great Migration of World War I had accustomed industrialists to employing African-Americans.

In 1921, a temporary measure restricted immigration from Europe to 357,000 per year (one-third of the annual average before the war). Three years later, Congress permanently limited European immigration to 150,000 per year, distributed according to a series of national quotas that severely restricted the numbers from southern and eastern Europe. The law aimed to ensure that descendants of the old immigrants forever outnumbered the children of the new. However, to satisfy the demands of large farmers in California who relied heavily on seasonal Mexican labor, the 1924 law established no limits on immigration from the Western Hemisphere.

The 1924 law did bar the entry of all those ineligible for naturalized citizenship—that is, the entire population of Asia, even though Japan had fought on the American side in World War I. The only Asians still able to enter the United States were residents of the Philippines, who were deemed to be "American nationals" (although not citizens) because the islands had been U.S. territory since the Spanish-American War. Largely to bar further Philippine immigration, Congress in 1934 established a timetable for the islands' independence, which was finally achieved in 1946. The 1934 law established an immigration quota of fifty Filipinos a year to the mainland United States, but allowed their continued entry into the Hawaiian Islands to work as plantation laborers.

Although a few Chinese had tried to enter the country in the past in spite of exclusion legislation, the law of 1924 established, in effect, for the first time a new category—the "illegal alien." With it came a new enforcement mechanism, the Border Patrol, charged with policing the land boundaries of the United States and empowered to arrest and deport persons who entered the country in violation of the new nationality quotas or other restrictions. Later associated almost exclusively with Latinos, "illegal aliens" at first referred mainly to southern and eastern Europeans who tried to sneak across the border from Mexico or Canada.

RACE AND THE LAW

The new immigration law reflected the heightened emphasis on "race" as a determinant of public policy. By the early 1920s, political leaders of both North and South agreed upon the relegation of blacks to second-class citizenship. In a speech in Alabama in 1921, President Harding unconsciously echoed W. E. B. Du Bois by affirming that the "problem" of race was a global one, not confined to the South. Unlike Du Bois, he believed the South showed the way to the problem's solution. "It would be helpful," he added, "to have that word 'equality' eliminated from this consideration." Clearly, the Republican Party of the Civil War era was dead.

But "race policy" meant far more than black-white relations. "America must be kept American," declared President Coolidge in signing the 1924 immigration law. His secretary of labor, James J. Davis, commented that immigration policy, once based on the need for labor and the notion of the United States as an asylum of liberty, must now rest on a biological definition of the ideal population. Although enacted by a highly conservative Congress strongly influenced by nativism, the 1924 immigration law also reflected the Progressive desire to improve the "quality" of democratic citizenship and to employ scientific methods to set public policy. It revealed how these aims were overlaid with pseudo-scientific assumptions about the superiority and inferiority of particular "races."

The seemingly "scientific" calculation of the new quotas—based on the "national origins" of the American population dating back to 1790—involved a highly speculative analysis of past census returns, with the results altered to increase allowable immigration by politically influential groups like Irish-Americans. Non-whites (one-fifth of the population in 1790) were excluded altogether when calculating quotas—otherwise, Africa would have received a far higher quota than the tiny number allotted to it. But then, the entire concept of race as a basis for public policy lacked any rational foundation. The Supreme Court admitted as much in 1923 when it rejected the claim of Bhagat Singh Thind, an Indian-born World War I veteran, who asserted that as a "pure Aryan," he was actually white and could therefore become an American citizen. "White," the Court declared, was not a scientific concept at all, but part of "common speech, to be interpreted with the understanding of the common man" (a forthright statement of what later scholars would call the "social construction" of race).

PLURALISM AND LIBERTY

During the 1920s, some Americans challenged the idea that southern and eastern Europeans were unfit to become citizens, or could only do so by abandoning their traditions in favor of Anglo-Saxon ways. Horace Kallen, himself of German-Jewish origin, in 1924 coined the phrase "cultural pluralism" to describe a society that gloried in ethnic diversity rather than attempting to suppress it. Toleration of difference was part of the "American Idea," Kallen wrote. Anthropologists like Franz Boas, Alfred Kroeber, and Ruth Benedict insisted that no scientific basis existed for theories of racial superiority or for the notion that societies and races could be ranked on a fixed scale running from "primitive" to "civilized."

These writings, however, had little immediate impact on public policy. In the 1920s, the most potent defense of a pluralist vision of American society came from the new immigrants themselves. Every major city still contained ethnic enclaves with their own civic institutions, theaters, churches, and foreign-language newspapers. Their sense of separate identity had been heightened by the emergence of independent nation-states in eastern Europe after the war. It would be wrong, to be sure, to view ethnic communities as united in opposition to Americanization. In a society increasingly knit together by mass culture and a consumer economy, few could escape the pull of assimilation. The department store, dance hall, and motion picture theater were as much agents of Americanization as the school and workplace. From the perspective of many immigrant women, moreover, assimilation often seemed not so much the loss of an inherited culture as a loosening of patriarchal bonds and an expansion of freedom. But most immigrants resented the coercive aspects of Americanization programs, so often based on the idea of the superiority of Protestant mainstream culture.

PROMOTING TOLERANCE

In the face of immigration restriction, Prohibition, a revived Ku Klux Klan, and widespread anti-Semitism and anti-Catholicism, immigrant groups asserted the validity of cultural diversity and identified toleration of difference—religious, cultural, and individual—as the essence of American freedom. In effect, they reinvented themselves as "ethnic" Americans, claiming an equal share in the nation's life but, in addition, the right to remain in many respects culturally distinct. The Roman Catholic Church urged immigrants to learn English and embrace "American principles," but it continued to maintain separate schools and other institutions. In 1924, the Catholic Holy Name Society brought 10,000 marchers to Washington to challenge the Klan and to affirm Catholics' loyalty to the nation. Throughout the country, organizations like the Anti-Defamation League of B'nai B'rith (founded in 1916 to combat anti-Semitism) and the National Catholic Welfare Council lobbied, in the name of "personal liberty," for laws prohibiting discrimination against immigrants by employers, colleges, and government agencies. The Americanization movement, declared a Polish newspaper in Chicago, had "not the smallest particle of the true American spirit, the spirit of freedom, the brightest virtue of which is the broadest possible tolerance."

The efforts of immigrant communities to resist coerced Americanization and of the Catholic Church to defend its school system broadened the definition of liberty for all Americans. In landmark decisions, the Supreme Court struck down Oregon's law, mentioned earlier, requiring all students to attend public schools and Nebraska's prohibiting teaching in a language other than English—one of the anti-German measures of World War I. "The protection of the Constitution," the decision in *Meyer v. Nebraska* (1923) declared, "extends to all, to those who speak other languages as well as to those born with English on the tongue," a startling rebuke to enforced Americanization. The decision expanded the freedom of all immigrant groups. In its aftermath, federal courts overturned various Hawaii laws imposing special taxes and regulations on private Japanese-language schools. In these cases, the Court also interpreted the Fourteenth Amendment's guarantee of equal liberty to include the right to "marry, establish a home and bring up children" and to practice religion as one chose, "without interference from the state." The decisions gave pluralism a constitutional foundation and paved the way for the Court's elaboration, two generations later, of a constitutional right to privacy.

THE EMERGENCE OF HARLEM

The 1920s also witnessed an upsurge of self-consciousness among black Americans, especially in the North's urban ghettos. With European immigration all but halted, the Great Migration of World War I continued apace. Nearly 1 million blacks left the South during the 1920s, and the black population of New York, Chicago, and other urban centers more than doubled. New York's Harlem gained an international reputation as the "capital" of black America, a mecca for migrants from the South and immigrants from the West Indies, 150,000 of whom entered the United States between 1900 and 1930. Unlike the southern newcomers, most of whom had been agricultural workers, the West Indians included a large number of well-educated professional and white-collar workers. Their encounter with American racism appalled them. "I had heard of prejudice in America," wrote the poet and novelist Claude McKay, who emigrated from Jamaica in 1912, "but never dreamed of it being so intensely bitter."

The 1920s became famous for "slumming," as groups of whites visited Harlem's dance halls, jazz clubs, and speakeasies in search of exotic adventure. The Harlem of the white imagination was a place of primitive passions, free from the puritanical restraints of mainstream American culture. The real Harlem was a community of widespread poverty, its residents confined to low-wage jobs and, because housing discrimination barred them from other neighborhoods, forced to pay exorbitant rents. Most Harlem businesses were owned by whites; even the famed Cotton Club excluded black customers and employed only light-skinned dancers in its renowned chorus line. Few blacks, North or South, shared in the prosperity of the 1920s.

THE HARLEM RENAISSANCE

But Harlem also contained a vibrant black cultural community that established links with New York's artistic mainstream. Poets and novelists like Countee Cullen, Langston Hughes, and Claude McKay were befriended and

A black family arriving in Chicago in 1922, as part of the Great Migration from the rural South.

sponsored by white intellectuals and published by white presses. Broadway for the first time presented black actors in serious dramatic roles, as well as shows like *Dixie to Broadway and Blackbirds* that featured great entertainers like the singers Florence Mills and Ethel Waters and the tap dancer Bill Robinson. At the same time, the theater flourished in Harlem, freeing black writers and actors from the constraints imposed by white producers.

The term "New Negro," associated in politics with pan-Africanism and the militancy of the Garvey movement, in art meant the rejection of established stereotypes and a search for black values to put in their place. This quest led the writers of what came to be called the Harlem Renaissance to the roots of the black experience—Africa, the rural South's folk traditions, and the life of the urban ghetto. Claude McKay made the major character of his novel *Home to Harlem* (1928) a free spirit who wandered from one scene of exotic life to another in search of a beautiful girl he had known. W. E. B. Du Bois feared that a novel like McKay's, with its graphic sex and violence, actually reinforced white prejudices about black life. Harlem Renaissance writings, however, also contained a strong element of protest. This mood was exemplified by McKay's poem "If We Must Die," a response to the race riots of 1919. The poem affirmed that blacks would no longer allow themselves to be murdered defenselessly by whites:

> If we must die, let it not be like hogs
> Hunted and penned in an inglorious spot,
> While round us bark the mad and hungry dogs,
> Making their mock at our accursed lot. . . .
> Like men we'll face the murderous, cowardly pack,
> Pressed to the wall, dying, but fighting back!

Winston Churchill would invoke McKay's words to inspire the British public during World War II. The celebrated case of Ossian Sweet, a black physician who moved into a previously all-white Detroit neighborhood in 1925, reflected the new spirit of assertiveness among many African-Americans. When a white mob attacked his home, someone (probably Sweet's brother) fired into the crowd, killing a man. Indicted for murder along with his two brothers, Sweet was defended by Clarence Darrow, fresh from his participation in the Scopes trial. The jury proved unable to agree on a verdict. A second prosecution, of Sweet's brother, ended in acquittal.

THE GREAT DEPRESSION

THE ELECTION OF 1928

Few men elected as president have seemed destined for a more successful term in office than Herbert Hoover. Born in Iowa in 1874, the son of a blacksmith and his schoolteacher wife, Hoover accumulated a fortune as a mining engineer working for firms in Asia, Africa, and Europe. During and immediately after World War I, he gained international fame by coordinating overseas food relief. The British economist John Maynard Keynes, a severe critic of the 1919 Versailles Treaty, called Hoover "the only man" to emerge from the peace conference "with an enhanced reputation." He "had never known failure," wrote the novelist Sherwood Anderson. Hoover seemed to exemplify what was widely called the "new era" of American capitalism. In 1922, while serving as secretary of commerce, he published *American Individualism*, which condemned government regulation as an interference with the economic opportunities of ordinary Americans, but also insisted that self-interest should be subordinated to public service. Hoover considered himself a Progressive, although he preferred what he called "associational action," in which private agencies directed regulatory and welfare policies, to government intervention in the economy.

After "silent Cal" Coolidge in 1927 handed a piece of paper to a group of reporters that stated, "I do not choose to run for president in 1928," Hoover quickly emerged as his successor. Accepting the Republican nomination, Hoover celebrated the decade's prosperity and promised that poverty would "soon be banished from this earth." His Democratic opponent was Alfred E. Smith, the first Catholic to be nominated by a major party. Born into poverty on New York's Lower East Side, Smith had become a fixture in Tammany Hall politics. Although he had no family connection with the new immigrants from southern and eastern Europe (his grandparents had emigrated from Ireland), Smith emerged as their symbolic spokesman. The Triangle fire of 1911 made him an advocate of Progressive social legislation. He served three terms as governor of New York, securing -passage of laws limiting the hours of working women and children and establishing widows' pensions. Smith denounced the Red Scare and called for the repeal of Prohibition. His bid for the Democratic nomination in 1924 had been blocked by delegates beholden to nativists and Klansmen, but he secured the nod four years later.

Given the prevailing prosperity and his own sterling reputation, Hoover's victory was inevitable. Other than on Prohibition, moreover, the Democratic platform did not differ much from the Republican one, leaving little to discuss except the candidates' personalities and religions. Smith's Catholicism became the focus of the race. Many Protestant ministers and religious publications denounced him for his faith. For the first time since Reconstruction, Republicans carried several southern states, reflecting the strength of anti-Catholicism and nativism among religious fundamentalists. "Hoover," wrote one previously Democratic southern newspaper editor, "is sprung from American soil and stock," while Smith represented "the aliens." On the other hand, Smith carried the nation's twelve largest cities and won significant support in economically struggling farm areas. With more than 58 percent of the vote, Hoover was elected by a landslide. But Smith's campaign helped to lay the foundation for the triumphant Democratic coalition of the 1930s, based on urban ethnic voters, farmers, and the South.

THE COMING OF THE DEPRESSION

On October 21, 1929, President Hoover traveled to Michigan to take part in the Golden Anniversary of the Festival of Light, organized by Henry Ford to commemorate the invention of the lightbulb by Thomas Edison fifty years earlier. Hoover's speech was a tribute to progress, and especially to the businessmen and scientists from whose efforts "we gain constantly in better standards of living, more stability of employment . . . and decreased suffering." Eight days later, on Black Tuesday, the stock market crashed. As panic selling set in, more than $10 billion in market value (equivalent to more than ten times that amount in today's money) vanished in five hours. Soon, the United States and, indeed, the entire world found itself in the grip of the Great Depression, the greatest economic disaster in modern history.

The stock market crash did not, by itself, cause the Depression. Even before 1929, signs of economic trouble had become evident. Southern California and Florida experienced frenzied real-estate speculation and then spectacular busts, with banks failing, land remaining undeveloped, and mortgages foreclosed. The highly unequal distribution of income and the prolonged depression in farm regions reduced American purchasing power. Sales of new autos and household consumer goods stagnated after 1926. European demand for American goods also declined, partly because industry there had recovered from wartime destruction.

A fall in the bloated stock market, driven ever higher during the 1920s by speculators, was inevitable. But it came with such severity that it destroyed many of the investment companies that had been created to buy and sell stock, wiping out thousands of investors, and it greatly reduced business and consumer confidence. Around 26,000 businesses failed in 1930. Those that survived cut back on further investment and began laying off workers. The global financial system, which was based on the gold standard, was ill-equipped to deal with the downturn. Germany defaulted on reparations payments to France and Britain, leading these governments to stop repaying debts to American banks. Throughout the industrial world, banks failed as depositors withdrew money, fearful that they could no longer count on the promise to redeem paper money in gold. Millions of families lost their life savings.

Although stocks recovered somewhat in 1930, they soon resumed their relentless downward slide. Between 1929 and 1932, the price of a share of U.S. Steel fell from $262 to $22, and General Motors from $73 to $8. Four-fifths of the Rockefeller family fortune disappeared. William C. Durant, one of the founders of General Motors, lost all his money and ended up running a bowling alley in Flint, Michigan. In 1932, the economy hit rock bottom. Since 1929, the gross national product (the value of all the goods and services in the country) had fallen by one-third, prices by nearly 40 percent, and more than 11 million Americans—25 percent of the labor force—could not find work. U.S. Steel, which had employed 225,000 full-time workers in 1929, had none at the end of 1932, when it was operating at only 12 percent of capacity. Those who retained their jobs confronted reduced hours and dramatically reduced wages. Every industrial economy suffered, but the United States, which had led the way in prosperity in the 1920s, was hit hardest of all.

AMERICANS AND THE DEPRESSION

The Depression transformed American life. Hundreds of thousands of people took to the road in search of work. Hungry men and women lined the streets of major cities. In Detroit, 4,000 children stood in bread lines each day seeking food. Thousands of families, evicted from their homes, moved into ramshackle shantytowns, dubbed Hoovervilles, that sprang up in parks and on abandoned land. Cities quickly spent the little money they had available for poor relief. In Chicago, where half the working population was unemployed at the beginning of 1932, Mayor Anton Cermak telephoned people individually, begging them to pay their taxes. "We saw want and despair walking the streets," wrote a Chicago social worker, "and our friends, sensible, thrifty families, reduced to poverty." When the Soviet Union advertised its need for skilled workers, it received more than 100,000 applications from the United States.

The Depression actually reversed the long-standing movement of population from farms to cities. Many Americans left cities to try to grow food for their families. In 1935, 33 million people lived on farms—more than at any previous point in American history. But rural areas, already poor, saw families reduce the number of meals per day and children go barefoot. With the future shrouded in uncertainty, the American suicide rate rose to the highest level in the nation's history, and the birthrate fell to the lowest.

"The American way of life," the confident slogan of the consumer culture, and common sayings like "safe as a bank" took on a hollow ring. The image of big business, carefully cultivated during the 1920s, collapsed as congressional investigations revealed massive irregularities committed by bankers and stockbrokers. Banks had knowingly sold worthless bonds. Prominent Wall Streeters had unloaded their own portfolios while advising small investors to maintain their holdings. Richard Whitney, the president of the New York Stock Exchange, was convicted of stealing funds from customers, including from a fund to aid widows and orphans. He ended up in jail.

The celebrated photographer Dorothea Lange took this photograph of an unemployed man on a San Francisco breadline in 1933.

RESIGNATION AND PROTEST

Many Americans reacted to the Depression with resignation or blamed themselves for economic misfortune. Others responded with protests that were at first spontaneous and uncoordinated, since unions, socialist organizations, and other groups that might have provided disciplined leadership had been decimated during the 1920s. In the spring of 1932, 20,000 unemployed World War I veterans descended on Washington to demand early payment of a bonus due in 1945, only to be driven away by federal soldiers led by the army's chief of staff, Douglas MacArthur. Throughout the country, the unemployed demonstrated for jobs and public relief. That summer, led by the charismatic Milo Reno, a former Iowa Populist, the National Farmers' Holiday Association protested low prices by temporarily blocking roads in the Midwest to prevent farm goods from getting to market.

Only the minuscule Communist Party seemed able to give a political focus to the anger and despair. "The most fully employed persons I met during the Depression," one labor leader later recalled, "were the Communists." They "brought misery out of hiding," forming unemployed councils, sponsoring marches and demonstrations for public assistance, and protesting the eviction of unemployed families from their homes. The press discussed the idea that the United States was on the verge of a revolution. The insurance firm Lloyd's of London reported an upsurge in American requests for riot insurance. The Hoover administration in 1931 opposed efforts to save money by reducing the size of the army, warning that this would "lessen our means of maintaining domestic peace and order."

HOOVER'S RESPONSE

In the eyes of many Americans, President Hoover's response to the Depression seemed inadequate and uncaring. Leading advisers, including Andrew Mellon, the wealthy secretary of the treasury, told Hoover that economic downturns were a normal part of capitalism, which weeded out unproductive firms and encouraged moral virtue among the less fortunate. Businessmen strongly opposed federal aid to the unemployed, and many publications called for individual "belt-tightening" as the road to recovery. Some initially saw a silver lining in the Depression. Wages had fallen so sharply, reported *Fortune* magazine, that "you can have your garden taken care of in Los Angeles for $1 a week" or hire an "affable Negro to fry your chicken and do your washing for $8 a month in Virginia."

The federal government had never faced an economic crisis as severe as the Great Depression. Few political leaders understood how important consumer spending had become in the American economy. Most held to the conventional view that government intervention to aid those who had lost their jobs would do little to spur economic recovery and would encourage Americans to rely on government charity to address misfortune. In 1931, Hoover quoted former president Grover Cleveland from four decades earlier: "The Government should not support the people. . . . Federal aid . . . weakens the sturdiness of our national character."

Strongly opposed on principle to direct federal intervention in the economy, Hoover remained committed to "associational action." He put his faith in voluntary steps by business to maintain investment and employment—something few found it possible to do—and efforts by local charity organizations to assist needy neighbors. He called numerous conferences of business and labor leaders and established commissions to encourage firms to cooperate in maintaining prices and wages without governmental dictation. Hoover attempted to restore public confidence, making frequent public statements that "the tide had turned." But these made him increasingly seem out of touch with reality. About the unemployed men who appeared on city streets offering apples at five cents apiece, Hoover would later write, "Many persons left their jobs for the more profitable one of selling apples."

THE WORSENING ECONOMIC OUTLOOK

Some administration remedies, like the Smoot-Hawley Tariff, which Hoover signed with some reluctance in 1930, made the economic situation worse. Raising the already high taxes on imported goods, it inspired similar increases abroad, further reducing international trade. A tax increase Hoover pushed through Congress in 1932 in an attempt to balance the federal budget further reduced Americans' purchasing power. Other initiatives inspired ridicule. When he approved funds to provide food for livestock, one observer remarked that the president would feed "jackasses but . . . not starving babies."

By 1932, Hoover had to admit that voluntary action had failed to stem the Depression. He signed laws creating the Reconstruction Finance Corporation, which loaned money to failing banks, railroads, and other businesses, and the Federal Home Loan Bank System, which offered aid to home owners threatened with foreclosure. Having vetoed previous bills to create employment through public-works projects like road and bridge construction, he now approved a measure appropriating nearly $2 billion for such initiatives and helping to fund local relief efforts. These were dramatic departures from previous federal economic policy. But further than this, Hoover would not go. He adamantly opposed offering direct relief to the unemployed—it would do them a "disservice," he told Congress.

FREEDOM IN THE MODERN WORLD

In 1927, the New School for Social Research in New York City organized a series of lectures on the theme of Freedom in the Modern World. Founded eight years earlier as a place where "free thought and intellectual integrity" could flourish in the wake of wartime repression, the school's distinguished faculty included the philosopher John Dewey and historian Charles Beard (who had resigned from Columbia University in 1917 to protest the dismissal of antiwar professors). The lectures painted a depressing portrait of American freedom on the eve of the Great Depression. "The idea of freedom," declared economist Walton H. Hamilton, had become "an intellectual instrument for looking backward.... Liberty of contract has been made the be-all and end-all of personal freedom; . . . the domain of business has been defended against control from without in the name of freedom." The free exchange of ideas, moreover, had not recovered from the crisis of World War I. The "sacred dogmas of patriotism and Big Business," said the educator Horace Kallen, dominated teaching, the press, and public debate. A definition of freedom reigned supreme that celebrated the unimpeded reign of economic enterprise yet tolerated the surveillance of private life and individual conscience.

The prosperity of the 1920s had reinforced this definition of freedom. With the economic crash, compounded by the ineffectiveness of the Hoover administration's response, it would be discredited. By 1932, the seeds had already been planted for a new conception of freedom that combined two different elements in a sometimes uneasy synthesis. One was the Progressive belief in a socially conscious state making what Dewey called "positive and constructive changes" in economic arrangements. The other, which arose in the 1920s, centered on respect for civil liberties and cultural pluralism and declared that realms of life like group identity, personal behavior, and the free expression of ideas lay outside legitimate state concern. These two principles would become the hallmarks of modern liberalism, which during the 1930s would redefine American freedom.

Chapter Review

REVIEW QUESTIONS

1. How did consumerism and the idea of the "American way of life" affect people's understanding of American values, including the meaning of freedom, in the 1920s?
2. Which groups did not share in the prosperity of the 1920s and why?
3. How did business practices and policies lead to a decline in union membership in the 1920s?
4. President Calvin Coolidge said that "the chief business of the American people is business." How did the federal government's policies and practices in the 1920s reflect this understanding of the importance of business interests?
5. Who supported restricting immigration in the 1920s and why? Why were they more successful in gaining federal legislation to limit immigration in these years?
6. Did U.S. society in the 1920s reflect the concept of cultural pluralism as explained by Horace Kallen? Why or why not?
7. Identify the causes of the Great Depression.
8. What principles guided President Hoover's response to the Great Depression, and how did this restrict his ability to help the American people?
9. What issues were of particular concern to religious fundamentalists in these years and why?
10. In what ways did the ideas about (and the reality of) proper roles for women change in these years?

KEY TERMS

Sacco-Vanzetti case
rise of the stock market
"welfare capitalism"
Equal Rights Amendment
the "flapper"
Adkins v. Children's Hospital
Teapot Dome scandal
McNary-Haugen farm bill
Hays code
American Civil Liberties Union

"clear and present danger"
fundamentalism
Scopes trial
second Ku Klux Klan
immigration restriction
"illegal alien"
the "New Negro"
stock market crash
bonus marchers
Reconstruction Finance Corporation

wwnorton.com/studyspace

VISIT STUDYSPACE FOR THESE RESOURCES AND MORE:

- Author Videos
- A chapter outline
- A practice quiz
- Interactive maps
- Multimedia documents

CHAPTER 6

THE NEW DEAL

From *Give Me Liberty! Seagull* *Fourth Edition*

Eric Foner

6

The New Deal 1932–1940

FOCUS QUESTIONS

- What were the major policy initiatives of the New Deal in the Hundred Days?
- Who were the main proponents of economic justice in the 1930s, and what measures did they advocate?
- What were the major initiatives of the Second New Deal, and how did they differ from the First New Deal?
- How did the New Deal recast the meaning of American freedom?
- How did New Deal benefits apply to women and minorities?
- How did the Popular Front influence American culture in the 1930s?

Early in 1941, the unemployed Woody Guthrie, soon to become one of the country's most popular songwriters and folk singers, brought his family to Portland, Oregon. He hoped to star in a film about the great public-works projects under way on the Columbia River. Given a temporary job by the Bonneville Power Authority, the public agency that controlled the Columbia dams, Guthrie produced a song every day for the next month. One, "Roll on, Columbia," became a popular statement of the benefits that resulted when government took the lead in improving the lot of ordinary citizens:

> And on up the river is the Grand Coulee Dam,
> The biggest thing built by the hand of a man,
> To run the great factories and water the land,

So, roll on, Columbia, roll on. . . .
Your power is turning our darkness to dawn.
So, roll on, Columbia, roll on. ©

The Columbia River winds its way on a 1,200-mile course from Canada through Washington and Oregon to the Pacific Ocean. Because of its steep descent from uplands to sea level, it produces an immense amount of energy. Residents of the economically underdeveloped Pacific Northwest had long dreamed of tapping this unused energy for electricity and irrigation. But not until the 1930s did the federal government launch the program of dam construction that transformed the region. The project created thousands of jobs for the unemployed, and the network of dams produced abundant cheap power.

When the Grand Coulee Dam went into operation in 1941, it was the largest man-made structure in world history. It eventually produced more than 40 percent of the nation's hydroelectric power. The dam provided the cheapest electricity in the country for towns that sprang up out of nowhere, farms on what had once been deserts in eastern Washington and Oregon,

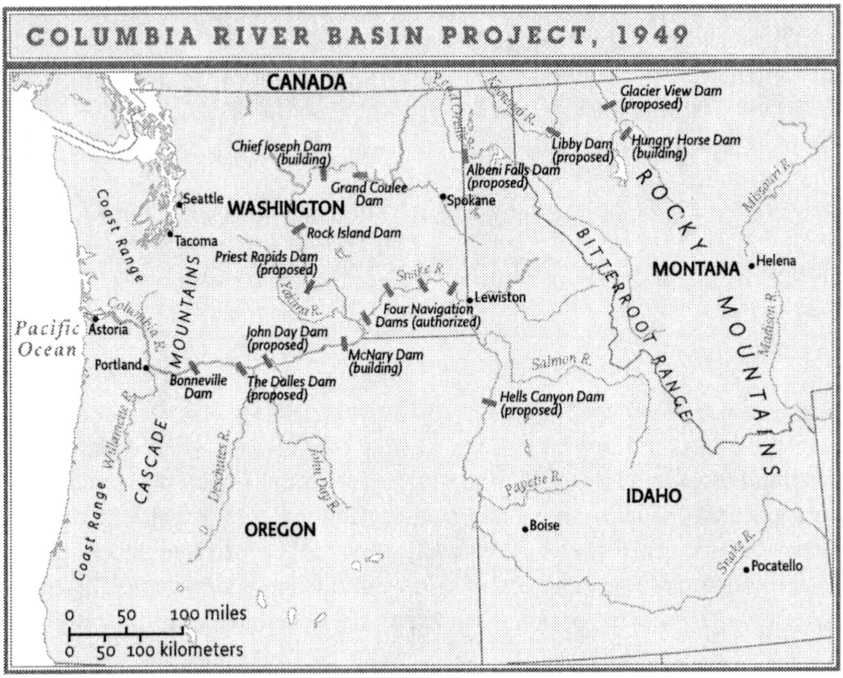

A 1949 map of the Columbia River project, showing its numerous dams, including the Grand Coulee, the largest man-made structure in the world at the time of its opening in 1941.

and factories that would soon be producing aluminum for World War II airplanes. The project also had less appealing consequences. From time immemorial, the Columbia River had been filled with salmon. But the Grand Coulee Dam made no provision for the passage of fish, and the salmon all but vanished. This caused little concern during the Depression but became a source of controversy later in the century as Americans became more concerned about preserving the natural environment.

The Grand Coulee Dam was part of what one scholar has called a "public works revolution" that transformed the American economy and landscape during the 1930s. The Roosevelt administration spent far more money on building roads, dams, airports, bridges, and housing than on any other activity.

Franklin D. Roosevelt believed regional economic development like that in the Northwest would promote economic growth, ease the domestic and working lives of ordinary Americans, and keep control of key natural resources in public rather than private hands. "It promises," one supporter wrote, "a world replete with more freedom and happiness than mankind has ever known."

The Columbia River project reflected broader changes in American life and thought during the New Deal of the 1930s. Roosevelt oversaw the transformation of the Democratic Party into a coalition of farmers, industrial workers, the reform-minded urban middle class, liberal intellectuals, northern African-Americans, and, somewhat incongruously, the white supremacist South, united by the belief that the federal government must provide Americans with protection against the dislocations caused by modern capitalism. "Liberalism," traditionally understood as limited government and free market economics, took on its modern meaning. Thanks to the New Deal, it now referred to active efforts by the national government to modernize and regulate the market economy and to uplift less fortunate members of society.

Freedom, too, underwent a transformation during the 1930s. The Depression had discredited the ideas that social progress rests on the unrestrained pursuit of wealth and that, apart from unfortunates like widows and orphans, most poverty is self-inflicted. The New Deal elevated a public guarantee of economic security to the forefront of American discussions of freedom. The 1930s were a decade of dramatic social upheaval. Social and political activists, most notably a revitalized labor movement, placed new issues on the political agenda. When one writer in 1941 published a survey of democratic thought beginning in the ancient world, he concluded that what distinguished his own time was its awareness of "the social conditions of freedom." Thanks to the New Deal, he wrote, "economic security" had "at last been recognized as a political condition of personal freedom." Regional economic development like that in the Northwest reflected this understanding of freedom. So did other New Deal measures, including the Social Security Act, which offered aid to the unemployed and aged, and the Fair Labor Standards Act, which established a national minimum wage.

Yet while the New Deal significantly expanded the meaning of freedom, it did not erase freedom's boundaries. Its benefits flowed to industrial workers but not tenant farmers, to men far more fully than to women, and to white Americans more than blacks, who, in the South, still were deprived of the basic rights of citizenship.

THE FIRST NEW DEAL

FDR AND THE ELECTION OF 1932

It is indeed paradoxical that Franklin D. Roosevelt, who had been raised in privilege on a New York country estate, came to be beloved as the symbolic representative of ordinary citizens. But like Lincoln, with whom he is often compared, Roosevelt's greatness lay in his willingness to throw off the "dogmas of the quiet past" (Lincoln's words) to confront an unprecedented national crisis. FDR, as he liked to be called, was born in 1882, a fifth cousin of Theodore Roosevelt. He graduated from Harvard in 1904 and six years later won election to the New York legislature from Dutchess County, site of his family's home at Hyde Park. After serving as undersecretary of the navy during World War I, he ran for vice president on the ill-fated Democratic ticket of 1920 headed by James M. Cox. In 1921, he contracted polio and lost the use of his legs, a fact carefully concealed from the public in that pre-television era. Very few Americans realized that the president who projected an image of vigorous leadership during the 1930s and World War II was confined to a wheelchair.

In his speech accepting the Democratic nomination for president in 1932, Roosevelt promised a "new deal" for the American people. But his campaign offered only vague hints of what this might entail. Roosevelt spoke of the government's responsibility to guarantee "every man . . . a right to make a comfortable living." But he also advocated a balanced federal budget and criticized his opponent, President Hoover, for excessive government spending. The biggest difference between the parties during the campaign was the Democrats' call for the repeal of Prohibition, although Roosevelt certainly suggested a greater awareness of the plight of ordinary Americans and a willingness to embark on new ways to address the Great Depression. Battered by the economic crisis, Americans in 1932 were desperate for new leadership, and Roosevelt won a resounding victory. He received 57 percent of the popular vote, and Democrats swept to a commanding majority in Congress.

THE COMING OF THE NEW DEAL

The Depression did not produce a single pattern of international public response. For nearly the entire decade of the 1930s, conservative governments ruled Britain and France. They were more interested in preserving public order than relieving suffering or embarking on policy innovations. In Germany, Adolf Hitler, leader of the Nazi Party, established one of the most brutal dictatorships in human history. Hitler banned all political opposition and launched a reign of terror against Jews and others deemed to be "un-German." In the Soviet Union, another tyrant, Joseph Stalin, embarked on successive five-year plans that at great social cost produced rapid industrialization and claimed to have eliminated unemployment. The militarist government of Japan invaded China in 1937, and hoped to extend its rule throughout Asia.

Roosevelt conceived of the New Deal as an alternative to socialism on the left, Nazism on the right, and the inaction of upholders of unregulated capitalism. He hoped to reconcile democracy, individual liberty, and economic recovery and development. "You have made

CHRONOLOGY

1931	Scottsboro case
1933	Franklin Roosevelt inaugurated president
	Bank holiday
	The Hundred Days and the First New Deal
	21st Amendment ratified
1934	Huey Long launches the Share Our Wealth movement
	American Liberty League established
	Herbert Hoover's *The Challenge to Liberty*
1934–1940	Height of the Dust Bowl
1935	Second New Deal launched
	Supreme Court rules the National Recovery Association unconstitutional
	John L. Lewis organizes the Congress of Industrial Organizations
1936	Supreme Court rules the Agricultural Adjustment Act unconstitutional
	New Deal coalition leads to Democratic landslide
	John Maynard Keynes's *The General Theory of Employment, Interest, and Money*
1936–1937	United Auto Workers sit-down strike

1938	House Un-American Activities Committee established
	Fair Labor Standards Act passed
1939	John Steinbeck's *The Grapes of Wrath*

yourself," the British economist John Maynard Keynes wrote to FDR, "the trustee for those in every country who seek to mend the evils of our condition by reasoned experiment within the framework of the existing social system." If Roosevelt failed, Keynes added, the only remaining choice would be "orthodoxy" (that is, doing nothing) or "revolution."

Roosevelt did not enter office with a blueprint for dealing with the Depression. At first, he relied heavily for advice on a group of intellectuals and social workers who took up key positions in his administration. They included Secretary of Labor Frances Perkins, a veteran of Hull House and the New York Consumers' League who had been among the eyewitnesses to the Triangle fire of 1911; Harry Hopkins, who had headed emergency relief efforts during Roosevelt's term as governor of New York; Secretary of the Interior Harold Ickes, a veteran of Theodore Roosevelt's Progressive campaign of 1912; and Louis Brandeis, who had advised Woodrow Wilson during the 1912 campaign and now offered political advice to FDR while serving on the Supreme Court.

The presence of these individuals reflected how Roosevelt drew on the reform traditions of the Progressive era. But Progressivism was hardly a unified movement, and Roosevelt's advisers did not speak with one voice. Brandeis believed that large corporations not only wielded excessive power but had contributed to the Depression by keeping prices artificially high and failing to increase workers' purchasing power. They should be broken up, he insisted, not regulated. But the "brains trust"—a group of academics that included a number of Columbia University professors—saw bigness as inevitable in a modern economy. The competitive marketplace, they argued, was a thing of the past, and large firms needed to be managed and directed by the government, not dismantled. Their view prevailed during what came to be called the First New Deal.

THE BANKING CRISIS

"This nation asks for action and action now," Roosevelt announced on taking office on March 4, 1933. The country, wrote the journalist and political commentator Walter Lippmann, "was in such a state of confused desperation that it would have followed almost any leader anywhere he chose to go." FDR spent much of 1933 trying to reassure the public. In his inaugural address, he declared that "the only thing we have to fear is fear itself."

Roosevelt confronted a banking system on the verge of collapse. As bank funds invested in the stock market and corporate bonds lost their value and panicked depositors withdrew their savings, bank after bank had closed its doors. By March 1933, banking had been suspended in a majority of the states—that is, people could not gain access to money in their bank accounts. Roosevelt declared a "bank holiday," temporarily halting all bank operations, and called Congress into special session. On March 9, it rushed to pass the Emergency Banking Act, which provided funds to shore up threatened institutions.

Further measures soon followed that transformed the American financial system. The Glass-Steagall Act barred commercial banks from becoming involved in the buying and selling of stocks. Until its repeal in the 1990s, the law prevented many of the irresponsible practices that had contributed to the stock market crash. The same law established the Federal Deposit Insurance Corporation (FDIC), a government system that insured the accounts of individual depositors. And Roosevelt took the United States off the gold standard—that is, he severed the link between the country's currency and its gold reserves, thus making possible the issuance of more money in the hope of stimulating business activity. Together, these measures rescued the financial system and greatly increased the government's power over it. About 5,000 banks—one-third of the nation's total—had failed between 1929 and 1933, representing a loss of tens of millions of dollars to depositors. In 1936, not a single bank failed in the United States.

THE NRA

The Emergency Banking Act was the first of an unprecedented flurry of legislation during the first three months of Roosevelt's administration, a period known as the "Hundred Days." Seizing on the sense of crisis and the momentum of his electoral victory, Roosevelt won rapid passage of laws he hoped would promote economic recovery. He persuaded Congress to create a host of new agencies, whose initials soon became part of the language of politics—NRA, AAA, CCC. Never in American history had a president exercised such power or so rapidly expanded the role of the federal government in people's lives.

The centerpiece of Roosevelt's plan for combating the Depression, the National Industrial Recovery Act, was to a large extent modeled on the government–business partnership established by the War Industries Board of World War I, although in keeping with FDR's nondogmatic approach, it also owed something to Herbert Hoover's efforts to build stronger government–business cooperation. Roosevelt called it "the most important and far-reaching legislation ever enacted by the American Congress." The act established the National Recovery Administration (NRA), which would work with groups of business leaders to establish industry codes that set standards for output, prices, and working conditions. Thus, "cutthroat" competition (in which companies took losses to drive competitors out of business) would be ended. These industry-wide arrangements would be exempt from antitrust laws.

The NRA reflected how even in its early days, the New Deal reshaped understandings of freedom. In effect, FDR had repudiated the older idea of liberty based on the idea that the best way to encourage economic activity and ensure a fair distribution of wealth was to allow market competition to operate, unrestrained by the government. And to win support from labor, section 7a of the new law recognized the workers' right to organize unions—a departure from the "open shop" policies of the 1920s and a step toward government support for what workers called "industrial freedom."

Headed by Hugh S. Johnson, a retired general and businessman, the NRA quickly established codes that set standards for production, prices, and wages in the textile, steel, mining, and auto industries. Johnson launched a publicity campaign to promote the NRA and its symbol, the Blue Eagle, which stores and factories that abided by the codes displayed. But after initial public enthusiasm, the NRA became mired in controversy. Large companies dominated the code-writing process. An inquiry conducted by the labor lawyer Clarence Darrow in 1934 concluded that they used the NRA to drive up prices, limit production, lay off workers, and divide markets among themselves at the expense of smaller competitors. Many anti-union employers ignored section 7a. The government lacked the manpower to police the 750 codes in effect by 1935. The NRA produced neither economic recovery nor peace between employers and workers. It did, however, help to undercut the pervasive sense that the federal government was doing nothing to deal with the economic crisis.

GOVERNMENT JOBS

The Hundred Days also brought the government into providing relief to those in need. Roosevelt and most of his advisers shared the widespread fear that direct government payments to the unemployed would undermine individual self-reliance. Indeed, one of the first measures of the Hundred Days had been the Economy Act, which reduced federal spending in an attempt to win the confidence of the business community. But with nearly a quarter of the workforce unemployed, spending on relief was unavoidable. In May 1933, Congress created the Federal Emergency Relief Administration, to make grants to local agencies that aided those impoverished by the Depression. FDR, however, much preferred to create temporary jobs, thereby combating unemployment while improving the nation's infrastructure of roads, bridges, public buildings, and parks.

In March 1933, Congress established the Civilian Conservation Corps (CCC), which set unemployed young men to work on projects like forest preservation, flood control, and the improvement of national parks and wildlife preserves. By the time the program ended in 1942, more than 3 million persons had passed through CCC camps, where they received government wages of $30 per month.

A Civilian Conservation Corps workforce in Yosemite National Park, 1935.

PUBLIC-WORKS PROJECTS

One section of the National Industrial Recovery Act created the Public Works Administration (PWA), with an appropriation of $3.3 billion. Directed by Secretary of the Interior Harold Ickes, it contracted with private construction companies to build roads, schools, hospitals, and other public facilities, including New York City's Triborough Bridge and the Overseas Highway between Miami and Key West, Florida. In November, yet another agency, the Civil Works Administration (CWA), was launched. Unlike the PWA, it directly hired workers for construction projects. By January 1934, it employed more than 4 million persons in the construction of highways, tunnels, courthouses, and airports. But as the cost spiraled upward and complaints multiplied that the New Deal was creating a class of Americans permanently dependent on government jobs, Roosevelt ordered the CWA dissolved.

Some New Deal public-works initiatives looked to government-planned economic transformation as much as economic relief. The Tennessee Valley Authority (TVA), another product of the Hundred Days, built a series of dams to prevent floods and deforestation along the Tennessee River and to provide cheap electric power for homes and factories in a seven-state region where many families still lived in isolated log cabins. The TVA put the federal government, for the first time, in the business of selling electricity in competition with private companies. It was a preview of the program of regional planning that spurred the economic development of the West.

THE NEW DEAL AND AGRICULTURE

Another policy initiative of the Hundred Days addressed the disastrous plight of American farmers. The Agricultural Adjustment Act (AAA) authorized the federal government to try to raise farm prices by setting production quotas for major crops and paying farmers to plant less. Many crops already in the field were destroyed. In 1933, the government ordered more than 6 million pigs slaughtered as part of the policy, a step critics found strange at a time of widespread hunger.

The AAA succeeded in significantly raising farm prices and incomes. But not all farmers benefited. Benefits flowed to property-owning farmers, ignoring the large number who worked on land owned by others. The AAA policy of paying landowning farmers not to grow crops encouraged the eviction of thousands of poor tenants and sharecroppers. Many joined the rural exodus to cities or to the farms of the West Coast.

The onset in 1930 of a period of unusually dry weather in the nation's heartland worsened the Depression's impact on rural America. By mid-decade, the region suffered from the century's most severe drought. Mechanized agriculture in this semiarid region had pulverized the topsoil and killed

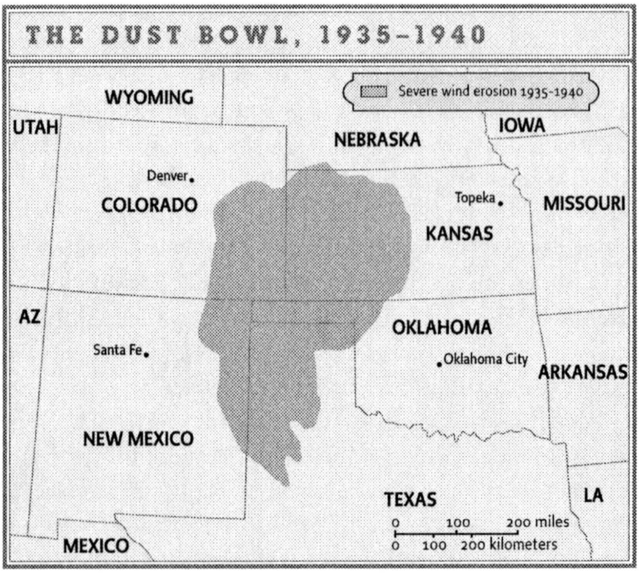

native grasses that prevented erosion. Winds now blew much of the soil away, creating the Dust Bowl, as the affected areas of Oklahoma, Texas, Kansas, and Colorado were called. A local newspaper described the situation in Cimarron County, Oklahoma: "Not a blade of wheat; cattle dying on the range, ninety percent of the poultry dead because of the sand storms, milk cows gone dry." One storm in 1934 carried dust as far as Washington, D.C. The drought and dust storms displaced more than 1 million farmers. John Steinbeck's novel *The Grapes of Wrath* (1939) and a popular film based on the book captured their plight, tracing a dispossessed family's trek from Oklahoma to California.

THE NEW DEAL AND HOUSING

Owning one's home had long been a widely shared American ambition. "A man is not a whole and complete man," Walt Whitman had written in the 1850s, "unless he owns a house and the ground it stands on." For many members of the middle class, home ownership had become a mark of respectability. For workers, it offered economic security at a time of low wages, erratic employment, and limited occupational mobility. On the eve of World War I, a considerably higher percentage of immigrant workers than the native-born middle class owned their homes.

The Depression devastated the American housing industry. The construction of new residences all but ceased, and banks and savings and loan associations that had financed home ownership collapsed or, to remain afloat, foreclosed on many homes (a quarter of a million in 1932 alone). In 1931, President Hoover convened a Conference on Home Building and Home Ownership to review the housing crisis. The president called owning a home an American "birthright," the embodiment of the spirit of "enterprise, of independence, and of . . . freedom." Rented apartments, he pointed out, did not inspire "immortal ballads" like *Home, Sweet Home* or *The Little Gray Home in the West.* Papers presented at the conference revealed that millions of Americans lived in overcrowded, unhealthy urban slums or in ramshackle rural dwellings. Private enterprise alone, it seemed clear, was unlikely to solve the nation's housing crisis.

Hoover's administration established a federally sponsored bank to issue home loans. Not until the New Deal, however, did the government systematically enter the housing market. Roosevelt spoke of "the security of the home" as a fundamental right akin to "the security of livelihood, and the security of social insurance." In 1933 and 1934, his administration moved energetically to protect home owners from foreclosure and to stimulate new construction. The Home Owners Loan Corporation and Federal Housing Administration (FHA) insured millions of long-term mortgages issued by private banks. At the same time, the federal government itself built thousands of units of low-rent housing. New Deal housing policy represented a remarkable departure from previous government practice. Thanks to the FHA and, later, the Veterans' Administration, home ownership came within the reach of tens of millions of families. It became cheaper for most Americans to buy single-family homes than to rent apartments.

Other important measures of Roosevelt's first two years in office included the ratification of the Twenty-first Amendment to the Constitution, which repealed Prohibition; the establishment of the Federal Communications Commission to oversee the nation's broadcast airwaves and telephone communications; and the creation of the Securities and Exchange Commission to regulate the stock and bond markets. Taken together, the First New Deal was a series of experiments, some of which succeeded and some of which did not. They transformed the role of the federal government, constructed numerous public facilities, and provided relief to millions of needy persons. But they did not end the Depression. Some 10 million Americans—more than 20 percent of the workforce—remained unemployed when 1934 came to an end.

THE COURT AND THE NEW DEAL

In 1935, the Supreme Court, still controlled by conservative Republican judges who held to the nineteenth-century understanding of freedom as liberty of contract, began to invalidate key New Deal laws. First came the NRA, declared unconstitutional in May in a case brought by the Schechter Poultry Company of Brooklyn, which had been charged with violating the code adopted by the chicken industry. In a unanimous decision, the Court declared the NRA unlawful because in its codes and other regulations it delegated legislative powers to the president and attempted to regulate local businesses that did not engage in interstate commerce. In January 1936, the AAA fell in *United States v. Butler*, which declared it an unconstitutional exercise of congressional power over local economic activities. In June, by a 5-4 vote, the justices ruled that New York could not establish a minimum wage for women and children.

Having failed to end the Depression or win judicial approval, the First New Deal ground to a halt. Meanwhile, pressures were mounting outside Washington that propelled the administration toward more radical departures in policy.

THE GRASSROOTS REVOLT

LABOR'S GREAT UPHEAVAL

The most striking development of the mid-1930s was the mobilization of millions of workers in mass-production industries that had successfully resisted unionization. "Labor's great upheaval," as this era of unprecedented militancy was called, came as a great surprise. Unlike in the past, however, the federal government now seemed to be on the side of labor, a commitment embodied in the National Industrial Recovery Act and in the Wagner Act (discussed later) of 1935, which granted workers the legal right to form unions. With the severe reduction of European immigration, ethnic differences among workers had diminished in importance. American-born children of the new immigrants now dominated the industrial labor force, and organizers no longer had to distribute materials in numerous languages as the IWW had done. And a cadre of militant labor leaders, many of them socialists and communists with long experience in organization, had survived the repression of the 1920s. They provided leadership to the labor upsurge.

American factories at the outset of the New Deal were miniature dictatorships in which unions were rare, workers could be beaten by supervisors and fired at will, and management determined the length of the workday and speed of the assembly line. In industrial communities scattered across the country, local government firmly supported the companies. "Jesus Christ couldn't speak in Duquesne for the union," declared the mayor of that Pennsylvania steel town. Workers' demands during the 1930s went beyond better wages. They included an end to employers' arbitrary power in the workplace, and basic civil liberties for workers, including the right to picket, distribute literature, and meet to discuss their grievances. All these goals required union recognition.

Roosevelt's election as president did much to rekindle hope among those who called themselves, in the words of a worker writing to Secretary of Labor Frances Perkins, "slaves of the depression." His inauguration unleashed a flood of poignant letters to the federal government describing what a Louisiana sugar laborer called the "terrible and inhuman condition" of many workers. Labor organizers spread the message that the "political liberty for which our forefathers fought" had been "made meaningless by economic inequality" and "industrial despotism." "We are free Americans," declared the Steel Workers Organizing Committee. "We shall exercise our inalienable rights to organize into a great industrial union."

Labor's great upheaval exploded in 1934, a year that witnessed no fewer than 2,000 strikes. Many produced violent confrontations between workers and the local police. In Toledo, Ohio, 10,000 striking auto workers surrounded the Electric Auto-Lite factory, where managers had brought strikebreakers to take their jobs, leading to a seven-hour fight with police and the National Guard. In Minneapolis, where an organization of businessmen known as the Citizens Alliance controlled the city government, a four-month strike by truck drivers led to pitched battles in the streets and the governor declaring martial law. San Francisco experienced the country's first general strike since 1919. It began with a walkout of dockworkers led by the fiery communist Harry Bridges.

Workers demanded recognition of the International Longshoremen's Association and an end to the hated "shape up" system in which they had to gather en masse each day to wait for work assignments. The year 1934 also witnessed a strike of 400,000 textile workers in states from New England to the Deep South, demanding recognition of the United Textile Workers. Many of these walkouts, including those in Toledo, Minneapolis, and San Francisco, won at least some of the workers' demands. But the textile strike failed.

THE RISE OF THE CIO

The labor upheaval posed a challenge to the American Federation of Labor's traditional policy of organizing workers by craft—welders or machine repairers, for example—rather than seeking to mobilize all the workers in a given industry, such as steel manufacturing. In 1934, thirty AFL leaders called for the creation of unions of industrial workers. When the AFL convention of 1935 refused, the head of the United Mine Workers, John L. Lewis, led a walkout that produced a new labor organization, the Congress of Industrial Organizations (CIO). It set out to create unions in the main bastions of the American economy. It aimed, said Lewis, at nothing less than to secure "economic freedom and industrial democracy" for American workers—a fair share in the wealth produced by their labor, and a voice in determining the conditions under which they worked.

In December 1936, unions, most notably the United Auto Workers (UAW), a fledgling CIO union, unveiled the sit-down, a strikingly effective tactic that the IWW had pioneered three decades earlier. Rather than walking out of a plant, thus enabling management to bring in strikebreakers, workers halted production but remained inside. In the UAW's first sit-down strike, 7,000 General Motors workers seized control of the Fisher Body Plant in Cleveland. Sit-downs soon spread to GM plants in Flint, Michigan, the nerve center of automobile production. When local police tried to storm the Flint plants, workers fought them off. Democratic governor Frank Murphy, who had been elected with strong support from the CIO, declared his unwillingness to use force to dislodge the strikers. The strikers demonstrated a remarkable spirit of unity. They cleaned the plant, oiled the idle machinery, settled disputes among themselves, prepared meals, and held concerts of labor songs. Workers' wives shuttled food into the plant. "They made a palace out of what had been their prison," wrote one reporter. On February 11, General Motors agreed to negotiate with the UAW. Not until 1941 would the bitterly anti-union Henry Ford sign a labor contract. But by the end of 1937, the UAW claimed 400,000 members.

The victory in the auto industry reverberated throughout industrial America. Steelworkers had suffered memorable defeats in the struggle for unionization, notably at Homestead in 1892 and in the Great Steel Strike of 1919.

Sit-down strike at a General Motors factory in Flint, Michigan, 1937.

U.S. Steel, the country's single most important business firm, owner of an industrial empire that stretched across several states and employed more than 200,000 workers, had been among the strongest opponents of unionization. But in March 1937, fearing a sit-down campaign and aware that it could no longer count on the aid of state and federal authorities, the company agreed to recognize the Steel Workers Organizing Committee (forerunner of the United Steelworkers of America). Smaller steel firms, however, refused to follow suit. On Memorial Day, 1937, company guards and Chicago police fired on a picnic of striking Republic Steel workers, killing ten persons. Not until 1942 would Republic sign a labor contract.

Union membership nonetheless reached 9 million by 1940, more than double the number in 1930. The coming of the union, said a member of New York City's transit workers' organization, enabled workers "to go to our bosses and talk to them like men, instead of . . . like slaves." Unions frequently demanded and won a say in workplace management, including the right to contest the amount and pace of work and the introduction of new technology. They gained new grievance procedures and seniority systems governing hiring, firing, and promotions. The CIO unions helped to stabilize a chaotic employment situation and offered members a sense of dignity and freedom.

LABOR AND POLITICS

Throughout the industrial heartland, the labor upsurge altered the balance of economic power and propelled to the forefront of politics labor's goal of a fairer, freer, more equal America. Unlike the AFL, traditionally hostile to government intervention in labor-management relations, the CIO put forward an ambitious program for federal action to shield Americans from economic and social insecurity, including public housing, universal health care, and unemployment and old age insurance.

Building on the idea, so prominent in the 1920s, that the key to prosperity lay in an American standard of living based on mass consumption, CIO leaders explained the Depression as the result of an imbalance of wealth and income. The role of unions, in cooperation with the government, they argued, was to "create a consumer's demand" by raising wages and redistributing wealth. Only in this way could society absorb the products that rolled off modern assembly lines. The pathbreaking 1937 agreement between the UAW and General Motors spoke of a "rate of pay commensurate with an American standard of living." By mid-decade, many New Dealers accepted the "underconsumptionist" explanation of the Depression, which saw lack of sufficient consumer demand as its underlying cause. They concluded that the government must act to raise dramatically wage earners' share of the national income.

VOICES OF PROTEST

Other popular movements of the mid-1930s also placed the question of economic justice on the political agenda. In California, the novelist Upton Sinclair won the Democratic nomination for governor in 1934 as the head of the End Poverty in California movement. Sinclair called for the state to use idle factories and land in cooperative ventures that would provide jobs for the unemployed. He lost the election after being subjected to one of the first modern "negative" media campaigns. Sinclair's opponents circulated false newsreels showing armies of unemployed men marching to California to support his candidacy and a fake endorsement from the Communist Party.

The rise to national prominence of Huey Long offered another sign of popular dissatisfaction with the slow pace of economic recovery. Long's career embodied both Louisiana's Populist and Socialist traditions (Winn Parish, his home, had voted for both of these third parties) and the state's heritage of undemocratic politics. Driven by intense ambition and the desire to help uplift the state's "common people," Long won election as governor in 1928 and in 1930 took a seat in the U.S. Senate. From Washington, he dominated every branch of state government. He used his dictatorial power to build roads, schools, and hospitals and to increase the tax burden on Louisiana's oil companies.

One of the most colorful characters in twentieth-century American politics, Long was referred to by both admirers and critics as the "Kingfish." In 1934, he launched the Share Our Wealth movement, with the slogan "Every Man a King." He called for the confiscation of most of the wealth of the richest Americans in order to finance an immediate grant of $5,000 and a guaranteed job and annual income for all citizens. In his inimitable style, Long explained his goal: "Let's pull down these huge piles of gold until there shall be a real job, not a little old sow-belly, black-eyed pea job but a real spending money, beefsteak and gravy . . . Ford in the garage . . . red, white, and blue job for every man." Long claimed a following of 5 million. He was on the verge of announcing a run for president when the son of a defeated political rival assassinated him in 1935.

Huey Long, the "Kingfish" of Louisiana politics, in full rhetorical flight. The photo was probably taken in 1934, when Long was in the Senate but still running the state government.

Dr. Francis Townsend, a California physician, meanwhile won wide support for a plan by which the government would make a monthly payment of $200 to older Americans, with the requirement that they spend it immediately. This, he argued, would boost the economy. By the end of 1934, Townsend Clubs claimed more than 2 million members. Along with the rise of the CIO, these signs of popular discontent helped to spark the Second New Deal.

RELIGION ON THE RADIO

Religious leaders of various denominations took advantage of the mass media to spread their beliefs. Ironically, many fundamentalists used the most modern techniques of communication, including the radio and popular entertainment, to promote their anti-modernist message. They found in the radio a way of bringing their views directly to ordinary Americans, bypassing established churches and their leaders. During the 1920s, Aimee Semple McPherson, a Los Angeles revivalist, had her own radio station, which broadcast sermons from the International Church of the Foursquare Gospel she had founded. McPherson also traveled the country as a revivalist preacher. Her sermons used elaborate sets, costumes, and special effects borrowed from the movie industry. By the 1940s, national religious broadcast networks emerged, with a reliable and dedicated listening audience. In later decades, fundamentalist Christians would take advantage of television and the Internet to disseminate their religious and political views.

Also in the mid-1930s, the "radio priest," Father Charles E. Coughlin, attracted millions of listeners with weekly broadcasts attacking Wall Street bankers and greedy capitalists, and calling for government ownership of key industries as a way of combating the Depression. Initially a strong supporter of FDR, Coughlin became increasingly critical of the president for what he considered the failure of the New Deal to promote social justice. His crusade would later shift to anti-Semitism and support for European fascism.

THE SECOND NEW DEAL

In 1935, President Roosevelt sent a message to 100,000 American clergymen asking about economic and social conditions in their communities. The responses indicated that their financially hard-pressed churches could not respond effectively via traditional charity to the massive needs of their congregations. This was one among many illustrations of the critical importance of government intervention in relieving the widespread hardship caused by the Depression.

Spurred by the failure of his initial policies to pull the country out of the Depression and the growing popular clamor for greater economic equality, and buoyed by Democratic gains in the midterm elections of 1934, Roosevelt in 1935 launched the Second New Deal. The first had focused on economic recovery. The emphasis of the second was economic security—a guarantee that Americans would be protected against unemployment and poverty. "Boys," Roosevelt's relief administrator, Harry Hopkins, told his staff, "this is our hour. We've got to get everything we want—a [public] works program, social security, wages and hours, everything—now or never."

The idea that lack of consumer demand caused the Depression had been popularized by Huey Long, Francis Townsend, and the CIO. By 1935, more and more New Dealers had concluded that the government should no longer try to plan business recovery but should try to redistribute the national income so as to sustain mass purchasing power in the consumer economy. A series of measures in 1935 attacked head-on the problem of weak demand and economic inequality. Congress levied a highly publicized tax on large fortunes and corporate profits—a direct response to the popularity of Huey Long's

Share Our Wealth campaign. It created the Rural Electrification Agency (REA) to bring electric power to homes that lacked it—80 percent of farms were still without electricity in 1934—in part to enable more Americans to purchase household appliances.

The REA proved to be one of the Second New Deal's most successful programs. By 1950, 90 percent of the nation's farms had been wired for electricity, and almost all now possessed radios, electric stoves, refrigerators, and mechanical equipment to milk cows. In addition, the federal government under the Second New Deal tried to promote soil conservation and family farming. This effort resulted from the belief that the country would never achieve prosperity so long as farmers' standard of living lagged well behind that of city dwellers, and that rural poverty resulted mainly from the poor use of natural resources. Thus, farmers received federal assistance in reducing soil loss in their fields. The federal government also purchased significant amounts of marginal and eroded land and converted these areas from farms into national grasslands and parks. It encouraged more environmentally conscious agricultural techniques. These measures (like those of the AAA) mainly benefited landowners, not sharecroppers, tenants, or migrant workers. In the long run, the Second New Deal failed to arrest the trend toward larger farms and fewer farmers.

THE WPA AND THE WAGNER ACT

In 1934, Roosevelt had severely curtailed federal employment for those in need. Now, he approved the establishment of the Works Progress Administration (WPA), which hired some 3 million Americans, in virtually every walk of life, each year until it ended in 1943. Under Harry Hopkins's direction, the WPA changed the physical face of the United States. It constructed thousands of public buildings and bridges, more than 500,000 miles of roads, and 600 airports. It built stadiums, swimming pools, and sewage treatment plants. Unlike previous work relief programs, the WPA employed many out-of-work white-collar workers and professionals, even doctors and dentists.

Perhaps the most famous WPA projects were in the arts. The WPA set hundreds of artists to work decorating public buildings with murals. It hired writers to produce local histories and guidebooks to the forty-eight states and to record the recollections of ordinary Americans, including hundreds of former slaves. Its Federal Theater Project put on plays, including an all-black production of *Macbeth* and Sinclair Lewis's drama *It Can't Happen Here*, about fascism coming to the United States. The Federal Music Project established orchestras and choral groups, and the Federal Dance Project sponsored ballet and modern dance programs. Thanks to the WPA, audiences across the country enjoyed their first glimpse of live musical and theatrical performances and their first opportunity to view exhibitions of American art. Also in 1935, Congress created the National Youth Administration to provide relief to American teenagers and young adults.

Another major initiative of the Second New Deal, the Wagner Act, was known at the time as "Labor's Magna Carta" (a reference to an early landmark in the history of freedom). This brought democracy into the American workplace by empowering the National Labor Relations Board to supervise elections in which employees voted on union representation. It also outlawed "unfair labor practices," including the firing and blacklisting of union organizers. The bill's main sponsor, Robert Wagner of New York, told the Senate that the ability of workers to pool their strength through collective bargaining represented the "next step" in "the evolution of American freedom." He also promised that unionization and higher wages would aid economic recovery by boosting the purchasing power of ordinary Americans.

THE AMERICAN WELFARE STATE

The centerpiece of the Second New Deal was the Social Security Act of 1935. It embodied Roosevelt's conviction that the national government had a responsibility to ensure the material well-being of ordinary Americans. It created a system of unemployment insurance, old age pensions, and aid to the disabled, the elderly poor, and families with dependent children.

None of these were original ideas. The Progressive platform of 1912 had called for old age pensions. Assistance to poor families with dependent children descended from the mothers' pensions promoted by maternalist reformers. Many European countries had already adopted national unemployment insurance plans. What was new, however, was that in the name of economic security, the American government would now supervise not simply temporary relief but a permanent system of social insurance.

The Social Security Act launched the American version of the welfare state—a term that originated in Britain during World War II to refer to a system of income assistance, health coverage, and social services for all citizens. The act illustrated both the extent and the limits of the changes ushered in by the Second New Deal. The American welfare state marked a radical departure from previous government policies, but compared with similar programs in Europe, it has always been far more decentralized, involved lower levels of public spending, and covered fewer citizens. The original Social Security bill, for example, envisioned a national system of health insurance. But Congress dropped this after ferocious opposition from the American Medical Association, which feared government regulation of doctors' activities and incomes.

THE SOCIAL SECURITY SYSTEM

Some New Dealers desired a program funded by the federal government's general tax revenues, and with a single set of eligibility standards administered by national officials. But Secretary of Labor Frances Perkins, along with powerful members of Congress, wished to keep relief in the hands of state and local authorities and believed that workers should contribute directly to the cost of their own benefits. Roosevelt himself preferred to fund Social Security by taxes on employers and workers, rather than out of general government revenues. He wanted to ensure that Social Security did not add to the federal deficit and believed that paying such taxes gave contributors "a legal, moral, and political right" to collect their old age pensions and unemployment benefits, which no future Congress could rescind.

As a result, Social Security emerged as a hybrid of national and local funding, control, and eligibility standards. Old age pensions were administered nationally but paid for by taxes on employers and employees. Such taxes also paid for payments to the unemployed, but this program was highly decentralized, with the states retaining considerable control over the level of benefits. The states paid most of the cost of direct poor relief, under the program called Aid to Dependent Children, and eligibility and the level of payments varied enormously from place to place. As will be discussed later, the combination of local administration and the fact that domestic and agricultural workers were not covered by unemployment and old age benefits meant that Social Security at first excluded large numbers of Americans, especially unmarried women and non-whites.

Nonetheless, Social Security represented a dramatic departure from the traditional functions of government. The Second New Deal transformed the relationship between the federal government and American citizens. Before the 1930s, national political debate often revolved around the question of *whether* the federal government should intervene in the economy. After the New Deal, debate rested on *how* it should intervene. In addition, the government assumed a responsibility, which it has never wholly relinquished, for guaranteeing Americans a living wage and protecting them against economic and personal misfortune. "Laissez-faire is dead," wrote Walter Lippmann, "and the modern state has become responsible for the modern economy [and] the task of insuring . . . the standard of life for its people."

A RECKONING WITH LIBERTY

The Depression made inevitable, in the words of one writer, a "reckoning with liberty." For too many Americans, Roosevelt proclaimed, "life was no longer free; liberty no longer real; men could no longer follow the pursuit of happiness." The 1930s produced an outpouring of books and essays on freedom. The large majority took for granted the need for a new definition. In a volume entitled *Land of the Free* (1938), the poet Archibald MacLeish used photographs of impoverished migrants and sharecroppers to question the reality of freedom in desperate times. "We told ourselves we were free," he wrote. Now, "we wonder if the liberty is done . . . or if there's something different men can mean by Liberty."

Like the Civil War, the New Deal recast the idea of freedom by linking it to the expanding power of the national state. "Our democracy," wrote Father John A. Ryan, a prominent Catholic social critic, "finds itself . . . in a new age where not political freedom but social and industrial freedom is the most insistent cry." Influenced by Ryan, the National Catholic Welfare Conference in 1935 declared that "social justice" required a government guarantee of continuous employment and a "decent livelihood and adequate security" for all Americans. A 1935 survey by *Fortune* magazine found that among poor respondents, 90 percent believed that the government should guarantee that "every man who wants work has a job."

FDR AND THE IDEA OF FREEDOM

Along with being a superb politician, Roosevelt was a master of political communication. At a time when his political opponents controlled most newspapers, he harnessed radio's power to bring his message directly into American homes. By the mid-1930s, more than two-thirds of American families owned radios. They listened avidly to Roosevelt's radio addresses, known as "fireside chats."

Roosevelt adeptly appealed to traditional values in support of new policies. He gave the term "liberalism" its modern meaning. In the nineteenth century, liberalism had been a shorthand for limited government and free-market economics. Roosevelt consciously chose to employ it to describe a large, active, socially conscious state. He reclaimed the word "freedom" from conservatives and made it a rallying cry for the New Deal. In his second fireside chat, Roosevelt juxtaposed his own definition of liberty as "greater security for the average man" to the older notion of liberty of contract, which served the interests of "the privileged few." Henceforth, he would consistently link freedom with economic security and identify entrenched economic inequality as its greatest enemy. "The liberty of a democracy," he declared in 1938, was not safe if citizens could not "sustain an acceptable standard of living."

Even as Roosevelt invoked the word to uphold the New Deal, "liberty"—in the sense of freedom from powerful government—became the fighting slogan of his opponents. Their principal critique of the New Deal was that its "reckless spending" undermined fiscal responsibility and its new government regulations restricted American freedom. When conservative businessmen and politicians in 1934 formed an organization to mobilize opposition to Roosevelt's policies, they called it the American Liberty League. Robert Taft of Ohio, leader of the Republicans in Congress, accused Roosevelt of sacrificing "individual freedom" in a misguided effort to "improve the conditions of the poor."

FDR delivering one of his "fireside chats" in 1938. Roosevelt was the first president to make effective use of the radio to promote his policies.

As the 1930s progressed, opponents of the New Deal invoked the language of liberty with greater and greater passion. The U.S. Chamber of Commerce charged FDR with attempting to "Sovietize" America. Even though his own administration had abandoned laissez-faire in the face of economic disaster, former president Hoover launched strident attacks on his successor for endangering "fundamental American liberties." In *The Challenge to Liberty* (1934), Hoover called the New Deal "the most stupendous invasion of the whole spirit of liberty" the nation had ever seen.

THE ELECTION OF 1936

By 1936, with working-class voters providing massive majorities for the Democratic Party and businesses large and small bitterly estranged from the New Deal, politics reflected class divisions more completely than at any other time in American history. Conceptions of freedom divided sharply as well. Americans, wrote George Soule, editor of *The New Republic*, confronted "two opposing systems of concepts about liberty," reflecting "the needs and purposes of two opposing [parts] of the population." One was the idea of "freedom for private enterprise," the other "socialized liberty" based on "an equitably shared abundance."

A fight for the possession of "the ideal of freedom," reported the *New York Times*, emerged as the central issue of the presidential campaign of 1936. The Democratic platform insisted that in a modern economy the government has an obligation to establish a "democracy of opportunity for all the people." In his speech accepting renomination, Roosevelt launched a blistering attack against "economic royalists" who, he charged, sought to establish a new

VOICES OF FREEDOM

From Franklin D. Roosevelt, "Fireside Chat" (1934)

President Roosevelt pioneered the use of the new mass medium of radio to speak directly to Americans in their homes. He used his "fireside chats" to mobilize support for New Deal programs, link them with American traditions, and outline his definition of freedom.

To those who say that our expenditures for public works and other means for recovery are a waste that we cannot afford, I answer that no country, however rich, can afford the waste of its human resources. Demoralization caused by vast unemployment is our greatest extravagance. Morally, it is the greatest menace to our social order. Some people try to tell me that we must make up our minds that in the future we shall permanently have millions of unemployed just as other countries have had them for over a decade. What may be necessary for those countries is not my responsibility to determine. But as for this country, I stand or fall by my refusal to accept as a necessary condition of our future a permanent army of unemployed. . . .

In our efforts for recovery we have avoided, on the one hand, the theory that business should and must be taken over into an all-embracing Government. We have avoided, on the other hand, the equally untenable theory that it is an interference with liberty to offer reasonable help when private enterprise is in need of help. The course we have followed fits the American practice of Government, a practice of taking action step by step, of regulating only to meet concrete needs, a practice of courageous recognition of change. I believe with Abraham Lincoln, that "the legitimate object of Government is to do for a community of people whatever they need to have done but cannot do at all or cannot do so well for themselves in their separate and individual capacities."

I am not for a return to that definition of liberty under which for many years a free people were being gradually regimented into the service of the privileged few. I prefer and I am sure you prefer that broader definition of liberty under which we are moving forward to greater freedom, to greater security for the average man than he has ever known before in the history of America.

From John Steinbeck, The Harvest Gypsies: On the Road to the Grapes of Wrath (1938)

John Steinbeck's popular novel *The Grapes of Wrath* (1939), and the film version that followed shortly thereafter, focused national attention on the plight of homeless migrants displaced from their farms as a result of the Great Depression. Before that book appeared, Steinbeck had published a series of newspaper articles based on eyewitness accounts of the migrants, which became the basis for his novel.

In California, we find a curious attitude toward a group that makes our agriculture successful. The migrants are needed, and they are hated. . . . The migrants are hated for the following reasons, that they are ignorant and dirty people, that they are carriers of disease, that they increase the necessity for police and the tax bill for schooling in a community, and that if they are allowed to organize they can, simply by refusing to work, wipe out the season's crops. . . .

Let us see what kind of people they are, where they come from, and the routes of their wanderings. In the past they have been of several races, encouraged to come and often imported as cheap labor. Chinese in the early period, then Filipinos, Japanese and Mexicans. These were foreigners, and as such they were ostracized and segregated and herded about. . . . But in recent years the foreign migrants have begun to organize, and at this danger they have been deported in great numbers, for there was a new reservoir from which a great quantity of cheap labor could be obtained.

The drought in the middle west has driven the agricultural populations of Oklahoma, Nebraska and parts of Kansas and Texas westward. . . . Thousands of them are crossing the borders in ancient rattling automobiles, destitute and hungry and homeless, ready to accept any pay so that they may eat and feed their children. . . .

The earlier foreign migrants have invariably been drawn from a peon class. This is not the case with the new migrants. They are small farmers who have lost their farms, or farm hands who have lived with the family in the old American way. . . . They have come from the little farm districts where democracy was not only possible but inevitable, where popular government, whether practiced in the Grange, in church organization or in local government, was the responsibility of every man. And they have come into the country where, because of the movement necessary to make a living, they are not allowed any vote whatever, but are rather considered a properly unprivileged class. . . .

As one little boy in a squatter's camp said, "When they need us they call us migrants, and when we've picked their crop, we're bums and we got to get out."

QUESTIONS

1. What does Roosevelt mean by the difference between the definition of liberty that has existed in the past and his own "broader definition of liberty"?

2. According to Steinbeck, how do Depression-era migrant workers differ from those in earlier periods?

3. Do the migrant workers described by Steinbeck enjoy liberty as Roosevelt understands it?

tyranny over the "average man." Economic rights, he went on, were the precondition of liberty—poor men "are not free men." Throughout the campaign, FDR would insist that the threat posed to economic freedom by the "new despotism" of large corporations was the main issue of the election.

As Roosevelt's opponent, Republicans chose Kansas governor Alfred Landon, a former Theodore Roosevelt Progressive. Landon denounced Social Security and other measures as threats to individual liberty. Opposition to the New Deal planted the seeds for the later flowering of an antigovernment conservatism bent on upholding the free market and dismantling the welfare state. But in 1936 Roosevelt won a landslide reelection, with more than 60 percent of the popular vote. He carried every state except Maine and Vermont. Roosevelt's victory was all the more remarkable in view of the heavy support most of the nation's newspapers and nearly the entire business community gave to the Republicans. His success stemmed from strong backing from organized labor and his ability to unite southern white and northern black voters, Protestant farmers and urban Catholic and Jewish ethnics, industrial workers and middle-class home owners. These groups made up the so-called New Deal coalition, which would dominate American politics for nearly half a century.

THE COURT FIGHT

Roosevelt's second inaugural address was the first to be delivered on January 20. In order to lessen a newly elected president's wait before taking office, the recently ratified Twentieth Amendment had moved inauguration day from March 4. FDR called on the nation to redouble its efforts to aid those "who have too little." The Depression, he admitted, had not been conquered: "I see one-third of a nation ill-housed, ill-clad, and ill-nourished." Emboldened by his electoral triumph, Roosevelt now made what many considered a serious political miscalculation. On the pretense that several members of the Supreme Court were too old to perform their functions, he proposed that the president be allowed to appoint a new justice for each one who remained on the Court past age seventy (an age that six of the nine had already surpassed). FDR's aim, of course, was to change the balance of power on a Court that, he feared, might well invalidate Social Security, the Wagner Act, and other measures of the Second New Deal.

The plan aroused cries that the president was an aspiring dictator. Congress rejected it. But Roosevelt accomplished his underlying purpose. The Supreme Court, it is sometimes said, follows the election returns. Coming soon after Roosevelt's landslide victory of 1936, the threat of "Court packing" inspired an astonishing about-face on the part of key justices. Beginning in March 1937, the Court suddenly revealed a new willingness to support economic regulation by both the federal government and the states. It upheld a minimum wage law of the state of Washington similar to the New York measure it had declared unconstitutional a year earlier. It turned aside challenges to Social Security and the Wagner Act. In subsequent cases, the Court affirmed federal power to regulate wages, hours, child labor, agricultural production, and numerous other aspects of economic life.

Announcing a new judicial definition of freedom, Chief Justice Charles Evans Hughes pointed out that the words "freedom of contract" did not appear in the Constitution. "Liberty," however, did, and this, Hughes continued, required "the protection of law against the evils which menace the health, safety, morals, and welfare of the people." The Court's new willingness to accept the New Deal marked a permanent change in judicial policy. Having declared dozens of economic laws unconstitutional in the decades leading up to 1937, the justices have rarely done so since.

THE END OF THE SECOND NEW DEAL

Even as the Court made its peace with Roosevelt's policies, the momentum of the Second New Deal slowed. The landmark United States Housing Act did pass in 1937, initiating the first major national effort to build homes for the poorest Americans. But the Fair Labor Standards bill failed to reach the floor for over a year. When it finally passed in 1938, it banned goods produced by child labor from interstate commerce, set forty cents as the minimum hourly wage, and required overtime pay for hours of work exceeding forty per week. This last major piece of New Deal legislation established the practice of federal regulation of wages and working conditions, another radical departure from pre-Depression policies.

The year 1937 also witnessed a sharp downturn of the economy. With economic conditions improving in 1936, Roosevelt had reduced federal funding for farm subsidies and WPA work relief. The result was disastrous. As government spending fell, so did business investment, industrial production, and the stock

Figure 1 UNEMPLOYMENT, 1925–1945

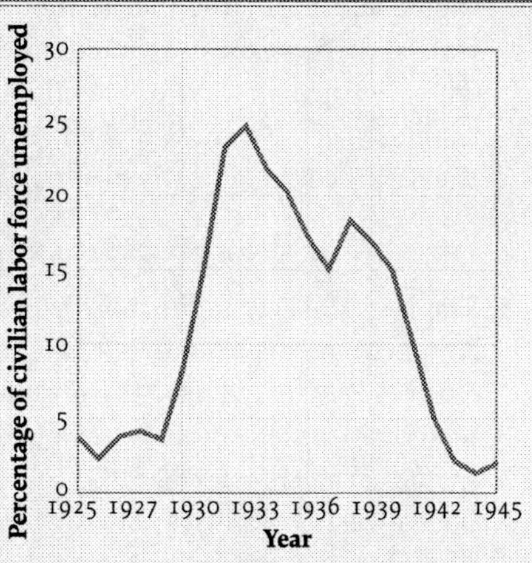

The New Deal did not really solve the problem of unemployment, which fell below 10 percent only in 1941, as the United States prepared to enter World War II.

market. Unemployment, still 14 percent at the beginning of 1937, rose to nearly 20 percent by year's end.

In 1936, in *The General Theory of Employment, Interest, and Money,* John Maynard Keynes had challenged economists' traditional belief in the sanctity of balanced budgets. Large-scale government spending, he insisted, was necessary to sustain purchasing power and stimulate economic activity during downturns. Such spending should be enacted even at the cost of a budget deficit (a situation in which the government spends more money than it takes in). By 1938, Roosevelt was ready to follow this prescription, which would later be known as Keynesian economics. In April, he asked Congress for billions more for work relief and farm aid. By the end of the year, the immediate crisis had passed. But the events of 1937–1938 marked a major shift in New Deal philosophy. Rather than economic planning, as in 1933–1934, or economic redistribution, as in 1935–1936, public spending would now be the government's major tool for combating unemployment and stimulating economic growth. The Second New Deal had come to an end.

THE LIMITS OF CHANGE

Roosevelt conceived of the Second New Deal, and especially Social Security, as expanding the meaning of freedom by extending assistance to broad groups of needy Americans—the unemployed, elderly, and dependent—as a right of citizenship, not charity or special privilege. But political realities, especially the power of inherited ideas about gender and black disenfranchisement in the South, powerfully affected the drafting of legislation. New Deal programs were justified as ways of bringing economic security to "the people" rather than to specific disadvantaged groups. But different Americans experienced the New Deal in radically different ways.

THE NEW DEAL AND AMERICAN WOMEN

The New Deal brought more women into government than ever before in American history. A number of talented women, including Secretary of Labor Frances Perkins, advised the president and shaped public policy. Most prominent of all was Eleanor Roosevelt, FDR's distant cousin whom he had married in 1905. She transformed the role of First Lady, turning a position with no formal responsibilities into a base for political action. She traveled widely, spoke out on public issues, wrote a regular newspaper column that sometimes disagreed openly with her husband's policies, and worked to enlarge the scope of the New Deal in areas like civil rights, labor legislation, and work relief.

But even as the New Deal increased women's visibility in national politics, organized feminism, already in disarray during the 1920s, disappeared as a political force. Indeed, the Depression inspired widespread demands for women to remove themselves from the labor market to make room for unemployed men. Because the Depression hit industrial employment harder than low-wage clerical and service jobs where women predominated, the proportion of the workforce made up of women rose. The government tried to reverse this trend. The Economy Act of 1933 prohibited both members of a married couple from holding federal jobs. Until its repeal in 1937, it led to the dismissal of numerous female civil service employees whose husbands worked for the government. Many states and localities prohibited the hiring of women whose husbands earned a "living wage," and employers from banks to public school systems barred married women from jobs. Although the CIO organized female workers, it, too, adhered to the idea that women should be supported by men. "The working wife whose husband is employed," said a vice president of the United Auto Workers, "should be barred from industry."

Most New Deal programs did not exclude women from benefits (although the CCC restricted its camps to men). But the ideal of the male-headed household powerfully shaped social policy. Since paying taxes on one's wages made one eligible for the most generous Social Security programs—old age pensions and unemployment insurance—they left most women uncovered, since they did not work outside the home. The program excluded the 3 million mostly female domestic workers altogether. "Those who need protection most are completely overlooked," the sister of a household worker complained to Secretary of Labor Perkins. "What about the poor domestics, both in private homes and private institutions. What have you done for them? Nothing."

THE SOUTHERN VETO

Roosevelt made the federal government the symbolic representative of all the people, including racial and ethnic groups generally ignored by previous administrations. Yet the power of the Solid South helped to mold the New Deal welfare state into an entitlement of white Americans. After the South's blacks lost the right to vote around the turn of the century, Democrats enjoyed a political monopoly in the region. Democratic members of Congress were elected again and again. With results predetermined, many whites did not bother to vote (only about 20 percent of eligible southern voters cast ballots in the election of 1920). But this tiny electorate had an enormous impact on national policy. Committee chairmanships in Congress rest on seniority—how many years a member has served in office. Beginning in 1933, when Democrats took control of Congress, southerners took the key leadership positions. Despite his personal popularity, Roosevelt felt he could not challenge the power of southern Democrats if he wished legislation to pass. At their insistence, the Social Security law excluded agricultural and domestic workers, the largest categories of black employment.

Roosevelt spoke of Social Security's universality, but the demand for truly comprehensive coverage came from the political left and black organizations. Congressman Ernest Lundeen of Minnesota in 1935 introduced a bill establishing a federally controlled system of old age, unemployment, and health benefits for all wage workers, plus support for female heads of households with dependents. Black organizations like the Urban League and the NAACP supported the Lundeen bill and lobbied strenuously for a system that enabled agricultural and domestic workers to receive unemployment and old age benefits and that established national relief standards. The Social Security Act, however, not Lundeen's proposal, became law. Its limitations, complained the *Pittsburgh Courier*, a black newspaper, reflected the power of "reactionary elements in the South who cannot bear the thought of Negroes getting pensions and compensations" and who feared that the inclusion of black workers would disrupt the region's low-wage, racially divided labor system.

THE STIGMA OF WELFARE

Because of the "southern veto," the majority of black workers found themselves confined to the least generous and most vulnerable wing of the new welfare state. The public assistance programs established by Social Security, notably aid to dependent children and to the poor elderly, were open to all Americans who could demonstrate financial need. But they set benefits at extremely low levels and authorized the states to determine eligibility standards, including "moral" behavior as defined by local authorities. As a result, public assistance programs allowed for widespread discrimination in the distribution of benefits. Because recipients did not pay Social Security taxes, they soon came to bear the humiliating stigma of dependency on government handouts, which would soon come to be known as "welfare."

In 1942, the National Resources Planning Board noted that because of their exclusion from programs "which give aid under relatively favorable conditions," blacks were becoming disproportionately dependent on welfare, a program widely viewed with popular disfavor. The situation, the report concluded, seemed certain to stigmatize blacks as recipients of unearned government assistance, and welfare as a program for minorities, thus dooming it forever to inadequate "standards of aid." Over time, this is precisely what happened, until the federal government abolished its responsibility for welfare in 1996, during the presidency of Bill Clinton.

THE INDIAN NEW DEAL

Overall, the Depression and New Deal had a contradictory impact on America's racial minorities. Under Commissioner of Indian Affairs John Collier, the administration launched an "Indian New Deal." Collier ended the policy of forced assimilation and allowed Indians unprecedented cultural autonomy. He replaced boarding schools meant to eradicate the tribal heritage of Indian children with schools on reservations, and dramatically increased spending on Indian health. He secured passage of the Indian Reorganization Act of 1934, ending the policy, dating back to the Dawes Act of 1887, of dividing Indian lands into small plots for individual families and selling off the rest. Federal authorities once again recognized Indians' right to govern their own affairs, except where specifically limited by national laws. Such limitations, however, could weigh heavily on Indian tribes. The Navajos, the nation's largest tribe, refused to cooperate with the Reorganization Act as a protest against a federal soil conservation program that required them to reduce their herds of livestock.

The New Deal marked the most radical shift in Indian policy in the nation's history. But living conditions on the desperately poor reservations did not significantly improve, and New Deal programs often ignored Indians' interests. The building of the Grand Coulee Dam on the Columbia River flooded thousands of acres where Indians had hunted and fished for centuries. But the government did not make any of the irrigation water available to the region's reservations.

THE NEW DEAL AND MEXICAN-AMERICANS

For Mexican-Americans, the Depression was a wrenching experience. With demand for their labor plummeting, more than 400,000 (one-fifth of the population of Mexican origin) returned to Mexico, some voluntarily, others at the strong urging of local authorities in the Southwest. A majority of those "encouraged" to leave the country were recent immigrants, but they included perhaps 200,000 Mexican-American children who had been born in the United States and were therefore citizens. Those who remained mostly worked in grim conditions in California's vegetable and fruit fields, whose corporate farms benefited enormously from New Deal dam construction that provided them with cheap electricity and water for irrigation. The Wagner and Social Security Acts did not apply to agricultural laborers. When the workers tried to organize a union as part of the decade's labor upsurge, they were brutally suppressed. In his 1939 book *Factories in the Field*, the writer Carey McWilliams exposed the low wages, inadequate housing, and political repression under which the migrant laborers suffered, which the New Deal did nothing to alleviate.

A large crowd of Mexican-Americans waiting to leave Los Angeles in 1932 as part of the repatriation campaign.

Mexican-American leaders struggled to develop a consistent strategy for their people. They sought greater rights by claiming to be white Americans—in order to not suffer the same discrimination as African-Americans—but also sought the backing of the Mexican government and promoted a mystical sense of pride and identification with Mexican heritage later given the name *la raza*.

LAST HIRED, FIRST FIRED

As the "last hired and first fired," African-Americans were hit hardest by the Depression. Even those who retained their jobs now faced competition from unemployed whites who had previously considered positions like waiter and porter beneath them. With an unemployment rate double that of whites, blacks benefited disproportionately from direct government relief and, especially in northern cities, jobs on New Deal public-works projects. Half of the families in Harlem received public assistance during the 1930s.

The Depression propelled economic survival to the top of the black agenda. Demonstrations in Harlem demanded jobs in the neighborhood's white-owned stores, with the slogan "Don't Buy Where You Can't Work." W. E. B. Du Bois abandoned his earlier goal of racial integration as unrealistic for the foreseeable future. Blacks, he wrote, must recognize themselves as "a nation within a nation." He called on blacks to organize for economic survival by building an independent, cooperative economy within their segregated communities, and to gain control of their own separate schools (a position reminiscent of that of Booker T. Washington, whom he had earlier condemned).

A NEW DEAL FOR BLACKS

Although Roosevelt seems to have had little personal interest in race relations or civil rights, he appointed Mary McLeod Bethune, a prominent black educator, as a special adviser on minority affairs and a number of other blacks to important federal positions. Key members of his administration, including his wife, Eleanor, and Secretary of the Interior Harold Ickes, a former president of the Chicago chapter of the NAACP, directed national attention to the injustices of segregation, disenfranchisement, and lynching. In 1939, Eleanor Roosevelt resigned from the Daughters of the American Revolution when the organization refused to allow the black singer Marian Anderson to present a concert at Constitution Hall in Washington. The president's wife arranged for Anderson to sing on the steps of the Lincoln Memorial and for the concert to be broadcast nationally on the radio.

Thanks to the New Deal, Bethune proclaimed, a "new day" had dawned when blacks would finally reach "the promised land of liberty." The decade witnessed a historic shift in black voting patterns. In the North and West, where they enjoyed the right to vote, blacks in 1934 and 1936 abandoned their allegiance to the party of Lincoln and emancipation in favor of Democrats and the New Deal. But their hopes for broad changes in the nation's race system were disappointed. Despite a massive lobbying campaign, southern congressmen prevented passage of a federal antilynching law. FDR offered little support. "I did not choose the tools with which I must work," he told Walter White of the NAACP; he could not jeopardize his economic programs by alienating powerful members of Congress. The CCC established segregated work camps. Because of the exclusion of agricultural and domestic workers, Social Security's old age pensions and unemployment benefits and the minimum wages established by the Fair Labor Standards Act left uncovered 60 percent of all employed blacks and 85 percent of black women.

FEDERAL DISCRIMINATION

Federal housing policy, which powerfully reinforced residential segregation, revealed the limits of New Deal freedom. As in the case of Social Security, local officials put national housing policy into practice in a way that reinforced existing racial boundaries. Nearly all municipalities, North as well as South, insisted that housing built or financially aided by the federal government be racially segregated. (In Texas, some communities financed three sets of housing projects—for whites, blacks, and Mexicans.) The Federal Housing Administration, moreover, had no hesitation about insuring mortgages that contained clauses barring future sales to non-white buyers, and it refused to channel money into integrated neighborhoods. In some cases, the presence of a single black family led the agency to declare an entire block off-limits for federal mortgage insurance. Along with discriminatory practices by private banks and real-estate companies, federal policy became a major factor in further entrenching housing segregation in the United States.

Federal employment practices also discriminated on the basis of race. As late as 1940, of the 150,000 blacks holding federal jobs, only 2 percent occupied positions other than clerk or custodian. In the South, many New Deal construction projects refused to hire blacks at all. "They give all the work to white people and give us nothing," a black resident of Mississippi wrote to FDR in 1935. The New Deal began the processof modernizing southern agriculture, but tenants, black and white, footed much of the bill. Tens of thousands of sharecroppers, as noted earlier, were driven offthe land as a result of the AAA policy of raising crop prices by paying landowners to reduce cotton acreage.

Support for civil rights would eventually become a test of liberal credentials. But in the 1930s, one could advocate Roosevelt's economic program and oppose antilynching legislation and moves to incorporate black workers within Social Security. Theodore Bilbo, the notoriously racist senator from Mississippi, was one of the New Deal's most loyal backers. Not until the Great Society of the 1960s would those left out of Social Security and other New Deal programs—racial minorities, many women, migrants and other less privileged workers—win inclusion in the American welfare state.

Nonetheless, in a society in which virtually all institutions, public and private, created and reinforced patterns of discrimination, the New Deal helped to create an atmosphere that made possible challenges to the racial and ethnic status quo and the rise of a new, more inclusive vision of American freedom.

A NEW CONCEPTION OF AMERICA

If the New Deal failed to dismantle the barriers that barred non-whites from full participation in American life, the 1930s witnessed the absorption of other groups into the social mainstream. With Catholics and Jews occupying prominent posts in the Roosevelt administration and new immigrant voters forming an important part of its electoral support, the New Deal made ethnic pluralism a living reality in American politics. One of Roosevelt's first acts on taking office had been to sign the Beer and Wine Revenue Act, an anticipation of the constitutional amendment repealing prohibition. While promoted as a way to revive employment in the liquor industry and boost tax revenues, it also represented a repudiation of the linkage of politics and Protestant morality. The election of the Italian-American Fiorello La Guardia as mayor of New York City in 1933 symbolized the coming to power of the new immigrants. Although elected as a Republican, La Guardia worked closely with FDR and launched his own program of spending on housing, parks, and public works. La Guardia's was one of numerous "little New Deals" that brought ethnic working-class voters to power in communities throughout the industrial heartland.

Thanks to the virtual cutoff of southern and eastern European immigration in 1924, the increasing penetration of movies, chain stores, and mass advertising into ethnic communities, and the common experience of economic crisis, the 1930s witnessed an acceleration of cultural assimilation. But the process had a different content from the corporate-sponsored Americanization plans of the preceding years. For the children of the new immigrants, labor and political activism became agents of a new kind of Americanization. One could participate fully in the broader society without surrendering one's ideals and ethnic identity. "Unionism is Americanism" became a CIO rallying cry. "The Mesabi Range," a Minnesota miner wrote to Secretary of Labor Perkins, complaining of low wages and management hostility to unions in the iron-rich region, "isn't Americanized yet."

THE HEYDAY OF AMERICAN COMMUNISM

In the mid-1930s, for the first time in American history, the left—an umbrella term for socialists, communists, labor radicals, and many New Deal liberals—enjoyed a shaping influence on the nation's politics and culture. The CIO and Communist Party became focal points for a broad social and intellectual impulse that helped to redraw the boundaries of American freedom. An obscure, faction-ridden organization when the Depression began, the Communist Party experienced remarkable growth during the 1930s. The party's membership never exceeded 100,000, but several times that number passed through its ranks.

The party's commitment to socialism resonated with a widespread belief that the Depression had demonstrated the bankruptcy of capitalism. But it was not so much the party's ideology as its vitality—its involvement in a mind-boggling array of activities, including demonstrations of the unemployed, struggles for industrial unionism, and a renewed movement for black civil rights—that for a time made it the center of gravity for a broad democratic upsurge. At the height of the Popular Front—a period during the mid-1930s when the Communist Party sought to ally itself with socialists and New Dealers in movements for social change, urging reform of the capitalist system rather than revolution—Communists gained an unprecedented respectability. Earl Browder, the party's leader, even appeared on the cover of *Time* magazine. It is one of the era's ironies that an organization with an undemocratic structure and closely tied to Stalin's dictatorial regime in Russia should have contributed to the expansion of freedom in the United States. But the Communist Party helped to imbue New Deal liberalism with a militant spirit and a more pluralistic understanding of Americanism.

REDEFINING THE PEOPLE

In theater, film, and dance, the Popular Front vision of American society sank deep roots and survived much longer than the political moment from which it sprang. In this broad left-wing culture, social and economic radicalism, not support for the status quo, defined true Americanism, ethnic and racial diversity was the glory of American society, and the "American way of life" meant unionism and social citizenship, not the unbridled pursuit of wealth. The American "people," viewed by many intellectuals in the 1920s as representing mean-spirited fundamentalism and crass commercialism, were suddenly rediscovered as embodiments of democratic virtue.

The "common man," Roosevelt proclaimed, embodied "the heart and soul of our country." During the 1930s, artists and writers who strove to create socially meaningful works eagerly took up the task of depicting the daily lives of ordinary farmers and city dwellers. Art about the people—such as Dorothea Lange's photographs of migrant workers and sharecroppers—and art created by the people—such as black spirituals—came to be seen as expressions of genuine Americanism. The Federal Music Project dispatched collectors with tape recorders to help preserve American folk music. Films celebrated populist figures who challenged and defeated corrupt businessmen and politicians, as in *Mr. Deeds Goes to Town* (1936) and *Mr. Smith Goes to Washington* (1939). New immigrants, especially Jews and Italians, played a prominent role in producing and directing Hollywood films of the 1930s. Their movies, however, glorified not urban ethnic communities but ordinary small-town middle-class Americans.

PROMOTING DIVERSITY

"A new conception of America is necessary," wrote the immigrant labor radical Louis Adamic in 1938. Despite bringing ethnic and northern black voters into its political coalition, the Democratic Party said little about ethno-cultural issues, fearful of rekindling the divisive battles of the 1920s. But the Popular Front forthrightly sought to promote the idea that the country's strength lay in diversity, tolerance, and the rejection of ethnic prejudice and class privilege. The CIO avidly promoted the idea of ethnic and racial inclusiveness. It broke decisively with the AFL's tradition of exclusionary unionism. The CIO embraced cultural pluralism—an idea previously associated with intellectuals like Horace Kallen and the self-defense of ethnic and Catholic communities against enforced Americanization. "We are the only Americans who take them into our organization as equals," wrote labor organizer Rose Pesotta, referring to the Mexican-Americans who flocked to the Cannery and Agricultural Workers union.

Popular Front culture presented a heroic but not uncritical picture of the country's past. Martha Graham's modern dance masterpiece *American Document* (1938), an embodiment of Popular Front aesthetics with its emphasis on America's folk traditions and multi-ethnic heritage, centered its account of history on the Declaration of Independence and the Gettysburg Address. Yet Graham did not neglect what her narrator called "things we are ashamed of," including the dispossession of the Indians and the plight of the unemployed. Graham's answer to Hector St. John de Crèvecoeur's old question, "What, then, is the American, this new man?" was that Americans were not only middle-class Anglo-Saxons but also blacks, immigrants, and the working class. Earl Robinson's song "Ballad for Americans," a typical expression of Popular Front culture that celebrated the religious, racial, and ethnic diversity of American society, became a national hit and was performed in 1940 at the Republican national convention.

CHALLENGING THE COLOR LINE

It was fitting that "Ballad for Americans" reached the top of the charts in a version performed by the magnificent black singer Paul Robeson. Popular Front culture moved well beyond New Deal liberalism in condemning racism as incompatible with true Americanism. In the 1930s, groups like the American Jewish Committee and the National Conference of Christians and Jews actively promoted ethnic and religious tolerance, defining pluralism as "the American way." But whether in Harlem or East Los Angeles, the Communist Party was the era's only predominantly white organization to make fighting racism a top priority. "The communists," declared Charles H. Houston, the NAACP's chief lawyer, "made it impossible for any aspirant to Negro leadership to advocate less than full economic, political and social equality."

Communist influence spread even to the South. The Communist-dominated International Labor Defense mobilized popular support for black defendants victimized by a racist criminal justice system. It helped to make the Scottsboro case an international cause célèbre. The case revolved around nine young black men arrested for the rape of two white women in Alabama in 1931.

The "Scottsboro boys," flanked by two prison guards, with their lawyer, Samuel Liebowitz.

Despite the weakness of the evidence against the "Scottsboro boys" and the fact that one of the two accusers recanted, Alabama authorities three times put them on trial and three times won convictions. Landmark Supreme Court decisions overturned the first two verdicts and established legal principles that greatly expanded the definition of civil liberties—that defendants have a constitutional right to effective legal representation, and that states cannot systematically exclude blacks from juries. But the Court allowed the third set of convictions to stand, which led to prison sentences for five of the defendants. In 1937, a defense lawyer worked out a deal whereby Alabama authorities released nearly all the defendants on parole, although the last of the Scottsboro boys did not leave prison until thirteen years had passed.

Despite considerable resistance from white workers determined to preserve their monopoly of skilled positions and access to promotions, the CIO welcomed black members and advocated the passage of antilynching laws and the return of voting rights to southern blacks. The CIO brought large numbers of black industrial workers into the labor movement for the first time and ran extensive educational campaigns to persuade white workers to recognize the interests they shared with their black counterparts. Black workers, many of them traditionally hostile to unions because of their long experience of exclusion, responded with enthusiasm to CIO organizing efforts. The union offered the promise of higher wages, dignity in the workplace, and an end to the arbitrary power of often racist foremen. Ed McRea, a white CIO organizer in Memphis, Tennessee, reported that he had little difficulty persuading black workers of the value of unionization: "You didn't have any trouble explaining this to blacks, with the kinds of oppression and conditions they had. It was a question of freedom."

LABOR AND CIVIL LIBERTIES

Another central element of Popular Front public culture was its mobilization for civil liberties, especially the right of labor to organize. The struggle to launch industrial unions encountered sweeping local restrictions on freedom of speech as well as repression by private and public police forces. Nationwide publicity about the wave of violence directed against the Southern Tenant Farmers Union in the South and the CIO in industrial communities in the North elevated the rights of labor to a central place in discussions of civil liberties. The American Civil Liberties Union, primarily concerned in the 1920s with governmental repression, by 1934 concluded that "the masters of property" posed as great a danger to freedom of speech and assembly as political authorities.

Beginning in 1936, a Senate subcommittee headed by Robert M. La Follette Jr. exposed the methods employers used to combat unionization, including spies and private police forces. Workers had "no liberties at all," an employee of General Motors wrote to the committee from Saginaw, Michigan. The extensive violence unleashed against strikers in California's cotton and lettuce fields made that state, the committee report concluded, seem more like a "European dictatorship" than part of the United States.

Labor militancy helped to produce an important shift in the understanding of civil liberties. Previously conceived of as individual rights that must be protected against infringement by the government, the concept now expanded to include violations of free speech and assembly by powerful private groups. As a result, just as the federal government emerged as a guarantor of economic security, it also became a protector of freedom of expression.

By the eve of World War II, civil liberties had assumed a central place in the New Deal understanding of freedom. In 1939, Attorney General Frank Murphy established a Civil Liberties Unit in the Department of Justice. "For the first time in our history," Murphy wrote the president, "the full weight of the Department will be thrown behind the effort to preserve in this country the blessings of liberty." Meanwhile, the same Supreme Court that in 1937 relinquished its role as a judge of economic legislation moved to expand its authority over civil liberties. The justices insisted that constitutional guarantees of free thought and expression were essential to "nearly every other form of freedom" and therefore deserved special protection by the courts. Thus, civil liberties replaced liberty of contract as the judicial foundation of freedom. In 1937, the Court overturned on free speech grounds the conviction of Angelo Herndon, a Communist organizer jailed in Georgia for "inciting insurrection." Three years later, it invalidated an Alabama law that prohibited picketing in labor disputes. Since 1937, the large majority of state and national laws overturned by the courts have been those that infringe on civil liberties, not on the property rights of business.

The new appreciation of free expression was hardly universal. In 1938, the House of Representatives established an Un-American Activities Committee to investigate disloyalty. Its expansive definition of "un-American" included communists, labor radicals, and the left of the Democratic Party, and its hearings led to the dismissal of dozens of federal employees on charges of subversion. Two years later, Congress enacted the Smith Act, which made it a federal crime to "teach, advocate, or encourage" the overthrow of the government. A similar pursuit of radical views took place at the state level. The New York legislature's Rapp-Coudert Committee held sweeping hearings investigating "subversive" influences in New York City's public colleges, resulting in the firing in 1941 of some sixty faculty members charged with communist sympathies.

THE END OF THE NEW DEAL

By then the New Deal, as an era of far-reaching social reform, had already begun to recede. One reason was that more and more southern Democrats were finding themselves at odds with Roosevelt's policies. In 1938, the administration released a "Report on Economic Conditions in the South," along with a letter by the president referring to the region as "the nation's No. 1 economic problem." The document revealed that the South lagged far behind other parts of the country in industrialization and investment in education and public health. Its per capita income stood at half that of the rest of the nation. Also in 1938, a new generation of homegrown radicals—southern New Dealers, black activists, labor leaders, communists, even a few elected officials—founded the Southern Conference for Human Welfare to work for unionization, unemployment relief, and racial justice.

Until the late 1930s, prominent southern Democrats had been strong supporters of the New Deal, while at the same time working to shape legislation to allow for the local administration of relief and the exclusion of most black workers. Now, southern business and political leaders feared that continuing federal intervention in their region would encourage unionization and upset race relations. Roosevelt concluded that the enactment of future New Deal measures required a liberalization of the southern Democratic Party. In 1938, he tried to persuade the region's voters to replace conservative congressmen with ones who would support his policies. The South's small electorate dealt him a stinging rebuke. In the North, where the economic downturn, the "Court-packing" plan, and the upsurge of CIO militancy alarmed many middle-class voters, Republicans increased their congressional representation.

A period of political stalemate followed the congressional election of 1938. For many years, a conservative coalition of southern Democrats and northern Republicans dominated Congress. Further reform initiatives became almost impossible, and Congress moved to abolish existing ones, beginning with the Federal Theater Project, which had alarmed conservatives because of the presence of radicals and homosexuals on its payroll. Congress repealed an earlier tax on corporate profits and rejected a proposed program of national medical insurance. The administration, moreover, increasingly focused its attention on the storm gathering in Europe. Even before December 1941, when the United States entered World War II, "Dr. Win the War," as Roosevelt put it, had replaced "Dr. New Deal."

THE NEW DEAL IN AMERICAN HISTORY

Given the scope of the economic calamity it tried to counter, the New Deal seems in many ways quite limited. Compared to later European welfare states, Social Security remained restricted in scope and modest in cost. The New Deal failed to address the problem of racial inequality, which in some ways it actually worsened.

Yet even as the New Deal receded, its substantial accomplishments remained. It greatly expanded the federal government's role in the American economy and made it an independent force in relations between industry and labor. The government influenced what farmers could and could not plant, required employers to deal with unions, insured bank deposits, regulated the stock market, loaned money to home owners, and provided payments to a majority of the elderly and unemployed. It transformed the physical environment through hydroelectric dams, reforestation projects, rural electrification, and the construction of innumerable public facilities. It restored faith in democracy and made the government an institution directly experienced in Americans' daily lives and directly concerned with their welfare. It redrew the map of American politics. It helped to inspire, and was powerfully influenced by, a popular upsurge that recast the idea of freedom to include a public guarantee of economic security for ordinary citizens and that identified economic inequality as the greatest threat to American freedom.

The New Deal certainly improved economic conditions in the United States. But it did not generate sustained prosperity. More than 15 percent of the workforce remained unemployed in 1940. Only the mobilization of the nation's resources to fight World War II would finally end the Great Depression.

Chapter Review

REVIEW QUESTIONS

1. Discuss how regional planning such as the Tennessee Valley Authority and the Columbia River project reflected broader changes in American life during the New Deal.
2. What actions did President Roosevelt and Congress take to help the banking system recover as well as to reform how it operated in the long run?
3. How did the actions of the AAA benefit many farmers, injure others, and provoke attacks by conservatives?
4. Explain what labor did in the 1930s to rise from being "slaves of the depression" to secure "economic freedom and industrial democracy" for American workers.
5. How did the emphasis of the Second New Deal differ from the First New Deal?
6. How did the entrenched power of southern white conservatives limit African-Americans' ability to enjoy the full benefits of the New Deal and eliminate racial violence and discrimination? Why did African-Americans still support the Democratic Party?
7. Analyze the effects of the Indian Reorganization Act of 1934 on Native Americans.
8. Explain how New Deal programs contributed to the stigma of blacks as welfare-dependent.
9. How did the New Deal build on traditional ideas about the importance of homeownership to Americans and how did it change Americans' ability to own their own homes?
10. What were the major characteristics of liberalism by 1939?

KEY TERMS

bank holiday
Emergency Banking Act
the Hundred Days
National Recovery Administration
Civilian Conservation Corps
Public Works Administration
Dust Bowl
Federal Housing Administration
sit-down strike

Congress of Industrial Organizations
Share Our Wealth movement
Works Progress Administration
welfare state
Social Security Act
court-packing plan
minimum wage laws
Indian New Deal
the Popular Front
"Scottsboro boys"
House Un-American Activities Committee

wwnorton.com/studyspace

VISIT STUDYSPACE FOR THESE RESOURCES AND MORE:

- Author Videos
- A chapter outline
- A practice quiz
- Interactive maps
- Multimedia documents

CHAPTER 7

FIGHTING FOR THE FOUR FREEDOMS: WORLD WAR II

From *Give Me Liberty! Seagull Fourth Edition*

Eric Foner

Credits: photo 1: Library of Congress; photo 2: Library of Congress; photo 3: Courtesy Northwestern University Library; photo 4: Library of Congress; photo 5: *Detroit Free Press*; photo 6: Library of Congress; photo 7: Courtesy of *Chicago Defender*.

7

Fighting for the Four Freedoms: World War II 1941–1945

FOCUS QUESTIONS

- What steps led to American participation in World War II?
- How did the United States mobilize economic resources and promote popular support for the war effort?
- What visions of America's postwar role began to emerge during the war?
- How did American minorities face threats to their freedom at home and abroad during World War II?
- How did the end of the war begin to shape the postwar world?

By far the most popular works of art produced during World War II were paintings of the Four Freedoms by the magazine illustrator Norman Rockwell. In his State of the Union Address, delivered before Congress on January 6, 1941, President Roosevelt spoke eloquently of a future world order founded on the "essential human freedoms": freedom of speech, freedom of worship, freedom from want, and freedom from fear. The Four Freedoms became Roosevelt's favorite statement of Allied aims. At various times, he compared them with the Ten Commandments, the Magna Carta, and the Emancipation Proclamation. They embodied, Roosevelt declared in a 1942 radio address, the "rights of men of every creed and every race, wherever they live," and made clear "the crucial difference between ourselves and the enemies we face today."

Rockwell's paintings succeeded in linking the Four Freedoms with the defense of traditional American values. "Words like *freedom* or *liberty*," declared one wartime advertisement, "draw close to us only when we break them down into the homely fragments of daily life." This insight helps to explain Rockwell's astonishing popularity. Born in New York City in 1894, Rockwell had lived in the New York area until 1939, when he and his family moved to Arlington, Vermont, where they could enjoy, as he put it, "the clean, simple country life, as opposed to the complicated world of the city." Drawing on the lives of his Vermont neighbors, Rockwell translated the Four Freedoms into images of real people situated in small-town America. Each of the paintings focuses on an instantly recognizable situation. An ordinary citizen rises to speak at a town meeting; members of different religious groups are seen at prayer; a family enjoys a Thanksgiving dinner; a mother and father stand over a sleeping child.

The immensely popular Office of War Information poster reproducing Norman Rockwell's paintings of the Four Freedoms, President Franklin D. Roosevelt's shorthand for American purposes in World War II.

The Four Freedoms paintings first appeared in the *Saturday Evening Post* early in 1943. Letters of praise poured in to the magazine's editors. The government produced and sold millions of reprints. The paintings toured the country as the centerpiece of the Four Freedoms Show, which included theatrical presentations, parades, and other events aimed at persuading Americans to purchase war bonds. By the end of its tour, the Four Freedoms Show had raised $133 million.

Even as Rockwell invoked images of small-town life to rally Americans to the war effort, however, the country experienced changes as deep as at any time in its history. Many of the economic trends and social movements that we associate with the last half of the twentieth century had their roots in the war years. As during World War I, but on a far larger scale, wartime mobilization expanded the size and scope of government and energized the economy. The gross national product more than doubled and unemployment disappeared as war production finally conquered the Depression. The demand for labor drew millions of women into the workforce and sent a tide of migrants from rural America to the industrial cities of the North and West, permanently altering the nation's social geography. Some 30 million Americans moved during the war, half going into military service and half taking up new jobs.

World War II gave the country a new and lasting international role and greatly strengthened the idea that American security was global in scope and could only be protected by the worldwide triumph of core American values. Government military spending sparked the economic development of the South and West, laying the foundation for the rise of the modern Sunbelt. The war created a close link between big business and a militarized federal government—a "military-industrial complex," as President Dwight D. Eisenhower would later call it—that long survived the end of fighting.

World War II also redrew the boundaries of American nationality. In contrast to World War I, the government recognized the "new immigrants" of the early twentieth century and their children as loyal Americans. Black Americans' second-class status assumed, for the first time since Reconstruction, a prominent place on the nation's political agenda. But toleration had its limits. With the United States at war with Japan, the federal government removed more than 100,000 Japanese-Americans, the majority of them American citizens, from their homes and placed them in internment camps.

As a means of generating support for the struggle, the Four Freedoms provided a crucial language of national unity. But this unity obscured divisions within American society that the war in some ways intensified, divisions reflected in debates over freedom. While some Americans looked forward to a worldwide New Deal, others envisioned "free enterprise" replacing government intervention in the economy. The war gave birth to the modern civil rights movement but strengthened the commitment of many white Americans to maintain the existing racial order. The movement of women into the labor force challenged traditional gender relations, but most men and not a few women longed for the restoration of family life with a male breadwinner and a wife responsible for the home.

Even Rockwell's popular paintings suggested some of the ambiguities within the idea of freedom. With the exception of *Freedom of Speech*, which depicts civic democracy in action, the paintings emphasized private situations. The message seemed to be that Americans were fighting to preserve freedoms enjoyed individually or within the family rather than in the larger public world. This emphasis on freedom as an element of private life would become more and more prominent in postwar America.

FIGHTING WORLD WAR II

GOOD NEIGHBORS

During the 1930s, with Americans preoccupied by the economic crisis, international relations played only a minor role in public affairs. From the outset of his administration, nonetheless, FDR embarked on a number of departures in foreign policy. In 1933, hoping to stimulate American trade, he exchanged ambassadors with the Soviet Union, whose government his Republican predecessors had stubbornly refused to recognize.

Roosevelt also formalized a policy initiated by Herbert Hoover by which the United States repudiated the right to intervene militarily in the internal affairs of Latin American countries. This Good Neighbor Policy, as it was called, had mixed results. During the 1930s, the United States withdrew its troops from Haiti and Nicaragua. FDR accepted Cuba's repeal of the Platt Amendment, which had authorized American military interventions on that island. These steps offered a belated recognition of the sovereignty of America's neighbors. But while Roosevelt condemned "economic royalists" (wealthy businessmen) at home, like previous presidents he felt comfortable dealing with undemocratic governments friendly to American business interests abroad. The United States lent its support to dictators like Anastasio Somoza in Nicaragua, Rafael Trujillo Molina in the Dominican Republic, and Fulgencio Batista in Cuba. "He may be a son of a bitch, but he's *our* son of a bitch," FDR said of Somoza.

However, as the international crisis deepened in the 1930s, the Roosevelt administration took steps to counter German influence in Latin America by expanding hemispheric trade and promoting respect for American culture. Nelson Rockefeller, the head of an office that hoped to expand cultural relations in the hemisphere, sent the artists of the American Ballet Caravan and the NBC Symphony Orchestra on Latin American tours. This was a far different approach to relations with Central and South America than the military interventions of the first decades of the century.

THE ROAD TO WAR

Ominous developments in Asia and Europe quickly overshadowed events in Latin America. By the mid-1930s, it seemed clear that the rule of law was disintegrating in international relations and that war was on the horizon. In 1931, seeking to expand its military and economic power in Asia, Japan invaded Manchuria, a province of northern China. Six years later, its troops moved farther into China. When the Japanese overran the city of Nanjing, they massacred an estimated 300,000 Chinese prisoners of war and civilians.

An aggressive power threatened Europe as well. After brutally consolidating his rule in Germany, Adolf Hitler embarked on a campaign to control the entire continent. In violation of the Versailles Treaty, he feverishly pursued German rearmament. In 1936, he sent troops to occupy the Rhineland, a demilitarized zone between France and Germany established after World War I. The failure of Britain, France, and the United States to oppose this action convinced Hitler that the democracies could not muster the will to halt his aggressive plans. Italian leader Benito Mussolini, the founder of fascism, a movement similar to Hitler's Nazism, invaded and conquered Ethiopia. When General Francisco Franco in 1936 led an uprising against the democratically elected government of Spain, Hitler poured in arms, seeing the conflict as a testing ground for new weaponry. In 1939, Franco emerged victorious from a bitter civil war, establishing yet another fascist government in Europe. As part of a campaign to unite all Europeans of German origin in a single empire, Hitler in 1938 annexed Austria

CHRONOLOGY

1931	Japan invades Manchuria
1933	U.S. recognizes Soviet Union
1935–1939	Congress passes Neutrality Acts
1937	Sino-Japanese War begins
1938	Munich agreement
1939	Germany invades Poland
1940	Draft established
1941	Four Freedoms speech Henry Luce's *The American Century* Lend-Lease Act Executive Order 8802 Atlantic Charter Pearl Harbor attacked
1942	Executive Order 9066 Battle of Midway Island Congress of Racial Equality (CORE) formed
1943	"Zoot" suit riots Detroit race riot Congress lifts Chinese Exclusion Act
1944	*Smith v. Allwright* D-Day GI Bill of Rights Bretton Woods conference *Korematsu v. United States* Battle of the Bulge
1945	Yalta conference Roosevelt dies; Harry Truman becomes president V-E Day (May) Atomic bombs dropped on Japan V-J Day (September)

and the Sudetenland, an ethnically German part of Czechoslovakia. Shortly thereafter, he gobbled up all of that country.

As the 1930s progressed, Roosevelt became more and more alarmed at Hitler's aggression as well as his accelerating campaign against Germany's Jews, whom the Nazis stripped of citizenship and property and began to deport to concentration camps. In a 1937 speech in Chicago, FDR called for international action to "quarantine" aggressors. But no further steps followed. Roosevelt had little choice but to follow the policy of "appeasement" adopted by Britain and France, who hoped that agreeing to Hitler's demands would prevent war. British prime minister Neville Chamberlain returned from the Munich conference of 1938, which awarded Hitler the Sudetenland, proclaiming that he had guaranteed "peace in our time."

ISOLATIONISM

To most Americans, the threat arising from Japanese and German aggression seemed very distant. Moreover, Hitler had more than a few admirers in the United States. Obsessed with the threat of communism, some Americans approved his expansion of German power as a counterweight to the Soviet Union. Businessmen did not wish to give up profitable overseas markets. Henry Ford did business with Nazi Germany throughout the 1930s. Indeed, Ford plants there employed slave labor provided by the German government. Trade with Japan also continued, including shipments of American trucks and aircraft and considerable amounts of oil. Until 1941, 80 percent of Japan's oil supply came from the United States.

Many Americans remained convinced that involvement in World War I had been a mistake. Senate hearings in 1934–1935 headed by Gerald P. Nye of North Dakota revealed that international bankers and arms exporters had pressed the Wilson administration to enter that war and had profited handsomely from it. Pacifism spread on college campuses, where tens of thousands of students took part in a "strike for peace" in 1935. Ethnic allegiances reinforced Americans' traditional reluctance to enter foreign conflicts. Many Americans of German and Italian descent celebrated the expansion of national power in their countries of origin, even when they disdained their dictatorial governments. Irish-Americans remained strongly anti-British.

Isolationism—the 1930s version of Americans' long-standing desire to avoid foreign entanglements—dominated Congress. Beginning in 1935, lawmakers passed a series of Neutrality Acts that banned travel on belligerents' ships and the sale of arms to countries at war. These policies, Congress hoped, would allow the United States to avoid the conflicts over freedom of the seas that had contributed to involvement in World War I. Despite the fact that the Spanish Civil War pitted a democratic government against an aspiring fascist dictator, the Western democracies, including the United States, imposed an embargo on arms shipments to both sides. Some 3,000 Americans volunteered to fight in the Abraham Lincoln Brigade on the side of the Spanish republic. But with Germany supplying the forces of Franco, the decision by democratic countries to abide by the arms embargo contributed substantially to his victory.

WAR IN EUROPE

In the Munich agreement of 1938, Britain and France had caved in to Hitler's aggression. In 1939, the Soviet Union proposed an international agreement to oppose further German demands for territory. Britain and France, who distrusted Stalin and saw Germany as a bulwark against the spread of communist influence in Europe, refused. Stalin then astonished the world by signing a nonaggression pact with Hitler, his former sworn enemy. On September 1, immediately after the signing of the Nazi–Soviet pact, Germany invaded Poland. This time, Britain and France, who had pledged to protect Poland against aggression, declared war. But Germany appeared unstoppable. Within a year, the Nazi *blitzkrieg* (lightning war) had overrun Poland and much of Scandinavia, Belgium, and the Netherlands. On June 14, 1940, German troops occupied Paris. Hitler now dominated nearly all of Europe, as well as North Africa. In September 1940, Germany, Italy, and Japan created a military alliance known as the Axis.

For one critical year, Britain stood virtually alone in fighting Germany. Winston Churchill, who became prime minister in 1940, vowed to resist a threatened Nazi invasion. In the Battle of Britain of 1940–1941, the German air force launched devastating attacks on London and other cities. The Royal Air Force eventually turned back the air assault. But Churchill pointedly called on the "new world, with all its power and might," to step forward to rescue the old.

TOWARD INTERVENTION

Roosevelt viewed Hitler as a mad gangster whose victories posed a direct threat to the United States. But most Americans remained desperate to remain out of the conflict. "What worries me, especially," FDR wrote to Kansas editor William Allen White, "is that public opinion over here is patting itself on the back every morning and thanking God for the Atlantic Ocean and the Pacific Ocean." After a tumultuous debate, Congress in 1940 agreed to allow the sale of arms to Britain on a "cash and carry" basis—that is, they had to be paid for in cash and transported in British ships. It also approved plans for military rearmament. But with a presidential election looming, Roosevelt was reluctant to go further. Opponents of involvement in Europe organized the America First Committee, with hundreds of thousands of members and a leadership that included well-known figures like Henry Ford, Father Coughlin, and Charles A. Lindbergh.

In 1940, breaking with a tradition that dated back to George Washington, Roosevelt announced his candidacy for a third term as president. The international situation was too dangerous and domestic recovery too fragile, he insisted, for him to leave office. Republicans chose as his opponent a political amateur, Wall Street businessman and lawyer Wendell Willkie. Differences between the candidates were far more muted than in 1936. Both supported the law, enacted in September 1940, that established the nation's first peacetime draft. Willkie endorsed New Deal social legislation. He captured more votes than Roosevelt's previous opponents, but FDR still emerged with a decisive victory. Soon after his victory, in a fireside chat in December 1940, Roosevelt announced that the United States would become the "great arsenal of democracy," providing Britain and China with military supplies in their fight against Germany and Japan.

During 1941, the United States became more and more closely allied with those fighting Germany and Japan. But with Britain virtually bankrupt, it could no longer pay for supplies. At Roosevelt's urging, Congress passed the Lend-Lease Act, which authorized military aid so long as countries promised somehow to return it all after the war. Under the law's provisions, the United States funneled billions of dollars' worth of arms to Britain and China, as well as the Soviet Union, after Hitler renounced his nonaggression pact and invaded that country in June 1941. FDR also froze Japanese assets in the United States, halting virtually all trade between the countries, including the sale of oil vital to Japan.

Those who believed that the United States must intervene to stem the rising tide of fascism tried to awaken a reluctant country to prepare for war. Interventionists popularized slogans that would become central to wartime mobilization. In June 1941, refugees from Germany and the occupied countries of Europe joined with Americans to form the Free World Association, which sought to bring the United States into the war against Hitler. The same year saw the formation of Freedom House. With a prestigious membership that included university presidents, ministers, businessmen, and labor leaders, Freedom House described the war raging in Europe as an ideological struggle between dictatorship and the "free world." In October 1941, it sponsored a "Fight for Freedom" rally at New York's Madison Square Garden, complete with a patriotic variety show entitled "It's Fun to Be Free." The rally ended by demanding an immediate declaration of war against Germany.

PEARL HARBOR

Until November 1941, the administration's attention focused on Europe. But at the end of that month, intercepted Japanese messages revealed that an assault in the Pacific was imminent. No one, however, knew where it would come. On December 7, 1941, Japanese planes, launched from aircraft carriers, bombed the naval base at Pearl Harbor in Hawaii, the first attack by a foreign power on

American soil since the War of 1812. Pearl Harbor was a complete and devastating surprise. In a few hours, more than 2,000 American servicemen were killed, and 187 aircraft and 18 naval vessels, including 8 battleships, had been destroyed or damaged. By a stroke of fortune, no aircraft carriers—which would prove decisive in the Pacific war—happened to be docked at Pearl Harbor on December 7.

To this day, conspiracy theories abound suggesting that FDR knew of the attack and did nothing to prevent it so as to bring the United States into the war. No credible evidence supports this charge. Indeed, with the country drawing ever closer to intervention in Europe, Roosevelt hoped to keep the peace in the Pacific. But Secretary of Labor Frances Perkins, who saw the president after the attack, remarked that he seemed calm—"his terrible moral problem had been resolved." Terming December 7 "a date which will live in infamy," Roosevelt asked Congress for a declaration of war against Japan. The combined vote in Congress was 388 in favor and 1 against—pacifist Jeanette Rankin of Montana, who had also voted against American entry into World War I. The next day, Germany declared war on the United States. America had finally joined the largest war in human history.

THE WAR IN THE PACIFIC

World War II has been called a "gross national product war," meaning that its outcome turned on which coalition of combatants could outproduce the other. In retrospect, it appears inevitable that the entry of the United States, with its superior industrial might, would ensure the defeat of the Axis powers. But the first few months of American involvement witnessed an unbroken string of military disasters. Having earlier occupied substantial portions of French Indochina (now Vietnam, Laos, and Cambodia), Japan in early 1942 conquered Burma (Myanmar) and Siam (Thailand). Japan also took control of the Dutch East Indies (Indonesia), whose extensive oil fields could replace supplies from the United States. And it occupied Guam, the Philippines, and other Pacific islands. At Bataan, in the Philippines, the Japanese forced 78,000 American and Filipino troops to lay down their arms—the largest surrender in American military history. Thousands perished on the ensuing "death march" to a prisoner-of-war camp, and thousands more died of disease and starvation after they arrived. At the same time, German submarines sank hundreds of Allied merchant and naval vessels during the Battle of the Atlantic.

Soon, however, the tide of battle began to turn. In May 1942, in the Battle of the Coral Sea, the American navy turned back a Japanese fleet intent on attacking Australia. The following month, it inflicted devastating losses on the Japanese navy in the Battle of Midway Island. These victories allowed American forces to launch the bloody campaigns that one by one drove the Japanese from fortified islands like Guadalcanal and the Solomons in the western Pacific and brought American troops ever closer to Japan.

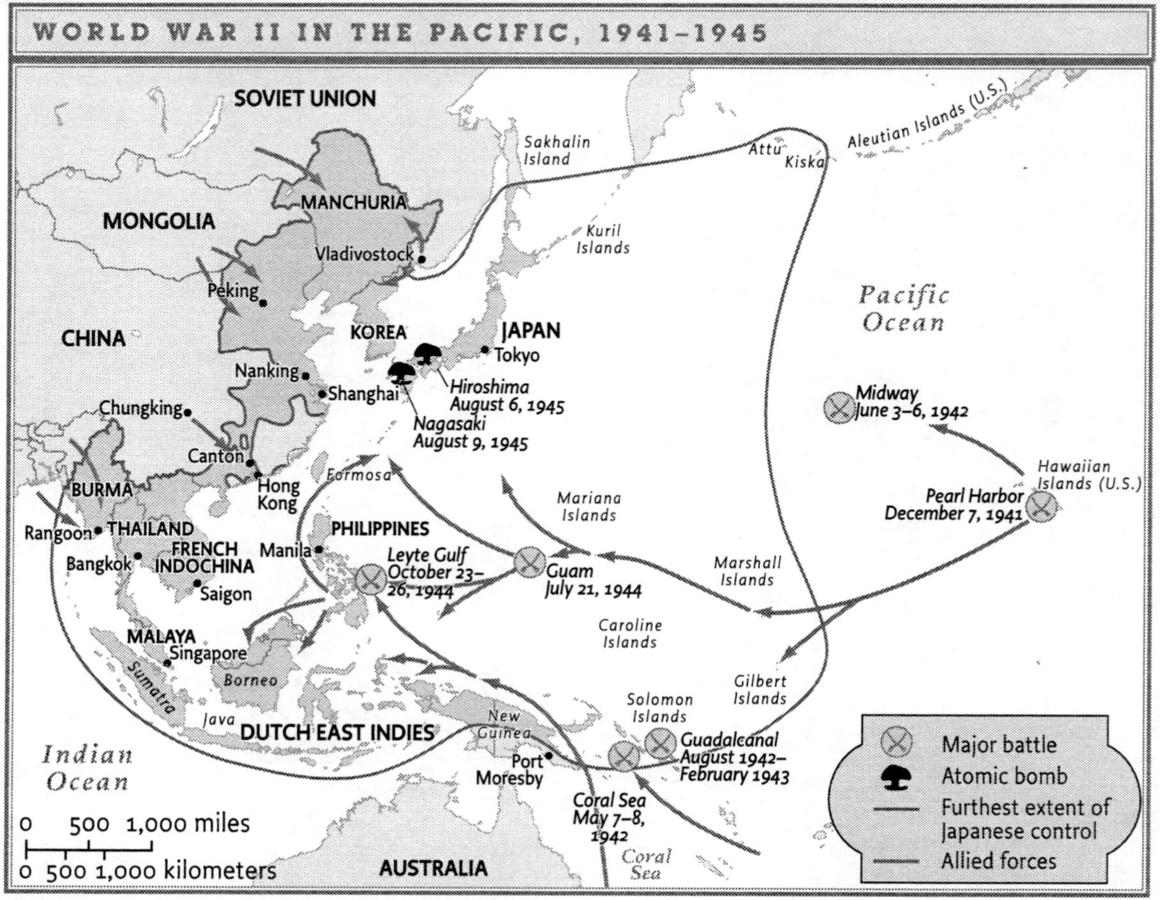

Although the Japanese navy never fully recovered from its defeats at the Coral Sea and Midway in 1942, it took three more years for American forces to near the Japanese homeland.

THE WAR IN EUROPE

In November 1942, British and American forces invaded North Africa and by May 1943 forced the surrender of the German army commanded by General Erwin Rommel. By the spring of 1943, the Allies also gained the upper hand in the Atlantic, as British and American destroyers and planes devastated the German submarine fleet. But even though Roosevelt was committed to liberating Europe from Nazi control, American troops did not immediately become involved on the European continent. As late as the end of 1944, more American military personnel were deployed in the Pacific than against Germany. In July 1943, American and British forces invaded Sicily, beginning the liberation of Italy. A popular uprising in Rome overthrew the Mussolini government, whereupon Germany occupied most of the country. Fighting there raged throughout 1944.

The major involvement of American troops in Europe did not begin until June 6, 1944. On that date, known as D-Day, nearly 200,000 American, British, and Canadian soldiers under the command of General Dwight D.Eisenhower landed in Normandy in northwestern France. More than a million troops followed them ashore in the next few weeks, in the most massive sea–land operation in history. After fierce fighting, German armies retreated eastward. By August, Paris had been liberated.

The crucial fighting in Europe, however, took place on the eastern front, the scene of an epic struggle between Germany and the Soviet Union. More than 3 million German soldiers took part in the 1941 invasion. After sweeping through western Russia, German armies in August 1942 launched a siege of Stalingrad, a city located deep inside Russia on the Volga River. This proved to be a catastrophic mistake. Bolstered by an influx of military supplies from the United States, the Russians surrounded the German troops and forced them to surrender. Some 800,000 Germans and 1.2 million Russians perished in the fighting. The German surrender at Stalingrad in January 1943 marked the turning point of the European war. Combined with a Russian victory at Kursk six months later in the greatest tank battle in history, the campaign in the east devastated Hitler's forces and sent surviving units on a long retreat back toward Germany.

Of 13.6 million German casualties in World War II, 10 million came on the Russian front. They represented only part of the war's vast toll in human lives. Millions of Poles and at least 20 million Russians, probably many more, perished—not only soldiers but civilian victims of starvation, disease, and massacres by German soldiers. After his armies had penetrated eastern Europe in 1941, moreover, Hitler embarked on the "final solution"—the mass extermination of "undesirable" peoples—Slavs, gypsies, homosexuals, and, above all, Jews. By 1945, 6 million Jewish men, women, and children had died

WORLD WAR II IN EUROPE, 1942–1945

Most of the land fighting in Europe during World War II took place on the eastern front between the German and Soviet armies.

in Nazi death camps. What came to be called the Holocaust was the horrifying culmination of the Nazi belief that Germans constituted a "master race" destined to rule the world.

THE HOME FRONT

MOBILIZING FOR WAR

At home, World War II transformed the role of the national government. FDR created federal agencies like the War Production Board, the War Manpower Commission, and the Office of Price Administration to regulate the allocation of labor, control the shipping industry, establish manufacturing quotas, and fix wages, prices, and rents. The number of federal workers rose from 1 million to 4 million, part of a tremendous growth in new jobs that pushed the unemployment rate down from 14 percent in 1940 to 2 percent three years later.

The government built housing for war workers and forced civilian industries to retool for war production. Michigan's auto factories now turned out trucks, tanks, and jeeps for the army. By 1944, American factories produced a ship every day and a plane every five minutes. The gross national product rose from $91 billion to $214 billion during the war, and the federal government's expenditures amounted to twice the combined total of the previous 150 years. The government marketed billions of dollars' worth of war bonds, increased taxes, and began the practice of withholding income tax directly from weekly paychecks. Before the war, only the 4 million wealthiest Americans paid income taxes; by 1945, more than 40 million did so. The government, one historian writes, moved during the war from "class taxation" to "mass taxation."

BUSINESS AND THE WAR

The relationship between the federal government and big business changed dramatically from the days of the Second New Deal. "If you are going to go to war in a capitalist country," observed Secretary of War Henry Stimson, "you had better let business make money out of the process." As corporate executives flooded into federal agencies concerned with war production, Roosevelt offered incentives to spur production—low-interest loans, tax concessions, and contracts with guaranteed profits. The great bulk of federal spending went to the largest corporations, furthering the long-term trend toward economic concentration. By the end of the war, the 200 biggest industrial companies accounted for almost half of all corporate assets in the United States.

Americans marveled at the achievements of wartime manufacturing. Thousands of aircraft, 100,000 armored vehicles, and 2.5 million trucks rolled off American assembly lines, and entirely new products like synthetic rubber replaced natural resources now controlled by Japan. Government-sponsored scientific research perfected inventions like radar, jet engines, and early computers that helped to win the war and would have a large impact on postwar life. These accomplishments not only made it possible to win a two-front war but also helped to restore the reputation of business and businessmen, which had reached a low point during the Depression.

Federal funds reinvigorated established manufacturing areas and created entirely new industrial centers. World War II saw the West Coast emerge as a focus of military-industrial production. The government invested billions of dollars in the shipyards of Seattle, Portland, and San Francisco and in the steel plants and aircraft factories of southern California. By the war's end,

M-5 tanks on the assembly line at a Detroit Cadillac plant, in a 1942 photograph. During the war, General Motors and other automakers produced vehicles for the armed forces rather than cars for consumers.

California had received one-tenth of all federal spending, and Los Angeles had become the nation's second largest manufacturing center. Nearly 2 million Americans moved to California for jobs in defense-related industries, and millions more passed through for military training and embarkation to the Pacific war.

In the South, the combination of rural out-migration and government investment in military-related factories and shipyards hastened a shift from agricultural to industrial employment. During the war, southern per capita income rose from 60 percent to 70 percent of the national average. But the South remained very poor when the war ended. Much of its rural population still lived in small wooden shacks with no indoor plumbing. The region had only two cities—Houston and New Orleans—with populations exceeding 500,000. Despite the expansion of war production, the South's economy still relied on agriculture and extractive industries—mining, lumber, oil—or manufacturing linked to farming, like the production of cotton textiles.

LABOR IN WARTIME

Organized labor repeatedly described World War II as a crusade for freedom that would expand economic and political democracy at home and abroad and win for unions a major voice in politics and industrial management. During the war, labor entered a three-sided arrangement with government and business that allowed union membership to soar to unprecedented levels. In order to secure industrial peace and stabilize war production, the federal government forced reluctant employers to recognize unions. In 1944, when Montgomery Ward, the large mail-order company, defied a pro-union order, the army seized its headquarters and physically evicted its president. For their part, union leaders agreed not to strike and conceded employers' right to "managerial prerogatives" and a "fair profit."

Despite the gains produced by labor militancy during the 1930s, unions only became firmly established in many sectors of the economy during World War II. By 1945, union membership stood at nearly 15 million, one-third of the non-farm labor force and the highest proportion in American history. But if labor became a partner in government, it was very much a junior partner. The decline of the New Deal, already evident in the late 1930s, proceeded during the war. Congress continued to be dominated by a conservative alliance of Republicans and southern Democrats. They left intact core New Deal programs like Social Security but eliminated agencies thought to be controlled by leftists, including the Civilian Conservation Corps, National Youth Administration, and Works Progress Administration. Congress rejected Roosevelt's call for a cap on personal incomes and set taxes on corporate profits at a level far lower than FDR requested. Despite the "no-strike" pledge, 1943 and 1944 witnessed numerous brief walkouts in which workers protested the increasing speed of assembly-line production and the disparity between wages frozen by government order and expanding corporate profits.

FIGHTING FOR THE FOUR FREEDOMS

Previous conflicts, including the Mexican War and World War I, had deeply divided American society. In contrast, World War II came to be remembered as the Good War, a time of national unity in pursuit of indisputably noble goals. But all wars require the mobilization of patriotic public opinion. By 1940, "To sell *goods*, we must sell *words*" had become a motto of advertisers. Foremost among the words that helped to "sell" World War II was "freedom."

Talk of freedom pervaded wartime America. To Roosevelt, the Four Freedoms expressed deeply held American values worthy of being spread worldwide. Freedom from fear meant not only a longing for peace but a more general desire for security in a world that appeared to be out of control. Freedom of speech and religion scarcely required detailed explanation. But their prominent place among the Four Freedoms accelerated the process by which First Amendment protections of free expression moved to the center of Americans' definition of liberty. In 1941, the administration celebrated with considerable fanfare the 150th anniversary of the Bill of Rights (the first ten amendments to the Constitution). FDR described their protections against tyrannical government as defining characteristics of American life, central to the rights of "free men and free women." In 1943, the Supreme Court reversed a 1940 ruling and, on First Amendment grounds, upheld the right of Jehovah's Witnesses to refuse to salute the American flag in public schools. The decision stood in sharp contrast to the coercive patriotism of World War I, and it affirmed the sanctity of individual conscience as a bedrock of freedom, even in times of crisis. The justices contrasted the American system of constitutional protection for unpopular minorities with Nazi tyranny.

FREEDOM FROM WANT

The "most ambiguous" of the Four Freedoms, *Fortune* magazine remarked, was freedom from want. Yet this "great inspiring phrase," as a Pennsylvania steelworker put it in a letter to the president, seemed to strike the deepest chord in a nation just emerging from the Depression. Roosevelt initially meant it to refer to the elimination of barriers to international trade. But he quickly came to link freedom from want to an economic goal more relevant to the average citizen—protecting the future "standard of living of the American worker and farmer" by guaranteeing that the Depression would not resume after the war. This, he declared, would bring "real freedom for the common man."

When Norman Rockwell's paintings of the Four Freedoms first appeared in the *Saturday Evening Post*, each was accompanied by a brief essay. Three of these essays, by the celebrated authors Stephen Vincent Benét, Booth Tarkington, and Will Durant, emphasized that the values Rockwell depicted were essentially American and the opposite of those of the Axis powers. For *Freedom from Want*, the editors chose an unknown Filipino poet, Carlos Bulosan, who had emigrated to the United States at the age of sixteen. Bulosan's essay showed how the Four Freedoms could inspire hopes for a better future as well as nostalgia for Rockwell's imagined small-town past. Bulosan wrote of those Americans still outside the social mainstream—migrant workers, cannery laborers, black victims of segregation—for whom freedom meant having enough to eat, sending their children to school, and being able to "share the promise and fruits of American life."

THE OFFICE OF WAR INFORMATION

The history of the Office of War Information (OWI), created in 1942 to mobilize public opinion, illustrates how the political divisions generated by the New Deal affected efforts to promote the Four Freedoms. The liberal Democrats who dominated the OWI's writing staff sought to make the conflict "a 'people's war' for freedom." The OWI feared that Americans had only a vague understanding of the war's purposes and that the populace seemed more fervently committed to paying back the Japanese for their attack on Pearl Harbor than ridding the world of fascism. They utilized radio, film, the press, and other media to give the conflict an ideological meaning, while seeking to avoid the nationalist hysteria of World War I.

Wartime mobilization drew on deep-seated American traditions. The portrait of the United States holding aloft the torch of liberty in a world overrun by oppression reached back at least as far as the American Revolution. The description of a world half slave and half free recalled the Great Emancipator. But critics charged that the OWI seemed most interested in promoting the definition of freedom Roosevelt had emphasized during the 1930s. One of its first pamphlets listed as elements of freedom the right to a job at fair pay and to adequate food, clothing, shelter, and medical care. Concerned that the OWI was devoting as much time to promoting New Deal social programs as to the war effort, Congress eliminated most of its funding.

Each side in World War II invoked history to rally support for its cause. This poster issued by the Office of War Information in the United States links the words of Abraham Lincoln to the struggle against Nazi tyranny.

THE FIFTH FREEDOM

After Congress curtailed the OWI, the "selling of America" became overwhelmingly a private affair. Under the watchful eye of the War Advertising Council, private companies joined in the campaign to promote wartime patriotism, while positioning themselves and their brand names for the postwar world. Alongside advertisements urging

Americans to purchase war bonds, guard against revealing military secrets, and grow "victory gardens" to allow food to be sent to the army, the war witnessed a burst of messages marketing advertisers' definition of freedom. Without directly criticizing Roosevelt, they repeatedly suggested that he had overlooked a fifth freedom. The National Association of Manufacturers and individual companies bombarded Americans with press releases, radio programs, and advertisements attributing the amazing feats of wartime production to "free enterprise."

Americans on the home front enjoyed a prosperity many could scarcely remember. Despite the rationing of scarce consumer items like coffee, meat, and gasoline, consumers found more goods available in 1944 than when the war began. With the memory of the Depression still very much alive, businessmen predicted a postwar world filled with consumer goods, with "freedom of choice" among abundant possibilities assured if only private enterprise were liberated from government controls. One advertisement for Royal typewriters, entitled "What This War Is All About," explained that victory would "hasten the day when you . . . can once more walk into any store in the land and buy anything you want." Certainly, ads suggested, the war did not imply any alteration in American institutions. "I'm fighting for freedom," said a soldier in an ad by the Nash-Kelvinator Corporation. "So don't anybody tell me I'll find America changed."

WOMEN AT WAR

During the war, the nation engaged in an unprecedented mobilization of "woman power" to fill industrial jobs vacated by men. OWI publications encouraged women to go to work, Hollywood films glorified the independent woman, and private advertising celebrated the achievements of Rosie the Riveter, the female industrial laborer depicted as muscular and self-reliant in Norman Rockwell's famous magazine cover. With 15 million men in the armed forces, women in 1944 made up more than one-third of the civilian labor force, and 350,000 served in auxiliary military units.

Even though most women workers still labored in clerical and service jobs, new opportunities suddenly opened in industrial, professional, and government positions previously restricted to men. On the West Coast, one-third of the workers in aircraft manufacturing and shipbuilding were women. For the first time in history, married women in their thirties outnumbered the young and single among female workers. Women forced unions like the United Auto Workers to confront issues like equal pay for equal work, maternity leave, and childcare facilities for working mothers. Defense companies sponsored swing bands and dances to boost worker morale and arranged dates between male and female workers. Having enjoyed what one wartime worker called "a taste

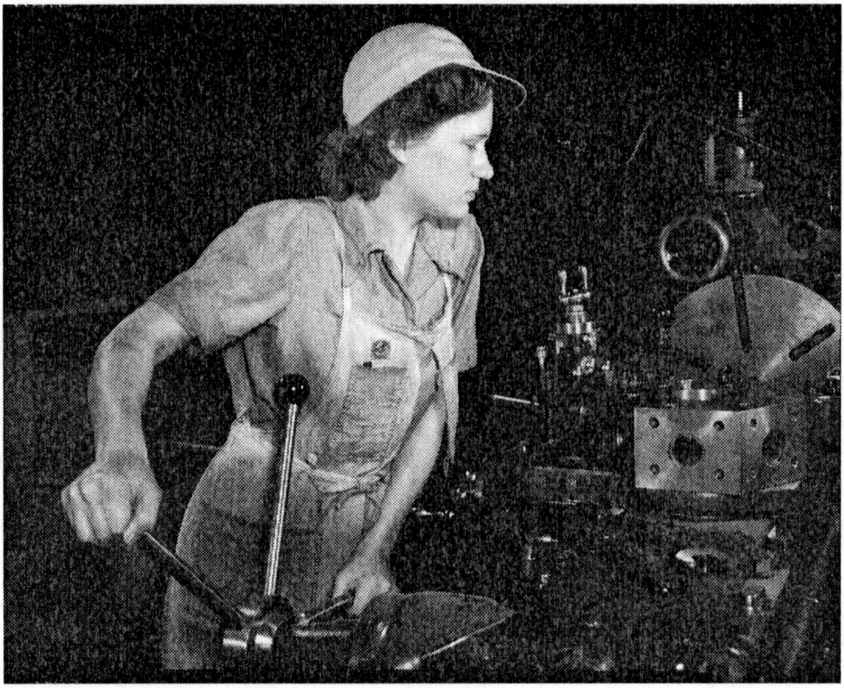

A female lathe operator in a Texas plant that produced transport planes.

of freedom"—doing "men's" jobs for men's wages and, sometimes, engaging in sexual activity while unmarried—many women hoped to remain in the labor force once peace returned.

WOMEN AT WORK

"We as a nation," proclaimed one magazine article, "must change our basic attitude toward the work of women." But change proved difficult. The government, employers, and unions depicted work as a temporary necessity, not an expansion of women's freedom. Advertisements assured women laboring in factories that they, too, were "fighting for freedom." But their language spoke of sacrifice and military victory, not rights, independence, or self-determination. One union publication even declared, "There should be a law requiring the women who have taken over men's jobs to be laid off after the war." When the war ended, most female war workers, especially those in better-paying industrial employment, did indeed lose their jobs.

Despite the upsurge in the number of working women, the advertisers' "world of tomorrow" rested on a vision of family-centered prosperity. Like Norman Rockwell's Four Freedoms paintings, these wartime discussions of freedom simultaneously looked forward to a day of material abundance and back to a time when the family stood as the bedrock of society. The "American way of life" celebrated during the war centered on the woman with "a husband to meet every night at the door," and a home stocked with household appliances and consumer goods. Advertisements portrayed working women dreaming of their boyfriends in the army and emphasized that with the proper makeup, women could labor in a factory and remain attractive to men. Men in the army seem to have assumed that they would return home to resume traditional family life. In one wartime radio program, a young man described his goal for peacetime: "Havin' a home and some kids, and breathin' fresh air out in the suburbs . . . livin' and workin' decent, like free people."

VISIONS OF POSTWAR FREEDOM

TOWARD AN AMERICAN CENTURY

The prospect of an affluent future provided a point of unity between New Dealers and conservatives, business and labor. And the promise of prosperity to some extent united two of the most celebrated blueprints for the postwar world. One was *The American Century*, publisher Henry Luce's 1941 effort to mobilize the American people both for the coming war and for an era of postwar world leadership. Americans, Luce's book insisted, must embrace the role history had thrust upon them as the "dominant power in the world." They must seize the opportunity to share with "all peoples" their "magnificent industrial products" and the "great American ideals," foremost among which stood "love of freedom." After the war, American power and American values would underpin a previously unimaginable prosperity—"the abundant life," Luce called it—produced by "free economic enterprise."

The idea of an American mission to spread democracy and freedom goes back to the Revolution. But traditionally, it had envisioned the country as an example, not an active agent imposing the American model throughout the globe. Luce's essay anticipated important aspects of the postwar world. But its bombastic rhetoric and a title easily interpreted as a call for an American imperialism aroused immediate opposition among liberals and the left. Henry Wallace offered their response in "The Price of Free World Victory," an address delivered in May 1942 to the Free World Association.

Wallace, secretary of agriculture during the 1930s and one of the more liberal New Dealers, had replaced Vice President John Nance Garner as Roosevelt's running mate in 1940. In contrast to Luce's American Century, a world of business dominance no less than of American power, Wallace predicted that the war would usher in a "century of the common man." The "march of freedom," said Wallace, would continue in the postwar world. That world, however, would be marked by international cooperation, not any single power's rule. Governments acting to "humanize" capitalism and redistribute economic resources would eliminate hunger, illiteracy, and poverty.

Luce and Wallace both spoke the language of freedom. Luce offered a confident vision of worldwide free enterprise, while Wallace anticipated a global New Deal. But they had one thing in common—a new conception of America's role in the world, tied to continued international involvement, the promise of economic abundance, and the idea that the American experience should serve as a model for all other nations. Neither took into account the ideas that other countries might have developed as to how to proceed once the war had ended.

"THE WAY OF LIFE OF FREE MEN"

Even as Congress moved to dismantle parts of the New Deal, liberal Democrats and their left-wing allies unveiled plans for a postwar economic policy that would allow all Americans to enjoy freedom from want. In 1942 and 1943, the reports of the National Resources Planning Board (NRPB) offered a blueprint for a peacetime economy based on full employment, an expanded welfare state, and a widely shared American standard of living. Economic security and full employment were the board's watchwords. It called for a "new bill of rights" that would include all Americans in an expanded Social Security system and guarantee access to education, health care, adequate housing, and jobs for able-bodied adults. Labor and farm organizations, church and civil rights groups, and liberal New Dealers hailed the reports as offering a "vision of freedom" for the postwar world. The NRPB's plan for a "full-employment economy" with a "fair distribution of income," said *The Nation*, embodied "the way of life of free men."

The reports continued a shift in liberals' outlook that dated from the late 1930s. Rather than seeking to reform the institutions of capitalism, liberals would henceforth rely on government spending to secure full employment, social welfare, and mass consumption, while leaving the operation of the economy in private hands. The reports appeared to reflect the views of British economist John Maynard Keynes, who had identified government spending as the best way to promote economic growth, even if it caused budget deficits. The war had, in effect, ended the Depression by implementing a military version of Keynesianism. In calling for massive spending on job creation and public works—urban redevelopment, rural electrification, an overhaul of the transportation system, and the like—the NRPB proposed the continuation of Keynesian spending in peacetime. But this went so far beyond what Congress was willing to support that it eliminated the NRPB's funding.

AN ECONOMIC BILL OF RIGHTS

Roosevelt had not publicized or promoted the NRPB reports of 1942 and 1943. Yet mindful that public-opinion polls showed a large majority of Americans favoring a guarantee of employment for those who could not find work, the president in 1944 called for an "Economic Bill of Rights." The original Bill of Rights restricted the power of government in the name of liberty. FDR proposed to expand its power in order to secure full employment, an adequate income, medical care, education, and a decent home for all Americans. "True individual freedom," he declared, "cannot exist without economic security and independence."

Already ill and preoccupied with the war, Roosevelt spoke only occasionally of the Economic Bill of Rights during the 1944 presidential campaign. The replacement of Vice President Henry Wallace by Harry S. Truman, then a little-known senator from Missouri, suggested that the president did not intend to do battle with Congress over social policy. Congress did not enact the Economic Bill of Rights. But in 1944, it extended to the millions of returning veterans an array of benefits, including unemployment pay, scholarships for further education, low-cost mortgage loans, pensions, and job training. The Servicemen's Readjustment Act, or GI Bill of Rights, was one of the most far-reaching pieces of social legislation in American history. Aimed at rewarding members of the armed forces for their service and preventing the widespread unemployment and economic disruption that had followed World War I, it profoundly shaped postwar society. By 1946, more than 1 million veterans were attending college under its provisions, making up half of total college enrollment. Almost 4 million would receive home mortgages, spurring the postwar suburban housing boom.

During 1945, unions, civil rights organizations, and religious groups urged Congress to enact the Full Employment Bill, which tried to do for the entire economy what the GI Bill promised veterans. The measure established a "right to employment" for all Americans and required the federal government to increase its level of spending to create enough jobs in case the economy failed to do so. The target of an intense business lobbying campaign, the bill only passed in 1946 with the word "Full" removed from its title and after its commitment to governmental job creation had been eliminated. But as the war drew to a close, most Americans embraced the idea that the government must continue to play a major role in maintaining employment and a high standard of living.

THE ROAD TO SERFDOM

The failure of the Full Employment Bill confirmed the political stalemate that had begun with the elections of 1938. It also revealed the renewed intellectual respectability of fears that economic planning represented a threat to liberty. When the *New Republic* spoke of full employment as the "road to freedom," it subtly acknowledged the impact of *The Road to Serfdom* (1944), a surprise best-seller by Friedrich A. Hayek, a previously obscure Austrian-born economist. Hayek claimed that even the best-intentioned government efforts to direct the economy posed a threat to individual liberty. He offered a simple message—"planning leads to dictatorship."

Coming at a time when the miracles of war production had reinvigorated belief in the virtues of capitalism, and with the confrontation with Nazism highlighting the danger of merging economic and political power, Hayek offered a new intellectual justification for opponents of active government. In a complex economy, he insisted, no single person or group of experts could possibly possess enough knowledge to direct economic activity intelligently. A free market, he wrote, mobilizes the fragmented and partial knowledge scattered throughout society far more effectively than a planned economy.

Unlike many of his disciples, Hayek was not a doctrinaire advocate of laissez-faire. His book endorsed measures that later conservatives would denounce as forms of socialism—minimum wage and maximum hours laws, antitrust enforcement, and a social safety net guaranteeing all citizens a basic minimum of food, shelter, and clothing. Hayek, moreover, criticized traditional conservatives for fondness for social hierarchy and authoritarian government. "I am not a conservative," he would later write. But by equating fascism, socialism, and the New Deal and by identifying economic planning with a loss of freedom, he helped lay the foundation for the rise of modern conservatism and a revival of laissez-faire economic thought. As the war drew to a close, the stage was set for a renewed battle over the government's proper role in society and the economy, and the social conditions of American freedom.

THE AMERICAN DILEMMA

The unprecedented attention to freedom as the defining characteristic of American life had implications that went far beyond wartime mobilization. World War II reshaped Americans' understanding of themselves as a people. The struggle against Nazi tyranny and its theory of a master race discredited ethnic and racial inequality. Originally promoted by religious and ethnic minorities in the 1920s and the Popular Front in the 1930s, a pluralist vision of American society now became part of official rhetoric. What set the United States apart from its wartime foes, the government insisted, was not only dedication to the ideals of the Four Freedoms but also the principle that Americans of all races, religions, and national origins could enjoy those freedoms equally. Racism was the enemy's philosophy; Americanism rested on toleration of diversity and equality for all. By the end of the war, the new immigrant groups had been fully accepted as loyal ethnic Americans, rather than members of distinct and inferior "races." And the contradiction between the principle of equal freedom and the actual status of blacks had come to the forefront of national life.

PATRIOTIC ASSIMILATION

Among other things, World War II created a vast melting pot, especially for European immigrants and their children. Millions of Americans moved out of urban ethnic neighborhoods and isolated rural enclaves into the army and industrial plants where they came into contact with people of very different backgrounds. What one historian has called their "patriotic assimilation" differed sharply from the forced Americanization of World War I. While the Wilson administration had established Anglo-Saxon culture as a national norm, Roosevelt promoted pluralism as the only source of harmony in a diverse society. The American way of life, wrote the novelist Pearl Buck in an OWI pamphlet, rested on brotherhood—the principle that "persons of many lands can live together . . . and if they believe in freedom they can become a united people."

Government and private agencies eagerly promoted equality as the definition of Americanism and a counterpoint to Nazism. Officials rewrote history to establish racial and ethnic tolerance as the American way. To be an American, FDR declared, had always been a "matter of mind and heart," and "never . . . a matter of race or ancestry"—a statement more effective in mobilizing support for the war than in accurately describing the nation's past. Mindful of the intolerance spawned by World War I, the OWI highlighted nearly every group's contributions to American life and celebrated the strength of a people united in respect for diversity. One OWI pamphlet described prejudice as a foreign import rather than a homegrown product and declared bigots more dangerous than spies—they were "fighting for the enemy."

Arthur Poinier's cartoon for the Detroit Free Press, *June 19, 1941, illustrates how, during World War II, white ethnics (of British, German, Irish, French, Polish, Italian,and Scandinanvian descent) were incorporated within the boundaries of American freedom.*

Horrified by the uses to which the Nazis put the idea of inborn racial difference, biological and social scientists abandoned belief in a link among race, culture, and intelligence, an idea only recently central to their disciplines. Ruth Benedict's *Races and Racism* (1942) described racism as "a travesty of scientific knowledge." In the same year, Ashley Montagu's *Man's Most Dangerous Myth: The Fallacy of Race* became a best-seller. By the war's end, racism and nativism had been stripped of intellectual respectability, at least outside the South, and were viewed as psychological disorders.

Hollywood, too, did its part, portraying fighting units whose members, representing various regional, ethnic, and religious backgrounds, put aside group loyalties and prejudices for the common cause. *Air Force* featured a bomber crew that included an Anglo-Saxon officer, a Jewish sergeant, and a Polish-American gunner. In the film *Bataan*, the ethnically balanced platoon included a black soldier, even though the real army was racially segregated. The war's most popular motion picture, *This Is the Army*, starring, among others, future president Ronald Reagan, offered a vision of postwar society that celebrated the ethnic diversity of the American people.

Intolerance, of course, hardly disappeared from American life. One correspondent complained to Norman Rockwell that he included too many "foreign-looking" faces in his *Freedom of Worship* painting. Many business and government circles still excluded Jews. Along with the fact that early reports of the Holocaust were too terrible to be believed, anti-Semitism contributed to the government's unwillingness to allow more than a handful of European Jews (21,000 during the course of the war) to find refuge in the United States. Roosevelt himself learned during the war of the extent of Hitler's "final solution" to the Jewish presence in Europe. But he failed to authorize air strikes that might have destroyed German death camps.

Nonetheless, the war made millions of ethnic Americans, especially the children of the new immigrants, feel fully American for the first time. During the war, one New York "ethnic" recalled, "the Italo-Americans stopped being Italo and started becoming Americans." But the event that inspired this comment, the Harlem race riot of 1943, suggested that patriotic assimilation stopped at the color line.

THE *BRACERO* PROGRAM

The war had a far more ambiguous meaning for non-white groups than for whites. On the eve of Pearl Harbor, racial barriers remained deeply entrenched in American life. Southern blacks were still trapped in a rigid system of segregation. Asians could not emigrate to the United States or become naturalized citizens. More than 400,000 Mexican-Americans had been "voluntarily" repatriated by local authorities in the Southwest during the Depression. Most American Indians still lived on reservations, in dismal poverty.

The war set in motion changes that would reverberate in the postwar years. Under the *bracero* program agreed to by the Mexican and American governments in 1942 (the name derives from *brazo*, the Spanish word for arm), tens of thousands of contract laborers crossed into the United States to take up jobs as domestic and agricultural workers. Initially designed as a temporary response to the wartime labor shortage, the program lasted until 1964. During the period of the *bracero* program, more than 4.5 million Mexicans entered the United States under government labor contracts (while a slightly larger number were arrested for illegal entry by the Border Patrol). *Braceros* were supposed to receive decent housing and wages. But since they could not become citizens and could be deported at any time, they found it almost impossible to form unions or secure better working conditions.

Although the *bracero* program reinforced the status of immigrants from Mexico as an unskilled labor force, wartime employment opened new opportunities for second-generation Mexican-Americans. Hundreds of thousands of men and women emerged from ethnic neighborhoods, or *barrios*, to work in defense industries and serve in the army (where, unlike blacks, they fought alongside whites). A new "Chicano" culture—a fusion of Mexican heritage and American experience—was being born. Contact with other groups led many to learn English and sparked a rise in interethnic marriages.

MEXICAN-AMERICAN RIGHTS

The "zoot suit" riots of 1943, in which club-wielding sailors and policemen attacked Mexican-American youths wearing flamboyant clothing on the streets of Los Angeles, illustrated the limits of wartime tolerance. "Our Latin American boys," complained one activist, "are not segregated at the front line. . . . They are dying that democracy may live." Yet when they return home, the activist continued, "they are not considered good enough to go into a café." But the contrast between the war's rhetoric of freedom and pluralism and the reality of continued discrimination inspired a heightened consciousness of civil rights. For example, Mexican-Americans brought complaints of discrimination before the Fair Employment Practices Commission (FEPC) to fight the practice in the Southwest of confining them to the lowest-paid work or paying them lower wages than white workers doing the same jobs.

Perhaps half a million Mexican-American men and women served in the armed forces. And with discrimination against Mexicans an increasing embarrassment in view of Roosevelt's Good Neighbor policy, Texas (the state with the largest population of Mexican descent) in 1943 unanimously passed the oddly named Caucasian Race—Equal Privileges resolution. It stated that since "all the nations of the North and South American continents" were united in the struggle against Nazism, "all persons of the Caucasian race" were entitled to equal treatment in places of public accommodation. Since Texas law had long defined Mexicans as white, the measure applied to them while not challenging the segregation of blacks. The resolution lacked an enforcement mechanism. Indeed, because of continued discrimination in Texas, the Mexican government for a time prohibited the state from receiving laborers under the *bracero* program.

INDIANS DURING THE WAR

The war also brought many American Indians closer to the mainstream of American life. Some 25,000 served in the army (including the famous Navajo "code-talkers," who transmitted messages in their complex native language, which the Japanese could not decipher). Insisting that the United States lacked the authority to draft Indian men into the army, the Iroquois issued their own declaration of war against the Axis powers. Tens of thousands of Indians left reservations for jobs in war industries. Exposed for the first time to urban life and industrial society, many chose not to return to the reservations after the war ended (indeed, the reservations did not share in wartime prosperity). Some Indian veterans took advantage of the GI Bill to attend college after the war, an opportunity that had been available to very few Indians previously.

ASIAN-AMERICANS IN WARTIME

Asian-Americans' war experience was paradoxical. More than 50,000—the children of immigrants from China, Japan, Korea, and the Philippines—fought in the army, mostly in all-Asian units. With China an ally in the Pacific war, Congress in 1943 ended decades of complete exclusion by establishing a nationality quota for Chinese immigrants. The annual limit of 105 hardly suggested a desire for a large-scale influx. But the image of the Chinese as gallant fighters defending their country against Japanese aggression called into question long-standing racial stereotypes. As in the case of Mexican-Americans, large numbers of Chinese-Americans moved out of ethnic ghettos to work alongside whites in jobs on the home front.

The experience of Japanese-Americans was far different. Many Americans viewed the war against Germany as an ideological struggle. But both sides saw the Pacific war as a race war. Japanese propaganda depicted Americans as a self-indulgent people contaminated by ethnic and racial diversity as opposed to the racially "pure" Japanese. In the United States, long-standing prejudices and the shocking attack on Pearl Harbor combined to produce an unprecedented hatred of Japan. "In all our history," according to one historian, "no foe has been detested as were the Japanese." Government propaganda and war films portrayed the Japanese foe as rats, dogs, gorillas, and snakes—bestial and subhuman. They blamed Japanese aggression on a violent racial or national character, not, as in the case of Germany and Italy, on tyrannical rulers.

About 70 percent of Japanese-Americans in the continental United States lived in California, where they dominated vegetable farming in the Los Angeles area. One-third were first-generation immigrants, or *issei*, but a substantial majority were *nisei*—American-born, and therefore citizens. Many of the latter spoke only English, had never been to Japan, and had tried to assimilate despite prevailing prejudice. But the Japanese-American community could not remain unaffected by the rising tide of hatred. The government bent over backward to include German-Americans and Italian-Americans in the war effort. It ordered the arrest of only a handful of the more than 800,000 German and Italian nationals in the United States when the war began. But it viewed every person of Japanese ethnicity as a potential spy.

JAPANESE-AMERICAN INTERNMENT

California had a long history of hostility toward the Japanese. Now, inspired by exaggerated fears of a Japanese invasion of the West Coast and pressured by whites who saw an opportunity to gain possession of Japanese-American property, the military persuaded FDR to issue Executive Order 9066. Promulgated in February 1942, this ordered the relocation of all persons of Japanese descent from the West Coast. That spring and summer, authorities removed more than 110,000 men, women, and children—nearly two-thirds of them American citizens—to camps far from their homes. The order did not apply to persons of Japanese descent living in Hawaii, where they represented nearly 40 percent of the population. Despite Hawaii's vulnerability, its economy could not function without Japanese-American labor. But the treatment of mainland Japanese-Americans provided ammunition for Japan's claim that its aggressions in Asia were intended to defend the rights of non-white peoples against colonial rule and a racist United States.

The internees were subjected to a quasi-military discipline in the camps. Living in former horse stables, makeshift shacks, or barracks behind barbed wire fences, they were awakened for roll call at 6:45 each morning and ate their meals (which rarely included the Japanese cooking to which they were accustomed) in giant mess halls. Armed guards patrolled the camps, and searchlights shone all night. Privacy was difficult to come by, and medical facilities were often nonexistent. Nonetheless, the internees did their best to create an atmosphere of home, decorating their accommodations with pictures, flowers, and curtains, planting vegetable gardens, and setting up activities like sports clubs and art classes for themselves.

Internment revealed how easily war can undermine basic freedoms. There were no court hearings, no due process, and no writs of habeas corpus. One searches the wartime record in vain for public protests among non-Japanese against the gravest violation of civil liberties since the end of slavery. The press supported the policy almost unanimously. In Congress, only Senator Robert Taft of Ohio spoke out against it. Groups publicly committed to fighting discrimination, from the Communist Party to the NAACP and the American Jewish Committee, either defended the policy or remained silent.

The courts refused to intervene. In 1944, in *Korematsu v. United States*, the Supreme Court denied the appeal of Fred Korematsu, a Japanese-American citizen who had been arrested for refusing to present himself for internment. Speaking for a 6-3 majority, Justice Hugo Black, usually an avid defender of civil liberties, upheld the legality of the internment policy, insisting that an order applying only to persons of Japanese descent was not based on race. The Court has never overturned the *Korematsu* decision. As Justice Robert H. Jackson warned in his dissent, it "lies about like a loaded weapon ready for the hand of any authority that can bring forward a plausible claim" of national security.

The government marketed war bonds to the internees. It established a loyalty oath program, expecting Japanese-Americans to swear allegiance to the government that had imprisoned them and to enlist in the army. Some young men refused, and about 200 were sent to prison for resisting the draft.

JAPANESE-AMERICAN INTERNMENT, 1942–1945

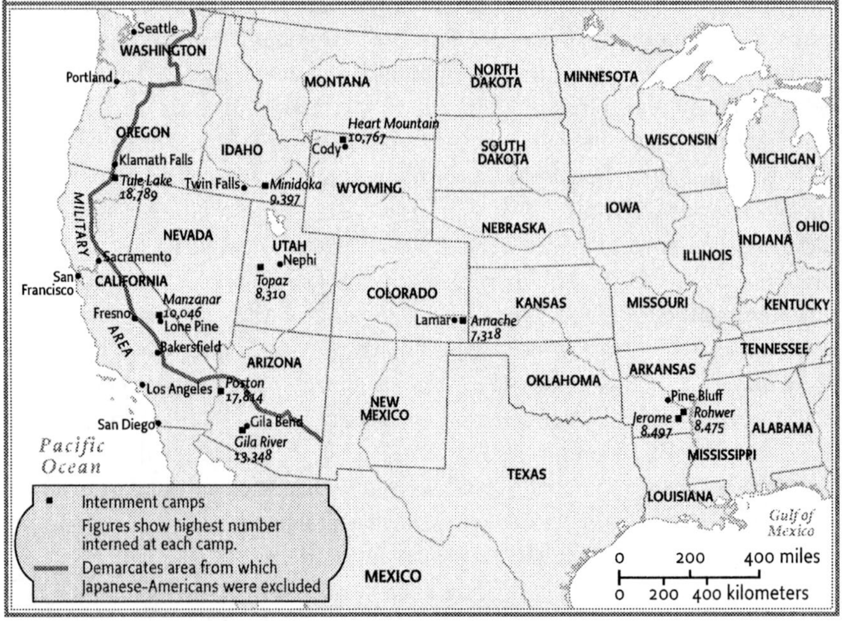

More than 100,000 Japanese-Americans—the majority American citizens—were forcibly moved from their homes to internment camps during World War II.

"Let us out and then maybe I'll think about risking my skin for 'the land of the free,'" one of the resisters remarked. But 20,000 Japanese-Americans joined the armed forces from the camps, along with another 13,000 from Hawaii. A long campaign for acknowledgment of the injustice done to Japanese-Americans followed the end of the war. In 1988, Congress apologized for internment and provided $20,000 in compensation to each surviving victim. President Bill Clinton subsequently awarded Fred Korematsu the Presidential Medal of Freedom.

BLACKS AND THE WAR

Although the treatment of Japanese-Americans revealed the stubborn hold of racism in American life, the wartime message of freedom portended a major transformation in the status of blacks. "There never has been, there isn't now, and there never will be," Roosevelt declared, "any race of people on the earth fit to serve as masters over their fellow men." Yet Nazi Germany cited American practices as proof of its own race policies. Washington remained a rigidly segregated city, and the Red Cross refused to mix blood from blacks and whites in its blood banks (thereby, critics charged, in effect accepting Nazi race theories). Charles Drew, the black scientist who pioneered the techniques of storing and shipping blood plasma—a development of immense importance to the treatment of wounded soldiers—protested bitterly against this policy, pointing out that it had no scientific basis. In 1940 and 1941, even as Roosevelt called for aid to the free peoples of Europe, thirteen lynchings took place in the United States.

The war spurred a movement of black population from the rural South to the cities of the North and West that dwarfed the Great Migration of World War I and the 1920s. About 700,000 black migrants poured out of the South on what they called "liberty trains," seeking jobs in the industrial heartland. They encountered sometimes violent hostility, nowhere more so than in Detroit, where angry white residents forced authorities to evict black tenants from a new housing project. In 1943, a fight at a Detroit city park spiraled into a race riot that left thirty-four persons dead, and a "hate strike" of 20,000 workers protested the upgrading of black employees in a plant manufacturing aircraft engines. The war failed to end lynching. Isaac Simmons, a black minister, was murdered in 1944 for refusing to sell his land to a white man who believed it might contain oil. The criminals went unpunished. This took place in Liberty, Mississippi.

BLACKS AND MILITARY SERVICE

When World War II began, the air force and marines had no black members. The army restricted the number of black enlistees and contained only five black officers, three of them chaplains. The navy accepted blacks only as waiters and cooks.

During the war, more than 1 million blacks served in the armed forces. They did so in segregated units, largely confined to construction, transport, and other noncombat tasks. Many northern black draftees were sent to the South for military training, where they found themselves excluded from movie theaters and servicemen's clubs on military bases and abused when they ventured into local towns. Black soldiers sometimes had to give up their seats on railroad cars to accommodate Nazi prisoners of war. "Nothing so lowers Negro morale," wrote the NAACP's magazine, *The Crisis*, "as the frequent preferential treatment of Axis prisoners of war in contrast with Army policy toward American troops who happen to be Negro."

When southern black veterans returned home and sought benefits through the GI Bill, they encountered even more evidence of racial discrimination. On the surface, the GI Bill contained no racial differentiation in offering benefits like health care, college tuition assistance, job training, and loans to start a business or purchase a farm. But local authorities who administered its provisions allowed southern black veterans to use its education benefits only at segregated colleges, limited their job training to unskilled work and low-wage service jobs, and limited loans for farm purchase to white veterans.

BIRTH OF THE CIVIL RIGHTS MOVEMENT

In 1942, a public-opinion survey sponsored by the army's Bureau of Intelligence found that the vast majority of white Americans were "unaware that there is any such thing as a 'Negro problem'??" and were convinced that blacks were satisfied with their social and economic conditions. They would soon discover their mistake.

The war years witnessed the birth of the modern civil rights movement. Angered by the almost complete exclusion of African-Americans from jobs in the rapidly expanding war industries (of 100,000 aircraft workers in 1940, fewer than 300 were blacks), the black labor leader A. Philip Randolph in July 1941 called for a March on Washington. His demands included access to defense employment, an end to segregation, and a national antilynching law. Randolph, who as founder of the Brotherhood of Sleeping Car Porters had long battled racism among both employers and unions, hurled Roosevelt's rhetoric back at the president. Randolph declared racial discrimination "undemocratic, un-American, and pro-Hitler."

The prospect of thousands of angry blacks descending on Washington, remarked one official, "scared the government half to death." To persuade Randolph to call off the march, Roosevelt issued Executive Order 8802, which banned discrimination in defense jobs and established a Fair Employment

Practices Commission (FEPC) to monitor compliance. The black press hailed the order as a new Emancipation Proclamation.

Essentially an investigative agency, the FEPC lacked enforcement powers. But its very existence marked a significant shift in public policy. Its hearings exposed patterns of racial exclusion so ingrained that firms at first freely admitted that their want ads asked for "colored" applicants for positions as porters and janitors and "white" ones for skilled jobs, and that they allowed black women to work only as laundresses and cooks. The first federal agency since Reconstruction to campaign for equal opportunity for black Americans, the FEPC played an important role in obtaining jobs for black workers in industrial plants and shipyards. In southern California, the aircraft manufacturer Lockheed ran special buses into black neighborhoods to bring workers to its plants. By 1944, more than 1 million blacks, 300,000 of them women, held manufacturing jobs. ("My sister always said that Hitler was the one that got us out of the white folks' kitchen," recalled one black woman.)

THE DOUBLE-V

When the president "said that we should have the Four Freedoms," a black steelworker declared, he meant to include "all races." During the war, NAACP membership grew from 50,000 to nearly 500,000. The Congress of Racial Equality (CORE), founded by an interracial group of pacifists in 1942, held sit-ins in northern cities to integrate restaurants and theaters. After a Firestone tire factory in Memphis fired a black woman for trying to enter a city bus before white passengers had been seated, black workers at the plant went on strike until she was reinstated.

In February 1942, the *Pittsburgh Courier* coined the phrase that came to symbolize black attitudes during the war—the "double-V." Victory over Germany and Japan, it insisted, must be accompanied by victory over segregation at home. While the Roosevelt administration and the white press saw the war as an expression of American ideals, black newspapers pointed to the gap between those ideals and reality. Side by side with ads for war bonds, *The Crisis* insisted that a segregated army "cannot fight for a free world."

Surveying wartime public opinion, a political scientist concluded that "symbols of national solidarity" had very different meanings to white and black Americans. To blacks, freedom from fear meant, among other things, an end to lynching, and freedom from want included doing away with "discrimination in getting jobs." If, in whites' eyes, freedom was a "possession to be defended," he observed, to blacks and other racial minorities it remained a "goal to be achieved." "*Our* fight for freedom," said a returning black veteran of the Pacific war, "begins when we get to San Francisco."

VOICES OF FREEDOM

From Henry R. Luce, *The American Century* (1941)

Even before the United States entered World War II, some Americans were thinking of a postwar world in which the United States would exert its influence throughout the globe. One influential call for Americans to accept the burden of world leadership was a short book by Henry R. Luce, the publisher of *Life* and *Time* magazines.

In the field of national policy, the fundamental trouble with America has been, and is, that whereas their nation became in the 20th Century the most powerful and the most vital nation in the world, nevertheless Americans were unable to accommodate themselves spiritually and practically to that fact. Hence they have failed to play their part as a world power—a failure which has had disastrous consequences for themselves and for all mankind. And the cure is this: to accept wholeheartedly our duty and our opportunity as the most powerful and vital nation in the world and in consequence to exert upon the world the full impact of our influence, for such purposes as we see fit and by such means as we see fit. . . .

Our world of 2,000,000,000 human beings is for the first time in history one world, fundamentally indivisible. . . . Our world, again for the first time in human history, is capable of producing all the material needs of the entire human family. . . . The world of the 20th Century, if it is to come to life in any nobility of health and vigor, must be to a significant degree an American Century. . . .

In postulating the indivisibility of the contemporary world, one does not necessarily imagine that anything like a world state—a parliament of men—must be brought about in this century. Nor need we assume that war can be abolished. . . . Large sections of the human family may be effectively organized into opposition to one another. Tyrannies may require a large amount of living space. But Freedom requires and will require far greater living space than Tyranny. . . . Justice will come near to losing all meaning in the minds of men unless Justice can have approximately the same fundamental meanings in many lands and among many peoples. . . .

As to the . . . promise of adequate production for all mankind, the "more abundant life," be it noted that this is characteristically an American promise. . . . What we must insist on is that the abundant life is predicated on Freedom. . . . Without Freedom, there will be no abundant life. With Freedom, there can be.

And finally there is the belief—shared let us remember by most men living—that the 20th Century must be to a significant degree an American Century. . . . As America enters dynamically upon the world scene, we need most of all to seek and to bring forth a vision of America as a world power and to bring forth a vision . . . which will guide us to the authentic creation of the 20th Century—our Century.

From Charles H. Wesley, "The Negro Has Always Wanted the Four Freedoms," in *What the Negro Wants* (1944)

In 1944, the University of North Carolina Press published *What the Negro Wants*, a book of essays by fourteen prominent black leaders. Virtually every contributor called for the right to vote in the South, the dismantling of segregation, and access to the "American standard of living." Several essays also linked the black struggle for racial justice with movements against European imperialism in Africa and Asia. When he read the manuscript, W. T. Couch, the director of the press, was stunned. "If this is what the Negro wants," he told the book's editor, "nothing could be clearer than what he needs, and needs most urgently, is to revise his wants." In this excerpt, the historian Charles H. Wesley explains that blacks are denied each of the Four Freedoms, and also illustrates how the war strengthened black internationalism.

[Negroes] have wanted what other citizens of the United States have wanted. They have wanted freedom and opportunity. They have wanted the pursuit of the life vouchsafed to all citizens of the United States by our own liberty documents. They have wanted freedom of speech, [but] they were supposed to be silently acquiescent in all aspects of their life.... They have wanted freedom of religion, for they had been compelled to "steal away to Jesus" ... in order to worship God as they desired.... They have wanted freedom from want.... However, the Negro has remained a marginal worker and the competition with white workers has left him in want in many localities of an economically sufficient nation. They have wanted freedom from fear. They have been cowed, browbeaten or beaten, as they have marched through the years of American life....

The Negro wants democracy to begin at home.... The future of our democratic life is insecure so long as the hatred, disdain and disparagement of Americans of African ancestry exist....

The Negro wants not only to win the war but also to win the peace.... He wants the peace to be free of race and color restrictions, of imperialism and exploitation, and inclusive of the participation of minorities all over the world in their own governments. When it is said that we are fighting for freedom, the Negro asks, "Whose freedom?" Is it the freedom of a peace to exploit, suppress, exclude, debase and restrict colored peoples in India, China, Africa, Malaya in the usual ways? ... Will Great Britain and the United States specifically omit from the Four Freedoms their minorities and subject peoples? The Negro does not want such a peace.

QUESTIONS

1. What values does Luce wish America to spread to the rest of the world?

2. Why does Wesley believe that black Americans are denied the Four Freedoms?

3. Do Luce and Wesley envision different roles for the United States in the postwar world?

WHAT THE NEGRO WANTS

During the war, a broad political coalition centered on the left but reaching well beyond it called for an end to racial inequality in America. The NAACP and American Jewish Congress cooperated closely in advocating laws to ban discrimination in employment and housing. Despite considerable resistance from rank-and-file white workers, CIO unions, especially those with strong left-liberal and communist influence, made significant efforts to organize black workers and win them access to skilled positions. AFL craft unions by and large continued their long tradition of excluding black workers. But during World War II, the CIO was probably more racially integrated than any labor organization since the Knights of Labor in the 1880s.

The new black militancy created a crisis for moderate white southerners. They now saw their middle ground evaporating as blacks demanded an end to segregation while southern politicians took up the cry of protecting white supremacy. The latter also spoke the language of freedom. Defenders of the racial status quo interpreted freedom to mean the right to shape their region's institutions without outside interference. The "war emergency," insisted Governor Frank Dixon of Alabama, "should not be used as a pretext to bring about the abolition of the color line." Even as the war gave birth to the modern civil rights movement, it also planted the seeds for the South's "massive resistance" to desegregation during the 1950s.

In the rest of the country, however, the status of black Americans assumed a place at the forefront of enlightened liberalism. Far more than in the 1930s, federal officials spoke openly of the need for a dramatic change in race relations. American democracy, noted Secretary of War Stimson, had not yet addressed "the persistent legacy of the original crime of slavery." Progress came slowly. But the National War Labor Board banned racial wage differentials. In *Smith v. Allwright* (1944), the Supreme Court outlawed all-white primaries, one of the mechanisms by which southern states deprived blacks of political rights. In the same year, the navy began assigning small numbers of black sailors to previously all-white ships. In the final months of the war, it ended segregation altogether, and the army established a few combat units that included black and white soldiers.

After a world tour in 1942 to rally support for the Allies, Wendell Willkie, Roosevelt's opponent of 1940, published *One World*. It sold 1 million copies, faster than any nonfiction work in American history. Willkie's travels persuaded him that Asia, Africa, and Latin America would play a pivotal role in the postwar era. But the book's great surprise came in Willkie's attack on "our imperialisms at home." Unless the United States addressed the "mocking paradox" of racism, he insisted, its claim to world leadership would lack moral authority. "If we want to talk about freedom," Willkie wrote, "we must mean freedom for everyone inside our frontiers."

AN AMERICAN DILEMMA

No event reflected the new concern with the status of black Americans more than the publication in 1944 of *An American Dilemma*, a sprawling account of the country's racial past, present, and future written by the Swedish social scientist Gunnar Myrdal. The book offered an uncompromising portrait of how deeply racism was entrenched in law, politics, economics, and social behavior. But Myrdal combined this sobering analysis with admiration for what he called the American Creed—belief in equality, justice, equal opportunity, and freedom. The war, he argued, had made Americans more aware than ever of the contradiction between this creed and the reality of racial inequality. He concluded that "there is bound to be a redefinition of the Negro's status as a result of this War."

Myrdal's notion of a conflict between American values and American racial policies was hardly new—Frederick Douglass and W. E. B. Du Bois had said much the same thing. But in the context of a worldwide struggle against Nazism and rising black demands for equality at home, his book struck a chord. It identified a serious national problem and seemed to offer an almost painless path to peaceful change, in which the federal government would take the lead in outlawing discrimination. This coupling of an appeal to American principles with federal social engineering established a liberal position on race relations that would survive for many years.

By 1945, support for racial justice had finally taken its place on the liberal-left agenda alongside full employment, civil liberties, and the expansion of the New Deal welfare state. Roosevelt himself rarely spoke out on racial issues. But many liberals insisted that racial discrimination must be confronted head-on through federal antilynching legislation, equal opportunity in the workplace, an end to segregated housing and schools, and the expansion of Social Security programs to cover agricultural and domestic workers. This wartime vision of a racially integrated full employment economy formed a bridge between the New Deal and the Great Society of the 1960s.

BLACK INTERNATIONALISM

In the nineteenth century, black radicals like David Walker and Martin Delany had sought to link the fate of African-Americans with that of peoples of African descent in other parts of the world, especially the Caribbean and Africa. In the first decades of the twentieth century, this kind of international consciousness was reinvigorated. In a sense, the global imposition of white supremacy brought forth a feeling of racial solidarity across national and geographic lines. Garveyism was one example; another was reflected in the five Pan-African Congresses that met between 1919 and 1945. Attended by black intellectuals from the United States, the Caribbean, Europe, and

Africa, these gatherings denounced the colonial rule of Africa and sought to establish a sense of unity among all people in the African diaspora (a term used to describe the scattering of a people with a single national, religious, or racial identity). At the home of George Padmore, a West Indian labor organizer and editor living in London, black American leaders like W. E. B. Du Bois and Paul Robeson came into contact with future leaders of African independence movements such as Jomo Kenyatta (Kenya), Kwame Nkrumah (Ghana), and Nnamdi Azikiwe (Nigeria). "I discovered Africa in London," Robeson remarked.

Through these gatherings, Du Bois, Robeson, and others developed an outlook that linked the plight of black Americans with that of people of color worldwide. Racism, they came to believe, originated not in irrational hatred but in the slave trade and slavery. In the modern age, it was perpetuated by colonialism. Thus, freeing Africa from colonial rule would encourage greater equality at home.

World War II stimulated among African-Americans an even greater awareness of the links between racism in the United States and colonialism abroad. In 1942, the *Pittsburgh Courier*, a major black newspaper, began publishing regular columns on events in India (where the British had imprisoned leaders of the movement for national independence) and China. In the same year, Robeson founded the Council on African Affairs, which tried to place colonial liberation at the top of the black American agenda.

THE END OF THE WAR

As 1945 opened, Allied victory was assured. In December 1944, in a desperate gamble, Hitler launched a surprise counterattack in France that pushed Allied forces back fifty miles, creating a large bulge in their lines. The largest single battle ever fought by the U.S. Army, the Battle of the Bulge produced more than 70,000 American casualties. But by early 1945 the assault had failed.

In March, American troops crossed the Rhine River and entered the industrial heartland of Germany. Hitler took his own life, and shortly afterward Soviet forces occupied Berlin. On May 8, known as V-E Day (for victory in Europe), came the formal end to the war against Germany. In the Pacific, American forces moved ever closer to Japan. They had reconquered Guam in August 1944 and landed in the Philippines two months later, where they destroyed most of the remainder of the enemy fleet in the naval battle of Leyte Gulf.

"THE MOST TERRIBLE WEAPON"

Franklin D. Roosevelt defeated Republican nominee Thomas E. Dewey, the governor of New York, to win an unprecedented fourth term in 1944. But FDR did not live to see the Allied victory. He succumbed to a stroke on April 12, 1945. To his successor, Harry S. Truman, fell one of the most momentous decisions ever confronted by an American president—whether to use the atomic bomb against Japan. Truman did not know about the bomb until after he became president. Then, Secretary of War Stimson informed him that the United States had secretly developed "the most terrible weapon ever known in human history."

The bomb was a practical realization of the theory of relativity, a rethinking of the laws of physics developed early in the twentieth century by the German scientist Albert Einstein. Energy and matter, Einstein showed, represented two forms of the same phenomenon. According to his famous equation $E = mc^2$, the energy contained in matter equals its mass times the speed of light squared—an enormous amount. By using certain forms of uranium, or the man-made element plutonium, an atomic reaction could be created that transformed part of the mass into energy. This energy could be harnessed to provide a form of controlled power, or it could be unleashed in a tremendous explosion.

Having fled to the United States from Hitler's Germany, Einstein in 1939 warned Roosevelt that Nazi scientists were trying to develop an atomic weapon and urged the president to do likewise. In the following year, FDR authorized what came to be known as the Manhattan Project, a top-secret program in which American scientists developed an atomic bomb during World War II. The weapon was tested successfully in New Mexico in July 1945.

THE DAWN OF THE ATOMIC AGE

On August 6, 1945, an American plane dropped an atomic bomb that detonated over Hiroshima, Japan—a target chosen because almost alone among major Japanese cities, it had not yet suffered damage. In an instant, nearly every building in the city was destroyed. Of the city's population of 280,000 civilians and 40,000 soldiers, approximately 70,000 died immediately. Because atomic bombs release deadly radiation, the death toll kept rising in the months that followed. By the end of the year, it reached at least 140,000. Thousands more perished over the next five years. On August 9, the United States exploded a second bomb over Nagasaki, killing 70,000 persons. On the same day, the Soviet Union declared war on Japan and invaded Manchuria. Within a week, Japan surrendered.

Because of the enormous cost in civilian lives—more than twice America's military fatalities in the entire Pacific war—the use of the bomb remains controversial. The Japanese had fought ferociously while being driven from one Pacific island after another. An American invasion of Japan, some advisers warned Truman, might cost as many as 250,000 American lives. No such invasion was planned, however, until 1946, and considerable evidence had accumulated that Japan was nearing surrender. Already some of its officials had communicated a willingness to end the war if Emperor Hirohito could remain on his throne. This fell short of the Allies' demand for "unconditional surrender," but the victors would, in the end, agree to Hirohito's survival.

Japan's economy had been crippled and its fleet destroyed, and it would now have to fight the Soviet Union as well as the United States. Some of the scientists who had worked on the bomb urged Truman to demonstrate its power to international observers. But Truman did not hesitate. The bomb was a weapon, and weapons are created to be used.

THE NATURE OF THE WAR

The dropping of the atomic bombs was the logical culmination of the way World War II had been fought. All wars inflict suffering on noncombatants. But never before had civilian populations been so ruthlessly targeted. Military personnel represented 90 percent of those who died in World War I. But of the estimated 50 million persons who perished during World War II (including 400,000 American soldiers), perhaps 20 million were civilians. Germany had killed millions of members of "inferior races." It had repeatedly bombed London and other cities. The Allies carried out even more deadly air assaults on civilian populations. Early in 1945, the firebombing of Dresden killed some 100,000 people, mostly women, children, and elderly men. On March 9, nearly the same number died in an inferno caused by the bombing of Tokyo.

Four years of war propaganda had dehumanized the Japanese in American eyes, and few persons criticized Truman's decision in 1945. But public doubts began to surface, especially after John Hersey published *Hiroshima* (1946), a graphic account of the horrors suffered by the civilian population. General Dwight D. Eisenhower, who thought the use of the bomb unnecessary, later wrote, "I hated to see our country be the first to use such a weapon."

PLANNING THE POSTWAR WORLD

Even as the war raged, a series of meetings between Allied leaders formulated plans for the postwar world. Churchill, Roosevelt, and Stalin met at Tehran, Iran, in 1943, and at Yalta, in the southern Soviet Union, early in 1945, to hammer out agreements. The final "Big Three" conference took place at Potsdam, near Berlin, in July 1945. It involved Stalin, Truman, and Churchill (replaced midway in the talks by Clement Attlee, who became prime minister when his Labour Party swept the British elections). At Potsdam, the Allied leaders established a military administration for Germany and agreed to place top Nazi leaders on trial for war crimes.

Relations among the three Allies were often uneasy, as each maneuvered to maximize its postwar power. Neither Britain nor the United States trusted Stalin. The delay in the Allied invasion of France until 1944, which left the Soviets to do the bulk of the fighting against Germany, angered the Russians. But since Stalin's troops had won the war on the eastern front, it was difficult to resist his demand that eastern Europe become a Soviet sphere of influence (a region whose governments can be counted on to do a great power's bidding).

The Big Three—Stalin, Roosevelt, and Churchill—at their first meeting, in Tehran, Iran, in 1943, where they discussed the opening of a second front against Germany in western Europe.

YALTA AND BRETTON WOODS

At Yalta, Roosevelt and Churchill entered only a mild protest against Soviet plans to retain control of the Baltic states (Estonia, Latvia, and Lithuania) and a large part of eastern Poland, in effect restoring Russia's pre–World War I western borders. Stalin agreed to enter the war against Japan later in 1945, to include noncommunists in the pro-Soviet government of Poland, and to allow "free and unfettered elections" there. But he was intent on establishing communism in eastern Europe. He believed, as he put it to Yugoslav communist leader Josip Broz ("Tito"), that in modern war, "whoever occupies a territory also imposes his own social system." Yalta saw the high-water mark of wartime American–Soviet cooperation. But it planted seeds of conflict, since the participants soon disagreed over the fate of eastern Europe.

Tension also existed between Britain and the United States. Churchill rejected American pressure to place India and other British colonies on the road to independence. He concluded private deals with Stalin to divide southern and eastern Europe into British and Soviet spheres of influence.

Britain also resisted, unsuccessfully, American efforts to reshape and dominate the postwar economic order. A meeting of representatives of forty-five nations at Bretton Woods, New Hampshire, in July 1944 replaced the British pound with the dollar as the main currency for international transactions. During the 1930s, FDR had taken the United States off the gold standard, allowing the government to issue more money in the hope of stimulating business activity. The Bretton Woods conference reestablished the link between the dollar and gold. It set the dollar's value at $35 per ounce of gold and gave other currencies a fixed relationship to the dollar. The conference also created two American-dominated financial institutions. The World Bank would provide money to developing countries and to help rebuild Europe. The International Monetary Fund would work to prevent governments from devaluing their currencies to gain an advantage in international trade, as many had done during the Depression.

Although the details took many years to emerge, Bretton Woods created the framework for the postwar capitalist economic system, based on a freer international flow of goods and investment and a recognition of the United States as the world's financial leader. Determined to avoid a recurrence of the Great Depression, American leaders believed that the removal of barriers to free trade would encourage the growth of the world economy, an emphasis that remains central to American foreign policy to this day.

THE UNITED NATIONS

Early in the war, the Allies also agreed to establish a successor to the League of Nations. In a 1944 conference at Dumbarton Oaks, near Washington, D.C., they developed the structure of the United Nations (UN). There would be a General Assembly—essentially a forum for discussion where each member enjoyed an equal voice—and a Security Council responsible for maintaining world peace. Along with ten rotating members, the council would have five permanent ones—Britain, China, France, the Soviet Union, and the United States—each with the power to veto resolutions. In June 1945, representatives of fifty-one countries met in San Francisco to adopt the UN Charter, which outlawed force or the threat of force as a means of settling international disputes. In July, the U.S. Senate endorsed the charter. In contrast to the bitter dispute over membership in the League of Nations after World War I, only two members of the U.S. Senate voted against joining the UN. At the conclusion of the San Francisco conference that established the United Nations, President Truman urged Americans to recognize that "no matter how great our strength, we must deny ourselves the license to do always as we please. This is the price which each nation will have to pay for world peace. . . . And what a reasonable price that is."

PEACE, BUT NOT HARMONY

World War II produced a radical redistribution of world power. Japan and Germany, the two dominant military powers in their regions before the war, were utterly defeated. Britain and France, though victorious, were substantially weakened. Only the United States and the Soviet Union were able to project significant influence beyond their national borders.

Overall, however, the United States was clearly the dominant world power. "What Rome was to the ancient world," wrote the journalist Walter Lippmann, "America is to be to the world of tomorrow." But peace did not usher in an era of international harmony. The Soviet occupation of eastern Europe created a division soon to be solidified in the Cold War. The dropping of the atomic bombs left a worldwide legacy of fear.

It remained to be seen how seriously the victorious Allies took their wartime rhetoric of freedom. In August 1941, four months before the United States entered the war, FDR and British prime minister Winston Churchill had met for a conference, on warships anchored off the coast of Newfoundland, and issued the Atlantic Charter. The charter promised that "the final destruction of Nazi tyranny" would be followed by open access to markets, the right of "all peoples" to choose their form of government, and a global extension of the New Deal so that people everywhere would enjoy "improved labor standards, economic advancement and social security." It referred specifically to two of

This 1943 cartoon from the Chicago Defender, *a black newspaper, questions whether non-white peoples will be accorded the right to choose their own government, as promised in the Atlantic Charter agreed to two years earlier by Franklin D. Roosevelt and Winston Churchill. Churchill insisted the principle only applied to Europeans.*

Roosevelt's Four Freedoms—freedom from want and freedom from fear. But freedom of speech and of worship had been left out because of British reluctance to apply them to its colonial possessions, especially India.

The Four Freedoms speech and the Atlantic Charter had been primarily intended to highlight the differences between Anglo-American ideals and Nazism. Nonetheless, they had unanticipated consequences. As one of Roosevelt's speechwriters remarked, "when you state a moral principle, you are stuck with it, no matter how many fingers you have kept crossed at the moment." The language with which World War II was fought helped to lay the foundation for postwar ideals of human rights that extend to all mankind.

During the war, Mahatma Gandhi, the Indian nationalist leader, wrote to Roosevelt that the idea "that the Allies are fighting to make the world safe for freedom of the individual and for democracy seems hollow, so long as India, and for that matter, Africa, are exploited by Great Britain, and America has the Negro problem in her own home." Allied victory saved mankind from a living nightmare—a worldwide system of dictatorial rule and slave labor in which peoples deemed inferior suffered the fate of European Jews and of the victims of Japanese outrages in Asia. But disputes over the freedom of colonial peoples overseas and non-whites in the United States foretold more wars and social upheavals to come.

Chapter Review

REVIEW QUESTIONS

1. Why did most Americans support isolationism in the 1930s?
2. What factors after 1939 led to U.S. involvement in World War II?
3. How did government, business, and labor work together to promote wartime production, and how did the war affect each group?
4. How did different groups understand or experience the Four Freedoms differently?
5. Explain how conservatives in Congress and business used the war effort to attack the goals and legacy of the New Deal.

6. How did the war alter the lives of women on the home front, and what did different groups think would happen to the status of women after the war?
7. How did a war fought to bring "essential human freedoms" to the world fail to protect the home front liberties of blacks, Indians, Japanese Americans, and Mexican Americans?
8. Explain how World War II promoted an awareness of the links between racism in the United States and colonialism around the world.
9. What was the impact of the GI Bill of Rights on American society including minorities?
10. Describe how the decisions made at the Bretton Woods conference in 1944 created the framework for postwar U.S. economic and foreign policy.

KEY TERMS

Four Freedoms
Good Neighbor Policy
Isolationism
Neutrality Acts
"Arsenal of Democracy"
Lend-Lease Act
Bataan "death march"
D-Day
Holocaust
Rosie the Riveter
GI Bill of Rights
"patriotic assimilation"
bracero program
zoot suit riots
Executive Order 9066
Korematsu v. United States
second Great Migration
Executive Order 8802
"double-V"
Manhattan Project
Yalta conference
Bretton Woods conference
United Nations
Atlantic Charter

wwnorton.com/studyspace

VISIT STUDYSPACE FOR THESE RESOURCES AND MORE:

- Author Videos
- A chapter outline
- A practice quiz
- Interactive maps
- Multimedia documents

CHAPTER 8

THE UNITED STATES AND THE COLD WAR

From *Give Me Liberty! Seagull Fourth Edition*

Eric Foner

8

The United States and the Cold War 1945–1953

FOCUS QUESTIONS

- What series of events and ideological conflicts prompted the Cold War?
- How did the Cold War reshape ideas of American freedom?
- What were the major initiatives of Truman's domestic policies?
- What effects did the anticommunism of the Cold War have on American politics and culture?

On September 16, 1947, the 160th anniversary of the signing of the Constitution, the Freedom Train opened to the public in Philadelphia. A traveling exhibition of 133 historical documents, the train, bedecked in red, white, and blue, soon embarked on a sixteen-month tour that took it to more than 300 American cities. Never before or since have so many cherished pieces of Americana—among them the Mayflower Compact, the Declaration of Independence, and the Gettysburg Address—been assembled in one place. After leaving the train, visitors were encouraged to rededicate themselves to American values by taking the Freedom Pledge and adding their names to a Freedom Scroll.

The idea for the Freedom Train, perhaps the most elaborate peacetime patriotic campaign in American history, originated in 1946 with the Department of Justice. President Harry S. Truman endorsed it as a way of contrasting American freedom with "the destruction of liberty by the Hitler tyranny." Since direct government funding raised fears of propaganda, however, the administration turned the project over to a nonprofit group, the American Heritage Foundation, headed by Winthrop W. Aldrich, chairman of Chase Manhattan Bank.

The cover of a comic book promoting the Freedom Train in 1948. The image links the train to Paul Revere's ride and, more broadly, the revolutionary era.

By any measure, the Freedom Train was an enormous success. It attracted more than 3.5 million visitors, and millions more took part in the civic activities that accompanied its journey, including labor-management forums, educational programs, and patriotic parades. The powerful grassroots response to the train, wrote *The New Republic*, revealed a popular hunger for "tangible evidence of American freedom." Behind the scenes, however, the Freedom Train demonstrated that the meaning of freedom remained as controversial as ever.

The liberal staff members at the National Archives who proposed the initial list of documents had included the Wagner Act of 1935, which guaranteed workers the right to form unions, as well as President Roosevelt's Four Freedoms speech of 1941, with its promise to fight "freedom from want." The more conservative American Heritage Foundation removed these documents. They also deleted from the original list the Fourteenth and Fifteenth Amendments, which had established the principle of equal civil and political rights regardless of race after the Civil War, and FDR's 1941 order establishing the Fair Employment Practices Commission, which Congress had recently allowed to expire. In the end, nothing on the train referred to organized labor or any twentieth-century social legislation. The only documents relating to blacks were the Emancipation Proclamation, the Thirteenth Amendment, and a 1776 letter by South Carolina patriot Henry Laurens criticizing slavery.

Many black Americans initially voiced doubts regarding the exhibit. On the eve of the train's unveiling, the poet Langston Hughes wondered whether there would be "Jim Crow on the Freedom Train." "When it stops in Mississippi," Hughes asked, "will it be made plain / Everybody's got a right to board the

Freedom Train?" In fact, with the Truman administration about to make civil rights a major priority, the train's organizers announced that they would not permit segregated viewing. In an unprecedented move, the American Heritage Foundation canceled visits to Memphis, Tennessee, and Birmingham, Alabama, when local authorities insisted on separating visitors by race. The Freedom Train visited forty-seven other southern cities without incident and was hailed in the black press for breaching, if only temporarily, the walls of segregation.

Even as the Freedom Train reflected a new sense of national unease about expressions of racial inequality, its journey also revealed the growing impact of the Cold War. Originally intended to contrast American freedom with Nazi tyranny, the train quickly became caught up in the emerging struggle with communism. In the spring of 1947, a few months before the train was dedicated, President Truman committed the United States to the worldwide containment of Soviet power and inaugurated a program to root out "disloyal" persons from government employment. Soon, Attorney General Tom C. Clark was praising the Freedom Train as a means of preventing "foreign ideologies" from infiltrating the United States and of "aiding the country in its internal war against subversive elements." The Federal Bureau of Investigation began compiling reports on those who found the train objectionable. The Freedom Train revealed how the Cold War helped to reshape freedom's meaning, identifying it ever more closely with anticommunism, "free enterprise," and the defense of the social and economic status quo.

ORIGINS OF THE COLD WAR

THE TWO POWERS

The United States emerged from World War II as by far the world's greatest power. Although most of the army was quickly demobilized, the country boasted the world's most powerful navy and air force. The United States accounted for half the world's manufacturing capacity. It alone possessed the atomic bomb. The Roosevelt administration was determined to avoid a retreat to isolationism like the one that followed World War I. It believed that the United States could lead the rest of the world to a future of international cooperation, expanding democracy, and ever-increasing living standards. New institutions like the United Nations and World Bank had been created to promote these goals. American leaders also believed that the nation's security depended on the security of Europe and Asia, and that American prosperity required global economic reconstruction.

CHRONOLOGY

1945	Yalta conference
1946	Philippines granted independence
1947	Truman Doctrine Federal Employee Loyalty program Jackie Robinson integrates major league baseball Marshall Plan Taft-Hartley Act Freedom Train exhibition House Un-American Activities Committee investigates Hollywood
1948	UN adopts Universal Declaration of Human Rights Truman desegregates military
1948–1949	Berlin blockade and airlift
1949	North Atlantic Treaty Organization established Soviet Union tests atomic bomb People's Republic of China established
1950	McCarthy's Wheeling, WV, speech NSC-68 issued McCarran Internal Security Act
1950–1953	Korean War
1951	*Dennis v. United States*
1953	Julius and Ethel Rosenberg executed for spying
1954	Army-McCarthy hearings
1955	Warsaw Pact organized

The only power that in any way could rival the United States was the Soviet Union, whose armies now occupied most of eastern Europe, including the eastern part of Germany. Its crucial role in defeating Hitler and its claim that communism had wrested a vast backward nation into modernity gave the Soviet Union considerable prestige in Europe and among colonial peoples struggling for independence. Like the United States, the Soviets looked forward to a world order modeled on their own society and values. Having lost more than 20 million dead and suffered vast devastation during the war, however, Stalin's government was in no position to embark on new military adventures. "Unless they were completely out of their minds," said American undersecretary of state Dean Acheson, the Russians were hardly likely to go to war with the far more powerful United States. But having done by far the largest amount of ground fighting in the defeat of Hitler, the Soviet government remained determined to establish a sphere of influence in eastern Europe, through which Germany had twice invaded Russia in the past thirty years.

THE ROOTS OF CONTAINMENT

FDR seems to have believed that the United States could maintain friendly relations with the Soviet Union once World War II ended. In retrospect, however, it seems all but inevitable that the two major powers to emerge from the war would come into conflict. Born of a common foe rather than common long-term interests, values, or history, their wartime alliance began to unravel almost from the day that peace was declared.

The first confrontation of the Cold War took place in the Middle East. At the end of World War II, Soviet troops had occupied parts of northern Iran, hoping to pressure that country to grant it access to its rich oil fields. Under British and American pressure, however, Stalin quickly withdrew Soviet forces. At the same time, the Soviets installed procommunist governments in Poland, Romania, and Bulgaria, a step they claimed was no different from American domination of Latin America or Britain's determination to maintain its own empire. But many Americans became convinced that Stalin was violating the promise of free elections in Poland that had been agreed to at the Yalta conference of 1945.

Early in 1946, in his famous Long Telegram from Moscow, American diplomat George Kennan advised the Truman administration that the Soviets could not be dealt with as a normal government. Communist ideology drove them to try to expand their power throughout the world, he claimed, and only the United States had the ability to stop them. While Kennan believed that the Russians could not be dislodged from control of eastern Europe, his telegram laid the foundation for what became known as the policy of "containment," according to which the United States committed itself to preventing any further expansion of Soviet power.

THE IRON CURTAIN

Shortly afterward, in a speech at Fulton, Missouri, Britain's former wartime prime minister Winston Churchill declared that an "iron curtain" had descended across Europe, partitioning the free West from the communist East. Churchill's speech helped to popularize the idea of an impending long-term struggle between the United States and the Soviets. But not until March 1947, in a speech announcing what came to be known as the Truman Doctrine, did the president officially embrace the Cold War as the foundation of American foreign policy and describe it as a worldwide struggle over the future of freedom.

THE TRUMAN DOCTRINE

Harry S. Truman never expected to become president. Until Democratic party leaders chose him to replace Henry Wallace as Roosevelt's running mate in 1944, he was an undistinguished senator from Missouri who had risen in politics through his connection with the boss of the Kansas City political machine, Tom Pendergast. When he assumed the presidency after Roosevelt's death in April 1945, Truman found himself forced to decide foreign policy debates in which he had previously played virtually no role.

Convinced that Stalin could not be trusted and that the United States had a responsibility to provide leadership to a world that he tended to view in stark, black-and-white terms, Truman soon determined to put the policy of containment into effect. The immediate occasion for this epochal decision came early in 1947 when Britain informed the United States that because its economy had been shattered by the war, it could no longer afford its traditional international role. Britain had no choice but to end military and financial aid to two crucial governments—Greece, a monarchy threatened by a communist-led rebellion, and Turkey, from which the Soviets were demanding joint control of the straits linking the Black Sea and the Mediterranean. Britain asked the United States to fill the vacuum.

The Soviet Union had little to do with the internal problems of Greece and Turkey, where opposition to corrupt, undemocratic regimes was largely homegrown. Neither had held truly free elections. But they occupied strategically important sites at the gateway to southeastern Europe and the oil-rich Middle East. Truman had been told by Senate leader Arthur Vandenberg that the only way a reluctant public and Congress would support aid to these governments was for the president to "scare hell" out of the American people. To rally popular backing, Truman rolled out the heaviest weapon in his rhetorical arsenal—the defense of freedom. As the leader of the "free world," the United States must now shoulder the responsibility of supporting "freedom-loving peoples" wherever communism threatened them. Twenty-four times in the eighteen-minute speech, Truman used the words "free" or "freedom."

Building on the wartime division of the globe into free and enslaved worlds, and invoking a far older vision of an American mission to defend liberty against the forces of darkness, the Truman Doctrine created the language through which most Americans came to understand the postwar world. More than any other statement a prominent senator would write, this speech established "the guiding spirit of American foreign policy." Truman succeeded in persuading both Republicans and Democrats in Congress to support his policy, beginning a long period of bipartisan support for the containment of communism. As Truman's speech to Congress suggested, the Cold War was, in part, an ideological conflict. Both sides claimed to be promoting freedom and social justice while defending their own security, and each offered its social system as a model the rest of the world should follow.

While his request to Congress was limited to $400 million in military aid to two governments (aid that enabled both Greece and Turkey to defeat their domestic foes), Truman's rhetoric suggested that the United States had assumed a permanent global responsibility. The speech set a precedent for American assistance to anticommunist regimes throughout the world, no matter how undemocratic, and for the creation of a set of global military alliances directed against the Soviet Union. There soon followed the creation of new national security bodies immune from democratic oversight, such as the Atomic Energy Commission, National Security Council, and Central Intelligence Agency (CIA), the last established in 1947 to gather intelligence and conduct secret military operations abroad.

THE MARSHALL PLAN

The language of the Truman Doctrine and the future it sketched of open-ended worldwide responsibilities for the United States alarmed many Americans. "Are we to shoulder the mantle of nineteenth-century British imperialism?" asked the *San Francisco Chronicle*. "Are we asking for a third world war?" But the threat of American military action overseas formed only one pillar of containment. Secretary of State George C. Marshall spelled out the other in a speech at Harvard University in June 1947. Marshall pledged the United States to contribute billions of dollars to finance the economic recovery of Europe. Two years after the end of the war, much of the continent still lay in ruins. Food shortages were widespread, and inflation was rampant. The economic chaos, exacerbated by the unusually severe winter of 1946–1947, had strengthened the communist parties of France and Italy. American policymakers feared that these countries might fall into the Soviet orbit.

The Marshall Plan offered a positive vision to go along with containment. It aimed to combat the idea, widespread since the Great Depression, that capitalism was in decline and communism the wave of the future. It defined the threat to American security not so much as Soviet military power but as economic and political instability, which could be breeding grounds for communism. Avoiding Truman's language of a world divided between free and unfree blocs, Marshall insisted, "Our policy is directed not against any country or doctrine, but against hunger, poverty, desperation, and chaos." Freedom meant more than simply anticommunism—it required the emergence of the "political and social conditions in which free institutions can exist." In effect, the Marshall Plan envisioned a New Deal for Europe, an extension to that continent of Roosevelt's wartime Four Freedoms. As a booklet explaining the idea to Europeans put it, the aim was "a higher standard of living for the entire nation; maximum employment for workers and farmers; greater production." Or, in the words of a slogan used to popularize the Marshall Plan, "Prosperity Makes You Free."

The Marshall Plan proved to be one of the most successful foreign aid programs in history. By 1950, western European production exceeded prewar levels and the region was poised to follow the United States down the road to a mass-consumption society. Since the Soviet Union refused to participate, fearing American control over the economies of eastern Europe, the Marshall Plan further solidified the division of the continent. At the same time, the United States worked out with twenty-three other Western nations the General Agreement on Tariffs and Trade (GATT), which proposed to stimulate freer trade among the participants, creating an enormous market for American goods and investment.

THE RECONSTRUCTION OF JAPAN

Under the guidance of General Douglas MacArthur, the "supreme commander" in Japan until 1948, the country adopted a new, democratic constitution and eliminated absentee landlordism so that most tenant farmers became owners of land. Thanks to American insistence, and against the wishes of most Japanese leaders, the new constitution gave women the right to vote for the first time in Japan's history. (A century after the Seneca Falls convention, women's suffrage had become an intrinsic part of American understandings of freedom.) Furthermore, Article 9 of the new constitution stated that Japan would renounce forever the policy of war and armed aggression, and would maintain only a modest self-defense force.

The United States also oversaw the economic reconstruction of Japan. Initially, the United States proposed to dissolve Japan's giant industrial corporations, which had contributed so much to the nation's war effort. But this plan was abandoned in 1948 in favor of an effort to rebuild Japan's industrial base as a bastion of anticommunist strength in Asia. By the 1950s, thanks to American economic assistance, the adoption of new technologies, and low spending on the military, Japan's economic recovery was in full swing.

THE BERLIN BLOCKADE AND NATO

Meanwhile, the Cold War intensified and, despite the Marshall Plan, increasingly took a militaristic turn. At the end of World War II, each of the four victorious powers assumed control of a section of occupied Germany, and of Berlin, located deep in the Soviet zone. In June 1948, the United States, Britain, and France introduced a separate currency in their zones, a prelude to the creation of a new West German government that would be aligned with them in the Cold War. In response, the Soviets cut off road and rail traffic from the American, British, and French zones of occupied Germany to Berlin (although Stalin kept supply routes open from the east, since Soviet forces occupied part of the divided city).

An eleven-month airlift followed, with Western planes supplying fuel and food to their zones of the city. When Stalin lifted the blockade in May 1949,

The division of Europe between communist and noncommunist nations, solidified by the early 1950s, would last for nearly forty years.

the Truman administration had won a major victory. Soon, two new nations emerged, East and West Germany, each allied with a side in the Cold War. Berlin itself remained divided. The city's western part survived as an isolated enclave within East Germany. Not until 1991 would Germany be reunified.

Also in 1949, the Soviet Union tested its first atomic bomb, ending the American monopoly of the weapon. In the same year, the United States, Canada, and ten western European nations established the North Atlantic Treaty Organization (NATO), pledging mutual defense against any future Soviet attack. Soon, West Germany became a crucial part of NATO. Many Europeans feared German rearmament. But France and other victims of Nazi aggression saw NATO as a kind of "double containment," in which West Germany would serve as a bulwark against the Soviets while integration into the Western alliance tamed and "civilized" German power. The North Atlantic Treaty was the first long-term military alliance between the United States and Europe since the Treaty of Amity and Commerce with France during the American Revolution. The Soviets formalized their own eastern European alliance, the Warsaw Pact, in 1955.

THE GROWING COMMUNIST CHALLENGE

In 1949, communists led by Mao Zedong emerged victorious in the long Chinese civil war—a serious setback for the policy of containment. Assailed by Republicans for having "lost" China (which, of course, the United States never "had" in the first place), the Truman administration refused to recognize the new government—the People's Republic of China—and blocked it from occupying China's seat at the United Nations. Until the 1970s, the United States insisted that the ousted regime, which had been forced into exile on the island of Taiwan, remained the legitimate government of China.

In the wake of Soviet-American confrontations over southern and eastern Europe and Berlin, the communist victory in China, and Soviet success in developing an atomic bomb, the National Security Council approved a call for a permanent military build-up to enable the United States to pursue a global crusade against communism. Known as NSC-68, this 1950 manifesto described the Cold War as an epic struggle between "the idea of freedom" and the "idea of slavery under the grim oligarchy of the Kremlin." At stake in the world conflict, it insisted, was nothing less than "the survival of the free world." One of the most important policy statements of the early Cold War, NSC-68 helped to spur a dramatic increase in American military spending.

THE KOREAN WAR

Initially, American postwar policy focused on Europe. But it was in Asia that the Cold War suddenly turned hot. Occupied by Japan during World War II, Korea had been divided in 1945 into Soviet and American zones. These soon evolved into two governments: communist North Korea, and anticommunist South Korea, undemocratic but aligned with the United States. In June 1950, the North Korean army invaded the south, hoping to reunify the country under communist control. North Korean soldiers soon occupied most of the peninsula. Viewing Korea as a clear test of the policy of containment, the Truman administration persuaded the United Nations Security Council to authorize the use of force to repel the invasion. (The Soviets, who could have vetoed the resolution, were boycotting Security Council meetings to protest the refusal to seat communist China.)

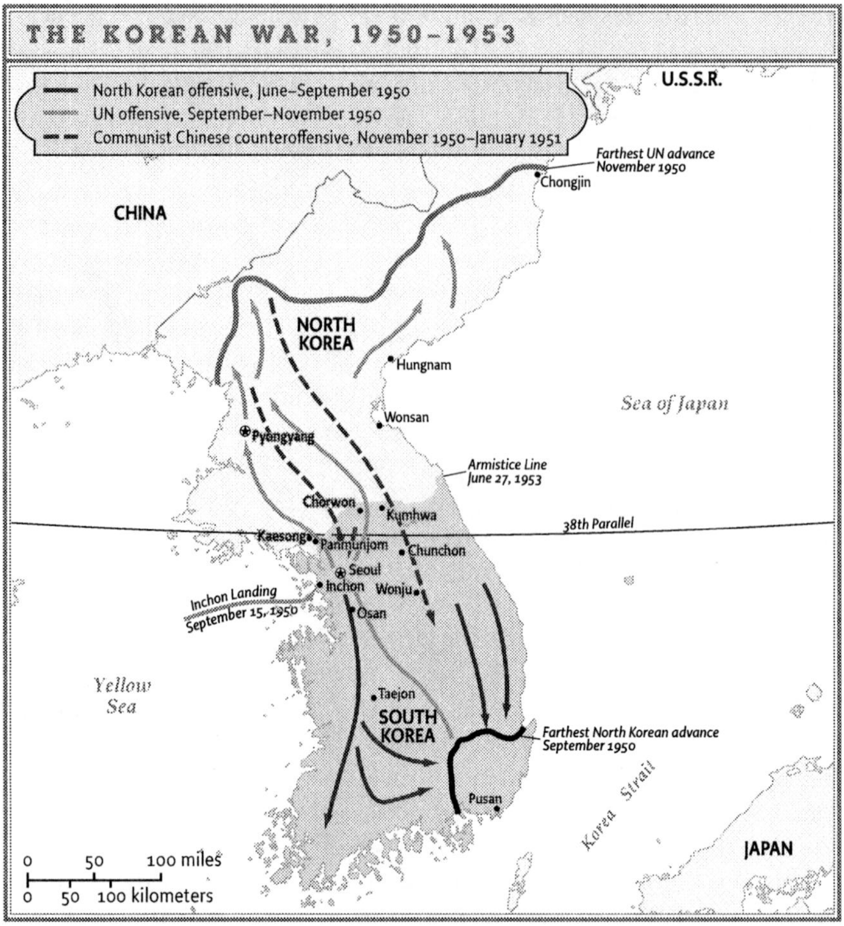

As this map indicates, when General Douglas MacArthur launched his surprise landing at Inchon, North Korean forces controlled nearly the entire Korean peninsula.

American troops did the bulk of the fighting on this first battlefield of the Cold War. In September 1950, General Douglas MacArthur launched a daring counterattack at Inchon, behind North Korean lines. The invading forces retreated northward, and MacArthur's army soon occupied most of North Korea. Truman now hoped to unite Korea under a pro-American government. But in October 1950, when UN forces neared the Chinese border, hundreds of thousands of Chinese troops intervened, driving them back in bloody fighting. MacArthur demanded the right to push north again and possibly even invade China and use nuclear weapons against it. But Truman, fearing an all-out war on the Asian mainland, refused. MacArthur did not fully accept the principle of civilian control of the military. When he went public with criticism of the president, Truman removed him from command. The war then settled into a stalemate around the thirty-eighth parallel, the original boundary between the two Koreas. Not until 1953 was an armistice agreed to, essentially restoring the prewar status quo. There has never been a formal peace treaty ending the Korean War.

More than 33,000 Americans died in Korea. The Asian death toll reached an estimated 1 million Korean soldiers and 2 million civilians (many of them victims of starvation after American bombing destroyed irrigation systems essential to rice cultivation), along with hundreds of thousands of Chinese troops. Korea made it clear that the Cold War, which began in Europe, had become a global conflict.

Taken together, the events of 1947–1953 showed that the world had moved very far from the hopes for global harmony symbolized by the founding of the United Nations in 1945. No longer did the United States speak of One World (the title of Wendell Willkie's influential wartime book). Instead, the world had been divided in two. The United States now stood as the undisputed leader of what was increasingly known as the West (although it included Japan, where permanent American military bases were established), or the Free World. NATO was soon followed by SEATO in Southeast Asia and CENTO in the Middle East, forming a web of military alliances that ringed the Soviet Union and China.

COLD WAR CRITICS

In the Soviet Union, Stalin had consolidated a brutal dictatorship that jailed or murdered millions of Soviet citizens. With its one-party rule, stringent state control of the arts and intellectual life, and government-controlled economy, the Soviet Union presented a stark opposite of democracy and "free enterprise." As a number of contemporary critics, few of them sympathetic to Soviet communism, pointed out, however, casting the Cold War in terms of a worldwide battle between freedom and slavery had unfortunate consequences. George Kennan, whose Long Telegram had inspired the policy of containment, observed that such language made it impossible to view international crises on a case-by-case basis, or to determine which genuinely involved either freedom or American interests.

In a penetrating critique of Truman's policies, Walter Lippmann, one of the nation's most prominent journalists, objected to turning foreign policy into an "ideological crusade." To view every challenge to the status quo as part of a contest with the Soviet Union, Lippmann correctly predicted, would require the United States to recruit and subsidize an "array of satellites, clients, dependents and puppets." It would have to intervene continuously in the affairs of nations whose political problems did not arise from Moscow and could not be easily understood in terms of the battle between freedom and slavery. World War II, he went on, had shaken the foundations of European empires. In the tide of revolutionary nationalism now sweeping the world, communists were certain to play an important role. It would be a serious mistake, Lippmann warned, for the United States to align itself against the movement for colonial independence in the name of anticommunism.

IMPERIALISM AND DECOLONIZATION

World War II had increased awareness in the United States of the problem of imperialism and had led many African-Americans to identify their own struggle for equality with the strivings of non-white colonial peoples overseas. Many movements for colonial independence borrowed the language of the American Declaration of Independence in demanding the right to self-government. Liberal Democrats and black leaders urged the Truman administration to take the lead in promoting worldwide decolonization, insisting that a Free World worthy of the name should not include colonies and empires. In 1946, the United States granted independence to the Philippines, a move hailed by nationalist movements in other colonies. But as the Cold War developed, the United States backed away from pressuring its European allies to move toward granting self-government to colonies like French Indochina, the Dutch East Indies, and British possessions like the Gold Coast and Nigeria in Africa and Malaya in Asia. Even after granting independence to India and Pakistan in 1947, Britain was determined to retain much of its empire.

In practice, geopolitical and economic interests shaped American foreign policy as powerfully as the idea of freedom. But American policymakers used the language of a crusade for freedom to justify actions around the world that had little to do with freedom by almost any definition. No matter how repressive to its own people, if a nation joined the worldwide anticommunist alliance led by the United States, it was counted as a member of the Free World. The Republic of South Africa, for example, was considered a part of the Free World even though its white minority had deprived the black population of nearly all their rights. Was there not some way, one critic asked, that the United States could accept "the aid of tyrants" on practical grounds "without corrupting our speeches by identifying tyranny with freedom"?

THE COLD WAR AND THE IDEA OF FREEDOM

Among other things, the Cold War was an ideological struggle, a battle, in a popular phrase of the 1950s, for the "hearts and minds" of people throughout the world. Like other wars, it required popular mobilization, in which the idea of freedom played a central role. During the 1950s, freedom became an inescapable theme of academic research, popular journalism, mass culture, and official pronouncements. Henry Luce, who had popularized the idea of an American Century, explained that "freedom" was the "one word out of the whole human vocabulary" through which *Time* magazine could best explain America to the rest of the world. In many ways, the Cold War established the framework for the discussion of freedom.

THE CULTURAL COLD WAR

One of the more unusual Cold War battlefields involved American history and culture. Many scholars read the American Creed of pluralism, tolerance, and equality back into the past as a timeless definition of Americanism, ignoring the powerful ethnic and racial strains with which it had always coexisted. Under the code name "Militant Liberty," national security agencies encouraged Hollywood to produce anticommunist movies, such as *The Red Menace* (1949) and *I Married a Communist* (1950), and urged that film scripts be changed to remove references to less-than-praiseworthy aspects of American history, such as Indian removal and racial discrimination.

The Central Intelligence Agency and Defense Department emerged as unlikely patrons of the arts. The federal government had openly financed all sorts of artistic works during the 1930s. But Cold War funding for the arts remained top-secret—in part because Congress proved reluctant to spend money for this purpose, in part because Americans charged communist governments with imposing artistic conformity. In an effort to influence public opinion abroad, the Soviet Union sponsored tours of its world-famous ballet companies, folk dance troupes, and symphony orchestras. To counteract the widespread European view of the United States as a cultural backwater, the CIA secretly funded an array of overseas publications, conferences, publishing houses, concerts, and art exhibits. And to try to improve the international image of American race relations, the government sent jazz musicians and other black performers abroad, especially to Africa and Asia.

A poster for The Red Menace, *one of numerous anticommunist films produced by Hollywood during the 1950s.*

Works produced by artists who considered themselves thoroughly nonpolitical became weapons in the cultural Cold War. The CIA promoted the so-called New York school of painters, led by Jackson Pollock. For Pollock, the essence of art lay in the process of creation, not the final product. His "action" paintings, made by spontaneously dripping and pouring paint over large canvases, produced works of vivid color and energy but without any recognizable subject matter. Many members of Congress much preferred Norman Rockwell's readily understandable illustrations of small-town life to Pollock's "abstract expressionism." Some called Pollock's works un-American and wondered aloud if they were part of a communist plot. But the CIA funded the Museum of Modern Art in New York, which championed the New York school, and helped arrange for exhibitions overseas. It hoped to persuade Europeans not only that these paintings demonstrated that the United States represented artistic leadership as well as military power, but that such art embodied the free, individual expression denied to artists in communist countries. Pollock's paintings, John Cage's musical compositions, which incorporated chance sounds rather than a fixed score, and the "graceful freedom" of George Balanchine's choreography were all described as artistic reflections of the essence of American life.

FREEDOM AND TOTALITARIANISM

Along with freedom, the Cold War's other great mobilizing concept was "totalitarianism." The term originated in Europe between the world wars to describe fascist Italy and Nazi Germany—aggressive, ideologically driven states that sought to subdue all of civil society, including churches, unions, and other voluntary associations, to their control. Such states, according to the theory of totalitarianism, left no room for individual rights or alternative values and therefore could never change from within. By 1950, the year the McCarran Internal Security Act barred "totalitarians" from entering the United States, the term had become a shorthand way of describing those on the other side in the Cold War. As the eventual collapse of communist governments in eastern Europe and the Soviet Union would demonstrate, the idea of totalitarianism greatly exaggerated the totality of government control of private life and thought in these countries. But its widespread use reinforced the view that the greatest danger to freedom lay in an overly powerful government.

Just as the conflict over slavery redefined American freedom in the nineteenth century and the confrontation with the Nazis shaped understandings of freedom during World War II, the Cold War reshaped them once again. Russia had already conquered America, the poet Archibald MacLeish complained in 1949, since politics was conducted "under a kind of upside-down Russian veto." Whatever Moscow stood for was by definition the opposite of freedom, including anything to which the word "socialized" could be attached. In the largest public relations campaign in American history, the American Medical Association raised the specter of "socialized medicine" to discredit and defeat Truman's proposal for national health insurance. The real-estate industry likewise mobilized against public housing, terming it "socialized housing," similar to policies undertaken by Moscow.

THE RISE OF HUMAN RIGHTS

The Cold War also affected the emerging concept of human rights. The idea that there are rights that are applicable to all of humanity originated during the eighteenth century in the Enlightenment and the American and French Revolutions. The atrocities committed during World War II, as well as the global language of the Four Freedoms and the Atlantic Charter, forcefully raised the issue of human rights in the postwar world. After the war, the victorious Allies put numerous German officials on trial before special courts at Nuremberg for crimes against humanity. For the first time, individuals were held directly accountable to the international community for violations of human rights. The trials resulted in prison terms for many Nazi officials and the execution of ten leaders.

The United Nations Charter includes strong language prohibiting discrimination on the basis of race, sex, or religion. In 1948, the UN General Assembly approved a far more sweeping document, the Universal Declaration of Human Rights, drafted by a committee chaired by Eleanor Roosevelt. It identified a broad range of rights to be enjoyed by people everywhere, including freedom of speech, religious toleration, and protection against arbitrary government, as well as social and economic entitlements like the right to an adequate standard of living and access to housing, education, and medical care. The document had no enforcement mechanism. Some considered it an exercise in empty rhetoric. But the core principle—that a nation's treatment of its own citizens should be subject to outside evaluation—slowly became part of the language in which freedom was discussed.

AMBIGUITIES OF HUMAN RIGHTS

The American and French Revolutions of the late eighteenth century had introduced into international relations the idea of basic rights belonging to all persons simply because they are human. In a sense, this was the origin of the idea of "human rights"—principles so fundamental that no government has a right to violate them. The antislavery movement had turned this idea into a powerful weapon against the legitimacy of slavery. Yet the debates over the Universal Declaration of Human Rights revealed the tensions inherent in the idea, tensions that persist to the present day. To what extent do human rights supersede national sovereignty? Who has the authority to enforce human rights that a government is violating? The United Nations? Regional bodies like the Organization of American States and the European Union? A single country (as the United States would claim to be doing in the Iraq War that began in 2003)? The Covenant of the League of Nations—the predecessor of the United Nations created after World War I—had contained a clause allowing the league to intervene when a government violated the rights of its own citizens.

One reason for the lack of an enforcement mechanism in the Universal Declaration of Human Rights was that both the United States and the Soviet Union refused to accept outside interference in their internal affairs or restraints on their ability to conduct foreign policy as they desired. John Foster Dulles, an American delegate to the conference that created the UN, opposed any statement affirming human rights out of fear that it would lead to an international investigation of "the Negro question in this country." In 1947, the NAACP did file a petition with the United Nations asking it to investigate racism in the United States as a violation of human rights. Conditions in states like Mississippi should be of concern to all mankind, it argued, because if democracy failed to function in "the leading democracy in the world," the prospects for democracy were weakened everywhere. But the UN decided that it lacked jurisdiction. Nonetheless, since the end of World War II, the enjoyment of human rights has increasingly taken its place in definitions of freedom across the globe, especially, perhaps, where such rights are flagrantly violated.

After the Cold War ended, the idea of human rights would play an increasingly prominent role in world affairs. But during the 1950s, Cold War imperatives shaped the concept. Neither the United States nor the Soviet Union could resist emphasizing certain provisions of the Universal Declaration while ignoring others. The Soviets claimed to provide all citizens with social and economic rights, but violated democratic rights and civil liberties. Many Americans condemned the nonpolitical rights as a step toward socialism. In 1950, Freedom House began yearly assessments of the status of freedom in the world's nations. It adopted purely political criteria, emphasizing citizens' rights to participate in open elections and to speak out on public issues. Considering access to employment, housing, education, medical care, and the like as part of the definition of freedom, the reports argued, would be a serious mistake.

Eleanor Roosevelt saw the Universal Declaration of Human Rights as an integrated body of principles, a combination of traditional civil and political liberties with the social conditions of freedom outlined in her husband's Economic Bill of Rights of 1944. But to make it easier for member states to ratify the document, the UN divided it into two "covenants"—Civil and Political Rights, and Economic, Social, and Cultural Rights. It took until 1992 for the U.S. Congress to ratify the first. It has never approved the second.

THE TRUMAN PRESIDENCY

THE FAIR DEAL

With the end of World War II, President Truman's first domestic task was to preside over the transition from a wartime to a peacetime economy. More than 12 million men remained in uniform in August 1945. They wanted nothing more than to return home to their families. Demobilization proceeded at a rapid pace. Within a year, the armed forces had been reduced to 3 million. Some returning soldiers found the adjustment to civilian life difficult. The divorce rate in 1945 rose to double its prewar level. Others took advantage of the GI Bill of Rights to obtain home mortgages, set up small businesses, and embark on college educations. The majority of returning soldiers entered the labor force—one reason why more than 2 million women workers lost their jobs. The government abolished wartime agencies that regulated industrial production and labor relations, and it dismantled wartime price controls, leading to a sharp rise in prices.

In the immediate aftermath of World War II, President Truman, backed by party liberals and organized labor, moved to revive the stalled momentum of the New Deal. Truman's program, which he announced in September 1945 and would later call the Fair Deal, focused on improving the social safety net and raising the standard of living of ordinary Americans. He called on Congress to increase the minimum wage, enact a program of national health insurance, and expand public housing, Social Security, and aid to education. Truman, complained one Republican leader, was "out–New Dealing the New Deal."

THE POSTWAR STRIKE WAVE

In 1946, a new wave of labor militancy swept the country. The AFL and CIO launched Operation Dixie, a campaign to bring unionization to the South and, by so doing, shatter the hold of anti-labor conservatives on the region's politics. More than 200 labor organizers entered the region, seeking support especially in the southern textile industry, the steel industry in the Birmingham region, and agriculture. With war production at an end, overtime work diminished even as inflation soared following the removal of price controls. The resulting drop in workers' real income sparked the largest strike wave in American history. Nearly 5 million workers—including those in the steel, auto, coal, and other key industries—walked off their jobs, demanding wage increases. The strike of 750,000 steelworkers represented the largest single walkout in American history to that date. Even Hollywood studios shut down because of a strike of actors and other employees of the movie industry that lasted for the better part of a year. One historian calls this period "the closest thing to a national general strike in industry in the twentieth century."

President Truman feared the strikes would seriously disrupt the economy. When railroad workers stopped work and set up picket lines, the infuriated president prepared a speech in which he threatened to draft them all into the army and "hang a few traitors"—language toned down by his advisers. The walkout soon ended, as did a coal strike after the Truman administration secured a court order requiring the miners to return to work. To resolve other strikes, Truman appointed federal "fact-finding boards," which generally recommended wage increases, although not enough to restore workers' purchasing power to wartime levels.

THE REPUBLICAN RESURGENCE

In the congressional elections of 1946, large numbers of middle-class voters, alarmed by the labor turmoil, voted Republican. Many workers, disappointed by Truman's policies, stayed at home. This was a lethal combination for the Democratic Party. For the first time since the 1920s, Republicans swept to control of both houses of Congress. Meanwhile, in the face of vigorous opposition from southern employers and public officials and the reluctance of many white workers to join interracial labor unions, Operation Dixie had failed to unionize the South or dent the political control of conservative Democrats in the region. The election of 1946 ensured that a conservative coalition of Republicans and southern Democrats would continue to dominate Congress.

Congress turned aside Truman's Fair Deal program. It enacted tax cuts for wealthy Americans and, over the president's veto, in 1947 passed the Taft-Hartley Act, which sought to reverse some of the gains made by organized labor in the past decade. The measure authorized the president to suspend strikes by ordering an eighty-day "cooling-off period," and it banned sympathy strikes and secondary boycotts (labor actions directed not at an employer but at those who did business with him). It outlawed the closed shop, which required a worker to be a union member when taking up a job, and authorized states to pass "right-to-work" laws, prohibiting other forms of compulsory union membership. It also forced union officials to swear that they were not communists. While hardly a "slave-labor bill," as the AFL and CIO called it, the Taft-Hartley Act made it considerably more difficult to bring unorganized workers into unions. Over time, as population and capital investment shifted to states with "right-to-work" laws like Texas, Florida, and North Carolina, Taft-Hartley contributed to the decline of organized labor's share of the nation's workforce.

POSTWAR CIVIL RIGHTS

During his first term, Truman reached out in unprecedented ways to the nation's black community. The war had inspired a new black militancy and led many whites to reject American racial practices as reminiscent of Hitler's theory of a master race. In the years immediately following World War II, the status of black Americans enjoyed a prominence in national affairs unmatched since Reconstruction.

Between 1945 and 1951, eleven states from New York to New Mexico established fair employment practices commissions, and numerous cities passed laws against discrimination in access to jobs and public accommodations. (Some of these measures addressed other racial groups besides blacks: for example, California in 1947 repealed its laws permitting local school districts to provide segregated education for children of Chinese descent and those barring aliens from owning land.) A broad civil rights coalition involving labor, religious groups, and black organizations supported these measures. The NAACP, its ranks swollen during the war, launched a voter registration campaign in the South. By 1952, 20 percent of black southerners were registered to vote, nearly a seven-fold increase since 1940. (Most of the gains took place in the Upper South—in Alabama and Mississippi, the heartland of white supremacy, the numbers barely budged.) Law enforcement agencies finally took the crime of lynching seriously. In 1952, for the first time since record keeping began seventy years earlier, no lynchings took place in the United States.

In another indication that race relations were in flux, the Brooklyn Dodgers in 1947 challenged the long-standing exclusion of black players from

Jackie Robinson sliding into third base, 1949.

major league baseball by adding Jackie Robinson to their team. Robinson, who possessed both remarkable athletic ability and a passion for equality, had been tried and acquitted for insubordination in 1944 when he refused to move to the back of a bus at Fort Hood, Texas, while serving in the army. But he promised Dodger owner Branch Rickey that he would not retaliate when subjected to racist taunts by opposing fans and players. His dignity in the face of constant verbal abuse won Robinson nationwide respect, and his baseball prowess earned him the Rookie of the Year award. His success opened the door to the integration of baseball and led to the demise of the Negro Leagues, to which black players had previously been confined.

TO SECURE THESE RIGHTS

In October 1947, a Commission on Civil Rights appointed by the president issued *To Secure These Rights*, one of the most devastating indictments ever published of racial inequality in America. It called on the federal government to assume the responsibility for abolishing segregation and ensuring equal treatment in housing, employment, education, and the criminal justice system. Truman hailed the report as "an American charter of human freedom." The impact of America's race system on the nation's ability to conduct the Cold War was not far from his mind. Truman noted that if the United States were to offer the "peoples of the world" a "choice of freedom or enslavement," it must "correct the remaining imperfections in our practice of democracy."

In February 1948, Truman presented an ambitious civil rights program to Congress, calling for a permanent federal civil rights commission, national laws against lynching and the poll tax, and action to ensure equal access to jobs and education. Congress, as Truman anticipated, approved none of his proposals. But in July 1948, just as the presidential campaign was getting under way, Truman issued an executive order desegregating the armed forces. The armed services became the first large institution in American life to promote racial integration actively and to attempt to root out long-standing racist practices. The Korean War would be the first American conflict fought by an integrated army since the War of Independence.

Truman genuinely despised racial discrimination. But his focus on civil rights also formed part of a strategy to win reelection by reinvigorating and expanding the political coalition Roosevelt had created. With calls for federal health insurance, the repeal of the Taft-Hartley Act, and aid to public education, the Democratic platform of 1948 was the most progressive in the party's history. Led by Hubert Humphrey, the young mayor of Minneapolis, party liberals overcame southern resistance and added a strong civil rights plank to the platform.

THE DIXIECRAT AND WALLACE REVOLTS

"I say the time has come," Humphrey told the Democratic national convention, "to walk out of the shadow of states' rights and into the sunlight of human rights." Whereupon numerous southern delegates—dubbed Dixiecrats by the press—walked out of the gathering. They soon formed the States' Rights Democratic Party and nominated for president Governor Strom Thurmond of South Carolina. Although his platform called for the "complete segregation of the races" and his campaign drew most of its support from those alarmed by Truman's civil rights initiatives, Thurmond denied charges of racism. The real issue of the election, Thurmond insisted, was freedom—the States' Rights Democratic Party, he declared, stood for "individual liberty and freedom, the right of people to govern themselves." Truman's plans for extending federal power into the South to enforce civil rights, Thurmond charged, would "convert America into a Hitler state."

Also in 1948, a group of left-wing critics of Truman's foreign policy formed the Progressive Party and nominated former vice president Henry A. Wallace for president. Wallace advocated an expansion of social welfare programs at home and denounced racial segregation even more vigorously than Truman. When he campaigned in the South, angry white crowds attacked him. But his real difference with the president concerned the Cold War. Wallace called for international control of nuclear weapons and a renewed effort to develop a relationship with the Soviet Union based on economic cooperation rather than military confrontation. He announced his willingness to accept support from all Americans who agreed with him, including socialists and communists. The influence of the now much-reduced Communist Party in Wallace's campaign led to an exodus of New Deal liberals and severe attacks on his candidacy. A vote for Wallace, Truman declared, was in effect a vote for Stalin.

THE 1948 CAMPAIGN

Wallace threatened to draw votes from Truman on the left, and Thurmond to undermine the president's support in the South, where whites had voted solidly for the Democrats throughout the twentieth century. But Truman's main opponent, fortunately for the president, was the colorless Republican Thomas A. Dewey. Certain of victory and an ineffective speaker and campaigner, Dewey seemed unwilling to commit himself on controversial issues. His speeches, wrote one hostile newspaper, amounted to nothing more than clichés: "Agriculture is important. Our rivers are full of fish. You cannot have freedom without liberty. Our future lies ahead." Truman, by contrast, ran an aggressive campaign. He crisscrossed the country by train, delivering fiery attacks on the Republican-controlled "do-nothing Congress." Truman revived New Deal rhetoric denouncing Wall Street and charged his opponent with threatening to undermine Social Security and other New Deal benefits. "Don't let them take it away," he repeated over and over.

The four-way 1948 campaign was the last before television put a premium on brief political advertisements and entertaining slogans rather than substantive debate, and the last in which a full spectrum of ideologies was presented to the American public. Virtually every public-opinion poll and newspaper report predicted a Dewey victory. Truman's success—by 303 to 189 electoral votes—represented one of the greatest upsets in American political history. For the first time since 1868, blacks (in the North, where they enjoyed the right to vote) played a decisive role in the outcome. Thurmond carried four Deep South states, demonstrating that the race issue, couched in terms of individual freedom, had the potential of leading traditionally Democratic white voters to desert their party. In retrospect, the States' Rights campaign offered a preview of the political transformation that by the end of the twentieth century would leave every southern state in the Republican column. As for Wallace, he suffered the humiliation of polling fewer popular votes (1.16 million) than Thurmond (1.17 million). His crushing defeat inaugurated an era in which public criticism of the foundations of American foreign policy became all but impossible.

THE ANTICOMMUNIST CRUSADE

For nearly half a century, the Cold War profoundly affected American life. There would be no return to "normalcy" as after World War I. The military-industrial establishment created during World War II would be permanent, not temporary. The United States retained a large and active federal government and poured money into weapons development and overseas bases. National security became the stated reason for a host of government projects, including aid to higher education and the building of a new national highway system (justified by the need to speed the evacuation of major cities in the event of nuclear war). The Cold War encouraged a culture of secrecy and dishonesty. Not until decades later was it revealed that during the 1950s and 1960s both the Soviet and American governments conducted experiments in which unwitting soldiers were exposed to chemical, biological, and nuclear weapons. American nuclear tests, conducted on Pacific islands and in Nevada, exposed thousands of civilians to radiation that caused cancer and birth defects.

Cold War military spending helped to fuel economic growth and support scientific research that not only perfected weaponry but also led to improved aircraft, computers, medicines, and other products with a large impact on civilian life. Since much of this research took place at universities, the Cold War promoted the rapid expansion of American higher education. The Cold

A postcard promoting tourism to Las Vegas highlights as one attraction the city's proximity to a nuclear test site. Witnessing nearby atomic explosions became a popular pastime in the city. The government failed to issue warnings of the dangers of nuclear fallout, and only years later did it admit that many onlookers had contracted diseases from radiation.

War reshaped immigration policy, with refugees from communism being allowed to enter the United States regardless of national-origin quotas. The international embarrassment caused by American racial policies contributed to the dismantling of segregation. And like other wars, the Cold War encouraged the drawing of a sharp line between patriotic Americans and those accused of being disloyal. Containment—not only of communism but of unorthodox opinions of all kinds—took place at home as well as abroad. At precisely the moment when the United States celebrated freedom as the foundation of American life, the right to dissent came under attack.

LOYALTY AND DISLOYALTY

Dividing the world between liberty and slavery automatically made those who could be linked to communism enemies of freedom. Although the assault on civil liberties came to be known as McCarthyism, it began before Senator Joseph R. McCarthy of Wisconsin burst onto the national scene in 1950. In 1947, less than two weeks after announcing the Truman Doctrine, the president established a loyalty review system in which government employees were required to demonstrate their patriotism without being allowed to confront accusers or, in some cases, knowing the charges against them. Along with persons suspected of disloyalty, the new national security system also targeted homosexuals who worked for the government. They were deemed particularly susceptible to blackmail by Soviet agents as well as supposedly lacking in the manly qualities needed to maintain the country's resolve in the fight against communism. Ironically, the government conducted an anti-gay campaign at the very time that gay men enjoyed a powerful presence in realms of culture and commercial life being promoted as expressions of American freedom—modern art and ballet, fashion, and advertising. The loyalty program failed to uncover any cases of espionage. But the federal government dismissed several hundred persons from their jobs, and thousands resigned rather than submit to investigation.

Also in 1947, the House Un-American Activities Committee (HUAC) launched a series of hearings about communist influence in Hollywood. Calling well-known screenwriters, directors, and actors to appear before the committee ensured it a wave of national publicity, which its members relished. Celebrities like producer Walt Disney and actors Gary Cooper and Ronald Reagan testified that the movie industry harbored numerous communists. But ten "unfriendly witnesses" refused to answer the committee's questions about their political beliefs or to "name names" (identify individual communists) on the grounds that the hearings violated the First Amendment's guarantees of freedom of speech and political association. The committee charged the Hollywood Ten, who included the prominent screenwriters Ring Lardner Jr. and Dalton Trumbo, with contempt of Congress, and they served jail terms of six months to a year. Hollywood studios blacklisted them (denied them employment), along with more than 200 others who were accused of communist sympathies or who refused to name names.

THE SPY TRIALS

A series of highly publicized legal cases followed, which fueled the growing anticommunist hysteria. Whittaker Chambers, an editor at *Time* magazine, testified before HUAC that during the 1930s, Alger Hiss, a high-ranking State Department official, had given him secret government documents to pass to agents of the Soviet Union. Hiss vehemently denied the charge, but a jury convicted him of perjury and he served five years in prison. A young congressman from California and a member of HUAC, Richard Nixon achieved national prominence because of his dogged pursuit of Hiss. In another celebrated case, the Truman administration put the leaders of the Communist Party on trial for advocating the overthrow of the government. In 1951, eleven of them were sentenced to five years in prison.

The most sensational trial involved Julius and Ethel Rosenberg, a working-class Jewish communist couple from New York City (quite different from Hiss, a member of the eastern Protestant "establishment"). In 1951, a jury convicted the Rosenbergs of conspiracy to pass secrets concerning the atomic bomb to Soviet agents during World War II (when the Soviets were American allies). Their chief accuser was David Greenglass, Ethel Rosenberg's brother, who had worked at the Los Alamos nuclear research center.

The case against Julius Rosenberg rested on highly secret documents that could not be revealed in court. (When they were released many years later, the scientific information they contained seemed too crude to justify the government's charge that Julius had passed along the "secret of the atomic bomb," although he may have helped the Soviets speed up their atomic program.) The government had almost no evidence against Ethel Rosenberg, and Greenglass later admitted that he had lied in some of his testimony about her. Indeed, prosecutors seem to have indicted her in the hope of pressuring Julius to confess and implicate others. But in the atmosphere of hysteria, their conviction was certain. Even though they had been convicted of conspiracy, a far weaker charge than spying or treason, Judge Irving Kaufman called their crime "worse than murder." They had helped, he declared, to "cause" the Korean War. Despite an international outcry, the death sentence was carried out in 1953. Controversy still surrounds the degree of guilt of both Hiss and the Rosenbergs, although almost no one today defends the Rosenbergs' execution. But these trials powerfully reinforced the idea that an army of Soviet spies was at work in the United States.

McCARTHY AND McCARTHYISM

In this atmosphere, a little-known senator from Wisconsin suddenly emerged as the chief national pursuer of subversives and gave a new name to the anticommunist crusade. Joseph R. McCarthy had won election to the Senate in 1946, partly on the basis of a fictional war record (he falsely claimed to have flown combat missions in the Pacific). In a speech at Wheeling, West Virginia, in February 1950, McCarthy announced that he had a list of 205 communists working for the State Department. The charge was preposterous, the numbers constantly changed, and McCarthy never identified a single person guilty of genuine disloyalty. But with a genius for self-promotion, McCarthy used the Senate subcommittee he chaired to hold hearings and level wild charges against numerous individuals as well as the Defense Department, the Voice of America, and other government agencies. Although many Republicans initially supported his rampage as a weapon against the Truman administration, McCarthy became an embarrassment to the party after the election of Republican Dwight D. Eisenhower as president in 1952. But McCarthy did not

"Fire!" *Cartoonist Herbert Block, known as "Herblock," offered this comment in 1949 on the danger to American freedom posed by the anticommunist crusade.*

halt his campaign. He even questioned Eisenhower's anticommunism.

McCarthy's downfall came in 1954, when a Senate committee investigated his charges that the army had harbored and "coddled" communists. The nationally televised Army-McCarthy hearings revealed McCarthy as a bully who browbeat witnesses and made sweeping accusations with no basis in fact. The dramatic high point came when McCarthy attacked the loyalty of a young lawyer in the firm of Joseph Welch, the army's chief lawyer. "Let us not assassinate this lad further," Welch pleaded. "You have done enough. Have you no sense of decency, sir?" After the hearings ended, the Republican-controlled Senate voted to "condemn" McCarthy for his behavior. He died three years later. But the word "McCarthyism" had entered the political vocabulary, a shorthand for character assassination, guilt by association, and abuse of power in the name of anticommunism.

AN ATMOSPHERE OF FEAR

By the early 1950s, the anticommunist crusade had created a pervasive atmosphere of fear. One commentator described Washington, D.C., as a city rife with "spying, suspicion, [and] defamation by rumor," with "democratic freedoms" at risk as power slipped into the hands of those "whose values are the values of dictatorship and whose methods are the methods of the police state." But anticommunism was as much a local as a national phenomenon. States created their own committees, modeled on HUAC, that investigated suspected communists and other dissenters. States and localities required loyalty oaths of teachers, pharmacists, and members of other professions, and they banned communists from fishing, holding a driver's license, and, in Indiana, working as a professional wrestler.

Private organizations like the American Legion, National Association of Manufacturers, and Daughters of the American Revolution also persecuted individuals for their beliefs. The Better America League of southern California gathered the names of nearly 2 million alleged subversives in the region. Previous membership in organizations with communist influence or even participation in campaigns in which communists had taken part, such as the defense of the government of Spain during the Spanish Civil War of the 1930s, suddenly took on sinister implications. Throughout the country in the late 1940s and 1950s, those who failed to testify about their past and present political beliefs and to inform on possible communists frequently lost their jobs.

Local anticommunist groups forced public libraries to remove from their shelves "un-American" books like the tales of Robin Hood, who took from the rich to give to the poor. Universities refused to allow left-wing speakers to appear on campus and fired teachers who refused to sign loyalty oaths or to testify against others.

As during World War I, the courts did nothing to halt the political repression, demonstrating once again James Madison's warning that popular hysteria could override "parchment barriers" like the Bill of Rights that sought to prevent infringements on freedom. In 1951, in *Dennis v. United States*, the Supreme Court upheld the jailing of Communist Party leaders even though the charges concerned their beliefs, not any actions they had taken. Even many liberals retreated from the idea that freedom of expression was a birthright of all Americans. The American Civil Liberties Union condemned McCarthy's tactics but refused to defend the indicted Communist Party leaders.

THE USES OF ANTICOMMUNISM

There undoubtedly were Soviet spies in the United States. Yet the tiny Communist Party hardly posed a threat to American security. And the vast majority of those jailed or deprived of their livelihoods during the McCarthy era were guilty of nothing more than holding unpopular beliefs and engaging in lawful political activities.

Anticommunism had many faces and purposes. A popular mass movement, it grew especially strong among ethnic groups like Polish-Americans, with roots in eastern European countries now dominated by the Soviet Union, and among American Catholics in general, who resented and feared communists' hostility to religion. Government agencies like the Federal Bureau of Investigation (FBI) used anticommunism to expand their power. Under director J. Edgar Hoover, the FBI developed files on thousands of American citizens, including political dissenters, homosexuals, and others, most of whom had no connection to communism.

Anticommunism also served as a weapon wielded by individuals and groups in battles unrelated to defending the United States against subversion. McCarthy and his Republican followers often seemed to target not so much Stalin as the legacy of Roosevelt and the New Deal. For many Democrats, aggressive anticommunism became a form of self-defense against Republican charges of disloyalty and a weapon in a struggle for the party's future. The campaign against subversion redrew the boundaries of acceptable Democratic liberalism to exclude both communists and those willing to cooperate with them as in the days of the Popular Front. Indeed, "sympathetic association" with communists—past or present—became grounds for dismissal from one's job under the government's loyalty program.

As the historian Henry Steele Commager argued in a 1947 magazine article, the anticommunist crusade promoted a new definition of loyalty—conformity. Anything other than "uncritical and unquestioning acceptance of America as it is," wrote Commager, could now be labeled unpatriotic. For business, anticommunism became part of a campaign to identify government intervention in the economy with socialism. White supremacists employed anticommunism against black civil rights, business used it against unions, and upholders of sexual morality and traditional gender roles raised the cry of subversion against feminism and homosexuality, both supposedly responsible for eroding the country's fighting spirit. (Those barred from government service now included homosexuals and members of nudist colonies.)

ANTICOMMUNIST POLITICS

At its height, from the late 1940s to around 1960, the anticommunist crusade powerfully structured American politics and culture. Especially after their unexpected defeat in 1948, Republicans in Congress used a drumbeat of charges of subversion to block Truman's political program. The most important actions of Congress were ones the president opposed. After launching the government's loyalty program in 1947, Truman had become increasingly alarmed at the excesses of the anticommunist crusade. He vetoed the McCarran Internal Security Bill of 1950, which required "subversive" groups to register with the government, allowed the denial of passports to their members, and authorized their deportation or detention on presidential order. But Congress quickly gave the measure the two-thirds majority necessary for it to become law.

The McCarran-Walter Act of 1952, the first major piece of immigration legislation since 1924, also passed over the president's veto. Truman had appointed a Commission on Immigration, whose report, *Whom Shall We Welcome?*, called for replacing the quotas based on national origins with a more flexible system taking into account family reunion, labor needs, and political asylum. But the McCarran-Walter Act kept the quotas in place. It also authorized the deportation of immigrants identified as communists, even if they had become citizens. But the renewed fear of aliens sparked by the anticommunist crusade went far beyond communists. In 1954, the federal government launched Operation Wetback, which employed the military to invade Mexican-American neighborhoods and round up and deport illegal aliens. Within a year, some 1 million Mexicans had been deported.

Truman did secure passage of a 1950 law that added previously excluded self-employed and domestic workers to Social Security. Otherwise, however, the idea of expanding the New Deal welfare state faded. In its place, private welfare arrangements proliferated. The labor contracts of unionized workers established health insurance plans, automatic cost of living wage increases, paid vacations, and pension plans that supplemented Social Security. Western European governments provided these benefits to all citizens. In the United States, union members in major industries enjoyed them, but not the nonunionized majority of the population, a situation that created increasing inequality among laboring Americans.

THE COLD WAR AND ORGANIZED LABOR

Every political and social organization had to cooperate with the anticommunist crusade or face destruction, a wrenching experience for movements like labor and civil rights, in which communists had been some of the most militant organizers. After the passage of the Taft-Hartley Act of 1947, which withdrew bargaining rights and legal protection from unions whose leaders failed to swear that they were not communists, the CIO expelled numerous left-wing officials and eleven communist-led unions, representing nearly 1 million workers. Organized labor emerged as a major supporter of the foreign policy of the Cold War. Internal battles over the role of communists and their allies led to the purging of some of the most militant union leaders, often the ones most committed to advancing equal rights to women and racial minorities in the workplace. This left organized labor less able to respond to the economy's shift to an emphasis on service rather than manufacturing, and to the rise of the civil rights movement.

COLD WAR CIVIL RIGHTS

The civil rights movement also underwent a transformation. At first, mainstream black organizations like the NAACP and Urban League protested the Truman administration's loyalty program. They wondered aloud why the program and congressional committees defined communism as "un-American," but not racism. Anticommunist investigators often cited attendance at interracial gatherings as evidence of disloyalty. But while a few prominent black leaders, notably the singer and actor Paul Robeson and the veteran crusader for equality W. E. B. Du Bois, became outspoken critics of the Cold War, most felt they had no choice but to go along. The NAACP purged communists from local branches. When the government deprived Robeson of his passport and indicted Du Bois for failing to register as an agent of the Soviet Union, few

VOICES OF FREEDOM

From Will Herberg, Protestant, Catholic, Jew (1955)

The Jewish philosopher Will Herberg was one of the more influential writers of the 1950s. In this excerpt, he analyzes the concept of the American Way of Life, a key slogan of the Cold War.

What is this American Way of Life that we have said constitutes the "common religion" of American society? . . . The American Way of Life is the symbol by which Americans define themselves and establish their unity. . . . On its political side it means the Constitution; on its economic side, "free enterprise"; on its social side, an equalitarianism which is not only compatible with but indeed actually implies vigorous economic competition and high mobility. . . .

The American Way of Life is humanitarian, "forward looking," optimistic. Americans are easily the most generous and philanthropic people in the world, in terms of their ready and unstinting response to suffering anywhere on the globe. The American believes in progress, in self-improvement, and quite fanatically in education. But above all, the American is idealistic. . . . And because they are so idealistic, Americans tend to be moralistic: they are inclined to see all issues as plain and simple, black and white, issues of morality. Every struggle in which they are seriously engaged becomes a "crusade." To Mr. Eisenhower, who in many ways exemplifies American religion in a particularly representative way, the second world war was a "crusade" (as was the first to Woodrow Wilson) . . . and so is his administration—a "battle for the republic" against "godless Communism" abroad and against "corruption and materialism" at home. . . . It is the secret of what outsiders must take to be the incredible self-righteousness of the American people, who tend to see the world divided into an innocent, virtuous America confronted with a corrupt, devious, and guileful Europe and Asia.

From Henry Steele Commager, "Who Is Loyal to America?" *Harper's* (September 1947)

In a sharply worded essay written in 1947, the prominent historian Henry Steele Commager commented on how the anticommunist crusade was stifling the expression of dissent and promoting an idea of patriotism that equated loyalty to the nation with the uncritical acceptance of American society and institutions.

Increasingly, Congress is concerned with the eradication of disloyalty and the defense of Americanism, and scarcely a day passes . . . that the outlines of the new loyalty and the new Americanism are not etched more sharply in public policy. . . . In the making is a revival of the red hysteria of the early 1920s, one of the shabbiest chapters in the history of American democracy, and more than a revival, for the new crusade is designed not merely to frustrate Communism but to formulate a positive definition of Americanism, and a positive concept of loyalty.

What is this new loyalty? It is, above all, conformity. It is the uncritical and unquestioning acceptance of America as it is—the political institutions, the social relationships, the economic practices. It rejects inquiry into the race question or socialized medicine, or public housing, or into the wisdom or validity of our foreign policy. It regards as particularly heinous any challenge to what is called "the system of private enterprise," identifying that system with Americanism. It abandons . . . the once popular concept of progress, and regards America as a finished product, perfect and complete.

It is, it must be added, easily satisfied. For it wants not intellectual conviction nor spiritual conquest, but mere outward conformity. In matters of loyalty, it takes the word for the deed, the gesture for the principle. It is content with the flag salute. . . . It is satisfied with membership in respectable organizations and, as it assumes that every member of a liberal organization is a Communist, concludes that every member of a conservative one is a true American. It has not yet learned that not everyone who saith Lord, Lord, shall enter into the kingdom of Heaven. It is designed neither to discover real disloyalty nor to foster true loyalty.

The concept of loyalty as conformity is a false one. It is narrow and restrictive, denies freedom of thought and of conscience. . . . What do men know of loyalty who make a mockery of the Declaration of Independence and the Bill of Rights?

QUESTIONS

1. What does Herberg think are the strengths and weaknesses of the American outlook?

2. Why does Commager feel that the new patriotism makes "a mockery" of the Bill of Rights?

3. How does Herberg's analysis help to explain the violations of civil liberties deplored by Commager?

prominent Americans, white or black, protested. (The charge against Du Bois was so absurd that even at the height of McCarthyism, the judge dismissed it.)

The Cold War caused a shift in thinking and tactics among civil rights groups. Organizations like the Southern Conference for Human Welfare, in which communists and noncommunists had cooperated in linking racial equality with labor organizing and economic reform, had been crucial to the struggles of the 1930s and war years. Their demise left a gaping hole that the NAACP, with its narrowly legalistic strategy, could not fill. Black organizations embraced the language of the Cold War and used it for their own purposes. They insisted that by damaging the American image abroad, racial inequality played into the Russians' hands. Thus, they helped to cement Cold War ideology as the foundation of the political culture, while complicating the idea of American freedom.

President Truman, as noted above, had called for greater attention to civil rights in part to improve the American image abroad. All in all, however, the height of the Cold War was an unfavorable time to raise questions about the imperfections of American society. In 1947, two months after the Truman Doctrine speech, Undersecretary of State Dean Acheson delivered a major address defending the president's pledge to aid "free peoples" seeking to preserve their "democratic institutions." Acheson chose as his audience the Delta Council, an organization of Mississippi planters, bankers, and merchants. He seemed unaware that to make the case for the Cold War, he had ventured into what one historian has called the "American Siberia," a place of grinding poverty whose black population (70 percent of the total) enjoyed neither genuine freedom nor democracy. Most of the Delta's citizens were denied the very liberties supposedly endangered by communism.

After 1948, little came of the Truman administration's civil rights flurry. State and local laws banning discrimination in employment and housing remained largely unenforced. In 1952, the Democrats showed how quickly the issue had faded by nominating for president Adlai Stevenson of Illinois, a candidate with little interest in civil rights, with southern segregationist John Sparkman as his running mate. The following year, Hortense Gabel, director of the eminently respectable New York State Committee Against Discrimination in Housing, reported that the shadow of fear hung over the civil rights movement. Given the persecution of dissent and the widespread sentiment that equated any criticism of American society with disloyalty, "a great many people are shying away from all activity in the civil liberties and civil rights fronts."

Time would reveal that the waning of the civil rights impulse was only temporary. But it came at a crucial moment, the late 1940s and early 1950s, when the United States experienced the greatest economic boom in its history. The rise of an "affluent society" transformed American life, opening new opportunities for tens of millions of white Americans in rapidly expanding suburbs. But it left blacks trapped in the declining rural areas of the South and urban ghettos of the North. The contrast between new opportunities and widespread prosperity for whites and continued discrimination for blacks would soon inspire a civil rights revolution and, with it, yet another redefinition of American freedom.

Chapter Review

REVIEW QUESTIONS

1. What major ideological conflicts, security interests, and events brought about the Cold War?
2. President Truman referred to the Truman Doctrine and the Marshall Plan as "two halves of the same walnut." Explain the similarities and differences between these two aspects of containment.
3. How did the tendency of both the United States and the Soviet Union to see all international events through the lens of the Cold War lessen each country's ability to understand what was happening in other countries around the world?
4. Why did the United States not support movements for colonial independence around the world?
5. How did the government attempt to shape public opinion during the Cold War?
6. Explain the differences between the United States' and the Soviet Union's application of the UN Universal Declaration of Human Rights.
7. How did the anticommunist crusade affect organized labor in the postwar period?
8. What accounts for the Republican resurgence in these years?
9. What were the major components of Truman's Fair Deal? Which ones were implemented and which ones not?
10. How did the Cold War affect civil liberties in the United States?

KEY TERMS

containment
Long Telegram
"iron curtain" speech
Truman Doctrine
Marshall Plan
National Security Council
General Agreement on Tariffs and Trade
North Atlantic Treaty Organization
NSC-68
decolonization
"Militant Liberty"
totalitarianism
the Fair Deal
Taft-Hartley Act
Dixiecrats
loyalty review system
Hollywood Ten
Army-McCarthy hearings
conformity
McCarran-Walter Act

wwnorton.com/studyspace

VISIT STUDYSPACE FOR THESE RESOURCES AND MORE:

- Author Videos
- A chapter outline
- A practice quiz
- Interactive maps
- Multimedia documents

CHAPTER 9

AN AFFLUENT SOCIETY

From *Give Me Liberty! Seagull Fourth Edition*

Eric Foner

Credits: photo 1: Howard Sochurek/Time Life Pictures/Getty Images; photo 2: Courtesy of Hagley Museum and Library; photo 3: Advertising Archive; photo 4: American Economic Foundation, "Man's Belief in God Is Personal," CU Libraries Exhibitions, accessed February 22, 2013, https://exhibitions.cul.columbia.edu/items/show/2829; photo 5: Bettmann/Corbis; photo 6: AP Photo; photo 7: Frank Driggs Collection; photo 8: AP Photo; photo 9: Collection of the Norman Rockwell Museum, Stockbridge, Massachusetts.

9

An Affluent Society 1953–1960

FOCUS QUESTIONS

- What were the main characteristics of the affluent society of the 1950s?
- How were the 1950s a period of consensus in both domestic policies and foreign affairs?
- What were the major thrusts of the civil rights movement in this period?
- What was the significance of the presidential election of 1960?

In 1958, during a "thaw" in the Cold War, the United States and the Soviet Union agreed to exchange national exhibitions in order to allow citizens of each "superpower" to become acquainted with life in the other. The Soviet Exhibition, unveiled in New York City in June 1959, featured factory machinery, scientific advances, and other illustrations of how communism had modernized a backward country. The following month, the American National Exhibition opened in Moscow. A showcase of consumer goods and leisure equipment, complete with stereo sets, a movie theater, home appliances, and twenty-two different cars, the exhibit, *Newsweek* observed, hoped to demonstrate the superiority of "modern capitalism with its ideology of political and economic freedom." Yet the exhibit's real message was not freedom but consumption—or, to be more precise, the equating of the two.

When Vice President Richard Nixon prepared for his trip to Moscow to launch the exhibition, a former ambassador to Russia urged him to emphasize American values: "We are idealists; they are materialists." But the events of the opening day seemed to reverse these roles. Nixon devoted his address, entitled "What Freedom Means to Us," not to freedom of expression or differing forms of government, but to the "extraordinarily high standard of living" in the United States, with its 56 million cars and 50 million television sets. The United States, he declared, had achieved what Soviets could only dream of—"prosperity for all in a classless society."

The Moscow exhibition became the site of a classic Cold War confrontation over the meaning of freedom—the "kitchen debate" between Nixon and Soviet premier Nikita Khrushchev. Twice during the first day Nixon and Khrushchev engaged in unscripted debate about the merits of capitalism and communism. The first took place in the kitchen of a model suburban ranch house, the second in a futuristic "miracle kitchen" complete with a mobile robot that swept the floors. Supposedly the home of an average steelworker, the ranch house was the exhibition's centerpiece. It represented, Nixon declared, the mass enjoyment of American freedom within a suburban setting—freedom of choice among products, colors, styles, and prices. It also implied a particular role for women. Throughout his exchanges with Khrushchev, Nixon used the words "women" and "housewives" inter-

Vice President Richard Nixon and Soviet premier Nikita Khrushchev during the "kitchen debate," a discussion, among other things, of the meaning of freedom, which took place in 1959 at the American National Exposition in Moscow. Khrushchev makes a point while a woman demonstrates a washing machine.

changeably. Pointing to the automatic floor sweeper, the vice president remarked that in the United States "you don't need a wife."

Nixon's decision to make a stand for American values in the setting of a suburban kitchen was a brilliant stroke. Nixon recognized that "soft power"—the penetration across the globe of American goods and popular culture—was an even more potent form of influence than military might. Indeed, his stance reflected the triumph during the 1950s of a conception of freedom centered on economic abundance and consumer choice within the context of traditional family life—a vision that seemed to offer far more opportunities for the "pursuit of happiness" to men than women. In reply, Khrushchev ridiculed consumer culture and the American obsession with household gadgets. "Don't you have a machine," he quipped, "that puts food in the mouth and pushes it down?" Many of the items on display, he continued, served "no useful purpose." Yet, in a sense, the Soviet leader conceded the debate when he predicted—quite incorrectly—that within seven years his country would surpass the United

CHRONOLOGY

1946	*Mendez v. Westminster*
1947	Levittown development starts
1950	David Riesman's *The Lonely Crowd*
1952	United States detonates first hydrogen bomb
1953	Soviet Union detonates hydrogen bomb
	CIA-led Iranian coup
1954	*Brown v. Board of Education*
	CIA-led Guatemalan coup
	Geneva Accords for Vietnam
1955	AFL and CIO merge
	Allen Ginsberg's *Howl*
1955–1956	Montgomery bus boycott
1956	"Southern Manifesto"
	Federal-Aid Highway Act
	Suez crisis
1957	Eisenhower Doctrine
	Southern Christian Leadership Conference organized
	Integration of Little Rock's Central High School
	Sputnik launched
	Jack Kerouac's *On the Road*
1958	National Defense Education Act
1959	Nixon-Khrushchev "kitchen debate"
1960	John F. Kennedy elected president
1962	Milton Friedman's *Capitalism and Freedom*

States in the production of consumer goods. For if material abundance was a battleground in the Cold War, American victory was certain.

THE GOLDEN AGE

The end of World War II was followed by what one scholar has called the "golden age" of capitalism, a period of economic expansion, stable prices, low unemployment, and rising standards of living that continued until 1973. Between 1946 and 1960, the American gross national product more than doubled and much of the benefit flowed to ordinary citizens in rising wages. In every measurable way—diet, housing, income, education, recreation—most Americans lived better than their parents and grandparents had. By 1960, an estimated 60 percent of Americans enjoyed what the government defined as a middle-class standard of living. The official poverty rate, 30 percent of all families in 1950, had declined to 22 percent a decade later (still, to be sure, representing more than one in five Americans).

Numerous innovations came into widespread use in these years, transforming Americans' daily lives. They included television, home air-conditioning, automatic dishwashers, inexpensive long-distance telephone calls, and jet air travel. Services like electricity, central heating, and indoor plumbing that within living memory had been enjoyed only by the rich and solidly middle class now became features of common life.

A CHANGING ECONOMY

Despite the economic recovery of western Europe and Japan after World War II, the United States remained the world's predominant industrial power. Major industries like steel, automobiles, and aircraft dominated the domestic and world markets for their products. Like other wars, the Cold War fueled industrial production and promoted a redistribution of the nation's population and economic resources. The West, especially the Seattle area, southern California, and the Rocky Mountain states, benefited enormously from government contracts for aircraft, guided missiles, and radar systems. The South became the home of numerous military bases and government-funded shipyards. Growth in the construction of aircraft engines and submarines counterbalanced the decline of New England's old textile and machinery industries, many of which relocated in the South to take advantage of low-cost nonunion labor.

In retrospect, the 1950s appear as the last decade of the industrial age in the United States. Since then, the American economy has shifted rapidly toward services, education, information, finance, and entertainment, while employment in manufacturing has declined. Even during the 1950s, the number of factory laborers fell slightly while clerical workers grew by nearly 25 percent and salaried employees in large corporate enterprises rose by 60 percent. Unions' very success in raising wages inspired employers to mechanize more and more elements of manufacturing in order to reduce labor costs. In 1956, for the first time in American history, white-collar workers outnumbered blue-collar factory and manual laborers.

The long-term trend toward fewer and larger farms continued. During the 1950s, the farm population fell from 23 million to 15 million, yet agricultural production rose by 50 percent, thanks to more efficient machinery, the application of chemical fertilizers and insecticides, increased use of irrigation to open land to cultivation in the West, and the development of new crop strains. The decade witnessed an acceleration of the transformation of southern life that had begun during World War II. New tractors and harvesting machinery and a continuing shift from cotton production to less labor-intensive soybean and poultry raising reduced the need for farm workers. More than 3 million black and white hired hands and sharecroppers migrated out of the region. The center of gravity of American farming shifted decisively to Texas, Arizona, and especially California. The large corporate farms of California, worked by Latino and Filipino migrant laborers, poured forth an endless supply of fruits and vegetables for the domestic and world markets. Items like oranges and orange juice, once luxuries, became an essential part of the American diet.

A SUBURBAN NATION

The main engines of economic growth during the 1950s, however, were residential construction and spending on consumer goods. The postwar baby boom (discussed later) and the shift of population from cities to suburbs created an enormous demand for housing, television sets, home appliances, and cars. By 1960, suburban residents of single-family homes outnumbered urban dwellers and those living in rural areas. (Today, they outnumber both combined.)

During the 1950s, the number of houses in the United States doubled, nearly all of them built in the suburbs that sprang up across the landscape. The dream of home ownership, the physical embodiment of hopes for a better life, came within reach of the majority of Americans. Developers pioneered inexpensive mass-building techniques, and government-backed low-interest loans to returning veterans allowed working-class men and women in large numbers to purchase homes. William and Alfred Levitt, who shortly after the war built the first Levittown on 1,200 acres of potato fields on Long Island near New York City, became the most famous suburban developers. Levittown's more than 10,000 houses were assembled quickly from prefabricated parts and priced well within the reach of most Americans. Levittown was soon home to 40,000 people. At the same time, suburbs required a new form of shopping center—the mall—to which people drove in their cars. In contrast to traditional mixed-use city centers crowded with pedestrians, malls existed solely for shopping and had virtually no public space.

THE GROWTH OF THE WEST

But it was California that became the most prominent symbol of the postwar suburban boom. Between World War II and 1975, more than 30 million Americans moved west of the Mississippi River. One-fifth of the population growth of the 1950s occurred in California alone. In 1963, it surpassed New York to become the nation's most populous state.

Most western growth took place in metropolitan areas, not on farms. But "centerless" western cities like Houston, Phoenix, and Los Angeles differed greatly from traditional urban centers in the East. Rather than consisting of downtown business districts linked to residential neighborhoods by public transportation, western cities were decentralized clusters of single-family homes and businesses united by a web of highways. The Los Angeles basin, the largest western suburban region, had once had an extensive system of trains, trolleys, and buses. But local governments dismantled these lines after World War II, and the state and federal governments replaced them with freeways for cars and trucks. Suburban growth spilled into farm regions like the San Fernando and San Bernardino valleys. By one estimate, one-third of southern California's land area (presumably not including mountains and deserts) was paved over with roads and parking lots. Life centered around the car; people drove to and from work and did their shopping at malls reachable only by driving. In other sections of the country as well, shopping shifted to suburban centers, and old downtown business districts stagnated. The spread of suburban homes created millions of new lawns. Today, more land is cultivated in grass than any agricultural crop in the United States.

A CONSUMER CULTURE

"The consumer is the key to our economy," declared Jack Straus, chairman of the board of Macy's, New York City's leading department store. "Our ability to consume is endless. The luxuries of today are the necessities of tomorrow." The roots of the consumer culture of the 1950s date back to the 1920s and even earlier. But never before had affluence, or consumerism, been so widespread. In a consumer culture, the measure of freedom became the ability to gratify market desires. Modern society, wrote Clark Kerr, president of the University of California, may well have reduced freedom "in the workplace" by subjecting workers to stringent discipline on the job, but it offered a far greater range of "goods and services," and therefore "a greater scope of freedom" in Americans' "personal lives."

A portrait of affluence: In this photograph by Alex Henderson, Steve Czekalinski, an employee of the DuPont Corporation, poses with his family and the food they consumed in a single year, 1951. The family spent $1,300 (around $11,000 in today's money) on food, including 699 bottles of milk, 578 pounds of meat, and 131 dozen eggs. Nowhere else in the world in 1951 was food so available and inexpensive.

In a sense, the 1950s represented the culmination of the long-term trend in which consumerism replaced economic independence and democratic participation as central definitions of American freedom. Attitudes toward debt changed as well. Low interest rates and the spread of credit cards encouraged Americans to borrow money to purchase consumer goods. Americans became comfortable living in never-ending debt, once seen as a loss of economic freedom.

Consumer culture demonstrated the superiority of the American way of life to communism and virtually redefined the nation's historic mission to extend freedom to other countries. From Coca-Cola to Levi's jeans, American consumer goods, once a status symbol for the rich in other countries, were now marketed to customers around the globe. The country's most powerful weapon in the Cold War, insisted a reporter for *House Beautiful* magazine, was "the freedom offered by washing machines and dishwashers, vacuum cleaners, automobiles, and refrigerators."

THE TV WORLD

Thanks to television, images of middle-class life and advertisements for consumer goods blanketed the country. By the end of the 1950s, nearly nine of ten American families owned a TV set. Television replaced newspapers as the most common source of information about public events, and TV watching became the nation's leading leisure activity. Television changed Americans' eating habits (the frozen TV dinner, heated and eaten while watching a program, went on sale in 1954), and it provided Americans of all regions and backgrounds with a common cultural experience.

With a few exceptions, like the Army-McCarthy hearings, TV avoided controversy and projected a bland image of middle-class life. Popular shows of the early 1950s, such as *The Goldbergs* (with Jewish immigrants as the central characters) and *The Honeymooners* (in which Jackie Gleason played a bus driver), featured working-class families living in urban apartments. By the end of the decade, they had been replaced as the dominant programs by quiz shows, westerns, and comedies set in suburban homes like *Leave It to Beaver* and *The Adventures of Ozzie and Harriet.* Television also became the most effective advertising medium ever invented. To polish their image, large corporations sponsored popular programs—*The General Electric Theater* (hosted for several years by Ronald Reagan), *Alcoa Presents*, and others. TV ads, aimed primarily at middle-class suburban viewers, conveyed images of the good life based on endless consumption.

A NEW FORD

"The concept of freedom," wrote one commentator in 1959, "has become as familiar to us as an old hat or a new Ford." And a new Ford—or Chrysler or Chevrolet—now seemed essential to the enjoyment of freedom's benefits. Along with a home and television set, the car became part of what sociologists called "the standard consumer package" of the 1950s. By 1960, 80 percent of American families owned at least one car, and 14 percent had two or more, nearly all manufactured in the United States. Most were designed to go out of style within a year or two, promoting further purchases.

Auto manufacturers and oil companies vaulted to the top ranks of corporate America. Detroit and its environs were home to immense auto factories. The River Rouge complex had 62,000 employees, Willow Run 42,000. Since the military increasingly needed high-technology goods rather than the trucks and tanks that had rolled off assembly lines in World War II, the region around the Great Lakes lagged in defense contracts. In the long term, the continued funneling of federal dollars from the North and Midwest to the Sunbelt would prove devastating to the old industrial heartland. But during the 1950s, the booming automobile industry, with its demand for steel, rubber, and other products, assured the region's continued prosperity.

The automobile, the pivot on which suburban life turned, transformed the nation's daily life, just as the interstate highway system (discussed later) transformed Americans' travel habits, making possible long-distance vacationing by car and commuting to work from ever-increasing distances. The result was an altered American landscape, leading to the construction of motels, drive-in movie theaters, and roadside eating establishments. The first McDonald's fast food restaurant opened in Illinois in 1954. Within ten years, having been franchised by California businessman Ray Kroc, approximately 700 McDonald's stands had been built, which had sold over 400 million hamburgers. The car symbolized the identification of freedom with individual mobility and private choice. On the road, Americans were constantly reminded in advertising, television shows, and popular songs, they truly enjoyed freedom. They could imagine themselves as modern versions of western pioneers, able to leave behind urban crowds and workplace pressures for the "open road."

WOMEN AT WORK AND AT HOME

The emergence of suburbia as a chief site of what was increasingly called the "American way of life" placed pressure on the family—and especially women—to live up to freedom's promise. After 1945, women lost most of the industrial jobs they had performed during the war. As during most of American history, women who worked outside the home remained concentrated in low-salary, nonunion jobs, such as clerical, sales, and service labor, rather than better-paying manufacturing positions. After a sharp postwar drop in female employment, the number of women at work soon began to rise. By 1955, it exceeded the level of World War II. But the nature and aims of women's work had changed. The modern woman, said *Look* magazine, worked part-time, to help support the family's middle-class lifestyle, not to help pull it out of poverty or to pursue personal fulfillment or an independent career. Working women in 1960 earned, on average, only 60 percent of the income of men.

Despite the increasing numbers of wage-earning women, the suburban family's breadwinner was assumed to be male, while the wife remained at home. Films, TV shows, and advertisements portrayed marriage as the most important goal of American women. And during the 1950s, men and women reaffirmed the virtues of family life. They married younger (at an average age of twenty-two for men and twenty for women), divorced less frequently than in the past, and had more children (3.2 per family). A "baby boom" that lasted into the mid-1960s followed the end of the war. At a time of low immigration, the American population rose by nearly 30 million (almost 20 percent) during the 1950s. The increase arose mostly from the large number of births, but it also reflected the fact that Americans now lived longer than in the past, thanks to the wide availability of "miracle drugs" like penicillin that had been developed during World War II to combat bacterial infections.

The family also became a weapon in the Cold War. The ability of women to remain at home, declared a government official, "separates us from the Communist world," where a high percentage of women worked. To be sure, the family life exalted during the 1950s differed from the patriarchal household of old. It was a modernized relationship, in which both partners reconciled family obligations with personal fulfillment through shared consumption, leisure activities, and sexual pleasure. Thanks to modern conveniences, the personal freedom once associated with work could now be found at home. Frozen and prepared meals, exulted one writer in 1953, offered housewives "freedom from tedium, space, work, and their own inexperience"—quite a change from the Four Freedoms of World War II.

Advertisers during the 1950s sought to convey the idea that women would enjoy their roles as suburban homemakers, as in this ad, which equates housework with a game of golf.

Like other forms of dissent, feminism seemed to have disappeared from American life or was widely dismissed as evidence of mental disorder. Prominent psychologists insisted that the unhappiness of individual women or even the desire to work for wages stemmed from a failure to accept the "maternal instinct." "The independent woman," declared the book *Modern Woman: The Lost Sex* (1947) "is a contradiction in terms." The idea of domestic life as a refuge and of full-time motherhood as a woman's "sphere" had a long history in the United States. But in the postwar suburbs, where family life was physically separated from work, relatives, and the web of social organizations typical of cities, it came close to realization.

A SEGREGATED LANDSCAPE

For millions of city dwellers, the suburban utopia fulfilled the dream, postponed by depression and war, of home ownership and middle-class incomes. For beneficiaries of postwar prosperity, in the words of a Boston worker who made heroic sacrifices to move his family to the suburbs, the home became "the center of freedom." The move to the suburbs also promoted Americanization, cutting residents off from urban ethnic communities and bringing them fully into the world of mass consumption. But if the suburbs offered a new site for the enjoyment of American freedom, they retained at least one familiar characteristic—rigid racial boundaries.

Suburbia has never been as uniform as either its celebrants or its critics claimed. There are upper-class suburbs, working-class suburbs, industrial suburbs, and "suburban" neighborhoods within city limits. But if the class uniformity of suburbia has been exaggerated, its racial uniformity was all too real. As late as the 1990s, nearly 90 percent of suburban whites lived in communities with non-white populations of less than 1 percent—the legacy of decisions by government, real-estate developers, banks, and residents.

During the postwar suburban boom, federal agencies continued to insure mortgages that barred resale of houses to non-whites, thereby financing housing segregation. Even after the Supreme Court in 1948 declared such provisions legally unenforceable, banks and private developers barred non-whites from the suburbs and the government refused to subsidize their mortgages except in segregated enclaves. In 1960, blacks represented less than 3 percent of the population of Chicago's suburbs. The vast new communities built by William Levitt refused to allow blacks, including army veterans, to rent or purchase homes. "If we sell one house to a Negro family," Levitt explained, "then 90 or 95 percent of our white customers will not buy into the community." After a lawsuit, Levitt finally agreed during the 1960s to sell homes to non-whites, but at a pace that can only be described as glacial. In 1990, his Long Island community, with a population of 53,000, included 127 black residents.

PUBLIC HOUSING AND URBAN RENEWAL

A Housing Act passed by Congress in 1949 authorized the construction of more than 800,000 units of public housing in order to provide a "decent home for every American family." But the law set an extremely low ceiling on the income of residents—a rule demanded by private contractors seeking to avoid competition from the government in building homes for the middle class. This regulation limited housing projects to the very poor. Since white urban and suburban neighborhoods successfully opposed the construction of public housing, it was increasingly confined to segregated neighborhoods in inner cities, reinforcing the concentration of poverty in urban non-white neighborhoods. At the same time, under programs of "urban renewal," cities demolished poor neighborhoods in city centers that occupied potentially valuable real estate. In their place, developers constructed retail centers and all-white middle-income housing complexes, and states built urban public universities like Wayne State in Detroit and the University of Illinois at Chicago. Los Angeles displaced a neighborhood of mixed ethnic groups in Chavez Ravine in order to build a stadium for the Dodgers, whose move in 1958 after sixty-eight years in Brooklyn seemed to symbolize the growing importance of California on the national scene. White residents displaced by urban renewal often moved to the suburbs. Non-whites, unable to do so, found housing in run-down city neighborhoods.

THE DIVIDED SOCIETY

Suburbanization hardened the racial lines of division in American life. Between 1950 and 1970, about 7 million white Americans left cities for the suburbs. Meanwhile, nearly 3 million blacks moved from the South to the North, greatly increasing the size of existing urban ghettos and creating entirely new ones. And half a million Puerto Ricans, mostly small coffee and tobacco farmers and agricultural laborers forced off the land when American sugar companies expanded their landholdings on the island, moved to the mainland. Most ended up in New York City's East Harlem, until then an Italian-American community. Although set in a different part of New York, the popular Broadway musical *West Side Story* dramatized the tensions between Puerto Rican newcomers and longtime urban residents. By the late 1960s, more Puerto Ricans lived in New York City than San Juan, the island's capital.

The process of racial exclusion became self-reinforcing. Non-whites remained concentrated in manual and unskilled jobs, the result of employment discrimination and their virtual exclusion from educational opportunities at public and private universities, including those outside the South. In 1950, only 12 percent of employed blacks held white-collar positions, compared with 45 percent of whites. As the white population and industrial jobs fled the old city centers for the suburbs, poorer blacks and Latinos remained trapped in urban ghettos, seen by many whites as places of crime, poverty, and welfare.

Suburbanites, for whom the home represented not only an emblem of freedom but the family's major investment, became increasingly fearful that any non-white presence would lower the quality of life and destroy property values. *Life* magazine quoted a white suburbanite discussing a prospective black neighbor: "He's probably a nice guy, but every time I see him, I see $2,000 drop off the value of my house." Residential segregation was reinforced by "blockbusting"—a tactic of real-estate brokers who circulated exaggerated warnings of an impending influx of non-whites, to persuade alarmed white residents to sell their homes hastily. Because of this practice, some all-white neighborhoods quickly became all-minority enclaves rather than places where members of different races lived side by side.

"Freedom is equal housing too" became a slogan in the campaign for residential integration. But suburban home ownership long remained a white entitlement, with the freedom of non-whites to rent or purchase a home where they desired overridden by the claims of private property and "freedom of association." Even as the old divisions between white ethnic Americans faded in the suburban melting pot, racial barriers in housing, and therefore in public education and jobs, were reinforced.

Cold War affluence coexisted with urban decay and racism, the seeds from which protest would soon flower. Yet to many observers in the 1950s it seemed that the ills of American society had been solved. Scholars celebrated the "end of ideology" and the triumph of a democratic, capitalist "consensus" in which all Americans except the maladjusted and fanatics shared the same liberal values of individualism, respect for private property, and belief in equal opportunity. If problems remained, their solutions required technical adjustments, not structural change or aggressive political intervention.

RELIGION AND ANTICOMMUNISM

Both Protestant and Roman Catholic religious leaders played crucial roles in the spread of anticommunism and Cold War culture. Official American values celebrated the nation's religiosity as opposed to "godless" communism. During the 1950s, a majority of Americans—the highest percentage in the nation's history—were affiliated with a church or synagogue. In 1954, to "strengthen our national resistance to communism," Congress added the words "under God" to the Pledge of Allegiance. In 1957, "In God We Trust" was included on paper money. Big-budget Hollywood films like *The Ten Commandments* and *Ben Hur* celebrated early Judaism and Christianity. Soviet domination of strongly Catholic eastern Europe inspired powerful currents of anticommunism among Catholic ethnic groups in the United States. Leading clerics like Bishop Fulton J. Sheen of the Catholic church and Protestant evangelist Billy Graham used radio and television to spread to millions a religious message heavily imbued with anticommunism. Communism, Graham declared, was not only an economic and political outlook but a religion—one "inspired, directed and motivated by the Devil himself."

As for religious differences, the source of persistent tension in American history, these were absorbed within a common "Judeo-Christian" heritage, a notion that became central to the cultural and political dialogue of the 1950s. This newly invented tradition sought to demonstrate that Catholics, Protestants, and Jews shared the same history and values and had all contributed to the evolution of American society. In the era of McCarthyism, ideological differences may have been un-American, but group pluralism reigned supreme, with the free exercise of religion yet another way of differentiating the American way of life from life under communism.

An image from a booklet issued by the American Economic Foundation illustrates the linkage of anticommunism and religious faith during the Cold War. The hairy hand in the bottom half of the drawing represents the communist threat, which endangers religious freedom in the United States. Most of the booklet, however, dealt with the superiority of free enterprise to communism.

The idea of a unified Judeo-Christian tradition overlooked the long history of hostility among religious denominations. But it reflected the decline of anti-Semitism and anti-Catholicism in the wake of World War II, as well as the ongoing secularization of American life. As Will Herberg argued in his influential book *Protestant-Catholic-Jew* (1955), religion now had less to do with spiritual activities or sacred values than with personal identity, group assimilation, and the promotion of traditional morality. In an affluent suburban society, Herberg argued, the "common religion" was the American way of life, a marriage of democratic values and economic prosperity—in a phrase, "free enterprise."

SELLING FREE ENTERPRISE

The economic content of Cold War freedom increasingly came to focus on consumer capitalism, or, as it was now universally known, "free enterprise." More than political democracy or freedom of speech, which many allies of the United States outside western Europe lacked, an economic system resting on private ownership united the nations of the Free World. A week before his Truman Doctrine speech, in a major address on economic policy, the president reduced Roosevelt's Four Freedoms to three. Freedom of speech and worship remained, but freedom from want and fear had been replaced by freedom of enterprise, "part and parcel," said Truman, of the American way of life.

Even more than during World War II, what one historian calls the "selling of free enterprise" became a major industry, involving corporate advertising, school programs, newspaper editorials, and civic activities. Convinced that ads represented "a new weapon in the world-wide fight for freedom," the Advertising Council invoked cherished symbols like the Statue of Liberty and the Liberty Bell in the service of "competitive free enterprise." To be sure, the free enterprise campaigners did not agree on every issue. Some businessmen believed that defending free enterprise required rolling back much of the power that labor unions had gained in the past decade, dismantling New Deal regulations, and restricting the economic role of government. Representing what might be called business's more liberal wing, the Advertising Council, in its "American Economic System" ad campaign of 1949, reaffirmed labor's right to collective bargaining and the importance of government–business cooperation. Indeed, despite talk of the glories of the free market, government policies played a crucial role in the postwar boom. The rapid expansion of the suburban middle class owed much to federal tax subsidies, mortgage guarantees for home purchases, dam and highway construction, military contracts, and benefits under the GI Bill.

PEOPLE'S CAPITALISM

Free enterprise seemed an odd way of describing an economy in which a few large corporations dominated key sectors. Until well into the twentieth century, most ordinary Americans had been deeply suspicious of big business, associating it with images of robber barons who manipulated politics, suppressed economic competition, and treated their workers unfairly. Americans, wrote David Lilienthal, chairman of the Atomic Energy Commission, must abandon their traditional fear that concentrated economic power endangered "our very liberties." Large-scale production was not only necessary to fighting the Cold War, but it enhanced freedom by multiplying consumer goods. "By freedom," wrote Lilienthal, "I mean essentially *freedom to choose*. . . . It means a maximum range of choice for the consumer when he spends his dollar." By the end of the 1950s, public-opinion surveys revealed that more than 80 percent of Americans believed that "our freedom depends on the free enterprise system."

The United States, declared *Fortune* magazine, anticipating Vice President Nixon's remark in the 1959 kitchen debate, had achieved the Marxist goal of a classless society. A sharp jump in the number of individuals investing in Wall Street inspired talk of a new "people's capitalism." In 1953, 4.5 million Americans—only slightly more than in 1928—owned shares of stock. By the mid-1960s, the number had grown to 25 million. In the face of widespread abundance, who could deny that the capitalist marketplace embodied individual freedom or that poverty would soon be a thing of the past? "It was American Freedom," proclaimed *Life* magazine, "by which and through which this amazing achievement of wealth and power was fashioned."

THE LIBERTARIAN CONSERVATIVES

During the 1950s, a group of thinkers began the task of reviving conservatism and reclaiming the idea of freedom from liberals. Although largely ignored outside their own immediate circle, they developed ideas that would define conservative thought for the next half-century. One was opposition to a strong national government, an outlook that had been given new political life in conservatives' bitter reaction against the New Deal. To these "libertarian" conservatives, freedom meant individual autonomy, limited government, and unregulated capitalism.

These ideas had great appeal to conservative entrepreneurs, especially in the rapidly growing South and West. Many businessmen who desired to pursue their economic fortunes free of government regulation, high taxes, and labor unions found intellectual reinforcement in the writings of the young economist Milton Friedman. In 1962, Friedman published *Capitalism and Freedom*, which identified the free market as the necessary foundation for individual liberty. This was not an uncommon idea during the Cold War, but Friedman pushed it to extreme conclusions. He called for turning over to the private sector virtually all government functions and the repeal of minimum wage laws, the graduated income tax, and the Social Security system. Friedman extended the idea of unrestricted free choice into virtually every realm of life. Government, he insisted, should seek to regulate neither the economy nor individual conduct.

THE NEW CONSERVATISM

Friedman was indirectly criticizing not only liberalism but also the "new conservatism," a second strand of thought that became increasingly prominent in the 1950s. Convinced that the Free World needed to arm itself morally and intellectually, not just militarily, for the battle against communism, "new conservatives" like writers Russell Kirk and Richard Weaver insisted that toleration of difference—a central belief of modern liberalism—offered no substitute for the search for absolute truth. Weaver's book, *Ideas Have Consequences* (1948), a rambling philosophical treatise that surprisingly became the most influential statement of this new traditionalism, warned that the West was suffering from moral decay and called for a return to a civilization based on values grounded in the Christian tradition and in timeless notions of good and evil.

The "new conservatives" understood freedom as first and foremost a moral condition. It required a decision by independent men and women to lead virtuous lives, or governmental action to force them to do so. Although they wanted government expelled from the economy, new conservatives trusted it to regulate personal behavior, to restore a Christian morality they saw as growing weaker and weaker in American society.

Here lay the origins of a division in conservative ranks that would persist into the twenty-first century. Unrestrained individual choice and moral virtue are radically different starting points from which to discuss freedom. Was the purpose of conservatism, one writer wondered, to create the "free man" or the "good man"? Libertarian conservatives spoke the language of progress and personal autonomy; the "new conservatives" emphasized tradition, community, and moral commitment. The former believed that too many barriers existed to the pursuit of individual liberty. The latter condemned an excess of individualism and a breakdown of common values.

Fortunately for conservatives, political unity often depends less on intellectual coherence than on the existence of a common foe. And two powerful enemies became focal points for the conservative revival—the Soviet Union abroad and the federal government at home. Anticommunism, however, did not clearly distinguish conservatives from liberals, who also supported the Cold War. What made conservatism distinct was its antagonism to "big government" in America, at least so long as it was controlled by liberals who, conservatives believed, tolerated or encouraged immorality. Republican control of the presidency did not lessen conservatives' hostility to the federal government, partly because they did not consider President Eisenhower one of their own.

THE EISENHOWER ERA

IKE AND NIXON

Dwight D. Eisenhower, or "Ike," as he was affectionately called, emerged from World War II as the military leader with the greatest political appeal, partly because his public image of fatherly warmth set him apart from other successful generals like the arrogant Douglas MacArthur. Eisenhower's party affiliation was unknown. In 1948, he voted for Truman, and he accepted

Truman's invitation to return to Europe as Supreme Commander of NATO forces. Both parties wanted him as their candidate in 1952. But Eisenhower became convinced that Senator Robert A. Taft of Ohio, a leading contender for the Republican nomination, would lead the United States back toward isolationism. Eisenhower entered the contest and won the Republican nomination.

As his running mate, Eisenhower chose Richard Nixon of California, a World War II veteran who had made a name for himself by vigorous anti-communism. In his first campaign for Congress, in 1946, Nixon attacked his opponent as an advocate of "state socialism." He gained greater fame by his pursuit of Alger Hiss while a member of the House Un-American Activities Committee. Nixon won election to the U.S. Senate in 1950 in a campaign in which he suggested that the Democratic candidate, Congresswoman Helen Gahagan Douglas, had communist sympathies.

These tactics gave Nixon a lifelong reputation for opportunism and dishonesty. But Nixon was also a shrewd politician, who pioneered efforts to transform the Republican Party's image from defender of business to champion of the "forgotten man"—the hardworking citizen burdened by heavy taxation and unresponsive government bureaucracies. "Freedom for the individual, for private enterprise," he insisted, had made America great. In using populist language to promote free market economics, Nixon helped to lay the foundation for the triumph of conservatism a generation later.

THE 1952 CAMPAIGN

Almost as soon as he won the vice-presidential nomination, Nixon ran into trouble over press reports that wealthy Californians had created a private fund for his family. Eisenhower considered dropping him from the ticket. But in an emotional nationally televised thirty-minute address in which he drew attention to his ordinary upbringing, war service, and close-knit family, Nixon denied the accusations. The "Checkers speech," named after the family dog—the one gift Nixon acknowledged receiving, but insisted he would not return—rescued his political career. It illustrated how television was beginning to transform politics by allowing candidates to bring a carefully crafted image directly into Americans' living rooms. The 1952 campaign became the first to make extensive use of TV ads. Parties, one observer complained, were "selling the president like toothpaste."

More important to the election's outcome, however, was Eisenhower's popularity (invoked in the Republican campaign slogan "I Like Ike") and the public's weariness with the Korean War. Ike's pledge to "go to Korea" in search of peace signaled his intention to bring the conflict to an end. He won a resounding victory over the Democratic candidate, Adlai Stevenson. Four years later, Eisenhower again defeated Stevenson, by an even wider margin.

His popularity, however, did not extend to his party. Republicans won a razor-thin majority in Congress in 1952, but Democrats regained control in 1954 and retained it for the rest of the decade. In 1956, Eisenhower became the first president to be elected without his party controlling either house of Congress.

In his two campaigns for president, the Texas-born Eisenhower made remarkable inroads in the Democratic South, a harbinger of the region's later political realignment. In 1952, he carried eight former slave states and won 48 percent of the votes cast in the states of the Confederacy. He ran strongly among moderate whites living in metropolitan and suburban areas of the upper South and border states. But his personal appeal did not translate into a "coattail" effect. For the time being, Democrats continued to control almost all southern state and local offices.

During the 1950s, voters at home and abroad seemed to find reassurance in selecting familiar, elderly leaders to govern them. At age sixty-two, Eisenhower was one of the oldest men ever elected president. But he seemed positively youthful compared with Winston Churchill, who returned to office as prime minister of Great Britain at age seventy-seven, Charles DeGaulle, who assumed the presidency of France at sixty-eight, and Konrad Adenauer, who served as chancellor of West Germany from age seventy-three until well into his eighties. In retrospect, Eisenhower's presidency seems almost uneventful, at least in domestic affairs—an interlude between the bitter party battles of the Truman administration and the social upheavals of the 1960s.

MODERN REPUBLICANISM

With a Republican serving as president for the first time in twenty years, the tone in Washington changed. Wealthy businessmen dominated Eisenhower's cabinet. Defense Secretary Charles Wilson, the former president of General Motors, made the widely publicized statement: "What is good for the country is good for General Motors, and vice versa." A champion of the business community and a fiscal conservative, Ike worked to scale back government spending, including the military budget. But while right-wing Republicans saw his victory as an invitation to roll back the New Deal, Eisenhower realized that such a course would be disastrous. "Should any political party attempt to abolish Social Security, unemployment insurance, and eliminate labor laws and farm programs," he declared, "you would not hear of that party again in our political history."

Eisenhower called his domestic agenda Modern Republicanism. It aimed to sever his party's identification in the minds of many Americans with Herbert Hoover, the Great Depression, and indifference to the economic conditions of ordinary citizens. The core New Deal programs not only remained in place, but expanded. In 1955, millions of agricultural workers became eligible for the first time for Social Security. Nor did Ike reduce the size and scope of government. Despite the use of "free enterprise" as a weapon in the Cold War, the idea of a "mixed economy" in which the government played a major role in planning economic activity was widely accepted throughout the Western world. America's European allies like Britain and France expanded their welfare states and nationalized key industries like steel, shipbuilding, and transportation (that is, the government bought them from private owners and operated and subsidized them).

The United States had a more limited welfare state than western Europe and left the main pillars of the economy in private hands. But it too used government spending to promote productivity and boost employment. Eisenhower presided over the largest public-works enterprise in American history, the building of the 41,000-mile interstate highway system. Cold War arguments—especially the need to provide rapid exit routes from cities in the event of nuclear war—justified this multibillion-dollar project. But automobile manufacturers, oil companies, suburban builders, and construction unions had very practical reasons for supporting highway construction regardless of any Soviet threat. When the Soviets launched *Sputnik*, the first artificial earth satellite, in 1957, the administration responded with the National Defense Education Act, which for the first time offered direct federal funding to higher education.

All in all, rather than dismantling the New Deal, Eisenhower's modern Republicanism consolidated and legitimized it. By accepting its basic premises, he ensured that its continuation no longer depended on Democratic control of the presidency.

THE SOCIAL CONTRACT

The 1950s also witnessed an easing of the labor conflict of the two previous decades. The passage of the Taft-Hartley Act in 1947 had reduced labor militancy. In 1955, the AFL and CIO merged to form a single organization representing 35 percent of all nonagricultural workers. In leading industries, labor and management hammered out what has been called a new "social contract." Unions signed long-term agreements that left decisions regarding capital investment, plant location, and output in management's hands, and they agreed to try to prevent unauthorized "wildcat" strikes. Employers stopped trying to eliminate existing unions and granted wage increases and fringe benefits such as private pension plans, health insurance, and automatic adjustments to pay to reflect rises in the cost of living.

Unionized workers shared fully in 1950s prosperity. Although the social contract did not apply to the majority of workers, who did not belong to unions, it did bring benefits to those who labored in nonunion jobs. For example, trade unions in the 1950s and 1960s were able to use their political power to win a steady increase in the minimum wage, which was earned mostly by nonunion workers at the bottom of the employment pyramid. But these "spillover effects" were limited. The majority of workers did not enjoy anything close to the wages, benefits, and job security of unionized workers in such industries as automobiles and steel.

Indeed, nonunion employers continued to fight vehemently against labor organization, and groups like the National Association of Manufacturers still viewed unions as an unacceptable infringement on the power of employers. Some firms continued to shift jobs to the less-unionized suburbs and South. By the end of the 1950s, the social contract was weakening. In 1959, the steel industry sought to tighten work rules and limit wage increases in an attempt to boost profits battered by a recession that hit two years earlier. The plan sparked a strike of 500,000 steelworkers, which successfully beat back the proposed changes.

MASSIVE RETALIATION

Soon after he entered office, Eisenhower approved an armistice that ended fighting in Korea. But this failed to ease international tensions. Ike took office at a time when the Cold War had entered an extremely dangerous phase. In 1952, the United States exploded the first hydrogen bomb—a weapon far more powerful than those that had devastated Hiroshima and Nagasaki. The following year, the Soviets matched this achievement. Both sides feverishly developed long-range bombers capable of delivering weapons of mass destruction around the world.

A professional soldier, Ike hated war, which he viewed as a tragic waste. "Every gun that is made," he said in 1953, "every warship launched . . . signifies a theft from those who hunger and are not fed." But his secretary of state, John Foster Dulles, was a grim Cold Warrior. In 1954, Dulles announced an updated version of the doctrine of containment. "Massive retaliation," as it was called, declared that any Soviet attack on an American ally would be countered by a nuclear assault on the Soviet Union itself. In some ways, this reliance on the nuclear threat was a way to enable the budget-conscious Eisenhower to reduce spending on conventional military forces. During his presidency, the size of the armed services fell by nearly half. But the number of American nuclear warheads rose from 1,000 in 1953 to 18,000 in 1960.

Massive retaliation ran the risk that any small conflict, or even a miscalculation, could escalate into a war that would destroy both the United States and the Soviet Union. Critics called the doctrine "brinksmanship," warning of the danger of Dulles's apparent willingness to bring the world to the brink of nuclear war. The reality that all-out war would result in "mutual assured destruction" (or MAD, in military shorthand) did succeed in making both great powers cautious in their direct dealings with one another. But it also inspired widespread fear of impending nuclear war. Government programs encouraging Americans to build bomb shelters in their backyards, and school drills that trained children to hide under their desks in the event of an atomic attack, aimed to convince Americans that nuclear war was survivable. But these measures only increased the atmosphere of fear.

IKE AND THE RUSSIANS

In his inaugural address, Eisenhower repeated the familiar Cold War formula: "Freedom is pitted against slavery; lightness against dark." But the end of the Korean War and the death of Stalin, both of which occurred in 1953, convinced him that rather than being blind zealots, the Soviets were reasonable and could be dealt with in conventional diplomatic terms. In 1955, Ike met in Geneva, Switzerland, with Nikita Khrushchev, the new Soviet leader, at the first "summit" conference since Potsdam a decade earlier. The following year, Khrushchev delivered a speech to the Communist Party Congress in Moscow that detailed Stalin's crimes, including purges of political opponents numbering in the millions. The revelations created a crisis of belief among communists throughout the world. In the United States, three-quarters of the remaining Communist Party members abandoned the organization, realizing that they had been blind to the nature of Stalin's rule.

A man helps his daughter into a backyard bomb shelter in Garden City, Long Island, New York, in a photograph from 1955. Manufacturers of such shelters assured purchasers that occupants could survive for five days after a nuclear attack.

Khrushchev's call in the same 1956 speech for "peaceful coexistence" with the United States raised the possibility of an easing of the Cold War. The "thaw" was abruptly shaken that fall, however, when Soviet troops put down an anticommunist uprising in Hungary. Many conservative Republicans had urged eastern Europeans to resist communist rule, and Secretary of State Dulles himself had declared "liberation," rather than containment, to be the goal of American policy. But Eisenhower refused to extend aid to the Hungarian rebels, an indication that he believed it impossible to "roll back" Soviet domination of eastern Europe.

In 1958, the two superpowers agreed to a voluntary halt to the testing of nuclear weapons. The pause lasted until 1961. It had been demanded by the National Committee for a Sane Nuclear Policy, which publicized the danger to public health posed by radioactive fallout from nuclear tests. In 1959, Khrushchev toured the United States and had a friendly meeting with Eisenhower at Camp David. But the spirit of cooperation ended abruptly in 1960, when the Soviets shot down an American U-2 spy plane over their territory. Eisenhower first denied that the plane had been involved in espionage and refused to apologize even after the Russians produced the captured pilot. The incident torpedoed another planned summit meeting.

THE EMERGENCE OF THE THIRD WORLD

Even as Europe, where the Cold War began, settled into what appeared to be a permanent division between a communist East and a capitalist West, an intense rivalry, which sometimes took a military form, persisted in what came to be called the Third World. The term was invented to describe developing countries aligned with neither of the two Cold War powers and desirous of finding their own model of development between Soviet centralized economic planning and free market capitalism. The Bandung Conference, which brought leaders of twenty-nine Asian and African nations together in Indonesia in 1955, seemed to announce the emergence of a new force in global affairs, representing a majority of the world's population. But none of these countries could avoid being strongly affected by the political, military, and economic contest of the Cold War.

The post–World War II era witnessed the crumbling of European empires. The "winds of change," said British prime minister Harold Macmillan, were sweeping Africa and Asia. Decolonization began when India and Pakistan (the latter carved out of India to give Muslims their own nation) achieved independence in 1947. Ten years later, Britain's Gold Coast colony in West Africa emerged as the independent nation of Ghana. Other new nations—including Indonesia, Malaysia, Nigeria, Kenya, and Tanzania—soon followed. In 1975, Portugal, which five centuries earlier had created the first modern overseas empire, granted independence to its African colonies of Mozambique and Angola.

Decolonization presented the United States with a complex set of choices. It created power vacuums in the former colonies into which, Americans feared, communists would move. The Soviet Union strongly supported the dissolution of Europe's overseas empires, and communists participated in movements for colonial independence. Many noncommunist leaders, like Jawaharlal Nehru of India and Kwame Nkrumah of Ghana, saw socialism of one sort or another as the best route to achieving economic independence and narrowing the social inequalities fostered by imperialism. Most of the new Third World nations resisted alignment with either major power bloc, hoping to remain neutral in the Cold War. On the other hand, many nationalists sincerely admired the United States and, indeed, saw the American struggle for independence as a model for their own struggles. Ho Chi Minh, the communist leader of the Vietnamese movement against rule by France, modeled his 1945 proclamation of nationhood on the American Declaration of Independence. He even requested that President Truman establish a protectorate over Vietnam to guarantee its independence.

THE COLD WAR IN THE THIRD WORLD

By the end of the 1950s, the division of Europe appeared to be set in stone. Much of the focus of the Cold War shifted to the Third World. The policy of containment easily slid over into opposition to any government, whether communist or not, that seemed to threaten American strategic or economic

The military junta installed in Guatemala by the CIA in 1954 enters Guatemala City in a Jeep driven by CIA agent Carlos Castillo Armas. Although hailed by the Eisenhower administration as a triumph for freedom, the new government suppressed democracy in Guatemala and embarked on a murderous campaign to stamp out opposition.

interests. Jacobo Arbenz Guzmán in Guatemala and Mohammed Mossadegh in Iran were elected, homegrown nationalists, not agents of Moscow. But they were determined to reduce foreign corporations' control over their countries' economies. Arbenz embarked on a sweeping land-reform policy that threatened the domination of Guatemala's economy by the American-owned United Fruit Company. Mossadegh nationalized the Anglo-Iranian Oil Company, whose refinery in Iran was Britain's largest remaining overseas asset. Their foes quickly branded both as communists. In 1953 and 1954, the Central Intelligence Agency organized the ouster of both governments—a clear violation of the UN Charter, which barred a member state from taking military action against another except in self-defense.

In 1956, Israel, France, and Britain—without prior consultation with the United States—invaded Egypt after the country's nationalist leader, Gamal Abdel Nasser, nationalized the Suez Canal, jointly owned by Britain and France. A furious Eisenhower forced them to abandon the invasion. After the Suez fiasco, the United States moved to replace Britain as the dominant Western power in the Middle East, and American companies increasingly dominated the region's oil fields. In 1957, Eisenhower extended the principle of containment to the region, issuing the Eisenhower Doctrine, which pledged the United States to defend Middle Eastern governments threatened by communism or Arab nationalism. A year later, Ike dispatched 5,000 American troops to Lebanon to protect a government dominated by pro-Western Christians against Nasser's effort to bring all Arab states into a single regime under his rule.

ORIGINS OF THE VIETNAM WAR

In Vietnam, the expulsion of the Japanese in 1945 led not to independence but to a French military effort to preserve their Asian empire, which dated to the late nineteenth century, against Ho Chi Minh's nationalist forces. Anticommunism led the United States into deeper and deeper involvement. Following a policy initiated by Truman, the Eisenhower administration funneled billions of dollars in aid to bolster French efforts. By the early 1950s, the United States was paying four-fifths of the cost of the war. Wary of becoming bogged down in another land war in Asia immediately after Korea, however, Ike declined to send in American troops when France requested them to avert defeat in 1954. He also rejected the National Security Council's advice to use nuclear weapons, leaving France no alternative but to agree to Vietnamese independence.

A peace conference in Geneva divided Vietnam temporarily into northern and southern districts, with elections scheduled for 1956 to unify the country. But the staunchly anticommunist southern leader Ngo Dinh Diem, urged on by the United States, refused to hold elections, which would almost certainly have resulted in a victory for Ho Chi Minh's communists. Diem's close ties to wealthy Catholic families—in predominantly Buddhist South Vietnam—and to landlords in a society dominated by small farmers who had been promised land by Ho alienated an increasing number of his subjects. American aid poured into South Vietnam in order to bolster the Diem regime. By the time Eisenhower left office, Diem nevertheless faced a full-scale guerrilla revolt by the communist-led National Liberation Front.

Events in Guatemala, Iran, and Vietnam, considered great successes at the time by American policymakers, cast a long shadow over American foreign relations. Little by little, the United States was becoming accustomed to intervention, both open and secret, in far-flung corners of the world. Despite the Cold War rhetoric of freedom, American leaders seemed more comfortable dealing with reliable military regimes than democratic governments. A series of military governments succeeded Arbenz. The shah of Iran replaced Mossadegh and agreed to give British and American oil companies 40 percent of his nation's oil revenues. He remained in office until 1979 as one of the world's most tyrannical rulers, until his overthrow in a revolution led by the fiercely anti-American radical Islamist Ayatollah Khomeini. In Vietnam, the American decision to prop up Diem's regime laid the groundwork for what would soon become the most disastrous military involvement in American history.

MASS SOCIETY AND ITS CRITICS

The fatherly Eisenhower seemed the perfect leader for the placid society of the 1950s. Consensus was the dominant ideal in an era in which McCarthyism had defined criticism of the social and economic order as disloyalty and most Americans located the enjoyment of freedom in private pleasures rather than the public sphere. With the mainstreams of both parties embracing the Cold War, political debate took place within extremely narrow limits. Even *Life* magazine commented that American freedom might be in greater danger from "disuse" than from communist subversion.

Dissenting voices could be heard. Some intellectuals wondered whether the celebration of affluence and the either-or mentality of the Cold War obscured the extent to which the United States itself fell short of the ideal of freedom. The sociologist C. Wright Mills challenged the self-satisfied vision of democratic pluralism that dominated mainstream social science in the 1950s. Mills wrote of a "power elite"—an interlocking directorate of corporate leaders, politicians, and military men whose domination of government and society had made political democracy obsolete. Freedom, Mills insisted, meant more than "the chance to do as one pleases." It rested on the ability "to formulate the available choices," and this most Americans were effectively denied.

Even as the government and media portrayed the United States as a beacon of liberty locked in a titanic struggle with its opposite, one strand of social analysis in the 1950s contended that Americans did not enjoy genuine freedom. These critics identified as the culprit not the unequal structure of power criticized by Mills, but the modern age itself, with its psychological and cultural discontents. Modern mass society, some writers worried, inevitably produced loneliness and anxiety, causing mankind to yearn for stability and authority, not freedom. In *The Lonely Crowd* (1950), the decade's most influential work of social analysis, the sociologist David Riesman described Americans as "other-directed" conformists who lacked the inner resources to lead truly independent lives. Other social critics charged that corporate bureaucracies had transformed employees into "organization men" incapable of independent thought.

Some commentators feared that the Russians had demonstrated a greater ability to sacrifice for common public goals than Americans. What kind of nation, the economist John Kenneth Galbraith asked in *The Affluent Society* (1958), neglected investment in schools, parks, and public services, while producing ever more goods to fulfill desires created by advertising? Was the spectacle of millions of educated middle-class women seeking happiness in suburban dream houses a reason for celebration or a waste of precious "woman power" at a time when the Soviets trumpeted the accomplishments of their female scientists, physicians, and engineers? Books like Galbraith's, along with William Whyte's *The Organization Man* (1956) and Vance Packard's *The Hidden Persuaders* (1957), which criticized the monotony of modern work, the emptiness of suburban life, and the pervasive influence of advertising, created the vocabulary for an assault on the nation's social values that lay just over the horizon. In the 1950s, however, while criticism of mass society became a minor industry among intellectuals, it failed to dent widespread complacency about the American way.

REBELS WITHOUT A CAUSE

The social critics did not offer a political alternative or have any real impact on the parties or government. Nor did other stirrings of dissent. With teenagers a growing part of the population thanks to the baby boom, the emergence of a popular culture geared to the emerging youth market suggested that significant generational tensions lay beneath the bland surface of 1950s life. J. D. Salinger's 1951 novel *Catcher in the Rye* and the 1955 films *Blackboard Jungle* and *Rebel without a Cause* (the latter starring James Dean as an aimlessly rebellious youth) highlighted the alienation of at least some young people from the world of adult respectability. These works helped to spur a mid-1950s panic about "juvenile delinquency." *Time* magazine devoted a cover story to

"Teenagers on the Rampage," and a Senate committee held hearings in 1954 on whether violent comic books caused criminal behavior among young people. (One witness even criticized Superman comics for arousing violent emotions among its readers.) To head off federal regulation, publishers—like movie producers in the 1920s—adopted a code of conduct for their industry that strictly limited the portrayal of crime and violence in comic books.

Cultural life during the 1950s seemed far more daring than politics. Indeed, many adults found the emergence of a mass-marketed teenage culture that rejected middle-class norms more alarming than the actual increase in juvenile arrests. Teenagers wore leather jackets and danced to rock-and-roll music that brought the hard-driving rhythms and sexually provocative movements of black musicians and dancers to enthusiastic young white audiences. They made Elvis Presley, a rock-and-roll singer with an openly sexual performance style, an immensely popular entertainment celebrity.

Challenges of various kinds also arose to the family-centered image of personal fulfillment. *Playboy* magazine, which began publication in 1953, reached a circulation of more than 1 million copies per month by 1960. It extended the consumer culture into the most intimate realms of life, offering men a fantasy world of sexual gratification outside the family's confines. Although considered sick or deviant by the larger society and subject to constant police harassment, gay men and lesbians created their own subcultures in major cities.

Elvis Presley's gyrating hips appealed to teenagers but alarmed many adults during the 1950s.

THE BEATS

In New York City and San Francisco, as well as college towns like Madison, Wisconsin, and Ann Arbor, Michigan, the Beats, a small group of poets and writers, railed against mainstream culture. The novelist Jack Kerouac coined the term "beat"—a play on "beaten down" and "beatified" (or saintlike). His *On the Road*, written in the early 1950s but not published until 1957, recounted in a seemingly spontaneous rush of sights, sounds, and images its main character's aimless wanderings across the American landscape. The book became a bible for a generation of young people who rejected the era's middle-class culture but had little to put in its place.

"I saw the best minds of my generation destroyed by madness, starving hysterical naked," wrote the Beat poet Allen Ginsberg in *Howl* (1955), a brilliant protest against materialism and conformism written while the author was under the influence of hallucinogenic drugs. Ginsberg became nationally known when San Francisco police in 1956 confiscated his book and arrested bookstore owners for selling an obscene work. (A judge later overturned the ban on the grounds that *Howl* possessed redeeming social value.) Rejecting the work ethic, the "desperate materialism" of the suburban middle class, and the militarization of American life by the Cold War, the Beats celebrated impulsive action, immediate pleasure (often enhanced by drugs), and sexual experimentation. Despite Cold War slogans, they insisted, personal and political repression, not freedom, were the hallmarks of American society.

THE FREEDOM MOVEMENT

Not until the 1960s would young white rebels find their cause, as the seeds of dissent planted by the social critics and Beats flowered in an outpouring of political activism, new attitudes toward sexuality, and a full-fledged generational rebellion. A more immediate challenge to the complacency of the 1950s arose from the twentieth century's greatest citizens' movement—the black struggle for equality.

ORIGINS OF THE MOVEMENT

Today, with the birthday of Martin Luther King Jr. a national holiday and the struggles of Montgomery, Little Rock, Birmingham, and Selma celebrated as heroic episodes in the history of freedom, it is easy to forget that at the time, the civil rights revolution came as a great surprise. Looking back, its causes seem clear: the destabilization of the racial system during World War II; the mass migration out of the segregated South that made black voters an increasingly important part of the Democratic Party coalition; and the Cold War and rise of independent states in the Third World, both of which made the gap

VOICES OF FREEDOM

From The Southern Manifesto (1956)

Drawn up early in 1956 and signed by 101 southern members of the Senate and House of Representatives, the Southern Manifesto repudiated the Supreme Court decision in *Brown v. Board of Education* and offered support to the campaign of resistance in the South.

The unwarranted decision of the Supreme Court in the public school cases is now bearing the fruit always produced when men substitute naked power for established law. . . .

We regard the decisions of the Supreme Court in the school cases as a clear abuse of judicial power. It climaxes a trend in the Federal Judiciary undertaking to legislate, in derogation [violation] of the authority of Congress, and to encroach upon the reserved rights of the States and the people.

The original Constitution does not mention education. Neither does the 14th Amendment nor any other amendment. The debates preceding the submission of the 14th Amendment clearly show that there was no intent that it should affect the system of education maintained by the States.

In the case of *Plessy v. Ferguson* in 1896 the Supreme Court expressly declared that under the 14th Amendment no person was denied any of his rights if the States provided separate but equal facilities. This decision . . . restated time and again, became a part of the life of the people of many of the States and confirmed their habits, traditions, and way of life. It is founded on elemental humanity and commonsense, for parents should not be deprived by Government of the right to direct the lives and education of their own children.

Though there has been no constitutional amendment or act of Congress changing this established legal principle almost a century old, the Supreme Court of the United States, with no legal basis for such action, undertook to exercise their naked judicial power and substituted their personal political and social ideas for the established law of the land.

This unwarranted exercise of power by the Court, contrary to the Constitution, is creating chaos and confusion in the States principally affected. It is destroying the amicable relations between the white and Negro races that have been created through 90 years of patient effort by the good people of both races. It has planted hatred and suspicion where there has been heretofore friendship and understanding.

With the gravest concern for the explosive and dangerous condition created by this decision and inflamed by outside meddlers: . . . we commend the motives of those States which have declared the intention to resist forced integration by any lawful means. . . .

From Martin Luther King Jr., Speech at Montgomery, Alabama (December 5, 1955)

On the evening of Rosa Parks's arrest for refusing to give up her seat on a Montgomery bus to a white passenger, a mass rally of local African-Americans decided to boycott city buses in protest. In his speech to the gathering, the young Baptist minister Martin Luther King Jr. invoked Christian and American ideals of justice and democracy—themes he would strike again and again during his career as the leading national symbol of the civil rights struggle.

We are here this evening . . . because first and foremost we are American citizens, and we are determined to apply our citizenship to the fullness of its means. We are here also because of our love for democracy. . . . Just the other day . . . one of the finest citizens in Montgomery—not one of the finest Negro citizens but one of the finest citizens in Montgomery—was taken from a bus and carried to jail and arrested because she refused to give her seat to a white person. . . .

Mrs. Rosa Parks is a fine person. And since it had to happen I'm happy that it happened to a person like Mrs. Parks, for nobody can doubt the boundless outreach of her integrity! Nobody can doubt the height of her character, nobody can doubt that depth of her Christian commitment and devotion to the teachings of Jesus. And I'm happy since it had to happen, it happened to a person that nobody can call a disturbing factor in the community. Mrs. Parks is a fine Christian person, unassuming, and yet there is integrity and character there. And just because she refused to get up, she was arrested.

I want to say, that we are not here advocating violence. We have never done that. . . . We believe in the teachings of Jesus. The only weapon that we have in our hands this evening is the weapon of protest. . . . There will be no white persons pulled out of their homes and taken out to some distant road and lynched. . . .

We are not wrong in what we are doing. If we are wrong, then the Supreme Court of this nation is wrong. If we are wrong, the Constitution of the United States is wrong. If we are wrong, God Almighty is wrong. . . . If we are wrong, justice is a lie. . . .

We, the disinherited of this land, we who have been oppressed so long, are tired of going through the long night of captivity. And now we are reaching out for the daybreak of freedom and justice and equality. . . . Right here in Montgomery when the history books are written in the future, somebody will have to say, "There lived a race of people, a *black* people, . . . a people who had the moral courage to stand up for their rights. And thereby they injected a new meaning into the veins of history and of civilization."

QUESTIONS

1. Why does the Southern Manifesto claim that the Supreme Court decision is a threat to constitutional government?
2. How do religious convictions shape King's definition of freedom?
3. How do these documents illustrate contrasting understandings of freedom in the wake of the civil rights movement?

between America's rhetoric and its racial reality an international embarrassment. Yet few predicted the emergence of the southern mass movement for civil rights.

In *An American Dilemma* (1944), Gunnar Myrdal had suggested that the challenge to racial inequality would arise in the North, where blacks had far greater opportunities for political organization than in the South. With blacks' traditional allies on the left decimated by McCarthyism, most union leaders unwilling to challenge racial inequalities within their own ranks, and the NAACP concentrating on court battles, new constituencies and new tactics were sorely needed. The movement found in the southern black church the organizing power for a militant, nonviolent assault on segregation.

The United States in the 1950s was still a segregated, unequal society. Half of the nation's black families lived in poverty. Because of labor contracts that linked promotions and firings to seniority, non-white workers, who had joined the industrial labor force later than whites, lost their jobs first in times of economic downturn. In the South, evidence of Jim Crow abounded—in separate public institutions and the signs "white" and "colored" at entrances to buildings, train carriages, drinking fountains, restrooms, and the like. In the North and West, the law did not require segregation, but custom barred blacks from many colleges, hotels, and restaurants, and from most suburban housing. Las Vegas, Nevada, for example, was as strictly segregated as any southern city. Hotels and casinos did not admit blacks except in the most menial jobs. Lena Horne, Sammy Davis Jr., Louis Armstrong, and other black entertainers played the hotel-casinos on the "strip" but could not stay as guests where they performed.

In 1950, seventeen southern and border states and Washington, D.C., had laws requiring the racial segregation of public schools, and several others permitted local districts to impose it. Around 40 percent of the nation's 28 million schoolchildren studied in legally segregated schools, and millions more attended classes in northern communities where housing patterns and school district lines created de facto segregation—separation in fact if not in law. Few white Americans felt any urgency about confronting racial inequality. "Segregation," the white writer John Egerton later recalled, "didn't restrict me in any way, so it was easy to accept things the way they were, to take my freedom for granted and not worry about anyone else's."

THE LEGAL ASSAULT ON SEGREGATION

With Truman's civil rights initiative having faded and the Eisenhower administration being reluctant to address the issue, it fell to the courts to confront the problem of racial segregation. In the Southwest, the League of United Latin American Citizens (LULAC), the equivalent of the NAACP, challenged restrictive housing, employment discrimination, and the segregation of Latino students. They won an important victory in 1946 in the case of *Mendez v. Westminster*, when the California Supreme Court ordered the schools of Orange County desegregated. In response, the state legislature repealed all school laws requiring racial segregation. The governor who signed the measure, Earl Warren, had presided over the internment of Japanese-Americans during World War II as the state's attorney general. After the war, he became convinced that racial inequality had no place in American life. When Chief Justice Fred Vinson died in 1953, Eisenhower appointed Earl Warren to replace him. Warren would play the key role in deciding *Brown v. Board of Education*, the momentous case that outlawed school segregation.

For years, the NAACP, under the leadership of attorneys Charles Hamilton Houston and Thurgood Marshall, had pressed legal challenges to the "separate but equal" doctrine laid down by the Court in 1896 in *Plessy v. Ferguson*. At first, the NAACP sought to gain admission to white institutions of higher learning for which no black equivalent existed. In 1938, the Supreme Court ordered the University of Missouri Law School to admit Lloyd Gaines, a black student, because the state had no such school for blacks. Missouri responded by setting up a segregated law school, satisfying the courts. But in 1950, the Supreme Court unanimously ordered Heman Sweatt admitted to the University of Texas Law School even though the state had established a "school" for him in a basement containing three classrooms and no library. There was no way, the Court declared, that this hastily constructed law school could be "equal" to the prestigious all-white institution.

THE *BROWN* CASE

Marshall now launched a frontal assault on segregation itself. He brought the NAACP's support to local cases that had arisen when black parents challenged unfair school policies. To do so required remarkable courage. In Clarendon County, South Carolina, Levi Pearson, a black farmer who brought a lawsuit on behalf of his children, saw his house burned to the ground. The Clarendon case attacked not segregation itself but the unequal funding of schools. The local school board spent $179 per white child and $43 per black, and unlike white pupils, black children attended class in buildings with no running water or indoor toilets and were not provided with buses to transport them to classes. Five such cases from four states and the District of Columbia were combined in a single appeal that reached the Supreme Court late in 1952.

When cases are united, they are listed alphabetically and the first case gives the entire decision its name. In this instance, the first case arose from a state outside the old Confederacy. Oliver Brown went to court because his daughter, a third grader, was forced to walk across dangerous railroad tracks each morning rather than being allowed to attend a nearby school restricted to whites. His lawsuit became *Brown v. Board of Education of Topeka, Kansas.*

Thurgood Marshall decided that the time had come to attack not the unfair applications of the "separate but equal" principle but the doctrine itself. Even with the same funding and facilities, he insisted, segregation was inherently unequal since it stigmatized one group of citizens as unfit to associate with others. Drawing on studies by New York psychologists Kenneth and Mamie Clark, Marshall argued that segregation did lifelong damage to black children, undermining their self-esteem. In its legal brief, the Eisenhower administration did not directly support Marshall's position, but it urged the justices to consider "the problem of racial discrimination . . . in the context of the present world struggle between freedom and tyranny." Other peoples, it noted, "cannot understand how such a practice can exist in a country which professes to be a staunch supporter of freedom, justice, and democracy."

The new chief justice, Earl Warren, managed to create unanimity on a divided Court, some of whose members disliked segregation but feared that a decision to outlaw it would spark widespread violence. On May 17, 1954, Warren himself read aloud the decision, only eleven pages long. Segregation in public education, he concluded, violated the equal protection of the laws guaranteed by the Fourteenth Amendment. "In the field of education, the doctrine of 'separate but equal' has no place. Separate educational facilities are inherently unequal."

The black press hailed the *Brown* decision as a "second Emancipation Proclamation." And like its predecessor it was in many ways a limited document. The decision did not address segregation in institutions other than public schools or ban all racial classifications in the law, such as statutes prohibiting interracial marriage. It did not address the de facto school segregation of the North, which rested on housing patterns rather than state law. It did not order immediate implementation but instead called for hearings as to how segregated schooling should be dismantled. But *Brown* marked the emergence of the "Warren Court" as an active agent of social change. And it inspired a wave of optimism that discrimination would soon disappear. "What a wonderful world of possibilities are unfolded for the children," wrote the black novelist Ralph Ellison.

THE MONTGOMERY BUS BOYCOTT

Brown did not cause the modern civil rights movement, which began during World War II and continued in cities like New York after the war. But the decision did ensure that when the movement resumed after waning in the early 1950s, it would have the backing of the federal courts. Mass action against Jim Crow soon reappeared. On December 1, 1955, Rosa Parks, a black tailor's assistant who had just completed her day's work in a Montgomery, Alabama, department store, refused to surrender her seat on a city bus to a white rider, as required by local law. Parks's arrest sparked a yearlong bus boycott, the beginning of the mass phase of the civil rights movement in the South. Within a decade, the civil rights revolution had overturned the structure of legal segregation and regained the right to vote for black southerners. In 2000, *Time* magazine named Rosa Parks one of the 100 most significant persons of the twentieth century.

The mug shot of Rosa Parks, taken in December 1955 at a Montgomery, Alabama, police station after she was arrested for refusing to give up her seat on a city bus to a white passenger.

Parks is widely remembered today as a "seamstress with tired feet," a symbol of ordinary blacks' determination to resist the daily injustices and indignities of the Jim Crow South. In fact, her life makes clear that the civil rights revolution built on earlier struggles. Parks was a veteran of black politics. During the 1930s, she took part in meetings protesting the conviction of the Scottsboro Boys. She served for many years as secretary to E. D. Nixon, the local leader of the NAACP. In 1943, she tried to register to vote, only to be turned away because she supposedly failed a literacy test. After two more attempts, Parks succeeded in becoming one of the few blacks in Montgomery able to cast a ballot. In 1954, she attended a training session for political activists at the Highlander School in Tennessee, a meeting ground for labor and civil rights radicals.

No one knows exactly why Parks decided not to give up her seat that day. Perhaps it was because an all-white jury in Mississippi had just acquitted the murderers of Emmett Till, a black teenager who had allegedly whistled at a white woman. Jo Ann Robinson, a professor at the all-black Alabama State University, had been calling for a boycott of public transportation since 1954. When news of Parks's arrest spread, hundreds of blacks gathered in a local church and vowed to refuse to ride the buses until accorded equal treatment. For 381 days, despite legal harassment and occasional violence, black maids, janitors, teachers, and students walked to their destinations or rode an informal network of taxis. Finally, in November 1956, the Supreme Court ruled segregation in public transportation unconstitutional. The boycott ended in triumph.

THE DAYBREAK OF FREEDOM

The Montgomery bus boycott marked a turning point in postwar American history. It launched the movement for racial justice as a nonviolent crusade based in the black churches of the South. It gained the support of northern liberals and focused unprecedented and unwelcome international attention on the country's racial policies. And it marked the emergence of twenty-six-year-old Martin Luther King Jr., who had recently arrived in Montgomery to become pastor of a Baptist church, as the movement's national symbol. On the night of the first protest meeting, King's call to action electrified the audience: "We, the disinherited of this land, we who have been oppressed so long, are tired of going through the long night of captivity. And now we are reaching out for the daybreak of freedom and justice and equality."

From the beginning, the language of freedom pervaded the black movement. It resonated in the speeches of civil rights leaders and in the hand-lettered placards of the struggle's foot soldiers. On the day of Rosa Parks's court appearance in December 1955, even before the bus boycott had officially been announced, a torn piece of cardboard appeared on a bus shelter in Montgomery's Court Square, advising passengers: "Don't ride the buses today. Don't ride it for freedom." During the summer of 1964, when civil rights activists established "freedom schools" for black children across Mississippi, lessons began with students being asked to define the word. Some gave specific answers ("going to public libraries"), some more abstract ("standing up for your rights"). Some insisted that freedom meant legal equality, others saw it as liberation from years of deference to and fear of whites. "Freedom of the mind," wrote one, was the greatest freedom of all.

For adults as well, freedom had many meanings. It meant enjoying the political rights and economic opportunities taken for granted by whites. It required eradicating historic wrongs such as segregation, disenfranchisement, confinement to low-wage jobs, and the ever-present threat of violence. It meant the right to be served at lunch counters and downtown department stores, central locations in the consumer culture, and to be addressed as "Mr.," "Miss," and "Mrs.," rather than "boy" and "auntie."

THE LEADERSHIP OF KING

In King's soaring oratory, the protesters' understandings of freedom fused into a coherent whole. For the title of his first book, relating the boycott's history, King chose the title *Stride Toward Freedom*. His most celebrated oration, the "I Have a Dream" speech of 1963, began by invoking the unfulfilled promise of emancipation ("one hundred years later, the Negro still is not free") and closed with a cry borrowed from a black spiritual: "Free at last! Free at last! Thank God Almighty, we are free at last!"

A master at appealing to the deep sense of injustice among blacks and to the conscience of white America, King presented the case for black rights in a vocabulary that merged the black experience with that of the nation. Having studied the writings on peaceful civil disobedience of Henry David Thoreau and Mohandas (Mahatma) Gandhi, as well as the nonviolent protests the Congress of Racial Equality had organized in the 1940s, King outlined a philosophy of struggle in which evil must be met with good, hate with Christian love, and violence with peaceful demands for change. "There will be no white persons pulled out of their homes and taken out to some distant road and lynched," he declared in his speech at the launching of the Montgomery bus boycott.

Echoing Christian themes derived from his training in the black church, King's speeches resonated deeply in both black communities and the broader culture. He repeatedly invoked the Bible to preach justice and forgiveness, even toward those "who desire to deprive you of freedom." Like Frederick Douglass before him, King appealed to white America by stressing the protesters' love of country and devotion to national values. The "daybreak of freedom," King made clear, meant a new dawn for the whole of American society. And like W. E. B. Du Bois, he linked the American "color line" with the degradation of non-white peoples overseas. "The great struggle of the Twentieth Century," he declared in a 1956 sermon, "has been between the exploited masses questing for freedom and the colonial powers seeking to maintain their domination." If Africa was gaining its freedom, he asked, why must black America lag behind?

MASSIVE RESISTANCE

Buoyed by success in Montgomery, King in 1956 took the lead in forming the Southern Christian Leadership Conference, a coalition of black ministers and civil rights activists, to press for desegregation. But despite the movement's success in popular mobilization, the fact that Montgomery's city fathers agreed to the boycott's demands only after a Supreme Court ruling indicated that without national backing, local action might not be enough to overturn Jim Crow. The white South's refusal to accept the *Brown* decision reinforced the conviction that black citizens could not gain their constitutional rights without Washington's intervention. This was not immediately forthcoming. When the Supreme Court finally issued its implementation ruling in 1955, the justices declared that desegregation should proceed "with all deliberate speed." This vague formulation unintentionally encouraged a campaign of "massive resistance" that paralyzed civil rights progress in much of the South.

In 1956, 82 of 106 southern congressmen—and every southern senator except Lyndon B. Johnson of Texas and Albert Gore and Estes Kefauver of

Tennessee—signed a Southern Manifesto, denouncing the *Brown* decision as a "clear abuse of judicial power," and calling for resistance to "forced integration" by "any lawful means." State after state passed laws to block desegregation. Some made it illegal for the NAACP to operate within their borders. Virginia pioneered the strategy of closing any public schools ordered to desegregate and offering funds to enable white pupils, but not black, to attend private institutions. Prince Edward County, Virginia, shut its schools entirely in 1959; not until 1964 did the Supreme Court order them reopened. Many states adopted "freedom of choice" plans that allowed white students to opt out of integrated schools. As a symbol of defiance, Georgia's legislature incorporated the Confederate battle flag into its state flag in 1956, and Alabama and South Carolina soon began flying the battle flag over their state capitol buildings.

The Problem We All Live With. *This 1964 painting by Norman Rockwell, which accompanied an article in* Look magazine, *depicts federal marshals escorting six-year-old Ruby Bridges to kindergarten in New Orleans in 1960 in accordance with a court order to integrate the city's schools. "There was a large crowd of people outside the school," she later recalled. "They were throwing things and shouting." But Rockwell, intent on focusing on the child, presents the mob only through their graffiti and tomatoes thrown against the wall, and does not show the faces of the marshals. Because of the decision to send her to the formerly white school, Bridges's father lost his job, and her grandparents, who worked as sharecroppers in Mississippi, were evicted from their land. In 2001, President Bill Clinton presented her with the Presidential Citizens Medal.*

EISENHOWER AND CIVIL RIGHTS

The federal government tried to remain aloof from the black struggle. Thanks to the efforts of Senate majority leader Lyndon B. Johnson, who hoped to win liberal support for a run for president in 1960, Congress in 1957 passed the first national civil rights law since Reconstruction. It targeted the denial of black voting rights in the South, but with weak enforcement provisions it added few voters to the rolls. President Eisenhower failed to provide moral leadership. He called for Americans to abide by the law, but he made it clear that he found the whole civil rights issue distasteful. He privately told aides that he disagreed with the Supreme Court's reasoning. Ike failed to act in 1956 when a federal court ordered that Autherine Lucy be admitted to the University of Alabama; a mob prevented her from registering and the board of trustees expelled her. The university remained all white into the 1960s.

In 1957, however, after Governor Orval Faubus of Arkansas used the National Guard to prevent the court-ordered integration of Little Rock's Central High School, Eisenhower dispatched federal troops to the city. In the face of a howling mob, soldiers of the 101st Airborne Division escorted nine black children into the school. Events in Little Rock showed that in the last instance, the federal government would not allow the flagrant violation of court orders. But because of massive resistance, the pace of the movement slowed in the final years of the 1950s. When Eisenhower left office, fewer than 2 percent of black students attended desegregated schools in the states of the old Confederacy.

THE WORLD VIEWS THE UNITED STATES

Ever since the beginning of the Cold War, American leaders had worried about the impact of segregation on the country's international reputation. President Truman had promoted his civil rights initiative, in part, by reminding Americans that they could not afford to "ignore what the world thinks of our record." The State Department filed a brief in the *Brown* case noting the damage segregation was doing to the country's image overseas.

Foreign nations and colonies paid close attention to the unfolding of the American civil rights movement. The global reaction to the *Brown* decision was overwhelmingly positive. "At Last! Whites and Blacks in the United States on the same school benches!" proclaimed a newspaper in Senegal, West Africa. But the slow pace of change led to criticism that embarrassed American diplomats seeking to win the loyalty of people in the non-white world. In a public forum in India, the American ambassador was peppered with questions about American race relations. Was it true that the Haitian ambassador to the United States had to live in a black ghetto in Washington? Why did no black person hold a high public office? Of course, the Soviet Union played up

American race relations as part of the global "battle for hearts and minds of men" that was a key part of the Cold War.

THE ELECTION OF 1960

KENNEDY AND NIXON

The presidential campaign of 1960 turned out to be one of the closest in American history. Republicans chose Vice President Richard Nixon as their candidate to succeed Eisenhower. Democrats nominated John F. Kennedy, a senator from Massachusetts and a Roman Catholic, whose father, a millionaire Irish-American businessman, had served as ambassador to Great Britain during the 1930s. Kennedy's chief rivals for the nomination were Hubert Humphrey, leader of the party's liberal wing, and Lyndon B. Johnson of Texas, the Senate majority leader, who accepted Kennedy's offer to run for vice president.

The atmosphere of tolerance promoted by World War II had weakened traditional anti-Catholicism. But as recently as 1949, Paul Blanshard's *American Freedom and Catholic Power*, which accused the church of being antidemocratic, morally repressive, and essentially un-American, had become a national best-seller. Many Protestants remained reluctant to vote for a Catholic, fearing that Kennedy would be required to support church doctrine on controversial public issues or, in a more extreme version, take orders from the pope. Kennedy addressed the question directly. "I do not speak for my church on public matters," he insisted, and "the church does not speak for me." His defeat of Humphrey in the Democratic primary in overwhelmingly Protestant West Virginia put the issue of his religion to rest. At age forty-three, Kennedy became the youngest major-party nominee for president in the nation's history.

THE PRESIDENTIAL ELECTION OF 1960

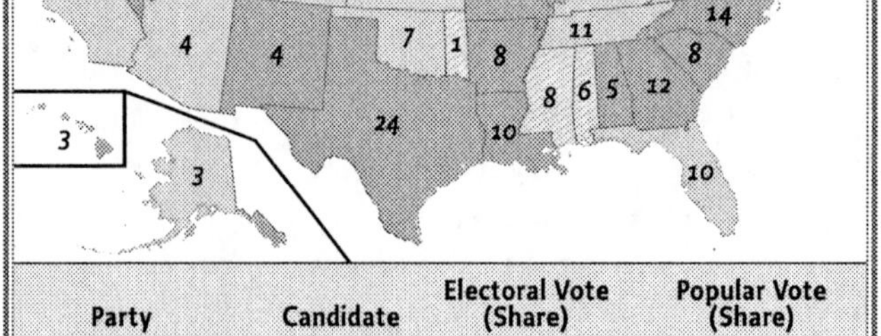

Party	Candidate	Electoral Vote (Share)	Popular Vote (Share)
Democrat	Kennedy	303 (56%)	34,227,096 (49.7%)
Republican	Nixon	219 (41%)	34,107,646 (49.6%)
Independent	Byrd	15 (3%)	501,643 (0.7%)

Both Kennedy and Nixon were ardent

Cold Warriors. But Kennedy pointed to Soviet success in putting *Sputnik*, the first earth satellite, into orbit and subsequently testing the first intercontinental ballistic missile (ICBM) as evidence that the United States had lost the sense of national purpose necessary to fight the Cold War. He warned that Republicans had allowed a "missile gap" to develop in which the Soviets had achieved technological and military superiority over the United States. In fact, as both Kennedy and Nixon well knew, American economic and military capacity far exceeded that of the Soviets. But the charge persuaded many Americans that the time had come for new leadership. The stylishness of Kennedy's wife, Jacqueline, which stood in sharp contrast to the more dowdy public appearance of Mamie Eisenhower and Pat Nixon, reinforced the impression that Kennedy would conduct a more youthful, vigorous presidency.

In the first televised debate between presidential candidates, judging by viewer response, the handsome Kennedy bested Nixon, who was suffering from a cold and appeared tired and nervous. Those who heard the encounter on the radio thought Nixon had won, but, on TV, image counted for more than substance. In November, Kennedy eked out a narrow victory, winning the popular vote by only 120,000 out of 69 million votes cast (and, Republicans charged, benefiting from a fraudulent vote count by the notoriously corrupt Chicago Democratic machine).

THE END OF THE 1950S

In January 1961, shortly before leaving office, Eisenhower delivered a televised Farewell Address, modeled to some extent on George Washington's address of 1796. Knowing that the missile gap was a myth, Ike warned against the drumbeat of calls for a new military buildup. He urged Americans to think about the dangerous power of what he called the "military-industrial complex"—the conjunction of "an immense military establishment" with a "permanent arms industry"—with an influence felt in "every office" in the land. "We must never let the weight of this combination," he advised his countrymen, "endanger our liberties or democratic processes." Few Americans shared Ike's concern—far more saw the alliance of the Defense Department and private industry as a source of jobs and national security rather than a threat to democracy. A few years later, however, with the United States locked in an increasingly unpopular war, Eisenhower's warning would come to seem prophetic.

By then, other underpinnings of 1950s life were also in disarray. The tens of millions of cars that made suburban life possible were spewing toxic lead, an additive to make gasoline more efficient, into the atmosphere. Penned in to the east by mountains that kept automobile emissions from being dispersed by the wind, Los Angeles had become synonymous with smog, a type of air pollution produced by cars. Chlorofluorocarbons, used in air conditioners, deodorants, and aerosol hair sprays, were releasing chemicals into the atmosphere that damaged the ozone layer, producing global warming and an increase in skin cancer. (Both leaded gasoline and chlorofluorocarbons had been invented by General Motors research scientist Thomas Midgley. He "had more impact on the atmosphere," writes one historian, "than any other single organism" in the history of the world.) The chemical insecticides that enabled agricultural conglomerates to produce the country's remarkable abundance of food were poisoning farm workers, consumers, and the water supply. Housewives were rebelling against a life centered in suburban dream houses. Blacks were increasingly impatient with the slow progress of racial change. The United States, in other words, had entered that most turbulent of decades, the 1960s.

Chapter Review

REVIEW QUESTIONS

1. Explain the meaning of the "American standard of living" during the 1950s.
2. Describe how the automobile transformed American communities and culture in the 1950s.
3. Identify the prescribed roles and aspirations for women during the social conformity of the 1950s.
4. How did governmental policies, business practices, and individual choices contribute to racially segregated suburbs?
5. Explain the ideological rifts between conservatives in the 1950s. Why did many view President Eisenhower as "not one of them"?
6. What was the new "social contract" between labor and management, and how did it benefit both sides as well as the nation as a whole?
7. How did the United States and Soviet Union shift the focus of the Cold War to the Third World?

8. What were the most significant factors that contributed to the growing momentum of the civil rights movement in the 1950s?
9. How did many southern whites, led by their elected officials, resist desegregation and civil rights in the name of "freedom"?
10. How and why did the federal government's concern with U.S. relations overseas shape its involvement with the *Brown v. Board of Education* case?

KEY TERMS

Levittown
"baby boom"
housing segregation
urban renewal
"In God We Trust"
Interstate highway system
Sputnik
National Defense Education Act
massive retaliation
Iranian coup
Geneva Accords
juvenile delinquency
rock-and-roll music
the Beats
League of United Latin American Citizens
Brown v. Board of Education
Montgomery bus boycott
"Southern Manifesto"
"missile gap"
military-industrial complex

wwnorton.com/studyspace

VISIT STUDYSPACE FOR THESE RESOURCES AND MORE:

- Author Videos
- A chapter outline
- A practice quiz
- Interactive maps
- Multimedia documents

CHAPTER 10

THE SIXTIES

From *Give Me Liberty! Seagull Fourth Edition*

Eric Foner

Credits: photo 1: © Cecil Williams; photo 2: Bettmann/Corbis; photo 3: Photo by Carl Mydans/Time Life Pictures/Getty Images; photo 4: Bettmann/Corbis; photo 5: Scurlock Studio Records, Archives Center, National Museum of American History, Smithsonian Institution; photo 6: Boston Globe via Getty Images; photo 7: © Grey Villet; photo 8: © 1963 Herbert Block.

Figure 1: *Congressional Quarterly, Civil Rights: A Progress Report* (1971), 46.

Young Americans for Freedom: The Sharon Statement, *National Review*, September 24, 1960. Reprinted by permission of Young Americans for Freedom/YAF Foundation.

Students for a Democratic Society: The Port Huron Statement, 1964, pp. 3–8. Reprinted by permission of Tom Hayden.

10

The Sixties 1960–1968

FOCUS QUESTIONS

- What were the major events in the civil rights movement of the early 1960s?
- What were the major crises and policy initiatives of the Kennedy presidency?
- What were the purposes and strategies of Johnson's Great Society programs?
- How did the civil rights movement change in the mid-1960s?
- How did the Vietnam War transform American politics and culture?
- What were the sources and significance of the rights revolution of the late 1960s?
- In what ways was 1968 a climactic year for the Sixties?

On the afternoon of February 1, 1960, four students from North Carolina Agricultural and Technical State University, a black college in Greensboro, North Carolina, entered the local Woolworth's department store. After making a few purchases, they sat down at the lunch counter, an area reserved for whites. Told that they could not be served, they remained in their seats until the store closed. They returned the next morning and the next. As the protest continued, other students, including a few local whites, joined in. Demonstrations spread across the country. After resisting for five months, Woolworth's in July agreed to serve black customers at its lunch counters.

The sit-in reflected mounting frustration at the slow pace of racial change. White Greensboro prided itself on being free of prejudice. In 1954, the city had been the first in the South to declare its intention of complying with the *Brown* decision. But by 1960 only a handful of black students had been admitted to all-white schools, the economic gap between blacks and whites had not narrowed, and Greensboro was still segregated.

More than any other event, the Greensboro sit-in launched the 1960s: a decade of political activism and social change. Sit-ins had occurred before, but never had they sparked so massive a response. Similar demonstrations soon took place throughout the South, demanding the integration not only of lunch counters but of parks, pools, restaurants, bowling alleys, libraries, and other facilities as well. By the end of 1960, some 70,000 demonstrators had taken part in sit-ins. Angry whites often assaulted them. But having been trained in nonviolent resistance, the protesters did not strike back.

Even more than elevating blacks to full citizenship, declared the writer James Baldwin, the civil rights movement challenged the United States to rethink "what it really means by freedom"—including whether freedom applied to all Americans or only to part of the population. With their freedom rides, freedom schools, freedom marches, and the insistent cry "freedom now," black Americans and their white allies made freedom once again the rallying cry of the dispossessed. Thousands of ordinary men and women—maids and laborers alongside students, teachers, businessmen, and ministers—risked physical and economic retribution to lay claim to freedom. Their courage inspired a host of other challenges to the status quo, including a student movement known as the New Left, the "second wave" of feminism, and activism among other minorities.

By the time the decade ended, these movements had challenged the 1950s' understanding of freedom linked to the Cold War abroad and consumer choice at home. They exposed the limitations of traditional New Deal liberalism. They forced a reconsideration of the nation's foreign policy and extended claims to freedom into the most intimate areas of life. They made American society confront the fact that certain groups, including students, women, members of racial minorities, and homosexuals, felt themselves excluded from full enjoyment of American freedom.

Reflecting back years later on the struggles of the 1960s, one black organizer in Memphis remarked, "All I wanted to do was to live in a free country." Of the movement's accomplishments, he added, "You had to fight for every inch of it. Nobody gave you anything. Nothing."

THE CIVIL RIGHTS REVOLUTION

THE RISING TIDE OF PROTEST

With the sit-ins, college students for the first time stepped onto the stage of American history as the leading force for social change. In April 1960, Ella Baker, a longtime civil rights organizer, called a meeting of young activists in Raleigh, North Carolina. About 200 black students and a few whites attended. Out of the gathering came the Student Non-Violent Coordinating Committee (SNCC), dedicated to replacing the culture of segregation with a "beloved community" of racial justice and to empowering ordinary blacks to take control of the decisions that affected their lives. "We can't count on adults," declared SNCC organizer Robert Moses. "Very few . . . are not afraid of the tremendous pressure they will face. This leaves the young people to be the organizers, the agents of social and political change."

Other forms of direct action soon followed the sit-ins. Blacks in Biloxi and Gulfport, Mississippi, engaged in "wade-ins," demanding access to segregated public beaches. Scores were arrested and two black teenagers were killed. In 1961, the Congress of Racial Equality (CORE) launched the Freedom Rides. Integrated groups traveled by bus into the Deep South to test compliance with court orders banning segregation on interstate buses and trains and in terminal facilities. Violent mobs assaulted them. Near Anniston, Alabama, a firebomb was thrown into the vehicle and the passengers beaten as they escaped. In Birmingham, Klansmen attacked riders with bats and chains, while police refused to intervene. Many of the Freedom Riders were arrested. But their actions led the Interstate Commerce Commission to order buses and terminals desegregated.

Civil rights demonstrators in Orangeburg, South Carolina, in 1960.

As protests escalated, so did the resistance of local authorities. Late in 1961, SNCC and other groups launched a campaign of nonviolent protests against racial discrimination in Albany, Georgia. The protests lasted a year, but despite filling the jails with demonstrators—a tactic adopted by the movement to gain national sympathy—they failed to achieve their goals. In September 1962, a court ordered the University of Mississippi to admit James Meredith, a black student. The state police stood aside as a mob, encouraged by Governor Ross Barnett, rampaged through the streets of Oxford, where the university is located.

Two bystanders lost their lives in the riot. President Kennedy was forced to dispatch the army to restore order.

BIRMINGHAM

The high point of protest came in the spring of 1963, when demonstrations took place in towns and cities across the South, dramatizing black discontent over inequality in education, employment, and housing. In one week in June, there were more than 15,000 arrests in 186 cities. The dramatic culmination came in Birmingham, Alabama, a citadel of segregation. Even for the Deep South, Birmingham was a violent city—there had been over fifty bombings of black homes and institutions since World War II. Local blacks had been demonstrating, with no result, for greater economic opportunities and an end to segregation by local businesses.

With the movement flagging, some of its leaders invited Martin Luther King Jr. to come to Birmingham. While serving a nine-day prison term in April 1963 for violating a ban on demonstrations, King composed one of his most eloquent pleas for racial justice, the "Letter from Birmingham Jail." Responding to local clergymen who counseled patience, King related the litany of abuses

CHRONOLOGY

1960	Greensboro, N.C., sit-in
	Young Americans for Freedom founded
1961	Bay of Pigs
	Freedom Rides
	Berlin Wall constructed
1962	Port Huron Statement
	University of Mississippi desegregated
	Rachel Carson's *Silent Spring*
	Cuban missile crisis
1963	Betty Friedan's *The Feminine Mystique*
	King's "Letter from Birmingham Jail"
	March on Washington
	Kennedy assassinated
1964	Freedom Summer
	Civil Rights Act passed
	Gulf of Tonkin resolution
1965–1967	Great Society
1965	Voting Rights Act
	Watts uprising
	Hart-Celler Act
1966	National Organization for Women organized
1968	Tet offensive
	Martin Luther King Jr. assassinated
	American Indian movement founded
	Richard Nixon elected
1969	Police raid on Stonewall Inn
	Woodstock festival
1973	*Roe v. Wade*

faced by black southerners, from police brutality to the daily humiliation of having to explain to their children why they could not enter amusement parks or public swimming pools. The "white moderate," King declared, must put aside fear of disorder and commit himself to racial justice.

In May, King made the bold decision to send black schoolchildren into the streets of Birmingham. Police chief Eugene "Bull" Connor unleashed his forces against the thousands of young marchers. The images, broadcast on television, of children being assaulted with nightsticks, high-pressure fire hoses, and attack dogs produced a wave of revulsion throughout the world and turned the Birmingham campaign into a triumph for the civil rights movement. It led President Kennedy, as will be related later, to endorse the movement's goals. Leading businessmen, fearing that the city was becoming an international symbol of brutality, brokered an end to the demonstrations that desegregated downtown stores and restaurants and promised that black salespeople would be hired.

But more than these modest gains, the events in Birmingham forced white Americans to decide whether they had more in common with fellow citizens demanding their basic rights or with violent segregationists. The question became more insistent in the following weeks. In June 1963, a sniper killed Medgar Evers, field secretary of the NAACP in Mississippi. In September, a bomb exploded at a black Baptist church in Birmingham, killing four young girls. (Not until the year 2002 was the last of those who committed this act of domestic terrorism tried and convicted.)

THE MARCH ON WASHINGTON

On August 28, 1963, two weeks before the Birmingham church bombing, 250,000 black and white Americans converged on the nation's capital for the March on Washington, often considered the high point of the nonviolent civil rights movement. Organized by a coalition of civil rights, labor, and church organizations led by A. Philip Randolph, the black unionist who had threatened a similar march in 1941, it was the largest public demonstration in the nation's history to that time. Calls for the passage of a civil rights bill pending before Congress took center stage. But the march's goals also included a public-works program to reduce unemployment, an increase in the minimum wage, and a law barring discrimination in employment. These demands, and the marchers' slogan, "Jobs and Freedom," revealed how the black movement had, for the moment, forged an alliance with white liberal groups. On the steps of the Lincoln Memorial, King delivered his most famous speech, including the words, "I have a dream that one day this nation will rise up and live out the true meaning of its creed: 'We hold these truths to be self-evident, that all men are created equal.'"

A fireman assaulting young African-American demonstrators with a high-pressure hose during the climactic demonstrations in Birmingham. Broadcast on television, such pictures proved a serious problem for the United States in its battle for the "hearts and minds" of people around the world and forced the Kennedy administration to confront the contradiction between the rhetoric of freedom and the reality of racism.

The March on Washington reflected an unprecedented degree of black-white cooperation in support of racial and economic justice. But it also revealed some of the movement's limitations, and the tensions within it. Even though female activists like Jo Ann Robinson and Ella Baker had played crucial roles in civil rights organizing, every speaker at the Lincoln Memorial was male. The organizers ordered SNCC leader John Lewis (later a congressman from Georgia) to tone down his speech, the original text of which called on blacks to "free ourselves of the chains of political and economic slavery" and march "through the heart of Dixie the way Sherman did . . . and burn Jim Crow to the ground." Lewis's rhetoric forecast the more militant turn many in the movement would soon be taking.

"Seek the freedom in 1963 promised in 1863," read one banner at the March on Washington. And civil rights activists resurrected the Civil War–era vision of national authority as the custodian of American freedom. Despite the fact that the federal government had for many decades promoted segregation, blacks' historical experience suggested that they had more hope for justice from national power than from local governments or civic institutions—home owners' associations, businesses, private clubs—still riddled with racism. It remained unclear whether the federal government would take up this responsibility.

THE KENNEDY YEARS

John F. Kennedy served as president for less than three years and, in domestic affairs, had few tangible accomplishments. But his administration is widely viewed today as a moment of youthful glamour, soaring hopes, and dynamic leadership at home and abroad. Later revelations of the sexual liaisons Kennedy obsessively pursued while in the White House have not significantly damaged his reputation among the general public.

Kennedy's inaugural address of January 1961 announced a watershed in American politics: "The torch has been passed," he declared, "to a new generation of Americans" who would "pay any price, bear any burden," to "assure the survival and success of liberty." The speech seemed to urge Americans to move beyond the self-centered consumer culture of the 1950s: "Ask not what your country can do for you; ask what you can do for your country." But while the sit-ins were by now a year old, the speech said nothing about segregation or race. At the outset of his presidency, Kennedy regarded civil rights as a distraction from his main concern—vigorous conduct of the Cold War.

KENNEDY AND THE WORLD

Kennedy's agenda envisioned new initiatives aimed at countering communist influence in the world. One of his administration's first acts was to establish the Peace Corps, which sent young Americans abroad to aid in the economic and educational progress of developing countries and to improve the image of the United States there. By 1966, more than 15,000 young men and women were serving as Peace Corps volunteers. When the Soviets in April 1961 launched a satellite carrying the first man into orbit around the earth, Kennedy announced that the United States would mobilize its resources to land a man on the moon by the end of the decade. The goal seemed almost impossible when announced, but it was stunningly accomplished in 1969.

Kennedy also formulated a new policy toward Latin America, the Alliance for Progress. A kind of Marshall Plan for the Western Hemisphere, although involving far smaller sums of money, it aimed, Kennedy said, to promote both "political" and "material freedom." Begun in 1961 with much fanfare about alleviating poverty and counteracting the appeal of communism, the Alliance for Progress failed. Unlike the Marshall Plan, military regimes and local elites controlled Alliance for Progress aid. They enriched themselves while the poor saw little benefit.

Like his predecessors, Kennedy viewed the entire world through the lens of the Cold War. This outlook shaped his dealings with Fidel Castro, who had led a revolution that in 1959 ousted Cuban dictator Fulgencio Batista. Until Castro took power, Cuba was an economic dependency of the United States. When his government began nationalizing American landholdings and other investments and signed an agreement to sell sugar to the Soviet Union, the Eisenhower administration suspended trade with the island. The CIA began training anti-Castro exiles for an invasion of Cuba.

In April 1961, Kennedy allowed the CIA to launch its invasion, at a site known as the Bay of Pigs. Military advisers predicted a popular uprising that would quickly topple the Castro government. But the assault proved to be a total failure. Of 1,400 invaders, more than 100 were killed and 1,100 captured. Cuba became ever more closely tied to the Soviet Union. The Kennedy administration tried other methods, including assassination attempts, to get rid of Castro's government.

THE MISSILE CRISIS

Meanwhile, relations between the two "superpowers" deteriorated. In August 1961, in order to stem a growing tide of emigrants fleeing from East to West Berlin, the Soviets constructed a wall separating the two parts of the city. Until its demolition in 1989, the Berlin Wall would stand as a tangible symbol of the Cold War and the division of Europe.

The most dangerous crisis of the Kennedy administration, and in many ways of the entire Cold War, came in October 1962, when American spy planes discovered that the Soviet Union was installing missiles in Cuba capable of reaching the United States with nuclear weapons. Rejecting advice from military leaders that he authorize an attack on Cuba, which would almost certainly have triggered a Soviet response in Berlin and perhaps a nuclear war, Kennedy imposed a blockade, or "quarantine," of the island and demanded the missiles' removal. After tense behind-the-scenes negotiations, Soviet premier Nikita Khrushchev agreed to withdraw the missiles; Kennedy pledged that the United States would not invade Cuba and secretly agreed to remove American Jupiter missiles from Turkey, from which they could reach the Soviet Union.

For thirteen days, the world teetered on the brink of all-out nuclear war. The crisis seems to have lessened Kennedy's passion for the Cold War. Indeed, he appears to have been shocked by the casual way military leaders spoke of "winning" a nuclear exchange in which tens of millions of Americans and Russians were certain to die. In 1963, Kennedy moved to reduce Cold War tensions. In a speech at American University, he called for greater cooperation with the Soviets. That summer, the two countries agreed to a treaty banning the testing of nuclear weapons in the atmosphere and in space. In announcing the agreement, Kennedy paid tribute to the small movement against nuclear weapons that had been urging such a ban for several years. He even sent word to Castro through a journalist that he desired a more constructive relationship with Cuba.

KENNEDY AND CIVIL RIGHTS

In his first two years in office, Kennedy was preoccupied with foreign policy. But in 1963, the crisis over civil rights eclipsed other concerns. Until then, Kennedy had been reluctant to take a forceful stand on black demands. He seemed to share FBI director J. Edgar Hoover's fear that the movement was inspired by communism. Attorney General Robert F. Kennedy, the president's brother, approved FBI wiretaps on King. Despite promising during the 1960 campaign to ban discrimination in federally assisted housing, Kennedy waited until the end of 1962 to issue the order. He used federal force when obstruction of the law became acute, as at the University of Mississippi. But he failed to protect civil rights workers from violence, insisting that law enforcement was a local matter.

Events in Birmingham in May 1963 forced Kennedy's hand. Kennedy realized that the United States simply could not declare itself the champion of freedom throughout the world while maintaining a system of racial inequality at home. In June, he went on national television to call for the passage of a law banning discrimination in all places of public accommodation, a major goal of the civil rights movement. The nation, he asserted, faced a moral crisis: "We preach freedom around the world, . . . but are we to say to the world, and much more importantly, to each other, that this is a land of the free except for Negroes?"

Kennedy did not live to see his civil rights bill enacted. On November 22, 1963, while riding in a motorcade through Dallas, Texas, he was shot and killed. Most likely, the assassin was Lee Harvey Oswald, a troubled former marine. Partly because Oswald was murdered two days later by a local nightclub owner while in police custody, speculation about a possible conspiracy continues to this day. In any event, Kennedy's death brought an abrupt and utterly unexpected end to his presidency. As with Pearl Harbor or September 11, 2001, an entire generation would always recall the moment when they first heard the news of Kennedy's death. It fell to his successor, Lyndon B. Johnson, to secure passage of the civil rights bill and to launch a program of domestic liberalism far more ambitious than anything Kennedy had envisioned.

New York City train passengers reading the news of President Kennedy's assassination, November 22, 1963.

LYNDON JOHNSON'S PRESIDENCY

Unlike John F. Kennedy, raised in a wealthy and powerful family, Lyndon Johnson grew up in one of the poorest parts of the United States, the central Texas hill country. Kennedy seemed to view success as his birthright; Johnson had to struggle ferociously to achieve wealth and power. By the 1950s, he had risen to become majority leader of the U.S. Senate. But Johnson never forgot the poor Mexican and white children he had taught in a Texas school in the early 1930s. Far more interested than Kennedy in domestic reform, he continued to hold the New Deal view that government had an obligation to assist less-fortunate members of society.

THE CIVIL RIGHTS ACT OF 1964

When he became president, nobody expected that Johnson would make the passage of civil rights legislation his first order of business or that he would come to identify himself with the black movement more passionately than any previous president. Just five days after Kennedy's assassination, however, Johnson called on Congress to enact the civil rights bill as the most fitting memorial to his slain predecessor. "We have talked long enough about equal rights in this country," he declared. "It is now time to write the next chapter and write it in the books of law."

In 1964, Congress passed the Civil Rights Act, which prohibited racial discrimination in employment, institutions like hospitals and schools, and privately owned public accommodations such as restaurants, hotels, and theaters. It also banned discrimination on the grounds of sex—a provision added by opponents of civil rights in an effort to derail the entire bill and embraced by liberal and female members of Congress as a way to broaden its scope. Johnson knew that many whites opposed the new law. After signing it, he turned to an aide and remarked, "I think we delivered the South to the Republican Party."

FREEDOM SUMMER

The 1964 law did not address a major concern of the civil rights movement—the right to vote in the South. That summer, a coalition of civil rights groups, including SNCC, CORE, and the NAACP, launched a voter registration drive in Mississippi. Hundreds of white college students from the North traveled to the state to take part in Freedom Summer. An outpouring of violence greeted the campaign, including thirty-five bombings and numerous beatings of civil rights workers. In June, three young activists—Michael Schwerner and Andrew Goodman, white students from the North, and James Chaney, a local black youth, were kidnapped by a group headed by a deputy sheriff and murdered near Philadelphia, Mississippi. Between 1961 and 1965, an estimated twenty-five black civil rights workers paid with their lives. But the deaths of the two white students focused unprecedented attention on Mississippi and on the apparent inability of the federal government to protect citizens seeking to enjoy their constitutional rights. (In June 2005, forty-one years after Freedom Summer, a Mississippi jury convicted a member of the Ku Klux Klan of manslaughter in the deaths of the three civil rights workers.)

Freedom Summer led directly to one of the most dramatic confrontations of the civil rights era—the campaign by the Mississippi Freedom Democratic Party (MFDP) to take the seats of the state's all-white official party at the 1964 Democratic national convention in Atlantic City, New Jersey. With blacks unable to participate in the activities of the Democratic Party or register to vote, the civil rights movement in Mississippi had created the MFDP, open to all residents of the state. At televised hearings before the credentials committee, Fannie Lou Hamer of the MFDP held a national audience spellbound with her account of growing up in poverty in the Yazoo-Mississippi Delta and of the savage beatings she had endured at the hands of police. Like many other black activists, Hamer was a deeply religious person who believed that

Christianity rested on the idea of freedom and that the movement had been divinely inspired. "Is this America," she asked, "the land of the free and home of the brave, where . . . we [are] threatened daily because we want to live as decent human beings?" Johnson feared a southern walkout, as had happened at the 1948 party convention, if the MFDP were seated. Party liberals, including Johnson's running mate, Hubert Humphrey, pressed for a compromise in which two black delegates would be granted seats. But the MFDP rejected the proposal.

THE 1964 ELECTION

The events at Atlantic City severely weakened black activists' faith in the responsiveness of the political system and forecast the impending breakup of the coalition between the civil rights movement and the liberal wing of the Democratic Party. For the moment, however, the movement rallied behind Johnson's campaign for reelection. Johnson's opponent, Senator Barry Goldwater of Arizona, had published *The Conscience of a Conservative* (1960), which sold more than 3 million copies. The book demanded a more aggressive conduct of the Cold War (he even suggested that nuclear war might be "the price of freedom"). But Goldwater directed most of his critique against "internal" dangers to freedom, especially the New Deal welfare state, which he believed stifled individual initiative and independence. He called for the substitution of private charity for public welfare programs and Social Security, and the abolition of the graduated income tax. Goldwater had voted against the Civil Rights Act of 1964. His acceptance speech at the Republican national convention contained the explosive statement, "Extremism in the defense of liberty is no vice."

Stigmatized by the Democrats as an extremist who would repeal Social Security and risk nuclear war, Goldwater went down to a disastrous defeat. Johnson received almost 43 million votes to Goldwater's 27 million. Democrats swept to two-to-one majorities in both houses of Congress. Although few realized it, the 1964 campaign marked a milestone in the resurgence of American conservatism. Goldwater's success in the Deep South, where he carried five states, coupled with the surprisingly strong showing of segregationist governor George Wallace of Alabama in Democratic primaries in Wisconsin, Indiana, and Maryland, suggested that politicians could strike electoral gold by appealing to white opposition to the civil rights movement.

One indication of problems for the Democrats came in California, with the passage by popular referendum of Proposition 14, which repealed a 1963 law banning racial discrimination in the sale of real estate. Backed by the state's realtors and developers, California conservatives made the "freedom" of home owners to control their property the rallying cry of the campaign against the fair housing law. Although Johnson carried California by more than 1 million votes, Proposition 14 received a considerable majority, winning three-fourths of the votes cast by whites.

THE CONSERVATIVE SIXTIES

The 1960s, today recalled as a decade of radicalism, clearly had a conservative side as well. With the founding in 1960 of Young Americans for Freedom (YAF), conservative students emerged as a force in politics. There were striking parallels between the Sharon Statement, issued by ninety young people who gathered at the estate of conservative intellectual William F. Buckley in Sharon, Connecticut, to establish YAF, and the Port Huron Statement of SDS of 1962 (discussed later in this chapter). Both manifestos portrayed youth as the cutting edge of a new radicalism, and both claimed to offer a route to greater freedom. The Sharon Statement summarized beliefs that had circulated among conservatives during the past decade—the free market underpinned "personal freedom," government must be strictly limited, and "international communism," the gravest threat to liberty, must be destroyed.

YAF aimed initially to take control of the Republican Party from leaders who had made their peace with the New Deal and seemed willing to coexist with communism. YAF members became Barry Goldwater's shock troops in

A 1967 rally by members of Young Americans for Freedom, a conservative group that flourished in the 1960s.

1964. Despite his landslide defeat in the general election, Goldwater's nomination was a remarkable triumph for a movement widely viewed as composed of fanatics out to "repeal the twentieth century."

Goldwater also brought new constituencies to the conservative cause. His campaign aroused enthusiasm in the rapidly expanding suburbs of southern California and the Southwest. Orange County, California, many of whose residents had recently arrived from the East and Midwest and worked in defense-related industries, became a nationally known center of grassroots conservative activism. The funds that poured into the Goldwater campaign from the Sunbelt's oilmen and aerospace entrepreneurs established a new financial base for conservatism. And by carrying five states of the Deep South, Goldwater showed that the civil rights revolution had redrawn the nation's political map, opening the door to a "southern strategy" that would eventually lead the entire region into the Republican Party.

Well before the rise of Black Power, a reaction against civil rights gains offered conservatives new opportunities and threatened the stability of the Democratic coalition. During the 1950s, many conservatives had responded favorably to southern whites' condemnation of the *Brown v. Board of Education* desegregation decision as an invasion of states' rights. The *National Review*, an influential conservative magazine, referred to whites as "the advanced race" and defended black disenfranchisement on the grounds that "the claims of civilization supersede those of universal suffrage." In 1962, YAF bestowed its Freedom Award on Senator Strom Thurmond of South Carolina, one of the country's most prominent segregationists. During the 1960s, most conservatives abandoned talk of racial superiority and inferiority. But conservative appeals to law and order, "freedom of association," and the evils of welfare often had strong racial overtones. Racial divisions would prove to be a political gold mine for conservatives.

THE VOTING RIGHTS ACT

One last legislative triumph, however, lay ahead for the civil rights movement. In January 1965, King launched a voting rights campaign in Selma, Alabama, a city where only 355 of 15,000 black residents had been allowed to register to vote. In March, defying a ban by Governor Wallace, King attempted to lead a march from Selma to the state capital, Montgomery. When the marchers reached the bridge leading out of the city, state police assaulted them with cattle prods, whips, and tear gas.

Once again, violence against nonviolent demonstrators flashed across television screens throughout the world, compelling the federal government to take action. Calling Selma a milestone in "man's unending search for freedom," Johnson asked Congress to enact a law securing the right to vote. He closed his speech by quoting the demonstrators' song, "We Shall Overcome." Never before had the movement received so powerful an endorsement from the federal government. Congress quickly passed the Voting Rights Act of 1965, which allowed federal officials to register voters. Black southerners finally regained the suffrage that had been stripped from them at the turn of the twentieth century. In addition, the Twenty-fourth Amendment to the Constitution outlawed the poll tax, which had long prevented poor blacks (and some whites) from voting in the South.

IMMIGRATION REFORM

By 1965, the civil rights movement had succeeded in eradicating the legal bases of second-class citizenship. The belief that racism should no longer serve as a basis of public policy spilled over into other realms. In 1965, the Hart-Celler Act abandoned the national-origins quota system of immigration, which had excluded Asians and severely restricted southern and eastern Europeans. The law established new, racially neutral criteria for immigration, notably family reunification and possession of skills in demand in the United States. On the other hand, because of growing hostility in the Southwest to Mexican immigration, the law established the first limit, 120,000, on newcomers from the Western Hemisphere. This created, for the first time, the category of "illegal aliens" from the Americas. The act set the quota for the rest of the world at 170,000. The total annual number of immigrants, 290,000, represented a lower percentage of the American population than had been admitted when the nationality quotas were established in 1924. However, because of special provisions for refugees from communist countries, immigration soon exceeded these caps.

The new law had many unexpected results. At the time, immigrants represented only 5 percent of the American population—the lowest proportion since the 1830s. No one anticipated that the new quotas not only would lead to an explosive rise in immigration but also would spark a dramatic shift in which newcomers from Latin America, the Caribbean, and Asia came to outnumber those from Europe. Taken together, the civil rights revolution and immigration reform marked the triumph of a pluralist conception of Americanism. By 1976, 85 percent of respondents to a public-opinion survey agreed with the statement, "The United States was meant to be . . . a country made up of many races, religions, and nationalities."

THE GREAT SOCIETY

After his landslide victory of 1964, Johnson outlined the most sweeping proposal for governmental action to promote the general welfare since the New Deal. Johnson's initiatives of 1965–1967, known collectively as the Great

Society, provided health services to the poor and elderly in the new Medicaid and Medicare programs and poured federal funds into education and urban development. New cabinet offices—the Departments of Transportation and of Housing and Urban Development—and new agencies, such as the Equal Employment Opportunity Commission, the National Endowments for the Humanities and for the Arts, and a national public broadcasting network, were created. These measures greatly expanded the powers of the federal government, and they completed and extended the social agenda (with the exception of national health insurance) that had been stalled in Congress since 1938.

Unlike the New Deal, however, the Great Society was a response to prosperity, not depression. The mid-1960s were a time of rapid economic expansion, fueled by increased government spending and a tax cut on individuals and businesses initially proposed by Kennedy and enacted in 1964. Johnson and Democratic liberals believed that economic growth made it possible to fund ambitious new government programs and to improve the quality of life.

THE WAR ON POVERTY

The centerpiece of the Great Society, however, was the crusade to eradicate poverty, launched by Johnson early in 1964. After the talk of universal affluence during the 1950s, economic deprivation had been rediscovered by political leaders, thanks in part to Michael Harrington's 1962 book *The Other America*. Harrington revealed that 40 to 50 million Americans lived in poverty, often in isolated rural areas or urban slums "invisible" to the middle class. The civil rights movement heightened the urgency of the issue, even though, as Harrington made clear, whites made up a majority of the nation's poor.

During the 1930s, Democrats had attributed poverty to an imbalance of economic power and flawed economic institutions. In the 1960s, the administration attributed it to an absence of skills and a lack of proper attitudes and work habits. Thus, the War on Poverty did not consider the most direct ways of eliminating poverty—guaranteeing an annual income for all Americans, creating jobs for the unemployed, promoting the spread of unionization, or making it more difficult for businesses to shift production to the low-wage South or overseas. Nor did it address the economic changes that were reducing the number of well-paid manufacturing jobs and leaving poor families in rural areas like Appalachia and decaying urban ghettos with little hope of economic advancement.

One of the Great Society's most popular and successful components, food stamps, offered direct aid to the poor. But, in general, the War on Poverty concentrated not on direct economic aid but on equipping the poor with skills and rebuilding their spirit and motivation. The new Office of Economic

Figure 1 PERCENTAGE OF POPULATION BELOW POVERTY LEVEL, BY RACE, 1959–1969*

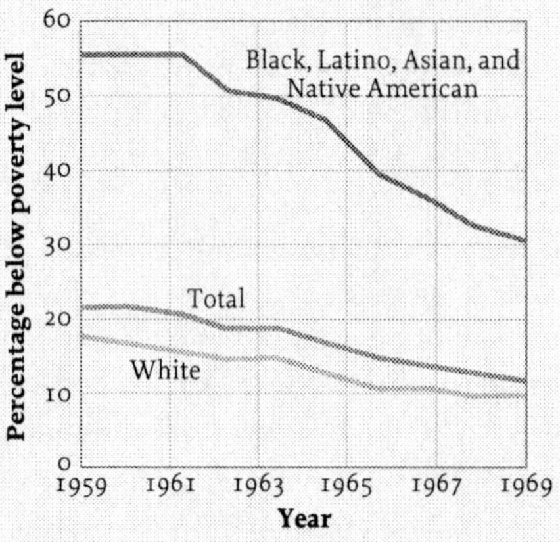

* The poverty threshold for a non-farm family of four was $3,743 in 1969 and $2,973 in 1959.

During the 1960s, an expanding economy and government programs assisting the poor produced a steady decrease in the percentage of Americans living in poverty.

Opportunity oversaw a series of initiatives designed to lift the poor into the social and economic mainstream. It provided Head Start (an early childhood education program), job training, legal services, and scholarships for poor college students. It also created VISTA, a domestic version of the Peace Corps for the inner cities. In an echo of SNCC's philosophy of empowering ordinary individuals to take control of their lives, the War on Poverty required that poor people play a leading part in the design and implementation of local policies, a recipe for continuing conflict with local political leaders accustomed to controlling the flow of federal dollars.

FREEDOM AND EQUALITY

Johnson defended the Great Society in a vocabulary of freedom derived from the New Deal, when his own political career began, and reinforced by the civil rights movement. Soon after assuming office in 1963, he resurrected the phrase "freedom from want," all but forgotten during the 1950s. Echoing FDR, Johnson told the 1964 Democratic convention, "The man who is hungry, who cannot find work or educate his children, who is bowed by want, that man is not fully free." Recognizing that black poverty was fundamentally different from white, since its roots lay in "past injustice and present prejudice," Johnson sought to redefine the relationship between freedom and equality. Economic liberty, he insisted, meant more than equal opportunity: "You do not wipe away the scars of centuries by saying: Now you are free to go where you want, do as you desire, and choose the leaders you please.... We seek... not just equality as a right and a theory, but equality as a fact and as a result."

Johnson's Great Society may not have achieved equality "as a fact," but it represented a remarkable reaffirmation of the idea of social citizenship. It was the most expansive effort in the nation's history to mobilize the powers of the national government to address the needs of the least-advantaged Americans, especially those, like blacks, largely excluded from the original New Deal entitlements such as Social Security.

Coupled with the decade's high rate of economic growth, the War on Poverty succeeded in reducing the incidence of poverty from 22 percent to 13 percent of American families during the 1960s. It has fluctuated around the latter figure ever since. The sum spent, however, was too low to end poverty altogether or to transform conditions of life in poor urban neighborhoods. By the 1990s, thanks to the civil rights movement and the Great Society, the historic gap between whites and blacks in education, income, and access to skilled employment narrowed considerably. But with deindustrialization and urban decay affecting numerous families and most suburbs still being off-limits to non-whites, the median wealth of white households remained ten times greater than that of blacks, and nearly a quarter of all black children still lived in poverty.

THE CHANGING BLACK MOVEMENT

Even at its moment of triumph, the civil rights movement confronted a crisis as it sought to move from access to schools, public accommodations, and the voting booth to the economic divide separating blacks from other Americans. In the mid-1960s, economic issues rose to the forefront of the civil rights agenda. Violent outbreaks in black ghettos outside the South drew attention to the national scope of racial injustice and to inequalities in jobs, education, and housing that the dismantling of legal segregation left intact. Much of the animosity that came to characterize race relations arose from the belief of many whites that the legislation of 1964 and 1965 had fulfilled the nation's obligation to assure blacks equality before the law, while blacks pushed for more government action, sparking fears of "reverse discrimination."

THE GHETTO UPRISINGS

The first riots—really, battles between angry blacks and the predominantly white police (widely seen by many ghetto residents as an occupying army)—erupted in Harlem in 1964. Far larger was the Watts uprising of 1965, which took place in the black ghetto of Los Angeles only days after Johnson signed the Voting Rights Act. An estimated 50,000 persons took part in this "rebellion," attacking police and firemen, looting white-owned businesses, and burning buildings. It required 15,000 police and National Guardsmen to restore order, by which time thirty-five people lay dead, 900 were injured, and $30 million worth of property had been destroyed.

By the summer of 1967, violence had become so widespread that some feared racial civil war. Urban uprisings in that year left twenty-three dead in Newark and forty-three in Detroit, where entire blocks went up in flames and property damage ran into the hundreds of millions of dollars. The violence led Johnson to appoint a commission headed by Illinois governor Otto Kerner to study the causes of urban rioting. Released in 1968, the Kerner Report blamed the violence on "segregation and poverty" and offered a powerful indictment of "white racism." It depicted a country in danger of being torn apart by racial antagonism: "Our nation is moving toward two societies, one black, one white—separate and unequal." But the report failed to offer any clear proposals for change.

With black unemployment twice that of whites and the average black family income little more than half the white norm, the movement looked for ways to "make freedom real" for black Americans. In 1964, King called for a "Bill of Rights for the Disadvantaged" to mobilize the nation's resources to abolish economic deprivation. His proposal was directed against poverty in general, but King also insisted that after "doing something special *against* the Negro for hundreds of years," the United States had an obligation to "do something special *for* him now"—an early call for what would come to be known as "affirmative action." A. Philip Randolph and civil rights veteran Bayard Rustin proposed a Freedom Budget, which envisioned spending $100 billion over ten years on a federal program of job creation and urban redevelopment.

In 1966, King launched the Chicago Freedom movement, with demands quite different from its predecessors in the South—an end to discrimination by employers and unions, equal access to mortgages, the integration of public housing, and the construction of low-income housing scattered throughout the region. Confronting the entrenched power of Mayor Richard J. Daley's political machine and the ferocious opposition of white home owners, the movement failed. King's tactics—marches, sit-ins, mass arrests—proved ineffective in the face of the North's less pervasive but still powerful system of racial inequality. As he came to realize the difficulty of combating the economic plight of black America, King's language became more and more radical. He called for nothing less than a "revolution in values" that would create a "better distribution of wealth" for "all God's children."

MALCOLM X

The civil rights movement's first phase had produced a clear set of objectives, far-reaching accomplishments, and a series of coherent if sometimes competitive organizations. The second witnessed political fragmentation and few significant victories. Even during the heyday of the integration struggle, the fiery orator Malcolm X had insisted that blacks must control the political and economic resources of their communities and rely on their own efforts rather than working with whites. Having committed a string of crimes as a youth, Malcolm Little was converted in jail to the teachings of the Nation of Islam, or Black Muslims, who preached a message of white evil and black self-discipline.

Malcolm dropped his "slave surname" in favor of "X," symbolizing blacks' separation from their African ancestry. On his release from prison he became a spokesman for the Muslims and a sharp critic of the ideas of integration and nonviolence, and of King's practice of appealing to American values. "I don't see any American dream," he proclaimed. "I see an American nightmare."

On a 1964 trip to Mecca, Saudi Arabia, Islam's spiritual home, Malcolm X witnessed harmony among Muslims of all races. He now began to speak of the possibility of interracial cooperation for radical change in the United States. But when members of the Nation of Islam assassinated him in February 1965 after he had formed his own Organization of Afro-American Unity, Malcolm X left neither a consistent ideology nor a coherent movement. Most whites considered him an apostle of racial violence. However, his call for blacks to rely on their own resources struck a chord among the urban poor and younger civil rights activists. His *Autobiography*, published in 1966, became a great best-seller. Today, streets, parks, and schools are named after him.

THE RISE OF BLACK POWER

Malcolm X was the intellectual father of "Black Power," a slogan that came to national attention in 1966 when SNCC leader Stokely Carmichael used it during a civil rights march in Mississippi. Black Power immediately became a rallying cry for those bitter over the federal government's failure to stop violence against civil rights workers, white attempts to determine movement strategy (as at the Democratic convention of 1964), and the civil rights movement's failure to have any impact on the economic problems of black ghettos.

One who embraced the idea proclaimed, "Black Power means Black Freedom"—freedom, especially, from whites who tried to dictate the movement's goals. A highly imprecise idea, Black Power suggested everything from the election of more black officials (hardly a radical notion) to the belief that black Americans were a colonized people whose freedom could be won only through a revolutionary struggle for self-determination. But however employed, the idea reflected the radicalization of young civil rights activists and sparked an explosion of racial self-assertion, reflected in the slogan "Black is beautiful." The abandonment of the word "Negro" in favor of "Afro-American" and the popularity of black beauty pageants, African styles of dress, and the "natural," or "Afro," hairdo among both men and women signified much more than a change in language and fashion. They reflected a new sense of racial pride and a rejection of white norms.

Inspired by the idea of black self-determination, SNCC and CORE repudiated their previous interracialism, and new militant groups sprang into existence. Most prominent of the new groups, in terms of publicity, if not

Female students on the campus of Howard University in Washington, D.C., sport the Afro, a hairstyle representative of the "black is beautiful" campaign of the 1960s.

numbers, was the Black Panther Party. Founded in Oakland, California, in 1966, it became notorious for advocating armed self-defense in response to police brutality. It demanded the release of black prisoners because of racism in the criminal justice system. The party's youthful members alarmed whites by wearing military garb, although they also ran health clinics, schools, and children's breakfast programs. But internal disputes and a campaign against the Black Panthers by police and the FBI, which left several leaders dead in shootouts, destroyed the organization.

By 1967, with the escalation of U.S. military involvement in Vietnam, the War on Poverty had ground to a halt. By then, with ghetto uprisings punctuating the urban landscape, the antiwar movement assuming massive proportions, and millions of young people ostentatiously rejecting mainstream values, American society faced its greatest crisis since the Depression.

VIETNAM AND THE NEW LEFT

OLD AND NEW LEFTS

To most Americans, the rise of a protest movement among white youth came as a complete surprise. For most of the century, colleges had been conservative institutions that drew their students from a privileged segment of the population. During the 1950s, young people had been called a "silent generation." If blacks' grievances appeared self-evident, those of white college students were difficult to understand. What persuaded large numbers of children of affluence to reject the values and institutions of their society? In part, the answer lay in a redefinition of the meaning of freedom by what came to be called the New Left.

What made the New Left new was its rejection of the intellectual and political categories that had shaped radicalism and liberalism for most of the twentieth century. It challenged not only mainstream America but also what it dismissively called the Old Left. Unlike the Communist Party, it did not take the Soviet Union as a model or see the working class as the main agent of social change. Instead of economic equality and social citizenship, the language of New Deal liberals, the New Left spoke of loneliness, isolation, and alienation, of powerlessness in the face of bureaucratic institutions and a hunger for authenticity that affluence could not provide. These discontents galvanized a mass movement among what was rapidly becoming a major sector of the American population. By 1968, thanks to the coming of age of the baby-boom generation and the growing number of jobs that required post–high school skills, more than 7 million students attended college, more than the number of farmers or steelworkers.

The New Left was not as new as it claimed. Its call for a democracy of citizen participation harked back to the American Revolution, and its critique of the contrast between American values and American reality, to the abolitionists. Its emphasis on authenticity in the face of conformity recalled the bohemians of the years before World War I, and its critique of consumer culture drew inspiration from 1950s writers on mass society. But the New Left's greatest inspiration was the black freedom movement. More than any other event, the sit-ins catalyzed white student activism.

Here was the unlikely combination that created the upheaval known as The Sixties—the convergence of society's most excluded members demanding full access to all its benefits, with the children of the middle class rejecting the social mainstream. The black movement and white New Left shared basic assumptions—that the evils to be corrected were deeply embedded in social institutions and that only direct confrontation could persuade Americans of the urgency of far-reaching change.

THE FADING CONSENSUS

The years 1962 and 1963 witnessed the appearance of several pathbreaking books that challenged one or another aspect of the 1950s consensus. James Baldwin's *The Fire Next Time* gave angry voice to the black revolution. Rachel Carson's *Silent Spring* exposed the environmental costs of economic growth. Michael Harrington's *The Other America* revealed the persistence of poverty amid plenty. *The Death and Life of Great American Cities*, by Jane Jacobs, criticized urban renewal, the removal of the poor from city centers, and the destruction of neighborhoods to build highways, accommodating cities to the needs of drivers rather than pedestrians. What made cities alive, she insisted, was density and diversity, the social interaction of people of different backgrounds encountering each other on urban streets.

Yet in some ways the most influential critique of all arose in 1962 from Students for a Democratic Society (SDS), an offshoot of the socialist League for Industrial Democracy. Meeting at Port Huron, Michigan, some sixty college students adopted a document that captured the mood and summarized the beliefs of this generation of student protesters.

The Port Huron Statement devoted four-fifths of its text to criticism of institutions ranging from political parties to corporations, unions, and the military-industrial complex. But what made the document the guiding spirit of a new radicalism was the remainder, which offered a new vision of social change. "We seek the establishment," it proclaimed, of "a democracy of individual participation, [in which] the individual shares in those social decisions determining the quality and direction of his life." Freedom, for the New Left, meant "participatory democracy." Although rarely defined with precision, this became a standard by which students judged existing social arrangements—workplaces, schools, government—and found them wanting.

THE RISE OF SDS

By the end of 1962, SDS had grown to 8,000 members. Then, in 1964, events at the University of California at Berkeley revealed the possibility for a far broader mobilization of students in the name of participatory democracy. A Cold War "multi-versity," Berkeley was an immense, impersonal institution where enrollments in many classes approached 1,000 students. The spark that set student protests alight was a new rule prohibiting political groups from using a central area of the campus to spread their ideas. Students—including conservatives outraged at being barred from distributing their own literature—responded by creating the Free Speech movement. Freedom of expression, declared Mario Savio, a student leader, "represents the very dignity of what a human being is. . . . That's what marks us off from the stones and the stars. You can speak freely." Likening the university to a factory, Savio called on students to "throw our body against the machines."

Thousands of Berkeley students became involved in the protests in the months that followed. Their program moved from demanding a repeal of the new rule to a critique of the entire structure of the university and of an education geared toward preparing graduates for corporate jobs. When the university gave in on the speech ban early in 1965, one activist exulted that the students had succeeded in reversing "the world-wide drift from freedom."

AMERICA AND VIETNAM

By 1965 the black movement and the emergence of the New Left had shattered the climate of consensus of the 1950s. But what transformed protest into a full-fledged generational rebellion was the war in Vietnam. What one historian has called "the greatest miscalculation in the history of American foreign relations" was a logical extension of Cold War policies and assumptions. The war tragically revealed the danger that Walter Lippmann had warned of at the outset of the Cold War—viewing the entire world and every local situation within it through the either-or lens of an anticommunist crusade. A Vietnam specialist in the State Department who attended a policy meeting in August 1963 later recalled "the abysmal ignorance around the table of the particular facts of Vietnam. . . . They made absolutely no distinctions between countries with completely different historical experiences. . . . They [believed] that we could manipulate other states and build nations; that we knew all the answers."

Few Americans had any knowledge of Vietnam's history and culture. Successive administrations reduced a complex struggle for national independence, led by homegrown communists who enjoyed widespread support throughout their country in addition to Soviet backing, to a test of "containment." The Truman and Eisenhower administrations had cast their lot with French colonialism in the region. After the French defeat, they financed the creation of a pro-American South Vietnamese government, in violation of the Geneva Accords of 1954 that had promised elections to unify Vietnam. By the 1960s, the United States was committed to the survival of this corrupt regime.

Fear that the public would not forgive them for "losing" Vietnam made it impossible for Presidents Kennedy and Johnson to remove the United States from an increasingly untenable situation. Kennedy's foreign policy advisers saw Vietnam as a test of whether the United States could, through "counterinsurgency"—intervention to counter internal uprisings in noncommunist countries—halt the spread of Third World revolutions. Despite the dispatch of increased American aid and numerous military advisers, South Vietnamese leader Ngo Dinh Diem lost control of the countryside to the communist-led Viet Cong. Diem resisted American advice to broaden his government's base of support. In October 1963, after large Buddhist demonstrations against his regime, the United States approved a military coup that led to Diem's death. When Kennedy was assassinated the following month, there were 17,000 American military advisers in South Vietnam. Shortly before his death, according to the notes of a White House meeting, Kennedy questioned "the wisdom of involvement in Vietnam." But he took no action to end the American presence.

LYNDON JOHNSON'S WAR

Lyndon B. Johnson came to the presidency with little experience in foreign relations. Johnson had misgivings about sending American troops to Vietnam. But he knew that Republicans had used the "loss" of China as a weapon against Truman. "I am not going to be the president," he vowed, "who saw Southeast Asia go the way China went."

In August 1964, North Vietnamese vessels encountered an American ship on a spy mission off its coast. When North Vietnamese patrol boats fired on the American vessel, Johnson proclaimed that the United States was a victim of "aggression." In response, Congress passed the Gulf of Tonkin resolution, authorizing the president to take "all necessary measures to repel armed attack" in Vietnam. Only two members—Senators Ernest Gruening of Alaska and Wayne Morse of Oregon—voted against giving Johnson this blank check. The nearest the United States ever came to a formal declaration of war, the resolution passed without any discussion of American goals and strategy in Vietnam. (Over forty years later, in December 2005, the National Security Agency finally released hundreds of pages of secret documents that made it clear that no North Vietnamese attack had actually taken place.)

During the 1964 campaign, Johnson insisted that he had no intention of sending American troops to Vietnam. But immediately after Johnson's reelection, the National Security Council recommended that the United States begin air strikes against North Vietnam and introduce American ground troops in the south. When the Viet Cong in February 1965 attacked an American air base in South Vietnam, Johnson put the plan into effect. At almost the same time, he intervened in the Dominican Republic. Here, military leaders in 1963 had overthrown the left-wing but noncommunist Juan Bosch, the country's first elected president since 1924. In April 1965, another group of military men attempted to restore Bosch to power but were defeated by the ruling junta. Fearing the unrest would lead to "another Cuba," Johnson dispatched 22,000 American troops. The intervention outraged many Latin Americans. But the operation's success seemed to bolster Johnson's determination in Vietnam.

By 1968, the number of American troops in Vietnam exceeded half a million, and the conduct of the war had become more and more brutal. The North Vietnamese mistreated American prisoners of war held in a camp known sardonically by the inmates as the Hanoi Hilton. (One prisoner of war, John McCain, who spent six years there, courageously refused to be exchanged unless his companions were freed with him. McCain later became a senator

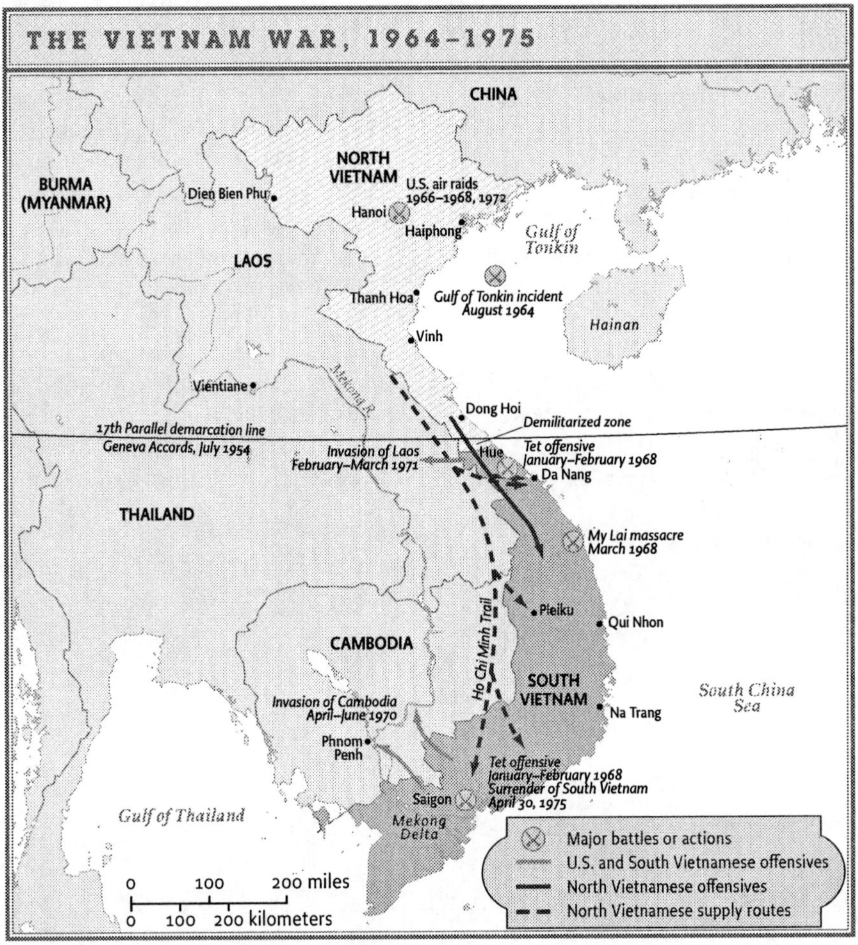

A war of aerial bombing and small guerilla skirmishes rather than fixed land battles, Vietnam was the longest war in American history and the only one the United States has lost.

VOICES OF FREEDOM

From Young Americans for Freedom, The Sharon Statement (September 1960)

Although the 1960s is usually thought of as a decade of youthful radicalism, it also witnessed the growth of conservative movements. The Sharon Statement marked the emergence of Young Americans for Freedom as a force for conservatism in American politics.

In this time of moral and political crisis, it is the responsibility of the youth of America to affirm certain eternal truths. We, as young conservatives, believe:

That foremost among the transcendent values is the individual's use of his God-given free will, whence derives his right to be free from the restrictions of arbitrary force;

That liberty is indivisible, and that political freedom cannot long exist without economic freedom;

That the purposes of government are to protect those freedoms through the preservation of internal order, the provision of national defense, and the administration of justice;

That when government ventures beyond these lawful functions, it accumulates power which tends to diminish order and liberty; . . .

That the market economy, allocating resources by the free play of supply and demand, is the single economic system compatible with the requirements of personal freedom and constitutional government, and that it is at the same time the most productive supplier of human needs; . . .

That the forces of international Communism are, at present, the greatest single threat to these liberties;

That the United States should stress victory over, rather than coexistence with, this menace.

From Tom Hayden and Others, The Port Huron Statement (June 1962)

One of the most influential documents of the 1960s emerged in 1962 from a meeting sponsored by the Students for a Democratic Society in Port Huron, Michigan. Its call for a "democracy of individual participation" inspired many of the social movements of the decade and offered a critique of institutions ranging from the government to universities that failed to live up to this standard.

We are the people of this generation, bred in at least modest comfort, housed now in universities, looking uncomfortably to the world we inherit. . . . Freedom and equality for each individual, government of, by, and for the people—these American values we found good principles by which we could live as men.

As we grew, however, our comfort was penetrated by events too troubling to dismiss. First, the . . . Southern struggle against racial bigotry compelled most of us from silence to activism. Second, . . . the proclaimed peaceful intentions of the United States contradicted its economic and military investments in the Cold War. . . . The conventional moral terms of the age, the politician moralities—"free world," "people's democracies"—reflect realities poorly if at all, and seem to function more as ruling myths than as descriptive principles. But neither has our experience in the universities brought us moral enlightenment. Our professors and administrators sacrifice controversy to public relations; . . . their skills and silence are purchased by investors in the arms race. . . .

We regard *men* as infinitely precious and possessed of unfulfilled capacities for reason, freedom, and love. In affirming these principles we are aware of countering perhaps the dominant conceptions of man in the twentieth century: that he is a thing to be manipulated, and that he is inherently incapable of directing his own affairs. We oppose the depersonalization that reduces human beings to the status of things—if anything, the brutalities of the twentieth century teach that means and ends are intimately related, that vague appeals to "posterity" cannot justify the mutilations of the present. . . . We see little reason why men cannot meet with increasing skill the complexities and responsibilities of their situation, if society is organized not for minority, but for majority, participation in decision-making.

We would replace power rooted in possession, privilege, or circumstance by power and uniqueness rooted in love, reflectiveness, reason, and creativity. As a social system we seek the establishment of a democracy of individual participation [so] that the individual [can] share in those social decisions determining the quality and direction of his life. . . . A new left must consist of younger people. . . . [It] must start controversy throughout the land, if national policies and national apathy are to be reversed.

QUESTIONS

1. How do the young conservatives who wrote the Sharon Statement understand freedom?

2. What do the authors of the Port Huron Statement appear to mean by participatory democracy?

3. What are the main differences, and are there any similarities, between the outlooks of the young conservatives and the young radicals?

from Arizona and the Republican candidate for president in 2008.) American planes dropped more tons of bombs on the small countries of North and South Vietnam than both sides used in all of World War II. They spread chemicals that destroyed forests to deprive the Viet Cong of hiding places and dropped bombs filled with napalm, a gelatinous form of gasoline that burns the skin of anyone exposed to it. The army pursued Viet Cong and North Vietnamese forces in "search and destroy" missions that often did not distinguish between combatants and civilians. Weekly reports of enemy losses or "body counts" became a fixation of the administration. But the United States could not break its opponents' ability to fight or make the South Vietnamese government any more able to survive on its own.

THE ANTIWAR MOVEMENT

As casualties mounted and American bombs poured down on North and South Vietnam, the Cold War foreign policy consensus began to unravel. By 1968, the war had sidetracked much of the Great Society and had torn families, universities, and the Democratic Party apart. With the entire political leadership, liberal no less than conservative, committed to the war for most of the 1960s, young activists lost all confidence in "the system."

Opposition to the war became the organizing theme that united people with all kinds of doubts and discontents. "We recoil with horror," said a SNCC position paper, "at the inconsistency of a supposedly 'free' society where responsibility to freedom is equated with the responsibility to lend oneself to military aggression." With college students exempted from the draft, the burden of fighting fell on the working class and the poor. In 1967, Martin Luther King Jr. condemned the administration's Vietnam policy as an unconscionable use of violence and for draining resources from needs at home. At this point, King was the most prominent American to speak out against the war.

As for SDS, the war seemed the opposite of participatory democracy, since American involvement had come through secret commitments and decisions made by political elites, with no real public debate. In April 1965, SDS invited opponents of American policy in Vietnam to assemble in Washington, D.C. The turnout of 25,000 amazed the organizers, offering the first hint that the antiwar movement would soon enjoy a mass constituency. At the next antiwar rally, in November 1965, SDS leader Carl Ogelsby openly challenged the foundations of Cold War thinking. He linked Vietnam to a critique of American interventions in Guatemala and Iran, support for South African apartheid, and Johnson's dispatch of troops to the Dominican Republic, all rooted in obsessive anticommunism. Some might feel, Ogelsby concluded, "that I sound mighty anti-American. To these, I say: 'Don't blame *me* for *that*! Blame those who mouthed my liberal values and broke my American heart.'"

An antiwar demonstrator offers a flower to Military Police stationed outside the Pentagon at a 1967 rally against the Vietnam War. Some 100,000 protesters took part in this demonstration.

The speech, observed one reporter, marked a "declaration of independence" for the New Left.

By 1967, young men were burning their draft cards or fleeing to Canada to avoid fighting in what they considered an unjust war. In October of that year, 100,000 antiwar protesters assembled at the Lincoln Memorial in Washington, D.C. Many marched across the Potomac River to the Pentagon, where photographers captured them placing flowers in the rifle barrels of soldiers guarding the nerve center of the American military.

THE COUNTERCULTURE

The New Left's definition of freedom initially centered on participatory democracy, a political concept. But as the 1960s progressed, young Americans' understanding of freedom increasingly expanded to include cultural freedom as well. Although many streams flowed into the generational rebellion known as the "counterculture," the youth revolt was inconceivable without the war's destruction of young Americans' belief in authority. By the late 1960s, millions of young people openly rejected the values and behavior of their elders. Their ranks included not only college students but also numerous young workers, even though most unions strongly opposed antiwar demonstrations and countercultural displays (a reaction that further separated young radicals from former allies on the traditional left). For the first time in American history, the flamboyant rejection of respectable norms in clothing, language, sexual behavior, and drug use, previously confined to artists and bohemians, became the basis of a mass movement. Its rallying cry was "liberation."

Here was John Winthrop's nightmare of three centuries earlier come to pass—a massive redefinition of freedom as a rejection of all authority. "Your sons and your daughters are beyond your command," Bob Dylan's song "The Times They Are A-Changin'" bluntly informed mainstream America. To be sure, the counterculture in some ways represented not rebellion but the fulfillment of the consumer marketplace. It extended into every realm of life the definition of freedom as the right to individual choice. Given the purchasing power of students and young adults, countercultural emblems—colorful clothing, rock music, images of sexual freedom, even symbols of black revolution and Native American resistance—were soon being mass-marketed as fashions of the day. Self-indulgence and self-destructive behavior were built into the counterculture. To followers of Timothy Leary, the Harvard scientist turned prophet of mind-expansion, the psychedelic drug LSD embodied a new freedom—"the freedom to expand your own consciousness." In 1967, Leary organized a Human Be-In in San Francisco, where he urged a crowd of 20,000 to "turn on, tune in, drop out."

PERSONAL LIBERATION AND THE FREE INDIVIDUAL

But there was far more to the counterculture than new consumer styles or the famed trio of sex, drugs, and rock and roll. To young dissenters, personal liberation represented a spirit of creative experimentation, a search for a way of life in which friendship and pleasure eclipsed the single-minded pursuit of wealth. It meant a release from bureaucratized education and work, repressive rules of personal behavior, and, above all, a militarized state that, in the name of freedom, rained destruction on a faraway people. It also encouraged new forms of radical action. "Underground" newspapers pioneered a personal and politically committed style of journalism. The Youth International Party, or "yippies," introduced humor and theatricality as elements of protest. From the visitor's gallery of the New York Stock Exchange, yippie founder Abbie

Hoffman showered dollar bills onto the floor, bringing trading to a halt as brokers scrambled to retrieve the money.

The counterculture emphasized the ideal of community, establishing quasi-independent neighborhoods in New York City's East Village and San Francisco's Haight-Ashbury district and, in an echo of nineteenth-century utopian communities like New Harmony, some 2,000 communes nationwide. Rock festivals, like Woodstock in upstate New York in 1969, brought together hundreds of thousands of young people to celebrate their alternative lifestyle and independence from adult authority. The opening song at Woodstock, performed by Richie Havens, began with eight repetitions of the single word "freedom."

FAITH AND THE COUNTERCULTURE

Religious conviction, as has been noted, helped to inspire the civil rights movement. A different religious development, the sweeping reforms initiated in Roman Catholic practice (such as the delivery of the Mass in local languages, not Latin) by the Second Vatican Council of 1962–65, led many priests, nuns, and lay Catholics to become involved in social justice movements. This produced a growing split in the church between liberals and conservatives. "Liberation theology," a movement that swept across parts of Latin America in which priests helped to mobilize rural peasants to combat economic inequality, also reverberated among some Catholics in the United States. Many members of the New Left were motivated by a quest for a new sense of brotherhood and social responsibility, which often sprang from Christian roots. Like adherents of the Social Gospel of the late nineteenth century, many young people came to see a commitment to social change as a fulfillment of Christian values.

The quest for personal authenticity, a feature of the counterculture, led to a flowering of religious and spiritual creativity and experimentation. The Jesus People (called by their detractors Jesus Freaks) saw the hippy lifestyle, with its long hair, unconventional attire, and quest for universal love, as an authentic expression of the outlook of the early church. Like nineteenth-century forebears, Jesus People created Christian communes; they also held religiously oriented rock concerts. The Sixties also witnessed a burgeoning interest in eastern religions. The Beats of the 1950s had been attracted to Buddhism as a religion that rejected violence and materialism—the antithesis of what they saw as key features of American society. Now, practices derived from Hinduism like yoga and meditation became popular with members of the counterculture and even in the suburban mainstream as a way of promoting spiritual and physical well-being. Some Americans traveled to Tibet and India to seek spiritual guidance from "gurus" (religious teachers) there.

More sinister was the emergence of religious cults based on single-minded devotion to a charismatic leader. The one with the most tragic outcome was the People's Temple, founded by Jim Jones, whose religious outlook combined intense spiritual commitment with strong criticism of racism. He attracted a racially mixed community of devout followers, whom he led from Indianapolis to San Francisco and finally to Guyana. There, in 1978 over 900 men, women, and children perished in a mass suicide/murder ordered by Jones.

THE NEW MOVEMENTS AND THE RIGHTS REVOLUTION

The civil rights revolution, soon followed by the rise of the New Left, inspired other Americans to voice their grievances and claim their rights. Many borrowed the confrontational tactics of the black movement and activist students, adopting their language of "power" and "liberation" and their rejection of traditional organizations and approaches. By the late 1960s, new social movements dotted the political landscape.

The counterculture's notion of liberation centered on the free individual. Nowhere was this more evident than in the place occupied by sexual freedom in the generational rebellion. Starting in 1960, the mass marketing of birth-control pills made possible what "free lovers" had long demanded—the separation of sex from procreation. By the late 1960s, sexual freedom had become as much an element of the youth rebellion as long hair and drugs. Rock music celebrated the free expression of sexuality. The musical *Hair*, which gave voice to the youth rebellion, flaunted nudity on Broadway. The sexual revolution was central to another mass movement that emerged in the 1960s—the "second wave" of feminism.

THE FEMININE MYSTIQUE

The achievement of the vote had not seemed to affect women's lack of power and opportunity. When the 1960s began, only a handful of women held political office, newspapers divided job ads into "male" and "female" sections, with the latter limited to low-wage clerical positions, and major universities limited the number of female students they accepted. In many states, husbands still controlled their wives' earnings. As late as 1970, the Ohio Supreme Court held that a wife was "at most a superior servant to her husband," without "legally recognized feelings or rights."

During the 1950s, some commentators had worried that the country was wasting its "woman power," a potential weapon in the Cold War. But the public reawakening of feminist consciousness did not get its start until the publication in 1963 of Betty Friedan's *The Feminine Mystique*. Friedan had written pioneering articles during the 1940s on pay discrimination against women workers and racism in the workplace for the newspaper of the United Electrical Workers' union. But, like other social critics of the 1950s, she now

In 1967, in a celebrated incident arising from the new feminism, a race official tried to eject Kathrine Switzer from the Boston Marathon, only to be pushed aside by other runners. Considered too fragile for the marathon (whose course covers more than twenty-six miles), women were prohibited from running. Switzer completed the race and today hundreds of thousands of women around the world compete in marathons each year.

took as her themes the emptiness of consumer culture and the discontents of the middle class. Her opening chapter, "The Problem That Has No Name," painted a devastating picture of talented, educated women trapped in a world that viewed marriage and motherhood as their primary goals. Somehow, after more than a century of agitation for access to the public sphere, women's lives still centered on the home. In Moscow in 1959, Richard Nixon had made the suburban home an emblem of American freedom. For Friedan, invoking the era's most powerful symbol of evil, it was a "comfortable concentration camp."

Few books have had the impact of *The Feminine Mystique*. Friedan was deluged by desperate letters from female readers relating how the suburban dream had become a nightmare. "Freedom," wrote an Atlanta woman, "was a word I had always taken for granted. [I now realized that] I had voluntarily enslaved myself." To be sure, a few of Friedan's correspondents insisted that for a woman to create "a comfortable, happy home for her family" was "what God intended." But the immediate result of *The Feminine Mystique* was to focus attention on yet another gap between American rhetoric and American reality.

The law slowly began to address feminist concerns. In 1963, Congress passed the Equal Pay Act, barring sex discrimination among holders of the same jobs. The Civil Rights Act of 1964, as noted earlier, prohibited inequalities based on sex as well as race. Deluged with complaints of discrimination by working women, the Equal Employment Opportunity Commission established by the law became a major force in breaking down barriers to female employment. The year 1966 saw the formation of the National Organization for Women (NOW), with Friedan as president. Modeled on civil rights organizations, it demanded equal opportunity in jobs, education, and political participation and attacked the "false image of women" spread by the mass media.

WOMEN'S LIBERATION

If NOW grew out of a resurgence of middle-class feminism, a different female revolt was brewing within the civil rights and student movements. As in the days of abolitionism, young women who had embraced an ideology of social equality and personal freedom and learned methods of political organizing encountered inequality and sexual exploitation. Women like Ella Baker and Fannie Lou Hamer had played major roles in grassroots civil rights organizing. But many women in the movement found themselves relegated to typing, cooking, and cleaning for male coworkers. Some were pressured to engage in sexual liaisons. Echoing the words of Abby Kelley a century earlier, a group of female SNCC activists concluded in a 1965 memorandum that "there seem to be many parallels that can be drawn between the treatment of Negroes and the treatment of women in our society as a whole." What bothered them most was the status of women within the movement, where assumptions of male supremacy seemed as deeply rooted as in society at large.

The same complaints arose in SDS. "The Movement is supposed to be for human liberation," wrote one student leader. "How come the condition of women inside it is no better than outside?" The rapidly growing number of women in college provided a ready-made constituency for the new feminism. By 1967, women throughout the country were establishing "consciousness-raising" groups to discuss the sources of their discontent. The time, many concluded, had come to establish a movement of their own, more radical than NOW. The new feminism burst onto the national scene at the Miss America beauty pageant of 1968, when protesters filled a "freedom trash can" with objects of "oppression"—girdles, brassieres, high-heeled shoes, and copies of *Playboy* and *Cosmopolitan*. (Contrary to legend, they did not set the contents on fire, which would have been highly dangerous on the wooden boardwalk. But the media quickly invented a new label for radical women—"bra burners.") Inside the hall, demonstrators unfurled banners carrying the slogans "Freedom for Women" and "Women's Liberation."

PERSONAL FREEDOM

The women's liberation movement inspired a major expansion of the idea of freedom by insisting that it should be applied to the most intimate realms of life. Introducing the terms "sexism" and "sexual politics" and the phrase "the personal is political" into public debate, they insisted that sexual relations, conditions of marriage, and standards of beauty were as much "political" questions as the war, civil rights, and the class tensions that had traditionally inspired the left to action. The idea that family life is not off-limits to considerations of power and justice repudiated the family-oriented public culture of the 1950s, and it permanently changed Americans' definition of freedom.

Radical feminists' first public campaign demanded the repeal of state laws that underscored women's lack of self-determination by banning abortions or leaving it up to physicians to decide whether a pregnancy could be terminated. Without the right to control her own reproduction, wrote one activist, "woman's other 'freedoms' are tantalizing mockeries that cannot be exercised." In 1969, a group of feminists disrupted legislative hearings on New York's law banning abortions, where the experts scheduled to testify consisted of fourteen men and a Roman Catholic nun.

The call for legalized abortions merged the nineteenth-century demand that a woman control her own body with the Sixties emphasis on sexual freedom. But the concerns of women's liberation went far beyond sexuality. *Sisterhood Is Powerful*, an influential collection of essays, manifestos, and personal accounts published in 1970, touched on a remarkable array of issues, from violence against women to inequalities in the law, churches, workplaces, and family life. By this time, feminist ideas had entered the mainstream. In 1962, a poll showed that two-thirds of American women did not feel themselves to be victims of discrimination. By 1974, two-thirds did.

GAY LIBERATION

In a decade full of surprises, perhaps the greatest of all was the emergence of the movement for gay liberation. Efforts of one kind or another for greater rights for racial minorities and women had a long history. Homosexuals, wrote Harry Hay, who in 1951 founded the Mattachine Society, the first gay rights organization, were "the one group of disadvantaged people who didn't even think of themselves as a group." Gay men and lesbians had long been stigmatized as sinful or mentally disordered. Most states made homosexual acts illegal, and police regularly harassed the gay subcultures that existed in major cities like San Francisco and New York. McCarthyism, which viewed homosexuality as a source of national weakness, made the discrimination to which gays were subjected even worse. Although homosexuals had achieved considerable success in the arts and fashion, most kept their sexual orientation secret, or "in the closet."

The Mattachine Society had worked to persuade the public that apart from their sexual orientation, gays were average Americans who ought not to be persecuted. But as with other groups, the Sixties transformed the gay movement. If one moment marked the advent of "gay liberation," it was a 1969 police raid on the Stonewall Bar in New York's Greenwich Village, a gathering place for homosexuals. Rather than bowing to police harassment, as in the past, gays fought back. Five days of rioting followed, and a militant movement was born. Gay men and lesbians stepped out of the "closet" to insist that sexual orientation is a matter of rights, power, and identity. Prejudice against homosexuals persisted. But within a few years, "gay pride" marches were being held in numerous cities.

LATINO ACTIVISM

As in the case of blacks, a movement for legal rights had long flourished among Mexican-Americans. But the mid-1960s saw the flowering of a new militancy challenging the group's second-class economic status. Like Black Power advocates, the movement emphasized pride in both the Mexican past and the new Chicano culture that had arisen in the United States. Unlike the Black Power movement and SDS, it was closely linked to labor struggles. Beginning in 1965, César Chavez, the son of migrant farm workers and a disciple of King, led a series of nonviolent protests, including marches, fasts, and a national boycott of California grapes, to pressure growers to agree to labor contracts with the United Farm Workers union (UFW). The UFW was as much a mass movement for civil rights as a campaign for economic betterment. The boycott mobilized Latino communities throughout the Southwest and drew national attention to the pitifully low wages and oppressive working conditions of migrant laborers. In 1970, the major growers agreed to contracts with the UFW.

In New York City, the Young Lords Organization, modeled on the Black Panthers, staged street demonstrations to protest the high unemployment rate among the city's Puerto Ricans and the lack of city services in Latino neighborhoods. (In one protest, they dumped garbage on city streets to draw attention to the city's failure to collect refuse in poor areas.) Like SNCC and SDS, the Latino movement gave rise to feminist dissent. Many Chicano and

Puerto Rican men regarded feminist demands as incompatible with the Latino heritage of *machismo* (an exaggerated sense of manliness, including the right to dominate women). Young female activists, however, viewed the sexual double standard and the inequality of women as incompatible with freedom for all members of *la raza* (the race, or people).

RED POWER

The 1960s also witnessed an upsurge of Indian militancy. The Truman and Eisenhower administrations had sought to dismantle the reservation system and integrate Indians into the American mainstream—a policy known as "termination," since it meant ending recognition of the remaining elements of Indian sovereignty. Many Indian leaders protested vigorously against this policy, and it was abandoned by President Kennedy. Johnson's War on Poverty channeled increased federal funds to reservations. But like other minority groups, Indian activists compared their own status to that of underdeveloped countries overseas. They demanded not simply economic aid but self-determination, like the emerging nations of the Third World. Using language typical of the late 1960s, Clyde Warrior, president of the National Indian Youth Council, declared, "We are not free in the most basic sense of the word. We are not allowed to make those basic human choices about our personal life and the destiny of our communities."

Founded in 1968, the American Indian movement staged protests demanding greater tribal self-government and the restoration of economic resources guaranteed in treaties. In 1969, a group calling itself "Indians of All Nations" occupied (or from their point of view, re-occupied) Alcatraz Island in San Francisco Bay, claiming that it had been illegally seized from its original inhabitants. The protest, which lasted into 1971, launched the Red Power movement. In the years that followed, many Indian tribes would win greater control over education and economic development on the reservations. Indian activists would bring land claims suits, demanding and receiving monetary settlements for past dispossession. As a result of a rising sense of self-respect, the number of Americans identifying themselves as Indians doubled between 1970 and 1990.

SILENT SPRING

Liberation movements among racial minorities, women, and gays challenged long-standing social inequalities. Another movement, environmentalism, called into question different pillars of American life—the equation of progress with endless increases in consumption and the faith that science, technology, and economic growth would advance the social welfare. Concern for preserving the natural environment dated back to the creation of national parks and other conservation efforts during the Progressive era. But in keeping with the spirit of the Sixties, the new environmentalism was more activist and youth-oriented, and it spoke the language of empowering citizens to participate in decisions that affected their lives. Its emergence reflected the very affluence celebrated by proponents of the American Way. As the "quality of life"—including physical fitness, health, and opportunities to enjoy leisure activities—occupied a greater role in the lives of middle-class Americans, the environmental consequences of economic growth received increased attention. When the 1960s began, complaints were already being heard about the bulldozing of forests for suburban development and the contamination produced by laundry detergents and chemical lawn fertilizers seeping into drinking supplies.

The publication in 1962 of *Silent Spring* by the marine biologist Rachel Carson brought home to millions of readers the effects of DDT, an insecticide widely used by home owners and farmers against mosquitoes, gypsy moths, and other insects. In chilling detail, Carson related how DDT killed birds and animals and caused sickness among humans. Chemical and pesticide companies launched a campaign to discredit her—some critics called the book part of a communist plot. *Time* magazine even condemned Carson as "hysterical" and "emotional"—words typically used by men to discredit women.

THE NEW ENVIRONMENTALISM

Carson's work launched the modern environmental movement. The Sierra Club, founded in the 1890s to preserve forests, saw its membership more than triple, and other groups sprang into existence to alert the country to the dangers of water contamination, air pollution, lead in paint, and the extinction of animal species. Nearly every state quickly banned the use of DDT. In 1969, television brought home to a national audience the death of birds and fish and the despoiling of beaches caused by a major oil spill off the coast of California, exposing the environmental dangers of oil transportation and ocean drilling for oil.

The postwar economic boom, with its seemingly limitless demand for resources like land, energy, and building materials, placed enormous stress on the natural environment. As highways and suburbs paved over the landscape, more and more Americans became committed to the survival of places of natural beauty.

Despite vigorous opposition from business groups that considered its proposals a violation of property rights, environmentalism attracted the broadest bipartisan support of any of the new social movements. Under Republican president Richard Nixon, Congress during the late 1960s and early 1970s passed a series of measures to protect the environment, including the Clean

Air and Clean Water Acts and the Endangered Species Act. On April 22, 1970, the first Earth Day, some 20 million people, most of them under the age of thirty, participated in rallies, concerts, and teach-ins.

Closely related to environmentalism was the consumer movement, spearheaded by the lawyer Ralph Nader. His book *Unsafe at Any Speed* (1965) exposed how auto manufacturers produced highly dangerous vehicles. General Motors, whose Chevrolet Corvair Nader singled out for its tendency to roll over in certain driving situations, hired private investigators to discredit him. When their campaign was exposed, General Motors paid Nader a handsome settlement, which he used to fund investigations of other dangerous products and of misleading advertising.

Nader's campaigns laid the groundwork for the numerous new consumer protection laws and regulations of the 1970s. Unlike 1960s movements that emphasized personal liberation, environmentalism and the consumer movement called for limiting some kinds of freedom—especially the right to use private property in any way the owner desired—in the name of a greater common good.

THE RIGHTS REVOLUTION

It is one of the more striking ironies of the 1960s that although the "rights revolution" began in the streets, it achieved constitutional legitimacy through the Supreme Court, historically the most conservative branch of government. Under the guidance of Chief Justice Earl Warren, the Court vastly expanded the rights enjoyed by all Americans and placed them beyond the reach of legislative and local majorities.

The Court's emergence as a vigorous guardian of civil liberties had been foreshadowed in 1937, when it abandoned its commitment to freedom of contract while declaring that the right of free expression deserved added protection. The McCarthy era halted progress toward a broader conception of civil liberties. It resumed on June 17, 1957, known as "Red Monday" by conservatives, when the Court moved to rein in the anticommunist crusade. The justices overturned convictions of individuals for advocating the overthrow of the government, failing to answer questions before the House Un-American Activities Committee, and refusing to disclose their political beliefs to state officials. The government, Warren declared, could prosecute illegal actions, but not "unorthodoxy or dissent." By the time Warren retired in 1969, the Court had reaffirmed the right of even the most unpopular viewpoints to First Amendment protection and had dismantled the Cold War loyalty security system.

Civil liberties had gained strength in the 1930s because of association with the rights of labor; in the 1950s and 1960s, they became intertwined with civil rights. Beginning with *NAACP v. Alabama* in 1958, the Court struck down southern laws that sought to destroy civil rights organizations by forcing them to make public their membership lists. In addition, in the landmark ruling in *New York Times v. -Sullivan* (1964), it overturned a libel judgment by an Alabama jury against the nation's leading newspaper for carrying an advertisement critical of how local officials treated civil rights demonstrators. The "central meaning of the First Amendment," the justices declared, lay in the right of citizens to criticize their government. For good measure, they declared the Sedition Act of 1798 unconstitutional over a century and a half after it had expired. Before the 1960s, few Supreme Court cases had dealt with newspaper publishing. *Sullivan* created the modern constitutional law of freedom of the press.

The Court in the 1960s continued the push toward racial equality, overturning numerous local Jim Crow laws. In *Loving v. Virginia* (1967), it declared unconstitutional the laws still on the books in sixteen states that prohibited interracial marriage. This aptly named case arose from the interracial marriage of Richard and Mildred Loving. Barred by Virginia law from marrying, they did so in Washington, D.C., and later returned to their home state. Two weeks after their arrival, the local sheriff entered their home in the middle of the night, roused the couple from bed, and arrested them. The Lovings were

Richard and Mildred Loving with their children in a 1965 photograph by Grey Villet. Their desire to live in Virginia as man and wife led to a Supreme Court decision declaring unconstitutional state laws that barred interracial marriages.

sentenced to five years in prison, although the judge gave them the option of leaving Virginia instead. They departed for Washington, but five years later, wishing to return, they sued in federal court, claiming that their rights had been violated. In 1968, in *Jones v. Alfred H. Mayer Co.*, the Court forbade discrimination in the rental or sale of housing. Eliminating "badges of slavery," such as unequal access to housing, the ruling suggested, was essential to fulfilling at long last the promise of emancipation.

POLICING THE STATES

The Court simultaneously pushed forward the process of imposing upon the states the obligation to respect the liberties outlined in the Bill of Rights. It required states to abide by protections against illegal search and seizure, the right of a defendant to a speedy trial, the prohibition against cruel and unusual punishment, and the right of poor persons accused of a crime to receive counsel from publicly supplied attorneys. Among the most important of these decisions was the 5-4 ruling in *Miranda v. Arizona* (1966). This held that an individual in police custody must be informed of the rights to remain silent and to confer with a lawyer before answering questions and must be told that any statements might be used in court. The decision made "Miranda warnings" standard police practice.

The Court also assumed the power to oversee the fairness of democratic procedures at the state and local levels. *Baker v. Carr* (1962) established the principle that districts electing members of state legislatures must be equal in population. This "one-man, one-vote" principle overturned apportionment systems in numerous states that had allowed individuals in sparsely inhabited rural areas to enjoy the same representation as residents of populous city districts.

The cartoonist Herblock's comment on critics of the Supreme Court's decision barring prayer in public schools.

The justices also moved to reinforce the "wall of separation" between church and state. In 1961, they unanimously declared unconstitutional a clause in Maryland's constitution requiring that public officials declare their belief "in the existence of God." In the following year, in *Engel v. Vitale*, they decreed that prayers and Bible readings in public schools also violated the First Amendment. President Kennedy pointed out that

Americans remained perfectly free to pray at home or in church, but these rulings proved to be the most unpopular of all the Warren Court's decisions. Polls showed that 80 percent of Americans favored allowing prayer in public schools.

THE RIGHT TO PRIVACY

The Warren Court not only expanded existing liberties but also outlined entirely new rights in response to the rapidly changing contours of American society. Most dramatic was its assertion of a constitutional right to privacy in *Griswold v. Connecticut* (1965), which overturned a state law prohibiting the use of contraceptives. Justice William O. Douglas, who wrote the decision, had once declared, "The right to be let alone is the beginning of all freedom." Apart from decisions of the 1920s that affirmed the right to marry and raise children without government interference, however, few legal precedents existed regarding privacy. The Constitution does not mention the word. Nonetheless, Douglas argued that a constitutionally protected "zone of privacy" within marriage could be inferred from the "penumbras" (shadows) of the Bill of Rights.

Griswold linked privacy to the sanctity of marriage. But the Court soon transformed it into a right of individuals. It extended access to birth control to unmarried adults and ultimately to minors—an admission by the Court that law could not reverse the sexual revolution. These decisions led directly to the most controversial decision that built on the rulings of the Warren Court (even though it occurred in 1973, four years after Warren's retirement). This was *Roe v. Wade*, which created a constitutional right to terminate a pregnancy. The Court declared access to abortion a fundamental freedom protected by the Constitution, a fulfillment of radical feminists' earliest demand. *Roe* provoked vigorous opposition, which has continued to this day. Only two states banned contraception when *Griswold* was decided; *Roe* invalidated the laws of no fewer than forty-six.

Griswold and *Roe* unleashed a flood of rulings and laws that seemed to accept the feminist view of the family as a collection of sovereign individuals rather than a unit with a single head. The legal rights of women within the domestic sphere expanded dramatically. Law enforcement authorities for the first time began to prosecute crimes like rape and assault by husbands against their wives. Today, some notion of privacy is central to most Americans' conception of freedom.

The rights revolution completed the transformation of American freedom from a set of entitlements enjoyed mainly by white men into an open-ended claim to equality, recognition, and self-determination. For the rest of the century, the government and legal system would be inundated by demands by aggrieved groups of all kinds, and the Supreme Court would devote much of its time to defining the rights of Americans.

1968

A YEAR OF TURMOIL

The Sixties reached their climax in 1968, a year when momentous events succeeded each other so rapidly that the foundations of society seemed to be dissolving. Late January 1968 saw the Tet offensive, in which Viet Cong and North Vietnamese troops launched well-organized uprisings in cities throughout South Vietnam, completely surprising American military leaders. The United States drove back the offensive and inflicted heavy losses. But the intensity of the fighting, brought into America's homes on television, shattered public confidence in the Johnson administration, which had repeatedly proclaimed victory to be "just around the corner." Leading members of the press and political establishment joined the chorus criticizing American involvement. Eugene McCarthy, an antiwar senator from Minnesota, announced that he would seek the Democratic nomination. In March, aided by a small army of student volunteers, McCarthy received more than 40 percent of the vote in the New Hampshire primary. With public support dissolving, Johnson rejected the military's request to send 200,000 more troops to Vietnam. In March, he stunned the nation by announcing that he had decided not to seek reelection. Peace talks soon opened in Paris.

Meanwhile, Martin Luther King Jr. was organizing a Poor People's March, hoping to bring thousands of demonstrators to Washington to demand increased anti-poverty efforts. On April 4, having traveled to Memphis to support a strike of the city's grossly underpaid black garbage collectors, King was killed by a white assassin. The greatest outbreak of urban violence in the nation's history followed in ghettos across the country. Washington, D.C., had to be occupied by soldiers before order was restored. As a gesture to King's memory, Congress passed its last major civil rights law, the Open Housing Act, which prohibited discrimination in the sale and rental of homes and apartments, although with weak enforcement mechanisms.

At the end of April, students protesting Columbia University's involvement in defense research and its plan to build a gymnasium in a public park occupied seven campus buildings. New York police removed them in an assault that left hundreds of protesters and bystanders injured and led to a strike that closed the campus. In June, a young Palestinian nationalist assassinated Robert F. Kennedy, who was seeking the Democratic nomination as an opponent of the war. In August, tens of thousands of antiwar activists descended on Chicago for protests at the Democratic national convention, where the delegates nominated Vice President Hubert Humphrey as their presidential candidate. The city's police, never known for restraint, assaulted the marchers with nightsticks, producing hundreds of injuries outside the convention hall and pandemonium inside it.

A later investigation called the event a "police riot." Nonetheless, the government indicted eight political radicals for conspiring to incite the violence. They included Tom Hayden of SDS, yippie leader Abbie Hoffman, and Bobby Seale of the Black Panthers. Five were found guilty after a tumultuous trial. But an appeals court overturned the convictions because Judge Julius Hoffman (no relation to Abbie Hoffman) had been flagrantly biased against the defendants.

THE GLOBAL 1968

Like 1848 and 1919, 1968 was a year of worldwide upheaval. In many countries, young radicals challenged existing power structures, often borrowing language and strategies from the decade's social movements in the United States and adapting them to their own circumstances. Television carried events in one country instantaneously across the globe.

Massive antiwar demonstrations took place in London, Rome, Paris, Munich, and Tokyo, leading to clashes with police and scores of injuries. In Italy, students occupied university buildings, bringing education to a halt. In Paris, a nationwide student uprising began in May 1968 that echoed American demands for educational reform and personal liberation. Unlike in the United States, millions of French workers soon joined the protest, adding their own demands for higher wages and greater democracy in the workplace. The result was a general strike that paralyzed the country and nearly led to the collapse of the government before it ended. In communist Czechoslovakia, leaders bent on reform came to power by promising to institute "socialism with a human face," only to be ousted by a Soviet invasion. Soldiers fired on students demonstrating for greater democracy on the eve of the opening of the Olympic Games in Mexico City, leading to more than 500 deaths. In Northern Ireland, which remained part of Great Britain after the rest of Ireland achieved independence, the police attacked a peaceful march of Catholics demanding an end to religious discrimination who were inspired by the American civil rights movement. This event marked the beginning of The Troubles, a period of both peaceful protest and violent conflict in the region that did not end until the turn of the twenty-first century.

And throughout the world, the second wave of American feminism found echoes among women who resented being relegated to unequal citizenship. American women influenced, and were influenced by, movements in other countries, particularly in Europe, which demanded equal rights and challenged demeaning representations of women in advertising and the mass media. As in the United States, personal liberation, including a woman's right to control her own body, became a rallying cry. In Catholic European countries like France and Italy, women's movements won significant legal changes, making it easier to obtain divorces and decriminalizing abortion. *Our Bodies, Ourselves*, a book originally published in 1973 by a group of Boston women, dealt frankly with widely misunderstood aspects of women's health, including pregnancy and childbirth, menopause, birth control, and sexually transmitted diseases. It was quickly translated into twenty languages.

NIXON'S COMEBACK

In the United States, instead of radical change, the year's events opened the door for a conservative reaction. Turmoil in the streets produced a demand for public order. Black militancy produced white "backlash," which played an increasing role in politics. The fact that the unelected Supreme Court was inventing and protecting "rights" fed the argument that faraway bureaucrats rode roughshod over local traditions.

In August, Richard Nixon capped a remarkable political comeback by winning the Republican nomination. He campaigned as the champion of the "silent majority"—ordinary Americans who believed that change had gone too far—and called for a renewed commitment to "law and order." Humphrey could not overcome the deep divide in his party. With 43 percent of the vote, Nixon had only a razor-thin margin over his Democratic rival. But George Wallace, running as an independent and appealing to resentments against blacks' gains, Great Society programs, and the Warren Court, received an additional 13 percent. Taken together, the Nixon and Wallace totals, which included a considerable number of former Democratic voters, indicated that four years after Johnson's landslide election ushered in the Great Society, liberalism was on the defensive.

The year 1968 did not mark the end of the 1960s. The Great Society would achieve an unlikely culmination during the Nixon administration. The second wave of feminism achieved its largest following during the 1970s. Nixon's election did, however, inaugurate a period of growing conservatism in American politics. The conservative ascendancy would usher in yet another chapter in the story of American freedom.

THE LEGACY OF THE SIXTIES

The 1960s transformed American life in ways unimaginable when the decade began. It produced new rights and new understandings of freedom. It made possible the entrance of numerous members of racial minorities into the mainstream of American life, while leaving unsolved the problem of urban poverty. It set in motion a transformation of the status of women. It changed what Americans expected from government—from clean air and water to medical coverage in old age. At the same time, it undermined public confidence in national leaders. Relations between young and old, men and women, and white and non-white, along with every institution in society, changed as a result.

Just as the Civil War and New Deal established the framework for future political debates, so, it seemed, Americans were condemned to refight the battles of the 1960s long after the decade had ended. Race relations, feminism, social policy, the nation's proper role in world affairs—these issues hardly originated in the 1960s. But the events of those years made them more pressing and more divisive. As the country became more conservative, the Sixties would be blamed for every imaginable social ill, from crime and drug abuse to a decline of respect for authority. Yet during the 1960s, the United States had become a more open, more tolerant—in a word, a freer—country.

Chapter Review

REVIEW QUESTIONS

1. How did the idea of a "zone of privacy" build on or change earlier notions of rights and freedom?
2. In what ways were President Kennedy's foreign policy decisions shaped by Cold War ideology?
3. How did immigration policies change in these years, and what were the consequences for the composition of the population in the United States?
4. Explain why many blacks, especially in the North, did not believe that the civil rights legislation went far enough in promoting black freedom.
5. What were the effects of President Johnson's Great Society and War on Poverty programs?
6. In what ways was the New Left not as new as it claimed?
7. How did the goals and actions of the United States in Vietnam cause controversy at home and abroad?

8. Discuss the impact of the Civil Rights movement on other movements for social change in the 1960s.
9. Identify the origins, goals, and composition of the feminist, or women's liberation, movement.
10. Describe how the social movement of the 1960s in the United States become part of global movements for change by 1968. How did those connections affect the United States' position in the world?
11. How did the counterculture expand the meaning of freedom in these years?

KEY TERMS

Student Non-Violent Coordinating Committee
Freedom Rides
March on Washington
Bay of Pigs
Berlin Wall
Cuban missile crisis
Civil Rights Act
Voting Rights Act
Hart-Celler Act
Great Society
War on Poverty
Black Power
Port Huron Statement
Gulf of Tonkin resolution
counterculture
The Feminine Mystique
National Organization for Women
Stonewall Inn
American Indian movement
Silent Spring
"zone of privacy"

wwnorton.com/studyspace

VISIT STUDYSPACE FOR THESE RESOURCES AND MORE:

- Author Videos
- A chapter outline
- A practice quiz
- Interactive maps
- Multimedia documents

CHAPTER 11

THE TRIUMPH OF CONSERVATISM

From *Give Me Liberty! Seagull Fourth Edition*

Eric Foner

Credits: photo 1: May 4 Collection. Kent State University Libraries, Special Collections and Archives; photo 2: © 1982 Doug Marlette; photo 3: © Mary Ellen Mark; photo 4: AP Photo.

Table 1: U.S. Bureau of the Census, *Statistical Abstract of the United States* (Washington D.C., 1982).

Redstockings of the Women's Liberation Movement: The Redstockings Manifesto was issued in New York City on July 7, 1969. It first appeared as a mimeographed flyer, designed for distribution at women's liberation events. Further information about the Manifesto and other materials from the 1960s rebirth years of feminism is available from the Redstockings Women's Liberation Archives for Action at www.redstockings.org. Reprinted with permission.

Jerry Falwell: From *Listen, America!* by Jerry Falwell, copyright © 1980 by Jerry Falwell. Used by permission of Doubleday, a division of Random House, Inc. * For on-line information about other Random House, Inc. books and authors, see the Internet web site at http://www.randomhouse.com.

11

The Triumph of Conservatism 1969–1988

FOCUS QUESTIONS

- What were the major policies of the Nixon administration on social and economic issues?
- How did Vietnam and the Watergate scandal affect popular trust in the government?
- In what ways did the opportunities of most Americans diminish in the 1970s?
- What were the roots of the rise of conservatism in the 1970s?
- How did the Reagan presidency affect Americans both at home and abroad?

Beginning with the dramatic 1960 contest between John F. Kennedy and Richard M. Nixon, the journalist Theodore White published best-selling accounts of four successive races for the presidency. Covering the 1964 election, White attended civil rights demonstrations and rallies for Barry Goldwater, the Republican nominee. White noticed something that struck him as odd: "The dominant word of these two groups, which loathe each other, is 'freedom.' Both demand either Freedom Now or Freedom for All. The word has such emotive power behind it that . . . a reporter is instantly denounced for questioning what they mean by the word 'freedom.' " The

United States, White concluded, sorely needed "a commonly agreed-on concept of freedom."

White had observed firsthand the struggle over the meaning of freedom set in motion by the 1960s, as well as the revival of conservatism in the midst of an era known for radicalism. Goldwater's campaign helped to crystallize and popularize ideas that would remain the bedrock of conservatism for years to come. To intense anticommunism, Goldwater added a critique of the welfare state for destroying "the dignity of the individual." He demanded a reduction in taxes and governmental regulations. Goldwater showed that with liberals in control in Washington, conservatives could claim for themselves the tradition of antigovernment populism, thus broadening their electoral base and countering their image as upper-crust elitists.

The second half of the 1960s and the 1970s would witness pivotal developments that reshaped American politics—the breakup of the political coalition forged by Franklin D. Roosevelt; an economic crisis that traditional liberal remedies seemed unable to solve; a shift of population and economic resources to conservative strongholds in the Sunbelt of the South and West; the growth of an activist, conservative Christianity increasingly aligned with the Republican Party; and a series of setbacks for the United States overseas. Together, they led to growing popularity for conservatives' ideas, including their understanding of freedom.

PRESIDENT NIXON

From the vantage point of the early twenty-first century, it is difficult to recall how marginal conservatism seemed at the end of World War II. Associated in many minds with conspiracy theories, anti-Semitism, and preference for social hierarchy over democracy and equality, conservatism seemed a relic of a discredited past. When conservative ideas did begin to spread, liberals explained them as a rejection of the modern world by the alienated or psychologically disturbed.

Nonetheless, the 1950s and 1960s witnessed a conservative rebirth. And in 1968, a "backlash" among formerly Democratic voters against both black assertiveness and antiwar demonstrations helped to propel Richard Nixon into the White House. But conservatives found Nixon no more to their liking than his predecessors. Nixon echoed conservative language, especially in his condemnation of student protesters and his calls for law and order, but in office he expanded the welfare state and moved to improve American relations with the Soviet Union and China. During his presidency, the social changes set in motion by the 1960s—seen by conservatives as forces of moral decay—continued apace.

NIXON'S DOMESTIC POLICIES

Having won the presidency by a very narrow margin, Nixon moved toward the political center on many issues. A shrewd politician, he worked to solidify his support among Republicans while reaching out to disaffected elements of the Democratic coalition. It is difficult to characterize Nixon's domestic agenda according to the traditional categories of liberal and conservative. Mostly interested in foreign policy, he had no desire to battle Congress, still under Democratic control, on domestic issues. Just as Eisenhower had helped to institutionalize the New Deal, Nixon accepted and even expanded many elements of the Great Society.

Conservatives applauded Nixon's New Federalism, which offered federal "block grants" to the states to spend as they saw fit, rather than for specific purposes dictated by Washington. On the other hand, the Nixon administration created a host of new federal agencies. The Environmental Protection Agency oversaw programs to combat

CHRONOLOGY

1968	Oil discovered in Alaska
	My Lai massacre
1970	U.S. invades Cambodia
1971	Pentagon Papers published
	U.S. goes off gold standard
1972	Nixon travels to the People's Republic of China
	Congress passes the ERA for ratification
	SALT is signed
	Congress approves Title IX
1973	Paris Peace Accords end U.S. involvement in Vietnam War
	CIA-aided Chilean coup
	War Powers Act
1974	Nixon resigns
1975	Collapse of South Vietnamese government
1976	Jimmy Carter elected
1978	*Regents of the University of California v. Bakke*
	Camp David Accords signed between Israel and Egypt
1979	Three Mile Island accident
	Sagebrush Rebellion
	Sixty-six Americans taken hostage in Iran
1980	Ronald Reagan elected
1981	Air traffic controllers' strike
1983	Strategic Defense Initiative
1985–1987	Iran-Contra affair
1986	*Bowers v. Hardwick*

water and air pollution, cleaned up hazardous wastes, and required "environmental impact" statements from any project that received federal funding. The Occupational Safety and Health Administration sent inspectors into the nation's workplaces. The National Transportation Safety Board instructed automobile makers on how to make their cars safer.

Nixon spent lavishly on social services and environmental initiatives. He abolished the Office of Economic Opportunity, which had coordinated Johnson's War on Poverty. But he signed congressional measures that expanded the food stamp program and indexed Social Security benefits to inflation—meaning that they would rise automatically as the cost of living increased. The Endangered Species Act prohibited spending federal funds on any project that might extinguish an animal species. The Clean Air Act set air quality standards for carbon monoxide and other chemicals released by cars and factories and led to a dramatic decline in air pollution.

NIXON AND WELFARE

Perhaps Nixon's most startling initiative was his proposal for a Family Assistance Plan, or "negative income tax," that would replace Aid to Families with Dependent Children (AFDC) by having the federal government guarantee a minimum income for all Americans. Universally known as "welfare," AFDC provided assistance, often quite limited, to poor families who met local eligibility requirements. Originally a New Deal program that mainly served the white poor, welfare had come to be associated with blacks, who by 1970 accounted for nearly half the recipients. The AFDC rolls expanded rapidly during the 1960s, partly because the federal government relaxed eligibility standards. This arose from an increase in births to unmarried women, which produced a sharp rise in the number of poor female-headed households, and from an aggressive campaign by welfare rights groups to encourage people to apply for benefits. Conservative politicians now attacked recipients of welfare as people who preferred to live at the expense of honest taxpayers rather than by working.

A striking example of Nixon's willingness to break the political mold, his plan to replace welfare with a guaranteed annual income failed to win approval by Congress. It proved too radical for conservatives, who saw it as a reward for laziness, while liberals denounced the proposed level of $1,600 per year for a needy family of four as inadequate.

NIXON AND RACE

Nixon's racial policies offer a similarly mixed picture. To consolidate support in the white South, he nominated to the Supreme Court Clement Haynsworth and G. Harold Carswell, conservative southern jurists with records of support for segregation. Both were rejected by the Senate. On the other hand, because the courts finally lost patience with southern delaying tactics, extensive racial integration at last came to public schools in the South. In Nixon's first three years in office, the proportion of southern black students attending integrated schools rose from 32 percent to 77 percent.

For a time, the Nixon administration also pursued "affirmative action" programs to upgrade minority employment. The Philadelphia Plan required that construction contractors on federal projects hire specific numbers of minority workers. Secretary of Labor George Shultz, who initiated the idea, sincerely hoped to open more jobs for black workers. Nixon seems to have viewed the plan mainly as a way of fighting inflation by weakening the power of the building trades unions. Their control over the labor market, he believed, pushed wages to unreasonably high levels, raising the cost of construction. And, he calculated, if the plan caused dissension between blacks and labor unions—two pillars of the Democratic coalition—Republicans could only benefit.

Trade unions of skilled workers like plumbers and electrical workers, which had virtually no black members, strongly opposed the Philadelphia Plan. After a widely publicized incident in May 1970, when a group of construction workers assaulted antiwar demonstrators in New York City, Nixon suddenly decided that he might be able to woo blue-collar workers in preparation for his 1972 reelection campaign. He soon abandoned the Philadelphia Plan in favor of an ineffective one that stressed voluntary local efforts toward minority hiring instead of federal requirements.

THE BURGER COURT

When Earl Warren retired as chief justice in 1969, Nixon appointed Warren Burger, a federal court-of-appeals judge, to succeed him. An outspoken critic of the "judicial activism" of the Warren Court—its willingness to expand old rights and create new ones by overturning acts of Congress and the states—Burger was expected to lead the justices in a conservative direction. But like Nixon, he surprised many of his supporters. While the pace of change slowed, the Burger Court, at least initially, consolidated and expanded many of the judicial innovations of the 1960s.

In 1971, in *Swann v. Charlotte-Mecklenburg Board of Education,* which arose from North Carolina, the justices unanimously approved a lower court's plan that required the extensive transportation of students to achieve school integration. The decision led to hundreds of cases in which judges throughout the country ordered the use of busing as a tool to achieve integration. With many white parents determined to keep their children in neighborhood schools and others willing to move to the suburbs or enroll them in private academies to avoid integration, busing became a lightning rod for protests. One of the most bitter fights took place in Boston in the mid-1970s. Residents of the tightly knit Irish-American community of South Boston demonstrated vociferously and sometimes violently against a busing plan decreed by a local judge.

The Supreme Court soon abandoned the idea of overturning local control of schools, or moving students great distances to achieve integration. In 1973, it rebuffed a group of Texas Latinos who sued to overturn the use of property taxes to finance public education. Because of the great disparity in wealth between districts, spending on predominantly Mexican-American schools stood far below that for white ones. But in *San Antonio Independent School District v. Rodriguez*, a 5-4 Court majority ruled that the Constitution did not require equality of school funding. In the following year, in *Milliken v. Bradley* (1974), the justices overturned a lower court order that required Detroit's predominantly white suburbs to enter into a regional desegregation plan with the city's heavily minority school system. By absolving suburban districts of responsibility for assisting in integrating urban schools, the decision guaranteed that housing segregation would be mirrored in public education. Indeed, by the 1990s, public schools in the North were considerably more segregated than those in the South.

THE COURT AND AFFIRMATIVE ACTION

Efforts to promote greater employment opportunities for minorities also spawned politically divisive legal issues. Many whites came to view affirmative action programs as a form of "reverse discrimination." Even as affirmative action programs quickly spread from blacks to encompass women, Latinos, Asian-Americans, and Native Americans, conservatives demanded that the Supreme Court invalidate all such policies. The justices refused, but they found it difficult to devise a consistent approach to this politically charged issue.

In *Griggs v. Duke Power Company* (1971), the Court ruled that even racially neutral job requirements such as a written examination were illegal if they operated to exclude a disproportionate number of non-white applicants and were not directly related to job performance. Later in the decade, in *United Steelworkers of America v. Weber* (1979), it upheld a program devised by the Kaiser Aluminum & Chemical Corporation and its union that set quotas for training and hiring non-white workers in skilled jobs. Since this private, voluntary agreement did not involve government action, the Court ruled, it did not violate the Fourteenth Amendment's ban on state policies that discriminated among citizens.

The justices, however, proved increasingly hostile to governmental affirmative action policies. In *Regents of the University of California v. Bakke* (1978), the Court overturned an admissions program of the University of California at Davis, a public university, which set aside 16 of 100 places in the entering medical school class for minority students. Justice Lewis F. Powell, a Nixon appointee who cast the deciding vote in the 5-4 decision, rejected the idea of fixed affirmative action quotas. He added, however, that race could be used as one factor among many in admissions decisions, so affirmative action continued at most colleges and universities.

THE CONTINUING SEXUAL REVOLUTION

To the alarm of conservatives, during the 1970s the sexual revolution passed from the counterculture into the social mainstream. The number of Americans who told public-opinion polls that premarital sex was wrong plummeted. The number of divorces soared, reaching more than 1 million in 1975, double the number ten years earlier. The age at which both men and women married rose dramatically. The figure for divorces in 1975 exceeded the number of first-time marriages. A popular 1978 film, *An Unmarried Woman,* portrayed the dissolution of a marriage as a triumph for the wife, who discovered her potential for individual growth only after being abandoned by her husband. As a result of women's changing aspirations and the availability of birth control and legal abortions, the American birthrate declined dramatically. By 1976, the average woman was bearing 1.7 children during her lifetime, less than half the figure of 1957 and below the level at which a population reproduces itself. A 1971 survey of the last five graduating classes at Bryn Mawr, an elite women's college, reported the birth of more than seventy children. A similar survey covering the classes of 1971 through 1975 found that only three had been born.

During the Nixon years, women made inroads into areas from which they had long been excluded. In 1972, Congress approved Title IX, which banned gender discrimination in higher education, and the Equal Credit Opportunity Act, which required that married women be given access to credit in their own name. The giant corporation American Telephone and Telegraph (AT&T) entered into a landmark agreement in which it agreed to pay millions of dollars to workers who had suffered gender discrimination and to upgrade employment opportunities for women. The number of women at work continued its upward climb. In 1960, only 20 percent of women with young children had been in the workforce. The figure reached 40 percent in 1980, and 55 percent in 1990. Working women were motivated by varied aims. Some sought careers in professions and skilled jobs previously open only to men. Others, spurred by the need to bolster family income as the economy faltered, flooded into the traditional, low-wage, "pink-collar" sector, working as cashiers, secretaries, and telephone operators.

In addition, the gay and lesbian movement, born at the end of the 1960s, expanded greatly during the 1970s and became a major concern of the right. In 1969, there had been about fifty local gay rights groups in the United States;

ten years later, their numbers reached into the thousands. They began to elect local officials, persuaded many states to decriminalize homosexual relations, and succeeded in convincing cities with large gay populations to pass antidiscrimination laws. They actively encouraged gay men and lesbians to "come out of the closet"—that is, to reveal their sexual orientation. During the 1970s, the American Psychiatric Association removed homosexuality from its list of mental diseases.

As pre–World War I bohemians saw many of their ideas absorbed into the mass culture of the 1920s, values and styles of the 1960s became part of 1970s America, dubbed by the writer Tom Wolfe the "Me Decade." When asked in a Gallup poll to rate a series of ideas, respondents gave the highest ranking not to "following God's will," "high income," or "a sense of accomplishment," but to "freedom to choose." The demand of student protesters that individuals be empowered to determine their own "lifestyle" emerged in depoliticized form in Americans' obsession with self-improvement through fitness programs, health food diets, and new forms of psychological therapy.

NIXON AND DÉTENTE

Just as domestic policies and social trends under Nixon disappointed conservatives, they viewed his foreign policy as dangerously "soft" on communism. To be sure, in the Third World, Nixon and Henry Kissinger, his national security adviser and secretary of state, continued their predecessors' policy of attempting to undermine governments deemed dangerous to American strategic or economic interests. Nixon funneled arms to dictatorial pro-American regimes in Iran, the Philippines, and South Africa. After Chile in 1970 elected socialist Salvador Allende as president, the CIA worked with his domestic opponents to destabilize the regime. On September 11, 1973, Allende was overthrown and killed in a military coup, which installed a bloody dictatorship under General Augusto Pinochet. Thousands of Allende backers, including a few Americans then in Chile, were tortured and murdered, and many others fled the country. The Nixon administration knew of the coup plans in advance but failed to warn Allende, and it continued to back Pinochet despite his brutal policies. Democracy did not return to Chile until the end of the 1980s.

In his relations with the major communist powers, however, Nixon fundamentally altered Cold War policies. Nixon had launched his political career as a fierce and, critics charged, unscrupulous anticommunist. But in the language of foreign relations, he and Kissinger were "realists." They had more interest in power than ideology and preferred international stability to relentless conflict. Nixon also hoped that if relations with the Soviet Union improved, the Russians would influence North Vietnam to agree to an end to the Vietnam War on terms acceptable to the United States.

Nixon realized that far from being part of a unified communist bloc, China had its own interests, different from those of the Soviet Union, and was destined to play a major role on the world stage. The policy of refusing to recognize China's communist government had reached a dead end. In 1971, Kissinger flew secretly to China, paving the way for Nixon's own astonishing public visit of February 1972. The trip led to the Beijing government's taking up China's seat at the United Nations, previously occupied by the exiled regime on Taiwan. Full diplomatic relations between the United States and the People's Republic of China were not established until 1979. But Nixon's visit sparked a dramatic increase in trade between the two countries.

Three months after his trip to Beijing, Nixon became the first American president to visit the Soviet Union, where he engaged in intense negotiations with his Soviet counterpart, Leonid Brezhnev. Out of this "summit" meeting came agreements for increased trade and two landmark arms-control treaties. SALT (named for the Strategic Arms Limitation Talks under way since 1969) froze each country's arsenal of intercontinental missiles capable of carrying nuclear warheads. The Anti–Ballistic Missile Treaty banned the development of systems designed to intercept incoming missiles, so that neither side would be tempted to attack the other without fearing devastating retaliation. Nixon and Brezhnev proclaimed a new era of "peaceful coexistence," in which "détente" (cooperation) would replace the hostility of the Cold War.

VIETNAM AND WATERGATE

NIXON AND VIETNAM

Despite Nixon's foreign policy triumphs, one issue would not go away—Vietnam. Nixon ran for president in 1968 declaring that he had a "secret plan" to end the war. On taking office, he announced a new policy, Vietnamization. Under this plan, American troops would gradually be withdrawn while South Vietnamese soldiers, backed by continued American bombing, did more and more of the fighting. But Vietnamization neither limited the war nor ended the antiwar movement. Hoping to cut North Vietnamese supply lines, Nixon in 1970 ordered American troops into neutral Cambodia. The invasion did not achieve its military goals, but it destabilized the Cambodian government and set in motion a chain of events that eventually brought to power the Khmer Rouge. Before being ousted by a Vietnamese invasion in 1979, this local communist movement attempted to force virtually all Cambodians into rural communes and committed widespread massacres in that unfortunate country.

As the war escalated, protests again spread on college campuses. In the wake of the killing of four antiwar protesters at Kent State University by the

Ohio National Guard and two by police at Jackson State University in Mississippi, the student movement reached its high-water mark. In the spring of 1970, more than 350 colleges and universities experienced strikes, and troops occupied 21 campuses. The protests at Kent State, a public university with a largely working-class student body, and Jackson State, a black institution, demonstrated how antiwar sentiment had spread far beyond elite campuses like Berkeley and Columbia.

Tear gas envelops the campus as members of the Ohio National Guard prepare to fire on student demonstrators at Kent State University. Shortly after this photo was taken, four students lay dead.

At the same time, troop morale in Vietnam plummeted. Although all young men were subject to the draft, for most of the war college students received exemptions. As a result, the army was predominantly composed of working-class whites and members of racial minorities. Unlike in previous wars, blacks complained not about exclusion from the army but about the high number of black soldiers among the casualties.

The same social changes sweeping the home front were evident among troops in Vietnam. Soldiers experimented with drugs, openly wore peace and black-power symbols, refused orders, and even assaulted unpopular officers. In 1971, thousands deserted the army, while at home Vietnam veterans held antiwar demonstrations. The decline of discipline within the army convinced increasing numbers of high-ranking officers that the United States must extricate itself from Vietnam.

Public support for the war was rapidly waning. In 1969, the *New York Times* published details of the My Lai massacre of 1968, in which a company of American troops had killed some 350 South Vietnamese civilians. After a military investigation, one soldier, Lieutenant William Calley, was found guilty of directing the atrocity. (The courts released him from prison in 1974.) In 1971, the *Times* began publishing the Pentagon Papers, a classified report prepared by the Defense Department that traced American involvement in Vietnam back to World War II and revealed how successive presidents had misled the American people about it. In a landmark freedom-of-the-press decision, the Supreme Court rejected Nixon's request for an injunction to halt publication. In 1973, Congress passed the War Powers Act. The most vigorous assertion of congressional control over foreign policy in the nation's history, it required the president to seek congressional approval for the commitment of American troops overseas.

THE END OF THE VIETNAM WAR

Early in 1973, Nixon achieved what had eluded his predecessors—a negotiated settlement in Vietnam. The Paris peace agreement, the result of five years of talks, made possible the final withdrawal of American troops. The compromise left in place the government of South Vietnam, but it also left North Vietnamese and Viet Cong soldiers in control of parts of the South. American bombing ceased, and the military draft came to an end. Henceforth, volunteers would make up the armed forces. But the agreement did not solve the basic issue of the war—whether Vietnam would be one country or two. That question was answered in the spring of 1975, when the North Vietnamese launched a final military offensive. The government of South Vietnam collapsed; the United States did not intervene except to evacuate the American embassy, and Vietnam was reunified under communist rule.

The only war the United States has ever lost, Vietnam was a military, political, and social disaster. By the time it ended, 58,000 Americans had been killed, along with 3 million to 4 million Vietnamese. The war cost the United States many hundreds of millions of dollars and diverted funds from needs at home. But the nonmonetary price was far higher. Vietnam undermined Americans' confidence in their own institutions and challenged long-standing beliefs about the country and its purposes. The divisions caused by the war continued in debates over its legacy that persisted for many years. The war's supporters blamed critics at home for undermining a successful and winnable military effort. Others took the lesson that the United States should be extremely reluctant to commit its armed forces overseas—an outlook sometimes called the Vietnam Syndrome.

Two decades after the war ended, former secretary of defense Robert McNamara published a memoir in which he admitted that the policy he had helped to shape had been "terribly wrong." Ignorance of the history and culture of Vietnam and a misguided belief that every communist movement in the world was a puppet of Moscow, he wrote, had led the country into a war that he now profoundly regretted. The *New York Times* rejected McNamara's apology. The "ghosts of those unlived lives," the young men sent to their death "for no purpose," it declared, could not so easily be wished away. But the *Times* itself, like the rest of the political establishment, had supported the war for most of its duration. For far too long, they had accepted its basic premise—that the United States had the right to decide the fate of a faraway people about whom it knew almost nothing.

WATERGATE

By the time the war ended, Richard Nixon was no longer president. His domestic policies and foreign policy successes had contributed greatly to his reelection in 1972. He won a landslide victory over liberal Democrat George McGovern, receiving 60 percent of the popular vote. Nixon made deep inroads into former Democratic strongholds in the South and among working-class white northerners. He carried every state but Massachusetts. But his triumph soon turned into disaster.

Nixon was obsessed with secrecy and could not accept honest difference of opinion. He viewed every critic as a threat to national security and developed an "enemies list" that included reporters, politicians, and celebrities unfriendly to the administration. When the Pentagon Papers were published, Nixon created a special investigative unit known as the "plumbers" to gather information about Daniel Ellsberg, the former government official who had leaked them to the press. The plumbers raided the office of Ellsberg's psychiatrist in search of incriminating records. In June 1972, five former employees of Nixon's reelection committee took part in a break-in at Democratic Party headquarters in the Watergate apartment complex in Washington, D.C. A security guard called police, who arrested the intruders.

No one knows precisely what the Watergate burglars were looking for (perhaps they intended to install listening devices), and the botched robbery played little role in the 1972 presidential campaign. But in 1973, Judge John J. Sirica, before whom the burglars were tried, determined to find out who had sponsored the break-in. A pair of *Washington Post* journalists began publishing investigative stories that made it clear that persons close to the president had ordered the burglary and then tried to "cover up" White House involvement. Congressional hearings followed that revealed a wider pattern of wiretapping, break-ins, and attempts to sabotage political opposition. When it became known that Nixon had made tape recordings of conversations in his office, Archibald Cox, a special prosecutor the president had reluctantly appointed to investigate the Watergate affair, demanded copies. In October 1973, Nixon proposed to allow Senator John C. Stennis of Mississippi to review the tapes, rather than releasing them. When Cox refused to agree, Nixon fired him, whereupon Attorney General Elliot Richardson resigned in protest. These events, known as the Saturday Night Massacre, further undermined Nixon's standing. The Supreme Court unanimously ordered Nixon to provide them—a decision that reaffirmed the principle that the president is not above the law.

NIXON'S FALL

Week after week, revelations about the scandal unfolded. By mid-1974, it had become clear that whether or not Nixon knew in advance of the Watergate break-in, he had become involved immediately afterward in authorizing payments to the burglars to remain silent or commit perjury, and he had ordered the FBI to halt its investigation of the crime. In August 1974, the House Judiciary Committee voted to recommend that Nixon be impeached for conspiracy to obstruct justice. His political support having evaporated, Nixon became the only president in history to resign.

Nixon's presidency remains a classic example of the abuse of political power. In 1973, his vice president, Spiro T. Agnew, resigned after revelations that he had accepted bribes from construction firms while serving as governor of Maryland. Nixon's attorney general, John Mitchell, and White House aides H. R. Haldeman and John Ehrlichman were convicted of obstruction of justice in the Watergate affair and went to jail. As for the president, he insisted that he had done nothing wrong—or at any rate, that previous presidents had also been guilty of lying and illegality.

Although it hardly excused his behavior, Nixon had a point. His departure from office was followed by Senate hearings headed by Frank Church of Idaho that laid bare a history of abusive actions that involved every administration since the beginning of the Cold War. In violation of the law, the FBI had spied on millions of Americans and had tried to disrupt the civil rights movement. The CIA had conducted secret operations to overthrow foreign governments and had tried to assassinate foreign leaders. It had even recruited a secret army to fight in Laos, a neighbor of Vietnam. Abuses of power, in other words, went far beyond the misdeeds of a single president.

Along with Watergate, the Pentagon Papers, and the Vietnam War itself, the Church Committee revelations seriously undermined Americans' confidence in their own government. They led Congress to enact new restrictions on the power of the FBI and CIA to spy on American citizens or conduct operations abroad without the knowledge of lawmakers. Congress also strengthened the Freedom of Information Act (FOIA), initially enacted in 1966. Since 1974, the FOIA has allowed scholars, journalists, and ordinary citizens to gain access to millions of pages of records of federal agencies.

Liberals, who had despised Nixon throughout his career, celebrated his downfall. They did not realize that the revulsion against Watergate undermined the foundations of liberalism itself, already weakened by the divisions of the 1960s. For liberalism rests, in part, on belief in the ability of government, especially the federal government, to solve social problems and promote both the public good and individual freedom. Nixon's fall and the revelations of years of governmental misconduct helped to convince many Americans that conservatives were correct when they argued that to protect liberty it was necessary to limit Washington's power over Americans' lives. The Watergate crisis also distracted attention from the economic crisis that began in the fall of 1973. Its inability to fashion a response to this crisis, which gripped the United States for much of the 1970s, dealt liberalism yet another blow.

THE END OF THE GOLDEN AGE

THE DECLINE OF MANUFACTURING

During the 1970s, the long period of postwar economic expansion and consumer prosperity came to an end, succeeded by slow growth and high inflation. For the only time in the twentieth century, other than the 1930s, the average American ended the 1970s poorer than when the decade began. There were many reasons for the end of capitalism's "golden age." With American prosperity seemingly unassailable and the military-industrial complex thriving, successive administrations had devoted little attention to the less positive economic consequences of the Cold War. To strengthen its anticommunist allies, the United States promoted the industrial reconstruction of Japan and Germany and the emergence of new centers of manufacturing in places like South Korea and Taiwan. It encouraged American companies to invest in overseas plants and did not complain when allies protected their own industries while seeking unrestricted access to the American market. Imports of foreign steel, for example, led to growing problems for this key industry at home. The strong dollar, linked to gold by the Bretton Woods agreement of 1944, made it harder to sell American goods overseas.

In 1971, for the first time in the twentieth century, the United States experienced a merchandise trade deficit—that is, it imported more goods than it exported. By 1980, nearly three-quarters of goods produced in the United States were competing with foreign-made products and the number of manufacturing workers, 38 percent of the American workforce in 1960, had fallen to 28 percent.

In 1971, Nixon announced the most radical change in economic policy since the Great Depression. He took the United States off the gold standard, ending the Bretton Woods agreement that fixed the value of the dollar and other currencies in terms of gold. Henceforth, the world's currencies would "float" in relation to one another, their worth determined not by treaty but by international currency markets. Nixon hoped that lowering the dollar's value in terms of the German mark and Japanese yen would promote exports by making American goods cheaper overseas and reduce imports since foreign products would be more expensive in the United States. But the end of fixed currency rates injected a new element of instability into the world economy. Nixon also ordered wages and prices frozen for ninety days.

STAGFLATION

These policies temporarily curtailed inflation and reduced imports. But in 1973, a brief war broke out between Israel and its neighbors Egypt and Syria. Middle Eastern Arab states retaliated for Western support of Israel by quadrupling the price of oil and suspending the export of oil to the United States for several months. Long lines of cars appeared at American gas stations, which either ran out of fuel or limited how much a customer could buy. A second "oil shock" occurred in 1979 as a result of the revolution that overthrew the shah of Iran, discussed later.

Because the rapidly growing demand for fuel by cars and factories outstripped domestic supplies, by 1973 the United States imported one-third of its oil. Europe and Japan depended even more heavily on oil imports. To promote energy conservation, Congress lowered the speed limit on interstate highways to fifty-five miles per hour, and many public buildings reduced heat and lighting.

The energy crisis of the 1970s drew increased attention to domestic energy resources like oil, coal, and natural gas. While the rest of the economy stagnated, western energy production grew apace. Oil was discovered in Alaska in 1968, and in 1977 a pipeline opened to facilitate its shipment to the rest of the country. Coal production in Wyoming boomed. Western energy companies

Table 1 THE MISERY INDEX, 1970–1980

Year	*Rate of Inflation (%)*	*Rate of Unemployment (%)*	*Misery Index (%)*
1970	5.9	4.9	10.8
1971	4.3	5.9	10.2
1972	3.3	5.6	8.9
1973	6.2	4.9	11.1
1974	11.0	5.6	16.6
1975	9.1	8.5	17.6
1976	5.8	7.7	13.5
1977	6.5	7.1	13.6
1978	7.7	6.1	13.8
1979	11.3	5.8	17.1
1980	13.5	7.1	20.6

benefited from the high oil prices set by OPEC—the Organization of Petroleum Exporting Countries.

But rising oil prices rippled through the world economy, contributing to the combination of stagnant economic growth and high inflation known as "stagflation." Between 1973 and 1981, the rate of inflation in developed countries was 10 percent per year, and the rate of economic growth only 2.4 percent, a sharp deterioration from the economic conditions of the 1960s. The so-called misery index—the sum of the unemployment and inflation rates—stood at 10.8 when the decade began. By 1980, it had almost doubled. As oil prices rose, many Americans shifted from large domestically produced cars, known for high gasoline consumption, to smaller, more fuel-efficient imports. By the end of the decade, Japan had become the world's leading automobile producer, and imports accounted for nearly 25 percent of car sales in the United States.

THE BELEAGUERED SOCIAL COMPACT

The economic crisis contributed to a breakdown of the postwar social compact. Faced with declining profits and rising overseas competition, corporations stepped up the trend, already under way before 1970, toward eliminating well-paid manufacturing jobs through automation and shifting production to low-wage areas of the United States and overseas. The effects on older industrial cities were devastating. By 1980, Detroit and Chicago had lost more than half the manufacturing jobs that had existed three decades earlier.

Smaller industrial cities suffered even sharper declines. As their tax bases shriveled, many found themselves unable to maintain public services. In Paterson, New Jersey, where great silk factories had arisen in the early twentieth century, deindustrialization left a landscape of abandoned manufacturing plants. The poverty rate reached 20 percent, the city sold off public library buildings to raise cash, and the schools became so run down and overcrowded that the state government took control. The accelerating flow of jobs, investment, and population to the nonunion, low-wage states of the Sunbelt increased the political influence of this conservative region. Of population growth in metropolitan areas, during the 1970s, 96 percent occurred in the South and West. San Jose and Phoenix, with populations around 100,000 in 1950, neared 1 million by 1990.

In some manufacturing centers, political and economic leaders welcomed the opportunity to remake their cities as finance, information, and entertainment hubs. In New York, the construction of the World Trade Center, completed in 1977, symbolized this shift in the economy. Until destroyed by terrorists twenty-four years later, the 110-story "twin towers" stood as a symbol of New York's grandeur. But to make way for the World Trade Center, the city displaced hundreds of small electronics, printing, and other firms, causing the loss of thousands of manufacturing jobs.

LABOR ON THE DEFENSIVE

Always a junior partner in the Democratic coalition, the labor movement found itself forced onto the defensive. It has remained there ever since. One example of the weakening of unions' power came in 1975 with the New York City fiscal crisis. Deeply in debt and unable to market its bonds, the city faced the prospect of bankruptcy. The solution to the crisis required a reduction of the city's workforce, severe cuts in the budgets of schools, parks, and the subway system, and an end to the century-old policy of free tuition at the City University. Even in this center of unionism, working-class New Yorkers had no choice but to absorb job losses and a drastic decline in public services.

The weakening of unions and the continuation of the economy's long-term shift from manufacturing to service employment had an adverse impact on ordinary Americans. Between 1953 and 1973, median family income had doubled. But beginning in 1973, real wages essentially did not rise for twenty years. The 1970s was one of only two decades in the twentieth century (the other being the 1930s) that ended with Americans on average poorer than when it began. The popular song "The River," by Bruce Springsteen, captured the woes of blue-collar workers: "Is a dream a lie if it don't come true / Or is it something worse?"

Figure 1 REAL AVERAGE WEEKLY WAGES, 1955–1990

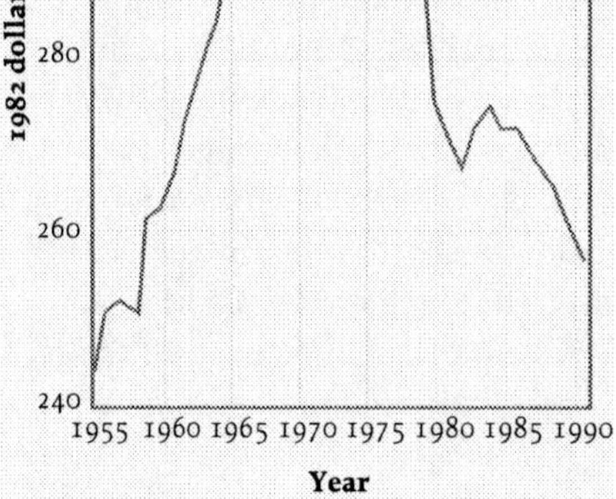

Because of economic dislocations and deindustrialization, Americans' real wages (wages adjusted to take account of inflation) peaked in the early 1970s and then began a sharp, prolonged decline.

FORD AS PRESIDENT

Economic problems dogged the presidencies of Nixon's successors. Gerald Ford, who had been appointed to replace Vice President Agnew, succeeded to the White House when Nixon resigned. Ford named Nelson Rockefeller of New York as his own vice president. Thus, for the only time in American history, both offices were occupied by persons for whom no one had actually voted. Among his first acts as president, Ford pardoned Nixon, shielding him from prosecution for obstruction of justice. Ford claimed that he wanted the country to put the Watergate scandal behind it. But the pardon proved to be widely unpopular.

In domestic policy, Ford's presidency lacked significant accomplishment. Ford and his chief economic adviser, Alan Greenspan, believed that Americans spent too much on consumption and saved too little, leaving business with insufficient money for investment. They called for cutting taxes on business and lessening government regulation of the economy. But the Democratic majority in Congress was in no mood to accept these traditional Republican policies. To combat inflation, Ford urged Americans to shop wisely, reduce expenditures, and wear WIN buttons (for "Whip Inflation Now"). Although inflation fell, joblessness continued to rise. During the steep recession of 1974–1975 unemployment exceeded 9 percent, the highest level since the Depression.

In the international arena, 1975 witnessed the major achievement of Ford's presidency. In a continuation of Nixon's policy of détente, the United States and Soviet Union signed an agreement at Helsinki, Finland, that recognized the permanence of Europe's post–World War II boundaries (including the division of Germany). In addition, both superpowers agreed to respect the basic liberties of their citizens. Secretary of State Kissinger and his Soviet counterpart, Andrey Gromyko, assumed that this latter pledge would have little practical effect. But over time, the Helsinki Accords inspired movements for greater freedom within the communist countries of eastern Europe.

THE CARTER ADMINISTRATION

In the presidential election of 1976, Jimmy Carter, a former governor of Georgia, narrowly defeated Ford. A graduate of the U.S. Naval Academy who later became a peanut farmer, Carter was virtually unknown outside his state when he launched his campaign for the Democratic nomination. But realizing that Watergate and Vietnam had produced a crisis in confidence in the federal government, he turned his obscurity into an advantage. Carter ran for president as an "outsider," making a virtue of the fact that he had never held federal office. A devout "born-again" Baptist, he spoke openly of his religious convictions. His promise, "I'll never lie to you," resonated with an electorate tired of official dishonesty.

Carter had much in common with Progressives of the early twentieth century. His passions were making government more efficient, protecting the environment, and raising the moral tone of politics. Unlike the Progressives, however, he embraced the aspirations of black Americans. As president, Carter appointed an unprecedented number of blacks to important positions, including Andrew Young, a former lieutenant of Martin Luther King Jr., as ambassador to the United Nations.

CARTER AND THE ECONOMIC CRISIS

The Democratic party found itself ill-equipped to deal with the economic crisis. The social upheavals of the 1960s had led to the emergence of politicians known as the New Democrats. Representing affluent urban and suburban districts, they viewed issues like race relations, gender equality, the environment, and improving the political process as more central than traditional economic matters. Although his party controlled both houses, Carter often found himself at odds with Congress. He viewed inflation, not unemployment, as the country's main economic problem, and to combat it he promoted cuts in spending on domestic programs. In the hope that increased competition would reduce prices, his administration deregulated the trucking and airline industries. Anticipating what would come to be called the supply-side economics of the Reagan administration, Carter in 1978 inaugurated tax cuts for wealthier Americans in the hope that this would stimulate investment and encourage economic growth. In 1980, with Carter's approval, Congress repealed usury laws—laws that limit how much interest lenders can charge—allowing credit card companies to push their interest rates up to 20 percent or even higher. Carter supported the Federal Reserve Bank's decision to raise interest rates to curtail economic activity until both wages and prices fell, traditionally a Republican policy. But oil prices kept rising, thanks to the overthrow of the shah of Iran, discussed later, and inflation did not decline.

Carter also believed that expanded use of nuclear energy could help reduce dependence on imported oil. For years, proponents of nuclear power had hailed it as an inexpensive way of meeting the country's energy needs. By the time Carter took office, more than 200 nuclear plants were operating or on order. But in 1979 the industry suffered a near-fatal blow when an accident at the Three Mile Island plant in Pennsylvania released a large amount of radioactive steam into the atmosphere. The rise of the environmental movement had promoted public skepticism about scientific experts who touted the miraculous promise of technological innovations without concern for their social consequences. The Three Mile Island mishap reinforced fears about the environmental hazards associated with nuclear energy and put a halt to the industry's expansion.

Since the New Deal, Democrats had presented themselves as the party of affluence and economic growth. But Carter seemed to be presiding over a period of national decline. It did not help his popularity when, in a speech in 1979, he spoke of a national "crisis of confidence" and seemed to blame it on the American people themselves and their "mistaken idea of freedom" as "self-indulgence and consumption."

THE EMERGENCE OF HUMAN RIGHTS POLITICS

Under Carter, a commitment to promoting human rights became a centerpiece of American foreign policy for the first time. He was influenced by the proliferation of information about global denials of human rights spread by nongovernmental agencies like Amnesty International and the International League for Human Rights. The American membership of Amnesty International, a London-based organization, grew from 6,000 to 35,000 between 1970 and 1976. Its reports marked a significant break with dominant ideas about international affairs since World War II, which had viewed the basic division in the world as between communist and noncommunist countries. Such reports, along with congressional hearings, fact-finding missions, and academic studies of human rights, exposed misdeeds not only by communist countries but also by American allies, especially the death squads of Latin American dictatorships. Amnesty International pressured the United States to try to do something to promote human rights abroad. In 1977, Amnesty International received the Nobel Peace Prize, an indication of the rapid emergence of human rights as an international issue.

In 1978, Carter cut off aid to the brutal military dictatorship governing Argentina, which in the name of anticommunism had launched a "dirty war" against its own citizens, kidnapping off the streets and secretly murdering an estimated 10,000 to 30,000 persons. Carter's action was a dramatic gesture, as Argentina was one of the most important powers in Latin America and previous American administrations had turned a blind eye to human rights abuses by Cold War allies. By the end of his presidency, the phrase "human rights" had acquired political potency. Its very vagueness was both a weakness and a strength. It was difficult to define exactly what rights should and should not be considered universally applicable, but various groups could and did unite under the umbrella of global human rights.

Carter believed that in the post–Vietnam era, American foreign policy should de-emphasize Cold War thinking. Combating poverty in the Third World, preventing the spread of nuclear weapons, and promoting human rights should take priority over what he called "the inordinate fear of communism that once led us to embrace any dictator who joined us in that fear." In one of his first acts as president, he offered an unconditional pardon to Vietnam-era draft resisters. In a 1977 address, he insisted that foreign policy could not be separated from "questions of justice, equity, and human rights."

Carter's emphasis on pursuing peaceful solutions to international problems and his willingness to think outside the Cold War framework yielded important results. In 1979, he brought the leaders of Egypt and Israel to the presidential retreat at Camp David and brokered a historic peace agreement between the two countries. He improved American relations with Latin America by agreeing to a treaty, ratified by the Senate in 1978, that provided for the transfer of the Panama Canal to local control by the year 2000. In 1979, he resisted calls for intervention when a popular revolution led by the left-wing Sandinista movement overthrew Nicaraguan dictator Anastasio Somoza, a longtime ally of the United States. Carter attempted to curb the murderous violence of death squads allied to the right-wing government of El Salvador, and in 1980 he suspended military aid after the murder of four American nuns by members of the country's army. He signed the SALT II agreement with the Soviets, which reduced the number of missiles, bombers, and nuclear warheads.

Both conservative Cold Warriors and foreign policy "realists" severely criticized Carter's emphasis on human rights. He himself found it impossible to translate rhetoric into action. He criticized American arms sales to the rest of the world. But with thousands of jobs and billions of dollars in corporate profits at stake, he did nothing to curtail them. The United States continued its support of allies with records of serious human rights violations such as the governments of Guatemala, the Philippines, South Korea, and Iran. Indeed, the American connection with the shah of Iran, whose secret police regularly jailed and tortured political opponents, proved to be Carter's undoing.

THE IRAN CRISIS AND AFGHANISTAN

Occupying a strategic location on the southern border of the Soviet Union, Iran was a major supplier of oil and an importer of American military equipment. At the end of 1977, Carter traveled there to help celebrate the shah's rule, causing the internal opposition to become more and more anti-American. Early in 1979, a popular revolution inspired by the exiled Muslim cleric Ayatollah Khomeini overthrew the shah and declared Iran an Islamic republic.

The Iranian revolution marked an ideological shift in opposition movements in the Middle East from socialism and Arab nationalism to religious fundamentalism. This would have important long-term consequences for the United States. More immediately, when Carter in November 1979 allowed the deposed shah to seek medical treatment in the United States, Khomeini's followers invaded the American embassy in Tehran and seized sixty-six hostages. Fourteen people (which included women, African-American men, and a white man in ill health) were soon released, leaving fifty-two captives. They did not regain their freedom until January 1981, on the day Carter's term as president ended. Events in Iran made Carter seem helpless and inept and led to a rapid fall in his popularity.

Another crisis that began in 1979 undermined American relations with Moscow. At the end of that year, the Soviet Union sent thousands of troops into Afghanistan to support a friendly government threatened by an Islamic rebellion. In the long run, Afghanistan became the Soviet Vietnam, an unwinnable conflict whose mounting casualties seriously weakened the government at home. Initially, however, it seemed another example of declining American power.

Declaring the invasion the greatest crisis since World War II (a considerable exaggeration), the president announced the Carter Doctrine, declaring that the United States would use military force, if necessary, to protect its interests in the Persian Gulf. He placed an embargo on grain exports to the Soviet Union and organized a Western boycott of the 1980 Olympics, which took place in Moscow. He withdrew the SALT II treaty from consideration by the Senate and dramatically increased American military spending. In a reversion to the Cold War principle that any opponent of the Soviet Union deserved American support, the United States funneled aid to fundamentalist Muslims in Afghanistan who fought a decade-long guerrilla war against the Soviets. The alliance had unforeseen consequences. A faction of Islamic fundamentalists known as the Taliban eventually came to power in Afghanistan. Tragically, they would prove as hostile to the United States as to Moscow.

In an unsuccessful attempt to bring down inflation, Carter had abandoned the Keynesian economic policy of increased government spending to combat recession in favor of high interest rates. He had cut back on social spending and the federal government's economic regulations, while projecting a major increase in the military budget. By 1980, détente had been eclipsed and the Cold War reinvigorated. Thus, many of the conservative policies associated with his successor, Ronald Reagan, were already in place when Carter's presidency ended.

THE RISING TIDE OF CONSERVATISM

The combination of domestic and international dislocations during the 1970s created a widespread sense of anxiety among Americans and offered conservatives new political opportunities. Economic problems heightened the appeal of lower taxes, reduced government regulation, and cuts in social spending to spur business investment. Fears about a decline of American power in the world led to calls for a renewal of the Cold War. The civil rights and sexual revolutions produced resentments that undermined the Democratic coalition. Rising urban crime rates reinforced demands for law and order and attacks on courts considered too lenient toward criminals. These issues brought new converts to the conservative cause.

As the 1970s went on, conservatives abandoned overt opposition to the black struggle for racial justice. The fiery rhetoric and direct confrontation tactics of Bull Connor, George Wallace, and other proponents of massive resistance were succeeded by appeals to freedom of association, local control, and resistance to the power of the federal government. This language of individual freedom resonated throughout the country, appealing especially to the growing, predominantly white, suburban population that was fleeing the cities and their urban problems. The suburbs would become one of the bastions of modern conservatism.

But it was not just a reaction to the 1960s and the spread of conservative ideas that nourished the movement. Like predecessors as diverse as the civil rights and labor movements, conservatives organized at the grass roots. In order to spread conservative doctrines, they ran candidates for office even when they had little chance of winning, and worked to change the policies of local institutions like school boards, town councils, and planning commissions.

One set of recruits was the "neoconservatives," a group of intellectuals who charged that the 1960s had produced a decline in moral standards and respect for authority. Once supporters of liberalism, they had come to believe that even well-intentioned government social programs did more harm than good. Welfare, for example, not only failed to alleviate poverty but also encouraged single motherhood and undermined the work ethic. High taxes and expensive government regulations drained resources from productive enterprises, stifling economic growth. Neoconservatives repudiated the attempts by Nixon, Ford, and Carter to reorient foreign policy away from the Cold War. Carter's focus on human rights and alleged blindness to the Soviet threat, they argued, endangered the "survival of freedom." Conservative "think tanks" created during the 1970s, like the Heritage Foundation and the American Enterprise Institute, refined and spread these ideas.

THE RELIGIOUS RIGHT

The rise of religious fundamentalism during the 1970s expanded conservatism's popular base. Challenged by the secular and material concerns of American society, some denominations tried to bring religion into harmony with these interests; others reasserted more traditional religious values. The latter approach seemed to appeal to growing numbers of Americans. Even as membership in mainstream denominations like Episcopalianism and Presbyterianism declined, evangelical Protestantism flourished. Some observers spoke of a Third Great Awakening (like those of the 1740s and early nineteenth century). The election of Carter, the first "born-again" Christian to become president, highlighted the growing influence of evangelical religion. But unlike Carter, most fundamentalists who entered politics did so as conservatives.

Of course, there was nothing new about the involvement of churches in political life. There is a long tradition in American history of moral stewardship—

devout Christians taking on responsibility for social reform and using political means to combat what they perceive as individual or collective sins. During the 1960s, many members of the burgeoning evangelical churches of the suburbs, South, and West had become more and more alienated from a culture that seemed to them to trivialize religion and promote immorality. Evangelicals of different denominations increasingly came to feel that they had more in common with each other than with more liberal coreligionists. They demanded the reversal of Supreme Court decisions banning prayer in public schools, protecting pornography as free speech, and legalizing abortion. Although it spoke of restoring traditional values, the Religious Right proved remarkably adept at using modern technology, including mass mailings and televised religious programming, to raise funds for their crusade and spread their message. In 1979, Jerry Falwell, a Virginia minister, created the self-styled Moral Majority, devoted to waging a "war against sin" and electing "pro-life, pro-family, pro-America" candidates to office. Falwell identified supporters of abortion rights, easy divorce, and "military unpreparedness" as the forces of Satan, who sought to undermine God's "special plans for this great, free country of ours."

Christian conservatives seemed most agitated by the ongoing sexual revolution, which they saw as undermining the traditional family and promoting immorality. As a result of the 1960s, they believed, American freedom was out of control. The growing assertiveness of the new gay movement spurred an especially fierce reaction. In 1977, after a campaign led by the popular singer Anita Bryant, a familiar fixture in televised orange juice commercials, Dade County, Florida, passed an anti-gay ordinance under the banner "Save Our Children."

THE BATTLE OVER THE EQUAL RIGHTS AMENDMENT

During the 1970s, "family values" moved to the center of conservative politics, nowhere more so than in the battle over the Equal Rights Amendment (ERA). Originally proposed during the 1920s by Alice Paul and the Women's Party, the ERA had been revived by second-wave feminists. In the wake of the rights revolution, the amendment's affirmation that "equality of rights under the law" could not be abridged "on account of sex" hardly seemed controversial. In 1972, with broad bipartisan support, Congress approved the ERA and sent it to the states for ratification. Designed to eliminate obstacles to the full participation of women in public life, it aroused unexpected protest from those who claimed it would discredit the role of wife and homemaker.

The ERA debate reflected a division among women as much as a battle of the sexes. To its supporters, the amendment offered a guarantee of women's freedom in the public sphere. To its foes, freedom for women still resided in the divinely appointed roles of wife and mother. Phyllis Schlafly, who

Doug Marlette's cartoon comments on the continuing gap in pay between men and women, the kind of inequality that inspired support for the proposed Equal Rights Amendment.

helped to organize opposition to the ERA, insisted that the "free enterprise system" was the "real liberator of women," since labor-saving home appliances offered more genuine freedom than "whining about past injustices" or seeking fulfillment outside the home. Opponents claimed that the ERA would let men "off the hook" by denying their responsibility to provide for their wives and children. Polls consistently showed that a majority of Americans, male and female, favored the ERA. But thanks to the mobilization of conservative women, the amendment failed to achieve ratification by the required thirty-eight states.

THE ABORTION CONTROVERSY

An even more bitter battle emerged in the 1970s over abortion rights, another example, to conservatives, of how liberals in office promoted sexual immorality at the expense of moral values. The movement to reverse the 1973 *Roe v. Wade* decision began among Roman Catholics, whose church condemned abortion under any circumstances. But it soon enlisted evangelical Protestants and social conservatives more generally. Life, the movement insisted, begins at conception, and abortion is nothing less than murder. Between this position and the feminist insistence that a woman's right to control her body includes the right to a safe, legal abortion, compromise was impossible. Ironically, both sides showed how the rights revolution had reshaped the language of politics. Defenders of abortion exalted "the right to choose" as the essence of freedom. Opponents called themselves the "right to life" movement and claimed to represent the rights of the "unborn child."

The abortion issue drew a bitter, sometimes violent line through American politics. It affected battles over nominees to judicial positions and led to demonstrations at family-planning and abortion clinics. The anti-abortion movement won its first victory in 1976 when Congress, over President Ford's veto, ended federal funding for abortions for poor women through the Medicaid program. By the 1990s, a few fringe anti-abortion activists were placing bombs at medical clinics and murdering doctors who terminated pregnancies. To the end of the century, most women would continue to have the legal right of access to abortion. But in many areas the procedure became more and more difficult to obtain as hospitals and doctors stopped providing it.

THE TAX REVOLT

With liberals unable to devise an effective policy to counteract deindustrialization and declining real wages, economic anxieties also created a growing constituency for conservative economics. Unlike during the Great Depression, economic distress inspired a critique of government rather than of business. New environmental regulations led to calls for less government intervention in the economy. These were most strident in the West, where measures to protect the environment threatened irrigation projects and private access to public lands. But everywhere, the economy's descent from affluence to "stagflation" increased the appeal of the conservative argument that government regulation raised business costs and eliminated jobs.

Economic decline also broadened the constituency receptive to demands for lower taxes. To conservatives, tax reductions served the dual purpose of enhancing business profits and reducing the resources available to government, thus making new social programs financially impossible.

In 1978, conservatives sponsored and California voters approved Proposition 13, a ban on further increases in property taxes. The vote demonstrated that the level of taxation could be a powerful political issue. Proposition 13 proved to be a windfall for businesses and home owners, while reducing funds available for schools, libraries, and other public services. Many voters, however, proved willing to accept this result of lower taxes. As anti-tax sentiment flourished throughout the country, many states followed California's lead.

A parallel upsurge of grassroots conservatism was reflected in the Sagebrush Rebellion (the name given to a bill passed by the Nevada legislature in 1979). Using the language of freedom from government tyranny, leaders in western states denounced control of large areas of land by the Bureau of Land Management in Washington, D.C., and insisted that the states themselves be given decision-making power over issues like grazing rights, mining development, and whether public lands should be closed to fishing and hunting. With the federal government reluctant to give up control over public lands in the West, the Sagebrush Rebellion had few concrete accomplishments, but it underscored the rising tide of antigovernment sentiment.

THE ELECTION OF 1980

By 1980, Carter's approval rating had fallen to 21 percent—lower than Nixon's at the time of his resignation. A conservative tide seemed to be rising throughout the Western world. In 1979, Margaret Thatcher became prime minister of Great Britain. She promised to restore economic competitiveness by curtailing the power of unions, reducing taxes, selling state-owned industries to private owners, and cutting back the welfare state. In the United States, Ronald Reagan's 1980 campaign for the presidency brought together the many strands of 1970s conservatism. He pledged to end stagflation and restore the country's dominant role in the world and its confidence in itself. "Let's make America great again," he proclaimed. "The era of self-doubt is over."

Reagan also appealed skillfully to "white backlash." He kicked off his campaign in Philadelphia, Mississippi, where three civil rights workers had been murdered in 1964, with a speech emphasizing his belief in states' rights. Many

THE PRESIDENTIAL ELECTION OF 1980

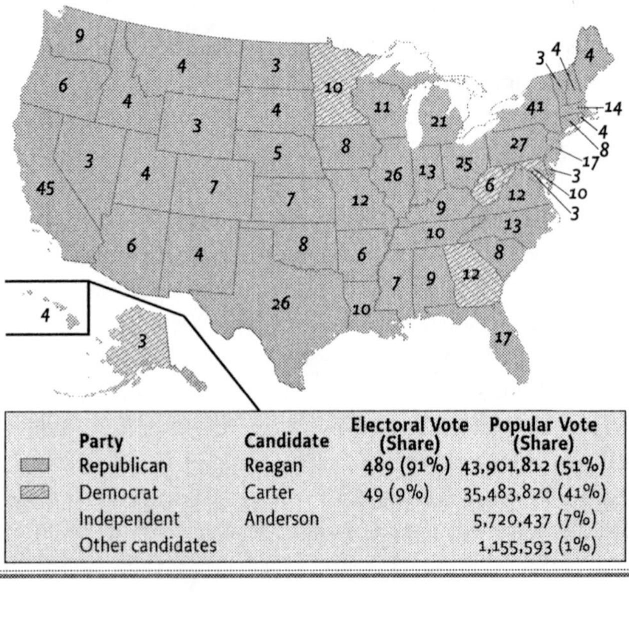

Party	Candidate	Electoral Vote (Share)	Popular Vote (Share)
Republican	Reagan	489 (91%)	43,901,812 (51%)
Democrat	Carter	49 (9%)	35,483,820 (41%)
Independent	Anderson		5,720,437 (7%)
Other candidates			1,155,593 (1%)

white southerners understood this doctrine as including opposition to federal intervention on behalf of civil rights. During the campaign, Reagan repeatedly condemned welfare "cheats," school busing, and affirmative action. The Republican platform reversed the party's long-standing support for the Equal Rights Amendment and condemned moral permissiveness. Although not personally religious and the first divorced man to run for president, Reagan won the support of the Religious Right and conservative upholders of "family values."

Riding a wave of dissatisfaction with the country's condition, Reagan swept into the White House. He carried such Democratic strongholds as Illinois, Texas, and New York. Because moderate Republican John Anderson, running for president as an independent, received about 7 percent of the popular vote, Reagan won only a bare majority, although he commanded a substantial margin in the electoral college. Carter received 41 percent, a humiliating defeat for a sitting president.

Jimmy Carter's reputation improved after he left the White House. He went to work for Habitat for Humanity, an organization that constructs homes for poor families. In the 1990s, he negotiated a cease-fire between warring Muslim and Serb forces in Bosnia and arranged a peaceful transfer of power from the military to an elected government in Haiti. In 2002, Carter was awarded the Nobel Peace Prize. His presidency, however, is almost universally considered a failure. And his defeat in 1980 launched the Reagan Revolution, which completed the transformation of freedom from the rallying cry of the left to a possession of the right.

THE REAGAN REVOLUTION

Ronald Reagan followed a most unusual path to the presidency. Originally a New Deal Democrat and head of the Screen Actors Guild (the only union leader ever to reach the White House), he emerged in the 1950s as a spokesman for the General Electric Corporation, preaching the virtues of unregulated capitalism. His nominating speech for Barry Goldwater at the 1964 Republican convention brought Reagan to national attention. Two years later, California voters elected Reagan as governor, establishing him as conservatives' best hope of capturing the presidency. In 1976, he challenged President Ford for the Republican nomination and came close to winning it. His victory in 1980 brought to power a diverse coalition of old and new conservatives: Sunbelt suburbanites and urban working-class ethnics; antigovernment crusaders and advocates of a more aggressive foreign policy; libertarians who believed in freeing the individual from restraint and the Christian Right, which sought to restore what they considered traditional moral values to American life.

VOICES OF FREEDOM

From Redstockings Manifesto (1969)

Redstockings was one of the radical feminist movements that arose in the late 1960s. Based in New York, it issued this manifesto, which, in language typical of the era, illustrates how at its most radical edge, feminism had evolved from demands for equal treatment for women to a total critique of male power and a call for women's "liberation."

After centuries of individual and preliminary political struggle, women are uniting to achieve their final liberation from male supremacy. Redstockings is dedicated to building this unity and winning our freedom.

Women are an oppressed class. Our oppression is total, affecting every facet of our lives. We are exploited as sex objects, breeders, domestic servants, and cheap labor. We are considered inferior beings, whose only purpose is to enhance men's lives. Our humanity is denied. Our prescribed behavior is enforced by the threat of physical violence.

Because we have lived so intimately with our oppressors, in isolation from each other, we have been kept from seeing our personal suffering as a political condition. . . .

We identify the agents of our oppression as men. Male supremacy is the oldest, most basic form of domination. . . . Men have controlled all political, economic, and cultural institutions and backed up this control with physical force. . . .

Our chief task at present is to develop female class consciousness through sharing experience and publicly exposing the sexist foundation of all our institutions. Consciousness-raising is not "therapy," which implies the existence of individual solutions and falsely assumes that the male-female relationship is purely personal, but the only method by which we can ensure that our program for liberation is based on the concrete realities of our lives. . . . The first requirement for raising class consciousness is honesty, in private and in public, with ourselves and other women.

We identify with all women. We define our best interest as that of the poorest, most brutally exploited women. . . .

We call on all our sisters to unite with us in struggle.

We call on all men to give up their male privileges and support women's liberation in the interest of our humanity and their own.

July 7, 1969, New York City

From Jerry Falwell, *Listen, America!* (1980)

The Reverend Jerry Falwell, a Virginia minister who in 1979 founded the self-proclaimed Moral Majority, was one of the leading conservative activists of the 1970s and 1980s. In language reminiscent of Puritan jeremiads about the decline of moral values, Falwell helped to mobilize evangelical Christians to ally with the Republican Party.

We must reverse the trend America finds herself in today. Young people between the ages of twenty-five and forty have been born and reared in a different world than Americans of years past. The television set has been their primary baby-sitter. From the television set they have learned situation ethics and immorality—they have learned a loss of respect for human life. They have learned to disrespect the family as God has established it. They have been educated in a public-school system that is permeated with secular humanism. They have been taught that the Bible is just another book of literature. They have been taught that there are no absolutes in our world today. They have been introduced to the drug culture. They have been reared by the family and the public school in a society that is greatly void of discipline and character-building. . . .

Every American who looks at the facts must share a deep concern and burden for our -country. . . . If Americans will face the truth, our nation can be turned around and can be saved from the evils and the destruction that have fallen upon every other nation that has turned its back on God. . . .

I personally feel that the home and the family are still held in reverence by the vast majority of the American public. I believe there is still a vast number of Americans who love their country, are patriotic, and are willing to sacrifice for her. . . . I believe that Americans want to see this -country come back to basics, back to values, back to biblical morality, back to sensibility, and back to patriotism. . . .

It is now time to take a stand on certain moral issues, and we can only stand if we have leaders. We must stand against the Equal Rights Amendment, the feminist revolution, and the homosexual revolution. . . . The hope of reversing the trends of decay in our republic now lies with the Christian public in America. We cannot expect help from the liberals. They certainly are not going to call our nation back to righteousness and neither are the pornographers, the smut peddlers, and those who are corrupting our youth. Moral Americans must be willing to put their reputations, their fortunes, and their very lives on the line for this great nation of ours. Would that we had the courage of our forefathers who knew the great responsibility that freedom carries with it.

QUESTIONS

1. How do the authors of the Redstockings Manifesto seem to define women's freedom?

2. What does Falwell see as the main threats to moral values?

3. How do the two documents differ in their views about the role of women in American society?

REAGAN AND AMERICAN FREEDOM

Reagan's opponents often underestimated him. By the time he left office at the age of seventy-seven, he had become the oldest man ever to serve as president. He "rose at the crack of noon," as one reporter put it, and relied on his wife to arrange his official schedule. Unlike most modern presidents, he was content to outline broad policy themes and leave their implementation to others.

Reagan, however, was hardly a political novice, having governed California during the turbulent 1960s. An excellent public speaker, his optimism and affability appealed to large numbers of Americans. Reagan made conservatism seem progressive, rather than an attempt to turn back the tide of progress. He frequently quoted Thomas Paine: "We have it in our power to begin the world over again." Reagan repeatedly invoked the idea that America has a divinely appointed mission as a "beacon of liberty and freedom." Freedom, indeed, became the watchword of the Reagan Revolution. In his public appearances and state papers, Reagan used the word more often than any president before him.

Reagan reshaped the nation's agenda and political language more effectively than any president since Franklin D. Roosevelt. Like FDR, he seized on the vocabulary of his opponents and gave it new meaning. Reagan promised to free government from control by "special interests," but these were racial minorities, unionists, and others hoping to use Washington's power to attack social inequalities, not businessmen seeking political favors, the traditional target of liberals. His Justice Department made the principle that the Constitution must be "color-blind"—a remark hurled at the Supreme Court majority by Justice John Marshall Harlan in 1896 to challenge a system of legal segregation—a justification for gutting civil rights enforcement.

Overall, Reagan proved remarkably successful at seizing control of the terms of public debate. On issues ranging from taxes to government spending, national security, crime, welfare, and "traditional values," he put Democrats on the defensive. But he also proved to be a pragmatist, recognizing when to compromise so as not to fragment his diverse coalition of supporters.

REAGANOMICS

Like Roosevelt and Johnson before him, Reagan spoke of "economic freedom" and proposed an "economic Bill of Rights." But in contrast to his predecessors, who used these phrases to support combating poverty and strengthening economic security, economic freedom for Reagan meant curtailing the power of unions, dismantling regulations, and radically reducing taxes. Taxation, he declared, violated the principle that "the right to earn your own keep and keep what you earn" was "what it means to be free."

In 1981, Reagan persuaded Congress to reduce the top tax rate from 70 percent to 50 percent and to index tax brackets to take inflation into account. Five years later, the Tax Reform Act reduced the rate on the wealthiest Americans to 28 percent. These measures marked a sharp retreat from the principle of progressivity (the idea that the wealthy should pay a higher percentage of their income in taxes than other citizens), one of the ways twentieth-century societies tried to address the unequal distribution of wealth. Reagan also appointed conservative heads of regulatory agencies, who cut back on environmental protection and workplace safety rules about which business had complained for years.

Since the New Deal, liberals had tried to promote economic growth by using the power of the government to bolster ordinary Americans' purchasing power. Reagan's economic program, known as "supply-side economics" by proponents and "trickle-down economics" by critics, relied on high interest rates to curb inflation and lower tax rates, especially for businesses and high-income Americans, to stimulate private investment. The policy assumed that cutting taxes would inspire Americans at all income levels to work harder, since they would keep more of the money they earned. Everyone would benefit from increased business profits, and because of a growing economy, government receipts would rise despite lower tax rates.

REAGAN AND LABOR

Reagan inaugurated an era of hostility between the federal government and organized labor. In August 1981, when 13,000 members of PATCO, the union of air traffic controllers, began a strike in violation of federal law, Reagan fired them all. He used the military to oversee the nation's air traffic system until new controllers could be trained. Reagan's action inspired many private employers to launch anti-union offensives. The hiring of workers to replace permanently those who had gone on strike, a rare occurrence before 1980, became widespread. Manufacturing employment, where union membership was concentrated, meanwhile continued its long-term decline. By the mid-1990s, the steel industry employed only 170,000 persons—down from 600,000 in 1973. When Reagan left office, both the service and retail sectors employed more Americans than manufacturing, and only 11 percent of workers with non-government jobs were union members.

"Reaganomics," as critics dubbed the administration's policies, initially produced the most severe recession since the 1930s. A long period of economic expansion, however, followed the downturn of 1981–1982. As companies "downsized" their workforces, shifted production overseas, and took advantage of new technologies such as satellite communications, they became more profitable. At the same time, the rate of inflation, 13.5 percent at the beginning of 1981, declined to 3.5 percent in 1988, partly because a period of expanded oil production that drove down prices succeeded the shortages of the 1970s.

THE PROBLEM OF INEQUALITY

Together, Reagan's policies, rising stock prices, and deindustrialization resulted in a considerable rise in economic inequality. By the mid-1990s, the richest 1 percent of Americans owned 40 percent of the nation's wealth, twice their share twenty years earlier. Most spent their income not on productive investments and charity as supply-side economists had promised, but on luxury goods, real-estate speculation, and corporate buyouts that often led to plant closings as operations were consolidated. The income of middle-class families, especially those with a wife who did not work outside the home, stagnated while that of the poorest one-fifth of the population declined. Because of falling investment in public housing, the release of mental patients from state hospitals, and cuts in welfare, homeless persons became a visible fixture on the streets of cities from New York to Los Angeles.

Deindustrialization and the decline of the labor movement had a particularly devastating impact on minority workers, who had only recently gained a foothold in better-paying manufacturing jobs. Thanks to the opening of colleges and professional schools to minority students as a result of the civil rights movement and affirmative action programs, the black middle class expanded considerably. But black workers, traditionally the last hired and first fired, were hard hit by economic changes.

During the 1970s, Jim Crow had finally ended in many workplaces and unions. But just as decades of painful efforts to obtain better jobs bore fruit, hundreds of thousands of black workers lost their jobs when factories closed their doors. In South Gate, a working-class suburb of Los Angeles, for example, the giant Firestone tire factory shut down in 1980, only a few years after black and Latino workers had made their first breakthroughs in employment. When the national unemployment rate reached 8.9 percent at the end of 1981, the figure for blacks exceeded 20 percent. Nor did black workers share fully in the recovery that followed. Few had the education to take advantage of job openings in growing "knowledge-based" industries like technology and information services. Overall,

A homeless Los Angeles family, forced to live in their car, photographed in 1983.

during the 1980s black males fell farther than any other group in the population in terms of wages and jobs.

THE SECOND GILDED AGE

In retrospect, the 1980s, like the 1890s, would be widely remembered as a decade of misplaced values. Buying out companies generated more profits than running them; making deals, not making products, became the way to get rich. The merger of Nabisco and R. J. Reynolds Tobacco Company in 1988 produced close to $1 billion in fees for lawyers, economic advisers, and stockbrokers.."Greed is healthy," declared Wall Street financier Ivan Boesky (who ended up in prison for insider stock trading). "Yuppie"—the young urban professional who earned a high income working in a bank or stock brokerage firm and spent lavishly on designer clothing and other trappings of the good life—became a household word.

Taxpayers footed the bill for some of the consequences. The deregulation of savings and loan associations—banks that had generally confined themselves to financing home mortgages—allowed these institutions to invest in unsound real-estate ventures and corporate mergers. Losses piled up, and the Federal Savings and Loan Insurance Corporation, which insured depositors' accounts, faced bankruptcy. After Reagan left office, the federal government bailed out the savings and loan institutions, at a cost to taxpayers estimated at $250 billion.

Supply-side advocates insisted that lowering taxes would enlarge government revenue by stimulating economic activity. But spurred by large increases in funds for the military, federal spending far outstripped income, producing large budget deficits, despite assurances by supply-siders that this would not happen. During Reagan's presidency, the national debt tripled to $2.7 trillion. Nonetheless, Reagan remained immensely popular. He took credit for economic expansion while blaming congressional leaders for the ballooning federal deficit. He won a triumphant reelection in 1984. His opponent, Walter Mondale (best remembered for choosing Congresswoman Geraldine Ferraro of New York as his running mate, the first woman candidate on a major-party presidential ticket), carried only his home state of Minnesota and the District of Columbia.

CONSERVATIVES AND REAGAN

While he implemented their economic policies, Reagan in some ways disappointed ardent conservatives. The administration sharply reduced funding for Great Society antipoverty programs such as food stamps, school lunches, and federal financing of low-income housing. But it left intact core elements of the welfare state, such as Social Security, Medicare, and Medicaid, which many conservatives wished to curtail significantly or repeal. The Reagan era did little to advance the social agenda of the Christian Right. Abortion remained legal, women continued to enter the labor force in unprecedented numbers, and Reagan even appointed the first female member of the Supreme Court, Sandra Day O'Connor. In 1986, in *Bowers v. Hardwick*, in a rare victory for cultural conservatives, the Supreme Court did uphold the constitutionality of state laws outlawing homosexual acts. (In 2003, the justices would reverse the *Bowers* decision, declaring laws that criminalized homosexuality unconstitutional.)

Reagan gave verbal support to a proposed constitutional amendment restoring prayer in public schools but did little to promote its passage. The administration launched a "Just Say No" campaign against illegal drug use. But this failed to halt the spread in urban areas of crack, a potent, inexpensive form of cocaine that produced an upsurge of street crime and family breakdown. Reagan's Justice Department cut back on civil rights enforcement and worked to curtail affirmative action programs. But to the end of Reagan's presidency, the Supreme Court continued to approve plans by private employers and city and state governments to upgrade minority employment.

REAGAN AND THE COLD WAR

In foreign policy, Reagan breathed new life into the rhetorical division of the world into a free West and unfree East. He resumed vigorous denunciation of the Soviet Union—calling it an "evil empire"—and sponsored the largest military buildup in American history, including new long-range bombers and missiles. In 1983, he proposed an entirely new strategy, the Strategic Defense Initiative, based on developing a space-based system to intercept and destroy enemy missiles. The idea was not remotely feasible technologically, and, if deployed, it would violate the Anti-Ballistic Missile Treaty of 1972. But it appealed to Reagan's desire to reassert America's worldwide power. He persuaded NATO, over much opposition, to introduce short-range nuclear weapons into Europe to counter Soviet forces. But the renewed arms race and Reagan's casual talk of winning a nuclear war caused widespread alarm at home and abroad. In the early 1980s, a movement for a nuclear freeze—a halt to the development of nuclear weapons—attracted millions of supporters in the United States and Europe. In 1983, half of the American population watched *The Day After*, a television program that unflinchingly depicted the devastation that would be caused by a nuclear war.

Reagan came into office determined to overturn the "Vietnam syndrome"—as widespread public reluctance to commit American forces overseas was called. He sent American troops to the Caribbean island of Grenada to oust a

THE UNITED STATES IN THE CARIBBEAN AND CENTRAL AMERICA, 1954–2004

As in the first part of the twentieth century, the United States intervened frequently in Caribbean and Central American countries during and immediately after the Cold War.

pro-Cuban government. In 1982, Reagan dispatched marines as a peacekeeping force to Lebanon, where a civil war raged between the Christian government, supported by Israeli forces, and Muslim insurgents. But he quickly withdrew them after a bomb exploded at their barracks, killing 241 Americans. The public, Reagan realized, would support minor operations like Grenada but remained unwilling to sustain heavy casualties abroad.

Reagan generally relied on military aid rather than American troops to pursue his foreign policy objectives. Abandoning the Carter administration's emphasis on human rights, Reagan embraced the idea, advanced in 1979 by neoconservative writer Jeane Kirkpatrick, that the United States should oppose "totalitarian" communists but assist "authoritarian" noncommunist regimes. Kirkpatrick became the American ambassador to the United Nations, and the United States stepped up its alliances with Third World anticommunist dictatorships like the governments of Chile and South Africa. The administration poured in funds to combat insurgencies against the governments of El Salvador and Guatemala, whose armies and associated death squads committed flagrant abuses against their own citizens. When El Salvador's army massacred hundreds of civilians in the town of El Mozote in 1981, the State Department denied that the event, widely reported in the press, had taken place.

THE IRAN-CONTRA AFFAIR

American involvement in Central America produced the greatest scandal of Reagan's presidency, the Iran-Contra affair. In 1984, Congress banned military aid to the Contras (derived from the Spanish word for "against") fighting the Sandinista government of Nicaragua, which, as noted earlier, had ousted the American-backed dictator Anastasio Somoza in 1979. In 1985, Reagan secretly authorized the sale of arms to Iran—now involved in a war with its neighbor, Iraq—in order to secure the release of a number of American hostages held by Islamic groups in the Middle East. CIA director William Casey and Lieutenant Colonel Oliver North of the National Security Council set up a system that diverted some of the proceeds to buy military supplies for the Contras in defiance of the congressional ban. The scheme continued for nearly two years.

In 1987, after a Middle Eastern newspaper leaked the story, Congress held televised hearings that revealed a pattern of official duplicity and violation of the law reminiscent of the Nixon era. Eleven members of the administration eventually were convicted of perjury or destroying documents, or pleaded guilty before being tried. Reagan denied knowledge of the illegal proceedings, but the Iran-Contra affair undermined confidence that he controlled his own administration.

REAGAN AND GORBACHEV

President Reagan visited Moscow in 1988, cementing his close relationship with Soviet leader Mikhail Gorbachev. They were photographed in Red Square.

In his second term, to the surprise of both his foes and supporters, Reagan softened his anticommunist rhetoric and established good relations with Soviet premier Mikhail Gorbachev. Gorbachev had come to power in 1985, bent on reforming the Soviet Union's repressive political system and reinvigorating its economy. The country had fallen further and further behind the United States in the production and distribution of consumer goods, and it relied increasingly on agricultural imports to feed itself. Gorbachev inaugurated policies known as *glasnost* (political openness) and *perestroika* (economic reform).

Gorbachev realized that significant change would be impossible without reducing his country's military budget. Reagan was ready to negotiate. A series of talks between 1985 and 1987 yielded more progress on arms control than in the entire postwar period to that point, including an agreement to eliminate intermediate- and short-range nuclear missiles in Europe. In 1988, Gorbachev began pulling Soviet troops out of Afghanistan. Having entered office as an ardent Cold Warrior, Reagan left with hostilities between the superpowers much diminished. He even repudiated his earlier comment that the Soviet Union was an "evil empire," saying that it referred to "another era."

REAGAN'S LEGACY

Reagan's presidency revealed the contradictions at the heart of modern conservatism. In some ways, the Reagan Revolution undermined the very values and institutions conservatives held dear. Intended to discourage reliance on government handouts by rewarding honest work and business initiative, Reagan's policies inspired a speculative frenzy that enriched architects of corporate takeovers and investors in the stock market while leaving in their wake plant closings, job losses, and devastated communities. Nothing proved more threatening to local traditions or family stability than deindustrialization, insecurity about employment, and the relentless downward pressure on wages. Nothing did more to undermine a sense of common national purpose than the widening gap between rich and poor.

Because of the Iran-Contra scandal and the enormous deficits the government had accumulated, Reagan left the presidency with his reputation somewhat tarnished. Nonetheless, few figures have so successfully changed the landscape and language of politics. Reagan's vice president, George H. W. Bush, defeated Michael Dukakis, the governor of Massachusetts, in the 1988 election partly because Dukakis could not respond effectively to the charge that he was a "liberal"—now a term of political abuse. Conservative assumptions about the virtues of the free market and the evils of "big government" dominated the mass media and political debates. Those receiving public assistance had come to be seen not as citizens entitled to help in coping with economic misfortune, but as a drain on taxes. During the 1990s, these and other conservative ideas would be embraced almost as fully by President Bill Clinton, a Democrat, as by Reagan and the Republicans.

THE ELECTION OF 1988

The 1988 election seemed to show politics sinking to new lows. Television advertisements and media exposés now dominated political campaigns. The race for the Democratic nomination had hardly begun before the front-runner, Senator Gary Hart of Colorado, withdrew after a newspaper reported that he had spent the night at his Washington town house with a woman other than his wife. Both parties ran negative campaigns. Democrats ridiculed the Republican vice-presidential nominee, Senator Dan Quayle of Indiana, for factual and linguistic mistakes. Republicans spread unfounded rumors that Michael Dukakis's wife had burned an American flag during the 1960s. The low point of the campaign came in a Republican television ad depicting the threatening image of Willie Horton, a black murderer and rapist who had been furloughed from prison during Dukakis's term as governor of Massachusetts. Rarely in the modern era had a major party appealed so blatantly to racial fears. Before his death in 1991, Lee Atwater, who masterminded Bush's campaign, apologized for the Horton ad.

Although he did not match Reagan's landslide victory of 1984, Bush achieved a substantial majority, winning 54 percent of the popular vote. Democratic success in retaining control of Congress suggested that an electoral base existed for a comeback. But this would occur only if the party fashioned a new appeal to replace traditional liberalism, which had been eclipsed by the triumph of conservatism.

Chapter Review

REVIEW QUESTIONS

1. Why were social issues associated with the sexual revolution so contested by all sides?
2. What were continuing challenges to the cohesiveness of the Democratic (New Deal) coalition? What were the consequences of those divisions?
3. What were the main features of Nixon's policy of "realism" in dealing with China and the Soviet Union?
4. Describe the basic events and the larger significance of the Watergate scandal.
5. What were the major causes for the decline of the U.S. economy in the 1970s?
6. What were the causes and consequences of the public's disillusionment with the federal government in the 1970s and 1980s?
7. Identify the groups and their agendas that combined to create the new conservative base in the 1970s and 1980s.
8. What impact did Ronald Reagan have on the American political scene?
9. Why was there growth in economic inequality in the 1980s?
10. How did various groups see the relationship between women's rights and freedom differently?

KEY TERMS

busing
affirmative action
"reverse discrimination"
Title IX
Strategic Arms Limitation Talks
détente
My Lai massacre
War Powers Act
Vietnam Syndrome
Watergate
oil embargo
stagflation
misery index
sunbelt
Helsinki Accords
Camp David Accords
Iran hostage crisis
neoconservatives

Reagan Revolution
Reaganomics
deregulation
Iran-Contra affair

wwnorton.com/studyspace

VISIT STUDYSPACE FOR THESE RESOURCES AND MORE:

- Author Videos
- A chapter outline
- A practice quiz
- Interactive maps
- Multimedia documents

FREDERICK JACKSON TURNER

The Significance of the Frontier in American History (1893)

In 1893, Chicago hosted a world's fair known as the Columbian Exposition to mark the 400th anniversary of Christopher Columbus's arrival in the New World. This historical and cultural milestone closely followed the announcement by the United States Census Bureau that the frontier no longer existed. Up until 1890, it had always been possible to draw a line on a map of the West connecting each area with a population of at least two per square mile. Anything beyond that line was deemed to be unsettled and by that definition constituted the frontier. By 1890, settlement beyond the Mississippi had advanced to the extent that an unbroken line of population advance was no longer visible, thereby prompting the official declaration of the end of the frontier. This was the context in which the historian Frederick Jackson Turner (1861–1932) delivered a famous address at the American Historical Association convention in Chicago the summer of its Exposition. The essay he read—on the frontier's importance in American history—is one of the most influential historical pieces ever written, provoking commentary and debate among generations of historians since.

Turner was himself a product of the West. He was born in Wisconsin at the beginning of the Civil War and graduated from the University of Wisconsin before going east for his doctoral studies; he earned his PhD in history at Baltimore's Johns Hopkins University in 1890. In the course of his training, Turner would have been exposed to the then-prevalent "germ theory," the notion that American political institutions like representative government were primarily European (Anglo-Saxon or Germanic) in origin, having been carried across the Atlantic with the initial colonizers. Turner's own essay on the American frontier ultimately developed into what is now known as the Frontier Thesis, which argues that the existence of a western frontier contributed to the development of a uniquely American culture and history. As you read Turner's essay, consider how boldly he challenged prevailing doctrines and how effectively he made his case for the West's predominant influence.

From Frederick Jackson Turner, "The Significance of the Frontier in American History," in *The Frontier in American History* (New York: Henry Holt and Company, 1940), 1–4, 22–23, 30–32, 37–38.

In a recent bulletin of the Superintendent of the Census for 1890 appear these significant words: "Up to and including 1880 the country had a frontier of settlement, but at present the unsettled area has been so broken into by isolated bodies of settlement that there can hardly be said to be a frontier line. In the discussion of its extent, its westward movement, etc., it can not, therefore, any longer have a place in the census reports." This brief official statement marks the closing of a great historic movement. Up to our own day American history has been in a large degree the history of the colonization of the Great West. The existence of an area of free land, its continuous recession, and the advance of American settlement westward, explain American development.

Behind institutions, behind constitutional forms and modifications, lie the vital forces that call these organs into life and shape them to meet changing conditions. The peculiarity of American institutions is, the fact that they have been compelled to adapt themselves to the changes of an expanding people—to the changes involved in crossing a continent, in winning a wilderness, and in developing at each area of this progress out of the primitive economic and political conditions of the frontier into the complexity of city life. Said Calhoun in 1817, "We are great, and rapidly—I was about to say fearfully—growing!" So saying, he touched the distinguishing feature of American life. All peoples show development; the germ theory of politics has been sufficiently emphasized. In the case of most nations, however, the development has occurred in a limited area; and if the nation has expanded, it has met other growing peoples whom it has conquered. But in the case of the United States we have a different phenomenon. Limiting our attention to the Atlantic coast, we have the familiar phenomenon of the evolution of institutions in a limited area, such as the rise of representative government; the differentiation of simple colonial governments into complex organs; the progress from primitive industrial society, without division of labor, up to manufacturing civilization. But we have in addition to this a recurrence of the process of evolution in each western area reached in the process of expansion. Thus American development has exhibited not merely advance along a single line, but a return to primitive conditions on a continually advancing frontier line, and a new development for that area. American social development has been continually beginning over again on the frontier. This perennial rebirth, this fluidity of American life, this expansion westward with its new opportunities, its continuous touch with the simplicity of primitive society, furnish the forces dominating American character. The true point of view in the history of this nation is not the Atlantic coast, it is the Great West. Even the slavery struggle occupies its important place in American history because of its relation to westward expansion.

In this advance, the frontier is the outer edge of the wave—the meeting point between savagery and civilization. Much has been written about the frontier from the point of view of border warfare and the chase, but as a field for the serious study of the economist and the historian it has been neglected.

The American frontier is sharply distinguished from the European frontier—a fortified boundary line running through dense populations. The most significant thing about the American frontier is, that it lies at the hither edge of free land. In the census reports it is treated as the margin of that settlement which has a density of two or more to the square mile. The term is an elastic one, and for our purposes does not need sharp definition. We shall consider the whole frontier belt, including the Indian country and the outer margin of the "settled area" of the census reports. This paper will make no attempt to treat the subject exhaustively; its aim is simply to call attention to the frontier as a fertile field for investigation, and to suggest some of the problems which arise in connection with it.

In the settlement of America we have to observe how European life entered the continent, and how America modified and developed that life and reacted on Europe. Our early history is the study of European germs developing in an American environment. Too exclusive attention has been paid by institutional students to the Germanic origins, too little to the American factors. The frontier is the line of most rapid and effective Americanization. The wilderness masters the colonist. It finds him a European in dress, industries, tools, modes of travel, and thought. It takes him from the railroad car and puts him in the birch canoe. (It strips off the garments of civilization and arrays him in the hunting shirt and the moccasin.) It puts him in the log cabin of the Cherokee and Iroquois and runs an Indian palisade around him. Before long he has gone to planting Indian corn and plowing with a sharp stick; he shouts the war cry and takes the scalp in orthodox Indian fashion. In short, at the frontier the environment is at first too strong for the man. He must accept the conditions which it furnishes, or perish, and so he fits himself into the Indian clearings and follows the Indian trails. Little by little he transforms the wilderness, but the outcome is not the old Europe, not simply the development of Germanic germs, any more than the first phenomenon was a case of reversion to the Germanic mark. The fact is, that here is a new product that is American. At first, the frontier was the Atlantic coast. It was the frontier of Europe in a very real sense. Moving westward, the frontier became more and more American. As successive terminal moraines result from successive glaciations, so each frontier leaves its traces behind it, and when it becomes a settled area the region still partakes of the frontier characteristics. Thus the advance of the frontier has meant a steady movement away from the influence of Europe, a steady growth of independence on American lines. And to study this advance, the men who grew up under these conditions, and the political, economic, and social results of it, is to study the really American part of our history.

* * *

We may next inquire what were the influences on the East and on the Old World. A rapid enumeration of some of the more noteworthy effects is all that I have time for.

First, we note that the frontier promoted the formation of a composite nationality for the American people. The coast was preponderantly English, but the later tides of continental immigration flowed across to the free lands. This was the case from the early colonial days. The Scotch-Irish and the Palatine Germans, or "Pennsylvania Dutch," furnished the dominant element in the stock of the colonial frontier. With these peoples were also the freed indented servants, or redemptioners, who at the expiration of their time of service passed to the frontier. Governor Spotswood of Virginia writes in 1717, "The inhabitants of our frontiers are composed generally of such as have been transported hither as servants, and, being out of their time, settle themselves where land is to be taken up and that will produce the necessarys of life with little labour." Very generally these redemptioners were of non-English stock. In the crucible of the frontier the immigrants were Americanized, liberated, and fused into a mixed race, English in neither nationality nor characteristics. The process has gone on from the early days to our own. Burke and other writers in the middle of the eighteenth century believed that Pennsylvania was "threatened with the danger of being wholly foreign in language, manners, and perhaps even inclinations." The German and Scotch-Irish elements in the frontier of the South were only less great. In the middle of the present century the German element in Wisconsin was already so considerable that leading publicists looked to the creation of a German state out of the commonwealth by concentrating their colonization. Such examples teach us to beware of misinterpreting the fact that there is a common English speech in America into a belief that the stock is also English.

* * *

But the most important effect of the frontier has been in the promotion of democracy here and in Europe. As has been indicated, the frontier is productive of individualism. Complex society is precipitated by the wilderness into a kind of primitive organization based on the family. The tendency is anti-social. It produces antipathy to control, and particularly to any direct control. The tax-gatherer is viewed as a representative of oppression. Prof. Osgood, in an able article, has pointed out that the frontier conditions prevalent in the colonies are important factors in the explanation of the American Revolution, where individual liberty was sometimes confused with absence of all effective government. The same conditions aid in explaining the difficulty of instituting a strong government in the period of the confederacy. The frontier individualism has from the beginning promoted democracy.

The frontier States that came into the Union in the first quarter of a century of its existence came in with democratic suffrage provisions, and had reactive effects of the highest importance upon the older States whose peoples were being attracted there. An extension of the franchise became essential. It was *western* New York that forced an extension of suffrage in the constitutional convention of that State in 1821; and it was *western* Virginia that compelled the tide-water region to put a more liberal suffrage provision in the constitution framed in 1830, and to give to the frontier region a more nearly proportionate representation with the tide-water aristocracy. The rise of democracy as an effective force in the nation came in with western preponderance under Jackson and William Henry Harrison, and it meant the triumph of the frontier—with all of its good and with all of its evil elements.

* * *

. . . The democracy born of free land, strong in selfishness and individualism, intolerant of administrative experience and education, and pressing individual liberty beyond its proper bounds, has its dangers as well as its benefits. Individualism in America has allowed a laxity in regard to governmental affairs which has rendered possible the spoils system and all the manifest evils that follow from the lack of a highly developed civic spirit. In this connection may be noted also the influence of frontier conditions in permitting lax business honor, inflated paper currency and wild-cat banking. The colonial and revolutionary frontier was the region whence emanated many of the worst forms of an evil currency. The West in the War of 1812 repeated the phenomenon on the frontier of that day, while the speculation and wild-cat banking of the period of the crisis of 1837 occurred on the new frontier belt of the next tier of States. Thus each one of the periods of lax financial integrity coincides with periods when a new set of frontier communities had arisen, and coincides in area with these successive frontiers, for the most part. The recent Populist agitation is a case in point. Many a State that now declines any connection with the tenets of the Populists, itself adhered to such ideas in an earlier stage of the development of the State. A primitive society can hardly be expected to show the intelligent appreciation of the complexity of business interests in a developed society. The continual recurrence of these areas of paper-money agitation is another evidence that the frontier can be isolated and studied as a factor in American history of the highest importance.

* * *

From the conditions of frontier life came intellectual traits of profound importance. The works of travelers along each frontier from colonial days onward describe certain common traits, and these traits have, while softening down, still persisted as survivals in the place of their origin, even when a higher social organization succeeded. The result is that to the frontier the American intellect owes its striking characteristics. That coarseness and strength combined with acuteness and inquisitiveness; that practical, inventive turn of mind, quick to find expedients; that masterful grasp of material things, lacking in the artistic but powerful to effect great ends; that restless, nervous energy; that dominant individualism, working for good and for evil, and withal that buoyancy and exuberance which comes with freedom—these are traits of the frontier, or traits called out elsewhere because of the existence of the frontier. Since the days when the fleet of Columbus sailed into the waters of the New World, America has been another name for opportunity, and the people of the United States have taken their tone from the incessant expansion which has not only been open but has even been forced upon them. He would be a rash prophet who should assert that the expansive character of American life has now entirely ceased. Movement has been its dominant fact, and, unless this training has no effect upon a people, the American energy will continually demand a wider field for its exercise. But never again will such gifts of free land offer themselves. For a moment, at the frontier, the bonds of custom are broken and unrestraint is triumphant. There is not *tabula rasa.*[1] The stubborn American environment is there with its imperious summons to accept its conditions; the inherited ways of doing things are also there; and yet, in spite of environment, and in spite of custom, each frontier did indeed furnish a new field of opportunity, a gate of escape from the bondage of the past; and freshness, and confidence, and scorn of older society, impatience of its restraints and its ideas, and indifference to its lessons, have accompanied the frontier. What the Mediterranean Sea was to the Greeks, breaking the bond of custom, offering new experiences, calling out new institutions and activities, that, and more, the ever retreating frontier has been to the United States directly, and to the nations of Europe more remotely. And now, four centuries from the discovery of America, at the end of a hundred years of life under the Constitution, the frontier has gone, and with its going has closed the first period of American history.

1. Blank slate (Latin).

Study Questions

1. How does Turner define the frontier? Where was it located at any given point in American history before 1890? What did he mean by saying "the wilderness masters the colonist"?
2. Turner argues the frontier's most important effect was "in promotion of democracy here and in Europe." What kinds of democracy did the frontier promote and why? How did it do so overseas as well as here?
3. Turner speaks of evil as well as beneficial influences of the frontier. What were some of the negative influences of the frontier on the American character? For example, is ongoing violence in American culture attributable to our frontier heritage?
4. Turner's Frontier Thesis has been debated by generations of historians. In the late 1980s Patricia Nelson Limerick, for example, advanced a "New Western history": rather than viewing the West as essential to the development of the East, Limerick argued that the West should be studied in its own right. Is there an essential difference between these two positions?
5. If Turner was right about the influence of the frontier, what did its closing imply for the future of the United States? Did Americans find new frontiers? Does the United States continue to be a distinctive country because of the frontier's lasting effects, or has it become more like the rest of the world since the frontier's disappearance?

VICTOR DRURY, JOHANN MOST, ALBERT PARSONS, JOSEPH REIFGRABER, AUGUST SPIES

The Pittsburgh Manifesto (1883)

In the late nineteenth century, anarchists were among the most persistent and well-publicized American opponents of industrial capitalism. Anarchists shared with socialists a commitment to equality, but they denied that radical, systemic change could be achieved through electoral action and that the government could be an agent of social justice. Instead, they claimed revolutionary or even violent tactics were necessary to destroy the central state and institute a worker-based society. Accordingly, anarchists were central participants in some of the bloodiest labor-management confrontations of the Gilded Age. Most shocking to the public was the assassination of President William McKinley in 1901 by the anarchist Leon Czolgosz, an outrage that led to Congress's passage of the Anarchist Exclusion Act of 1903, prohibiting the entry of anarchist immigrants into the United States.

When hundreds of anarchists gathered in Pittsburgh in October 1883 to decide on a program of common action, an ongoing economic recession meant increased hardships of layoffs and wage cuts for the industrial workers who were their primary constituency. Delegates from twenty-six cities adopted what the conference termed the Manifesto of the International Working Peoples' Association. Two of the major authors of this document, the German immigrant August Spies (1855–1887) and a Confederate veteran from Texas, Albert Parsons (1848–1887), would later be hanged for their involvement in the May 1886 Haymarket Riot in which a bomb thrower killed eight police attempting to break up an anarchist-led demonstration. As you read this statement, commonly referred to as the Pittsburgh Manifesto, look for the sources of anarchy's appeal to many working-class Americans.

From "Manifesto of the International Working Peoples' Association" (KSL: Bulletin of the Kate Sharpley Library No. 22, May 2000), http://www.katesharpleylibrary.net.

Fellow-workmen: The Declaration of Independence says:

> ". . . But when a long train of abuses and usurpations, pursuing invariably the same object, evinces a design to reduce them (the people) under absolute Despotism, it is their right, it is their duty to throw off such government and provide new guards for their future security."

This thought of Thomas Jefferson was the justification for armed resistance by our forefathers, which gave birth to our Republic, and do not the necessities of our present time compel us to reassert their declaration?

Fellow-Workmen, we ask you to give us your attention for a few moments. We ask you candidly to read the following manifesto issued in your behalf, in the behalf of your wives and children, in behalf of humanity and progress.

Our present society is founded on the exploitation of the propertyless classes by the propertied. This exploitation is such that the propertied (capitalists) buy the working force body and soul of the propertyless, for the price of the mere costs of existence (wages), and take for themselves, i.e., steal, the amount of new values (products) which exceeds this price, whereby wages are made to represent the necessities instead of the earnings of the wage-laborer.

As the non-possessing classes are forced by their poverty to offer for sale to the propertied their working forces, and as our present production on a grand scale enforces technical development with immense rapidity, so that by the application of an always decreasing number of human working forces, an always increasing amount of products is created; so does the supply of working forces increase constantly, while the demand therefore decreases. This is the reason why the workers compete more and more intensely in selling themselves, causing their wages to sink, or at least on the average, never raising them above the margin necessary for keeping intact their working ability.

Whilst by this process the propertyless are entirely debarred from entering the ranks of the propertied, even by the most strenuous exertions, the propertied, by means of the ever-increasing plundering of the working class, are becoming richer day by day, without in any way being themselves productive.

If now and then one of the propertyless class become rich, it is not by their own labor, but from opportunities which they have to speculate upon, and absorb the labor-product of others.

With the accumulation of individual wealth, the greed and power of the propertied grows. They use all the means for competing among themselves for the robbery of the people. In this struggle, generally, the less-propertied (middle class) are overcome, while the great capitalists, par excellence, swell their wealth enormously, concentrate entire branches of production, as well as trade and intercommunication, into their hands, and develop into monopolists. The increase of products, accompanied by simultaneous decrease of the average income of the working mass of the people, leads to so-called "business" and "commercial" crises, when the misery of the wage-workers is forced to the extreme.

For illustration, the last census of the United States shows that after deducting the cost of raw material, interest, rent, risks, etc., the propertied class have absorbed—i.e., stolen—more than five-eighths of all products, leaving scarcely three-eighths to the producers. The propertied class, being scarcely one-tenth of our population, and in spite of their luxury and extravagance, unable to consume their enormous "profits," and the producers, unable to consume more than they receive—three-eighths—so-called "over-productions" must necessarily take place. The terrible results of panics are well known.

The increasing eradication of working forces from the productive process, annually increases the percentage of the propertyless population, which becomes pauperized, and is driven to "crime," vagabondage, prostitution, suicide, starvation, and general depravity. This system is unjust, insane, and murderous. It is therefore necessary to totally destroy it with and by all means, and with the greatest energy on the part of every one who suffers by it, and who does not want to be made culpable for its continued existence by their inactivity.

Agitation for the purpose of organization; organization for the purpose of rebellion. In these few words the ways are marked, which the workers must take if they want to be rid of their chains, as the economic condition is the same in all countries of so-called "civilization," as the governments of all Monarchies and Republics work hand in hand for the purpose of opposing all movements of the thinking part of the workers, as finally the victory in the decisive combat of the proletarians against their oppressors can only be gained by the simultaneous struggle along the whole line of the bourgeois (capitalistic) society, so therefore the international fraternity of peoples, as expressed in the International Working People's Association, presents itself a self-evident necessity.

True order should take its place. This can only be achieved when all implements of labor, the soil and other premises of production, in short, capital produced by labor, is changed into societary property. Only by this presupposition is destroyed every possibility of the future spoliation of man by man. Only by common, undivided capital can all be enabled to enjoy in their fullness the fruits of the common toil. Only by the impossibility of accumulating individual (private) capital can every one be compelled to work who makes a demand to live.

This order of things allows production to regulate itself according to the demand of the whole people, so that nobody need work more than a few hours a day, and that all nevertheless can satisfy their needs. Hereby time and opportunity are given for opening to the people the way to the highest possible civilization; the privileges of higher intelligence fall with the privileges of wealth and birth. To the achievement of such a system the political organizations of the capitalistic classes—be they Monarchies or Republics—form the barriers. These political structures (States), which are completely in the hands of the propertied, have no other purpose than the upholding of the present order of exploitation.

All laws are directed against the working people. In so far as the opposite appears to be the case, they serve on one hand to blind the worker, while on the other hand they are simply evaded. Even the school serves only the purpose of furnishing the offspring of the wealthy with those qualities necessary to uphold their class domination. The children of the poor get scarcely a formal elementary training, and this, too, is mainly directed to such branches as tend to producing prejudices, arrogance and servility; in short, want of sense. The Church finally seeks to make complete idiots out of the mass and to make them forego the paradise on earth by promising a fictitious heaven. The capitalistic press, on the other hand, takes care of the confusion of spirits in public life. All these institutions, far from aiding in the education of the masses, have for their object the keeping in ignorance of the people. They are all in the pay and under the direction of the capitalistic classes. The workers can therefore expect no help from any capitalistic party in their struggle against the existing system. They must achieve their liberation by their own efforts. As in former times a privileged class never surrendered its tyranny, neither can it be expected that the capitalists of this age will give up their rulership without being forced to do it.

If there ever could have been any question on this point, it should long ago have been dispelled by the brutalities which the bourgeoisie of all countries—in America as well as in Europe—constantly commit, as often as the proletariat anywhere energetically move to better their condition. It becomes, therefore, self-evident that the struggle of the proletariat with the bourgeoisie must have a violent revolutionary character.

We could show by scores of illustrations that all attempts in the past to reform this monstrous system by peaceable means, such as the ballot, have been futile, and all such efforts in the future must necessarily be so, for the following reasons:

The political institutions of our times are the agencies of the propertied class; their mission is the upholding of the privileges of their masters; any reform in your own behalf would curtail these privileges. To this they will not and cannot consent, for it would be suicidal to themselves.

That they will not resign their privileges voluntarily we know; that they will not make any concessions to us we likewise know. Since we must then rely upon the kindness of our masters for whatever redress we have, and knowing that from them no good may be expected, there remains but one recourse—FORCE! Our forefathers have not only told us that against despots force is justifiable, because it is the only means, but they themselves have set the immemorial example.

By force our ancestors liberated themselves from political oppression, by force their children will have to liberate themselves from economic bondage. "It is, therefore, your right; it is your duty," says Jefferson—"to arm!"

What we would achieve is, therefore, plainly and simply:

First: Destruction of the existing class rule, by all means, i.e., by energetic, relentless, revolutionary, and international action.

Second: Establishment of a free society based upon cooperative organization of production.

Third: Free exchange of equivalent products by and between the productive organizations without commerce and profit-mongery.

Fourth: Organization of education on a secular, scientific, and equal basis for both sexes.

Fifth: Equal rights for all without distinction to sex or race.

Sixth: Regulation of all public affairs by free contracts between the autonomous (independent) communes and associations, resting on a federalistic basis.

Whoever agrees with this ideal let him grasp our outstretched brother hands!

Proletarians of all countries, unite! Fellow workingmen, all we need for the achievement of this great end is ORGANIZATION and UNITY!

There exists now no great obstacle to that unity. The work of peaceful education and revolutionary conspiracy well can and ought to run in parallel lines.

The day has come for solidarity. Join our ranks! Let the drum beat defiantly the roll of battle: "Workmen of all lands, unite! You have nothing to lose but your chains; you have a world to win!"[1]

Tremble, oppressors of the world! Not far beyond your purblind sight there dawn the scarlet and sable[2] lights of the JUDGMENT DAY!

1. The concluding words of *The Communist Manifesto*, written in 1848 by Karl Marx and Frederick Engels.
2. Red and black were the colors of the European and American revolutionary movements.

Study Questions

1. How do the anarchists view government, both monarchies and republics? How would society function in government's absence?
2. Why does this manifesto quote Thomas Jefferson? What would Jefferson think of the anarchist program? Fully explain.
3. How do the anarchists explain low wage levels, periodic depressions, and rising crime rates? What is their view of organized religion?
4. In what sense were the anarchists truly revolutionary? What might have kept anarchy from becoming a more powerful movement in the United States?

SAMUEL GOMPERS

What Does Labor Want? (1893)

Samuel Gompers (1850–1924) is revered as one of the transcendent figures in the history of American labor, primarily for his leadership of the American Federation of Labor (AFL) from its founding in 1886 until his death almost forty years later. Gompers was born in England of Dutch-Jewish descent, immigrating to New York City in 1863. As a young man, he became a cigar maker, a skilled trade which nonetheless, due to its repetitious nature, allowed workers to read and talk to one another and otherwise educate themselves in the course of the workday. Gompers became president of the Cigarmakers Union, which would become one of the original components of the AFL.

Gompers took a practical approach to trade-unionism, believing that groups of workers organized by skilled craft or trade could pressure employers to improve working conditions. While rejecting revolution, Gompers did share with anarchists a cynical view about the trustworthiness of government or legislation as the source of labor's deliverance, and so he argued that the AFL as an organization should remain nonpolitical. The following speech was delivered by Gompers in Chicago during a time of depression and massive labor unrest. As you read it, see why Gompers believed the trade union movement to be the real hope of civilization.

From Samuel Gompers, "What Does Labor Want? A Paper Read Before the International Labor Congress," (Amer. Federation of Labor, 1893).

A legend of ancient Rome relates that while the capitol was building, there came one day to the tyrannical king Tarquin the Proud, a poor old woman, carrying nine books of prophecies of the Sibyl,[1] which she offered to sell for three hundred pieces of gold. The king laughingly bade her go away, which she did; but after burning three of the books, she returned and asked the same price for the remaining six. Again treated with scorn, she retired, burnt three more of the volumes, and then came back demanding the same sum for the three which were left. Astonished at this conduct, the king consulted his wise men, who answered him that in those nine books, six of which had been lost, were contained the fate of the city and the Roman people.

1. Legends of prophetesses known as sibyls date back to ancient Greece.

To-day the marvellous Sibyl, who grows the grain, yet goes a-hungered; who weaves the silken robes of pride, yet goes threadbare; who mines the coal and precious ores, yet goes cold and penniless; who rears the gorgeous palaces, yet herds in noisome basements, she again appears. This old, yet ever young Sibyl, called labor, offers to modern society the fate of civilization. What is her demand? Modern society, the most complex organization yet evolved by the human race, is based on one simple fact, the practical separation of the capitalistic class from the great mass of the industrious.

If this separation were only that resulting from a differentiation in the functions of directions of industrial operations and their execution in detail then that separation would be regarded as real, direct progress. But the separation between the capitalistic class and the laboring mass is not so much a difference in industrial rank as it is a difference in social status, placing the laborers in a position involving a degradation of mind and body.

This distinction, scarcely noticeable in the United States before the previous generation, rapidly became more and more marked, increasing day by day, until at length, it has widened into a veritable chasm; economic, social and moral. On each side of this seemingly impassable chasm, we see the hostile camps of rich and poor. On one side, a class in possession of all the tools and means of labor; on the other, an immense mass begging for the opportunity to labor. In the mansion, the soft notes betokening ease and security; in the tenement the stifled wail of drudgery and poverty. The arrogance of the rich ever mounting in proportion to the debasement of the poor.

* * *

The state of industrial anarchy produced by the capitalist system is first strongly illustrated in the existence of a class of wealthy social parasites; those who do no work, never did any work and never intend to work. This class of parasites devours incomes derived from many sources; from the stunted babies employed in the mills, mines and factories to the lessees of the gambling hells and the profits of fashionable brothels; from the lands which the labor of others has made valuable; from royalties on coal and other minerals beneath the surface and from rent of houses above the surface, the rent paying all cost of the houses many times over and the houses coming back to those who never paid for them.

Then we have the active capitalists; those engaged in business. This number must be divided into two classes; the first consisting of those legitimately using their capital in the production of utilities and honest goods. The second, those misusing their capital in the production of "bogus" imitations of luxuries; of adulterations and of useless goods, the miserable makeshifts specially produced for the consumption of underpaid workers. With this "bogus" class must be included not only the jerry builders and the shoddy clothiers, but also the quack doctors and the shyster lawyers, also the mass of insurance and other agents and middlemen.

* * *

In spite of all opposition, the Trade Unions have grown until they have become a power that none can hope to annihilate.

To-day modern society is beginning to regard the Trade Unions as the only hope of civilization; to regard them as the only power capable of evolving order out of the social-chaos. But will the Sibyl's demand be re-regarded or heeded before it is too late? Let us hope so. The Trade Unions having a thorough knowledge of the origin and development of the capitalist class entertain no desire for revenge or retaliation. The Trade Unions have deprecated the malevolent and unjust spirit with which they have had to contend in their protests and struggles against the abuse of the capitalist system, yet while seeking justice have not permitted their movement to become acrid by the desire of revenge. Their methods were always conservative, their steps evolutionary.

* * *

What does labor want? It wants the earth and the fulness thereof. There is nothing too precious, there is nothing too beautiful, too lofty, too ennobling, unless it is within the scope and comprehension of labor's aspirations and wants. But to be more specific: The expressed demands of labor are first and foremost a reduction of the hours of daily labor to eight hours to-day, fewer to-morrow.

Is labor justified in making this demand? Let us examine the facts.

Within the past twenty-five years more inventions and discoveries have been made in the method of producing wealth than in the entire history of the world before. Steam power has been applied on the most extensive scale. The improvement of tools, the consequent division and sub-division of labor, the force of electricity, so little known a few years ago, is now applied to an enormous extent. As a result, the productivity of the toiler with these new improved machines and forces has increased so many fold as to completely overshadow the product of the joint masses of past ages. Every effort, every ingenious device has been utilized to cultivate the greater productivity of the worker.

The fact that in the end the toilers must be the great body of the consumers, has been given little or no consideration at all. The tendency to employ the machines continuously (the worker has been made part of the machines) and the direction has been in the line of endeavoring to make the wealth producers work longer hours.

On the other hand, the organized labor movement, the Trade Unions, have concentrated all their forces upon the movement to reduce the hours of daily toil not only as has been often said, to lighten the burdens of drudgery and severe toil, but also to give the great body of the people more time, more opportunity and more leisure in order to create and increase their consumptive power; in other words, to relieve the choked and glutted condition of industry and commerce.

The prosperity of a nation, the success of a people, the civilizing influence of our era, can always be measured by the comparative consuming power of a people.

If as it has often been said, cheap labor and long hours of toil are necessary to a country's prosperity, commercially and industrially, China should necessarily be at the height of civilization.

Millions of willing heads, hands and hearts are ready to frame and to fashion the fabrics and supply the necessities as well as the desires of the people. There are hundreds of thousands of our fellow men and women who cannot find the opportunity to employ their powers, their brain and brawn to satisfy their commonest and barest necessities to sustain life. In every city and town through this broad land of plenty, gaunt figures, hungry men and women with blanched faces and children having the mark of premature age and emaciated conditions indelibly impressed upon their countenances, stalk through the streets and highways. It does not require a philanthropist nor even a humanitarian to evidence deep concern or to give deep thought in order to arrive at the conclusion that in the midst of plenty, such results are both unnatural and wrong. The ordinary man may truly inquire why it is that the political economist answers our demand for work by saying that the law of supply and demand, from which they say there is no relief, regulates these conditions. Might we not say fails to regulate them?

The organized working men and women, the producers of the wealth of the world, declare that men, women and children with human brains and human hearts, should have a better consideration than inanimate and dormant things, usually known under the euphonious title of "Property." We maintain that it is both inhuman, barbaric and retrogressive to allow the members of the human family to suffer for want, while the very things that could and would contribute to their wants and comforts as well as to the advantage of the entire people, are allowed to decay.

We demand a reduction of the hours of labor which would give a due share of work and wages to the reserve army of labor and eliminate many of the worst abuses of the industrial system now filling our poor houses and jails. The movement for the reduction of the hours of labor is contemporaneous with the introduction of labor saving machinery and has been the most faithful of all reformatory attempts of modern times, since it has clearly revealed the power of the working people to realize an improved industrial system and raises the hope that we may yet be able to stem the tide of economic, social and moral degradations, robbing those who work of four-fifths of their natural wages and keeping the whole of society within a few months of destitution.

Labor demands and insists upon the exercise of the right to organize for self and mutual protection. The toilers want the abrogation of all laws discriminating against them in the exercise of those functions which make our organizations in the economic struggle a factor and not a farce.

That the lives and limbs of the wage-workers shall be regarded as sacred as those of all others of our fellow human beings; that an injury or destruction of either by reason of negligence or maliciousness of another, shall not leave him without redress simply because he is a wage worker. We demand equality before the law, in fact as well as in theory.

The right to appear by counsel guaranteed by the constitution of our country is one upon which labor is determined.

To prescribe narrower limits to the wage workers and urge as a special plea that right is accorded before the courts, is insufficient. The counsel of the toilers have earned their diplomas by sacrifices made and scars received in the battle for labor's rights rather than the mental acquirements of legends and musty precedents of semi-barbaric ages. The diplomas of labor's counsel are not written on parchment, they are engraved in heart and mind. The court our counsels file their briefs in and make their pleas for justice, right and equality in are the offices of the employers. The denial to labor of the right to be heard by counsel—their committees—is a violation of the spirit of a fundamental principle of our republic.

And by no means the least demand of the Trade Unions is for adequate wages.

The importance of this demand is not likely to be under-estimated. Adam Smith[2] says: "It is but equity that they who feed, clothe and lodge the whole body of the people, should have such a share of the produce of their labor as to be themselves tolerably well fed, clothed and lodged." But the Trade Unions' demand is for better pay than [that] which Adam Smith deemed equitable. The Trade Unions taking normal conditions as its point of view, regards the workman as the producer of the wealth of the world and demands that wages (as long as the wage system may last), shall be sufficient to enable him to support his family in a manner consistent with existing civilization and all that is required for maintaining and improving physical and mental health and the self respect of human beings.

Render our lives while working as safe and healthful as modern science demonstrates it is possible. Give us better homes is just as potent a cry to-day as when Dickens[3] voiced the yearnings of the people of a generation ago.

Save our children in their infancy from being forced into the maelstrom of wage slavery. See to it that they are not dwarfed in body and mind or brought to a premature death by early drudgery. Give them the sunshine of the school and playground instead of the factory, the mine and the workshop.

We want more school houses and less jails; more books and less arsenals; more learning and less vice; more constant work and less crime; more leisure and less greed; more justice and less revenge; in fact, more of the opportunities to cultivate

2. An intellectual founder of capitalism based on his 1776 classic, *The Wealth of Nations*.

3. English writer Charles Dickens sympathetically depicted the plight of the working class in novels such as *Oliver Twist* and *Hard Times*.

our better natures, to make manhood more noble, womanhood more beautiful and childhood more happy and bright.

These in brief are the primary demands made by the Trade Unions in the name of labor.

These are the demands made by labor upon modern society and in their consideration is involved the fate of civilization.

Study Questions

1. According to Gompers, what are the "primary demands" of organized labor? How can they be achieved? Why does he describe labor's methods as "always conservative"?
2. According to Gompers, who are the productive members of society? Who are the nonproductive? What does this imply about an ideal distribution of wealth and income in the United States? Was Gompers opposed to capitalism?
3. Commentators often allege that Gompers's answer to the question "what does labor want" was simply "more." To what degree is that a fair representation of what Gompers says in this speech? Why would someone characterize Gompers's perspective this way?
4. What would Samuel Gompers think of the state of organized labor today? Why are contemporary American unions not as strong as he certainly would have liked them to be?

ANDREW CARNEGIE

Wealth (1889)

Andrew Carnegie (1835–1919) is by any measure one of the most important figures in the business and cultural history of the United States. Carnegie, son of a poor Scottish weaver, migrated from Scotland to Pittsburgh with his family at age twelve. Displaying an astonishing drive and work ethic, Carnegie worked in textiles, telegraphy, and the railroad industry. After a successful tenure as an executive with the Pennsylvania Railroad, Carnegie went into the steel business in the early 1870s. By introducing the new Bessemer process, an inexpensive method for manufacturing steel that had been patented in England in 1855, Carnegie transformed steelmaking in the United States. By the time he sold his firm, Carnegie Steel, to the Wall Street financial titan J. P. Morgan in 1901 (thereby enabling the creation of U.S. Steel), Carnegie had amassed a fortune that, adjusted to contemporary dollars, made him the second-richest American—behind only John D. Rockefeller—who ever lived.

Carnegie used the last years of his life to engage in extensive philanthropy, essentially giving his fortune away by the time of his death in 1919. His well-thought-out philosophy justifying this activity was articulated in a widely read article, "Wealth," published in the North American Review, *a prestigious literary magazine, in June 1889. As you read it, consider Carnegie's views on the social responsibilities of the wealthy and how he distinguished himself from many elite Americans of the period. Carnegie's perspective would soon become known as the "Gospel of Wealth" due to the wording he employed in the last sentence of this essay. That phrase would come to embody the dominant values of the Gilded Age.*

From Andrew Carnegie, *North American Review,* 148 no. 391 (June 1889), 656–664.

The problem of our age is the proper administration of wealth, so that the ties of brotherhood may still bind together the rich and poor in harmonious relationship. The conditions of human life have not only been changed, but revolutionized, within the past few hundred years. In former days there was little difference between the dwelling, dress, food, and environment of the chief and those of his retainers. The Indians are to-day where civilized man then was. When visiting the Sioux, I was led to the wigwam of the chief. It was just like the others in external appearance, and even within the difference was trifling between it and those of the poorest of his braves. The contrast between the palace of the millionaire and the cottage of the laborer with us to-day measures the change which has come with civilization.

This change, however, is not to be deplored, but welcomed as highly beneficial. It is well, nay, essential for the progress of the race, that the houses of some should be homes for all that is highest and best in literature and the arts, and for all the refinements of civilization, rather than that none should be so. Much better this great irregularity than universal squalor. Without wealth there can be no Maecenas.[1] The "good old times" were not good old times. Neither master nor servant was as well situated then as to-day. A relapse to old conditions would be disastrous to both—not the least so to him who serves—and would sweep away civilization with it. But whether the change be for good or ill, it is upon us, beyond our power to alter, and therefore to be accepted and made the best of. It is a waste of time to criticise the inevitable.

It is easy to see how the change has come. One illustration will serve for almost every phase of the cause. In the manufacture of products we have the whole story. It applies to all combinations of human industry, as stimulated and enlarged by the inventions of this scientific age. Formerly articles were manufactured at the domestic hearth or in small shops which formed part of the household. The master and his apprentices worked side by side, the latter living with the master, and therefore subject to the same conditions. When these apprentices rose to be masters, there was little or no change in their mode of life, and they, in turn, educated in the same routine succeeding apprentices. There was, substantially, social equality, and even political equality, for those engaged in industrial pursuits had then little or no political voice in the State.

But the inevitable result of such a mode of manufacture was crude articles at high prices. To-day the world obtains commodities of excellent quality at prices which even the generation preceding this would have deemed incredible. In the commercial world similar causes have produced similar results, and the race is benefited thereby. The poor enjoy what the rich could not before afford. What were the luxuries have become the necessaries of life. The laborer has now more comforts than the farmer had a few generations ago. The farmer has more luxuries than the landlord had, and is more richly clad and better housed. The landlord has books and pictures rarer, and appointments more artistic, than the King could then obtain.

The price we pay for this salutary change is, no doubt, great. We assemble thousands of operatives in the factory, in the mine, and in the counting-house, of whom the employer can know little or nothing, and to whom the employer is little better than a myth. All intercourse between them is at an end. Rigid Castes are formed, and, as usual, mutual ignorance breeds mutual distrust. Each Caste is without

1. Wealthy Roman famed as a friend of emperors and a patron of poets.

sympathy for the other, and ready to credit anything disparaging in regard to it. Under the law of competition, the employer of thousands is forced into the strictest economies, among which the rates paid to labor figure prominently, and often there is friction between the employer and the employed, between capital and labor, between rich and poor. Human society loses homogeneity.

The price which society pays for the law of competition, like the price it pays for cheap comforts and luxuries, is also great; but the advantages of this law are also greater still, for it is to this law that we owe our wonderful material development, which brings improved conditions in its train. But, whether the law be benign or not, we must say of it, as we say of the change in the conditions of men to which we have referred: It is here; we cannot evade it; no substitutes for it have been found; and while the law may be sometimes hard for the individual, it is best for the race, because it insures the survival of the fittest in every department. We accept and welcome, therefore, as conditions to which we must accommodate ourselves, great inequality of environment, the concentration of business, industrial and commercial, in the hands of a few, and the law of competition between these, as being not only beneficial, but essential for the future progress of the race. Having accepted these, it follows that there must be great scope for the exercise of special ability in the merchant and in the manufacturer who has to conduct affairs upon a great scale. That this talent for organization and management is rare among men is proved by the fact that it invariably secures for its possessor enormous rewards, no matter where or under what laws or conditions. The experienced in affairs always rate the man whose services can be obtained as a partner as not only the first consideration, but such as to render the question of his capital scarcely worth considering, for such men soon create capital; while, without the special talent required, capital soon takes wings. Such men become interested in firms or corporations using millions; and estimating only simple interest to be made upon the capital invested, it is inevitable that their income must exceed their expenditures, and that they must accumulate wealth. Nor is there any middle ground which such men can occupy, because the great manufacturing or commercial concern which does not earn at least interest upon its capital soon becomes bankrupt. It must either go forward or fall behind; to stand still is impossible. It is a condition essential for its successful operation that it should be thus far profitable, and even that, in addition to interest on capital, it should make profit. It is a law, as certain as any of the others named, that men possessed of this peculiar talent for affairs, under the free play of economic forces, must, of necessity, soon be in receipt of more revenue than can be judiciously expended upon themselves; and this law is as beneficial for the race as the others.

Objections to the foundations upon which society is based are not in order, because the condition of the race is better with these than it has been with any others which have been tried. Of the effect of any new substitutes proposed we cannot be sure. The Socialist or Anarchist who seeks to overturn present conditions is to be regarded as attacking the foundation upon which civilization itself rests, for civilization took its start from the day that the capable, industrious workman said to his incompetent and lazy fellow," If thou dost not sow, thou shalt not reap,"[2] and thus ended primitive Communism by separating the drones from the bees. One who studies this subject will soon be brought face to face with the conclusion that upon the sacredness of property civilization itself depends—the right of the laborer to his hundred dollars in the savings bank, and equally the legal right of the millionaire to his millions. To those who propose to substitute Communism for this intense Individualism the answer, therefore, is: The race has tried that. All progress from that barbarous day to the present time has resulted from its displacement. Not evil, but good, has come to the race from the accumulation of wealth by those who have the ability and energy that produce it. But even if we admit for a moment that it might be better for the race to discard its present foundation, Individualism—that it is a nobler ideal that man should labor, not for himself alone, but in and for a brotherhood of his fellows, and share with them all in common, realizing Swedenborg's[3] idea of Heaven, where, as he says, the angels derive their happiness, not from laboring for self, but for each other—even admit all this, and a sufficient answer is, This is not evolution, but revolution. It necessitates the changing of human nature itself—a work of eons, even if it were good to change it, which we cannot know.

It is not practicable in our day or in our age. Even if desirable theoretically, it belongs to another and long-succeeding sociological stratum. Our duty is with what is practicable now; with the next step possible in our day and generation. It is criminal to waste our energies in endeavoring to uproot, when all we can profitably or possibly accomplish is to bend the universal tree of humanity a little in the direction most favorable to the production of good fruit under existing circumstances. We might as well urge the destruction of the highest existing type of man because he failed to reach our ideal as to favor the destruction of Individualism, Private Property, the Law of Accumulation of Wealth, and the Law of Competition; for these are the highest results of human experience, the soil in which society so far has produced the best fruit. Unequally or unjustly, perhaps, as these laws sometimes operate, and imperfect as they appear to the Idealist, they are, nevertheless, like the highest type of man, the best and most valuable of all that humanity has yet accomplished.

We start, then, with a condition of affairs under which the best interests of the race are promoted, but which inevitably gives wealth to the few. Thus far, accepting conditions as they exist, the situation can be surveyed and pronounced good. The question then arises—and, if the foregoing be correct, it is the only question

2. Carnegie's adaptation of Micah 6:15 from the Bible: "Thou shalt sow, but thou shall not reap."

3. Emanuel Swedenborg (1688–1722), Swedish scientist and Christian theologian whose teachings emphasized the importance of good works as well as faith.

with which we have to deal—What is the proper mode of administering wealth after the laws upon which civilization is founded have thrown it into the hands of the few? And it is of this great question that I believe I offer the true solution. It will be understood that fortunes are here spoken of, not moderate sums saved by many years of effort, the returns from which are required for the comfortable maintenance and education of families. This is not wealth, but only competence, which it should be the aim of all to acquire.

There are but three modes in which surplus wealth can be disposed of. It can be left to the families of the decedents; or it can be bequeathed for public purposes; or, finally, it can be administered during their lives by its possessors. Under the first and second modes most of the wealth of the world that has reached the few has hitherto been applied. Let us in turn consider each of these modes. The first is the most injudicious. In monarchical countries, the estates and the greatest portion of the wealth are left to the first son,[4] that the vanity of the parent may be gratified by the thought that his name and title are to descend to succeeding generations unimpaired. The condition of this class in Europe to-day teaches the futility of such hopes or ambitions. The successors have become impoverished through their follies or from the fall in the value of land. Even in Great Britain the strict law of entail[5] has been found inadequate to maintain the status of an hereditary class. Its soil is rapidly passing into the hands of the stranger. Under republican institutions the division of property among the children is much fairer, but the question which forces itself upon thoughtful men in all lands is: Why should men leave great fortunes to their children? If this is done from affection, is it not misguided affection? Observation teaches that, generally speaking, it is not well for the children that they should be so burdened. Neither is it well for the state. Beyond providing for the wife and daughters moderate sources of income, and very moderate allowances indeed, if any, for the sons, men may well hesitate, for it is no longer questionable that great sums bequeathed oftener work more for the injury than for the good of the recipients. Wise men will soon conclude that, for the best interests of the members of their families and of the state, such bequests are an improper use of their means.

It is not suggested that men who have failed to educate their sons to earn a livelihood shall cast them adrift in poverty. If any man has seen fit to rear his sons with a view to their living idle lives, or, what is highly commendable, has instilled in them the sentiment that they are in a position to labor for public ends without reference to pecuniary considerations, then, of course, the duty of the parent is to see that such are provided for in moderation. There are instances of millionaires' sons unspoiled by wealth, who, being rich, still perform great services in the community. Such are the very salt of the earth, as valuable as, unfortunately, they are

4. The practice known as primogeniture.

5. Entail requires that a man's estate during his lifetime be kept intact.

rare; still it is not the exception, but the rule, that men must regard, and, looking at the usual result of enormous sums conferred upon legatees, the thoughtful man must shortly say, "I would as soon leave to my son a curse as the almighty dollar," and admit to himself that it is not the welfare of the children, but family pride, which inspires these enormous legacies.

As to the second mode, that of leaving wealth at death for public uses, it may be said that this is only a means for the disposal of wealth, provided a man is content to wait until he is dead before it becomes of much good in the world. Knowledge of the results of legacies bequeathed is not calculated to inspire the brightest hopes of much posthumous good being accomplished. The cases are not few in which the real object sought by the testator is not attained, nor are they few in which his real wishes are thwarted. In many cases the bequests are so used as to become only monuments of his folly. It is well to remember that it requires the exercise of not less ability than that which acquired the wealth to use it so as to be really beneficial to the community. Besides this, it may fairly be said that no man is to be extolled for doing what he cannot help doing, nor is he to be thanked by the community to which he only leaves wealth at death. Men who leave vast sums in this way may fairly be thought men who would not have left it at all, had they been able to take it with them. The memories of such cannot be held in grateful remembrance, for there is no grace in their gifts. It is not to be wondered at that such bequests seem so generally to lack the blessing.

The growing disposition to tax more and more heavily large estates left at death is a cheering indication of the growth of a salutary change in public opinion. The State of Pennsylvania now takes—subject to some exceptions—one-tenth of the property left by its citizens. The budget presented in the British Parliament the other day proposes to increase the death-duties; and, most significant of all, the new tax is to be a graduated one. Of all forms of taxation, this seems the wisest. Men who continue hoarding great sums all their lives, the proper use of which for public ends would work good to the community, should be made to feel that the community, in the form of the state, cannot thus be deprived of its proper share. By taxing estates heavily at death the state marks its condemnation of the selfish millionaire's unworthy life.

It is desirable that nations should go much further in this direction. Indeed, it is difficult to set bounds to the share of a rich man's estate which should go at his death to the public through the agency of the state, and by all means such taxes should be graduated, beginning at nothing upon moderate sums to dependents, and increasing rapidly as the amounts swell, until of the millionaire's hoard, as of Shylock's, at least

> The other half
> Comes to the privy coffer of the state.[6]

6. Lines spoken by Portia about the fortune amassed by Shylock, the villainous moneylender, in Shakespeare's *The Merchant of Venice* (4.1.351–2).

This policy would work powerfully to induce the rich man to attend to the administration of wealth during his life, which is the end that society should always have in view, as being that by far most fruitful for the people. Nor need it be feared that this policy would sap the root of enterprise and render men less anxious to accumulate, for to the class whose ambition it is to leave great fortunes and be talked about after their death, it will attract even more attention, and, indeed, be a somewhat nobler ambition to have enormous sums paid over to the state from their fortunes.

There remains, then, only one mode of using great fortunes; but in this we have the true antidote for the temporary unequal distribution of wealth, the reconciliation of the rich and the poor a reign of harmony—another ideal, differing, indeed, from that of the Communist in requiring only the further evolution of existing conditions, not the total overthrow of our civilization. It is founded upon the present most intense individualism, and the race is prepared to put it in practice by degrees whenever it pleases. Under its sway we shall have an ideal state, in which the surplus wealth of the few will become, in the best sense, the property of the many, because administered for the common good, and this wealth, passing through the hands of the few, can be made a much more potent force for the elevation of our race than if it had been distributed in small sums to the people themselves. Even the poorest can be made to see this, and to agree that great sums gathered by some of their fellow-citizens and spent for public purposes, from which the masses reap the principal benefit, are more valuable to them than if scattered among them through the course of many years in trifling amounts.

If we consider what results flow from the Cooper Institute, for instance, to the best portion of the race in New York not possessed of means, and compare these with those which would have arisen for the good of the masses from an equal sum distributed by Mr. Cooper[7] in his lifetime in the form of wages, which is the highest form of distribution, being for work done and not for charity, we can form some estimate of the possibilities for the improvement of the race which lie embedded in the present law of the accumulation of wealth. Much of this sum, if distributed in small quantities among the people, would have been wasted in the indulgence of appetite, some of it in excess, and it may be doubted whether even the part put to the best use, that of adding to the comforts of the home, would have yielded results for the race, as a race, at all comparable to those which are flowing and are to flow from the Cooper Institute from generation to generation. Let the advocate of violent or radical change ponder well this thought.

We might even go so far as to take another instance, that of Mr. Tilden's[8] bequest of five millions of dollars for a free library in the city of New York, but in

7. Peter Cooper (1791–1883), wealthy industrialist and founder of the Cooper Union, a free college for the working class of New York City.

8. Samuel J. Tilden (1814–86), governor of New York, Democratic presidential candidate, and a founding benefactor of the New York Public Library.

referring to this one cannot help saying involuntarily, How much better if Mr. Tilden had devoted the last years of his own life to the proper administration of this immense sum; in which case neither legal contest nor any other cause of delay could have interfered with his aims. But let us assume that Mr. Tilden's millions finally become the means of giving to this city a noble public library, where the treasures of the world contained in books will be open to all forever, without money and without price. Considering the good of that part of the race which congregates in and around Manhattan Island, would its permanent benefit have been better promoted had these millions been allowed to circulate in small sums through the hands of the masses? Even the most strenuous advocate of Communism must entertain a doubt upon this subject. Most of those who think will probably entertain no doubt whatever.

Poor and restricted are our opportunities in this life; narrow our horizon; our best work most imperfect; but rich men should be thankful for one inestimable boon. They have it in their power during their lives to busy themselves in organizing benefactions from which the masses of their fellows will derive lasting advantage, and thus dignify their own lives. The highest life is probably to be reached, not by such imitation of the life of Christ as Count Tolstoy[9] gives us, but, while animated by Christ's spirit, by recognizing the changed conditions of this age, and adopting modes of expressing this spirit suitable to the changed conditions under which we live; still laboring for the good of our fellows, which was the essence of his life and teaching, but laboring in a different manner.

This, then, is held to be the duty of the man of Wealth: First, to set an example of modest, unostentatious living, shunning display or extravagance; to provide moderately for the legitimate wants of those dependent upon him; and after doing so to consider all surplus revenues which come to him simply as trust funds, which he is called upon to administer, and strictly bound as a matter of duty to administer in the manner which, in his judgment, is best calculated to produce the most beneficial results for the community—the man of wealth thus becoming the mere agent and trustee for his poorer brethren, bringing to their service his superior wisdom, experience, and ability to administer, doing for them better than they would or could do for themselves.

We are met here with the difficulty of determining what are moderate sums to leave to members of the family; what is modest, unostentatious living; what is the test of extravagance. There must be different standards for different conditions. The answer is that it is as impossible to name exact amounts or actions as it is to define good manners, good taste, or the rules of propriety; but, nevertheless, these are verities, well known although undefinable. Public sentiment is quick to know

9. That is, Leo Tolstoy (1828–1910), Russian aristocrat famed for his novels *War and Peace* and *Anna Karenina* and to his ardent devotion to an ascetic life inspired by Jesus Christ.

and to feel what offends these. So in the case of wealth. The rule in regard to good taste in the dress of men or women applies here. Whatever makes one conspicuous offends the canon. If any family be chiefly known for display, for extravagance in home, table, equipage, for enormous sums ostentatiously spent in any form upon itself—if these be its chief distinctions, we have no difficulty in estimating its nature or culture. So likewise in regard to the use or abuse of its surplus wealth, or to generous, freehanded co-operation in good public uses, or to unabated efforts to accumulate and hoard to the last, whether they administer or bequeath. The verdict rests with the best and most enlightened public sentiment. The community will surely judge, and its judgments will not often be wrong.

The best uses to which surplus wealth can be put have already been indicated. Those who would administer wisely must, indeed, be wise, for one of the serious obstacles to the improvement of our race is indiscriminate charity. It were better for mankind that the millions of the rich were thrown into the sea than so spent as to encourage the slothful, the drunken, the unworthy. Of every thousand dollars spent in so called charity to-day, it is probable that $950 is unwisely spent; so spent, indeed, as to produce the very evils which it proposes to mitigate or cure. A well-known writer of philosophic books admitted the other day that he had given a quarter of a dollar to a man who approached him as he was coming to visit the house of his friend, He knew nothing of the habits of this beggar; knew not the use that would be made of this money, although he had every reason to suspect that it would be spent improperly. This man professed to be a disciple of Herbert Spencer;[1] yet the quarter-dollar given that night will probably work more injury than all the money which its thoughtless donor will ever be able to give in true charity will do good. He only gratified his own feelings, saved himself from annoyance—and this was probably one of the most selfish and very worst actions of his life, for in all respects he is most worthy.

In bestowing charity, the main consideration should be to help those who will help themselves; to provide part of the means by which those who desire to improve may do so; to give those who desire to rise the aids by which they may rise; to assist, but rarely or never to do all. Neither the individual nor the race is improved by alms-giving. Those worthy of assistance, except in rare cases, seldom require assistance. The really valuable men of the race never do, except in cases of accident or sudden change. Every one has, of course, cases of individuals brought to his own knowledge where temporary assistance can do genuine good, and these he will not overlook. But the amount which can be wisely given by the individual for individuals is necessarily limited by his lack of knowledge of the circumstances connected with each. He is the only true reformer who is as careful

1. Spencer (1820–1903) was the English biologist and philosopher who popularized the notion that Charles Darwin's principles of natural selection applied to human society as well as the plant and animal kingdom.

and as anxious not to aid the unworthy as he is to aid the worthy, and, perhaps, even more so, for in alms-giving more injury is probably done by rewarding vice than by relieving virtue.

The rich man is thus almost restricted to following the examples of Peter Cooper, Enoch Pratt of Baltimore,[2] Mr. Pratt of Brooklyn,[3] Senator Stanford,[4] and others, who know that the best means of benefiting the community is to place within its reach the ladders upon which the aspiring can rise—free libraries, parks, and means of recreation, by which men are helped in body and mind; works of art, certain to give pleasure and improve the public taste, and public institutions of various kinds, which will improve the general condition of the people; in this manner returning their surplus wealth to the mass of their fellows in the forms best calculated to do them lasting good.

Thus is the problem of Rich and Poor to be solved. The laws of accumulation will be left free; the laws of distribution free. Individualism will continue, but the millionaire will be but a trustee for the poor; intrusted for a season with a great part of the increased wealth of the community, but administering it for the community far better than it could or would have done for itself. The best minds will thus have reached a stage in the development of the race in which it is clearly seen that there is no mode of disposing of surplus wealth creditable to thoughtful and earnest men into whose hands it flows save by using it year by year for the general good. This day already dawns. Men may die without incurring the pity of their fellows, still sharers in great business enterprises from which their capital cannot be or has not been withdrawn, and is left chiefly at death for public uses, yet the day is not far distant when the man who dies leaving behind him millions of available wealth, which was his to administer during life, will pass away "unwept, unhonored, and unsung,"[5] no matter to what uses he leaves the dross which he cannot take with him. Of such as these the public verdict will then be: The man who dies thus rich dies disgraced.

Such, in my opinion, is the true Gospel concerning Wealth, obedience to which is destined some day to solve the problem of the Rich and the Poor, and to bring "Peace on earth, among men Good-Will."[6]

2. Businessman and philanthropist (1808–96), founder of a still-functioning public library system in Baltimore.

3. Oil millionaire Charles Pratt, (1830–91) founder of an industrial college in Brooklyn, the Pratt Institute, in 1887.

4. Railroad tycoon Leland Stanford (1824–93), who served as U.S. senator from California and established the elite university in Palo Alto, California, that bears his name.

5. From the poem "Breathes There the Man" by Scottish novelist Sir Walter Scott (1771–1832).

6. From the Christmas story, Luke 2:14.

Study Questions

1. How does Carnegie believe that industrial capitalism has "revolutionized" American life? What are the benefits and shortcomings of this change? How does he feel about doctrines like socialism that address the ills of industrial society?
2. Analyze Carnegie's claim that the American economic system "inevitably gives wealth to the few." Why would he advise rich men to practice "unostentatious living"? How would they likely respond?
3. According to Carnegie, what are the three methods of disposing of surplus wealth? Which does he favor and why? On what grounds does he reject the other approaches?
4. How does Carnegie think wealthy philanthropists can best benefit society? What are his thoughts on charitable contributions to the poor?
5. At the time of Carnegie's writing, Social Darwinist ideas of survival of the fittest were commonplace among men of his class. To what degree is Carnegie's "gospel of wealth" compatible with Social Darwinist thinking? Fully explain.
6. Why did Carnegie oppose aristocracy of the type that existed in Europe? Do American aristocrats exist today? If so, what might Carnegie advocate to correct the situation?

THE NEW YORK SUN

A Typical Base-Ball Crowd (1884)

One by-product of Gilded Age urbanization was the growing popularity of spectator sports. By the late nineteenth century, industrial cities in the Northeast and Midwest had sufficient populations to provide the fan base for professional baseball teams. The growth of an urban middle class and a slow rise in real wages meant that increasing numbers of residents had the time and money to attend games. The Cincinnati Red Stockings organized as the first professional baseball club in 1869 and were charter members of the National League upon its formation in 1876. By 1883 New York had a permanent team of its own, the Giants. This franchise played at an Upper Manhattan stadium called the Polo Grounds, which would be the site of such legendary moments in the national pastime as Bobby Thomson's dramatic pennant-winning home run in 1951 and Willie Mays's epic deep centerfield catch in the 1954 World Series. The Polo Grounds was home to a variety of professional baseball and football teams until its eventual demolition in 1964.

The following document describes a trip to the Polo Grounds in the summer of 1884, by which time major league baseball teams have clearly begun to draw regular crowds. As you read it, look for the sources of baseball's popularity in that era and the continuities between the spectator experience then and today.

From Benjamin H. Day, pub., "Those Who Like Base-ball: A Study of the Daily Multitude at the Polo Grounds," *The New York Sun*, June 1, 1884, 9.

The first thing that impresses one on a visit to the Polo Grounds on any day of the week is the number of spectators. It makes no difference what day it is or which clubs are to compete, there are always crowds on hand to witness a match. On Fridays and Saturdays there are more persons than on other days. But a match between two of the more prominent nines of the League will call out 7,000 or 8,000 persons, no matter what the day may be. The wonder to a man who works for his living is how so many people can spare the time for the sport. They are obliged to leave their offices down town at 2 or 3 o'clock in order to get to the Polo Grounds in time, and very many of them are constant attendants on the field. The next thing that impresses the visitor is the absolute and perfect knowledge of base-ball which every visitor at the grounds possesses. Nearly every boy and man keeps his own score, registering base hits, runs and errors as the game goes along, and the slightest hint of unfairness on the part of the umpire will bring a yell from thousands of throats instantaneously. The third notable characteristic . . . is the good nature, affability, and friendliness of the crowd. The slim schoolboy ten years of age, and the fat, lager-beer saloon proprietor of fifty talk gracefully about the game as it progresses as though they had known each other for years. Men exchange opinions freely about the game with persons they never saw before and everybody seems good-natured and happy.

THE MAJORITY OF THE MEN are intensely interested in the game. Most of them come well provided with their own cigars, and sedulously evade the eye of the man who peddles "sody-water, sarss-a-parilla lemonade, pea-nuts and seegars." There is little drinking of any sort and much smoking. . . . At times when the umpire renders a decision that does not meet with popular approval, there will be a terrific outbreak, and for the next ten minutes the offending one is guyed unmercifully. Every decision he renders is received with jeers, and sarcastic comments are made upon the play. The good sense of the crowd gets the better of this boyishness, however, and unless the umpire is decidedly biased, which rarely occurs, the crowd soon settles back into its accustomed condition of contentment.

Perhaps the most enthusiastic and expert spectators at the Polo Grounds are the stockily built young Irishmen. They may be bartenders, light porters, expressmen, clerks, loungers, policemen off duty, or merchants out on a holiday. One of them is a type of a thousand others. He is usually square shouldered and well built. Probably he has had a taste of athletics himself and plays. . . .

It has often been remarked that there are at the Polo Grounds every day AN EXTRAORDINARY NUMBER OF FAT MEN. No one can tell why this is. It is said that men of extraordinary avoirdupois[1] who find it impractical, inelegant, and more or less sensational to throw hand-springs, steal base, and run swiftly at 250 pounds weight, enjoy the spectacle of the cat-like and rapid movements of the athletes on the field. . . .

A good many gray heads and gray beards are to be seen on the grand stand. They belong to men who have been base-ball enthusiasts from boyhood up. They enjoy the sport more than they would any play, horse or boat race, and they are full of reminiscences of the game. Scattered in among them are bright-face boys, who are well dressed, well mannered and intelligent. They are looked upon by the men as of enough importance to warrant sober treatment, and their opinions are as gravely accepted as those of men. Another pronounced type is the young business man. Hundreds of spruce, well-dressed and wide-awake young men who are apparently clerks, brokers or business men from downtown are to be seen about the grounds. They talk balls and strike, but principally ball. They do not

1. Weight.

know as much about it as . . . the solid young Irishmen, but they make up in enthusiasm what they lack in knowledge. Their interest in the game consists largely in the money [they] have on it. They always bet freely among themselves, and return home happy or crestfallen, according to their winnings.

There are among the ladies who attend ball matches a few, perhaps a dozen in all, who thoroughly understand the game and are actually and warmly interested in the sport. Most of them, however have such a superficial knowledge of the game that they grow tired before the ninth inning is reached, and conceal their weariness when they leave early, by expressing a desire to avoid the crowd.

Study Questions

1. What impresses the reporter so much about the number and types of spectators at the Polo Grounds? What are the sources of entertainment at the ballpark other than the action on the field?
2. What does this document indicate about when games were played or not played? How would this have influenced who was attending? What does the presence of what the writer terms "an extraordinary number of fat men" reveal about the fan base of the New York team?
3. How is it that this writer is able to identify so many of the spectators as Irish? Why might the environment of the ballpark be less attractive to women?
4. Earlier in the nineteenth century, baseball was often called *town ball*, explicitly linking the sport to urbanization. Why did the game naturally develop in cities? What made a trip to a baseball park especially appealing to residents of an industrial city?

THE NATION

Corruption in College Football: The Athletic Craze (1893)

American football has its roots in the "foot ball" games of England that evolved into what Americans now call rugby and soccer. The first football game in the United States pitted Rutgers against Princeton (then the College of New Jersey) in 1869. Rutgers prevailed, 6 goals to 4, in a contest that assembled 25 players on each team. The game developed further in 1874 when McGill University of Montreal introduced its own version of English rugby football—which allowed players to pick up and advance the ball—in a series at Harvard in 1874. Walter Camp, a player-coach at Yale, made essential changes in the early 1880s by introducing the line of scrimmage and the downs system, which made the American game distinct from any of its English counterparts.

By the 1890s college football had spread beyond the Northeast, with the teams at elite institutions like Harvard and Princeton remaining dominant. It seemed to be a game uniquely suited for a rapidly industrializing nation, because of its division of labor among the players and the fact that, unlike baseball, it was played against a time clock. Like workers in a factory, football players each had their own specialized role (though at this stage in the sport's history, most of them played both offense and defense). Concerns were arising, however, about the physical danger of the sport and the possibility that its popularity might corrupt the scholarly missions of the universities that fielded prominent teams. As you read this editorial from the Nation *(December 7, 1893), consider why its writers were so disturbed by the growing popularity of what would become a national obsession.*

From "The Athletic Craze," *The Nation* (7 December 1893): 422–23.

We are glad that the Harvard Overseers have appointed a committee to investigate the game of football in its various aspects. We are also glad to learn that there is to be this winter a convention of the deities of the football world, to revise the rules, and probably abolish the "flying wedge"[1] and other dangerous features of the present game. So far so good. But

1. A tactic by which the ball carrier advances inside a tightly packed group of running blockers.

we would respectfully ask the college faculties whether they propose this winter to take any action looking to the reform of the game, and indeed all college games, on the moral side.

We refer them to some paragraphs in *Harper's Weekly* on Phillips Exeter Academy, which show the effect that the inordinate attention given to athletics in college is having on young boys in the preparatory schools. How many of them who have the size and weight qualifying to row or play football now think of the college to which they are going as a seat of learning? The practice, on the part of the athletic element in the colleges, of seeking them out, and bribing them by offers of a free education to come to one college rather than another, has become unhappily common, and has ceased to seem discreditable; that is, very young boys are invited to become professionals, and to take what is in reality a salary for acting as football players in the guise of students.

That the faculties play into the hands of these debauchers of youth by being easy with these young professionals in examinations and recitations is at least generally believed. Can nothing be done to suppress or make disgraceful this abuse of allowing professional athletes to haunt the college buildings as sham students? Is not the presence of such men at all in colleges highly demoralizing, and likely to confuse the minds of freshmen as to the ends for which colleges exist?

We are informed on good authority that Yale spent last year about $47,000 on athletics, and the team went to Springfield the other day with three drawing-room cars and fifty men as substitutes, doctors, trainers, rubbers, and cooks. The receipts from the gate-money in New York cannot have fallen far short of $50,000. It was earned by exhibiting feats of strength and agility by scholars and gentlemen before an enormous city crowd, in which the gambling fraternity and the prostitutes were very prominent.

We are not inveighing against athletic games. If the colleges were to-morrow to make football compulsory for every man in them, we should not say a word in objection. We are simply asking for moderation and decency. It seems to be the weakness of the American people to take nearly everything in "crazes." There was the greenback craze, and the silver craze, and the granger craze, and the cholera craze, and now there is the athletic craze, and the leading colleges are becoming huge training-grounds for young gladiators, around whom nearly as many spectators roar as roared in the Flavian amphitheater.[2]

One of its worst results is, however, that it frightens "the plain people" away from the colleges. The modest father who is willing to pinch himself and wife and daughters in order to give a son a college education, is appalled by what he hears and sees of the results of a football match. Debt, drink, debauchery rise up before his mind's eye as a probable concomitant of "college training," and he decides to keep his pet lamb at home. The colleges are not drawing as they ought for this

2. The Colosseum in ancient Rome, which could accommodate 50,000 spectators.

class. The wealthy men are going to them in greater and greater numbers, but it is not they who keep alive the traditions of American scholarship, or show the world what a college education can do by way of preparation for life. Of the effect on the members of the various teams of the conspicuousness in which they pass some months of every year, of the interviews, the newspaper gossip, and portraits, we will not speak, as nothing definite can be known about it. But if much remains of "the modest stillness and humility" which is, the poet says, so becoming in time of peace, after training for two or three matches, they must be almost more than human.

Study Questions

1. According to the article, how is college football corrupting higher education? In what sense are its players actually professional athletes?
2. Analyze the reference to the "young gladiators" in the "Flavian amphitheater." What is the historical allusion? How might the role of football in Gilded Age America mirror that of spectator sports in ancient times?
3. What sort of people in American society do the editorialists believe most need a college education? Why? Why might football discourage pursuit of a college career?
4. To what extent is football inherently dangerous? Is the sport more or less safe now than in 1893? What if anything could be done to lessen the number and degree of football-related injuries?

BOOKER T. WASHINGTON

Atlanta Exposition Address (1895)

Booker T. Washington (1856–1915) lived the first nine years of his life as a slave on a Virginia plantation. After emancipation, he enrolled at Hampton Institute in Virginia, a teacher-training college founded just after the Civil War for the benefit of former slaves. Washington later catapulted to prominence among African Americans as a result of his leadership at Tuskegee Institute, a school he established in Alabama in 1881 that reflected Washington's pragmatic approach to black uplift with its heavily industrial-vocational curriculum.

Due to Washington's prominence as an educator and black spokesman, he was invited to deliver a major address on the opening day of the Atlanta Cotton States and International Exposition on September 18, 1895. The white business leaders who had organized the event hoped to project a New South image of racial harmony by asking Washington to share their platform. The image concealed a darker reality: the exposition occurred just as black enfranchisement was being stripped away by poll taxes and literacy tests and shortly before the Supreme Court validated segregation laws in the Plessy *ruling of 1896. Nonetheless, Washington's speech was a tremendous success. As you read it, consider Washington's cautious strategy for black progress against a backdrop of racial oppression.*

From Booker T. Washington, *Up from Slavery: The Autobiography of Booker T. Washington* (New York: Doubleday, 1959), 153–58.

One-third of the population of the South is of the Negro race. No enterprise seeking the material, civil, or moral welfare of this section can convey to you, Mr. President and Directors, the sentiment of the masses of my race when I say that in no way have the value and manhood of the American Negro been more fittingly and generously recognized than by the managers of this magnificent Exposition at every stage of its progress. It is a recognition that will do more to cement the friendship of the two races than any occurrence since the dawn of our freedom.

Not only this, but the opportunity here afforded will awaken among us a new era of industrial progress. Ignorant and inexperienced, it is not strange that in the first years of our new life we began at the top instead of at the bottom; that a seat in Congress or the State Legislature was more sought than real estate or industrial skill; that the political convention or stump speaking had more attractions than starting a dairy farm or truck garden.

A ship lost at sea for many days suddenly sighted a friendly vessel. From the mast of the unfortunate vessel was seen a signal: "Water, water, we die of thirst." The answer from the friendly vessel at once came back, "Cast down your bucket where you are." A second time the signal, "Water, water, send us water," ran up from the distressed vessel and was answered, "Cast down your bucket where you are." The captain of the distressed vessel, at last heeding the injunction, cast down his bucket and it came up full of fresh, sparkling water from the mouth of the Amazon River. To those of my race who depend on bettering their condition in a foreign land, or who underestimate the importance of cultivating friendly relations with the Southern white man who is their next-door neighbor, I would say: Cast down your bucket where you are; cast it down in making friends, in every manly way, of the people of all races by whom we are surrounded.

Cast it down in agriculture, mechanics, in commerce, in domestic service, and in the professions. And in this connection it is well to bear in mind that whatever other sins the South may be called upon to bear, when it comes to business pure and simple, it is in the South that the Negro is given a man's chance in the commercial world, and in nothing is this Exposition more eloquent than in emphasizing this chance. Our greatest danger is that, in the great leap from slavery to freedom, we may overlook the fact that the masses of us are to live by the productions of our hands and fail to keep in mind that we shall prosper in the proportion as we learn to dignify and glorify common labor, and put brains and skill into the common occupations of life; shall prosper in proportion as we learn to draw the line between the superficial and the substantial, the ornamental gewgaws of life and the useful. No race can prosper until it learns that there is as much dignity in tilling a field as in writing a poem. It is at the bottom of life we must begin, and not at the top. Nor should we permit our grievances to overshadow our opportunities.

To those of the white race who look to the incoming of those of foreign birth and strange tongue and habits for the prosperity of the South, were I permitted I would repeat what I say to my own race, "Cast down your bucket where you are." Cast it down among the 8,000,000 Negroes whose habits you know, whose fidelity and love you have tested in days when to have proved treacherous meant the ruin of your firesides. Cast down your bucket among these people who have, without strikes and labor wars, tilled your fields, cleared your forests, built your railroads and cities, and brought forth treasures from the bowels of the earth and helped make possible this magnificent representation of the progress of the South. Casting down your bucket among my people, helping and encouraging them as you are doing on these grounds, and, with education of head, hand and heart, you will find that they will buy your surplus land, make blossom the waste places in your fields, and run your factories. While doing this, you can be sure in the future, as in the past, that you and your families will be surrounded by the most patient, faithful, law-abiding and unresentful people that the world has seen. As we have proved our loyalty to you in the past, in nursing your children, watching by the sick-bed of your mothers and fathers, and often following them with tear-dimmed eyes to their graves, so in the future, in our humble way, we shall stand by you with a devotion that no foreigner can approach, ready to lay down our lives, if need be, in defense of yours; interlacing our industrial, commercial, civil, and religious life with yours in a way that shall make the interest of both races one. In all things that are purely social we can be as separate as the fingers, yet one as the hand in all things essential to mutual progress.

There is no defense or security for any of us except in the highest intelligence and development of all. If anywhere there are efforts tending to curtail the fullest growth of the Negro, let these efforts be turned into stimulating, encouraging, and making him the most useful and intelligent citizen. Effort or means so invested will pay a thousand per cent interest. These efforts will be twice blessed—"blessing him that gives and him that takes."[1]

There is no escape, through law of man or God, from the inevitable:

> The laws of changeless justice bind
> Oppressor with oppressed,
> And close as sin and suffering joined
> We march to fate abreast.[2]

Nearly sixteen million hands will aid you in pulling the load upward, or they will pull against you the load downward. We shall constitute one-third and more of the ignorance and crime of the South, or one-third its intelligence and progress; we shall contribute one-third to the business and industrial prosperity of the South, or we shall prove a veritable body of death, stagnating, depressing, retarding every effort to advance the body politic.

Gentlemen of the Exposition: As we present to you our humble effort at an exhibition of our progress, you must not expect over much. Starting thirty years ago with ownership here and there in a few quilts and pumpkins and chickens (gathered from miscellaneous sources), remember: the path that has led us from these to the invention and production of agricultural implements, buggies, steam engines, newspapers, books, statuary carving, paintings, the management of drugstores and banks, has not been trodden without contact, with thorns and thistles. While we take pride in what we exhibit as a result of our independent efforts, we do not for a moment forget that our part in this exhibition would fall far

1. Slightly altered quotation of Matthew 5:7, as well as Portia's "quality of mercy" speech in Shakespeare's *The Merchant of Venice*.

2. From the 1862 poem "Song of the Negro Boatmen" by the New England poet and abolitionist John Greenleaf Whittier.

short of your expectations but for the constant help that has come to our educational life, not only from the Southern states, but especially from Northern philanthropists who have made their gifts a constant stream of blessing and encouragement.

The wisest among my race understand that the agitation of questions of social equality is the extremist folly, and that progress in the enjoyment of all the privileges that will come to us must be the result of severe and constant struggle rather than of artificial forcing. No race that has anything to contribute to the markets of the world is long in any degree ostracized. It is important and right that all privileges of the law be ours, but it is vastly more important that we be prepared for the exercise of those privileges. The opportunity to earn a dollar in a factory just now is worth infinitely more than the opportunity to spend a dollar in an opera house.

In conclusion, may I repeat that nothing in thirty years has given us more hope and encouragement, and drawn us so near to you of the white race, as this opportunity offered by the Exposition; and here bending, as it were, over the altar that represents the results of the struggles of your race and mine, both starting practically empty-handed three decades ago, I pledge that, in your effort to work out the great and intricate problem which God has laid at the door of the South, you shall have at all times the patient, sympathetic help of my race; only let this be constantly in mind that, while from representations in these buildings of the product of field, of forest, or mine, of factory, letters and art, much good will come—yet far above and beyond material benefits, will be that higher good, that let us pray God will come, in a blotting out of sectional difference and racial animosities and suspicions, in a determination to administer absolute justice, in a willing obedience among all classes to the mandates of law. This, coupled with material prosperity, will bring into our beloved South a new heaven and a new earth.

Study Questions

1. What mistake does Washington believe many blacks made in their initial years of freedom? What does he mean for blacks in advising them to "cast down your bucket where you are"? What does he mean by giving exactly the same advice to whites?
2. In what ways does the speech allude to tensions over foreign immigration and unionization in the 1890s? What is Washington's purpose in making such references?
3. What does Washington have to say about segregation laws or voting rights? What if any strategy did he have for eventually securing black equality?
4. Why did so many white leaders warmly receive Washington's speech? Was Washington justified in his attempt to win their favor?

★

W. E. B. DU BOIS

Of the Training of Black Men (1903)

FROM *The Souls of Black Folk*

W. E. B. Du Bois (1868–1963), the first African American to earn a doctorate from Harvard University, was born in the Reconstruction Era in Great Barrington, Massachusetts. Du Bois argued for an African American identity and full equal rights for blacks. His activism included anti-lynching and anti-war efforts as well as Pan-Africanism, the opposition to European colonialism in Africa. In 1909, he co-founded the National Association for the Advancement of Colored People (NAACP). Among his early writing was a positive account of Reconstruction that ran counter to prevailing views. By 1945, he was a member of the NAACP delegation to the new United Nations, and as an anti-war activist he ran afoul of the government during the McCarthy era. He died in Ghana, where he had become a citizen after the United States denied his passport.

Du Bois is often compared with Booker T. Washington (1856–1915), who promoted vocational training for blacks and delivered the Atlanta Address of 1895, which advocated accommodation with southern whites. As you read this excerpt, consider how Du Bois's own background shaped his thinking, and why he might advocate a leap to higher education rather than a gradual climb to it.

From W. E. B. Du Bois, "Of the Training of Black Men," in *The Souls of Black Folk* (Chicago: A.C. McClurg & Co., 1903), 21–39.

Why, if the Soul can fling the Dust aside.
And naked on the Air of Heaven ride,
  Were't not a Shame—were't not a Shame for him
In this clay carcase crippled to abide?

OMAR KHAYYÁM (FITZGERALD)[1]

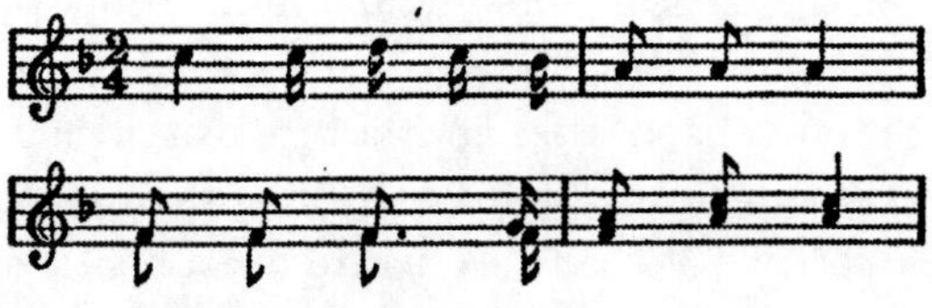

1. Each chapter of *The Souls of Black Folk* (1903) begins with a poem stanza and musical notes from a spiritual; the notes in this excerpt are from the spiritual "March On."

From the shimmering swirl of waters where many, many thoughts ago the slave-ship first saw the square tower of Jamestown, have flowed down to our day three streams of thinking: one swollen from the larger world here and over-seas, saying, the multiplying of human wants in culture-lands calls for the world-wide coöperation of men in satisfying them. Hence arises a new human unity, pulling the ends of earth nearer, and all men, black, yellow, and white. The larger humanity strives to feel in this contact of living Nations and sleeping hordes a thrill of new life in the world, crying. "If the contact of Life and Sleep be Death, shame on such Life." To be sure, behind this thought lurks the afterthought of force and dominion,—the making of brown men to delve when the temptation of beads and red calico cloys.

The second thought streaming from the death-ship and the curving river is the thought of the older South,—the sincere and passionate belief that somewhere between men and cattle, God created a *tertiumquid*, and called it a Negro,—a clownish, simple creature, at times even lovable within its limitations, but straitly foreordained to walk within the Veil. To be sure, behind the thought lurks the afterthought,—some of them with favoring chance might become men, but in sheer self-defence we dare not let them, and we build about them walls so high, and hang between them and the light a veil so thick, that they shall not even think of breaking through.

And last of all there trickles down that third and darker thought,—the thought of the things themselves, the confused, half-conscious mutter of men who are black and whitened, crying "Liberty, Freedom, Opportunity—vouchsafe to us, O boastful World, the chance of living men!" To be sure, behind the thought lurks the afterthought,—suppose, after all, the World is right and we are less than men? Suppose this mad impulse within is all wrong, some mock mirage from the untrue?

So here we stand among thoughts of human unity, even through conquest and slavery; the inferiority of black men, even if forced by fraud; a shriek in the night for the freedom of men who themselves are not yet sure of their right to demand it. This is the tangle of thought and afterthought wherein we are called to solve the problem of training men for life.

Behind all its curiousness, so attractive alike to sage and *dilettante*, lie its dim dangers, throwing across us shadows at once grotesque and awful. Plain it is to us that what the world seeks through desert and wild we have within our threshold,—a stalwart laboring force, suited to the semi-tropics; if, deaf to the voice of the Zeitgeist, we refuse to use and develop these men, we risk poverty and loss. If, on the other hand, seized by the brutal afterthought, we debauch the race thus caught in our talons, selfishly sucking their blood and brains in the future as in the past, what shall save us from national decadence? Only that saner selfishness, which Education teaches, can find the rights of all in the whirl of work.

Again, we may decry the color-prejudice of the South, yet it remains a heavy fact. Such curious kinks of the human mind exist and must be reckoned with soberly. They cannot be laughed away, nor always successfully stormed at, nor easily abolished by act of legislature. And yet they must not be encouraged by being let alone. They must be recognized as facts, but unpleasant facts; things that stand in the way of civilization and religion and common decency. They can be met in but one way,—by the breadth and broadening of human reason, by catholicity of taste and culture. And so, too, the native ambition and aspiration of men, even though they be black, backward, and ungraceful, must not lightly be dealt with. To stimulate wildly weak and untrained minds is to play with mighty fires; to flout their striving idly is to welcome a harvest of brutish crime and shameless lethargy in our very laps. The guiding of thought and the deft coordination of deed is at once the path of honor and humanity.

And so, in this great question of reconciling three vast and partially contradictory streams of thought, the one panacea of Education leaps to the lips of all:—such human training as will best use the labor of all men without enslaving or brutalizing; such training as will give us poise to encourage the prejudices that bulwark society, and to stamp out those that in sheer barbarity deafen us to the wail of prisoned souls within the Veil, and the mounting fury of shackled men.

* * *

In rough approximation we may point out four varying decades of work in Southern education since the Civil War. From the close of the war until 1876, was the period of uncertain groping and temporary relief. There were army schools, mission schools, and schools of the Freedman's Bureau in chaotic disarrangement seeking system and cooperation. Then followed ten years of constructive definite effort toward the building of complete school systems in the South. Normal schools[2] and colleges were founded for the freedmen, and teachers trained there to man the public schools. There was the inevitable tendency of war to underestimate the prejudices of the master and the ignorance of the slave, and all seemed clear sailing out of the wreckage of the storm. Meantime, starting in this decade yet especially developing from 1885 to 1895, began the industrial revolution of the South. The land saw glimpses of a new destiny and the stirring of new ideals. The educational system striving to complete itself saw new obstacles and a field of work ever broader and deeper. The Negro colleges, hurriedly founded, were inadequately equipped, illogically distributed, and of varying efficiency and grade; the normal and high schools were doing little more than common-school work, and the common schools were training but a third of the children who ought to be in them, and training these too often poorly. At the same time the white South by reason of its sudden conversion from the slavery ideal, by so much the more

2. Two-year colleges, for training elementary school teachers.

became set and strengthened in its racial prejudice, and crystallized it into harsh law and harsher custom; while the marvellous pushing forward of the poor white daily threatened to take even bread and butter from the mouths of the heavily handicapped sons of the freedmen. In the midst, then, of the larger problem of Negro education sprang up the more practical question of work, the inevitable economic quandary that faces a people in the transition from slavery to freedom, and especially those who make that change amid hate and prejudice, lawlessness and ruthless competition.

The industrial school springing to notice in this decade, but coming to full recognition in the decade beginning with 1895, was the proffered answer to this combined educational and economic crisis, and an answer of singular wisdom and timeliness. From the very first in nearly all the schools some attention had been given to training in handiwork, but now was this training first raised to a dignity that brought it in direct touch with the South's magnificent industrial development, and given an emphasis which reminded black folk that before the Temple of Knowledge swing the Gates of Toil.

Yet after all they are but gates, and when turning our eyes from the temporary and the contingent in the Negro problem to the broader question of the permanent uplifting and civilization of black men in America, we have a right to inquire, as this enthusiasm for material advancement mounts to its height, if after all the industrial school is the final and sufficient answer in the training of the Negro race; and to ask gently, but in all sincerity, the ever-recurring query of the ages, Is not life more than meat, and the body more than raiment? And men ask this to-day all the more eagerly because of sinister signs in recent educational movements. The tendency is here, born of slavery and quickened to renewed life by the crazy imperialism of the day, to regard human beings as among the material resources of a land to be trained with an eye single to future dividends. Race-prejudices, which keep brown and black men in their "places," we are coming to regard as useful allies with such a theory, no matter how much they may dull the ambition and sicken the hearts of struggling human beings. And above all, we daily hear that an education that encourages aspiration, that sets the loftiest of ideals and seeks as an end culture and character rather than bread-winning, is the privilege of white men and the danger and delusion of black.

Especially has criticism been directed against the former educational efforts to aid the Negro. In the four periods I have mentioned, we find first, boundless, planless enthusiasm and sacrifice; then the preparation of teachers for a vast public-school system; then the launching and expansion of that school system amid increasing difficulties; and finally the training of workmen for the new and growing industries. This development has been sharply ridiculed as a logical anomaly and flat reversal of nature. Soothly we have been told that first industrial and manual training should have taught the Negro to work, then simple schools should have taught him to read and write, and finally, after years, high and normal schools could have completed the system, as intelligence and wealth demanded.

That a system logically so complete was historically impossible, it needs but a little thought to prove. Progress in human affairs is more often a pull than a push, a surging forward of the exceptional man, and the lifting of his duller brethren slowly and painfully to his vantage-ground. Thus it was no accident that gave birth to universities centuries before the common schools, that made fair Harvard the first flower of our wilderness. So in the South: the mass of the freedmen at the end of the war lacked the intelligence so necessary to modern workingmen. They must first have the common school to teach them to read, write, and cipher; and they must have higher schools to teach teachers for the common schools. The white teachers who flocked South went to establish such a common-school system. Few held the idea of founding colleges; most of them at first would have laughed at the idea. But they faced, as all men since them have faced, that central paradox of the South,—the social separation of the races. At that time it was the sudden volcanic rupture of nearly all relations between black and white, in work and government and family life. Since then a new adjustment of relations in economic and political affairs has grown up,—an adjustment subtle and difficult to grasp, yet singularly ingenious, which leaves still that frightful chasm at the color-line across which men pass at their peril.[3] Thus, then and now, there stand in the South two separate worlds; and separate not simply in the higher realms of social intercourse, but also in church and school, on railway and street-car, in hotels and theatres, in streets and city sections, in books and newspapers, in asylums and jails, in hospitals and graveyards. There is still enough of contact for large economic and group coöperation, but the separation is so thorough and deep that it absolutely precludes for the present between the races anything like that sympathetic and effective group-training and leadership of the one by the other, such as the American Negro and all backward peoples must have for effectual progress.

This the missionaries of '68 soon saw; and if effective industrial and trade schools were impracticable before the establishment of a common-school system, just as certainly no adequate common schools could be founded until there were teachers to teach them. Southern whites would not teach them; Northern whites in sufficient numbers could not be had. If the Negro was to learn, he must teach himself, and the most effective help that could be given him was the establishment of schools to train Negro teachers. This conclusion was slowly but surely reached by every student of the situation until simultaneously, in widely separated regions, without consultation or systematic plan, there arose a series of institutions designed to furnish teachers for the untaught. Above the sneers of critics at the obvious

3. Du Bois begins *The Souls of Black Folk* by clearly stating, "The problem of the Twentieth Century is the problem of the color line."

defects of this procedure must ever stand its one crushing rejoinder: in a single generation they put thirty thousand black teachers in the South; they wiped out the illiteracy of the majority of the black people of the land, and they made Tuskegee possible.

Such higher training-schools tended naturally to deepen broader development: at first they were common and grammar schools, then some became high schools. And finally, by 1900, some thirty-four had one year or more of studies of college grade. This development was reached with different degrees of speed in different institutions: Hampton is still a high school, while Fisk University started her college in 1871, and Spelman Seminary about 1896. In all cases the aim was identical,—to maintain the standards of the lower training by giving teachers and leaders the best practicable training; and above all, to furnish the black world with adequate standards of human culture and lofty ideals of life. It was not enough that the teachers of teachers should be trained in technical normal methods; they must also, so far as possible, be broad-minded, cultured men and women, to scatter civilization among a people whose ignorance was not simply of letters, but of life itself.

It can thus be seen that the work of education in the South began with higher institutions of training, which threw off as their foliage common schools, and later industrial schools, and at the same time strove to shoot their roots ever deeper toward college and university training. That this was an inevitable and necessary development, sooner or later, goes without saying; but there has been, and still is, a question in many minds if the natural growth was not forced, and if the higher training was not either overdone or done with cheap and unsound methods. Among white Southerners this feeling is widespread and positive. A prominent Southern journal voiced this in a recent editorial.

"The experiment that has been made to give the colored students classical training has not been satisfactory. Even though many were able to pursue the course, most of them did so in a parrot-like way, learning what was taught, but not seeming to appropriate the truth and import of their instruction, and graduating without sensible aim or valuable occupation for their future. The whole scheme has proved a waste of time, efforts, and the money of the state."

While most fair-minded men would recognize this as extreme and overdrawn, still without doubt many are asking. Are there a sufficient number of Negroes ready for college training to warrant the undertaking? Are not too many students prematurely forced into this work? Does it not have the effect of dissatisfying the young Negro with his environment? And do these graduates succeed in real life? Such natural questions cannot be evaded, nor on the other hand must a Nation naturally skeptical as to Negro ability assume an unfavorable answer without careful inquiry and patient openness to conviction. We must not forget that most Americans answer all queries regarding the Negro *a priori*, and that the least that human courtesy can do is to listen to evidence.

The advocates of the higher education of the Negro would be the last to deny the incompleteness and glaring defects of the present system: too many institutions have attempted to do college work, the work in some cases has not been thoroughly done, and quantity rather than quality has sometimes been sought. But all this can be said of higher education throughout the land; it is the almost inevitable incident of educational growth, and leaves the deeper question of the legitimate demand for the higher training of Negroes untouched. And this latter question can be settled in but one way,—by a first-hand study of the facts. If we leave out of view all institutions which have not actually graduated students from a course higher than that of a New England high school, even though they be called colleges; if then we take the thirty-four remaining institutions, we may clear up many misapprehensions by asking searchingly, What kind of institutions are they? what do they teach? and what sort of men do they graduate?

And first we may say that this type of college, including Atlanta, Fisk, and Howard, Wilberforce and Claflin, Shaw, and the rest is peculiar, almost unique.

* * *

The teachers in these institutions came not to keep the Negroes in their place, but to raise them out of the defilement of the places where slavery had wallowed them. The colleges they founded were social settlements; homes where the best of the sons of the freedmen came in close and sympathetic touch with the best traditions of New England. They lived and ate together, studied and worked, hoped and harkened in the dawning light. In actual formal content their curriculum was doubtless old-fashioned, but in educational power it was supreme, for it was the contact of living souls.

From such schools about two thousand Negroes have gone forth with the bachelor's degree. The number in itself is enough to put at rest the argument that too large a proportion of Negroes are receiving higher training. If the ratio to population of all Negro students throughout the land, in both college and secondary training, be counted, Commissioner Harris assures us "it must be increased to five times its present average" to equal the average of the land.

Fifty years ago the ability of Negro students in any appreciable numbers to master a modern college course would have been difficult to prove. To-day it is proved by the fact that four hundred Negroes, many of whom have been reported as brilliant students, have received the bachelor's degree from Harvard, Yale, Oberlin, and seventy other leading colleges. Here we have, then, nearly twenty-five hundred Negro graduates, of whom the crucial query must be made, How far did their training fit them for life?

* * *

Fifty-three per cent of these graduates were teachers,—presidents of institutions, heads of normal schools, principals of city school-systems, and the like.

Seventeen per cent were clergymen; another seventeen per cent were in the professions, chiefly as physicians. Over six per cent were merchants, farmers, and artisans, and four per cent were in the government civil-service. Granting even that a considerable proportion of the third unheard from are unsuccessful, this is a record of usefulness.

* * *

With all their larger vision and deeper sensibility, these men have usually been conservative, careful leaders. They have seldom been agitators, have withstood the temptation to head the mob, and have worked steadily and faithfully in a thousand communities in the South. As teachers, they have given the South a commendable system of city schools and large numbers of private normal-schools and academies. Colored college-bred men have worked side by side with white college graduates at Hampton; almost from the beginning the backbone of Tuskegee's teaching force has been formed of graduates from Fisk and Atlanta. And to-day the institute is filled with college graduates, from the energetic wife of the principal down to the teacher of agriculture, including nearly half of the executive council and a majority of the heads of departments. In the professions, college men are slowly but surely leavening the Negro church, are healing and preventing the devastations of disease, and beginning to furnish legal protection for the liberty and property of the toiling masses. All this is needful work. Who would do it if Negroes did not? How could Negroes do it if they were not trained carefully for it? If white people need colleges to furnish teachers, ministers, lawyers, and doctors, do black people need nothing of the sort?

* * *

No secure civilization can be built in the south with the Negro as an ignorant, turbulent proletariat. Suppose we seek to remedy this by making them laborers and nothing more: they are not fools, they have tasted of the Tree of Life, and they will not cease to think, will not cease attempting to read the riddle of the world. By taking away their best equipped teachers and leaders, by slamming the door of opportunity in the faces of their bolder and brighter minds, will you make them satisfied with their lot? or will you not rather transfer their leading from the hands of men taught to think to the hands of untrained demagogues? We ought not to forget that despite the pressure of poverty, and despite the active discouragement and even ridicule of friends, the demand for higher training steadily increases among Negro youth: there were, in the years from 1875 to 1880, 22 Negro graduates from Northern colleges; from 1885 to 1890 there were 43, and from 1895 to 1900, nearly 100 graduates. From Southern Negro colleges there were, in the same three periods, 143, 413, and over 500 graduates. Here, then, is the plain thirst for training; by refusing to give this Talented Tenth the key to knowledge, can any sane man imagine that they will lightly lay aside their yearning and contentedly become hewers of wood and drawers of water?

No. The dangerously clear logic of the Negro's position will more and more loudly assert itself in that day when increasing wealth and more intricate social organization preclude the South from being, as it so largely is, simply an armed camp for intimidating black folk. Such waste of energy cannot be spared if the South is to catch up with civilization. And as the black third of the land grows in thrift and skill, unless skilfully guided in its larger philosophy, it must more and more brood over the red past and the creeping, crooked present, until it grasps a gospel of revolt and revenge and throws its new-found energies athwart the current of advance. Even to-day the masses of the Negroes see all too clearly the anomalies of their position and the moral crookedness of yours. You may marshal strong indictments against them, but their counter-cries, lacking though they be in formal logic, have burning truths within them which you may not wholly ignore, O Southern Gentlemen! If you deplore their presence here, they ask, Who brought us? When you cry, Deliver us from the vision of intermarriage, they answer that legal marriage is infinitely better than systematic concubinage and prostitution. And if in just fury you accuse their vagabonds of violating women, they also in fury quite as just may reply: The rape which your gentlemen have done against helpless black women in defiance of your own laws is written on the foreheads of two millions of mulattoes, and written in ineffaceable blood. And finally, when you fasten crime upon this race as its peculiar trait, they answer that slavery was the arch-crime, and lynching and lawlessness its twin abortions; that color and race are not crimes, and yet it is they which in this land receive most unceasing condemnation, North, East, South, and West.

I will not say such arguments are wholly justified,—I will not insist that there is no other side to the shield; but I do say that of the nine millions of Negroes in this nation, there is scarcely one out of the cradle to whom these arguments do not daily present themselves in the guise of terrible truth. I insist that the question of the future is how best to keep these millions from brooding over the wrongs of the past and the difficulties of the present, so that all their energies may be bent toward a cheerful striving and coöperation with their white neighbors toward a larger, juster, and fuller future. That one wise method of doing this lies in the closer knitting of the Negro to the great industrial possibilities of the South is a great truth. And this the common schools and the manual training and trade schools are working to accomplish. But these alone are not enough. The foundations of knowledge in this race, as in others, must be sunk deep in the college and university if we would build a solid, permanent structure.

* * *

The function of the Negro college, then, is clear: it must maintain the standards of popular education, it must seek the social regeneration of the Negro, and it must help in the solution of problems of race contact and coöperation. And finally, beyond all this, it must develop men. Above our modern socialism, and out of the worship of the mass, must persist and evolve that higher individualism which the centres of culture protect; there must come a loftier respect for the sovereign human soul that seeks to know itself and the world about it; that seeks a freedom for expansion and self-development; that will love and hate and labor in its own way, untrammeled alike by old and new. Such souls aforetime have inspired and guided worlds, and if we be not wholly bewitched by our Rhinegold,[4] they shall again. Herein the longing of black men must have respect: the rich and bitter depth of their experience, the unknown treasures of their inner life, the strange rendings of nature they have seen, may give the world new points of view and make their loving, living, and doing precious to all human hearts. And to themselves in these the days that try their souls, the chance to soar in the dim blue air above the smoke is to their finer spirits boon and guerdon for what they lose on earth by being black.

I sit with Shakespeare and he winces not. Across the color line I move arm in arm with Balzac and Dumas, where smiling men and welcoming women glide in gilded halls. From out the caves of evening that swing between the strong-limbed earth and the tracery of the stars, I summon Aristotle and Aurelius and what soul I will, and they come all graciously with no scorn nor condescension. So, wed with Truth, I dwell above the Veil. Is this the life you grudge us, O knightly America? Is this the life you long to change into the dull red hideousness of Georgia? Are you so afraid lest peering from this high Pisgah, between Philistine and Amalekite, we sight the Promised Land?

Study Questions

1. How does Du Bois describe the history of education for African Americans?
2. What type of training does Du Bois advocate for black men?
3. What rationale does Du Bois offer to support his view?
4. What opposition would Du Bois have faced? What were the alternatives to his views and what arguments would he have encountered?

4. A reference to corrupting wealth.

H. L. MENCKEN

Homo Neanderthalensis (1925)

In 1925, lawyers, journalists, and the curious converged on the small town of Dayton, Tennessee, for what was called in some quarters the "Monkey Trial." A young high-school biology teacher, John Scopes (1900–1970), was on trial for illegally teaching the theory of evolution in public school. William Jennings Bryan (1860–1925), a leading Populist and three-time Democratic presidential candidate, led the prosecution. The famous Chicago lawyer Clarence Darrow (1857–1938) agreed to defend Scopes. The trial lasted two weeks, but the jury deliberated for only a few minutes before finding Scopes guilty—as indeed he was, in that he readily admitted to teaching evolution in order to force a test case. A year later the Tennessee Supreme Court reversed the decision on a technicality.

The Scopes Trial can be seen as part of a broader cultural struggle in the 1920s. Many Americans, particularly younger Americans living in urban centers, embraced science and secularism, changing gender roles and sexual mores, mass culture and consumerism, and increased racial and ethnic mixing. Other Americans, however, felt threatened by these modernist trends, and the decade also saw a surge in religious fundamentalism and "traditional" values, particularly in the South.

No individual more embodied the modernist side of this cultural divide than the magazine editor and columnist H. L. Mencken. Known for his acerbic wit, Mencken once wrote that he was a "theological moron," someone "absolutely devoid of what is called religious feeling." Titling his essay "Homo Neanderthalensis"—the scientific term for Neanderthals, a now-extinct species of homonid closely related to modern humans—Mencken published this piece in the Baltimore Evening Sun *on June 29, 1925, not quite two weeks before the Scopes trial began. As you read it, think about how Mencken portrayed progress, religion, and "the great masses of men."*

Such obscenities as the forthcoming trial of the Tennessee evolutionist, if they serve no other purpose, at least call attention dramatically to the fact that enlightenment, among mankind, is very narrowly dispersed. It is common to assume that human progress affects everyone—that even the dullest man, in these bright days, knows more than any man of, say, the Eighteenth Century, and is far more civilized. This assumption is quite erroneous. The men of the educated minority, no doubt, know more than their predecessors, and of some of them, perhaps, it may be said that they are more civilized—though I should not like to be put to giving names—but the great masses of men, even in this inspired republic, are precisely where the mob was at the dawn of history. They are ignorant, they are dishonest, they are cowardly, they are ignoble. They know little if anything that is worth knowing, and there is not the slightest sign of a natural desire among them to increase their knowledge.

Such immortal vermin, true enough, get their share of the fruits of human progress, and so they may be said, in a way, to have their part in it. The most ignorant man, when he is ill, may enjoy whatever boons and usufructs modern medicine may offer—that is, provided he is too poor to choose his own doctor. He is free, if he wants to, to take a bath. The literature of the world is at his disposal in public libraries. He may look at works of art. He may hear good music. He has at hand a thousand devices for making life less wearisome and more tolerable: the telephone, railroads, bichloride tablets,[1] newspapers, sewers, correspondence schools, delicatessen. But he had no more to do with bringing these things into the world than the horned cattle in the fields, and he does no more to increase them today than the birds of the air.

On the contrary, he is generally against them, and sometimes with immense violence. Every step in human progress, from the first feeble stirrings in the abyss of time, has been opposed by the great majority of men. Every valuable thing that has been added to the store of man's possessions has been derided by them when it was new, and destroyed by them when they had the power. They have fought every new truth ever heard of, and they have killed every truth-seeker who got into their hands.

The so-called religious organizations which now lead the war against the teaching of evolution are nothing more, at bottom, than conspiracies of the inferior man against his betters. They mirror very accurately his congenital hatred of knowledge, his bitter enmity to the man who knows more than he does, and so gets more out of life. Certainly it cannot have gone unnoticed that their membership is recruited, in the overwhelming main, from the lower orders—that no man of any education or other human dignity belongs to them. What they propose to do, at bottom and in brief, is to make the superior man infamous—by mere abuse if it is sufficient, and if it is not, then by law.

Such organizations, of course, must have leaders; there must be men in them whose ignorance and imbecility are measurably less abject than the ignorance

1. Mercury bichloride tablets were widely available in the early decades of the twentieth century. Dissolved in water, they formed a topical antiseptic and were used in both the treatment of syphilis and as a form of birth control. The tablets, however, were extremely poisonous if ingested and led to numerous accidental deaths and suicides in the 1920s.

and imbecility of the average. These super-Chandala[2] often attain to a considerable power, especially in democratic states. Their followers trust them and look up to them; sometimes, when the pack is on the loose, it is necessary to conciliate them. But their puissance cannot conceal their incurable inferiority. They belong to the mob as surely as their dupes, and the thing that animates them is precisely the mob's hatred of superiority. Whatever lies above the level of their comprehension is of the devil. A glass of wine delights civilized men; they themselves, drinking it, would get drunk. Ergo, wine must be prohibited. The hypothesis of evolution is credited by all men of education; they themselves can't understand it. Ergo, its teaching must be put down.

This simple fact explains such phenomena as the Tennessee buffoonery. Nothing else can. We must think of human progress, not as of something going on in the race in general, but as of something going on in a small minority, perpetually beleaguered in a few walled towns. Now and then the horde of barbarians outside breaks through, and we have an armed effort to halt the process. That is, we have a Reformation, a French Revolution, a war for democracy, a Great Awakening.[3] The minority is decimated and driven to cover. But a few survive—and a few are enough to carry on.

The inferior man's reasons for hating knowledge are not hard to discern. He hates it because it is complex—because it puts an unbearable burden upon his meager capacity for taking in ideas. Thus his search is always for shortcuts. All superstitions are such shortcuts. Their aim is to make the unintelligible simple, and even obvious. So on what seem to be higher levels. No man who has not had a long and arduous education can understand even the most elementary concepts of modern pathology. But even a hind at the plow can grasp the theory of chiropractic in two lessons. Hence the vast popularity of chiropractic among the submerged—and of osteopathy, Christian Science and other such quackeries with it. They are idiotic, but they are simple—and every man prefers what he can understand to what puzzles and dismays him.

The popularity of Fundamentalism among the inferior orders of men is explicable in exactly the same way. The cosmogonies that educated men toy with are all inordinately complex. To comprehend their veriest outlines requires an immense stock of knowledge, and a habit of thought. It would be as vain to try to teach to peasants or to the city proletariat as it would be to try to teach them to strepto-

2. Chandala is a Sanskrit word for a low caste of Indians once known as "untouchables."

3. The Reformation was the sixteenth-century schism in Western Christianity that led to the formation of Protestant churches. "French Revolution" generally refers to a period of political and social upheaval that occurred in France between 1789 and 1799, although France experienced revolutions in 1830 and 1848 as well. President Woodrow Wilson (1856–1924) called World War I "a war for democracy." The term "Great Awakening" refers to several waves of religious revival in America between the early eighteenth century and the late nineteenth century.

cocci. But the cosmogony of Genesis[4] is so simple that even a yokel can grasp it. It is set forth in a few phrases. It offers, to an ignorant man, the irresistable reasonableness of the nonsensical. So he accepts it with loud hosannas, and has one more excuse for hating his betters.

Politics and the fine arts repeat the story. The issues that the former throw up are often so complex that, in the present state of human knowledge, they must remain impenetrable, even to the most enlightened men. How much easier to follow a mountebank with a shibboleth—a Coolidge, a Wilson or a Roosevelt![5] The arts, like the sciences, demand special training, often very difficult. But in jazz there are simple rhythms, comprehensible even to savages.

What all this amounts to is that the human race is divided into two sharply differentiated and mutually antagonistic classes, almost two genera—a small minority that plays with ideas and is capable of taking them in, and a vast majority that finds them painful, and is thus arrayed against them, and against all who have traffic with them. The intellectual heritage of the race belongs to the minority, and to the minority only. The majority has no more to do with it than it has to do with ecclesiastic politics on Mars. In so far as that heritage is apprehended, it is viewed with enmity. But in the main it is not apprehended at all.

That is why Beethoven[6] survives. Of the 110,000,000 so-called human beings who now live in the United States, flogged and crazed by Coolidge, Rotary, the Ku Klux and the newspapers, it is probable that at least 108,000,000 have never heard of him at all. To these immortals, made in God's image, one of the greatest artists the human race has ever produced is not even a name. So far as they are concerned he might as well have died at birth. The gorgeous and incomparable beauties that he created are nothing to them. They get no value out of the fact that he existed. They are completely unaware of what he did in the world, and would not be interested if they were told.

The fact saves good Ludwig's bacon. His music survives because it lies outside the plane of the popular apprehension, like the colors beyond violet or the concept of honor. If it could be brought within range, it would at once arouse hostility. Its complexity would challenge; its lace of moral purpose would affright. Soon there would be a movement to put it down, and Baptist clergymen would range the land denouncing it, and in the end some poor musician, taken in the un-American act of playing it, would be put on trial before a jury of Ku Kluxers, and railroaded to the calaboose.

4. The first book of the Hebrew Bible and the Christian Old Testament, which lays out the Judeo-Christian creation story.

5. Calvin Coolidge (1872–1933), president of the United States from 1923 to 1929; Woodrow Wilson (1856–1924), president of the United States from 1913 to 1921; and Theodore "Teddy" Roosevelt (1858–1919), president of the United States from 1901 to 1909.

6. Ludwig van Beethoven (1770–1827), German composer and pianist.

Study Questions

1. How did Mencken view "the great majority of men"? What nouns and adjectives did he use to describe them?
2. Who did Mencken think was responsible for progress?
3. How did Mencken explain the appeal of religion?
4. In the 1920s Darwin's theory of evolution was used by American supporters of eugenics to argue for immigration restrictions and the sterilization of "inferior stock." In fact, the biology textbook used by John Scopes included a section advocating eugenics. Given this, can you imagine how William Jennings Bryan or another supporter of Tennessee's law might have responded to Mencken's column?

FREDERICK LEWIS ALLEN

The Revolution in Manners and Morals (1931)

Frederick Lewis Allen (1890–1954), a popular magazine editor, author, and historian wrote Only Yesterday, *a sweeping and often humorous depiction of events in the 1920s that was published in 1931. The account received national attention as a Book of the Month Club selection. While the turn of the century had marked the era of the "New Woman," when some women sought higher education and careers, the 1920s witnessed a more widespread change in expectations, manners, and morals for both men and women. Allen's narrative covers a wide range of developments linked to this loosening of old restrictions—some technological, some scientific, and some political.*

In this chapter from Only Yesterday, *Allen focuses on a radical change in young women's sexual mores in the decade following World War I. As you read, think about the historical developments that contributed to the new manners and morals of the 1920s. Why do you think technological and political change led to more freedom for women in the United States in this period? What were the particular social, religious, and economic circumstances that caused many people to reject more-rigid sexual codes? Consider also whether the author might be exaggerating the change in morals.*

A first-class revolt against the accepted American order was certainly taking place during those early years of the Post-war Decade, but it was one with which Nikolai Lenin[1] had nothing whatever to do. The shock troops of the rebellion were not alien agitators, but the sons and daughters of well-to-do American families, who knew little about Bolshevism[2] and cared distinctly less, and their defiance was expressed not in obscure radical publications or in

1. Vladimir Lenin (1870–1924), born Vladimir Ilyich Ulyanov, communist revolutionary and leader of Russia, 1917–24. Some American writers referred to him as Nikolai Lenin.
2. Like "Red Menace," a term for communism, i.e., government or communal ownership of property.

soap-box speeches, but right across the family breakfast table into the horrified ears of conservative fathers and mothers. Men and women were still shivering at the Red Menace when they awoke to the no less alarming Problem of the Younger Generation, and realized that if the constitution were not in danger, the moral code of the country certainly was.

This code, as it currently concerned young people, might have been roughly summarized as follows: Women were the guardians of morality; they were made of finer stuff than men and were expected to act accordingly. Young girls must look forward in innocence (tempered perhaps with a modicum of physiological instruction) to a romantic love match which would lead them to the altar and to living-happily-ever-after; and until the "right man" came along they must allow no male to kiss them. It was expected that some men would succumb to the temptations of sex, but only with a special class of outlawed women; girls of respectable families were supposed to have no such temptations. Boys and girls were permitted large freedom to work and play together, with decreasing and well-nigh nominal chaperonage, but only because the code worked so well on the whole that a sort of honor system was supplanting supervision by their elders; it was taken for granted that if they had been well brought up they would never take advantage of this freedom. And although the attitude toward smoking and drinking by girls differed widely in different strata of society and different parts of the country, majority opinion held that it was morally wrong for them to smoke and could hardly imagine them showing the effects of alcohol.

The war had not long been over when cries of alarm from parents, teachers, and moral preceptors began to rend the air. For the boys and girls just growing out of adolescence were making mincemeat of this code.

The dresses that the girls—and for that matter most of the older women—were wearing seemed alarming enough. In July, 1920, a fashion-writer reported in the *New York Times* that "the American woman . . . has lifted her skirts far beyond any modest limitation," which was another way of saying that the hem was now all of nine inches above the ground. It was freely predicted that skirts would come down again in the winter of 1920–21, but instead they climbed a few scandalous inches farther. The flappers wore thin dresses, short-sleeved and occasionally (in the evening) sleeveless; some of the wilder young things rolled their stockings below their knees, revealing to the shocked eyes of virtue a fleeting glance of shin-bones and knee-cap; and many of them were visibly using cosmetics. "The intoxication of rouge," earnestly explained Dorothy Speare in *Dancers in the Dark*, "is an insidious vintage known to more girls than mere man can ever believe." Useless for frantic parents to insist that no lady did such things; the answer was that the daughters of ladies were doing it, and even retouching their masterpieces in public. Some of them, furthermore, were abandoning their corsets. "The men won't dance with you if you wear a corset," they were quoted as saying.

The current mode in dancing created still more consternation. Not the romantic violin but the barbaric saxophone now dominated the orchestra, and to its passionate crooning and wailing the fox-trotters moved in what the editor of the Hobart College *Herald* disgustedly called a "syncopated embrace." No longer did even an inch of space separate them; they danced as if glued together, body to body, cheek to cheek. Cried the *Catholic Telegraph* of Cincinnati in righteous indignation, "The music is sensuous, the embracing of partners—the female only half dressed—is absolutely indecent; and the motions—they are such as may not be described, with any respect for propriety, in a family newspaper. Suffice it to say that there are certain houses appropriate for such dances; but those houses have been closed by law."

Supposedly "nice" girls were smoking cigarettes—openly and defiantly, if often rather awkwardly and self-consciously. They were drinking—somewhat less openly but often all too efficaciously. There were stories of daughters of the most exemplary parents getting drunk—"blotto," as their companions cheerfully put it—on the contents of the hip-flasks of the new prohibition régime, and going out joyriding with men at four in the morning. And worst of all, even at well-regulated dances they were said to retire where the eye of the most sharp-sighted chaperon could not follow, and in darkened rooms or in parked cars to engage in the unspeakable practice of petting and necking.

It was not until F. Scott Fitzgerald, who had hardly graduated from Princeton and ought to know what his generation was doing, brought out *This Side of Paradise* in April, 1920, that fathers and mothers realized fully what was afoot and how long it had been going on. Apparently the "petting party" had been current as early as 1916, and was now widely established as an indoor sport. "None of the Victorian mothers—and most of the mothers were Victorian—had any idea how casually their daughters were accustomed to be kissed," wrote Mr. Fitzgerald. ". . . Amory saw girls doing things that even in his memory would have been impossible: eating three-o'clock, after-dance suppers in impossible cafés, talking of every side of life with an air half of earnestness, half of mockery, yet with a furtive excitement that Amory considered stood for a real moral let-down. But he never realized how widespread it was until he saw the cities between New York and Chicago as one vast juvenile intrigue." The book caused a shudder to run down the national spine; did not Mr. Fitzgerald represent one of his well-nurtured heroines as brazenly confessing, "I've kissed dozens of men. I suppose I'll kiss dozens more"; and another heroine as saying to a young man (*to a young man!*). "Oh, just one person in fifty has any glimmer of what sex is. I'm hipped on Freud[3] and all that, but it's rotten that every bit of *real* love in the world is ninety-nine per cent passion and one little *soupçon* of jealousy."

It was incredible. It was abominable. What did it all mean? Was every decent standard being thrown over? Mothers read the scarlet words and wondered if

3. Sigmund Freud (1856–1939), Austrian psychologist who pioneered psychoanalysis and formulated theories relating to sexual repression.

they themselves "had any idea how often their daughters were accustomed to be kissed." . . . But no, this must be an exaggerated account of the misconduct of some especially depraved group. Nice girls couldn't behave like that and talk openly about passion. But in due course other books appeared to substantiate the findings of Mr. Fitzgerald: *Dancers in the Dark, The Plastic Age, Flaming Youth.* Magazine articles and newspapers reiterated the scandal. To be sure, there were plenty of communities where nice girls did not, in actual fact, "behave like that"; and even in the more sophisticated urban centers there were plenty of girls who did not. Nevertheless, there was enough fire beneath the smoke of these sensational revelations to make the Problem of the Younger Generation a topic of anxious discussion from coast to coast.

The forces of morality rallied to the attack. Dr. Francis E. Clark, the founder and president of the Christian Endeavor Society, declared that the modern "indecent dance" was "an offense against womanly purity, the very fountainhead of our family and civil life." The new style of dancing was denounced in religious journals as "impure, polluting, corrupting, debasing, destroying spirituality, increasing carnality," and the mothers and sisters and church members of the land were called upon to admonish and instruct and raise the spiritual tone of these dreadful young people. President Murphy of the University of Florida cried out with true Southern warmth, "The low-cut gowns, the rolled hose and short skirts are born of the Devil and his angels, and are carrying the present and future generations to chaos and destruction." A group of Episcopal churchwomen in New York, speaking with the authority of wealth and social position (for they included Mrs. J. Pierpont Morgan, Mrs. Borden Harriman, Mrs. Henry Phipps, Mrs. James Roosevelt, and Mrs. E. H. Harriman), proposed an organization to discourage fashions involving an "excess of nudity" and "improper ways of dancing." The Y. W. C. A.[4] conducted a national campaign against immodest dress among high-school girls, supplying newspapers with printed matter carrying headlines such as "Working Girls Responsive to Modesty Appeal" and "High Heels Losing Ground Even in France." In Philadelphia a Dress Reform Committee of prominent citizens sent a questionnaire to over a thousand clergymen to ask them what would be their idea of a proper dress, and although the gentlemen of the cloth showed a distressing variety of opinion, the committee proceeded to design a "moral gown" which was endorsed by ministers of fifteen denominations. The distinguishing characteristics of this moral gown were that it was very loose-fitting, that the sleeves reached just below the elbows, and that the hem came within seven and a half inches of the floor.

Not content with example and reproof, legislators in several states introduced bills to reform feminine dress once and for all. The *New York American* reported in

4. Young Women's Christian Association. The YWCA sponsored hotels with strict rules and curfews that would serve as safe and chaperoned locations for women in urban areas.

1921 that a bill was pending in Utah providing fine and imprisonment for those who wore on the streets "skirts higher than three inches above the ankle." A bill was laid before the Virginia legislature which would forbid any woman from wearing shirtwaists or evening gowns which displayed "more than three inches of her throat." In Ohio the proposed limit of decolletage was two inches; the bill introduced in the Ohio legislature aimed also to prevent the sale of any "garment which unduly displays or accentuates the lines of the female figure," and to prohibit any "female over fourteen years of age" from wearing "a skirt which does not reach to that part of the foot known as the instep."

Meanwhile innumerable families were torn with dissension over cigarettes and gin and all-night automobile rides. Fathers and mothers lay awake asking themselves whether their children were not utterly lost; sons and daughters evaded questions, lied miserably and unhappily, or flared up to reply rudely that at least they were not dirty-minded hypocrites, that they saw no harm in what they were doing and proposed to go right on doing it. From those liberal clergymen and teachers who prided themselves on keeping step with all that was new came a chorus of reassurance: these young people were at least franker and more honest than their elders had been; having experimented for themselves, would they not soon find out which standards were outworn and which represented the accumulated moral wisdom of the race? Hearing such hopeful words, many good people took heart again. Perhaps this flare-up of youthful passion was a flash in the pan, after all. Perhaps in another year or two the boys and girls would come to their senses and everything would be all right again.

They were wrong, however. For the revolt of the younger generation was only the beginning of a revolution in manners and morals that was already beginning to affect men and women of every age in every part of the country.

A number of forces were working together and interacting upon one another to make this revolution inevitable.

First of all was the state of mind brought about by the war and its conclusion. A whole generation had been infected by the eat-drink-and-be-merry-for-tomorrow-we-die spirit which accompanied the departure of the soldiers to the training camps and the fighting front. There had been an epidemic not only of abrupt war marriages, but of less conventional liaisons. In France, two million men had found themselves very close to filth and annihilation and very far from the American moral code and its defenders; prostitution had followed the flag and willing mademoiselles from Armentières[5] had been plentiful; American girls sent over as nurses and war workers had come under the influence of continental manners and standards without being subject to the rigid protections thrown

5. An allusion to the song "Mademoiselle from Armentières," which was popular with British and American soldiers during World War I.

about their continental sisters of the respectable classes; and there had been a very widespread and very natural breakdown of traditional restraints and reticences and taboos. It was impossible for this generation to return unchanged when the ordeal was over. Some of them had acquired under the pressure of wartime conditions a new code which seemed to them quite defensible; millions of them had been provided with an emotional stimulant from which it was not easy to taper off. Their torn nerves craved the anodynes of speed, excitement, and passion. They found themselves expected to settle down into the humdrum routine of American life as if nothing had happened, to accept the moral dicta of elders who seemed to them still to be living in a Pollyanna[6] land of rosy ideals which the war had killed for them. They couldn't do it, and they very disrespectfully said so.

"The older generation had certainly pretty well ruined this world before passing it on to us," wrote one of them (John F. Carter in the *Atlantic Monthly*, September, 1920), expressing accurately the sentiments of innumerable contemporaries. "They give us this thing, knocked to pieces, leaky, red-hot, threatening to blow up; and then they are surprised that we don't accept it with the same attitude of pretty, decorous enthusiasm with which they received it, way back in the 'eighties."

The middle generation was not so immediately affected by the war neurosis. They had had time enough, before 1917, to build up habits of conformity not easily broken down. But they, too, as the let-down of 1919 followed the war, found themselves restless and discontented, in a mood to question everything that had once seemed to them true and worthy and of good report. They too had spent themselves and wanted a good time. They saw their juniors exploring the approaches to the forbidden land of sex, and presently they began to play with the idea of doing a little experimenting of their own. The same disillusion which had defeated Woodrow Wilson and had caused strikes and riots and the Big Red Scare furnished a culture in which the germs of the new freedom could grow and multiply.

The revolution was accelerated also by the growing independence of the American woman. She won the suffrage in 1920. She seemed, it is true, to be very little interested in it once she had it; she voted, but mostly as the unregenerate men about her did, despite the efforts of women's clubs and the League of Women Voters to awaken her to womanhood's civic opportunity; feminine candidates for office were few, and some of them—such as Governor Ma Ferguson[7] of Texas—scarcely seemed to represent the starry-eyed spiritual influence which, it had

6. The heroine of Eleanor H. Porter's best-selling 1913 novel *Pollyanna*; the name soon became a byword meaning "goody-goody."

7. Miriam Amanda "Ma" Ferguson (1875–1961), twice served a governor of Texas (1925–27, 1932–35); her husband, James Edward "Pa" Ferguson, had held that office before being impeached and removed from office in 1917, and his wife's administration was dogged by charges that both "Ma" and "Pa" Ferguson accepted bribes from bootleggers in exchange for pardons.

been promised, would presently ennoble public life. Few of the younger women could rouse themselves to even a passing interest in politics: to them it was a sordid and futile business, without flavor and without hope. Nevertheless, the winning of the suffrage had its effect. It consolidated woman's position as man's equal.

Even more marked was the effect of woman's growing independence of the drudgeries of housekeeping. Smaller houses were being built, and they were easier to look after. Families were moving into apartments, and these made even less claim upon the housekeeper's time and energy. Women were learning how to make lighter work of the preparation of meals. Sales of canned foods were growing, the number of delicatessen stores had increased three times as fast as the population during the decade 1910–20, the output of bakeries increased by 60 per cent during the decade 1914–24. Much of what had once been housework was now either moving out of the home entirely or being simplified by machinery. The use of commercial laundries, for instance, increased by 57 per cent between 1914 and 1924. Electric washing-machines and electric irons were coming to the aid of those who still did their washing at home; the manager of the local electric power company at "Middletown," a typical small American city, estimated in 1924 that nearly 90 per cent of the homes in the city already had electric irons. The housewife was learning to telephone her shopping orders, to get her clothes ready-made and spare herself the rigors of dress-making, to buy a vacuum cleaner and emulate the lovely carefree girls in the magazine advertisements who banished dust with such delicate fingers. Women were slowly becoming emancipated from routine to "live their own lives."

And what were these "own lives" of theirs to be like? Well, for one thing, they could take jobs. Up to this time girls of the middle classes who had wanted to "do something" had been largely restricted to school-teaching, social-service work, nursing, stenography, and clerical work in business houses. But now they poured out of the schools and colleges into all manner of new occupations. They besieged the offices of publishers and advertisers; they went into tea-room management until there threatened to be more purveyors than consumers of chicken patties and cinnamon toast; they sold antiques, sold real estate, opened smart little shops, and finally invaded the department stores. In 1920 the department store was in the mind of the average college girl a rather bourgeois institution which employed "poor shop girls"; by the end of the decade college girls were standing in line for openings in the misses' sports-wear department and even selling behind the counter in the hope that some day fortune might smile upon them and make them buyers or stylists. Small-town girls who once would have been contented to stay in Sauk Center[8] all their days were now borrowing from father to go to New

8. That is, Sauk Centre, Minnesota, author Sinclair Lewis's birthplace and the inspiration for the fictional town Gopher Prairie in his novel *Main Street* (1920).

York or Chicago to seek their fortunes—in Best's or Macy's or Marshall Field's[9] Married women who were encumbered with children and could not seek jobs consoled themselves with the thought that home-making and child-rearing were really "professions," after all. No topic was so furiously discussed at luncheon tables from one end of the country to the other as the question whether the married woman should take a job, and whether the mother had a right to. And as for the unmarried woman, she no longer had to explain why she worked in a shop or an office; it was idleness, nowadays, that had to be defended.

With the job—or at least the sense that the job was a possibility—came a feeling of comparative economic independence. With the feeling of economic independence came a slackening of husbandly and parental authority. Maiden aunts and unmarried daughters were leaving the shelter of the family roof to install themselves in kitchenette apartments of their own. For city-dwellers the home was steadily becoming less of a shrine, more of a dormitory—a place of casual shelter where one stopped overnight on the way from the restaurant and the movie theater to the office. Yet even the job did not provide the American woman with that complete satisfaction which the management of a mechanized home no longer furnished. She still had energies and emotions to burn; she was ready for the revolution.

Like all revolutions, this one was stimulated by foreign propaganda. It came, however, not from Moscow, but from Vienna. Sigmund Freud had published his first book on psychoanalysis at the end of the nineteenth century, and he and Jung[1] had lectured to American psychologists as early as 1909, but it was not until after the war that the Freudian gospel began to circulate to a marked extent among the American lay public. The one great intellectual force which had not suffered disrepute as a result of the war was science; the more-or-less educated public was now absorbing a quantity of popularized information about biology and anthropology which gave a general impression that men and women were merely animals of a rather intricate variety, and that moral codes had no universal validity and were often based on curious superstitions. A fertile ground was ready for the seeds of Freudianism, and presently one began to hear even from the lips of flappers that "science taught" new and disturbing things about sex. Sex, it appeared, was the central and pervasive force which moved mankind. Almost every human motive was attributable to it: if you were patriotic or liked the violin, you were in the grip of sex—in a sublimated form. The first requirement of mental health was to have an uninhibited sex life. If you would be well and happy, you must obey your libido. Such was the Freudian gospel as it imbedded itself in the American

9. Major urban department stores. Regional and national chain stores multiplied in the 1920s.

1. Carl Jung (1875–1961), Swiss psychologist known for his theories of archetypes and the collective unconscious.

mind after being filtered through the successive minds of interpreters and popularizers and guileless readers and people who had heard guileless readers talk about it. New words and phrases began to be bandied about the cocktail-tray and the Mah Jong[2] table—inferiority complex, sadism, masochism, Œdipus complex.[3] Intellectual ladies went to Europe to be analyzed; analysts plied their new trade in American cities, conscientiously transferring the affections of their fair patients to themselves; and clergymen who preached about the virtue of self-control were reminded by outspoken critics that self-control was out-of-date and really dangerous.

The principal remaining forces which accelerated the revolution in manners and morals were all 100 per cent American. They were prohibition, the automobile, the confession and sex magazines, and the movies.

When the Eighteenth Amendment was ratified, prohibition seemed, as we have already noted, to have an almost united country behind it. Evasion of the law began immediately, however, and strenuous and sincere opposition to it—especially in the large cities of the North and East—quickly gathered force. The results were the bootlegger, the speakeasy, and a spirit of deliberate revolt which in many communities made drinking "the thing to do." From these facts in turn flowed further results: the increased popularity of distilled as against fermented liquors, the use of the hip-flask, the cocktail party, and the general transformation of drinking from a masculine prerogative to one shared by both sexes together. The old-time saloon had been overwhelmingly masculine; the speakeasy usually catered to both men and women. As Elmer Davis[4] put it, "The old days when father spent his evenings at Cassidy's bar with the rest of the boys are gone, and probably gone forever; Cassidy may still be in business at the old stand and father may still go down there of evenings, but since prohibition mother goes down with him." Under the new régime not only the drinks were mixed, but the company as well.

Meanwhile a new sort of freedom was being made possible by the enormous increase in the use of the automobile, and particularly of the closed car. (In 1919 hardly more than 10 per cent of the cars produced in the United States were closed; by 1924 the percentage had jumped to 43, by 1927 it had reached 82.8.) The automobile offered an almost universally available means of escaping temporarily from the supervision of parents and chaperons, or from the influence of neighborhood opinion. Boys and girls now thought nothing, as the Lynds[5] pointed

2. Game originating in China and played with tiles.

3. Psychological term for a son's sexual attraction to his mother, a condition named by Freud after the Sophocles's tragedy *Oedipus the King*.

4. Elmer Davis (1890–1958), well-known national journalist.

5. Robert Staughton Lynd (1879–1949) and Helen Merrell Lynd (1896–1982), authors of the pioneering sociological study *Middletown: A Study in Contemporary American Culture* (1929).

out in *Middletown*, of jumping into a car and driving off at a moment's notice—without asking anybody's permission—to a dance in another town twenty miles away, where they were strangers and enjoyed a freedom impossible among their neighbors. The closed car, moreover, was in effect a room protected from the weather which could be occupied at any time of the day or night and could be moved at will into a darkened byway or a country lane. The Lynds quoted the judge of the juvenile court in "Middletown" as declaring that the automobile had become a "house of prostitution on wheels," and cited the fact that of thirty girls brought before his court in a year on charges of sex crimes, for whom the place where the offense had occurred was recorded, nineteen were listed as having committed it in an automobile.

Finally, as the revolution began, its influence fertilized a bumper crop of sex magazines, confession magazines, and lurid motion pictures, and these in turn had their effect on a class of readers and movie-goers who had never heard and never would hear of Freud and the libido. The publishers of the sex adventure magazines, offering stories with such titles as "What I Told My Daughter the Night Before Her Marriage," "Indolent Kisses," and "Watch Your Step-Ins," learned to a nicety the gentle art of arousing the reader without arousing the censor. The publishers of the confession magazines, while always instructing their authors to provide a moral ending and to utter pious sentiments, concentrated on the description of what they euphemistically called "missteps." Most of their fiction was faked to order by hack writers who could write one day "The Confessions of a Chorus Girl" and the next day recount, again in the first person, the temptations which made it easy for the taxidriver to go wrong. Both classes of magazines became astonishingly numerous and successful. Bernarr Macfadden's *True-Story*, launched as late as 1919, had over 300,000 readers by 1923; 848,000 by 1924; over a million and a half by 1925; and almost two million by 1926—a record of rapid growth probably unparalleled in magazine publishing.

Crowding the news stands along with the sex and confession magazines were motion-picture magazines which depicted "seven movie kisses" with such captions as "Do you recognize your little friend, Mae Busch? She's had lots of kisses, but she never seems to grow *blasé*. At least you'll agree that she's giving a good imitation of a person enjoying this one." The movies themselves, drawing millions to their doors every day and every night, played incessantly upon the same lucrative theme. The producers of one picture advertised "brilliant men, beautiful jazz babies, champagne baths, midnight revels, petting parties in the purple dawn, all ending in one terrific smashing climax that makes you gasp"; the venders of another promised "neckers, petters, white kisses, red kisses, pleasure-mad daughters, sensation-craving mothers, . . . the truth—bold, naked, sensational." Seldom did the films offer as much as these advertisements promised, but there was enough in some of them to cause a sixteen-year-old girl (quoted by Alice

Miller Mitchell)[6] to testify. "Those pictures with hot love-making in them, they make girls and boys sitting together want to get up and walk out, go off somewhere, you know. Once I walked out with a boy before the picture was even over. We took a ride. But my friend, she all the time had to get up and go out with her boyfriend."

A storm of criticism from church organizations led the motion-picture producers, early in the decade, to install Will H. Hays, President Harding's Postmaster-General, as their arbiter of morals and of taste, and Mr. Hays promised that all would be well. "This industry must have," said he before the Los Angeles Chamber of Commerce, "toward that sacred thing, the mind of a child, toward that clean virgin thing, that unmarked slate, the same responsibility, the same care about the impressions made upon it, that the best clergyman or the most inspired teacher of youth would have." The result of Mr. Hays's labors in behalf of the unmarked slate was to make the moral ending as obligatory as in the confession magazines, to smear over sexy pictures with pious platitudes, and to blacklist for motion-picture production many a fine novel and play which, because of its very honesty, might be construed as seriously or intelligently questioning the traditional sex ethics of the small town. Mr. Hays, being something of a genius, managed to keep the churchmen at bay. Whenever the threats of censorship began to become ominous he would promulgate a new series of moral commandments for the producers to follow. Yet of the practical effects of his supervision it is perhaps enough to say that the quotations given above all date from the period of his dictatorship. Giving lip-service to the old code, the movies diligently and with consummate vulgarity publicized the new.

Each of these diverse influences—the post-war disillusion, the new status of women, the Freudian gospel, the automobile, prohibition, the sex and confession magazines, and the movies—had its part in bringing about the revolution. Each of them, as an influence, was played upon by all the others; none of them could alone have changed to any great degree the folkways of America; together their force was irresistible.

6. Author of the sociological study *Children and Movies* (1929).

Study Questions

1. What were the signs of a moral revolution in the 1920s? What changes took place in the lives of average women in the 1920s?
2. How does the author explain the reasons for changes in morals and manners? What political, social, and technological developments contributed to the change?
3. How does the author connect the moral revolution to World War I? Do you think the moral revolution would have occurred if it were not for World War I?
4. What does the author's tone convey about his opinion of the change in manners? How do you think other types of Americans would have written about the change in morals?

FRANKLIN DELANO ROOSEVELT

First Inaugural Address (1933)

When Franklin Delano Roosevelt (1882–1945) delivered his first inaugural address on March 4, 1933, the Great Depression had been underway for three years. Stock prices had plunged by about 80 percent from their highs in September of 1929; industrial production had fallen by about half; and low crop prices had pushed farm foreclosures to record levels. One in four American workers—more than 13 million people in all—were unemployed, and those who had jobs were often forced to work for rock-bottom wages. Perhaps most damaging of all to the economy, the nation's banking system hovered on the verge of collapse. Many banks had loaned money to stock market investors, farmers, and others who were unable to repay. When word spread that banks had huge loans on their books that they could not collect, panicky depositors rushed to withdraw their savings, triggering bank runs. Between 1929 and 1933, more than 5,000 American banks failed. Even more would have collapsed had governors across the country not declared "bank holidays," temporarily closing the banks' doors. On the day Roosevelt took office, such proclamations had closed all banks in thirty-two states and most banks in six others.

Roosevelt's first inaugural address was delivered to a crowd of over 100,000 in Washington, D.C., and to millions more Americans listening on the radio. As you read this speech, think about how the nation's economic distress and the president's audience shaped his tone.

From Franklin D. Roosevelt, "First Inaugural Address," March 4, 1933 (Joint Congressional Committee on Inaugural Ceremonies).

I am certain that my fellow Americans expect that on my induction into the presidency I will address them with a candor and a decision which the present situation of our nation impels. This is preeminently the time to speak the truth, the whole truth, frankly and boldly. Nor need we shrink from honestly facing conditions in our country today, This great nation will endure as it has endured, will revive and will prosper. So, first of all, let me assert my firm belief that the only thing we have to fear is fear itself—nameless, unreasoning, unjustified terror which paralyzes needed efforts to convert retreat into advance. In every dark hour of our national life a leadership of frankness and vigor has met with that understanding and support of the people themselves which is essential to victory. I am convinced that you will again give that support to leadership in these critical days.

In such a spirit on my part and on yours we face our common difficulties. They concern, thank God, only material things. Values have shrunken to fantastic levels; taxes have risen; our ability to pay has fallen; government of all kinds is faced by serious curtailment of income; the means of exchange are frozen in the currents of trade; the withered leaves of industrial enterprise lie on every side; farmers find no markets for their produce; the savings of many years in thousands of families are gone.

More important, a host of unemployed citizens face the grim problem of existence, and an equally great number toil with little return. Only a foolish optimist can deny the dark realities of the moment.

Yet our distress comes from no failure of substance. We are stricken by no plague of locusts. Compared with the perils which our forefathers conquered because they believed and were not afraid, we have still much to be thankful for. Nature still offers her bounty and human efforts have multiplied it. Plenty is at our doorstep, but a generous use of it languishes in the very sight of the supply. Primarily this is because the rulers of the exchange of mankind's goods have failed, through their own stubbornness and their own incompetence, have admitted their failure, and abdicated. Practices of the unscrupulous money changers stand indicted in the court of public opinion, rejected by the hearts and minds of men.

True they have tried, but their efforts have been cast in the pattern of an outworn tradition. Faced by failure of credit they have proposed only the lending of more money. Stripped of the lure of profit by which to induce our people to follow their false leadership, they have resorted to exhortations, pleading tearfully for restored confidence. They know only the rules of a generation of self-seekers. They have no vision, and when there is no vision the people perish.

The money changers have fled from their high seats in the temple of our civilization. We may now restore that temple to the ancient truths. The measure of the restoration lies in the extent to which we apply social values more noble than mere monetary profit.

Happiness lies not in the mere possession of money; it lies in the joy of achievement, in the thrill of creative effort. The joy and moral stimulation of work no longer must be forgotten in the mad chase of evanescent profits. These dark days will be worth all they cost us if they teach us that our true destiny is not to be ministered unto but to minister to ourselves and to our fellow men.

Recognition of the falsity of material wealth as the standard of success goes hand in hand with the abandonment of the false belief that public office and high political position are to be valued only by the standards of pride of place and personal profit; and there must be an end to a conduct in banking and in business which too often has given to a sacred trust the likeness of callous and selfish wrongdoing. Small wonder that confidence languishes, for it thrives only on honesty, on honor, on the sacredness of obligations, on faithful protection, on unselfish performance; without them it cannot live.

Restoration calls, however, not for changes in ethics alone. This nation asks for action, and action now.

Our greatest primary task is to put people to work. This is no unsolvable problem if we face it wisely and courageously. It can be accomplished in part by direct recruiting by the government itself, treating the task as we would treat the emergency of a war, but at the same time, through this employment, accomplishing greatly needed projects to stimulate and reorganize the use of our natural resources.

Hand in hand with this we must frankly recognize the overbalance of population in our industrial centers and, by engaging on a national scale in a redistribution, endeavor to provide a better use of the land for those best fitted for the land. The task can be helped by definite efforts to raise the values of agricultural products and with this the power to purchase the output of our cities. It can be helped by preventing realistically the tragedy of the growing loss through foreclosure of our small homes and our farms. It can be helped by insistence that the federal, state, and local governments act forthwith on the demand that their cost be drastically reduced. It can be helped by the unifying of relief activities which today are often scattered, uneconomical, and unequal. It can be helped by national planning for and supervision of all forms of transportation and of communications and other utilities which have a definitely public character. There are many ways in which it can be helped, but it can never be helped merely by talking about it. We must act and act quickly.

Finally, in our progress toward a resumption of work we require two safeguards against a return of the evils of the old order: there must be a strict supervision of all banking and credits and investments, so that there will be an end to speculation with other people's money; and there must be provision for an adequate but sound currency.

These are the lines of attack. I shall presently urge upon a new Congress, in special session, detailed measures for their fulfillment, and I shall seek the immediate assistance of the several states.

Through this program of action we address ourselves to putting our own national house in order and making income balance outgo. Our international trade relations, though vastly important, are in point of time and necessity secondary to the establishment of a sound national economy. I favor as a practical policy the putting of first things first. I shall spare no effort to restore world trade by international economic readjustment, but the emergency at home cannot wait on that accomplishment.

The basic thought that guides these specific means of national recovery is not narrowly nationalistic. It is the insistence, as a first consideration, upon the interdependence of the various elements in all parts of the United States—a recognition of the old and permanently important manifestation of the American spirit of the pioneer. It is the way to recovery. It is the immediate way. It is the strongest assurance that the recovery will endure.

In the field of world policy I would dedicate this nation to the policy of the good neighbor—the neighbor who resolutely respects himself and, because he does so, respects the rights of others—the neighbor who respects his obligations and respects the sanctity of his agreements in and with a world of neighbors.

If I read the temper of our people correctly, we now realize as we have never realized before our interdependence on each other; that we cannot merely take but we must give as well; that if we are to go forward, we must move as a trained and loyal army willing to sacrifice for the good of a common discipline, because without such discipline no progress is made, no leadership becomes effective. We are, I know, ready and willing to submit our lives and property to such discipline, because it makes possible a leadership which aims at a larger good. This I propose to offer, pledging that the larger purposes will bind upon us all as a sacred obligation with a unity of duty hitherto evoked only in time of armed strife.

With this pledge taken, I assume unhesitatingly the leadership of this great army of our people dedicated to a disciplined attack upon our common problems.

Action in this image and to this end is feasible under the form of government which we have inherited from our ancestors. Our Constitution is so simple and practical that it is possible always to meet extraordinary needs by changes in emphasis and arrangement without loss of essential form. That is why our constitutional system has proved itself the most superbly enduring political mechanism the modern world has produced. It has met every stress of vast expansion of territory, of foreign wars, of bitter internal strife, of world relations.

It is to be hoped that the normal balance of executive and legislative authority may be wholly adequate to meet the unprecedented task before us. But it may be that an unprecedented demand and need for undelayed action may call for temporary departure from that normal balance of public procedure.

I am prepared under my constitutional duty to recommend the measures that a stricken nation in the midst of a stricken world may require. These measures, or such other measures as the Congress may build out of its experience and wisdom, I shall seek, within my constitutional authority, to bring to speedy adoption.

But in the event that the Congress shall fail to take one of these two courses, and in the event that the national emergency is still critical, I shall not evade the clear course of duty that will then confront me. I shall ask the Congress for the one remaining instrument to meet the crisis—broad executive power to wage a war against the emergency, as great as the power that would be given to me if we were in fact invaded by a foreign foe.

For the trust reposed in me I will return the courage and the devotion that befit the time. I can do no less.

We face the arduous days that lie before us in the warm courage of the national unity; with the clear consciousness of seeking old and precious moral values; with the clean satisfaction that comes from the stern performance of duty by old and young alike. We aim at the assurance of a rounded and permanent national life.

We do not distrust the future of essential democracy. The people of the United States have not failed. In their need they have registered a mandate that they want direct, vigorous action. They have asked for discipline and direction under leadership. They have made me the present instrument of their wishes. In the spirit of the gift I take it.

In this dedication of a nation we humbly ask the blessing of God. May He protect each and every one of us. May He guide me in the days to come.

Study Questions

1. Who or what does Roosevelt blame for the nation's economic devastation? What does he propose to do about it?
2. What policies passed during the first two years of Roosevelt's presidency are foreshadowed in this speech?
3. This speech is best remembered for a single line: "[T]he only thing we have to fear is fear itself." What does Roosevelt mean by this, and why might it have resonated with the American public? How was fear contributing to the ongoing banking crisis?
4. In this speech, Roosevelt refers to the American people as a "great army" and calls for "wag[ing] a war" against the economic emergency. Why does he use this martial language? What policy or approach is he trying to justify?

FRANKLIN DELANO ROOSEVELT

Fireside Chat on the Works Relief Program and Social Security (1935)

Franklin Delano Roosevelt (1882–1945) launched his presidency with an unparalleled burst of legislative activism. Relying on a broad coalition of Democrats (his party) and liberal Republicans, he persuaded Congress to pass laws designed to buoy the economy, regulate the banking industry, and help farmers, workers, and the unemployed. Nevertheless, by early 1935 the country's optimism was waning. Two years into the New Deal, the economic crisis had abated, but unemployment still hovered near 20 percent. Growing impatience with the slow pace of recovery fueled dissident political movements on both the right and the left. Roosevelt feared such movements would fracture his coalition and lead to political paralysis.

To stem such discontent and to sell a second wave of legislation to the public, Roosevelt took to the radio. On April 28, 1935, he delivered a "fireside chat," the seventh of thirty such broadcasts he made during his presidency. (The nickname "fireside chat" pointedly suggests the warm, cozy intimacy of a family parlor rather than an audience of 60 million radio listeners, and though it wasn't coined by Roosevelt himself, it certainly does reflect his intuitive mastery of this new medium.) Using simple vocabulary and concrete analogies, Roosevelt explained how he planned to deal with the complex issues facing the nation. One measure of his success was the millions of letters that flooded into the White House from Americans of every sort. Many addressed the president as if he were a personal friend. As you read the published text of his broadcast, consider what Roosevelt was trying to accomplish and why Americans responded as they did.

From Franklin D. Roosevelt, "Fireside Chat 7," April 28, 1935 (Miller Center, University of Virginia), www.millercenter.org.

Since my annual message to the Congress on January fourth, last, I have not addressed the general public over the air. In the many weeks since that time the Congress has devoted itself to the arduous task of formulating legislation necessary to the country's welfare. It has made and is making distinct progress.

Before I come to any of the specific measures, however, I want to leave in your minds one clear fact. The Administration and the Congress are not proceeding in any haphazard fashion in this task of government. Each of our steps has a definite relationship to every other step. The job of creating a program for the nation's welfare is, in some respects, like the building of a ship. At different points on the coast where I often visit they build great seagoing ships. When one of these ships is under construction and the steel frames have been set in the keel, it is difficult for a person who does not know ships to tell how it will finally look when it is sailing the high seas.

It may seem confused to some, but out of the multitude of detailed parts that go into the making of the structure the creation of a useful instrument for man ultimately comes. It is that way with the making of a national policy. The objective of the nation has greatly changed in three years. Before that time individual self-interest and group selfishness were paramount in public thinking. The general good was at a discount.

Three years of hard thinking have changed the picture. More and more people, because of clearer thinking and a better understanding, are considering the whole rather than a mere part relating to one section or to one crop, or to one industry, or to an individual private occupation. That is a tremendous gain for the principles of democracy. The overwhelming majority of people in this country know how to sift the wheat from the chaff in what they hear and what they read. They know that the process of the constructive rebuilding of America cannot be done in a day or a year, but that it is being done in spite of the few who seek to confuse them and to profit by their confusion. Americans as a whole are feeling a lot better—a lot more cheerful than for many, many years.

The most difficult place in the world to get a clear, open perspective of the country as a whole is Washington. I am reminded sometimes of what President Wilson once said: "So many people come to Washington who know things that are not so, and so few people who know anything about what the people of the United States are thinking about." That is why I occasionally leave this scene of action for a few days to go fishing or back home to Hyde Park, so that I can have a chance to think quietly about the country as a whole. "To get away from the trees," as they say, "and to look at the whole forest." This duty of seeing the country in a long-range perspective is one which, in a very special manner, attaches to this office to which you have chosen me. Did you ever stop to think that there are, after all, only two positions in the nation that are filled by the vote of all of the voters—the president and the vice president? That makes it particularly necessary for the vice president and for me to conceive of our duty toward the entire country. I speak, therefore, tonight, to and of the American people as a whole.

My most immediate concern is in carrying out the purposes of the great work program just enacted by the Congress. Its first objective is to put men and women now on the relief rolls to work and, incidentally, to assist materially in our already unmistakable march toward recovery. I shall not confuse my discussion by a multitude of figures. So many figures are quoted to prove so many things. Sometimes it depends upon what paper you read and what broadcast you hear. Therefore, let us keep our minds on two or three simple, essential facts in connection with this problem of unemployment. It is true that while business and industry are definitely better our relief rolls are still too large. However, for the first time in five years the relief rolls have declined instead of increased during the winter months. They are still declining. The simple fact is that many million more people have private work today than two years ago today or one year ago today, and every day that passes offers more chances to work for those who want to work. In spite of the fact that unemployment remains a serious problem here as in every other nation, we have come to recognize the possibility and the necessity of certain helpful remedial measures. These measures are of two kinds. The first is to make provisions intended to relieve, to minimize, and to prevent future unemployment; the second is to establish the practical means to help those who are unemployed in this present emergency. Our social security legislation is an attempt to answer the first of these questions. Our work relief program the second.

The program for social security now pending before the Congress is a necessary part of the future unemployment policy of the government. While our present and projected expenditures for work relief are wholly within the reasonable limits of our national credit resources, it is obvious that we cannot continue to create governmental deficits for that purpose year after year. We must begin now to make provision for the future. That is why our social security program is an important part of the complete picture. It proposes, by means of old age pensions, to help those who have reached the age of retirement to give up their jobs and thus give to the younger generation greater opportunities for work and to give to all a feeling of security as they look toward old age.

The unemployment insurance part of the legislation will not only help to guard the individual in future periods of lay-off against dependence upon relief, but it will, by sustaining purchasing power, cushion the shock of economic distress. Another helpful feature of unemployment insurance is the incentive it will give to employers to plan more carefully in order that unemployment may be prevented by the stabilizing of employment itself.

Provisions for social security, however, are protections for the future. Our responsibility for the immediate necessities of the unemployed has been met by the Congress through the most comprehensive work plan in the history of the nation. Our problem is to put to work three and one-half million employable persons now on the relief rolls. It is a problem quite as much for private industry as for the government.

We are losing no time getting the government's vast work relief program under way, and we have every reason to believe that it should be in full swing by autumn. In directing it, I shall recognize six fundamental principles:

1. The projects should be useful.
2. Projects shall be of a nature that a considerable proportion of the money spent will go into wages for labor.
3. Projects which promise ultimate return to the federal treasury of a considerable proportion of the costs will be sought.
4. Funds allotted for each project should be actually and promptly spent and not held over until later years.
5. In all cases projects must be of a character to give employment to those on the relief rolls.
6. Projects will be allocated to localities or relief areas in relation to the number of workers on relief rolls in those areas.

I next want to make it clear exactly how we shall direct the work.

1. I have set up a Division of Applications and Information to which all proposals for the expenditure of money must go for preliminary study and consideration.
2. After the Division of Applications and Information has sifted those projects, they will be sent to an Allotment Division composed of representatives of the more important governmental agencies charged with carrying on work relief projects. The group will also include representatives of cities, and of labor, farming, banking, and industry. This Allotment Division will consider all of the recommendations submitted to it and such projects as they approve will be next submitted to the president who under the act is required to make final allocations.
3. The next step will be to notify the proper government agency in whose field the project falls, and also to notify another agency which I am creating—a Progress Division. This division will have the duty of coordinating the purchases of materials and supplies and of making certain that people who are employed will be taken from the relief rolls. It will also have the responsibility of determining work payments in various localities, of making full use of existing employment services and to assist people engaged in relief work to move as rapidly as possible back into private employment when such employment is available. Moreover, this division will be charged with keeping projects moving on schedule.
4. I have felt it to be essentially wise and prudent to avoid, so far as possible, the creation of new governmental machinery for supervising this work. The national government now has at least sixty different agencies with the staff and the experience and the competence necessary to carry on the two hundred and fifty or three hundred kinds of work that will be undertaken. These agencies, therefore, will simply be doing on a somewhat enlarged scale the same sort of things that they have been doing. This will make certain that

the largest possible portion of the funds allotted will be spent for actually creating new work and not for building up expensive overhead organizations here in Washington.

For many months preparations have been under way. The allotment of funds for desirable projects has already begun. The key men for the major responsibilities of this great task already have been selected. I well realize that the country is expecting before this year is out to see the "dirt fly," as they say, in carrying on the work, and I assure my fellow citizens that no energy will be spared in using these funds effectively to make a major attack upon the problem of unemployment.

Our responsibility is to all of the people in this country. This is a great national crusade to destroy enforced idleness, which is an enemy of the human spirit generated by this depression. Our attack upon these enemies must be without stint and without discrimination. No sectional, no political distinctions can be permitted. It must, however, be recognized that when an enterprise of this character is extended over more than three thousand counties throughout the nation, there may be occasional instances of inefficiency, bad management, or misuse of funds. When cases of this kind occur, there will be those, of course, who will try to tell you that the exceptional failure is characteristic of the entire endeavor. It should be remembered that in every big job there are some imperfections. There are chiselers in every walk of life; there are those in every industry who are guilty of unfair practices, every profession has its black sheep, but long experience in government has taught me that the exceptional instances of wrong-doing in government are probably less numerous than in almost every other line of endeavor. The most effective means of preventing such evils in this work relief program will be the eternal vigilance of the American people themselves. I call upon my fellow citizens everywhere to cooperate with me in making this the most efficient and the cleanest example of public enterprise the world has ever seen. It is time to provide a smashing answer for those cynical men who say that a democracy cannot be honest and efficient. If you will help, this can be done. I, therefore, hope you will watch the work in every corner of this nation. Feel free to criticize. Tell me of instances where work can be done better, or where improper practices prevail. Neither you nor I want criticism conceived in a purely fault-finding or partisan spirit, but I am jealous of the right of every citizen to call to the attention of his or her government examples of how the public money can be more effectively spent for the benefit of the American people.

I now come, my friends, to a part of the remaining business before the Congress. It has under consideration many measures which provide for the rounding out of the program of economic and social reconstruction with which we have been concerned for two years. I can mention only a few of them tonight, but I do not want my mention of specific measures to be interpreted as lack of interest in or disapproval of many other important proposals that are pending.

The National Industrial Recovery Act expires on the sixteenth of June. After careful consideration, I have asked the Congress to extend the life of this useful agency of government. As we have proceeded with the administration of this act, we have found from time to time more and more useful ways of promoting its purposes. No reasonable person wants to abandon our present gains—we must continue to protect children, to enforce minimum wages, to prevent excessive hours, to safeguard, define, and enforce collective bargaining, and, while retaining fair competition, to eliminate, so far as humanly possible, the kinds of unfair practices by selfish minorities which unfortunately did more than anything else to bring about the recent collapse of industries.

There is likewise pending before the Congress legislation to provide for the elimination of unnecessary holding companies in the public utility field.

I consider this legislation a positive recovery measure. Power production in this country is virtually back to the 1929 peak. The operating companies in the gas and electric utility field are by and large in good condition. But under holding company domination the utility industry has long been hopelessly at war within itself and with public sentiment. By far the greater part of the general decline in utility securities had occurred before I was inaugurated. The absentee management of unnecessary holding company control has lost touch with and has lost the sympathy of the communities it pretends to serve. Even more significantly, it has given the country as a whole an uneasy apprehension of over-concentrated economic power.

A business that loses the confidence of its customers and the good will of the public cannot long continue to be a good risk for the investor. This legislation will serve the investor by ending the conditions which have caused that lack of confidence and good will. It will put the public utility operating industry on a sound basis for the future, both in its public relations and in its internal relations.

This legislation will not only in the long run result in providing lower electric and gas rates to the consumer, but it will protect the actual value and earning power of properties now owned by thousands of investors who have little protection under the old laws against what used to be called frenzied finance. It will not destroy values.

Not only business recovery, but the general economic recovery of the nation will be greatly stimulated by the enactment of legislation designed to improve the status of our transportation agencies. There is need for legislation providing for the regulation of interstate transportation by buses and trucks, to regulate transportation by water, new provisions for strengthening our merchant marine and air transport, measures for the strengthening of the Interstate Commerce Commission to enable it to carry out a rounded conception of the national transportation system in which the benefits of private ownership are retained, while the public stake in these important services is protected by the public's government.

Finally, the reestablishment of public confidence in the banks of the nation is one of the most hopeful results of our efforts as a nation to reestablish public confidence in private banking. We all know that private banking actually exists by virtue of the permission of and regulation by the people as a whole, speaking through their government. Wise public policy, however, requires not only that banking be safe but that its resources be most fully utilized, in the economic life of the country. To this end it was decided more than twenty years ago that the government should assume the responsibility of providing a means by which the credit of the nation might be controlled, not by a few private banking institutions, but by a body with public prestige and authority. The answer to this demand was the Federal Reserve System. Twenty years of experience with this system have justified the efforts made to create it, but these twenty years have shown by experience definite possibilities for improvement. Certain proposals made to amend the Federal Reserve Act deserve prompt and favorable action by the Congress. They are a minimum of wise readjustment of our Federal Reserve System in the light of past experience and present needs.

These measures I have mentioned are, in large part, the program which under my constitutional duty I have recommended to the Congress. They are essential factors in a rounded program for national recovery. They contemplate the enrichment of our national life by a sound and rational ordering of its various elements and wise provisions for the protection of the weak against the strong. Never since my inauguration in March, 1933, have I felt so unmistakably the atmosphere of recovery. But it is more than the recovery of the material basis of our individual lives. It is the recovery of confidence in our democratic processes and institutions. We have survived all of the arduous burdens and the threatening dangers of a great economic calamity. We have in the darkest moments of our national trials retained our faith in our own ability to master our destiny. Fear is vanishing and confidence is growing on every side, renewed faith in the vast possibilities of human beings to improve their material and spiritual status through the instrumentality of the democratic form of government. That faith is receiving its just reward. For that we can be thankful to the God who watches over America.

Study Questions

1. Roosevelt argued that "[t]he objective of the nation has greatly changed" since he took office. How did he think it had changed? How did he portray his role as president?
2. According to Roosevelt, why did the United States need a work relief program? Why did it need a social security program?
3. Early in his speech, Roosevelt compared the steps taken by his administration "for the nation's welfare" to the process of building a ship. What was the purpose of this analogy?
4. Although Roosevelt was not the first president to use the radio, he made far greater use of it than any of his predecessors, and his fireside chats were unique. Why do you think Roosevelt broadcast these informal addresses to the public rather than relying simply on formal speeches and news coverage?

CLAYTON B. VOGEL

Memo Recommending the Recruitment of Navajo Code Talkers (1942)

During World War II, the U.S. military struggled with how to send and receive messages on the battlefield without running the risk that the enemy would intercept and decipher them. One approach was to encrypt and then decode each message, but this could be very time consuming. The U.S. Marine Corps used another approach in the Pacific Theater. It enlisted some 400 Navajo "code talkers" who transmitted messages over radios and walkie talkies in their tribal language, Since the Navajo language had no equivalent of many modern military terms, the code talkers improvised: their word for turtle (chay-da-gahi) *stood in for tank, while a dive bomber was called a chicken hawk* (gini). *The code talkers also spelled out terms and place names, using Navajo words that represented English letters. In February 1945, a Navajo code talker used the Navajo words for sheep, Ute, rabbit, ice, bear, ant, cat, horse and itch to tell the Pacific high command that the marines had planted a U.S. flag on Mount Suribachi on the Japanese island of Iwo Jima, an event commemorated by the Marine Corps War Memorial sculpture near Arlington National Cemetery in Virginia.*

The idea for recruiting Navajo code talkers originated with Philip Johnston (1892–1978), a civil engineer working in Los Angeles. The son of missionaries, Johnston had grown up on the Navajo reservation and knew the language. As a World War I veteran, he also understood military needs. In late February 1942, he demonstrated his idea to Major General Clayton B. Vogel (1882–1964), the commanding general of the Pacific Fleet's Amphibious Force. Vogel was so impressed by the demonstration that he wrote this memo recommending the program to the Marine Corps commandant. As you read this memo, think about the light it sheds on military priorities and concerns.

From "Maj. Gen. Clayton B. Vogel's Recommendation Letter," National Archives and Records Administration, Records of the United States Marine Corps, Record Group 127.

HEADQUARTERS,
AMPHIBIOUS FORCE, PACIFIC FLEET,
CAMP ELLIOTT, SAN DIEGO, CALIFORNIA

March 6, 1942

From: The Commanding General.
To: The Commandant, U.S. Marine Corps.

Subject: Enlistment of Navaho[1] Indians.

Enclosures: (A) Brochure by Mr. Philip Johnston, with maps.
(B) Messages used in demonstration.

1. Mr. Philip Johnston of Los Angeles recently offered his services to this force to demonstrate the use of Indians for the transmission of messages by telephone and voice-radio. His offer was accepted and the demonstration was held for the Commanding General and his staff.

2. The demonstration was interesting and successful. Messages were transmitted and received almost verbatim. In conducting the demonstration messages were written by a member of the staff and handed to the Indian; he would transmit the messages in his tribal dialect and the Indian on the other end would write them down in English. The text of messages as written and received are enclosed. The Indians do not have many military terms in their dialect so it was necessary to give them a few minutes, before the demonstration, to improvise words for dive-bombing, anti-tank gun, etc.

3. Mr. Johnston stated that the Navaho is the only tribe in the United States that has not been infested with German students during the past twenty years. These Germans, studying the various tribal dialects under the guise of art students, anthropologists, etc., have undoubtedly attained a good working knowledge of all tribal dialects except Navaho. For this reason the Navaho is the only tribe available offering complete security for the type of work under consideration. It is noted in Mr. Johnston's article (enclosed) that the Navaho is the largest tribe but the lowest in literacy. He stated, however, that 1,000—if that many were needed—could be found with the necessary qualifications. It should also be noted that the Navaho tribal dialect is completely unintelligible to all other tribes and all other people, with the possible exception of as many as 26 Americans who have made a study of the dialect. This dialect is thus equivalent to a secret code to the enemy, and admirably suited for rapid, secure communication.

1. Navajo.

4. It is therefore recommended that an effort be made to enlist 200 Navaho Indians for this force. In addition to linguistic qualifications in English and their tribal dialect they should have the physical qualifications necessary for messengers.

CLAYTON B. VOGEL

Study Questions

1. According to Johnston and Vogel, what qualities made the Navajo particularly well suited to this endeavor?
2. What kind of language did Vogel use to describe the activities of German students in this memo? What does this suggest about his attitudes toward Germans?
3. The Navajo code talker program remained classified until 1968. Why might the military have wanted to keep this program secret long after the end of World War II?
4. How do you think the Navajo recruits felt about this program? What concerns might they have had about participating? What would have motivated their participation?

THE NEW YORK TIMES

Zoot-Suit Fighting Spreads on Coast (1943)

The Japanese attack on Pearl Harbor ensured that Americans entered World War II riding a high tide of national unity. Government propaganda reinforced this sentiment and encouraged Americans on the home front to sacrifice for the war effort just as U.S. servicemen were doing abroad. By 1943, however, Americans' sense of national unity had begun to fade. Rising labor discontent led to massive strikes by workers in an array of vital industries. The Federal Bureau of Investigation reported growing problems with draft dodging. Newspapers noted a surge in juvenile delinquency, and major race riots broke out in cities from New York and Detroit to Beaumont, Texas.

Racial tensions in Los Angeles exploded in June 1943. By then, the city had emerged as a wartime boomtown and a staging area for the conflict with Japan. Diverse Americans poured into Los Angeles to work in aircraft plants and shipyards. Meanwhile, thousands of sailors and soldiers passed through military bases in Southern California en route to the Pacific theater of war. These servicemen increasingly clashed with civilian youth, particularly with Mexican Americans who wore flamboyant outfits called "zoot suits"—balloon trousers and outsize jackets that were a deliberate challenge to wartime austerities, including the rationing of fabric. On the evening of June 3, scores of club-wielding sailors organized a systematic attack on zoot-suiters, some of whom were only twelve years old. That attack triggered more than a week of rioting, during which mobs of sailors, soldiers, and marines rampaged through minority parts of the city. More than 150 people were injured before military and civilian officials were able to regain control. As you read this report, consider how it accounts for the conflict and portrays the various participants.

The City Council voted late today to have an ordinance drawn up which would provide a thirty-day jail sentence for the wearing of a zoot suit in Los Angeles, in an attempt to stop open warfare between service men and teen-age hoodlums which had made the reat pleat and stuff cuff the mark of the outlaw.

The action came as the rioting spread to Los Angeles suburbs and a Vernon policeman suffered a severe back injury when he was deliberately run over by an automobile filled with zoot-suited ruffians.

After hours of debate, in which one Councilman insisted that the action was unconstitutional, the City Council adopted a resolution asking its attorneys to draw up such an ordinance.

The Council argued that by removing the identifying garb the attacks by sailors on the zoot-suited hoodlums would be halted. However, the Council did not say whether such action would stop the gangs from beating and stabbing service men.

Governer Orders Inquiry

Governor Earl Warren conferred with Attorney General Robert W. Kenny at Sacramento and issued a general appeal asking the service men and zoot-suiters to end their fighting. Governor Warren ordered Mr. Kenny and a citizens' committee of five to investigate the disturbances.

The fighting in the first five days of the undeclared war between the service men and the youths—mostly Mexicans and Negroes whose uniform is the drape shape coat with the reat pleat—had been confined to the Skidrow area of Los Angeles. But early today the action spread to Vernon, where Patrolman C. D. Medley suffered a broken back when he fell into a trap he said the hoodlums had set for a serviceman.

Patrolman Medley saw a man prostrate in the street. When he went to help him a parked car shifted into gear and ran him down. The man in the street jumped up and ran and the youths in the car sped away.

"They were all Mexicans," he said. "Even the decoy in the street."

400 Sailors Hunt Handlooms

A crowd of nearly 400 sailors roamed the Pike, amusement zone in Long Beach, in search for Mexican and Negro youths sporting reat pleats. They ran one into a theatre and stripped him of his pants while the audience cheered.

In Watts, an interurban electric street car bound for the Los Angeles Harbor and loaded largely with sailors, was stoned by a group of youths whom police described as "pachucos," Mexican wearers of the pancake hat and other fancy clothing.

San Diego police were ordered to keep a close watch for carloads and truckloads of zoot-suited youngsters after receiving reports that they planned to "clean

A young man wears a typical zoot-suit. *AP Photo.*

up" on sailors and marines stationed at the naval and marina bases there.

In El Monte, South Gate, Compton and Lynwood crowds of sailors and soldiers raided pool halls, dance halls and other places frequented by the zoot-suit wearers, but found that they had gone into hiding.

Police in Colton summoned emergency reinforcements from San Bernardino and Redlands to cope with taxicab-loads of soldiers from March Field and Camp Haan seeking revenge for the beating of a soldier in Colton on Monday night. Police broke up crowds of fighting men.

Mexican Consulate Reports

Meanwhile, the Mexican consulate made an official report on the disturbances to the Washington embassy and the foreign office at Mexico City.

The Mexican consul, Alfredo Calles, son of the former Mexican president, distributed circulars throughout the Mexican district last night advising all Mexican nationals to stay indoors after dark.

"Remain at home after dark to avoid unpleasant happenings," said the circulars, printed in Spanish. "Stay at home during these days of unrest. We are confident that civil and military authorities will soon remedy this unpleasant situation."

County supervisors officially deplored the outbreaks, unanimously adopting a resolution stating that "a general cordial relation exists between residents of Anglo and Latin ancestry, many of whom have lived side by side for years." They said the situation "calls for both a sympathetic understanding and a firm insistence on an impartial administration of justice," he added:

"We deplore the instances of lawlessness and racial discrimination and of efforts of various groups to take the law into their own hands."

Study Questions

1. According to this story, what happened during the zoot-suit riots? Who or what caused the rampaging and who sought to calm the situation? How did U.S. and Mexican officials react?
2. What kinds of words does this *New York Times* article use to describe the minority teenagers involved in the confrontation? What does this suggest about the reporter's sympathies?
3. During World War II, the federal government urged consumers to conserve fabric, as wool, silk, and other materials were needed for everything from military uniforms to parachutes. Zoot suits, however, had high-waisted, wide-legged pants and long coats with wide lapels and broad padded shoulders; in other words, they used an enormous amount of fabric. Why might minority teenagers have chosen to wear zoot suits? Why do you think these oversized outfits—and their wearers—became the target of servicemen's rage?
4. How might an account of the zoot-suit riots appearing in the Spanish-language press differ from the account offered here?

U.S. SUPREME COURT

Korematsu v. United States (1944)

In late May 1942, Fred Korematsu (1919–2005), a twenty-two-year-old American citizen whose parents were Japanese immigrants, was arrested for refusing to leave his home in San Leandro, California. Some six months earlier Japanese warplanes had attacked the American naval base at Pearl Harbor, bringing the United States into World War II and triggering widespread fears of domestic espionage. During the hysteria that followed, President Franklin Delano Roosevelt (1882–1945) issued Executive Order 9066, which authorized military commanders to exclude individuals from areas of the country deemed essential to national security. The military soon used this power to ban "all persons of Japanese ancestry" from a swath of the West Coast stretching from Washington State to southern Arizona—an area that had long been a hotbed of anti-Japanese nativism. The order affected some 120,000 people, two-thirds of them American citizens. Those who had not left before the military order was issued were required to report to assembly centers. Most were then relocated to hastily constructed "relocation camps" in the nation's interior.

Korematsu was convicted of violating the evacuation order and sent to a relocation camp in Topaz, Utah. Attorneys for the American Civil Liberties Union, hoping to challenge the constitutionality of the government's policy, persuaded Korematsu to appeal his conviction. In December 1944, a bitterly divided Supreme Court finally issued its decision upholding Korematsu's conviction. As you read the majority decision, written by Justice Hugo Black (1886–1971), think about how the Court balances issues of racial discrimination, civil liberties, and military necessity.

From *Korematsu v. United States*, 323 U.S. 214.

Mr. Justice Black delivered the opinion of the Court.

The petitioner, an American citizen of Japanese descent, was convicted in a federal district court for remaining in San Leandro, California, a "Military Area," contrary to Civilian Exclusion Order No. 34 of the Commanding General of the Western Command, U.S. Army, which directed that, after May 9, 1942, all persons of Japanese ancestry should be excluded from that area. No question was raised as to petitioner's loyalty to the United States. The Circuit

Court of Appeals affirmed, and the importance of the constitutional question involved caused us to grant certiorari.[1]

It should be noted, to begin with, that all legal restrictions which curtail the civil rights of a single racial group are immediately suspect. That is not to say that all such restrictions are unconstitutional. It is to say that courts must subject them to the most rigid scrutiny. Pressing public necessity may sometimes justify the existence of such restrictions; racial antagonism never can.

In the instant case, prosecution of the petitioner was begun by information charging violation of an Act of Congress, of March 21, 1942, 56 Stat. 173, which provides that

> . . . whoever shall enter, remain in, leave, or commit any act in any military area or military zone prescribed, under the authority of an Executive order of the President, by the Secretary of War, or by any military commander designated by the Secretary of War, contrary to the restrictions applicable to any such area or zone or contrary to the order of the Secretary of War or any such military commander, shall, if it appears that he knew or should have known of the existence and extent of the restrictions or order and that his act was in violation thereof, be guilty of a misdemeanor and upon conviction shall be liable to a fine of not to exceed $5,000 or to imprisonment for not more than one year, or both, for each offense.

Exclusion Order No. 34, which the petitioner knowingly and admittedly violated, was one of a number of military orders and proclamations, all of which were substantially based upon Executive Order No. 9066, 7 Fed. Reg. 1407. That order, issued after we were at war with Japan, declared that

> the successful prosecution of the war requires every possible protection against espionage and against sabotage to national defense material, national defense premises, and national defense utilities . . .

One of the series of orders and proclamations, a curfew order, which, like the exclusion order here, was promulgated pursuant to Executive Order 9066, subjected all persons of Japanese ancestry in prescribed West Coast military areas to remain in their residences from 8 p.m. to 6 a.m. As is the case with the exclusion order here, that prior curfew order was designed as a "protection against espionage and against sabotage." In *Hirabayashi v. United States, 320 U.S. 81*, we sustained a conviction obtained for violation of the curfew order. The Hirabayashi conviction and this one thus rest on the same 1942 Congressional Act and the same basic executive and military orders, all of which orders were aimed at the twin dangers of espionage and sabotage.

1. A writ from a superior court requiring a lower court to deliver records of a case under review.

The 1942 Act was attacked in the *Hirabayashi* case as an unconstitutional delegation of power; it was contended that the curfew order and other orders on which it rested were beyond the war powers of the Congress, the military authorities, and of the President, as Commander in Chief of the Army, and, finally, that to apply the curfew order against none but citizens of Japanese ancestry amounted to a constitutionally prohibited discrimination solely on account of race. To these questions, we gave the serious consideration which their importance justified. We upheld the curfew order as an exercise of the power of the government to take steps necessary to prevent espionage and sabotage in an area threatened by Japanese attack.

In the light of the principles we announced in the *Hirabayashi* case, we are unable to conclude that it was beyond the war power of Congress and the Executive to exclude those of Japanese ancestry from the West Coast war area at the time they did. True, exclusion from the area in which one's home is located is a far greater deprivation than constant confinement to the home from 8 p.m. to 6 a.m. Nothing short of apprehension by the proper military authorities of the gravest imminent danger to the public safety can constitutionally justify either. But exclusion from a threatened area, no less than curfew, has a definite and close relationship to the prevention of espionage and sabotage. The military authorities, charged with the primary responsibility of defending our shores, concluded that curfew provided inadequate protection and ordered exclusion. They did so, as pointed out in our *Hirabayashi* opinion, in accordance with Congressional authority to the military to say who should, and who should not, remain in the threatened areas.

In this case, the petitioner challenges the assumptions upon which we rested our conclusions in the *Hirabayashi* case. He also urges that, by May, 1942, when Order No. 34 was promulgated, all danger of Japanese invasion of the West Coast had disappeared. After careful consideration of these contentions, we are compelled to reject them.

Here, as in the *Hirabayashi* case, *supra*,[2] at p. 99,

> . . . we cannot reject as unfounded the judgment of the military authorities and of Congress that there were disloyal members of that population, whose number and strength could not be precisely and quickly ascertained. We cannot say that the war-making branches of the Government did not have ground for believing that, in a critical hour, such persons could not readily be isolated and separately dealt with, and constituted a menace to the national defense and safety which demanded that prompt and adequate measures be taken to guard against it.

Like curfew, exclusion of those of Japanese origin was deemed necessary because of the presence of an unascertained number of disloyal members of the group,

2. Above (Latin).

most of whom we have no doubt were loyal to this country. It was because we could not reject the finding of the military authorities that it was impossible to bring about an immediate segregation of the disloyal from the loyal that we sustained the validity of the curfew order as applying to the whole group. In the instant case, temporary exclusion of the entire group was rested by the military on the same ground. The judgment that exclusion of the whole group was, for the same reason, a military imperative answers the contention that the exclusion was in the nature of group punishment based on antagonism to those of Japanese origin. That there were members of the group who retained loyalties to Japan has been confirmed by investigations made subsequent to the exclusion. Approximately five thousand American citizens of Japanese ancestry refused to swear unqualified allegiance to the United States and to renounce allegiance to the Japanese Emperor, and several thousand evacuees requested repatriation to Japan.

We uphold the exclusion order as of the time it was made and when the petitioner violated it. *Cf. Chastleton Corporation v. Sinclair, 264 U.S.* 543, 547; *Block v. Hirsh, 256 U.S.* 135, 155. In doing so, we are not unmindful of the hardships imposed by it upon a large group of American citizens. *Cf. Ex parte Kawato, 317 U.S.* 69, 73. But hardships are part of war, and war is an aggregation of hardships. All citizens alike, both in and out of uniform, feel the impact of war in greater or lesser measure. Citizenship has its responsibilities, as well as its privileges, and, in time of war, the burden is always heavier. Compulsory exclusion of large groups of citizens from their homes, except under circumstances of direst emergency and peril, is inconsistent with our basic governmental institutions. But when, under conditions of modern warfare, our shores are threatened by hostile forces, the power to protect must be commensurate with the threatened danger.

It is argued that, on May 30, 1942, the date the petitioner was charged with remaining in the prohibited area, there were conflicting orders outstanding, forbidding him both to leave the area and to remain there. Of course, a person cannot be convicted for doing the very thing which it is a crime to fail to do. But the outstanding orders here contained no such contradictory commands.

There was an order issued March 27, 1942, which prohibited petitioner and others of Japanese ancestry from leaving the area, but its effect was specifically limited in time "until and to the extent that a future proclamation or order should so permit or direct." 7 Fed.Reg. 2601. That "future order," the one for violation of which petitioner was convicted, was issued May 3, 1942, and it did "direct" exclusion from the area of all persons of Japanese ancestry before 12 o'clock noon, May 9; furthermore, it contained a warning that all such persons found in the prohibited area would be liable to punishment under the March 21, 1942, Act of Congress. Consequently, the only order in effect touching the petitioner's being in the area on May 30, 1942, the date specified in the information against him, was the May

3 order which prohibited his remaining there, and it was that same order which he stipulated in his trial that he had violated, knowing of its existence. There is therefore no basis for the argument that, on May 30, 1942, he was subject to punishment, under the March 27 and May 3 orders, whether he remained in or left the area.

It does appear, however, that, on May 9, the effective date of the exclusion order, the military authorities had already determined that the evacuation should be effected by assembling together and placing under guard all those of Japanese ancestry at central points, designated as "assembly centers," in order

> to insure the orderly evacuation and resettlement of Japanese voluntarily migrating from Military Area No. 1, to restrict and regulate such migration.

Public Proclamation No. 4, 7 Fed.Reg. 2601. And on May 19, 1942, eleven days before the time petitioner was charged with unlawfully remaining in the area, Civilian Restrictive Order No. 1, 8 Fed.Reg. 982, provided for detention of those of Japanese ancestry in assembly or relocation centers. It is now argued that the validity of the exclusion order cannot be considered apart from the orders requiring him, after departure from the area, to report and to remain in an assembly or relocation center. The contention is that we must treat these separate orders as one and inseparable; that, for this reason, if detention in the assembly or relocation center would have illegally deprived the petitioner of his liberty, the exclusion order and his conviction under it cannot stand.

We are thus being asked to pass at this time upon the whole subsequent detention program in both assembly and relocation centers, although the only issues framed at the trial related to petitioner's remaining in the prohibited area in violation of the exclusion order. Had petitioner here left the prohibited area and gone to an assembly center, we cannot say, either as a matter of fact or law, that his presence in that center would have resulted in his detention in a relocation center. Some who did report to the assembly center were not sent to relocation centers, but were released upon condition that they remain outside the prohibited zone until the military orders were modified or lifted. This illustrates that they pose different problems, and may be governed by different principles. The lawfulness of one does not necessarily determine the lawfulness of the others. This is made clear when we analyze the requirements of the separate provisions of the separate orders. These separate requirements were that those of Japanese ancestry (1) depart from the area; (2) report to and temporarily remain in an assembly center; (3) go under military control to a relocation center, there to remain for an indeterminate period until released conditionally or unconditionally by the military authorities. Each of these requirements, it will be noted, imposed distinct duties in connection with the separate steps in a complete evacuation program.

Had Congress directly incorporated into one Act the language of these separate orders, and provided sanctions for their violations, disobedience of any one would have constituted a separate offense. *Cf. Blockburger v. United States, 284 U.S. 299*, 304. There is no reason why violations of these orders, insofar as they were promulgated pursuant to Congressional enactment, should not be treated as separate offenses.

The *Endo* case[3] graphically illustrates the difference between the validity of an order to exclude and the validity of a detention order after exclusion has been effected.

Since the petitioner has not been convicted of failing to report or to remain in an assembly or relocation center, we cannot in this case determine the validity of those separate provisions of the order. It is sufficient here for us to pass upon the order which petitioner violated. To do more would be to go beyond the issues raised, and to decide momentous questions not contained within the framework of the pleadings or the evidence in this case. It will be time enough to decide the serious constitutional issues which petitioner seeks to raise when an assembly or relocation order is applied or is certain to be applied to him, and we have its terms before us.

Some of the members of the Court are of the view that evacuation and detention in an Assembly Center were inseparable. After May 3, 1942, the date of Exclusion Order No. 34, Korematsu was under compulsion to leave the area not as he would choose, but via an Assembly Center. The Assembly Center was conceived as a part of the machinery for group evacuation. The power to exclude includes the power to do it by force if necessary. And any forcible measure must necessarily entail some degree of detention or restraint, whatever method of removal is selected. But whichever view is taken, it results in holding that the order under which petitioner was convicted was valid.

It is said that we are dealing here with the case of imprisonment of a citizen in a concentration camp solely because of his ancestry, without evidence or inquiry concerning his loyalty and good disposition towards the United States. Our task would be simple, our duty clear, were this a case involving the imprisonment of a loyal citizen in a concentration camp because of racial prejudice. Regardless of the true nature of the assembly and relocation centers—and we deem it unjustifiable to call them concentration camps, with all the ugly connotations that term implies—we are dealing specifically with nothing but an exclusion order. To cast this case into outlines of racial prejudice, without reference to the real military

3. In the *Ex parte Endo* case, which the Supreme Court decided on the same day as *Korematsu v. U.S.*, the Court ruled unanimously that the federal government could not continue to detain a citizen whom the government itself conceded was loyal. The Court did not condemn the original evacuation order, but by banning the continued detention of loyal citizens, the *Endo* case effectively reopened the West Coast to people of Japanese ancestry.

dangers which were presented, merely confuses the issue. Korematsu was not excluded from the Military Area because of hostility to him or his race. He was excluded because we are at war with the Japanese Empire, because the properly constituted military authorities feared an invasion of our West Coast and felt constrained to take proper security measures, because they decided that the military urgency of the situation demanded that all citizens of Japanese ancestry be segregated from the West Coast temporarily, and, finally, because Congress, reposing its confidence in this time of war in our military leaders—as inevitably it must—determined that they should have the power to do just this. There was evidence of disloyalty on the part of some, the military authorities considered that the need for action was great, and time was short. We cannot—by availing ourselves of the calm perspective of hindsight—now say that, at that time, these actions were unjustified.

Affirmed.

Study Questions

1. According to the majority decision, why was the evacuation order justified?
2. How does the Court majority treat the issue of race? Does it believe that the civil rights of a single racial group may ever be curtailed? If so, when?
3. Despite the Japanese attack on Pearl Harbor, no one ever proposed evacuating people of Japanese descent from the Hawaiian islands. Such residents made up about one-third of the islands' population in 1942, whereas they constituted only about 1 percent of the population of the West Coast. U.S. officials also imposed no similar sweeping ban on Americans of German or Italian descent. What light do these facts shed on the Supreme Court's contention that "Korematsu was not excluded from the Military Area because of hostility to him or his race"?
4. In a dissenting opinion, Justice Robert Jackson argued that the majority's decision to uphold the evacuation order was "a far more subtle blow to liberty than the [military's] promulgation of the order itself." Why might this be? What does Jackson's statement suggest about the role of Supreme Court decisions in American society?

U.S. SUPREME COURT

Brown v. Board of Education (1954)

On May 17, 1954, the U.S. Supreme Court issued a landmark ruling in Brown v. Board of Education, *a case challenging state-sanctioned racial segregation in public schools. The case originated in Topeka, Kansas, where the father of a third-grader challenged a school district board-sanctioned policy that required his daughter to walk to a distant "black" elementary school even though a "white" school was nearby. Such legal segregation might appear to violate the "equal protection" clause of the Fourteenth Amendment; but in* Plessy v. Ferguson *(1896), the Supreme Court had held that separate facilities were legal as long as they were equal in quality, a ruling that opened the door to widespread segregation of schools and other public facilities for more than half a century. After World War II, the National Association for the Advancement of Colored People filed a series of lawsuits challenging the "separate but equal" doctrine in various arenas. The Supreme Court sided with the N.A.A.C.P. in some of these challenges, but not until the* Brown *decision did it explicitly overturn its earlier ruling and declare that segregated public schools were inherently unequal. The unanimous decision, drafted by Chief Justice Earl Warren (1891–1974), marked a legal turning point and helped launch the best-known phase of the civil rights movement.*

As you read this decision, think carefully about the reasons the Court offers for rejecting the "separate but equal" doctrine in 1954. What had changed since 1896?

From *Brown v. Board of Education*, 347 US 483 (1954).

MR. CHIEF JUSTICE WARREN delivered the opinion of the Court.

These cases come to us from the States of Kansas, South Carolina, Virginia, and Delaware.[1] They are premised on different facts and different local conditions, but a common legal question justifies their consideration together in this consolidated opinion.

In each of the cases, minors of the Negro race, through their legal representatives, seek the aid of the courts in obtaining admission to the public schools of

1. The Court consolidated the lead case, which originated in Topeka, Kansas, with school desegregation cases from South Carolina, Virginia, and Delaware.

their community on a nonsegregated basis. In each instance, they had been denied admission to schools attended by white children under laws requiring or permitting segregation according to race. This segregation was alleged to deprive the plaintiffs of the equal protection of the laws under the Fourteenth Amendment. In each of the cases other than the Delaware case, a three-judge federal district court denied relief to the plaintiffs on the so-called "separate but equal" doctrine announced by this Court in *Plessy v. Ferguson*. Under that doctrine, equality of treatment is accorded when the races are provided substantially equal facilities, even though these facilities be separate. In the Delaware case, the Supreme Court of Delaware adhered to that doctrine, but ordered that the plaintiffs be admitted to the white schools because of their superiority to the Negro schools.

The plaintiffs contend that segregated public schools are not "equal" and cannot be made "equal," and that hence they are deprived of the equal protection of the laws. Because of the obvious importance of the question presented, the Court took jurisdiction. Argument was heard in the 1952 Term, and reargument was heard this Term on certain question propounded by the Court.

Reargument was largely devoted to the circumstances surrounding the adoption of the Fourteenth Amendment in 1868. It covered exhaustively consideration of the Amendment in Congress, ratification by the states, then-existing practices in racial segregation, and the views of proponents and opponents of the Amendment. This discussion and our own investigation convince us that, although these sources cast some light, it is not enough to resolve the problem with which we are faced. At best, they are inconclusive. The most avid proponents of the post-War Amendments[2] undoubtedly intended them to remove all legal distinctions among "all persons born or naturalized in the United States." Their opponents, just as certainly, were antagonistic to both the letter and the spirit of the Amendments and wished them to have the most limited effect. What others in Congress and the state legislatures had in mind cannot be determined with any degree of certainty.

An additional reason for the inconclusive nature of the Amendment's history with respect to segregated schools is the status of public education at that time. In the South, the movement toward free common schools, supported by general taxation, had not yet taken hold. Education of white children was largely in the hands of private groups. Education of Negroes was almost nonexistent, and practically all of the race were illiterate. In fact, any education of Negroes was forbidden by law in some states. Today, in contrast, many Negroes have achieved outstand-

2. The Thirteenth, Fourteenth, and Fifteenth Amendments, which were passed immediately after the Civil War. The Thirteenth Amendment abolished slavery. The Fourteenth Amendment granted citizenship to all persons born in the United States and guaranteed all citizens "due process" and "equal protection" before the law. The Fifteenth Amendment barred both the federal and state governments from denying any citizen the right to vote because of race.

ing success in the arts and sciences, as well as in the business and professional world. It is true that public school education at the time of the Amendment had advanced further in the North, but the effect of the Amendment on Northern States was generally ignored in the congressional debates. Even in the North, the conditions of public education did not approximate those existing today. The curriculum was usually rudimentary; ungraded schools were common in rural areas; the school term was but three months a year in many states, and compulsory school attendance was virtually unknown. As a consequence, it is not surprising that there should be so little in the history of the Fourteenth Amendment relating to its intended effect on public education.

In the first cases in this Court construing the Fourteenth Amendment, decided shortly after its adoption, the Court interpreted it as proscribing all state-imposed discriminations against the Negro race. The doctrine of "separate but equal" did not make its appearance in this Court until 1896 in the case of *Plessy v. Ferguson*, involving not education but transportation. American courts have since labored with the doctrine for over half a century.

* * *

There are findings below that the Negro and white schools involved have been equalized, or are being equalized, with respect to buildings, curricula, qualifications and salaries of teachers, and other "tangible" factors. Our decision, therefore, cannot turn on merely a comparison of these tangible factors in the Negro and white schools involved in each of the cases. We must look instead to the effect of segregation itself on public education.

In approaching this problem, we cannot turn the clock back to 1868, when the Amendment was adopted, or even to 1896, when *Plessy v. Ferguson* was written. We must consider public education in the light of its full development and its present place in American life throughout the Nation. Only in this way can it be determined if segregation in public schools deprives these plaintiffs of the equal protection of the laws.

Today, education is perhaps the most important function of state and local governments. Compulsory school attendance laws and the great expenditures for education both demonstrate our recognition of the importance of education to our democratic society. It is required in the performance of our most basic public responsibilities, even service in the armed forces. It is the very foundation of good citizenship. Today it is the principal instrument in awakening the child to cultural values, in preparing him for later professional training, and in helping him to adjust normally to his environment. In these days, it is doubtful that any child may reasonably be expected to succeed in life if he is denied the opportunity of an education. Such an opportunity, where the state has undertaken to provide it, is a right which must be made available to all on equal terms.

We come then to the question presented: Does segregation of children in public schools solely on the basis of race, even though the physical facilities and other "tangible" factors may be equal, deprive the children of the minority group of equal educational opportunities? We believe that it does.

In *Sweatt v. Painter*[3] in finding that a segregated law school for Negroes could not provide them equal educational opportunities, this Court relied in large part on "those qualities which are incapable of objective measurement but which make for greatness in a law school." In *McLaurin v. Oklahoma State Regents*,[4] the Court, in requiring that a Negro admitted to a white graduate school be treated like all other students, again resorted to intangible considerations: ". . . his ability to study, to engage in discussions and exchange views with other students, and, in general, to learn his profession." Such considerations apply with added force to children in grade and high schools. To separate them from others of similar age and qualifications solely because of their race generates a feeling of inferiority as to their status in the community that may affect their hearts and minds in a way unlikely ever to be undone. The effect of this separation on their educational opportunities was well stated by a finding in the Kansas case by a court which nevertheless felt compelled to rule against the Negro plaintiffs:

> Segregation of white and colored children in public schools has a detrimental effect upon the colored children. The impact is greater when it has the sanction of the law, for the policy of separating the races is usually interpreted as denoting the inferiority of the negro group. A sense of inferiority affects the motivation of a child to learn. Segregation with the sanction of law, therefore, has a tendency to [retard] the educational and mental development of negro children and to deprive them of some of the benefits they would receive in a racial[ly] integrated school system.

Whatever may have been the extent of psychological knowledge at the time of *Plessy v. Ferguson*, this finding is amply supported by modern authority. Any language in *Plessy v. Ferguson* contrary to this finding is rejected.

We conclude that, in the field of public education, the doctrine of "separate but equal" has no place. Separate educational facilities are inherently unequal. Therefore, we hold that the plaintiffs and others similarly situated for whom the actions have been brought are, by reason of the segregation complained of, deprived of the equal protection of the laws guaranteed by the Fourteenth Amendment. . . .

3. A 1950 case in which the Supreme Court ruled that the University of Texas could not deny an African American man admission to law school simply because of his race.

4. A 1950 case in which the Supreme Court ruled that the University of Oklahoma could not deny an African American man admission to a Ph.D. program in education simply because of his race.

Study Questions

1. According to the *Brown* decision, why do the circumstances surrounding the adoption of the Fourteenth Amendment have limited bearing on this case?
2. Why does the Supreme Court reject its own precedent in *Plessy v. Ferguson*? On what kind of evidence or logic does its argument rest?
3. In 1954 the United States was in the midst of a cold war and less than ten years removed from World War II. How might this have affected the Court's judgment about the role of education in American society?
4. Chief Justice Warren thought it essential that the Court issue a unanimous decision in *Brown*. (He considered this so critical, in fact, that he agreed to postpone a ruling on the decision's implementation and eventually accepted vague language on this point.) Why do you think Warren considered unanimity in this case so crucial?

The Southern Manifesto (1956)

In 1956, 101 members of Congress, including 19 senators and 82 representatives from 11 Southern states, signed a resolution that became known as the Southern Manifesto. Formally titled "Declaration of Constitutional Principles," the resolution condemned the Supreme Court's landmark 1954 decision in Brown v. Board of Education, *which declared that segregated public schools were inherently unequal. The* Brown *decision had been unanimous, but the price of that unanimity was a certain vagueness about implementation; the Court declared only that the decision should be implemented "with all deliberate speed." Federal authorities initially did little to enforce the ruling. While some southern communities moved in the direction of desegregation, others decided to push back. The Southern Manifesto urged states not to implement the court mandate, and the resolution helped to build support for a campaign of "massive resistance" across the South.*

The senators who took the lead in drafting and circulating the Southern Manifesto—including Strom Thurmond (1902–2003) of South Carolina and Harry Byrd (1887–1966) of Virginia—hoped to coerce moderate southern politicians into supporting a regional campaign of defiance. They believed that efforts to grant southern blacks full civil rights would founder in the face of united opposition by a "solid South." As you read this document, think about the rhetorical devices the authors use, and the way they portray the relationship between segregation and southern culture.

From "Declaration of Constitutional Principles," Congressional Record, 84th Cong,. 2nd sess., 1956, 102: 4459–60.

The unwarranted decision of the Supreme Court in the public school cases is now bearing the fruit always produced when men substitute naked power for established law.

The Founding Fathers gave us a Constitution of checks and balances because they realized the inescapable lesson of history that no man or group of men can be safely entrusted with unlimited power. They framed this Constitution with its provisions for change by amendment in order to secure the fundamentals of government against the dangers of temporary popular passion or the personal predilections of public officeholders.

We regard the decision of the Supreme Court in the school cases as clear abuse of judicial power. It climaxes a trend in the federal judiciary undertaking to legislate, in derogation of the authority of Congress, and to encroach upon the reserved rights of the states and the people.

The original Constitutional does not mention education. Neither does the Fourteenth Amendment nor any other amendment. The debates preceding the submission of the Fourteenth Amendment clearly show that there was no intent that it should affect the systems of education maintained by the states.

The very Congress which proposed the amendment subsequently provided for segregated schools in the District of Columbia.

When the amendment was adopted in 1868, there were thirty-seven states of the Union. Every one of the twenty-six states that had any substantial racial differences among its people either approved the operation of segregated schools already in existence or subsequently established such schools by action of the same lawmaking body which considered the Fourteenth Amendment.

As admitted by the Supreme Court in the public school case (*Brown v. Board of Education*), the doctrine of separate but equal schools "apparently originated in *Roberts v. City of Boston* (1849), upholding school segregation against attack as being violative of a state constitutional guarantee of equality." This constitutional doctrine began in the North—not in the South—and it was followed not only in Massachusetts but in Connecticut, New York, Illinois, Indiana, Michigan, Minnesota, New Jersey, Ohio, Pennsylvania, and other northern states until they, exercising their rights as states through the constitutional processes of local self-government, changed their school systems.

In the case of *Plessy v. Ferguson* in 1896 the Supreme Court expressly declared that under the Fourteenth Amendment no person was denied any of his rights if the states provided separate but equal public facilities. This decision has been followed in many other cases. It is notable that the Supreme Court, speaking through Chief Justice Taft, a former president of the United States, unanimously declared in 1927 in *Lum v. Rice* that the "separate but equal" principle is . . . within the discretion of the state in regulating its public schools and does not conflict with the Fourteenth Amendment."

This interpretation, restated time and again, became a part of the life of the people of many of the states and confirmed their habits, customs, traditions, and way of life. It is founded on elemental humanity and common sense, for parents should not be deprived by Government of the right to direct the lives and education of their own children.

Though there has been no constitutional amendment or act of Congress changing this established legal principle almost a century old, the Supreme Court of the United States, with no legal basis for such action, undertook to exercise their naked judicial power and substituted their personal political and social ideas for the established law of the land.

This unwarranted exercise of power by the court, contrary to the Constitution, is creating chaos and confusion in the states principally affected. It is destroying the amicable relations between the white and Negro races that have been created through ninety years of patient effort by the good people of both races. It has planted hatred and suspicion where there has been heretofore friendship and understanding.

Without regard to the consent of the governed, outside agitators are threatening immediate and revolutionary changes in our public school systems. If done, this is certain to destroy the system of public education in some of the states.

With the gravest concern for the explosive and dangerous condition created by this decision and inflamed by outside meddlers:

We reaffirm our reliance on the Constitution as the fundamental law of the land.

We decry the Supreme Court's encroachments on rights reserved to the states and to the people, contrary to established law and to the Constitution.

We commend the motives of those states which have declared the intention to resist forced integration by any lawful means.

We appeal to the states and people who are not directly affected by these decisions to consider the constitutional principles involved against the time when they too, on issues vital to them, may be the victims of judicial encroachment.

Even though we constitute a minority in the present congress, we have full faith that a majority of the American people believe in the dual system of government which has enabled us to achieve our greatness and will in time demand that the reserved rights of the states and of the people be made secure against judicial usurpation.

We pledge ourselves to use all lawful means to bring about a reversal of this decision which is contrary to the Constitution and to prevent the use of force in its implementation.

In this trying period, as we all seek to right this wrong, we appeal to our people not to be provoked by the agitators and troublemakers invading our states and to scrupulously refrain from disorder and lawless acts.

Signed by:
Members of the United States Senate:
Alabama—John Sparkman and Lister Hill.
Arkansas—J. W. Fulbright and John L. McClellan.
Florida—George A. Smathers and Spessard L. Holland.
Georgia—Walter F. George and Richard B. Russell.
Louisiana—Allen J. Ellender and Russell B. Lono.
Mississippi—John Stennis and James O. Eastland.
North Carolina—Sam J. Ervin Jr. and W. Kerr Scott.
South Carolina—Strom Thurmon [sic] and Olin D. Johnston.
Texas—Price Daniel.
Virginia—Harry F. Bird [sic] and A. Willis Robertson.

Members of the United States House of Representatives:

Alabama—Frank J. Boykin, George M. Grant, George M. Andrews, Kenneth R. Roberts, Albert Rains, Armistead I. Selden Jr., Carl Elliott, Robert E. Jones and George Huddleston Jr.

Arkansas—E. C. Gathings, Wilbur D. Mills, James W. Trimble, Oren Harris, Brooks Hays, F. W. Norrell.

Florida—Charles E. Bennett Robert L. Sikes, A. S. Her Jr., Paul G. Rogers, James A. Haley, D. R. Matthews.

Georgia—Prince H. Preston, John L. Pilcher, E. L. Forrester, John James Flint Jr., James C. Davis, Carl Vinson, Henderson Lanham, Iris F. Blitch, Phil M. Landrum, Paul Brown.

Louisiana—F. Edward Hebert, Hale Boggs, Edwin E. Willis, Overton Brooks, Otto E. Passman, James H. Morrison, T. Ashton Thompson, George S. Long.

Mississippi—Thomas G. Abernethy, Jamie L. Whitten, Frank E. Smith, John Bell Williams, Arthur Winsted, William M. Colmer.

North Carolina—Herbert C. Bonner, L. H. Fountain, Graham A. Barden, Carl T. Durham, F. Ertel Carlyle, Hugh Q. Alexander, Woodrow W. Jones, George A. Shuford.

South Carolina—L. Mendel Rivers, John J. Riley, W. J. Bryan Dorn, Robert T. Ashmore, James P. Richards, John L. McMillan.

Tennessee—James B. Frazier Jr., Tom Murray, Jere Cooper, Clifford Davis.

Texas—Wright Patman, John Dowdy, Walter Rogers, O. C. Fisher.

Virginia—Edward J. Robeson Jr., Porter Hardy Jr., J. Vaughan Gary, Watkins M. Abbitt, William M. Tuck, Richard H. Poff, Burr P. Harrison, Howard W. Smith, W. Pat Jennings, Joel T. Brothill.

Study Questions

1. Why do the signers of the Southern Manifesto say the Supreme Court decision is an "abuse of judicial power"? What do they predict will be the results of that decision?
2. The signers of the Southern Manifesto portray civil rights activists as "outside agitators" and "troublemakers invading our states." Why do you think they portray them in this way?
3. How do the signers of the Southern Manifesto seek to appeal to those living outside the South? How did they want outsiders to understand their position?
4. The Southern Manifesto charges the Supreme Court with destroying "the amicable relations between the white and Negro races" and "plant[ing] hatred and suspicion where there has been heretofore friendship and understanding." How do you think Southern blacks would have responded to this argument?

ANNE MOODY

High School (1968)

FROM *Coming of Age in Mississippi*

In August 1955, the brutal murder of a young black teenager in Mississippi by two white men shocked many Americans and focused international attention on the racial violence that reinforced white supremacy in the South. Systematic racial terror had claimed the lives of hundreds of black southerners since the end of Reconstruction; in Mississippi alone, at least thirty-three African Americans were lynched between 1930 and 1950. The murder of Emmett Till (1941–1955) was different, however. The victim, a fourteen-year-old from Chicago who didn't understand the South's unwritten racial codes, had allegedly whistled at a white woman in a grocery store. For that, he was dragged from his great-uncle's home, beaten, and shot. Till's bloated and mutilated body was eventually pulled from the Tallahatchie River and returned to Chicago for an open-casket funeral. Thousands attended the service and millions more saw a photo of Till's corpse that was reprinted in Jet *magazine. The men who committed the murder were quickly acquitted by an all-white jury; a few months later, in an interview with* Look *magazine, they vividly described how they had lynched Till.*

Anne Moody (b. 1940) was just fourteen when Till's murder made international headlines. In this excerpt from her acclaimed autobiography, she recounts how news of the lynching reverberated through her small town in rural Mississippi. As you read her account, think about how race, age, and other factors affected the reactions of different individuals to the news.

Not only did I enter high school with a new name,[1] but also with a completely new insight into the life of Negroes in Mississippi. I was now working for one of the meanest white women in town, and a week before school started Emmett Till was killed.

Up until his death, I had heard of Negroes found floating in a river or dead somewhere with their bodies riddled with bullets. But I didn't know the mystery behind these killings then. I remember once when I was only seven I heard Mama and one of my aunts talking about some Negro who had been beaten to death. "Just like them low-down skunks killed him they will do the same to us," Mama had said. When I asked her who killed the man and why, she said, "An Evil Spirit killed him. You gotta be a good girl or it will kill you too." So since I was seven, I had lived in fear of that "Evil Spirit." It took me eight years to learn what that spirit was.

I was coming from school the evening I heard about Emmett Till's death. There was a whole group of us, girls and boys, walking down the road headed home. A group of about six high school boys were walking a few paces ahead of me and several other girls. We were laughing and talking about something that had happened in school that day. However, the six boys in front of us weren't talking very loud. Usually they kept up so much noise. But today they were just walking and talking among themselves. All of a sudden they began to shout at each other.

"Man, what in the hell do you mean?"

"What I mean is these goddamned white folks is gonna start some shit here you just watch!"

"That boy wasn't but fourteen years old and they killed him. Now what kin a fourteen-year-old boy do with a white woman? What if he did whistle at her, he might have thought the whore was pretty."

"Look at all these white men here that's fucking over our women. Everybody knows it too and what's done about that? Look how many white babies we got walking around in our neighborhoods. Their mamas ain't white either. That boy was from Chicago, shit, everybody fuck everybody up there. He probably didn't even think of the bitch as white."

What they were saying shocked me. I knew all of those boys and I had never heard them talk like that. We walked on behind them for a while listening. Questions about who was killed, where, and why started running through my mind. I walked up to one of the boys.

"Eddie, what boy was killed?"

"Moody, where've you been?" he asked me. "Everybody talking about that fourteen-year-old boy who was killed in Greenwood by some white men. You don't know nothing that's going on besides what's in them books of yours, huh?"

1. Anne Moody was born Essie Mae Moody. When she graduated from eighth grade she had to obtain a copy of her birth certificate, which mistakenly gave her name as Anne Mae Moody. Anne took this as an opportunity to change her name, although her white employer continued to call her Essie.

Standing there before the rest of the girls, I felt so stupid. It was then that I realized I really didn't know what was going on all around me. It wasn't that I was dumb. It was just that ever since I was nine, I'd had to work after school and do my lessons on lunch hour. I never had time to learn anything, to hang around with people my own age. And you never were told anything by adults.

That evening when I stopped off at the house on my way to Mrs. Burke's,[2] Mama was singing. Any other day she would have been yelling at Adline and Junior them[3] to take off their school clothes. I wondered if she knew about Emmett Till. The way she was singing she had something on her mind and it wasn't pleasant either.

I got a shoe, you got a shoe,
All of God's chillun got shoes;
When I get to hebben, I'm gonna put on my shoes,
And gonna tromp all over God's hebben.
When I get to hebben I'm gonna put on my shoes,
And gonna walk all over God's hebben.

Mama was dishing up beans like she didn't know anyone was home. Adline, Junior, and James[4] had just thrown their books down and sat themselves at the table. I didn't usually eat before I went to work. But I wanted to ask Mama about Emmett Till. So I ate and thought of some way of asking her.

"These beans are some good, Mama," I said, trying to sense her mood.

"Why is you eating anyway? You gonna be late for work. You know how Miss Burke is," she said to me.

"I don't have much to do this evening. I kin get it done before I leave work," I said.

The conversation stopped after that. Then Mama started humming that song again.

When I get to hebben, I'm gonna put on my shoes,
And gonna tromp all over God's hebben.

She put a plate on the floor for Jennie Ann and Jerry.

"Jennie Ann! You and Jerry sit down here and eat and don't put beans all over this floor."

Ralph, the baby, started crying, and she went in the bedroom to give him his bottle. I got up and followed her.

"Mama, did you hear about that fourteen-year-old Negro boy who was killed a little over a week ago by some white men?" I asked her.

2. The white woman in whose house Anne worked.
3. In this dialect, "them" can be understood to mean "and the others."
4. Anne has six younger siblings: Adline, Junior, James, Jennie Ann, Jerry, and Ralph.

"Where did you hear that?" she said angrily.

"Boy, everybody really thinks I am dumb or deaf or something. I heard Eddie them talking about it this evening coming from school."

"Eddie them better watch how they go around here talking. These white folks git a hold of it they gonna be in trouble," she said.

"What are they gonna be in trouble about, Mama? People got a right to talk, ain't they?"

"You go on to work before you is late. And don't you let on like you know nothing about that boy being killed before Miss Burke them. Just do your work like you don't know nothing," she said. "That boys a lot better off in heaven than he is here," she continued and then started singing again.

On my way to Mrs. Burke's that evening, Mama's words kept running through my mind. "Just do your work like you don't know nothing." "Why is Mama acting so scared?" I thought. "And what if Mrs. Burke knew we knew? Why must I pretend I don't know? Why are these people killing Negroes? What did Emmett Till do besides whistle at that woman?"

By the time I got to work, I had worked my nerves up some. I was shaking as I walked up on the porch. "Do your work like you don't know nothing." But once I got inside, I couldn't have acted normal if Mrs. Burke were paying me to be myself.

I was so nervous, I spent most of the evening avoiding them going about the house dusting and sweeping. Everything went along fairly well until dinner was served.

"Don, Wayne, and Mama, y'all come on to dinner. Essie, you can wash up the pots and dishes in the sink now. Then after dinner you won't have as many," Mrs. Burke called to me.

If I had the power to mysteriously disappear at that moment, I would have. They used the breakfast table in the kitchen for most of their meals. The dining room was only used for Sunday dinner or when they had company. I wished they had company tonight so they could eat in the dining room while I was at the kitchen sink.

"I forgot the bread," Mrs. Burke said when they were all seated. "Essie, will you cut it and put it on the table for me?"

I took the cornbread, cut it in squares, and put it on a small round dish. Just as I was about to set it on the table, Wayne yelled at the cat. I dropped the plate and the bread went all over the floor.

"Never mind, Essie," Mrs. Burke said angrily as she got up and got some white bread from the breadbox.[5]

I didn't say anything. I picked up the cornbread from around the table and went back to the dishes. As soon as I got to the sink, I dropped a saucer on the floor and broke it. Didn't anyone say a word until I had picked up the pieces.

5. A container used for storing bread and other baked goods in order to keep them fresh.

"Essie, I bought some new cleanser today. It's setting on the bathroom shelf. See if it will remove the stains in the tub," Mrs. Burke said.

I went to the bathroom to clean the tub. By the time I got through with it, it was snow white. I spent a whole hour scrubbing it. I had removed the stains in no time but I kept scrubbing until they finished dinner.

When they had finished and gone into the living room as usual to watch TV, Mrs. Burke called me to eat. I took a clean plate out of the cabinet and sat down. Just as I was putting the first forkful of food in my mouth, Mrs. Burke entered the kitchen.

"Essie, did you hear about that fourteen-year-old boy who was killed in Greenwood?" she asked me, sitting down in one of the chairs opposite me.

"No, I didn't hear that," I answered, almost choking on the food.

"Do you know why he was killed?" she asked and I didn't answer.

"He was killed because he got out of his place with a white woman. A boy from Mississippi would have known better than that. This boy was from Chicago. Negroes up North have no respect for people. They think they can get away with anything. He just came to Mississippi and put a whole lot of notions in the boys' heads here and stirred up a lot of trouble," she said passionately.

"How old are you, Essie?" she asked me after a pause.

"Fourteen. I will soon be fifteen though," I said.

"See, that boy was just fourteen too. It's a shame he had to die so soon." She was so red in the face, she looked as if she was on fire.

When she left the kitchen I sat there with my mouth open and my food untouched. I couldn't have eaten now if I were starving. "Just do your work like you don't know nothing" ran through my mind again and I began washing the dishes.

I went home shaking like a leaf on a tree. For the first time out of all her trying, Mrs. Burke had made me feel like rotten garbage. Many times she had tried to instill fear within me and subdue me and had given up. But when she talked about Emmett Till there was something in her voice that sent chills and fear all over me.

Before Emmett Till's murder, I had known the fear of hunger, hell, and the Devil. But now there was a new fear known to me—the fear of being killed just because I was black. This was the worst of my fears. I knew once I got food, the fear of starving to death would leave. I also was told that if I were a good girl, I wouldn't have to fear the Devil or hell. But I didn't know what one had to do or not do as a Negro not to be killed. Probably just being a Negro period was enough, I thought.

A few days later, I went to work and Mrs. Burke had about eight women over for tea. They were all sitting around in the living room when I got there. She told me she was having a "guild meeting," and asked me to help her serve the cookies and tea.

After helping her, I started cleaning the house. I always swept the hallway and porch first. As I was sweeping the hall, I could hear them talking. When I heard the word "nigger," I stopped sweeping and listened. Mrs. Burke must have sensed this, because she suddenly came to the door.

"Essie, finish the hall and clean the bathroom," she said hesitantly. "Then you can go for today. I am not making dinner tonight." Then she went back in the living room with the rest of the ladies.

Before she interrupted my listening, I had picked up the words "NAACP" and "that organization."[6] Because they were talking about niggers, I knew NAACP had something to do with Negroes. All that night I kept wondering what could that NAACP mean?

Later when I was sitting in the kitchen at home doing my lessons, I decided to ask Mama. It was about twelve-thirty. Everyone was in bed but me. When Mama came in to put some milk in Ralph's bottle, I said, "Mama, what do NAACP mean?"

"Where did you git that from?" she asked me, spilling milk all over the floor.

"Mrs. Burke had a meeting tonight—"

"What kind of meeting?" she asked, cutting me off.

"I don't know. She had some women over—she said it was a guild meeting," I said.

"A guild meeting," she repeated.

"Yes, they were talking about Negroes and I heard some woman say 'that NAACP' and another 'that organization,' meaning the same thing."

"What else did they say?" she asked me.

"That's all I heard. Mrs. Burke must have thought I was listening, so she told me to clean the bathroom and leave."

"Don't you ever mention that word around Mrs. Burke or no other white person, you heah! Finish your lesson and cut that light out and go to bed," Mama said angrily and left the kitchen.

"With a Mama like that you'll never learn anything," I thought as I got into bed. All night long I thought about Emmett Till and the NAACP. I even got up to look up NAACP in my little concise dictionary. But I didn't find it.

The next day at school, I decided to ask my homeroom teacher Mrs. Rice the meaning of NAACP. When the bell sounded for lunch, I remained in my seat as the other students left the room.

"Are you going to spend your lunch hour studying again today, Moody?" Mrs. Rice asked me.

"Can I ask you a question, Mrs. Rice?" I asked her.

"You *may* ask me a question, yes, but I don't know if you *can* or not," she said.

"What does the word NAACP mean?" I asked.

"Why do you want to know?"

"The lady I worked for had a meeting and I overheard the word mentioned."

"What else did you hear?"

"Nothing. I didn't know what NAACP meant, that's all." I felt like I was on the witness stand or something.

6. The National Association for the Advancement of Colored People, the nation's oldest civil rights organization.

"Well, next time your boss has another meeting you listen more carefully. NAACP is a Negro organization that was established a long time ago to help Negroes gain a few basic rights," she said.

"What's it gotta do with the Emmett Till murder?" I asked.

"They are trying to get a conviction in Emmett Till's case. You see the NAACP is trying to do a lot for the Negroes and get the right to vote for Negroes in the South. I shouldn't be telling you all this. And don't you dare breathe a word of what I said. It could cost me my job if word got out I was teaching my students such. I gotta go to lunch and you should go outside too because it's nice and sunny out today," she said leaving the room. "We'll talk more when I have time."

About a week later, Mrs. Rice had me over for Sunday dinner, and I spent about five hours with her. Within that time, I digested a good meal and accumulated a whole new pool of knowledge about Negroes being butchered and slaughtered by whites in the South. After Mrs. Rice had told me all this, I felt like the lowest animal on earth. At least when other animals (hogs, cows, etc.) were killed by man, they were used as food. But when man was butchered or killed by man, in the case of Negroes by whites, they were left lying on a road or found floating in a river or something.

Mrs. Rice got to be something like a mother to me. She told me anything I wanted to know. And made me promise that I would keep all this information she was passing on to me to myself. She said she couldn't, rather didn't, want to talk about these things to the other teachers, that they would tell Mr. Willis and she would be fired. At the end of that year she was fired. I never found out why. I haven't seen her since then.

Study Questions

1. How does Anne Moody react to the news of Emmett Till's death? How do Anne's mother and Mrs. Burke react to the news?
2. Moody recalls asking her mother about a man who was beaten to death and being told that he was killed by an "Evil Spirit." What is that "Evil Spirit"? What does Moody's mother mean when she warns Anne to be a "good girl" so as not to be killed?
3. Why does Moody's mother get angry when Anne asks her about the NAACP? Why does Mrs. Rice react differently?
4. Anne Moody published her memoir in 1968, thirteen years after the events described here. By then, she had spent years working as a civil rights activist in Mississippi, had seen friends and family members beaten or killed, and had herself received threats. How might all this have affected the way she told this story? Do you think she would have told it in the same way in 1955?

LYNDON B. JOHNSON

Speech Proposing a War on Poverty (1964)

Lyndon B. Johnson (1908–1973) was thrust into the presidency by the assassination of John F. Kennedy (1917–1963) in November 1963. The following year Johnson won a landslide reelection victory, in part by promising to implement what he called the "Great Society." Invoking the memory of his slain predecessor and deploying his own formidable legislative skills, Johnson persuaded Congress to pass the greatest outpouring of legislation since the New Deal. Great Society legislation included Medicare and Medicaid, which provided health care for the elderly and the poor; federal funds for education, urban redevelopment, low-income housing, and a national public broadcasting network; and new laws aimed at curbing pollution and setting automobile safety standards.

The centerpiece of Johnson's Great Society initiative was the War on Poverty, which he introduced in a special message to Congress delivered on March 16, 1964. During the 1950s, many Americans had assumed that every citizen enjoyed a share of the nation's growing affluence, but in the early 1960s journalists and political leaders reawakened to the fact that roughly one-fifth of Americans remained poor. Johnson hoped to stamp out poverty wherever it existed, from rural Appalachia to urban slums, by providing poor Americans with food stamps, early childhood education, job training, legal services, and work-study scholarships. His administration also established community-based anti-poverty programs designed to give the poor a voice in shaping housing, education, and welfare programs at the local level. As you read Johnson's message to Congress, consider his belief that the nation can—and must—work to eliminate poverty.

From Lyndon B. Johnson: "Special Message to the Congress Proposing a Nationwide War on the Sources of Poverty," March 16, 1964. Online by Gerhard Peters and John T. Woolley, *The American Presidency Project*, http://www.presidency.ucsb.edu.

To the Congress of the United States:

We are citizens of the richest and most fortunate nation in the history of the world. One hundred and eighty years ago we were a small country struggling for survival on the margin of a hostile land. Today we have established a civilization of free men which spans an entire continent. With the growth of our country has come opportunity for our people—opportunity to educate our children, to use our energies in productive work, to increase our leisure opportunity for almost every American to hope that through work and talent he could create a better life for himself and his family.

The path forward has not been an easy one. But we have never lost sight of our goal: an America in which every citizen shares all the opportunities of his society, in which every man has a chance to advance his welfare to the limit of his capacities. We have come a long way toward this goal. We still have a long way to go. The distance which remains is the measure of the great unfinished work of our society.

To finish that work I have called for a national war on poverty. Our objective: total victory.

There are millions of Americans—one-fifth of our people—who have not shared in the abundance which has been granted to most of us, and on whom the gates of opportunity have been closed. What does this poverty mean to those who endure it? It means a daily struggle to secure the necessities for even a meager existence. It means that the abundance, the comforts, the opportunities they see all around them are beyond their grasp.

Worst of all, it means hopelessness for the young. The young man or woman who grows up without a decent education, in a broken home, in a hostile and squalid environment, in ill health or in the face of racial injustice—that young man or woman is often trapped in a life of poverty. He does not have the skills demanded by a complex society. He does not know how to acquire those skills. He faces a mounting sense of despair which drains initiative and ambition and energy.

Our tax cut will create millions of new jobs—new exits from poverty. But we must also strike down all the barriers which keep many from using those exits. The war on poverty is not a struggle simply to support people, to make them dependent on the generosity of others. It is a struggle to give people a chance. It is an effort to allow them to develop and use their capacities, as we have been allowed to develop and use ours, so that they can share, as others share, in the promise of this nation.

We do this, first of all, because it is right that we should. From the establishment of public education and land-grant colleges through agricultural extension and encouragement to industry, we have pursued the goal of a nation with full and increasing opportunities for all its citizens. The war on poverty is a further step in that pursuit.

We do it also because helping some will increase the prosperity of all. Our fight against poverty will be an investment in the most valuable of our resources—the skills and strength of our people. And in the future, as in the past, this investment will return its cost many fold to our entire economy. If we can raise the annual earnings of 10 million among the poor by only $1,000 we will have added $14 billion a year to our national output. In addition we can make important reductions in public assistance payments which now cost us $4 billion a year, and in the large costs of fighting crime and delinquency, disease and hunger. This is only part of the story. Our history has proved that each time we broaden the base of abundance, giving more people the chance to produce and consume, we create new industry, higher production, increased earnings and better income for all. Giving new opportunity to those who have little will enrich the lives of all the rest.

Because it is right, because it is wise, and because, for the first time in our history, it is possible to conquer poverty, I submit, for the consideration of the Congress and the country, the Economic Opportunity Act of 1964.[1] The Act does not merely expand old programs or improve what is already being done. It charts a new course. It strikes at the causes, not just the consequences of poverty. It can be a milestone in our one-hundred-eighty year search for a better life for our people.

This Act provides five basic opportunities:

It will give almost half a million underprivileged young Americans the opportunity to develop skills, continue education, and find useful work.

It will give every American community the opportunity to develop a comprehensive plan to fight its own poverty—and help them to carry out their plans.

It will give dedicated Americans the opportunity to enlist as volunteers in the war against poverty.

It will give many workers and farmers the opportunity to break through particular barriers which bar their escape from poverty.

It will give the entire nation the opportunity for a concerted attack on poverty through the establishment, under my direction, of the Office of Economic Opportunity,[2] a national headquarters for the war against poverty.

This is how we propose to create these opportunities.

First we will give high priority to helping young Americans who lack skills, who have not completed their education or who cannot complete it because they are too poor. The years of high school and college are the most critical stage of a young person's life. If they are not helped then, many will be condemned to a life of poverty which they, in turn, will pass on to their children. I therefore recommend the creation of a Job Corps, a Work-Training Program, and a Work Study Program.

A new national Job Corps will build toward an enlistment of 100,000 young men. They will be drawn from those whose background, health and education make them least fit for useful work. Those who volunteer will enter more than 100 Camps and Centers around the country. Half of these young men will work, in the first year, on special conservation projects to give them education, useful

1. The legislation that established most of the programs included in the War on Poverty.

2. The agency responsible for administering most of the War on Poverty programs.

work experience and to enrich the natural resources of the country. Half of these young men will receive, in the first year, a blend of training, basic education and work experience in Job Training Centers. These are not simply camps for the underprivileged. They are new educational institutions, comparable in innovation to the land-grant colleges. Those who enter them will emerge better qualified to play a productive role in American society.

A new national Work-Training Program operated by the Department of Labor will provide work and training for 200,000 American men and women between the ages of 16 and 21. This will be developed through state and local governments and nonprofit agencies. Hundreds of thousands of young Americans badly need the experience, the income, and the sense of purpose which useful full or part-time work can bring. For them such work may mean the difference between finishing school or dropping out. Vital community activities from hospitals and playgrounds to libraries and settlement houses are suffering because there are not enough people to staff them. We are simply bringing these needs together.

A new national Work-Study Program operated by the Department of Health, Education, and Welfare will provide federal funds for part-time jobs for 140,000 young Americans who do not go to college because they cannot afford it. There is no more senseless waste than the waste of the brainpower and skill of those who are kept from college by economic circumstance. Under this program they will, in a great American tradition, be able to work their way through school. They and the country will be richer for it.

Second, through a new Community Action program we intend to strike at poverty at its source—in the streets of our cities and on the farms of our countryside among the very young and the impoverished old. This program asks men and women throughout the country to prepare long-range plans for the attack on poverty in their own local communities. These are not plans prepared in Washington and imposed upon hundreds of different situations. They are based on the fact that local citizens best understand their own problems, and know best how to deal with those problems. These plans will be local plans striking at the many untilled needs which underlie poverty in each community, not just one or two. Their components and emphasis will differ as needs differ. These plans will be local plans calling upon all the resources available to the community—federal and state, local and private, human and material. And when these plans are approved by the Office of Economic Opportunity, the federal government will finance up to 90 percent of the additional cost for the first two years.

The most enduring strength of our nation is the huge reservoir of talent, initiative and leadership which exists at every level of our society. Through the Community Action Program we call upon this, our greatest strength, to overcome our greatest weakness.

Third, I ask for the authority to recruit and train skilled volunteers for the war against poverty. Thousands of Americans have volunteered to serve the needs of other lands. Thousands more want the chance to serve the needs of their own land. They should have that chance. Among older people who have retired, as well as among the young, among women as well as men, there are many Americans who are ready to enlist in our war against poverty. They have skills and dedication. They are badly needed. If the State requests them, if the community needs and will use them, we will recruit and train them and give them the chance to serve.

Fourth, we intend to create new opportunities for certain hard-hit groups to break out of the pattern of poverty. Through a new program of loans and guarantees we can provide incentives to those who will employ the unemployed. Through programs of work and retraining for unemployed fathers and mothers we can help them support their families in dignity while preparing themselves for new work. Through funds to purchase needed land, organize cooperatives, and create new and adequate family farms we can help those whose life on the land has been a struggle without hope.

Fifth, I do not intend that the war against poverty become a series of uncoordinated and unrelated efforts—that it perish for lack of leadership and direction. Therefore this bill creates, in the Executive Office of the President, a new Office of Economic Opportunity. Its Director will be my personal Chief of Staff for the war against poverty. I intend to appoint Sargent Shriver[3] to this post. He will be directly responsible for these new programs. He will work with and through existing agencies of the government.

This program—the Economic Opportunity Act—is the foundation of our war against poverty. But it does not stand alone. For the past three years this government has advanced a number of new proposals which strike at important areas of need and distress. I ask the Congress to extend those which are already in action, and to establish those which have already been proposed. There are programs to help badly distressed areas such as the Area Redevelopment Act,[4] and the legislation now being prepared to help Appalachia. There are programs to help those without training find a place in today's complex society—such as the Manpower Development Training Act and the Vocational Education Act for youth.[5] There are programs to protect those who are specially vulnerable to the ravages of poverty—hospital insurance for the elderly, protection for migrant farm workers, a food stamp program for the needy, coverage for millions not now protected by a minimum wage, new and expanded unemployment benefits for men out of work,

3. Robert Sargent Shriver Jr. (1915–2011), John F. Kennedy's brother-in-law, had founded the Peace Corps and served as its first director during the Kennedy administration. As director of the Office of Economic Opportunity, he founded and oversaw many of the programs established by the War on Poverty.

4. Passed in 1961, the Area Redevelopment Act provided nearly $400 million to stimulate job creation in urban and depressed rural areas.

5. The Manpower Development and Training Act of 1962 authorized a three-year program aimed at retraining workers displaced by new technology. The Vocational Education Act of 1963 called for the expansion of existing high-school vocational education programs and the creation of new ones.

a Housing and Community Development bill for those seeking decent homes. Finally there are programs which help the entire country, such as aid to education which, by raising the quality of schooling available to every American child, will give a new chance for knowledge to the children of the poor.

I ask immediate action on all these programs. What you are being asked to consider is not a simple or an easy program. But poverty is not a simple or an easy enemy. It cannot be driven from the land by a single attack on a single front. Were this so we would have conquered poverty long ago. Nor can it be conquered by government alone. For decades American labor and American business, private institutions and private individuals have been engaged in strengthening our economy and offering new opportunity to those in need. We need their help, their support, and their full participation. Through this program we offer new incentives and new opportunities for cooperation, so that all the energy of our nation, not merely the efforts of government, can be brought to bear on our common enemy.

Today, for the first time in our history, we have the power to strike away the barriers to full participation in our society. Having the power, we have the duty. The Congress is charged by the Constitution to "provide . . . for the general welfare of the United States." Our present abundance is a measure of its success in fulfilling that duty. Now Congress is being asked to extend that welfare to all our people. The President of the United States is President of all the people in every section of the country. But this office also holds a special responsibility to the distressed and disinherited, the hungry and the hopeless of this abundant nation. It is in pursuit of that special responsibility that I submit this Message to you today.

The new program I propose is within our means. Its cost of $970 million is 1 percent of our national budget—and every dollar I am requesting for this program is already included in the budget I sent to Congress in January. But we cannot measure its importance by its cost. For it charts an entirely new course of hope for our people. We are fully aware that this program will not eliminate all the poverty in America in a few months or a few years. Poverty is deeply rooted and its causes are many. But this program will show the way to new opportunities for millions of our fellow citizens. It will provide a lever with which we can begin to open the door to our prosperity for those who have been kept outside. It will also give us the chance to test our weapons, to try our energy and ideas and imagination for the many battles yet to come. As conditions change, and as experience illuminates our difficulties, we will be prepared to modify our strategy.

And this program is much more than a beginning. Rather it is a commitment. It is a total commitment by this President, and this Congress, and this nation, to pursue victory over the most ancient of mankind's enemies. On many historic occasions the President has requested from Congress the authority to move against forces which were endangering the well-being of our country. This is such an occasion. On similar occasions in the past we have often been called upon to wage war against foreign enemies which threatened our freedom. Today we are asked to declare war on a domestic enemy which threatens the strength of our nation and the welfare of our people. If we now move forward against this enemy—if we can bring to the challenges of peace the same determination and strength which has brought us victory in war—then this day and this Congress will have won a secure and honorable place in the history of the nation, and the enduring gratitude of generations of Americans yet to come.

Study Questions

1. During the New Deal, many liberals saw poverty as the result of a flawed political and economic system that gave too much power to corporations. How did President Johnson describe the causes of poverty in the United States?
2. According to President Johnson, who besides the poor would benefit from the elimination of poverty? Why?
3. Notice President Johnson's use of male pronouns throughout this speech. What does this suggest about his view of American workers and citizens? How do you think his gendered perception might have shaped anti-poverty programs?
4. President Johnson used martial language throughout this speech, declaring "war" on poverty and referring to enemies, weapons, battles, and "total victory." What might have been the advantage of using such military metaphors, particularly at a time when many Americans still remembered the experience of World War II? Are there disadvantages to using such language?

INDIANS OF ALL TRIBES

The Alcatraz Proclamation (1969)

With some important exceptions, American Indian protests in the eighteenth and nineteenth centuries were tribally based and focused on issues specific to particular tribes or regions. This started to change in the twentieth century, as government-run boarding schools brought together American Indians from diverse tribal backgrounds. The trend toward pan-Indian political activism accelerated further in the late 1960s, in part because of a postwar shift in federal policy that encouraged American Indians from many tribes to relocate from reservations to urban areas, where jobs were supposedly more plentiful. Many young urban Indians were also inspired by the civil rights and Black Power movements. In 1968, activists in Minnesota's Twin Cities organized the American Indian Movement. That same year Mohawks blockaded an international bridge linking Canada and New York, arguing that the Canadian requirement that they pay tolls and customs violated their treaty rights to free passage between the two countries.

In November 1969, another group seized Alcatraz Island in San Francisco Bay in the name of "Indians of All Tribes." Alcatraz, the site of a former federal prison, had been declared surplus property by the federal government. Local Indians had planned to request use of the island, but their plans gained urgency after an Indian cultural center in San Francisco burned down and word spread that San Francisco officials might allow private development of the island. The activists issued a proclamation to explain their occupation, which ultimately lasted nineteen months. As you read this document, think about how and why the authors made use of the language of old treaties.

To the Great White Father and All His People:

We, the native Americans, re-claim the land known as Alcatraz Island in the name of all American Indians by right of discovery.

We wish to be fair and honorable in our dealings with the Caucasian inhabitants of this land, and hereby offer the following treaty:

We will purchase said Alcatraz Island for twenty-four dollars ($24) in glass beads and red cloth, a precedent set by the white man's purchase of a similar island about 300 years ago. We know that $24 in trade goods for these 16 acres is more than was paid when Manhattan Island was sold, but we know that land values have risen over the years. Our offer of $1.24 per acre is greater than the 47 cents per acre the white men are now paying the California Indians for their land.[1]

We will give to the inhabitants of this island a portion of that land for their own, to be held in trust by the American Indian Government—for as long as the sun shall rise and the rivers go down to the sea[2]—to be administered by the Bureau of Caucasian Affairs (BCA). We will further guide the inhabitants in the proper way of living. We will offer them our religion, our education, our life-ways, in order to help them achieve our level of civilization and thus raise them and all their white brothers up from their savage and unhappy state. We offer this treaty in good faith and wish to be fair and honorable in our dealings with all white men.

We feel that this so-called Alcatraz Island is more than suitable for an Indian Reservation, as determined by the white man's own standards. By this we mean that this place resembles most Indian reservations, in that:

1. It is isolated from modern facilities, and without adequate means of transportation.
2. It has no fresh running water.
3. It has inadequate sanitation facilities.
4. There are no oil or mineral rights.
5. There is no industry so unemployment is great.
6. There are no health care facilities.
7. The soil is rocky and non-productive; and the land does not support game.
8. There are no educational facilities.
9. The population has always exceeded the land base.
10. The population has always been held as prisoners and kept dependent upon others.

Further, it would be fitting and symbolic that ships from all over the world, entering the Golden Gate, would first see Indian land, and thus be reminded of the true history of this nation. This tiny island would be a symbol of the great lands once ruled by free and noble Indians.

1. In 1968, the federal government agreed to pay California Indians $29.1 million dollars, or the equivalent of 47 cents per acre, as compensation for land that had been determined by the Indian Claims Commission to belong to them in 1853.

2. A mocking allusion to the phraseology of treaties between Indian tribes and the U.S. government during the eighteenth and nineteenth centuries.

USE TO BE MADE OF ALCATRAZ ISLAND

What use will be made of this land?

Since the San Francisco Indian Center burned down, there is no place for Indians to assemble and carry on our tribal life here in the white man's city. Therefore, we plan to develop on this island several Indian institutes:

1. A Center for Native American Studies will be developed which will train our young people in the best of our native cultural arts and sciences, as well as educate them to the skills and knowledge relevant to improve the lives and spirits of all Indian peoples. Attached to this center will be traveling universities, managed by Indians, which will go to the Indian Reservations in order to learn the traditional values from the people, which are now absent in the Caucasian higher educational system.
2. An American Indian Spiritual center will be developed which will practice our ancient tribal religious ceremonies and medicine. Our cultural arts will be featured and our young people trained in music, dance, and medicine.
3. An Indian Center of Ecology will be built which will train and support our young people in scientific research and practice in order to restore our lands and waters to their pure and natural state. We will seek to de-pollute the air and the water of the Bay Area. We will seek to restore fish and animal life, and to revitalize sea life which has been threatened by the white man's way. Facilities will be developed to de-salt sea water for human use.
4. A Great Indian Training School will be developed to teach our peoples how to make a living in the world, improve our standards of living, and end hunger and unemployment among all our peoples. This training school will include a center for Indian arts and crafts, and an Indian restaurant serving native foods and training Indians in culinary arts. This center will display Indian arts and offer the Indian foods of all tribes to the public, so they all may know of the beauty and spirit of the traditional Indian ways.
5. Some of the present buildings will be taken over to develop an American Indian Museum, which will depict our native foods and other cultural contributions we have given to all the world. Another part of the museum will present some of the things the white man has given to the Indians, in return for the land and the life he took: disease, alcohol, poverty, and cultural decimation (as symbolized by old tin cans, barbed wire, rubber tires, plastic containers, etc.). Part of the museum will remain a dungeon, to symbolize both Indian captives who were incarcerated for challenging white authority, and those who were imprisoned on reservations. The museum will show the noble and the tragic events of Indian history, including the broken treaties, the documentary of the Trail of Tears, the Massacre of Wounded Knee, as well as the victory over Yellow-Hair Custer and his army.

In the name of all Indians, therefore, we re-claim this island for Indian nations, for all these reasons. We feel this claim is just and proper, and that this land should rightfully be granted to us for as long as the rivers shall run and the sun shall shine.

Signed,
Indians of All Tribes
November 1969
San Francisco, California

Study Questions

1. To whom was this Proclamation addressed?
2. On what grounds did the Indians of All Tribes lay claim to Alcatraz Island? According to them, what was the symbolic importance of seizing Alcatraz? How did they plan to use the island?
3. What can you infer about American Indian grievances from reading this Proclamation?
4. How would you describe the tone of this document? Why do you think the authors adopted this tone? The opening sentence of the Proclamation speaks of "native Americans" rather than "Native Americans." Why is this significant?

California Voters Pamphlet (1978)

In 1978 California voters sparked a nationwide tax revolt. That year, anti-tax activists succeeded in getting an initiative known as Proposition 13 onto the California state ballot. Proposition 13 called for slashing property taxes, capping the rate at which they could rise in the future, and amending the state constitution to make it more difficult to increase state taxes of any kind. The initiative, if passed threatened to wreak havoc with the state's education and welfare systems, and politicians in both parties, as well as the state's major media outlets, opposed it. But although tax revolts had failed in the past, this time voters felt differently. By the late 1970s, runaway inflation was boosting property values and hence property taxes, while wages and salaries barely kept up. All this threatened to drive many working- and middle-class families from their homes. On June 6, 1978, voters passed Proposition 13 by a two-to-one margin. Politicians, pollsters, and pundits took note, and anti-tax conservatives across the country felt emboldened. Over the next few years more than a dozen states followed California's lead and forced limits on government spending. In California, Proposition 13 resulted in stable, predictable tax rates for homeowners and a slower rate of growth in property tax revenues, leading to budget constraints in public services and public education. Thus the state came to rely more heavily on other types of taxes—income, capital gains, and special assessments.

The battle over Proposition 13 marked a significant shift in American politics. In the past, those who favored limited government had focused on cutting programs rather than limiting government revenue. In 1978, however, California conservatives reframed the debate in ways that continued to resonate long after the inflation of that era abated. As you read the arguments offered by proponents and opponents of Proposition 13, think about how each side tried to appeal to voters.

From "California Voter's Pamphlet—Primary Election" (California: State of California, 1978), 56–60.

OFFICIAL TITLE AND SUMMARY PREPARED BY THE ATTORNEY GENERAL

Tax Limitation—Initiative Constitutional Amendment. Limits ad valorem taxes on real property to 1% of value except to pay indebtedness previously approved by voters. Establishes 1975–76 assessed valuation base for property tax purposes. Limits annual increases in value. Provides for reassessment after sale, transfer, or construction. Requires ⅔ vote of Legislature to enact any change in state taxes designed to increase revenues. Prohibits imposition by state of new ad valorem, sales, or transaction taxes on real property. Authorizes imposition of special taxes by local government (except on real property) by ⅔ vote of qualified electors. Financial impact: Commencing with fiscal year beginning July 1, 1978, would result in annual losses of local government property tax revenues (approximately $7 billion in 1978–79 fiscal year), reduction in annual state costs (approximately $600 million in 1978–79 fiscal year), and restriction on future ability of local governments to finance capital construction by sale of general obligation bonds.

* * *

Proposal:

This initiative would: (1) place a limit on the amount of property taxes that could be collected by local governments, (2) restrict the growth in the assessed value of property subject to taxation, (3) require a two-thirds vote of the Legislature to increase state tax revenues, and (4) authorize local governments to impose certain nonproperty taxes if two-thirds of the voters give their approval in a local election. . . .

The following is a summary of the main provisions of this initiative:

1. *Property tax limit.* Beginning with the 1978–79 fiscal year, this measure would limit the amount of property taxes that could be collected from an owner of county assessed *real* property to 1 percent of the property's full cash value.

* * *

The limit on property taxes plus the restrictions on assessed values noted below, would substantially reduce local property tax revenues.

2. *Distribution of remaining property tax revenues.* The reduced property tax revenues which could be raised under the 1 percent limit would be collected by the counties and then distributed "according to law to the districts within the counties."

* * *

3. *Restrictions on the growth in assessed values.* Initially this measure would roll back the current assessed values of real property to the values shown on the 1975–76 assessment roll. However county assessors could adjust the values shown on the 1975–76 assessment roll if these values were lower than the estimated market value as of March 1, 1975. The adjusted values could then be increased by no more than 2 percent per year as long as the same taxpayer continued to own the property. For property which is sold or newly constructed after March 1, 1975, the assessed value would be set at the appraised (or market) value at the time of sale or construction. As a result, two identical properties with the same market value could have different assessed values for tax purposes if one of them has been sold since March 1, 1975.

4. *Increases in state taxes.* Currently state taxes can be increased by a majority vote of both houses of the Legislature and approval by the Governor (that is, if the

Governor signs the measure increasing taxes). This initiative would require a two-thirds vote by the Legislature to increase state taxes and would prohibit the Legislature from enacting any new taxes based on the value or sale of real property.

5. *Alternative local taxes.* This measure would authorize cities, counties, special districts and school districts to impose unspecified "special" taxes only if they receive approval by two-thirds of the voters. Such taxes could not be based on the value or sale of real property.

The Legislative Counsel advises us that provisions in the existing Constitution would prohibit general law cities,[1] counties, school districts and special districts from imposing new "special taxes" without specific approval by the Legislature. Such restrictions limit the ability of these local governments, even with local voter approval, to replace property tax losses resulting from the adoption of this initiative.

Fiscal Effect:

This measure would have the following direct impact on the state and local governments:

1. Local governments would lose about $7 billion in property tax revenues during the 1978–79 fiscal year. This is because the measure would reduce local property tax revenues (estimated at $12.4 billion under current law) by 57 percent, statewide. Some counties would lose more, and others would lose less.

2. The ability of local governments to sell general obligation bonds in the future would be severely restricted. These bonds are used to finance the construction of new schools, local government buildings, and a variety of other facilities such as parks and sewage treatment plants.

ARGUMENTS IN FAVOR OF PROPOSITION 13

Limits property tax to 1% of market value, requires two-thirds vote of both houses of the legislature to raise any other taxes, limits yearly market value tax raises to 2% per year, and requires all other tax raises to be approved by the people. Why then the amendment? President Carter[2] said "our tax system is a National disgrace".

Our audit figures show loss to local governments at about $5 billion, not $7 billion as claimed by the state finance director.

Assembly leader Paul Priolo said "it's a tough amendment but the state can live with it. It means public officials will have to go to work."

Noted UCLA tax expert Dr. Neil Jacoby writes "This unjust process must be brought to an end." A 1% limit would still leave property tax revenue *far above* the

1. California cities fall into three categories: general law cities, charter cities, and one consolidated city and county (San Francisco). The majority of California cities are general law cities, deriving power from an act of the state legislature rather than from a charter.
2. James Earl "Jimmy" Carter (b. 1924) was president of the United States from 1977 to 1981.

level required to pay for property-related governmental services, street lighting maintenance, sewers, trash collection and *POLICE* AND *FIRE PROTECTION*."

According to the State Controller's office, state agencies will still collect more than 33 thousand million tax dollars every year after this amendment passes. We think this is more than enough. *The people will save 7 thousand million dollars every year* for *themselves.*

This amendment will make rent reductions *probable.* Otherwise *rent raises are certain as property taxes go up.* It will help farmers and keep business in California. It will make home and building improvements possible *and create thousands of new jobs.*

The amendment DOES NOT reduce property tax exemptions for senior citizens. DOES NOT remove tax exemptions for churches or charities. DOES NOT prohibit the use of property tax money for schools.

To make California taxes FAIR, EQUAL and WITHIN THE ABILITY OF THE TAXPAYERS TO PAY, vote YES on Proposition 13.

HOWARD JARVIS
Chairman, United Organizations of Taxpayers

PAUL GANN
President, Peoples Advocate

The Legislature will not act to reduce your property taxes. As a Senator and Legislator for 11 years, I, like you, have been totally frustrated with the Legislature's failure to enact a meaningful property tax relief and reform bill.

What Ronald Reagan[3] describes as the "spenders coalition" of spendthrift politicians and powerful special interests are spending millions to defeat Proposition 13.

Your Yes vote will NOT require a reduction of vital services like police or fire, nor any tax increase. Your Yes vote will require a tough Governor take the lead in cutting wasteful, unnecessary government spending 10 to 15%.

More than 15% of all governmental spending is wasted! Wasted on huge pensions for politicians which sometimes approach $80,000 per year! Wasted on limousines for elected officials or taxpayer paid junkets. Now we have the opportunity to trade waste for property tax relief!

If we want to permanently cut property taxes about 67%, we must do it ourselves. Join Democratic Senator Robert "Bob" Wilson and me, a Republican Senator, in voting Yes on Proposition 13.

JOHN V. BRIGGS
State Senator, 35th District

3. Ronald Reagan (1911–2004), a former movie actor, was the Republican governor of California from 1967 to 1975. He was elected president of the United States in 1980, in part because of conservative momentum generated by the tax revolt.

REBUTTAL TO ARGUMENTS IN FAVOR OF PROPOSITION 13

PROPOSITION 13:

GIVES nearly two-thirds of the tax relief to BUSINESS, INDUSTRIAL property owners and apartment house LANDLORDS;

TRANSFERS your LOCAL CONTROL over neighborhood and community program funding to state and federal government bureaucracies;

PROVIDES absolutely NO TAX RELIEF for RENTERS;

REDUCES drastically police patrol services and fire protection while INCREASING home insurance COSTS by 50% to 300%;

REQUIRES new taxes to preserve CRITICAL SERVICES. Doubling the sales tax, substantially increasing the income tax or increasing the bank and corporation tax by 500% are the potential alternatives;

SLASHES current local funding for PARKS, BEACHES, MUSEUMS, LIBRARIES and PARAMEDIC PROGRAMS;

PENALIZES our school CHILDREN by CUTTING operating school budgets by nearly $4 billion, further lowering the quality of education;

PLACES a disproportionate and unfair tax burden on anyone purchasing a home after July 1, 1978;

INCREASES your state and federal INCOME TAXES and HANDS the IRS nearly $2 BILLION of your tax dollars.

Check the FACTS. Talk to your local officials; talk to your schools and talk to your business and labor organizations and demand to know what cutbacks in essential services would occur if Proposition 13 passes.

JOIN the LEAGUE OF WOMEN VOTERS
CALIFORNIA TAXPAYERS ASSOCIATION
LOS ANGELES CHAMBER OF COMMERCE
LEAGUE OF CITIES
COUNTY SUPERVISORS ASSOCIATION
CALIFORNIA RETAILERS ASSOCIATION

and countless others who are opposed to this IRRESPONSIBLE MEASURE which CUTS $7 BILLION from critical services.

VOTE NO ON 13!

HOUSTON I. FLOURNOY
Dean, Center for Public Affairs,
University of Southern California
Former State Controller

TOM BRADLEY
Mayor, City of Los Angeles

GARY SIRBU
State Chairman, California Common Cause

ARGUMENT AGAINST PROPOSITION 13

Proposition 13 invites economic and governmental chaos in California. It will drastically cut police and fire protection and bankrupt schools unless massive new tax burdens are imposed on California taxpayers. It will take decision-making away from the local level and weaken home rule.

Proposition 13 is a vague, poorly drafted and incomplete proposal which will seriously damage the economic stability of state and local governments. Shocking increases in state and local taxes are virtually inevitable. Many homeowners who expect to benefit will actually suffer a net tax increase.

Homeowners will be in for several unpleasant economic surprises if Proposition 13 is adopted. They will be paying higher federal income taxes, yet at the same time the community they live in will lose its rightful share of federal revenue sharing funds. Homeowners living in identical side-by-side houses will pay vastly different property tax bills.

Millions of renters will be doubly jeopardized. Renters have no guarantee that their landlord's property tax savings will be voluntarily passed through to them. But they can be certain they will be forced to pay the new or additional taxes necessary to keep our local governments out of bankruptcy.

Passage of Proposition 13 will slash $7 billion from school and local government budgets—an amount nearly equal to one-half of the General Fund budget for the entire State of California. This crippling blow simply cannot be absorbed. For example, it would require a doubling of your present income tax, or the sales tax to simply replace the lost revenues.

Homeowners and renters are most in need of property tax relief. But Proposition 13 gives two-thirds of the property tax decrease to commercial and industrial property owners.

Proposition 13 will seriously cripple local government services, including police and fire protection. Proposition 13 will force default on many redevelopment and revenue bond issues and prohibit future general obligation bond issues to pay for needed schools, hospitals, and water facilities. Business will not locate or expand in California if the local services necessary for economic development and new jobs are slashed.

This irresponsible initiative is not a solution. Proposition 13 goes too far. It is an invitation to poor community services, less local control and inequitable taxation for all Californians.

Vote "no" on Proposition 13.

HOUSTON I. FLOURNOY
Dean, Center for Public Affairs,
University of Southern California
Former State Controller

TOM BRADLEY
Mayor, City of Los Angeles

GARY SIRBU
State Chairman, California Common Cause

REBUTTAL TO ARGUMENT AGAINST PROPOSITION 13

We who own homes, farms, property or rent must not let the political horror stories scare us. We must vote proposition 13 into law June 6, 1978. We must not let the spendthrift politicians continue to tax us into poverty. *Proposition 13 will NOT cut fire protection, police protection, sewers, streets, and lighting or garbage collection. All property related services. It will cut spending about 15%.*

Proposition 13 will NOT give business a NEW WINDFALL. It does NOT change the tax ratio between residences and business property in effect for 75 years. It will stop business from leaving California and bring new companies to California, creating thousands of new jobs. Proposition 13 will *NOT* prohibit the use of property taxes to finance schools.

Proposition 13 will make property taxes FAIR, EQUAL and within the *ABILITY to pay for all Californians.*

Proposition 13 will make lower rents certain. It will reduce the monthly impound tax payments on home mortgages.

As expected, the opposition to proposition 13 is signed by 2 persons long on the taxpayers payroll and one person from a tax free foundation. *Proposition 13 makes sense for California. Means thousands of extra dollars for you and your family each and every year. Restores government of, for and by the people.*

Also for 13: Assemblymen Robert Cline (R), Wm. Dannemeyer (R), Mike Antonovich (R) and Senator Bob Wilson (D).

VOTE YES ON PROPOSITION 13, YOUR LAST CHANCE FOR PERMANENT TAX RELIEF.

HOWARD JARVIS
Chairman, United Organizations of Taxpayers

PAUL GANN
President, Peoples Advocate

JOHN V. BRIGGS
State Senator, 35th District

Study Questions

1. What were the key provisions of Proposition 13?
2. According to the opponents of Proposition 13, what government services would have to be cut if property taxes were slashed? What aspects of government did the proponents of the initiative propose to cut?
3. How did the proponents of Proposition 13 characterize their opponents? Who did they suggest was leading the opposition to the initiative?
4. Those who favored Proposition 13 argued that it would make property taxes "FAIR [and] EQUAL." How might opponents of the measure have responded to this statement? What aspects of the amendment did they suggest were unfair?

INDEX

E

G

H

I

K

M

S

T

U

W

Y

Z